GW01018454

THE SKYSCRAPER AND THE CITY

GAIL FENSKE

THE SKYSCRAPER AND THE CITY

The Woolworth Building and the Making of Modern New York

THE UNIVERSITY OF CHICAGO PRESS

CHICAGO AND LONDON

GAIL FENSKE is professor of architecture at Roger Williams University.

The University of Chicago Press, Chicago 60637
The University of Chicago Press, Ltd., London

Printed in the United States of America

17 16 15 14 13 12 11 10 2 3 4 5

ISBN-13: 978-0-226-24141-8 (cloth)
ISBN-10: 0-226-24141-6 (cloth)

Published with the generous support of Furthermore: a program of the J. M. Kaplan Fund.

LIBRARY OF CONGRESS
CATALOGING-IN-PUBLICATION DATA

Fenske, Gail.

The skyscraper and the city : the Woolworth Building and the making of modern New York / Gail Fenske.

p. cm.

Includes bibliographical references and index.
ISBN-13: 978-0-226-24141-8 (cloth : alk. paper)
ISBN-10: 0-226-24141-6 (cloth : alk. paper) 1. Woolworth Building (New York, N.Y.). 2. Architecture, Gothic—Influence. 3. Architecture and society—New York (State)—New York—History—20th century. 4. Gilbert, Cass, 1859–1934. 5. Woolworth, Frank Winfield, 1852–1919. 6. New York (N.Y.)—Buildings, structures, etc. I. Title.
NA6233.N5W664 2008
725'.2097471—dc22

2007029171

∞ The paper used in this publication meets the minimum requirements of the American National Standard for Information Sciences—Permanence of Paper for Printed Library Materials, ANSI Z39.48-1992.

for Don

CONTENTS

ACKNOWLEDGMENTS

It is easy enough to see something of New York in the Woolworth Building—its collections of the historical and rare, atmosphere of ceaseless change, spirit of excitement, and renown as a city of possibility. This I discovered during one of my walks down Broadway and across City Hall Park, and this has kept my interest alive down to the day I write these words. The Woolworth Building anchors this book, but more largely its subject is New York.

Given the complexity of the skyscraper as well as the city, this project has benefited greatly from the engagement of other minds in addition to my own. Gifted teachers, fellow scholars, friends, and the acquaintances one makes through chance encounters have inspired my intellectual quest—beginning with its origins in a simple set of questions and then continuing through its refinement over the years as the conceptual framework that structures and informs the argument of this book.

When I began the project as a graduate student in MIT's program in the history, theory, and criticism of architecture, the program's chair, Stanford Anderson, suggested that I examine the tensions between architecture and consumer values. I am grateful that I had his example as a scholar and to have learned from his advice. Equally important, Mardges Bacon, David Friedman, and Leo Marx contributed the finest expertise in guiding the project as a dissertation. Previous work on tall buildings with James Becker in civil engineering and with Robert Bruegmann, then a visiting professor at MIT, sparked my interest in the skyscraper's many technologies as well as processes of construction. Conversations with Henry Millon, Anne Wagner, William Porter, and at Wellesley with James O'Gorman further stimulated my thinking about the skyscraper, alternative conceptions of the modern, and Gilbert's distinctive approach as a Beaux-Arts architect.

Among all of the advisers who generously offered their guidance and support, I owe my greatest debt to Leo Marx. It was my good fortune to count as one among many students who have benefited—initially as a participant in his seminar on cultural criticism, and later as I reshaped the project—from his strong sense of commitment to the development of young scholars. Without his deep knowledge of American culture and its critics, along with his guidance, skepticism, and astute criticism of my research and writing, this study might well have materialized, but certainly not in its present form.

I am also deeply grateful to colleagues who read all or parts of the manuscript, and who offered observations and criticism at key stages in its development while providing all kinds of important related advice. Katherine Solomonson sharpened my perspective on consumer culture as well as the "skyscraper Gothic," Robert Bruegmann emphasized the value of contextually explaining key engineering features and methods of construction, and Richard Longstreth made discerning observations about Woolworth and his retailing empire as well as about Gilbert as artist and professional. During the early stages of the project, Robert Fogelson urged me to "get the building built"; Richard Chafee shared detailed comments based on his knowledge of the École des Beaux-Arts; and Sharon Irish contributed important insights on Gilbert. Mary Ellen Lepionka generously read major parts of the manuscript up to three times and offered trenchant editorial advice. I am further thankful to Jeffrey Howe, Michael Lewis, Sarah Wermiel, and the two anonymous readers for the University of Chicago Press.

Sarah Landau offered valuable advice on Woolworth's commercial objectives, and Carol Willis served as an excellent sounding board. Susan Tunick and Theodore Prudon provided important materials on terra cotta and all aspects of its production. Mike Radow kept me abreast of the Woolworth Building's recent changes and renovations, sharing his own keen perceptions based on "inside news" gleaned from his regular visits to the building's mezzanine and later, ninth-story, barbershop. In addition, Deryck Holdsworth, Nancy Stieber, Joseph Siry, Mark Jarzombek, Hilary Ballon, Michael Leja, Isabelle Gournay, Alice Friedman, Gwendolyn Wright, Andrew Dolkart, Thomas Hubka, Bernice Thomas, Bernice Buresh, Lois Marie Fink, William R. Taylor, Neil Levine, and the late William Jordy made provocative suggestions during important stages of the project's development. Any faults or shortcomings that remain are mine.

Opportunities provided by colleagues to present my research supported the testing of my arguments publicly. David Ward and Olivier Zunz invited my participation in the Social Science Research Council's 1990 symposium on early twentieth-century New York, a stimulating interdisciplinary exchange that led to my fortuitous collaboration with Deryck Holdsworth for *The Landscape of Modernity*. Symposiums on Cass Gilbert sponsored by the Second Judicial Court of the United States's Committee on Cass Gilbert Projects in 1998 and by the New-York Historical Society in 2000, both of which were accompanied by publications on Gilbert, provided forums for exchanging ideas with other Gilbert scholars—Sharon Irish, Barbara Christen, Mary Beth Betts, and the late Geoffrey Blodgett—whose knowledge of Gilbert as a person and professional has greatly enhanced my own. More recently, I am thankful to Roberta Moudry for inviting my contribution to *The American Skyscraper: Cultural Histories*, which prompted my scrutiny of Gilbert's relations with his consulting engineers and builders.

Participating as a guest lecturer in Kevin Murphy and Lisa Reilly's seminar at the University of Virginia on the "skyscraper Gothic" and David Friedman's seminar on historical city views at MIT opened new lines of inquiry. Serving on the advisory committee for the Liberty Science Center's permanent exhibition on the skyscraper, The Skyscraper: Achievement and Impact, exposed me to a broader array of perspectives on tall buildings and their associated urban environments. Teaching seminars on the skyscraper at MIT, Wellesley, and Roger Williams University provided opportunities to be challenged by students' questions and to engage the methodological complexities of my topic. Advising Tom Lee's M.Arch. thesis project with Andrew Scott at MIT—an innovative contemporary skyscraper—only further inspired me.

At the former Woolworth Corporation, William Barry Thomson generously provided invaluable assistance with navigating the informal system of storage that at the time constituted the company's archive. Joseph Grabowski showed me every square inch of the building, taking me on countless tours extending from the depths of the subbasement mechanical rooms to the pinnacled heights of the tower's crowning observatory. Jennifer Vickery identified a cache of valuable photographs, and Barbara Pedone, important company publications. More recently, Roy Suskin of the Witkoff Group—the current owner of the building after its sale by the Woolworth Corporation in 1998—has shared his detailed knowledge of construction-related discoveries exposed by the skyscraper's latest renovations.

Throughout the course of the study, certain individuals and staffs at institutions and archives have worked hard at identifying and excavating the materials essential to my research. I am especially grateful to C. Ford Peatross, curator of the architecture, design, and engineering collections at the Library of Congress; Helena Zinkham, Wendy Shadwell, and Mary Beth Betts and later Matthew Murphy and Kelly McAnnaney in the Department of Prints, Photographs, and Architectural Collections at the New-York Historical Society and Jill Reichenbach in Rights and Reproductions; Melanie Bower, manager of collections access at the Museum of the City of New York; Dana Twersky, collections manager at the National Building Museum; Tony P. Wrenn, former archivist at the American Institute of Architects Archives; William Worthington, former curator in the Division of Mechanical and Civil Engineering at the Smithsonian's Museum of American History; Herbert Mitchell, former rare book librarian, and Janet Parks, curator of drawings and archives, at the Avery Architectural and Fine Arts Library, Columbia University; Franz Jantzen in the Office of the Curator, Supreme Court of the United States; Janice Chadbourne, curator of the Fine Arts Library, Boston Public Library, and Aaron Schmidt, curator of photographs in the library's Print Department; the staff of New York Public Library; the staffs of Hayden and Rotch libraries and Rotch Visual Collections at MIT; John Schlinke, architecture librarian of Roger Williams University; and Franklin and Alex McCann. For the production of tables, maps, and digital scans, I am grateful to Dennis McClendon, Marcio Tavares, Donna McLaren, Hal Reynolds, Barbara Hanna, John Cook, and Carol Smith.

I have the greatest appreciation for Susan Bielstein, my editor at the University of Chicago Press, for her support of the project, advice, and perceptiveness and sense of humor about securing the illustrations and permissions so essential to any scholarly endeavor in art and architectural history. Her assistant, Anthony Burton, carefully shepherded the project through all phases of the publication process, and Erik Carlson's sharp editorial eye improved the manuscript. Maia Wright envisioned the book's design.

The project could not have been completed without substantial support for writing as well as research and travel. The School of Architecture, Art, and Historic Preservation at Roger Williams University and the Roger Williams University Foundation to Promote Scholarship and Teaching contributed both leave time and funding. I am also grateful to MIT's Department of Architecture, the American Institute of Architects, the National Endowment for the Humanities, the Smithsonian Institution, and the Hagley and Winterthur museums. The Writers' Room of Boston continues to provide inspiring space for writers of all genres, including myself, amid the skyscrapers of Boston's State Street. The quality of the book's illustration program would not have been possible without a substantial grant from the Graham Foundation for Advanced Studies in the Fine Arts. The J. M. Kaplan Fund supported the book's production through a grant made directly to the University of Chicago Press.

I am deeply appreciative of my family, particularly of my parents, whose contribution to the project is inestimable. My father, Paul, a research professor, taught me the value of asking original questions. My brother Roderick provided me with a place to stay in New York, and my brother Jon read the final draft. I am further grateful to my grandmother, the late Emma Fenske, and to Jean Perry and Kate Morse Fenske.

From the project's very outset, my husband, Don Cecich, participated in every step of the research and writing, sharing my passion for discovery. He listened carefully as I tested for the first time arguments and stories, then further as I wove them together to create the chapters of the book, asking penetrating questions, offering keen perceptions, and providing insights from his own field of engineering. He traveled with me as I traced the steps of Woolworth and Gilbert from the remote regions around Watertown, New York, to Lancaster, Pennsylvania, and Washington, D.C., and then across western Europe, from Rome north to the Loire Valley, through Normandy and Paris's surrounding cathedral towns, to Malines, Bruges, Louvain, and Audenaarde, and then on to London, Wells, Salisbury, and Ely. The book is as much his as it is mine. I will always be grateful for his unfailing support—and I will never be able to thank him enough for the continuing adventure of our shared lives.

THE SKYSCRAPER AND THE CITY

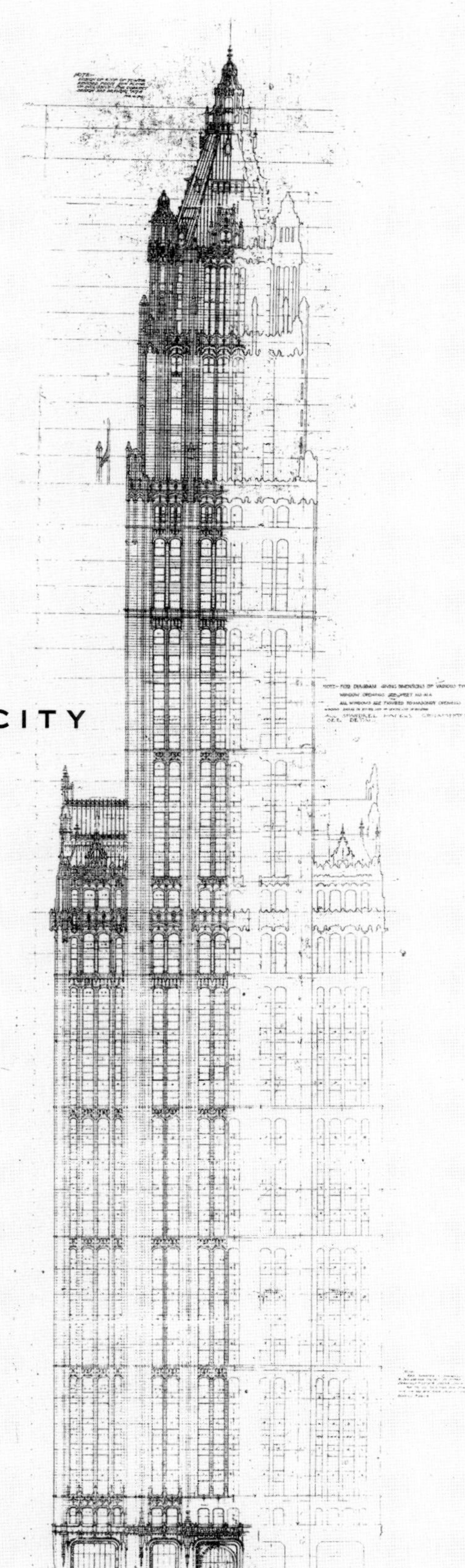

Cass Gilbert, Woolworth Building, Broadway elevation, drawn by Frederick Stickel, 1911. Collection of the New-York Historical Society, negative 79623d.

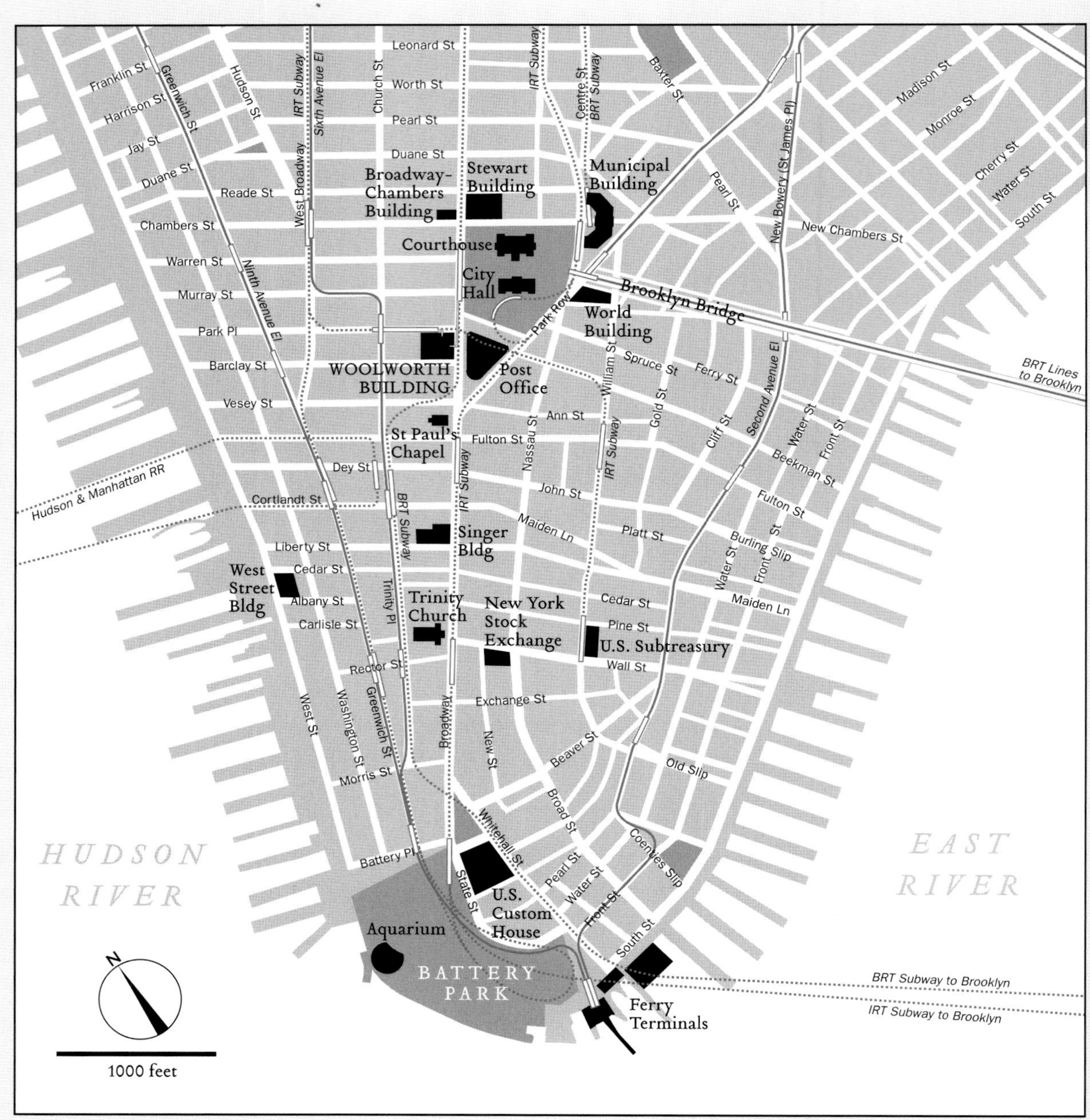

Lower Manhattan, 1918. Map by Dennis McClendon.

INTRODUCTION

From its completion in 1913 down to the present, the Woolworth Building has enhanced our experience of the city, and this suggests the importance of urban aspirations to its creators (fig. 1). Although the building's pinnacled tower no longer dominates the skyline, it still retains the visual identity of a singular Gothic spire, commanding the attention of spectators from multiple locations within the metropolis and beyond. Especially striking vistas can be secured from the Brooklyn Bridge, from the Municipal Building diagonally across City Hall Park, and from vantage points north or south along lower Broadway. In the Broadway views, the tower's piers and colonnettes soar straight upward from the street toward its pinnacle, imparting to the sidewalk observer an experience of sheer vertical ascent unrivaled by the taller but stepped-back skyscrapers of the 1920s.

At the base of the Woolworth Building, the visitor encounters shops and show windows. These set up a sidewalk path culminating at the main entrance, a Tudor Gothic portal located on the central axis of the tower. Just inside the entrance, a tall, vaulted Romanesque lobby-arcade rivaling a cathedral in scale unfolds, with an impressive brilliance of color, gilded Gothic tracery, walls of variegated marble, and sparkling Byzantine mosaics. On the main axis with the entrance and closing the space's perspective, a flight of marble steps rises to the entrance of the former Irving National Exchange Bank. Beneath this stair, another stair descends to tall, bronze gates; these once opened grandly onto the platforms of the IRT and BRT subway lines. From the lobby-arcade, the visitor could ride a high-speed elevator to the tower's pinnacle observatory,

FIGURE 1
Woolworth Building on lower Broadway, looking south, New York, 1913. Photograph by Irving Underhill. Prints and Photographs Division, Library of Congress.

stand in the octagonal peak's encircling balcony, and take in a panoramic view of the city. Those who experienced the Woolworth Building, especially during the height of its popularity as a tourist destination in the 1920s, were more than merely observers; they had become, rather, active participants in a modern social, spatial, and visual dynamic which involved the urban surroundings in complex ways.

Such an experience of the skyscraper, connected as it is to the experience of the city, raises questions about the Woolworth Building's relationship to its historic urban setting. It is difficult to sum up that setting, and even more so the cultural complexities of early twentieth-century New York.[1] Still, it is possible to define some important themes. Well established at the time as the nation's chief metropolis, New York had a generation earlier developed a vigorous commercial culture. Its status as one of the world's leading emporiums of consumer enticement encouraged the development of new forms of display and spectatorship. The city was also a site of intensive modernization, both technological and social. The fast-paced construction of large-scale works of engineering paralleled expanding immigration, ethnic heterogeneity, and sharpening class divides. In 1904, Henry James described New York's "mood of the moment . . . an expression of things lately and currently *done*, done on a large impersonal stage and on the basis of inordinate gain."[2] He had discovered an equally prominent but less tangible aspect of the city's culture: the unbridled forces of capital and atmosphere of temporal instability that characterized the experience of modernity.

The cultural critic Marshall Berman and others have defined "modernity" as the social experience of modernization, an experience perhaps most deeply felt in world metropolises such as New York and Paris during the late nineteenth and early twentieth centuries. The rise of industrialization, prodigious scientific and technological advances, and new and dynamic systems of mass communication such as daily newspapers, telegraphs, and telephones contributed to the experience. So did new political and economic forms, among them the growth of the nation-state and the triumph of an "ever expanding, drastically fluctuating capitalist world market."[3] The Woolworth Building, as New York's paradigmatic skyscraper of the early twentieth century, was bound up with these wholly unprecedented material conditions and related cultural processes and, in view of that, can be strongly identified with the experience of modernity.

The history of early twentieth-century New York is documented in recent scholarship on the city. Broadly conceived studies, particularly those of Kenneth Jackson and, more recently, Edwin G. Burrows and Mike Wallace, are complemented by more focused studies that delineate a specific aspect of the city's modern urban culture.[4] Among the latter are William Taylor's study of the city as a "showcase" designed for "the stimulation and gratification of a mass of consumers" composing a newly spectatorial "public" and Peter Hall's of the technological modernization of the city through bold and imaginative works of engineering. Neil Harris has analyzed the tourist as both a sightseer and consumer in the period after the city emerged in the early 1890s as a major travel destination, and Alan Trachtenberg, avant-garde photographers' efforts to find a "principle of picturing" that would order a city made unintelligible and discontinuous by the forces of modernity.[5] The Woolworth Building—part Beaux-Arts architecture, part setting for consumer pleasure, part feat of modern engineering and construction, part office environment for paperwork, and part a tourist attraction—encompasses in intriguing ways these and other telling urban cultural themes.

The Woolworth Building's contradictory architectural hybrid of fanciful Gothic ornamental features—tracery, tourelles, gables, gargoyles, and finials—and technologically audacious steel-framed engineering calls attention to the jarring discontinuities, startling proximities, and unpredictability of the modern urban experience. When the critic Charles Baudelaire described "modernity" in 1863 as "the ephemeral, the fugitive, the contingent, the half of art whose other half is the eternal and immutable," he showed an awareness of such disparities.[6] Berman has described another type of modern artist that "throws himself into parodies of the past," thereby expressing modernity's sense of "inner dichotomy" or of "living in two worlds simultaneously." By contrast to modernism, with its "quest for the pure, self-referential art object" and severing of the relationship between art and social life, modernity was by its very nature dialectical, dynamic, and "capable of everything except solidity and stability."[7] It is in this light that the Woolworth Building and its contradictions are best examined and understood—as opposed to within the intellectual framework of the canonic modernism later identified in architecture with the 1920s European avant-garde.

What was Frank Woolworth's relationship to the dynamic urban culture of early twentieth-century New York? Woolworth, the founder of the famous chain of five- and ten-cent stores, had already conceived city sidewalks as environments conducive to the stimulation of consumer desire. His strong orientation toward the sidewalk shopper had from the beginnings of his enterprise influenced not only his choices of profitable sites for stores, but also his use of architecture to showcase commodities and to catch the eye of the spectator. He had fabricated theatrical store-opening extravaganzas for the purpose of entertaining, even dazzling, sidewalk crowds. Throughout the Woolworth Building's sequential stages of design, construction, and completion, not surprisingly, Woolworth wove into the project architectural and urban decisions informed by such earlier experiences. More generally, he based the project on his thorough understanding—given his role as a retailing innovator—of modern consumer practices.

In studying the origins of the consumer culture in which Woolworth participated, the historians William Leach, Jackson Lears, and Christine Boyer have clarified the culture's values and visual character. During the 1890s, according to Leach, the corporate and institutional proponents of consumer capitalism began to assert their future-oriented "one vision of the good life" against "the earlier traditions of republicanism and Christian virtue" to create the reigning culture of the United States. Leach goes on to identify the cardinal features of this new culture: "acquisition and consumption as a means of achieving happiness; the cult of the new; the democratization of desire; and money value as the predominant measure of all value in society."[8] In a parallel vein, Lears has illuminated the transition from a nineteenth-century producer's ethic, which emphasized thrift, hard work, character, and "authenticity," to a new, twentieth-century consumer's ethic, which emphasized instead fashion and style, superficiality, and "artifice."[9] The new set of values identified with this cultural shift had by the 1870s already begun inscribing itself within New York's built environment, as

Boyer has shown—from Ladies' Mile as a sidewalk setting to major works of commercial and entertainment architecture such as department stores and theaters. Together, this new consumer setting and its architecture engendered an "out-of-doors spectacle" of promenaders, display windows, and advertisements.[10]

Other scholars have examined consumerism's relation to the late nineteenth-century city's emerging mass culture, whether that of the culture's fabricators or that of its participating audiences. According to Vanessa Schwartz, this new culture entailed "mass production by industrial techniques and mass consumption by most of the people, most of the time"—a process that at a "particular cultural moment" turned consumers into spectators. Schwartz contrasts Paris's new "society of spectators" with the city's previously dangerous and potentially violent crowd, an analysis that suggests important parallels for New York.[11] New forms of mass communication such as the daily newspaper became saturated with images, abetted by developments in photography and lithography, allowing the new mass audience to participate visually in a broadly shared and now spectacularized metropolitan culture.[12] Similarly, John Kasson has identified the simultaneous emergence of a mass "cultural upheaval," or revolt, on New York's Coney Island, where the diverse populace of the industrial metropolis achieved through participation in consumer spectacles a new form of social unity by challenging nineteenth-century genteel cultural values.[13] The architect Rem Koolhaas has in a complementary way characterized Coney Island as spectacle of exotic architecture, illusion, electricity, mechanical marvels, and stage-set theatricality, an "urbanism of the fantastic" that served as a "laboratory for Manhattan."[14] Indeed, in New York electric lighting functioned equally spectacularly as a "symbol of modernity." According to David Nye, "promoters and public alike demanded ever-greater public displays" as electric lighting became "a central part of the representation of the city."[15] All point to the vibrant urban culture of mass entertainment, mass spectatorship, and technological theatrics in which Woolworth and his skyscraper both competed and triumphed.

But did these phenomena of consumerism, mass culture, and urban spectatorship have any positive value for architecture? In his work on antebellum New York, Dell Upton has examined the linkages between the city's "economic efflorescence" and the material culture of commodities display, commercial pleasures, and privatized spectacle, showing how the critical examination of such values can deepen our understanding of American architecture as a social and material phenomenon.[16] Another especially instructive and germane example for this study—given that it entails the analysis of a landmark skyscraper in relation to consumerism and the mass phenomena of advertising and newspaper publicity—is Katherine Solomonson's recent examination of the Chicago Tribune Tower competition (1922). Solomonson's subject is a landmark skyscraper built as a competitive challenge to the architectural beauty and renown of the Woolworth Building. Although the Tribune Company's mission differed markedly from that of Woolworth's retailing enterprise, Solomonson's emphasis on how it turned "what might have been a quiet competition for the design of an office building into a spectacle that reached well over a million people" illuminates the ways in which it, too, "engaged in the production of a consumer culture" during the 1920s.[17]

Of greatest importance to this study,

then, is the illumination of the many strategies—some obvious and some subtle—by which the values of New York's vigorous commercial culture inscribed themselves in Woolworth's skyscraper. Woolworth had designed the skyscraper as a setting for office work, to be sure, but soon enough the project evolved under his direction into one of the city's most prominent sites for high-style consumption. Through the project's integration of the newest fashionable consumer enticements—among them an interior shopping arcade, a health club with a swimming pool, a giant barbershop, a restaurant, a proposed downtown club, and a pinnacle observatory—Woolworth's skyscraper provided an evocative architectural setting for his tenants' high-style entertainment and amusement. Earlier, Woolworth had carefully timed his release to the city's newspapers of Cass Gilbert's colorful perspective illustrating the skyscraper's final design, seeking to achieve the greatest media impact. At the skyscraper's completion, he contrived a breathtaking electrical opening using a giant flash of illumination that exploited New York's City Hall Park as a grand setting for spectatorship and printed media publicity. Finally, he promoted the skyscraper's observatory as a sensational tourist attraction. All pointed to a newly powerful role for the skyscraper in the city.

New York's commercial culture exerted a forceful and inescapable influence over Woolworth and Gilbert, but both also aspired to design the Woolworth Building as something higher: an architectural monument of great artistic refinement and beauty, an unassailable Gothic landmark. Woolworth pointed to the Victoria Tower at the Houses of Parliament in London as his model and Gilbert culled from among photographs, etchings, and his own sketches countless Gothic motifs for the skyscraper's ornamental features. While designing the Woolworth Building as what he called "only a skyscraper," Gilbert also envisioned the project as a culturally significant work of Beaux-Arts architecture on the order of his recently completed Minnesota State Capitol and United States Custom House.[18] Among Gilbert's professional contemporaries, "Beaux-Arts" referred to the methods of design and the academic principles espoused by the École des Beaux-Arts in Paris. Historically sanctioned and founded on "composition"—or the ordered disposition of spaces in plan and elevation—Beaux-Arts principles established the basis for the choice of "style."[19] For both Woolworth and Gilbert, then, the skyscraper as a Beaux-Arts monument in the Gothic style, with associations of gentility founded on western European traditions, would serve to legitimize their status socially while also dignifying culturally the alliance between art and capital that their architect-client collaboration represented. If for Woolworth the skyscraper functioned primarily as a conspicuous form of elite, high-style consumption, for Gilbert it proclaimed an architectural commitment, however tentative, to the loftier ideals of urbanity associated with the City Beautiful movement.

Gilbert's effort to create a Beaux-Arts masterpiece within the most commercial of the world's cities raises questions about issues of architectural authenticity. His use of the Gothic for commercial purposes strongly challenged the well-established nexus of nineteenth-century moral and ethical beliefs embedded in the Gothic Revival. In addition, Gilbert employed in the Woolworth Building the respected conventions of mural and sculptural decoration he had used only a few years earlier to craft memorable identities for key institutions of state and national government. Today, it may seem unusual that Gilbert believed Woolworth's enterprise deserved such an association with the Gothic's ethical values, or with the decorated public building's evocations of lofty political ideals. Yet both Gilbert and Woolworth had also attempted to reign in overly spectacular advertising and publicity; in particular, they expressed strong reservations about the popular perceptions of the Woolworth Building as a "cathedral of commerce." Their skyscraper was already a product of the expanding milieu of commodities exchange, display, and advertising and, more generally, of the city's mass culture. But in conceiving it as a Beaux-Arts masterpiece, Gilbert and Woolworth also resisted the forces of sensationalism and spectacle with which they and others strongly identified that milieu.

Woolworth and Gilbert also aspired to build and to publicize the highest skyscraper in the world.[20] As documentation of the project shows, they envisioned the Woolworth Building as the day's most up-to-date work of steel-framed construction, and they prided themselves on commissioning such a modern feat of technology. Gunvald Aus, the project's structural engineer, had proposed inventive solutions for Gilbert's earlier projects. Louis Horowitz, head of the Thompson-Starrett Construction Company, had devised new methods for further rationalizing the construction industry under the single-contract system—with the objective of speed in completing big projects—echoing the modern obsessions with "scientific management" and the standardization of time.[21] Other engineers also contributed the newest expertise, making the Woolworth Building a benchmark in the sophisticated application of a range of innovative building technologies. These included a water supply system incorporating six separate but interconnected subsystems, an independent plant for generating electrical power, high-speed electric elevators providing express and local service, and the first prominent use of architectural floodlighting in the world.[22] Woolworth, furthermore, designed the skyscraper to compete with the city's contemporary and widely noted colossal, innovative works of engineering, among them the Pennsylvania and Grand Central railroad stations and the new IRT and BRT subway systems. The recently completed Singer and Metropolitan Life Insurance towers only fueled his ambition to engineer a still more spectacular feat of steel-framed construction.

Gilbert's designs for the Woolworth Building began at twenty stories but ended up at fifty-five stories. Thomas A. P. van Leeuwen refers to "the lurking presence of the Tower of Babel" as the impetus behind architects' and builders' putting technology in the service of scaling the heavens, or "the realization of ancient dreams and visions."[23] Such an impulse to conquer vertical space, however, can be explained just as compellingly in local historical terms. The obsession with "big spatial ideas," whether vertical or horizontal, marked the contemporary impulse toward imperial expansion.[24] The United States's recent forays into the Pacific and the Carribean mirrored the rise to power of the vigorous corporate economy headquartered in the towering skyscrapers of lower Manhattan, where Wall Street bankers, brokers, and investors set the goal of identifying and securing new foreign outlets for investment.[25] More specifically, Woolworth's interest in undertaking his skyscraper as a bold technological feat reflected the retailing world's longstanding attachment to novel materials, building methods, and inventions—among them iron, plate glass, and electricity.[26] In deploying steel-framed construction and, eventually, electrical illumination for the purpose of achieving height and prominence, Woolworth took to a new level of spectacularization the methods he and other retailers had long ago developed to catch the eye, to stimulate desire, and to theatrically entertain sidewalk crowds.

Whether ennobling the city with a work of art or modernizing it with a technologically marvelous feat of construction, Woolworth adhered to the more pragmatic notion that his skyscraper should function as a solid investment in New York urban real estate. Recently, Carol Willis has stressed the determining influence of the real estate industry on the design of skyscrapers. She has analyzed how widely accepted formulas of real estate finance, along with height and zoning regulations, shaped the two historic centers of skyscraper construction, Chicago and New York.[27] Yet despite the centrality of such economic and legal determinants in shaping the early twentieth-century built environment, this study argues that human aspirations—even those informed by types of market forces other than real estate—played an equally powerful role. Woolworth rigorously adhered to some of the real estate rules and broke others. In the end, he manipulated those rules to create a first-class office building that would by virtue of its height, visual distinction, and other amenities outshine all others in the metropolis. Consequently, Woolworth showed a keener understanding than most speculators of the complex array of market dynamics inciting development and change in the modern city.

If early twentieth-century New York functioned as a kind of urban stage for Woolworth's and Gilbert's ambitious goals, then who composed the audience for the Woolworth Building? Actually, Woolworth intended to reach many audiences, whose individuality and diversity echoed the city's modern, heterogeneous social character. In creating a distinctive, iconic headquarters for F. W. Woolworth and Company, he envisioned one key audience as the corporation's rank and file—his inner circle of executives, store managers, and sales clerks. Woolworth, however, also aimed to advertise. Hence, another key audience comprised his five- and ten-cent stores' shoppers and prospective shoppers, many of whom numbered among New York's and the nation's ethnically varied population of recent immigrants. Finally, he resolved to construct a profitable office building, so a third important audience consisted of the many anticipated tenants who would occupy the skyscraper's office interiors, paying the rents essential to its success as a financial enterprise.

Woolworth, however, also had in mind a much larger, broader, and more diffuse audience. Through publications of various kinds, he envisioned the skyscraper as a form of cultural edification and urban entertainment for New Yorkers and visitors to the city alike—at the very moment the city emerged as one of the world's leading tourist centers. The publications ranged from the high-toned *Woolworth Building*, which featured an essay by the noted architectural critic Montgomery Schuyler, to publicity booklets such as the popular *Cathedral of Commerce*, with an introduction by the noted Methodist clergyman S. Parkes Cadman, and the guide written specifically for tourists, *Above the Clouds and Old New York*.[28] In these publications and others, Woolworth presented his skyscraper to audiences both high and low as one of the city's finest works of art and most spectacular sites for visitation.

My most basic working assumption as a historian is that architectural issues cannot be separated from urban issues—especially when the subject is the skyscraper. In this study, I bring together tools of analysis from both architectural and urban history to construct a narrative illuminating the Woolworth Building's planning, design, construction, and reception in early twentieth-century New York—a cradle of consumerism, mass culture, and modernity—and beyond. The narrative describes, as Neil Harris has put it, the "life" of the building from birth to maturity.[29] It is divided into three sequential stages. In the first part (chaps. 1 and 2), I analyze Woolworth's objectives for his skyscraper, his choice of a site on Broadway at City Hall Park, formation of a partnership with Irving National Exchange Bank, and choice of Gilbert as the project's architect. All were inflected by his retailing practices and by the visually competitive commercial environment of early twentieth-century New York. In the second part (chaps. 3–5), I assess Gilbert's Beaux-Arts imagery, his distinctive approach to the skyscraper, and his responses to the visual dynamics of New York's spectatorial and printed-publicity-oriented urban environment. As the skyscraper's construction begins, I show how Louis Horowitz of the Thompson-Starrett Company rationalized the process, set a record for speed, and evaded labor conflict—all of which facilitated the project's completion but also served Woolworth's aim of spectacularization with the well-timed theatrics of the world's highest skyscraper. The third part of the book (chaps. 6 and 7) describes and analyzes the completed Woolworth Building—how tenants used, experienced, and perceived the skyscraper as a place of work and a fantasy setting for a European-inspired, cosmopolitan, and high-style form of consumption, and how Woolworth promoted it as a "cathedral of commerce." It also examines the skyscraper's reception, that is, its contribution to the contemporary processes of perceiving, understanding, and investing the urban experience with meaning. This includes the skyscraper's afterlife as a trademark, a putative catalyst for community at New York's civic center, a heroic feat of technology rivaling the Eiffel Tower, a site conducive to modern viewing experiences, and an emblem in the imaging of the world's first "signature skyline."

The human presence behind the design, construction, and reception of Woolworth's skyscraper strongly informs this account of the life of the building.[30] In addition to Woolworth and Gilbert, the project's key collaborators included Gilbert's chief designer, Thomas R. Johnson, the structural engineer Gunvald Aus, the builder Louis Horowitz, the real estate agent Edward Hogan, and the publicity agent Hugh McAtamney. Among the project's minor collaborators numbered the draftsmen working in Gilbert's office, those working in Aus's office and for the Atlantic Terra Cotta Company, and immigrant craftsmen such as John Donnelly and Elisio V. Ricci, who modeled the building's stone, terra cotta, and copper ornamentation. This presence also included the building's tenants, a diverse white-collar population of professionals, entrepreneurs, governmental institutions, and businesses large and small; the range of critics who assessed Gilbert's design as a work of architectural art, a feat of technology, and a distinctive visual feature in the modern city; and the array of avant-garde painters and photographers that perceived in the Woolworth Building's modernity evocations of a future twentieth-century world.

The question of whether the Woolworth Building is, indeed, a great work of architecture may still be open to debate. Yet Woolworth and Gilbert's project represented in the eyes of contemporaries more than a vulgar contraption for producing a profit, and more than a dubious expression of corporate power, egregious advertising, or an aggressive assault on New York's new signature skyline. Subsequent accounts of the building focused on formal criteria—with these shifting from the Beaux-Arts appreciation for composition to the modernist touchstones of structure and function, then for a moment back again. Today's historian, however, seeks explanations for the modern that reach beyond such criteria to integrate analyses of material conditions, cultural processes, and social relations and experiences. Consequently, the Woolworth Building's importance, it could be argued, resides not simply in its aesthetic distinction, but rather in its capacity to shine a light on New York's broader historical context: A brilliant cynosure for the modernity of its times, it reflected and refracted the many dreams and obsessions of the urban society that produced it.

CHAPTER ONE

Woolworth's Skyscraper

Reportedly, Frank Woolworth built his skyscraper to house the executive offices of F. W. Woolworth and Company in New York. In actuality, however, the amount of space the company's headquarters' functions required was minimal—only a single story in what would eventually become a skyscraper of fifty-five stories. The real explanation for Woolworth's skyscraper lies elsewhere, and is complex, but one thing is certain: Woolworth aspired to build a spectacular urban landmark. The landmark, for which he chose Cass Gilbert as the architect, would serve a range of personal and business purposes. It would be a testimonial to Woolworth's power as a merchant in America's new mass consumer economy, the capital of a recently incorporated international retailing empire, and a work of flamboyant architectural advertising directed toward New York's newly spectatorial sidewalk crowds.[1] Woolworth shrewdly exploited the dynamics of New York's real estate market as the mere expedient for achieving these grander, theatrical ends. The market would provide the practical excuse as well as the financial wherewithal for raising a skyscraper on so impractical a scale.

Woolworth's aspirations for his skyscraper were bound up with his entrepreneurial objectives as an American retailing innovator. With his five- and ten-cent store he modernized American shopping practices, providing consumers with new types of commodities at bargain prices, and through his chain of stores he promoted the late nineteenth century's rising culture of consumerism.[2] From the scale of the individual store interior to the larger geographic landscape of the towns and cities in which he chose to locate his stores, Woolworth strategically assessed by trial and error the functional contribution of both architectural and urban criteria to the vitality of his consumer enterprise. In shaping the built environment with his stores, Woolworth responded on the one hand to clear-cut merchandising needs: He identified well-traveled locations on the main streets of towns and cities, and he arranged store interiors to maximize the display and sale of his commodities. Equally important, however, Woolworth contrived an array of visual strategies for advertising those commodities—comprising storefronts, show windows, trademarks, and signs. With these, he aimed to attract the eye of the sidewalk spectator, to create a consistent identity for his chain, and to inspire consumer loyalty.

Beyond the catalog of architectural and urban strategies that Woolworth deployed in the design and siting of his stores, his perspective on consumer practices implicated itself in the skyscraper in countless subtler and more intricate ways. From the first Woolworth Building in Lancaster, Pennsylvania, to the music room of his Fifth Avenue chateau, Woolworth manipulated the boundaries between the nineteenth century's genteel conceptions of art and architecture and his own passion for theater and spectacle. As an indefatigable tourist, he sought out notable works of high-style architecture on his European buying trips. But he also orchestrated store openings as popular theatrical entertainments and celebrated the growth of his enterprise with dazzling commemorative extravaganzas. The full range of Woolworth's early experiences as a merchant, then, would be of the highest importance to the creation of his spectacular landmark skyscraper—not only for how he conceived it as a work of architecture, but also for how he envisioned its role within the twentieth-century metropolis.

The Commercial Architecture of F. W. Woolworth and Company

In 1919, Woolworth called his new landmark skyscraper a "monument to the Woolworth business," the enterprise that he had built from a single five- and ten-cent store into a $65 million multinational private stock corporation in a little more than three decades.[3] In a similar vein, one New York journalist called the skyscraper a "fitting crown to a remarkable career."[4] The chronicle of Woolworth's retailing career, recounted innumerable times by both him and contemporary writers, echoed the rags-to-riches narrative of the day's popular Horatio Alger stories. Alger's "rags," did, in fact, signify Woolworth's simple rural background. Woolworth's parents, John Hubbell Woolworth and Fanny McBrier Woolworth were farmers, as their ancestors had been.[5] According to his younger brother, Charles Sumner Woolworth, the "struggle to make ends meet was never absent."[6] The Alger-inspired biographers further suggested the centrality of character traits such as thrift and honesty to Woolworth's attainment of "riches." Such traits may have been grounded in Woolworth's Methodist upbringing, the influence of which he later acknowledged, writing that he held his Sunday school teacher, Emery J. Pennock, "in affection and regard for life . . . his example has done more good than is generally realized."[7] Regardless of the Alger-inspired biographers' view, however, there existed a strong parallel between Woolworth's rapid ascent as a merchant and the equally rapid growth of the United States during the 1880s and 1890s as a wealthy, urbanized, consumption-oriented society. It is within such a changing social context that Woolworth cultivated his shoppers' desires and sought their loyalty as consumers.

MAIN STREET AND THE FIVE- AND TEN-CENT STORE

Woolworth's conviction that goods should literally "sell themselves" would be of greatest importance to his founding of the five- and ten-cent store. All of Woolworth's early employers—Augsbury and Moore, A. Bushnell and Company, and Moore and Smith—had instantly recognized him as an outstandingly inept salesman. Woolworth, as a consequence, appreciated the significance of the "five-cent counter craze," about which he heard during the late 1870s; it demonstrated that the traditional shopkeeper had little relation to the counter's volume of sales. If instead goods were simply placed on the counter with a sign reading "five cents," consumers flocked to the goods. That flocking, along with the goods' visual appeal and five-cent price, stimulated spontaneous purchases. Woolworth's favorite employer, William Harvey Moore, tried out the counter in Watertown, New York during fall 1878.[8] Woolworth decided shortly afterward that if the five-cent idea worked for a counter, it might also work for a store: "Naturally some of Moore & Smith's clerks got the fever, and I was one of them. Day after day and week after week I saw the five-cent tide grow. Every train brought buyers from the surrounding towns. And it fired me with a desire to get into the game myself."[9] Two years earlier, Woolworth had married the seamstress Jennie Creighton, of Ontario, Canada. In early 1878, the young couple's first child, Helena, was born. Later that year, Woolworth's mother died. Yet despite the highs and lows in his personal life, Woolworth's determination never wavered. He relentlessly forged ahead with his plan. He opened his first five-cent store in Utica, New York, in January 1879.

From the start, Woolworth recognized the importance of choosing the right location for a store, which for him meant the right town or city, the right street, and the right address. He identified Utica after exploring potential sites for stores in Syracuse, Rochester, Auburn, and Rome. He observed Utica's pedestrian traffic and then chose a thirteen-by-twenty-foot space in the Arcade Building on Bleecker Street in February 1879. The store thrived during the first few weeks, but over a period of four months, Woolworth noticed a pattern of steadily declining sales. Woolworth closed the store in May, attributing its failure to a fault in his observational skills: He had in fact sited the store off the beat of the town's heaviest pedestrian traffic.[10]

Within a month, Woolworth made a new attempt at implementing his five-cent idea in a second location, Lancaster, Pennsylvania, selecting a deep, fourteen-by-thirty-five-foot space near the Pennsylvania Railroad depot on 170 North Queen Street (fig. 1.1). Lancaster, a manufacturing and agricultural center, had attracted him because of its "amazing air of business and prosperity." Woolworth further observed that the store's part of town had a liveliness of street traffic contrasting with that of his former Utica site. "The plain people who wore Quaker's garb or the black of Shakers," moreover, "knew the value of a nickel."[11] Woolworth signed a lease for the new retailing space, began paying thirty dollars a month in rent, and employed three clerks at $1.50 per week.[12] He supplemented his old Utica stock of utilitarian objects, most of it "Yankee notions," with

FIGURE 1.1 Woolworth's Five and Ten Cent Store, Lancaster, Pennsylvania, 1879, exterior. Unidentified photographer. Woolworth Collection, National Building Museum.

fresh purchases to create a new stock, some twenty thousand items in all, among them recently available, inexpensive, and enticing commodities: fire shovels, boot blacking, jelly cake tins, school book straps, tin pepper boxes, police whistles, pencils, and "turkey red" napkins.[13] Woolworth's Lancaster store instantly turned a profit and over a period of several months continued to thrive. Woolworth had developed a viable formula for choosing store locations: First, he identified a town with a prospering economy, and second, he chose a visible site on a well-traveled main street within the commercial heart of that town.

The success of Woolworth's Lancaster experiment can also be credited to his methods of heightening the visual allure and seeming availability of his low-priced commodities among a main street's sidewalk crowds. In doing so, Woolworth broke with the practices of what he and others called "the old country store" in two important ways. First, following the example of the "five-cent counter craze," he displayed goods temptingly on open tables rather than consigning them to storage out of sight behind inaccessible counters. Second, he sold those goods for a standardized fixed cash price, rather than expecting customers to bargain with clerks over prices. For lessons on standardized fixed cash prices, Woolworth looked to the big urban dry goods stores.[14] A. T. Stewart had used standardized prices in his New York stores from the early 1820s and eventually in his Marble Palace, and John Wanamaker had done the same in his Grand Depot in Philadelphia, which opened in 1876. Woolworth's pricing strategy, however, entailed not only selling goods at a fixed cash price, but also showcasing them within a standardized single-price store.[15] By 1880, Woolworth had elaborated upon his single price strategy, adding a new ten-cent line at a new store in Scranton, Pennsylvania, now making his stores a standardized two-price phenomenon. The ten-cent line brought still greater variety to Woolworth's stock, thereby increasing the illusion—and hence consumer appeal—of a more diversified array of inexpensively priced commodities.

Woolworth publicly expressed his ambition to create a chain of five- and ten-cent stores the day he opened his first successful store in Lancaster. "Were I to let myself dream," he told a local reporter, "I could visualize a whole chain of Woolworth stores someday."[16] Aiming to become as prosperous as large department store merchants such as A. T. Stewart or John Wanamaker, Woolworth envisioned expanding geographically by locating multiple outlets for his low-priced commodities on the main streets of several towns and cities. Given his objective of selling a lot for a very little, such a chain of stores would function as an efficient instrument for producing a wider diversity of commodities at bargain prices, for supporting a still larger "stock turn," and, as a consequence, for generating still larger profits.[17] Rather than expecting his customers to seek out a single large store in a big city, then, Woolworth—in the spirit of a true mass retailer—instead would take his stores to the people. Through enticingly exhibiting his commodities on main streets, he would "create" demand. In conceiving his chain, Woolworth followed the example of George Huntington Hartford, the founder along with George F. Gilman of the Great Atlantic and Pacific Tea Company in 1859. By 1880, Hartford owned a chain of approximately one hundred grocery stores between Norfolk, Virginia, and St. Paul, Minnesota. Woolworth's chain in turn inspired competitors, among them S. H. Kress and Sebastian S.

Kresge, in 1896 and 1899.[18] Still, he would be the first to engage in mass retailing practices on the scale that came to typify the twentieth-century chains.

Within a month after opening his Lancaster store, Woolworth attempted to implement his chain idea. He began by evaluating sites on the main streets of neighboring small towns. In July 1879 he negotiated a lease in Harrisburg, Pennsylvania, in collaboration with his brother, Charles Sumner Woolworth. The Harrisburg store failed eight months later, however, and Woolworth then continued to fail repeatedly in his attempts to expand into other towns and cities in Pennsylvania. A store that he eventually sold to his brother in Scranton, a small industrial city dominated by the Lackawanna Iron and Coal Company, thrived briefly but then numbered among the failures. Finally, in 1884, Woolworth established a profitable store in Reading, another center of iron production and manufacturing, this time in partnership with his cousin Seymour Horace Knox. Altogether, it had taken Woolworth five years to discover by trial and error that his greatest challenge involved finding the right locations for his stores—not only the right city or town, but also the right street and right address.

During the mid-1880s, Woolworth continued to refine his observations of the economic vigor of various town and city locations, of real estate values, and of street traffic: "From that time on, I got ahead so rapidly that actually, it made me dizzy. I have never been able to fully realize how rapidly I was making money. I couldn't tell you myself how it is that my stores have increased in number. When my bank first notified me that my cash balance had reached $50,000, I could hardly believe it."[19] Woolworth opened two more profitable stores in 1885 and three more in 1886. By the end of 1886, he owned a total of eight stores along with Knox and other partners. That year, he set up a headquarters and central buying office in New York for the Woolworth Syndicate of Stores.

From his New York headquarters, Woolworth increased the size of his chain at a steady pace throughout the late 1880s and early 1890s. The chain rapidly took shape geographically as a pattern of widely scattered units located in the Northeast, and by 1891 in the South, after Woolworth opened stores in Richmond and Norfolk, Virginia. Woolworth continued to hone his methods of selecting locations for stores. In 1889, for example, he analyzed United States census figures to determine more accurately the growth of selected towns and cities and then made a list of one hundred possible new locations.[20] Woolworth initially acted in New York as the Woolworth Syndicate's principal buyer and chief financial officer. Functioning as an absentee owner, he chose trustworthy men to open, supply the capital for, partly own, and manage each of his stores—creating a "partner-manager system." Many were friends and relations from the vicinity of Watertown, beginning with Knox at the Reading store in 1884. Woolworth quickly discovered, however, that these partner-managers might also become his future competitors. Consequently, in 1888, after accumulating enough of his own capital, he sold his interest in the stores he owned with Knox and replaced the original partner-manager system with a profit-sharing system.[21]

By 1895, Woolworth had become the owner and sole proprietor of a chain of twenty-five stores in the Northeast and the South with annual sales of more than $1 million, among them a store in Worcester, Massachusetts (fig. 1.2). Once he had established himself securely in such a geo-

FIGURE 1.2 *(left)* F. W. Woolworth and Company, Five and Ten Cent Store, Worcester, Massachusetts, view of ca. 1910. Photograph by Herbert L. Green. Woolworth Collection, National Building Museum.

FIGURE 1.3 *(right)* F. W. Woolworth and Company, Five and Ten Cent Store, Brooklyn, New York, view of ca. 1910. Unidentified photographer. Woolworth Collection, National Building Museum.

graphically broad array of small cities and towns, he felt financially secure in competing with the department stores of big cities. That year, he launched the first of his two "big city" stores in Washington, D.C., followed by a store in Brooklyn, New York (fig. 1.3). By 1900, Woolworth's chain comprised fifty-nine stores, with sales of more than $5 million.

Of instrumental consequence to his expansion geographically, Woolworth aimed to thoroughly control and to dominate the production and distribution of his many five- and ten-cent commodities. First, he drove prices down by squeezing out his middleman competitors, or jobbers, and buying directly from manufacturers, a practice already in place at midcentury in dry goods stores connected with wholesaling operations such as A. T. Stewart.[22] To facilitate this objective, he developed his own buying organization. Second, he arranged exclusive one-year contracts with manufacturers, beginning in 1887 with D. Arnould, a candy maker, and Bernard Wilmsen, a fabricator of Christmas tree ornaments, while also ruthlessly negotiating lower prices.[23] At the same time, he convinced those manufacturers to employ time-saving processes and new mechanical devices to standardize and increase the production of items from hardware to white china cups and saucers. Through his control of production and distribution networks, Woolworth was able to acquire a still wider diversity of commodities at still lower prices, and to ship them in greater volume to the multiplying outlets of his chain (fig. 1.4). Woolworth, then, had engaged in an aggressive form of vertical integration, one of the two characteristic patterns—the other being horizontal

FIGURE 1.4
F. W. Woolworth and Company, Five and Ten Cent Store, Minneapolis, Minnesota, second story of interior, view of ca. 1910. Photograph by C. J. Hibbard. Woolworth Collection, National Building Museum.

integration—that facilitated the rise of big business in the late nineteenth-century United States.[24]

Determined to implement his mass retailing practices on a still grander scale, both geographically and financially, Woolworth shortly after 1900 adopted a policy of acquiring the smaller chains of competitors. Woolworth's strongest competitors, J. G. McCrory, Kresge, and Kress, the latter with twelve stores, refused to be acquired and held their ground. Meanwhile, Woolworth purchased several five- and ten-cent chains from various owners in the East, the Midwest, and the West—among them Pfohl and Smith, S. D. Rider, and George B. Carey—to create an enlarged retailing "empire" of 120 stores. In February 1905, he incorporated F. W. Woolworth and Company.[25] By the time he proposed the Woolworth Building as his New York headquarters in 1910, Woolworth had either founded himself or acquired almost 300 stores in varying locations throughout all regions of the United States, including the Far West and, beginning in 1909, in his first transatlantic location—England (fig. 1.5).

Altogether, Woolworth's entrepreneurial method of building up his geographically expansive retailing empire—the development of the five- and ten-cent idea, the exploitation of the idea through a chain, the squeezing out of his middleman competitors for the purpose of controlling goods manufacturing and distribution, and finally, his acquisition of competitors' chains—resulted in his reorganization, and eventually, in his dominance of the entire low-priced segment of the American retailing industry.[26] Woolworth later credited the success of his entrepreneurial strategies to his vigorous pursuit of "one idea" and to his own "broad view of things."[27] Just as crucially, however, the large-scale structural changes occurring within the nation's economy provided a favorable environment for Woolworth. First, the United States had experienced its own version of the international "great depression" between 1873 and 1896, with a continual pattern of falling prices brought about by declining costs of production.[28] As a consequence, Woolworth could purchase still greater quantities of "large and fine goods" for his stores at still lower prices. This he frankly acknowledged; his business secured a solid financial foothold precisely at the moment economic conditions became depressed and troublesome for everyone else, and especially during the financial panic of 1893.[29] Second, the large-scale revolutions in transportation and communication—supported by the completion in the mid-1890s of the nation's far-flung railroad and, before that, of its telegraphic infrastructure—facilitated Woolworth's expansion of goods production and distribution.[30] Consequently, Woolworth and his main street five- and ten-cent stores, along with the enterprises of other mass retailers who prospered during the 1890s, among them big department stores such as Wanamaker's and Siegel-Cooper's and large mail order houses such as Sears Roebuck and Company and Montgomery Ward's, were enmeshed in a larger trend of vigorous economic and infrastructural expansion.[31] This expansion, in turn, was feeding the fastest-growing mass consumer market of all industrial nations.[32]

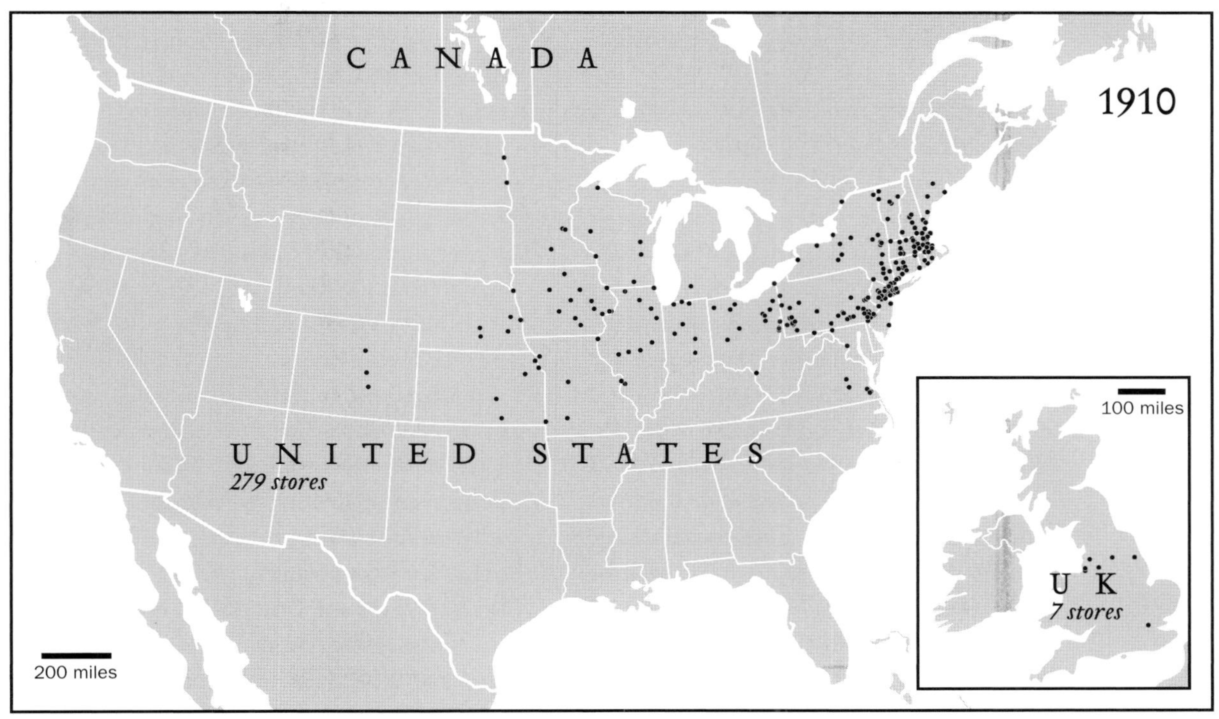

FIGURE 1.5 Location of Woolworth stores, national headquarters, and district headquarters in the United States, Canada, and England, 1910. Map by Dennis McClendon.

THE HEADQUARTERS AS AN URBAN LANDMARK

Woolworth's decision to build in celebration of his dominant position as a retailer within America's new mass consumer economy constituted the most obvious of personal reasons for his skyscraper. Just as important, however, he incorporated F. W. Woolworth in 1905 and that year developed an executive hierarchy to manage the new corporate structure. Woolworth's skyscraper, as a consequence, would also serve as a powerful persuasive tool for promoting the identity of the corporation among the members of this executive hierarchy, and in turn among store managers and store employees. Between 1906 and 1908, Woolworth continued to shape and to refine the hierarchy, adding a new managerial layer at the regional level to streamline the coordination of his ever more widely dispersed chain of stores. All of Woolworth's decisions facilitated the rapid maturing of a corporate character that before 1910 had come into increasingly sharper focus. Each would have important implications for the architecture of his skyscraper headquarters in New York.

In creating the new F. W. Woolworth and Company, Woolworth legally established a $10 million privately held stock corporation.[33] He and his inner circle of executives controlled half the stock, or the common stock, and the other half Woolworth offered at par to store managers and selected employees as preferred stock. Woolworth told his executives and managers that incorporation insured the permanency of the five- and ten-cent business.[34] In fact, Woolworth and other mass retailers had identified in the corporation the supreme mechanism for generating capital—through the shared ownership of stock—and, consequently, for augmenting profits. The corporation's administrative efficiencies, furthermore, would facilitate Woolworth's squeezing out of competition, allowing his firmer control over the prices and the production of commodities along with the cost of labor.[35] Both, in turn, solidified his position of dominance in the mass retailing industry, auguring his enterprise's continued profitability and continued growth.

Woolworth's decision to incorporate suggested a commensurate architectural identity for the new F. W. Woolworth and Company's headquarters in New York. Woolworth, consequently, undertook in 1905 an ambitious program of improvement in his offices in the Stewart Building at 280 Broadway (fig. 1.6). Formerly the famous A. T. Stewart Department Store (Joseph Trench and Company, 1845–46), the Stewart Building had functioned as a distinctive downtown office building after its renovation and addition of two new stories in 1884.[36] Woolworth had already relocated his headquarters to the Chambers Street side of the Stewart Building from the Reade Street side in 1892. In 1905, however, Woolworth relocated once again, moving his offices from the Stewart Building's second story to its fifth story. Woolworth's new offices had an impressive lobby, a luxurious paneled suite for himself with teak floors and gilded mahogany furniture, and large offices adjacent to his own for his inner circle of executives. As F. W. Woolworth and Company's chief executive, moreover, Woolworth aimed to secure from his office a sweeping view—today's "power view"—embracing the broad expanse of City Hall Park and the skyscrapers of lower Manhattan beyond.

Altogether, F. W. Woolworth and Company's new headquarters comprised five rooms in the Stewart Building, which it secured at an annual rental rate of $6,150.

FIGURE 1.6 A. T. Stewart Building, 280 Broadway, view north from Chambers Street, New York, ca. 1850. Lithograph published by Henry Hoff. Collection of the New-York Historical Society, negative 878.

Woolworth expected to impress every visitor with what he described as his new corporation's "system" and "magnificence."[37] In doing so, he identified with A. T. Stewart and his legendary dry goods store, or Marble Palace, the most opulent in mid-nineteenth-century New York. Yet Woolworth also argued to his managers that the headquarters' sudden opulence indeed reflected sound financial practice. It showed those with whom the company negotiated—manufacturers, bankers, and salesmen—that they had entered the realm of a "successful and important concern." F. W. Woolworth and Company, furthermore, sold goods to the wealthy "carriage trade" as well as to the middle classes, so it no longer could be considered a "cheap John affair."[38]

F. W. Woolworth and Company continued to expand after Woolworth had incorporated, and within a period of five years, the volume of its sales doubled. The growth in the company's administrative and supporting staff—managers and buyers, typists, bill clerks, and bookkeepers—paralleled this rapid financial growth. To accommodate the new personnel, Woolworth added more office space within the Stewart Building. By 1909, his headquarters housed a workforce of sixty. Among the newest members of the staff were a financial manager, several more buyers, both domestic and foreign, more bookkeepers, inspectors of stores, and a sizable force of stenographers.[39] Woolworth, as a consequence, drove up his yearly rental payments.[40] Such a program of rapid internal expansion, along with Woolworth's growing concern for the image of his headquarters, provided the most compelling reasons for constructing his skyscraper as a landmark headquarters in 1910.

If incorporating F. W. Woolworth and Company caused Woolworth to focus on the architecture of his Stewart Building headquarters, then his related decision of 1906 to build up his executive hierarchy with an additional layer of eight "district superintendents" suggested architectural changes of a wholly different order. Woolworth placed the superintendents in charge of regional groupings of stores, housing them in eight new regional subheadquarters.[41] By 1908, he had leased space for the subheadquarters in prominent office blocks in Manhattan, Buffalo, Boston, Wilkes-Barre, Chicago, St. Louis, San Francisco, and Toronto, including offices in the Railway Exchange Building in Chicago.[42] The regional subheadquarters served the purpose of administratively buttressing the company's executive headquarters in New York. Given the chain's unwieldiness due to rapid expansion, Woolworth aimed to bring a new order to the operation of his 189 stores scattered across the United States, with annual sales of $20 million.

Woolworth's corporate hierarchy traced origins back to 1890, when Woolworth hired a right-hand man, Carson Peck, to work on designing a pattern of promotion from within the company, to ensure the proper training of store managers and executives.[43] Over subsequent years, the pattern crystallized as a pyramidal hierarchy of men. The hierarchy stepped upward from the lowest tier, that of the stockroom boys who unpacked goods in the store basement as "learners," or apprentices, to the next tier of assistant store managers. The store managers occupied a higher tier still, and were allocated approximately 25 per cent of a store's total profits. Near the top of the hierarchy stood the corporation's new regional executives, who received a fixed percentage of profits from several stores. The corporation's inner circle of executives claimed the hierarchy's apex. Headquartered in New York, they split among themselves a fixed percentage of the corporation's total profits.

Woolworth for the most part excluded women from his corporate hierarchy—regardless of their importance to the day-to-day functioning of his stores. Two exceptions to the rule were Mary Ann Creighton, Woolworth's sister-in-law, and Mrs. A. E. Coons, who had formerly worked with Woolworth at Moore and Smith's in Watertown. Woolworth had selected both women as store managers before 1889; he seemed willing to professionally accommodate those with whom he had established close personal relationships. Otherwise, "men only," Woolworth advised his male store managers, should be trained as future managers.[44] If Woolworth had faith in his own ability to choose women for such positions, he had little faith in theirs. Not surprisingly, Woolworth promoted "men only" to the executive levels of the corporation's hierarchy, creating an inner circle that functioned independently from the "domestic" realm of the stores. The vast sums of money available through profit sharing provided a fail-safe incentive for the male manager's upward climb.[45] Woolworth conceived the company's managerial structure as having a boundless future, given the certainty of continuing profits. He could "leave it for a day or forever and it would go on and on."[46]

Woolworth carefully selected his white-collar store managers—as he put it, he "could always size up a man at a glance."[47] He also worked tirelessly among those managers to inculcate a strongly sales-oriented corporate culture. Beginning in the mid-1890s, Woolworth called his managers "one big united family."[48] He cultivated a collective identity through his national "store conventions," which actually functioned as managerial training seminars, the first of which he held in Darlington, New Jersey, in 1894, and through his regularly issued "General Letter to All Stores."[49] The letters he wrote by hand and then had typed, multigraphed, and mailed every two to three days from his New York headquarters, beginning in 1886. After the turn of the century, Woolworth further cultivated such a shared managerial identity through the staging of dazzling commemorative celebrations. A reception and dinner he held in Utica in 1904, "The First Five and Ten Cent Store: Twenty-Fifth Anniversary of Its Formation Properly Celebrated," stood out for the publicity it received. The celebration featured talks by Woolworth and his original employer, W. H. Moore, beneath a large *W* illuminated with electric lights.[50]

After Woolworth began creating the F. W. Woolworth and Company's new regional hierarchy in 1906, he also began holding special regional training seminars in addition to the regularly held, nationally oriented "store conventions."[51] The seminars, together with the subheadquarters housed in prominent office blocks, brought considerable attention to the corporation's new regional tier. As a consequence, it began to overshadow the company's national headquarters in New York—its center of command and "home." The latter remained buried in the low and unassertive mass of the Stewart Building. Recreating F. W. Woolworth and Company's national headquarters as a skyscraper, that is, as a visually salient vertical landmark, would return its executive office to its formerly unchallenged position of prominence.

Woolworth's decision in 1909 to open a chain of five-and-tens in England, beginning with a store in Liverpool, served as the final event that crystallized the new F. W. Woolworth and Company's corporate identity. By 1890, Woolworth envisioned the five-and-ten as a lucrative novelty on foreign shores.[52] He could establish his English "three-and-sixpence stores," however, only after the world "shrank," that is, after the passenger-carrying steamships of the 1880s began making the trip across the Atlantic in five to six days and the transatlantic telegraphic cable began functioning reliably in 1886.[53] Later, Woolworth would boast about his desire "to open a store in every civilized town throughout the world."[54] Such dreams of global conquest epitomized Alexis de Tocqueville's earlier observation that what ambitious men in a democracy "most covet is empire."[55] Woolworth had already asserted that America, although "hardly out of her swaddling clothes," would with a little time "rule the world."[56]

In the larger sense, Woolworth's effort to expand internationally could be considered part of what the historian Eric Hobsbawm has called the "confident conquest of the globe by the capitalist economy," which came to an end with World War I.[57] Woolworth and other American capitalists, supported by official government policy, had aggressively opened up foreign markets, seeking through such access to expand the scale and profitability of their enterprises. In 1909, President William Howard Taft reorganized the State Department to make it an "efficient instrument" for furthering foreign trade and American expansion abroad, following the United States Navy's seizure of Cuba, Puerto Rico, and the Philippines during the Spanish-American War of 1898.[58] Still, F. W. Woolworth and Company had numbered among the last to spearhead the "American invasion" overseas. In the mid-1860s, the Singer Manufacturing Company had established branch offices in Germany and Sweden. Singer was followed by the Western Union Telegraph Company, Bell Telephone, General Electric, Standard Oil, and, in the mid-1880s, the insurance industry's "big three," the Equitable, the Mutual, and the New York Life insurance companies. By World War I, American corporate enterprise had become a formidable presence abroad.[59] Like the industrial and service enterprises preceding him, Woolworth had identified in the foreign markets future outlets for the sale of his commodities, surpluses of which had been generated through the newly industrialized processes of production. Both he and they catered to—and stimulated—foreign consumer demand.

Woolworth's vision of F. W. Woolworth and Company as an international retailing empire also resonated with the identity he crafted for himself as an American business entrepreneur. This identity derived from the mythology he and contemporaries in business fabricated around Napoleon Bonaparte—whom Ralph Waldo Emerson described as the "representative" for America and Europe's "class of business men," or "the young and poor who have fortunes to make"—and Napoleon's French Empire.[60] During Woolworth's youth, stories about Joseph Bonaparte, Napoleon's exiled older brother and former king of Spain and the Indies, circulated in the Watertown area. Seeking refuge in America, Bonaparte settled in "North Country" in 1818, about twenty-five miles northeast of Watertown. There, he and lesser Bonapartist expatriates built at least four houses on four hundred thousand acres near today's Lake Bonaparte. According to the local stories, the houses functioned as brilliantly furnished settings for Bonaparte's private entertainments, hunting expeditions, and gondola trips on the lake. Woolworth reportedly visited the houses, being especially impressed by the house of Joseph Bonaparte's American wife, Annette Savage. This may have compelled him to read a biography of Napoleon.[61]

Whatever the origins of Woolworth's personal fascination with Napoleon, it is clear that shortly after conceiving his retailing enterprise as a chain, he had begun modeling his career on that of the French emperor. Fellow members of New York's Hardware Club, it was rumored, affectionately called Woolworth the "Napoleon of Commerce," even though Woolworth, who was tall, did not at all resemble Napoleon in stature.[62] Later, the builder Louis Horowitz spoke frankly of Woolworth's "kingly affliction."[63] On his buying trips in Europe, Woolworth made a point of visiting sights associated with Napoleon's military conquests or architectural ambitions. In 1890, for example, he toured Napoleon's battlefields at Leipzig, Jena, and Ulm; the emperor's Paris projects, the Arc de Triomphe and the Madeleine; the Coronation Room and Battle Gallery at Versailles; and the Schönbrunn palace and gardens in Vienna. Woolworth's pursuit of what he called "the scenes of Napoleon" culminated in a visit to the emperor's tomb, housed within the Dome des Invalides in Paris, which he described as "situated in a beautiful part of the city . . .

magnificent; no expense had been saved whatsoever."[64] Even Woolworth openly admitted to his admiration for Napoleon, "the man who has probably done more and accomplished more than any other one man in the world."[65] Woolworth further argued—like many chiefs of America's earliest corporations—that F. W. Woolworth and Company's corporate hierarchy had the strategic efficiencies of a military organization. He viewed selecting middle and top managers as a matter of finding "able lieutenants" and "good generals."[66] Equally significant, the trajectory of Woolworth's entrepreneurial career offered a vivid parallel to that of Napoleon's—each had risen from humble origins to command a vast empire of his own making.

By 1910, then, Woolworth had envisioned a landmark skyscraper that would serve to identify a rapidly maturing, more rigidly hierarchical, still continually expanding, and newly international corporate enterprise. He and his Napoleonic brigade had carved out one of the nation's—and the world's—most expansive retailing empires. By constructing such a landmark in New York, Woolworth would be responding not only to external expectations, but also to F. W. Woolworth and Company's internal needs. He would be forging an imperial identity with the goals of both national and international visibility in mind.

ARCHITECTURE AS ADVERTISING

F. W. Woolworth and Company's new skyscraper had another important purpose to fulfill, beyond that of calling attention to Woolworth's dominance of the five- and ten-cent retailing industry and establishing a salient corporate identity. It would also function as a showy piece of architectural promotion, or as he told a contemporary, a "giant signboard to advertise around the world his spreading chain of five- and ten-cent stores."[67] As such, the skyscraper had to be competitive and publicity seeking, a work of architecture designed for the sake of conspicuous architectural display. Woolworth later recalled that the 612-foot Singer Tower, completed in 1908 as the world's tallest skyscraper, "gave me an idea"; while traveling in Europe, he heard business associates talking excitedly about the tower's effectiveness as advertising (fig. 1.7).[68] The crowns of such towers—here a showy French Second Empire mansard recalling Visconti and Lefuel's "new" Louvre in Paris—functioned on the skyline like trademarks.[69] The Singer Manufacturing Company, like Woolworth's enterprise, had an important relationship to maintain with the millions of consumers who purchased sewing machines in both domestic and foreign markets.

Building a skyscraper for the purpose of advertising a chain of stores before a broad urban populace might have been expected of Woolworth. He and his managers had long relied on storefronts and show windows to advertise the bargain-priced commodities from which the company's substantial profits derived: "You can pull customers into your stores and they won't know it. Draw them in with attractive window displays and when you get them in have a plentiful showing of the window goods on the counters. . . . Remember our advertisements are in our show windows and on our counters."[70] Woolworth had, furthermore, meticulously documented the growth of American towns and cities, in effect creating his own census, concluding that more sidewalk shoppers had more money to spend on the consumption of goods.[71] Some twenty-three million new

FIGURE 1.7
Ernest Flagg, Singer Tower, New York, 1906–8. Rendering by Hughson Hawley. Collection of the New-York Historical Society, negative 64107.

immigrants, in fact, had arrived in the United States between 1880 and 1919, most coming from southern and eastern Europe. This fueled the growth of American cities, the population of which multiplied fivefold between 1870 and 1910. The nation's per capita income, following a similar pattern, doubled between 1897 and 1911.[72] Woolworth, who had already earned a reputation for enticing show window design, envisioned his storefronts displaying and advertising commodities so seductively that such an expanding population of new arrivals along with the increasingly prosperous local population simply would not be able to resist buying them. He also drew on his own experiences in Europe. Of Vienna, he wrote, "The store windows make the finest display of any city I ever was in, and it is all I can do to keep my money in my pocket."[73] As a keen observer of crowds of shoppers and settings for shopping, Woolworth fully understood the visual logic of consumption.

Woolworth refined the design of his show windows as the advertisers of commodities throughout the early years of his career. As what William Leach has called "eye-level devices for capturing consumers," he appreciated the show windows' capacity for altering the way that people related to goods and for fabricating a "public environment of desire."[74] In the early 1890s, Woolworth began employing the latest technologies in plate glass manufacturing along with mirrors and the new incandescent illumination to heighten the viewers' experience of the show windows' allure. In his general letters and at store conventions, Woolworth instructed his store managers in detail about the art of show window display.[75]

Rivaling the show windows in importance to his storefronts was the large and visually striking billboardlike sign Woolworth devised in 1886, probably modeled on the "red fronts" of the Great Atlantic and Pacific Tea Company.[76] Bright carmine red with gilded lettering and moldings, Woolworth's sign was bigger than those of a main street's comparably scaled stores. By 1900, he had completely standardized the sign's design, refitting all stores with signs of a uniform size, shape, and color. In addition to the stores' show windows and signs, Woolworth also designed the company's trademark, the "diamond W," which he used to brand his commodities and which he placed over the entrance to his headquarters in the Stewart Building in 1886.[77] In designing such a wide array of commercial signs and symbols, Woolworth aimed to strengthen the visual identity of his five- and ten-cent chain of stores, making their image consistent in all locations, and so suggesting a consumer's version of an "institution."[78]

Woolworth devoted a comparable energy to the refinement of his store interiors, which he continued to view as efficient enclosures for heightening the allure and expediting the sale of his low-priced commodities. Between 1896 and 1900, he undertook an ambitious "beautification program" as part of a competitive strategy inspired by New York's newest big department stores, among them lavish consumer emporiums such as Sixth Avenue's Siegel-Cooper's. Woolworth proudly told his managers that the program had increased sales in some stores by as much as 100 percent (fig. 1.8).[79] Woolworth's beautification effort followed on the heels of his decision to open the "big city" stores. Whereas Woolworth's earliest stores had small and simple interiors of a narrow, deep configuration with a single central aisle, by 1900 he had designed a number of stores

FIGURE 1.8 *(above)* F. W. Woolworth and Company, Five and Ten Cent Store, Reading, Massachusetts, interior, ca. 1910. Unidentified photographer. Woolworth Collection, National Building Museum.

FIGURE 1.9 *(below)* F. W. Woolworth Company, Five and Ten Cent Store, Cincinnati, Ohio, view of ca. 1920. Unidentified photographer. Woolworth Collection, National Building Museum.

around a long central counter flanked by parallel side aisles. The big-city stores had several long counters and aisles.[80] Woolworth, consequently, had adapted the scale of his store interiors to emulate the department stores' more spacious proportions and to correspond to the larger size of his anticipated sidewalk crowd.

As part of his beautification program, Woolworth developed a list of rules in 1900, through which he exerted a strong control over all aspects of his stores' visual character. The 1906 version, *Rules for Management of Stores*, covered everything from the salesladies' clothing ("black waists" from October 1 to May 1, and "white waists" from May 1 to October 1) to precise specifications with measurements down to the half-inch for the length of counters and the display of goods in counter boxes. The rules also specified the exact size and placement of glass signs, the height and type of the signs' lettering, and the type of paint to be used for "fixtures" such as ceilings (to be painted white), awnings (to be painted gold), and columns (also gold).[81] Altogether, Woolworth's rules demonstrated the importance he placed on visually enticing sidewalk shoppers through store entrances, on directing their path among rationally organized and identified displays of five- and ten-cent commodities, and, ultimately, on forging a relationship between the consumer and the commodities, which he exhibited as tantalizing objects of desire.

Shortly after Woolworth incorporated his chain, he further crystallized his desired "institutional" image with the design of a singular, representative, and infinitely replicable store type. His store in Cincinnati, Ohio, which he acquired and remodeled in 1908, shows that Woolworth's storefronts and store interiors now advertised more than just his commodities to the consumer (fig. 1.9). In their consistency as a type, they advertised the chain as a whole. Given Woolworth's ambition to build a landmark skyscraper, however, it is clear that by 1910 he had decided such localized advertising, directed toward the street and passersby, could no longer fulfill such institutional advertising needs. Woolworth had envisioned instead a new kind of advertising with national as well as international impact. A conspicuous landmark headquarters, or "giant signboard"—that is, the still grander equivalent of his stores' billboardlike signs—would reach a far broader audience than a main street's sidewalk crowds.

Well before Woolworth asked Gilbert to design his skyscraper, then, he had a vague if not yet fully articulated notion of the varied purposes that the project would fulfill. Woolworth later acknowledged that the "structure had been taking form in my mind for a great many years."[82] Woolworth's landmark, if it were to serve as a monument to his dominance within the retailing industry and as an impressive corporate headquarters for a far-flung retailing empire, would have to suggest a distinctive, memorable, and salient presence in the city. At the same time, if the skyscraper were to succeed as advertising, it would need to brandish before crowds a seductive and fashionable image, like that of the Singer Tower. As a giant signboard and trademark, it would have to dazzle and impress the eye, competing for the spectator's attention within the strident and showcaselike visual environment of the modern city. Yet regardless of how Woolworth ultimately reconciled such disparate objectives, he also faced the equally important question of how—in strictly practical terms—he would realize those objectives with the construction of a skyscraper.

THE SPECULATIVE SKYSCRAPER AS A COMMEMORATIVE ATTRACTION

Woolworth's practical means for fulfilling his dream of building a landmark headquarters and advertising cynosure in New York called for adding a final ingredient to the mix—the profit-producing speculative office uses that would make the project's construction financially feasible. To build a speculative office building had never been Woolworth's sole and primary objective.[83] Speculative office uses, furthermore, would count among the least harmonious of elements making up Woolworth's building program. Still, he could not escape them. They provided the practical means and financial wherewithal to the end of constructing a skyscraper with great height and prominence in the city—of a size far exceeding that required by F. W. Woolworth and Company. The company's widely dispersed management hierarchy did not begin to suggest a central headquarters of a size that filled the interior of such a skyscraper.

Woolworth had previously utilized such a strategy of financing height in his first Woolworth Building, completed in Lancaster, Pennsylvania in 1900 (fig. 1.10). In its siting, pattern of uses, and prominence in the city, moreover, Woolworth's Lancaster project would serve as an important model for his much grander skyscraper in New York. Located at 21 North Queen Street, the project had five stories plus a roof garden. As a "modern store and office building," it stood out as the city's tallest; later accounts judged it a "skyscraper."[84] Significantly, Woolworth built the skyscraper for a commemorative purpose: Queen Street in Lancaster had served as the site for his first successful five-cent store.

Determined to show contemporaries that his five- and ten-cent retail enterprise had indeed since its origins prospered and come of age, Woolworth modeled the Lancaster Woolworth Building on New York's newest department stores. Recalling the interiors of those stores, which housed settings for social activity that ranged from theaters to tearooms, Woolworth's skyscraper incorporated a diverse array of uses in addition to speculative office space.[85] On the ground floor, it featured a large five- and ten-cent store with tall show windows, which Woolworth called "the handsomest store in the syndicate," other stores, and a restaurant.[86] Rising above the cornice line, it sported an electrically illuminated roof garden theater for "high-class entertainments," which in actuality ranged from symphony orchestras to variety shows featuring the stage acts constituting vaudeville.[87] Such roof-garden theaters had recently risen to popularity among shoppers; since 1900 they had appeared with increasing frequency in New York's department stores. Woolworth employed his own manager for the theater and treated it in financial statements as his own successful enterprise.[88] Most important, Woolworth had the Lancaster Woolworth Building designed to look like a department store; its urban silhouette sported festive gold-domed cupolas echoing those of famous Parisian department stores, among them Les Magasins du Printemps (Paul Sedille, 1882–85) (fig. 1.11). Woolworth, like his American merchant rivals, looked to Paris and its grand emporiums as signifying the epitome of "enlightened consumption," that is, the all at once worldly, fashionable, and glamorous.[89]

Given Woolworth's objective of rivaling Paris and New York department stores with the design of his Lancaster Woolworth Building, it is not surprising that he

FIGURE 1.10 Woolworth Building, Lancaster, Pennsylvania, 1900–1901, as illustrated in *The Woolworth Building, Lancaster, Pa.* Woolworth Collection, National Building Museum.

FIGURE 1.11 Paul Sedille, Les Magasins du Printemps, Paris, 1882–85. Unidentified photographer. Reproduced by permission of the Bibliothèque Nationale de France.

selected William Schickel of the New York firm Schickel and Ditmars as the project's architect. Schickel had by the early 1890s conceived additions for three major New York department stores—Arnold Constable, Ehrlich Brothers, and Stern Brothers.[90] Schickel's "Parisian" design for Woolworth's Lancaster project, given its exuberant ornamental scheme, indeed looked more like a department store than an office building. It also alluded to New York's contemporary venues of mass amusement, among them the recently completed Olympia Theater on Broadway (J. B. McElfatrick and Son, 1895) and Madison Square Garden (McKim, Mead, and White, 1889–90). Costing in total about $300,000, the Lancaster Woolworth Building outshone the buildings of its Lancaster surroundings—among them the spatially more expansive but architecturally much more staid Watt and Shand department store a block away—as the town's most exuberantly ornamented commercial structure.[91]

Long before Woolworth undertook his first Woolworth Building in Lancaster, the Woolworth Syndicate had begun heavily investing in speculative urban real estate. Woolworth had selected hundreds of properties and negotiated hundreds of leases for stores, but after he began acquiring competitors' smaller five- and ten-cent chains in the early 1900s, the syndicate's financial stake in rental properties doubled.[92] Yet even within such a larger context of real estate investment, Woolworth's Lancaster "skyscraper" represented a wholly unprecedented, and far more ambitious, architectural phenomenon. Instead of paying rent as a tenant, Woolworth had now decided to collect that rent from others, using the project's projected future rental income to build on a scale that he might not have attempted otherwise. The formula worked; subsequently, Woolworth invested in a series of similar store and speculative office building projects in Paterson, New Jersey (1900); Trenton, New Jersey (1907); and Troy, New York (1911). In each of the projects, Woolworth established a five- and ten-cent store with large show windows on the ground floor, and then rented out the offices that rose in three to five stories above.[93] Yet by contrast to these purely speculative projects, the Lancaster Woolworth Building—a speculative as well as commemorative "skyscraper"—would predict the character of Woolworth's practical yet showy skyscraper in New York.

Woolworth unveiled the completed Lancaster Woolworth Building at his "Five and Ten Cent Store Convention," which he held in the city in June 1901. He welcomed the Woolworth Syndicate's store managers to the event, describing his commemorative landmark as "a monument to the wonderful success of the five and ten cent business." Sales had recently passed the $5 million mark, Woolworth pointed out, and now his five- and ten-cent enterprise reflected "a more prosperous condition than ever before."[94] Woolworth had "Woolworth Building" inscribed in stone over the "skyscraper's" main entrance and a "diamond W" trademark emblazoned in gold high over the ground-floor store's interior. Adages such as "This is the oldest 5 and 10 cent store in the world" appeared on the interior's side walls, and twenty-six relief panels illustrated in detail the history of the Woolworth stores throughout the country.[95] The exterior's gold-domed cupolas, when illuminated at night by electricity, could be seen for "several miles."[96] Through such strategies of exuberant architecture and didactic ornamentation, Woolworth aimed not only to celebrate the growth of his enterprise, but also to invest the entire Woolworth Syndicate with a new social importance.

Woolworth understood that the Lancaster Woolworth Building's viability as a commemorative structure depended strongly upon the "sale" to tenants of its income-producing office space. To that end, the project's rental brochure highlighted the skyscraper's location in the heart of the business district at Queen and Grant streets; modern services such as electric lighting, steam heating, and two electric elevators with the latest safety devices; and fully equipped toilet rooms for ladies and gentlemen on each floor. After hours, the project's tenants could frequent the roof garden.[97] In providing such conveniences, comforts, and pleasures, Woolworth, like his department store rivals, aimed to attract and to cultivate the loyalty of his "customers." Such standards of "service" he, like they, regarded as indispensable to an enterprise's success.[98]

Woolworth spoke to journalists with pride about the Lancaster Woolworth Building, showing confidence in the soundness of his financial strategy, even while his business associates in the city called it "a most daring speculation."[99] Regardless of his contemporaries' doubts, Woolworth presumably assumed that the financial risk would be worth the payoff: the confirmation to his store managers, to fellow merchants, and to the Lancaster business community that his five- and ten-cent enterprise had indeed achieved a stature worthy of such commemoration.

Five years after Woolworth completed his Lancaster Woolworth Building, the Singer Manufacturing Company built in New York the record-setting trademark tower that Woolworth considered especially successful advertising (see fig. 1.7). As the first American enterprise to expand abroad, by 1890 Singer controlled 80 percent of the world market for sewing machines; later, it opened franchises in India, China, Russia, Japan, Spain, Australia, Turkey, and Germany. Between 1902 and 1914, Singer's growth in Russia alone increased its sales by 44.7 percent and accounted for at least three-quarters of its profits. To finance the Singer Tower, Singer leased all of its offices to tenants—with the exception of the company's executive headquarters on the thirty-fourth floor—using the proceeds from rental returns as projected future income.[100] Woolworth, who was able to watch the tower's construction on lower Broadway from his headquarters on the fifth floor of the Stewart Building, may well have viewed its advertising potentials as excelling those of the Lancaster Woolworth Building's. Key features from the Lancaster Woolworth Building as well as the Singer Tower would predict the character of his New York skyscraper's design.

Woolworth, the Landmarks of Europe, and the Theater

That Woolworth considered architecture and urban design worthy interests in their own right can be credited largely to their importance in facilitating the sale of his five- and ten-cent commodities. Beginning in 1890, however, he made new discoveries about those interests during his yearly buying trips in Europe. In the process of seeking out, assessing, and bargaining for his European commodities, he toured noted European cities, historic towns, and their architectural landmarks, often receiving instruction from knowledgeable guides. Woolworth's European travels, as a consequence, pointed to a new and competing architectural and urban standard: historically based, high style, and, for him, evoking an Old World luxury and grandeur. For this reason, his skyscraper would stand out among other skyscrapers in New York. Its design would be inspired by the landmarks, but equally important, it would be the site of a cosmopolitan, and specifically European, high style of consumption, not only for Woolworth and his corporate executives and tenants, but also for the city's tourists.

Woolworth's educational background, ironically, provided little clue to his later interest in touring European cities and their architecture. He boasted at the end of his career that "the education I got in two terms in a business college at Watertown, New York, did me more good than any classical education I might have got."[101] Still, his earliest biographers noted that as a young man Woolworth aspired conscientiously to improve his surroundings. He undertook two beautification projects along the road adjoining his family's farmhouse—installing running white picket fences on both sides of the road and then planting a straight line of small trees adjacent to the nearest of them.[102] While in Europe as well as in New York, furthermore, Woolworth regularly attended the opera, taking note of performances, theater seating capacities, balcony and box arrangements, and orchestras.[103] Altogether, then, Woolworth's early experiences with landscape beautification and the opera pointed to a predilection for a skyscraper that would rival the most memorable of tourist attractions: It would be enticing and grand, and it would elevate the beauty of its surroundings. But it would also engage viewers with an opera-influenced version of theater: Woolworth would employ techniques of flamboyant showmanship as the skyscraper's design and construction progressed.

Woolworth took the first of his European buying trips between February and May of 1890. He had embarked on the steamer *The City of Paris* in search of a broader range of "high-quality" inexpensive handcrafted objects from the German and Austrian cottage industries—among them rocking horses, clowns, "china-limb dolls," dominoes, and other commodities important to the profitability of his stores, notably blown-glass Christmas tree ornaments.[104] The latter he moved through his stores in such large quantities that after 1900 he was reputed to be the largest importer in the United States.[105] B. F. Hunt, a partner in Horace Partridge and Company, a major American importer of toys, served as Woolworth's guide.[106] Woolworth followed an ambitious touring itinerary; it included overnight stays in London, Frankfurt, Sonneberg, Nuremburg, Munich, Vienna, Dresden, Leipzig, Berlin, and Paris. He had his photograph taken in Berlin and mailed letters back to store managers effusing with enthusiasm for the cities and buildings he encountered as a sightseer (fig. 1.12).

FIGURE 1.12 Frank Woolworth, in a photograph taken in Berlin on his first European buying trip, 1890. Unidentified photographer. Woolworth Collection, National Building Museum.

Paris ranked at the top of Woolworth's itinerary as a tourist. "It has been the height of my ambition to see Paris. I have heard so much about it and read so much about it."[107] Woolworth identified the city with Napoleon III and Georges-Eugène Haussmann's modern, tree-lined boulevards as settings for social display, and also with the elite form of consumption represented by spectacular emporiums such as Aristide Boucicaut's Au Bon Marché (Alexandre Laplanche, 1869, and Louis-Charles Boileau, 1873, 1876) (fig. 1.13).[108] Woolworth arranged for a personal tour of what he called Boucicaut's "world famous store," and compared it to Wanamaker's in Philadelphia, noting that it employed some four thousand people and sold three hundred thousand dollars' worth of goods a day.[109] The monumentality and grandeur of Paris's boulevards also made a forceful impression on Woolworth: "The more one sees of Paris, the larger and more magnificent it looks." He further described the boulevards as places

FIGURE 1.13 Alexandre Laplanche, Au Bon Marché, Paris, 1869, extended by Louis-Charles Boileau in 1873, 1876 (Gustav Eiffel, engineer), interior. From *Paris Projet* 8 (Paris: Atelier parisien d'urbanisme, 1972).

to "see style"; they offered public gardens, cafés, and a thriving culture of leisure, or what he called "a city of pleasure" in cabarets, theaters, circuses, and related mass amusements.[110] In breaking down the boundaries between the commercial and the public, the boulevards' show windows enticed sidewalk crowds to pause before commodities displays so abundant as to create in themselves a spectacle. Well before Woolworth's visit, Paris had begun its transformation into the world's modern capital of stylish consumption.[111]

Judging by the enthusiasm, length, and detail of Woolworth's descriptions, Paris's "wonderful Eiffel Tower," or "most famous sight," as he put it—completed only the year before as the world's tallest structure—counted among the high points of his 1890 tour (fig. 1.14). The tower's platforms and summit accommodated crowds of tourists—according to Woolworth, "5000 persons an hour."[112] Among all the sights of Paris, however, Woolworth judged its most prominent Beaux-Arts landmark, the Opéra (Charles Garnier, 1862–75), the very pinnacle of architecture—a judgement that reflected his passion for theater (fig. 1.15). He called the Opéra "a beautiful place of amusement" and assessed its lobby as "the finest in Europe": "The magnificent lobby where people go out between the acts is the finest work of art that can be imagined—one magnificent room with very high ceilings and large chandeliers, elegant paintings, beautiful frescoes, and inlaid floors."[113] Woolworth's eye as a retailer for the lobby's craftsmanship in fine materials, for color, and for ornamental detail showed especially in his description of the Opéra's central stair: "one of the finest works of its kind in the world . . . built of white marble with balustrades of red antique marble, and handrails of Algerian onyx." In the foyer that opened onto the stair, Woolworth made note of "gold and bronze decorations" and "elegant statuary on all sides."[114] He emphasized the Opéra's relationship with its Paris surroundings. As an urban focal point, it stood alone, "free from any buildings," and its "simply grand" facade commanded "the head of one of the broadest avenues in Paris," the Avenue of the Opéra.[115]

In Woolworth's evaluation of Europe's architectural landmarks, imposing scale stood out as an important criterion of value. The Opéra could be considered great architecture in part because it was "the largest theater in the world."[116] Woolworth, furthermore, assessed the landmarks in terms of dollars and cents, like the commodities he had traveled to Europe to select, assess, and bargain for with hard cash, firmly situating the most culturally significant among them within the realm of modern commercial exchange. St. Paul's Cathedral in London, for example, "cost over $3,815,000." In Vienna, Woolworth visited "several fine churches that were simply grand and must have cost a mint

FIGURE 1.14 *Vue Generale prise du Trocadero*, showing Eiffel Tower (Gustav Eiffel, engineer), Exposition Universelle, Paris, 1889. Photograph by Napoleon Dufeu, 1889. (Courtesy of the Boston Public Library, Print Department.)

FIGURE 1.15 Charles Garnier, Opéra, Paris (1861) 1862–75. Photograph by M. Leon and J. Levy. (Courtesy of the Boston Public Library, Print Department.)

of money; there was a large altar in one of them that was solid silver."[117] He called Westminster Abbey "the greatest site in London," describing its "tomb after tomb" and "statuary after statuary," all "very expensive," as if a dazzling display of the finest commodities. During a brief stop in Cologne, he sought out "the Great Cathedral," and in Paris, he admired the "fine carvings" in the portals of Notre Dame.[118]

Woolworth's fascination with the landmarks of Europe, or "the European fever," as he called it, echoed the larger, and growing, American attraction to European cities and their art and architecture, which culminated in the day's preeminent spectacle of European-inspired, Beaux-Arts architecture and planning, the World's Columbian Exposition in Chicago of 1893.[119] Woolworth, among other American retailers, made a special trip to Chicago that September to see and report to his store managers on the exposition. Later, in the summer of 1901, he visited the Pan-American Exposition in Buffalo, and in 1904, the Louisiana Purchase Exposition in St. Louis.[120] Such expositions served at least two purposes for Woolworth. First, in viewing their Beaux-Arts architecture and planning, he continued the program of touring and self-instruction he had begun in Europe. Second, he appreciated the expositions' abundant displays of exotic commodities imported from Europe and around the world. Like his contemporaries in retailing, he discovered in the displays a new and elevated standard of variety, quality, and fashionableness. The expositions had, in fact, opened the floodgates not only to a surging wave of remarkable and enticing commodities, but also to fantasies about their consumption, both of which rapidly permeated all aspects of American life.[121]

Woolworth's desire to replicate his experiences of cosmopolitan travel found their most vivid expression in the French Renaissance chateau he built at 990 Fifth Avenue in 1901. Designed by C. P. H. Gilbert (unrelated to Cass Gilbert), Woolworth's mansion stood on the corner of Eightieth Street in the heart of the city's so-called Billionaire District (fig. 1.16).[122] Richard Morris Hunt's William K. Vanderbilt house (1879–82) at Fifty-second Street had served as the district's architectural pacesetter since the 1880s, and most recently as the model for C. P. H. Gilbert's Isaac D. Fletcher house (1899), at the corner of Seventy-ninth Street, directly across from Woolworth's site.[123] In choosing Gilbert for the design of an ambitious mansion in the Vanderbilt mold, Woolworth positioned himself conspicuously in the city among the Vanderbilts, as well as among other members of New York's older, established financial and industrial elite—the Astors, Carnegies, and Fricks. Woolworth aimed to fit in with this elite by means of what Thorstein Veblen called "pecuniary emulation," that is, to show that he, like they, had achieved "a reputable degree of success."[124]

Altogether, Woolworth's Fifth Avenue chateau, like those surrounding it, projected an image of monumentality, timelessness, and repose graced with exquisitely crafted ornamental refinements: delicately carved projecting bays, continuous balconies supported on sculpted brackets, and an entrance flanked by layers of pilasters. Its composition exuded what the architectural critic Montgomery Schuyler called an exemplary "quietness," with this foiled by a skyline bristling picturesquely with chimneys, projecting dormers, crockets, and finials, and a steep slate roof sprouting ornate copper cresting.[125]

The Woolworth mansion's interior, by contrast, revealed a private world that suggested less deference to Fifth Avenue's time-honored conventions. Its stylistically differentiated array of period rooms, while typical, showed a scenographic thinness of decoration and an unusual degree of eclecticism by comparison to those of its progenitors. Woolworth had Gilbert design a spacious entrance hall for the ground floor, flanked by a "medieval German" smoking room and a billiard room (figs. 1.17, 1.18). The foyer's main axis led to a generous stair, the first landing of which opened into a Louis XIV reception hall. The hall led in turn to a dining room with an iron and glass "palm gardern" beyond or, alternatively, into a "French eighteenth-century" drawing room with a Louis XV mantle. A grandly proportioned music room adjoined the drawing room and featured a distinctive curved bay window, balcony, and medieval fireplace. Such a contrasting array of period styles provided Woolworth, like the owners of Fifth Avenue's older chateaux, with the fiction that he could, indeed, master historical space and time—a prerogative open only to those with substantial financial resources.[126]

The well-known interior designer William Baumgarten—reputed to be one of "the number of interior decorators on Fifth Avenue, who are interested only in the most expensive class of work, and whose agents are scouring Europe, not only for old fabrics and wood work, but for columns, mantlepieces, floors, and ceilings"—may have been responsible for conceiving the Woolworth mansion's widely diverse array of period rooms.[127]

FIGURE 1.16 C. P. H. Gilbert, F. W. Woolworth house, 990 Fifth Avenue, New York, 1901 (demolished 1927), exterior. From *Architecture*, vol. 4 (November 15, 1901). Avery Architectural and Fine Arts Library, Columbia University.

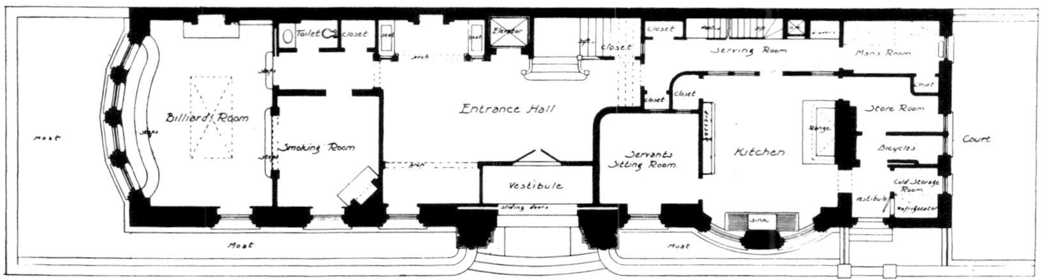

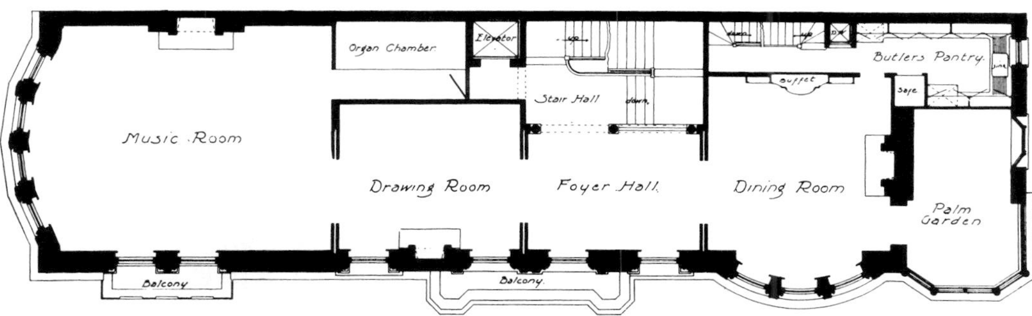

FIGURE 1.17 C. P. H. Gilbert, F. W. Woolworth house, 1901, plans of ground floor and first floor. From *Architecture*, vol. 4 (November 15, 1901). Avery Architectural and Fine Arts Library, Columbia University.

FIGURE 1.18 C. P. H. Gilbert, F. W. Woolworth house, 1901, view of entrance hall. From *Architecture*, vol. 4 (November 15, 1901). (Courtesy of the Trustees of the Boston Public Library.)

Woolworth's wife, Jennie Creighton, may have also had a hand in the design, but little evidence remains to suggest that she asserted herself nearly as strongly as, for example, Alva Smith Vanderbilt.[128] Woolworth's contribution was clear: He wanted in his private life "the scenes of Europe." Yet despite his firsthand experience with European cities and their architecture, he could not escape the provocative world of European-inspired consumerist fantasy associated with New York's 1890s department stores—among them Siegel-Cooper and Company, which featured a replication of the World's Columbian Exposition's Roman and Renaissance architecture and sculpture, and Macy's, with its English Palladian details.[129] For Woolworth, architecture would always be linked to such compelling worlds of consumer splendor.

Sequestered behind his Fifth Avenue chateau's genteel exterior, Woolworth contrived in the private music room of its main story an extravagant, colorful, and garish world of electrical showmanship—not unlike that of the roof garden "variety entertainments" featured at his new Lancaster Woolworth Building. With himself as the audience—and little in the way of a true social life—Woolworth improvised flamboyant, possibly Richard Wagner–inspired "concerts," using "his favorite mechanical toy," a specially designed roll-playing mechanical pipe organ.[130] Woolworth's spectacles opened with oil portraits of composers, among them Wagner and Beethoven, which became brighter as a musical piece progressed, followed by dramatic sound and lighting effects, which echoed thunder, lightning, and rain. He invented special mechanical and electrical features, and used colored lighting in even brighter shades of amber, green, and mauve to seemingly amplify sound in synchrony with the music.[131] Such pipe organs had appeared elsewhere in the Billionaire District, notably in Joseph Pulitzer's mansion, but the ingenious contrivances and "infernal" character of Woolworth's instrument placed it in a special class by itself.[132]

One friend of Woolworth's called him a "lover of color" in every aspect of life.[133] Woolworth, in fact, had begun featuring ten-piece orchestras in his stores' Saturday opening extravaganzas by the late 1880s. In 1900, he added a specially commissioned "Woolworth March" to the extravaganzas; later, he incorporated pipe organs, piano players, and performances by popular soloists.[134] Such luminous musical spectacles, whether manufactured privately within the walls of his chateau or publicly for his store openings, suggested that Woolworth had begun to view himself as a flamboyant theatrical impresario.

During his 1890 European buying tour, Woolworth had aspired to see as many different operas in as many different cities as possible, showing a ritualistic devotion to the opera that only further betrayed his love of spectacle. He attended performances in Nuremburg, Munich, Vienna, Dresden, and Berlin, as well as in Paris, finding especially impressive the fanfare, drama, and colorful scenography featured in Richard Wagner's operas. He saw *Lohengrin* in Munich and *Tristan and Isolde* in Dresden.[135] Shortly after his arrival in New York, Woolworth secured a grand-tier box at the Metropolitan Opera. In his attendance at the opera, he emulated New York's financial and industrial elite, for whom operagoing had attained the status of an important social rite. By the 1890s, the glittery "Four Hundred" had begun gathering at the Metropolitan Opera House, making the experience a grand occasion for seeing and being seen, accompanied by a lavish display of riches and physical beauty.[136] Yet Woolworth, who at least initially did not hold stock in one of the Metropolitan Opera's more opulent parterre boxes, predicated his attendance on the theatrical qualities he valued most as a retailer—bright color, light, music, scenography, and "show."

Creating a European-inspired, theatrical, and spectacular site for consumption would become one of Woolworth's principal objectives for his skyscraper, reflecting his own modern consumerist tastes, his imagined popular audience, and the flashier side of his personality. For this, he relied little on the precedent of New York's old wealth to guide him.[137] J. Pierpont Morgan, among others, could have built a spectacular skyscraper for J. P. Morgan and Company on the expensive site that he had acquired by 1912 at Broad and Wall streets, at the time occupied by the five-story Drexel Building. Instead, he had Trowbridge and Livingston design a reticent, classical four-story headquarters in solid marble. He aspired to the prestige of an "aristocratic" building for his own exclusive occupancy, as opposed to a showy, eye-catching, and towering headquarters for which tenants footed part of the bill.[138] Morgan had little need for Woolworth's consumer-oriented aesthetic, which, as evidenced by the merchant's shop fronts and show window displays, competed for the attention of sidewalk crowds.

Woolworth's long-established passion for the theatrical and the spectacular starkly contrasted with the cold, uncompromising pragmatism with which he administered F. W. Woolworth and Company's financial affairs. Woolworth espoused the exaction of the "smallest practicable margin of profit" from the sale of each commodity as his central business principle.[139] Woolworth's profits on each five- and ten-cent item, while excruciatingly small, formed when multiplied thousands of times in hundreds of stores the financial bedrock of the future F. W. Woolworth Company. Ultimately, they constituted the very substance of his own immense personal wealth.

Even after incorporating F. W. Woolworth and Company in 1905, Woolworth continued to exert a hegemonic control over the company's finances. With the assistance of Carson Peck, he developed meticulous and sophisticated cost-accounting practices, employed a central financial manager to keep daily ledgers, and through his store inspectors relentlessly monitored store managers on matters of record-keeping and costs. He prescribed strict ratios governing the proportion of goods ordered to goods sold, seeking to guarantee the highest efficiency of "stock turn" in each of his stores.[140] Every week he reported to managers the previous week's sales figures as contrasted with the same week's totals from earlier years.[141] He kept a constant watch on the ratio between total expenses and total profits, which he presented monthly to all managers in tabular form, and purposely stirred up rivalries among managers by citing disparities between the total profit figures of various stores.[142]

Woolworth watched especially closely the weekly salaries of the stores' "salesgirls." Each week he calculated the ratio of all salaries paid to all sales generated. He refused to compromise on the meager three-dollar-per-week minimum wage he set in 1902, at the time far below the official "poverty line indicator," despite his managers' repeated requests to raise the wage and the clerks' strikes of 1892 and 1897.[143] Regardless of the incalculable value of the young women's efficient and friendly service to the success of his stores, Woolworth insisted that "we must have cheap help to sell cheap goods." For women who went on strike for higher wages,

Woolworth firmly instructed his managers to "give them the bounce" once the summer, or the "slow season," arrived.[144] Salaries absorbed at least one-third of Woolworth's annual expenses, and inexpensive female labor—at the turn of the century widely available and always new in supply—insured that Woolworth kept his operating expenses low and profits high.[145]

At a time when retailers began extending credit to customers as a standard business practice, Woolworth stringently applied a "cash only" policy throughout his chain. He also refused to shoulder debt. "I believe in doing business by and with cash. . . . Large credit is a temptation to careless buying."[146] As a consequence, the growth of Woolworth's chain proceeded slowly, following a strictly pay-as-you-go basis. Woolworth used profits from existing stores to finance new stores. He cautiously established a secure financial footing in small towns, seeking out and exploiting "unsuspected markets," before risking competition during the mid-1890s with a big city's palatial department stores.[147] Woolworth's skyscraper, it turned out, would capture something of the striking duality of his existence—a life spent longing for the European world of aristocratic splendor on the one hand, a life devoted to applying the exacting stringencies of finance on the other.

When Woolworth decided to build his landmark skyscraper, then, his inclinations as a client for a major work of architecture were already well established. Woolworth's life as a retailing entrepreneur had demanded vision, imagination, and perception, but also, paradoxically, a cold, uncompromising, and at times inhuman business acumen. As a tourist, he prized the historical cities and landmarks of Europe, but he also deeply understood all cities as settings for modern consumerism. He aspired to attract his shoppers and stimulate desire with an evocative dream world of fantasy, theater, and spectacle, but he also shrewdly tracked their movements on main streets spread across the American continent and abroad. It is only fitting, then, that the Woolworth Building would be part fantastical dream and part ordinary place of business. Woolworth called himself a believer in dreams, but only if those dreams could be translated into tangible results. "Dreaming never hurts [a man] if he keeps working right behind the dream to make as much of it come real as he can."[148]

CHAPTER TWO

Woolworth, Modernity, and the City

Woolworth resolved to build his landmark skyscraper in January or February 1910, although he did not officially announce the project until November 10 of that year.[1] He faced the prospect of identifying a building site, arranging a scheme of financing, and selecting an architect—hardly simple matters. The proposed skyscraper's contradictory programmatic requirements imposed competing demands on Woolworth's decision-making process. It was to function not only as a landmark headquarters, eye-catching architectural advertising, and commemorative attraction for sidewalk spectators, but also as a solid investment in urban real estate. In aiming to reconcile such competing demands, Woolworth employed his merchant's experience with the locational, spatial, and visual decisions influencing consumption. These included selecting sites for stores in the right part of town, catching the sidewalk spectator's attention with bold signage and well-placed show window displays, and fabricating theatrical opening extravaganzas that transformed those spectators into consumers.

Woolworth made his decisions about the skyscraper's site, scheme of financing, and architect within a particular urban environment, that of New York around 1900. Woolworth's Stewart Building headquarters had from the early 1880s firmly situated him within the composite of local sites and thoroughfares that composed "his" New York: the showy department stores of Broadway and Ladies' Mile, the steel-framed and electrified "skyscraper city" centered on lower Broadway, Wall Street as a bastion of banking and finance, New York's monumental civic center at City Hall Park, and the publicity-inspired architecture of Newspaper Row. Collectively, the sites and thoroughfares exemplified the marked heterogeneity that by 1900 had come to distinguish the city's physical character. As the art historian John Van Dyke put it in his *New New York* of 1909, "Nothing shall conform except by law of contrariety. . . . Hence the difficulty of trying to summarize either the place or the people."[2] Each facet of Woolworth's surroundings signified a distinctive urban condition, but together they composed a complex and dynamic metropolitan culture marked by the dominant impulses of consumerism, technological modernization, and escalating land values. In the early 1900s, champions of the City Beautiful movement aimed to restore the order and dignity of the city as a public realm, but new types of communities had already been reconfiguring that realm with skyscrapers and spaces dedicated to consumption. Architectural advertising, the strident graphics of signage, commodities displays, and spectacular printed media publicity engendered new forms of urban spectatorship. Woolworth's decisions, as a consequence, would reflect to varying degrees the competing values of these New York surroundings.

In choosing a site for his skyscraper in lower Manhattan at Broadway and Park Place, Woolworth signaled F. W. Woolworth and Company's transition from a mere participant in the city's diverse array of physical and cultural settings to an active, assertive presence. Within a matter of days, Gilbert's design for his "Woolworth Bank and Office Building" became simply "Woolworth Building." Woolworth's bold assertion of his name and hence his identity in the city echoed Van Dyke's assessment of its architecture: "this cry of the individual in brick and stone and steel, this strain for novelty or peculiarity or mere 'loudness.'"[3] Similarly, Woolworth and Gilbert's coming together as a client and architect in the first place reflected the values of an urban environment that prized salesmanship, advertising, and competition in the marketplace. This is not to say that Gilbert marginalized the ideal of architecture as a high art. Through the promotion of his Beaux-Arts designs within the city's modern, commercial context, however, utilizing the techniques of salesmanship and the speculative real estate developer's savvy, Gilbert, like Woolworth, also engaged in diffusing the boundaries between the realms of high culture and the competitive urban marketplace. As a result, even before Woolworth and Gilbert set out to design the Woolworth Building, the modernizing and fragmented cultural milieu of New York engendered the question of which values the skyscraper was to represent and to whom.

A Site in Lower Manhattan on Broadway at City Hall Park

Woolworth briefly considered a site for his skyscraper at West Broadway and Reade Street, two blocks west of his Stewart Building headquarters. By late March 1910, however, he had begun negotiations on the site at Broadway and Park Place, opposite the southwestern corner of City Hall Park. Directly across Broadway from the Post Office, and across Barclay Street from the Astor House, the site had a high visibility from points along the Brooklyn Bridge (figs. 2.1, 2.2).[4] Woolworth later recounted that in selecting the site, he rigorously applied his already proven techniques of store siting. He studied the circulation of New York's crowds as they crossed the bridge and moved along lower Broadway; he watched where they turned onto side streets; and he observed the densest traffic

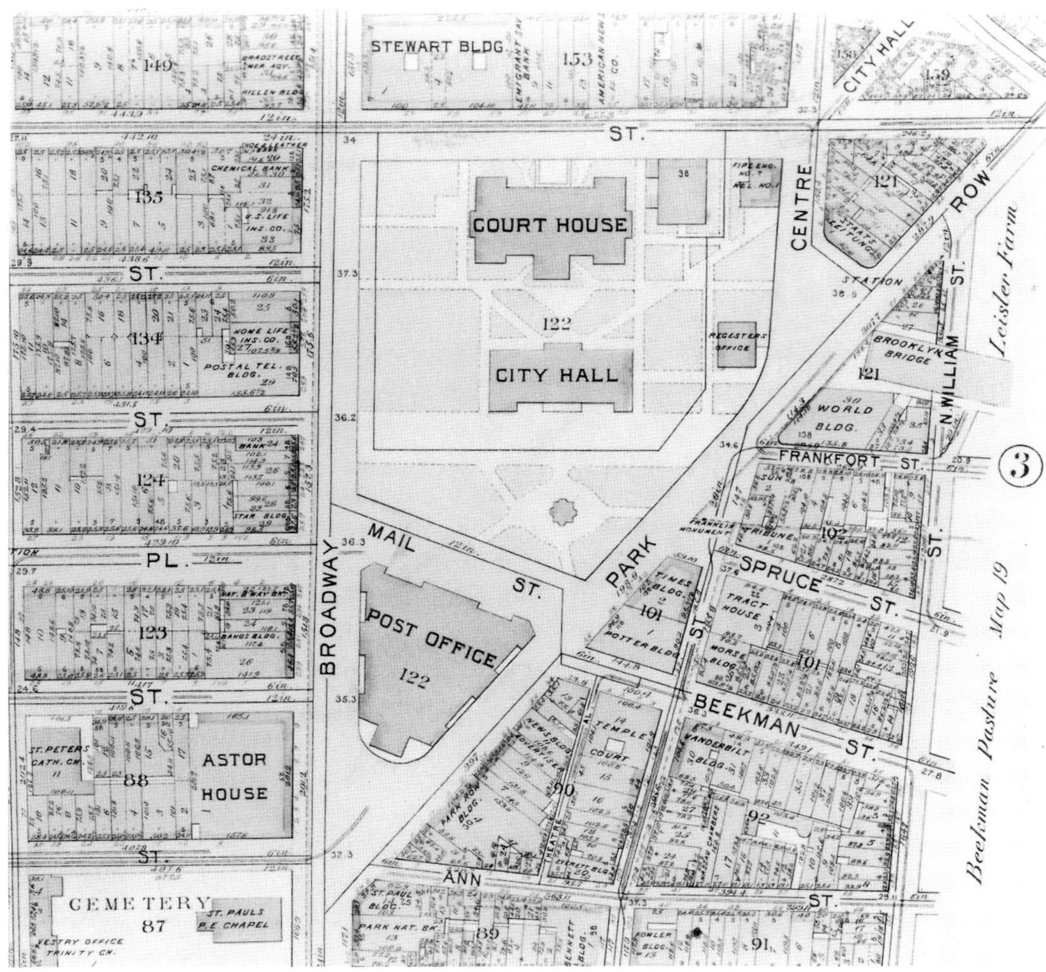

FIGURE 2.1 *(above)* Lower Manhattan, showing future site of Woolworth Building at Broadway and Park Place, opposite Post Office and north of Astor House. From G. W. Bromley, *Atlas of the City of New York, Manhattan Island, from Actual Surveys and Official Plans* (Philadelphia, G. W. Bromley, 1897). Map Division, New York Public Library, Astor, Lenox and Tilden Foundations.

FIGURE 2.2 *(below)* *Broadway and City Hall Park South*, 1908. Photograph by Irving Underhill. Prints and Photographs Division, Library of Congress.

occurring at Broadway's intersection with Park Place.[5] Having noticed Broadway's teeming pedestrian traffic might have been expected of Woolworth. He had also, however, refined to a nearly scientific precision his technique for locating stores by pinpointing exactly where the greatest number of people passed on a sidewalk during a specific period of time. The volume of sidewalk traffic in any city or town, he had already discovered, depended upon adjacent patterns of land use and transportation lines.[6] If such a siting technique influenced the financial success of his stores, then Woolworth—regardless of the differences between his shoppers and downtown's "peculiar crowd," as Van Dyke described the city's white-collar work force ("its hands are white, its body is fragile but active, its head is somewhat feverish")—also valued the technique's implications for assessing all urban real estate, including the location of his future skyscraper.[7]

LOWER MANHATTAN

When Woolworth established the Woolworth Syndicate's central buying office at 104 Chambers Street in 1886, New York had already achieved renown as the undisputed economic capital of the United States and as a world metropolis rivaling London and Paris.[8] The busy banks and merchant exchanges of lower Manhattan—in particular, the New York Stock Exchange on Wall Street—had by the mid-nineteenth century won for the city an unrivaled supremacy in the financial world. As the nation's major retailing and manufacturing center, moreover, New York decisively dominated the import and export trade. Serving as a key hub in ocean freight and rail systems, it commanded wholesale and retail markets that would by 1910 extend "to all quarters of the United States."[9] As a consequence, it is only natural that Woolworth considered New York the best location for his headquarters. He would be positioning his syndicate's administrative and buying functions strategically close to the nation's capital markets and customs offices and to the warehousing facilities of its most important port.

Woolworth's move to New York in 1886 represented but a single example of a much larger economic trend. The increasing involvement of private investment bankers in issuing securities had turned Wall Street into what one contemporary described as a "vortex" for "the entire circulation of capital, currency, and exchange" and, as a consequence, "a kind of corporate headquarters for the nation."[10] By 1895, the number of corporate headquarters concentrated in New York had reached a disproportionate size compared to the number in other American cities. The city had more than three times the headquarters found in Chicago, where reportedly "the taxes and legal restrictions [were] burdensome."[11] Among New York's corporate headquarters, moreover, nearly three hundred firms boasted assets of more than $1 million dollars each.[12] Woolworth's syndicate of stores, although not yet incorporated at the time, ranked among them in size, having recorded sales of more than $1 million in 1895.

A number of the New York corporations' chief executive officers, notably John D. Rockefeller of Cleveland and Andrew Carnegie of Pittsburgh, established factories elsewhere but attended to their finances from executive headquarters in lower Manhattan. Locating in the vicinity of Wall Street and the New York Stock Exchange, they and their business rivals secured ready access to the city's investment bankers and to expanding pools of international capital. The prospect of capitalization fueled their drive to further expand and consolidate their corporate enterprises; they absorbed new companies, then exchanged securities and reissued stock. By the early 1890s, some of the executives had converted the enterprises into still larger corporate holding companies, a strategy they and their lawyers devised to circumvent the Sherman Antitrust Act of 1890. Their aggressive pattern of corporate growth and consolidation culminated in what is known today as the great merger movement of 1897–1904.[13] Mass retailers such as Woolworth, although slower than the industrial firms to incorporate, had by the early twentieth century profited nearly as strongly from New York's unrivaled position as the nation's financial clearinghouse. By 1906, the merger movement had spawned a second wave of consolidation, this time among the mass retailers, producing that year a still large Sears, Roebuck, and Company and then, in 1911, the newly enlarged F. W. Woolworth Company.[14]

New York's status as the nation's economic capital had an allure powerful enough to attract entrepreneurs as ambitious as Woolworth. Woolworth's initial decision to move to New York, however, also stemmed from his practical need to establish a central buying office for his syndicate. He sought adjacency to the wholesalers and small manufacturers of his five- and ten-cent commodities, many of whom occupied loft buildings to the west of lower Broadway, flanking the side streets in today's Tribeca. Later, he would find his lower Manhattan location convenient to the companies on whose boards of directors he served, including the New York National Exchange Bank, later Irving National Exchange Bank, the Merchant's Refrigerating Company, and the Guardian Trust Company.[15] After he incorporated F. W. Woolworth and Company in 1905, Woolworth, like the city's other corporate executives, valued his proximity to the major banks and securities markets concentrated on Wall Street, and his adjacency to the New York Stock Exchange.

BROADWAY

In selecting a site for his skyscraper on Broadway, Woolworth chose an address on New York's most historically renowned consumer thoroughfare. By the early 1890s, Broadway had established a world reputation for its abundant mix of consumer diversions—theaters, restaurants, cafés, and, prominently, department stores.[16] The opulent architecture of the department stores exuberantly showcased the finest of commodities, flaunting the avenue's reputation for a high style of consumption. As Van Dyke put it, "In Europe things of fineness and value are hidden in the secret places of the shop . . . but in America they are often openly displayed; this does not mean jewels and goldsmith's work alone, but rare rugs, rich silks, fine porcelains, Japanese embroideries, works of art."[17] As the city's widest, longest, and most prominent retail axis, Broadway had from the midfifties streamed with crowds by day and by gaslight at night. In 1890, *Scribner's* described the emergence of the avenue's leisurely promenade: "The Flaneur," it noted, "made his appearance."[18] As the premier site of this activity, Broadway functioned brilliantly as "an extension of the stores, a stage for the fashion conscious."[19]

Woolworth's choice of the former A. T. Stewart store, Broadway's first and, when it was built, biggest and most luxurious dry goods store, for his headquarters in 1888 had reflected his desire to link the Woolworth Syndicate with the monument that signified the avenue's reputation for wealth and lavish commodities display. The Stewart store's "trappings of nobility" and image of a "public institution" dated back to Stewart's decision in 1845 to model its exterior on a Renaissance palazzo and to construct it with gleaming white marble, echoing that of the adjacent City Hall (see fig. 1.6).[20] Beyond doubt, Woolworth identified with Stewart as New York's wealthiest dry goods retailer and as the builder of such a showy but fine commercial "palace" on Broadway.

Broadway was also renowned for Ladies' Mile, the fashionable shopping district whose construction between the 1860s and 1880s extended northward along the avenue, then spilled onto Sixth Avenue between Fourteenth and Twenty-fourth streets and Union and Madison Squares. Ladies' Mile functioned emblematically as the city's classic elite shopping district, conspicuously featuring a variety of elaborately decorated department stores, the architecture of which, like clothing or furnishings, suggested the heights of fashion. In 1862, A. T. Stewart built a new "palace" of white cast iron and glass on Broadway at Tenth Street, stylishly updating the image of his retailing enterprise while also initiating the move of Broadway's dry goods establishments uptown. On Sixth Avenue, the R. H. Macy Department Store served as an anchor for Ladies' Mile. Clustered nearby were Lord and Taylor, Brooks Brothers, Arnold Constable, and B. Altman. Many of the stores' owners built with cast iron of such an ornamental showiness that the critic Leopold Eidlitz assessed them as aberrant, that is, lacking in their ostentation the proper urban decorum.[21]

In the 1870s, the R. H. Macy Department Store featured a catalog of consumer-oriented theatrical strategies, which Macy inaugurated to heighten shopping's appeal as an attraction, marking a turning point in the history of retailing. A friend of the showman P. T. Barnum, Macy counted among the first to imagine didactic exhibits, Christmas extravaganzas featuring a store Santa Claus, and gas-lit show window displays. He boldly modernized his emporium in the early 1880s—another first—by enveloping and unifying its many departments and piecemeal expansion with the most delicate of facades in ornamental cast iron and glass (fig. 2.3).[22] Macy, like Aristide Boucicaut in conceiving his nearly contemporary Au Bon Marché, recognized the commercial value of the new, exceedingly open, and light-admitting facades. Technologically inventive while also decorative, Macy's light but ornate construction invited the eye of the sidewalk spectator. More important, the facades publicized architecturally a "modern" style of consumption, which made the showcased commodities seem more abundant and more apparently available to all.

In the mid-1890s, Ladies' Mile took on a still greater monumentality with the arrival of a new group of large department stores, beginning with Siegel-Cooper and Company of Chicago in 1896 and culminating in 1906 in John Wanamaker's acquisition, expansion, and redesign of the former A. T. Stewart Department Store (fig. 2.4). Woolworth's Stewart Building headquarters had already established his association with Broadway, but the new department stores may have inspired him to strengthen that association. In 1896, he opened his first Manhattan store, which he called "the New York Store," in the heart of Ladies' Mile.[23] In choosing a site at Sixth Avenue and Seventeenth Street, beneath the Sixth Avenue elevated and just one block south of the new Siegel-Cooper and Company, he firmly established his five- and ten-cent style of mass retailing among the district's bastions of elite consumption (fig. 2.5). He also directly profited from the association, exploiting his adjacency of location to offer

FIGURE 2.3 *(above left)* R. H. Macy's, Sixth Avenue and Fourteenth Street, Ladies' Mile, ca. 1885, exterior.

FIGURE 2.4 *(above right)* De Lemos and Cordes, Siegel Cooper and Company Department Store, Sixth Avenue between Eighteenth and Nineteenth streets, 1896, view from the northwest with the Sixth Avenue elevated in the foreground. Photograph by the Byron Company. Museum of the City of New York.

FIGURE 2.5 *(below)* F. W. Woolworth store, "the New York Store," Sixth Avenue at Seventeenth Street, 1896. Diorama by Ned J. Burns showing store interior as it appeared in 1897. Museum of the City of New York.

at bargain prices commodities not typically available in the big stores. But above all else, the cachet of Broadway counted for Woolworth. Even after Ladies' Mile began to decline with R. H. Macy's relocation northward to Thirty-fourth Street in 1902, Woolworth judged his headquarters' address on Broadway important enough to make it a priority when choosing a site for the Woolworth Building.

After incorporating F. W. Woolworth and Company in 1905, Woolworth was well positioned as the new corporation's chief executive to appreciate the architectural significance of an equally striking and recently more renowned aspect of Broadway. Around 1900, the lower part of the avenue exploded with energy as the site of intensive infrastructural and superstructural modernization fueled by speculative building activity (see fig. 2.2). Skyscrapers soared to unprecedented heights. The Manhattan Life, Adams Express, Washington Life, Commercial Cable, American Surety, and Standard Oil companies—all of which exploited to the fullest the new steel-framed technology with the aim of achieving great height, had by 1901 built unusually "tall and slender" towers, extending vertically lower Manhattan's characteristically small parcels of land.[24] The crowns of the slender towers, given their visibility and their frequently eye-catching designs, functioned collectively but competitively in views of the city as trademarks.[25] Soon enough, the nation's newspapers and mass-market journals would call further attention to the towers as trademarks in their printed advertising, identifying a particular corporation by an image of its headquarters. In the words of a contemporary handbook that described trademarks, "just the fleeting glance" at either the trademark or an advertisement featuring it would set the name of a corporation "vibrating in the mind."[26] The trademark towers, then, effectively created as well as advertised a brand identity for a corporation and for the products it produced and sold. This, in turn, caused the towers to proliferate still more widely as symbols.

In the wake of the economic transformation wrought by modern industrial capitalism, and just as a wave of corporate consolidations was occurring at the turn of the century, Broadway became the preferred address for the nation's biggest and most notoriously aggressive enterprises and, as such, the site for their most conspicuous architectural advertising. As a writer for *Harper's Weekly* put it in 1902, "The captains of industry have come to New York to finance their vast undertakings and to live. They have helped build the towering structures that almost bewilder themselves. . . . The entire town has felt the inspiring power of this prosperity."[27] It is not surprising, then, that Woolworth, who frequently tabulated the profits of the nation's large railroad corporations, and who closely followed the colossal financial manipulations of powerful investment bankers such as J. P. Morgan, aspired to build and to advertise on a comparably ambitious scale.[28]

As a consequence of the steel-framed construction rising in a flurry around the axis of lower Broadway, by 1900 lower Manhattan's business district housed "the world's largest and densest concentration of workplaces located on an island." Seeking to make the workplaces function efficiently, the city's politicians, private investors, engineers, and builders developed countless brilliant and complex technological solutions, creating a "new kind of city," or "the quintessence of the early 20th-century metropolis."[29] By 1910, the engineers had refined not only the design of steel-framed skyscrapers, but, along with it, new techniques of protection against fire and corrosion as well as wind bracing, all of which had within a decade facilitated the doubling of the skyline's former height. At the same time, they had conceived new systems of mechanical movement that speeded access to, from, and through the densely-built-up cluster of skyscrapers—high-speed electric elevators in skyscraper interiors and express and local subway lines leading north and south beneath the city's streets.

In 1891, the city's Rapid Transit Commission and its chief engineer, Willam Barclay Parsons, proposed a plan for an electric-powered subway running beneath lower Broadway. The subway would link with and thereby facilitate the development of the city's still broader transportation infrastructure. During the 1890s, this infrastructure incorporated electric street railways and elevated lines and, after the turn of the century, the rail connections provided by the Pennsylvania and Grand Central stations. Under the supervision of Parsons, the Interborough Rapid Transit Company began construction of the first subway line by 1900, which ran beneath Broadway from City Hall Park north to 145th Street. In 1904, it extended the line southward from the park through the first tunnel below the East River, joining lower Manhattan with downtown Brooklyn. By 1906, it had extended the line still farther northward, constructing a new branch to connect with 180th Street in the Bronx, and by 1908, it added another branch extending to 242nd Street. Under William McAdoo, the engineers and builders completed two new tunnels below the Hudson River by 1910, joining by rail the Hudson Terminal Buildings at Church Street and Fulton with stations in Newark, New Jersey. Farther uptown, the new Queensborough (1909) and Manhattan bridges (1910) linked Manhattan with Queens and Brooklyn.[30] Ironically, the city's ambitious and ingenious engineering of such a transportation infrastructure, aimed at relieving lower Manhattan's congestion of workplaces, only further propelled Broadway's speculative development and energetic dynamic of vertical construction. The increasing height of the steel-framed structures bordering Broadway on both sides, then, correlated decisively with the spreading, horizontal growth of the city's layered network of infrastructural modernization.

In choosing to construct a steel-framed skyscraper on lower Broadway, Woolworth staked his own claim in the technological modernization of New York. Earlier, he had voiced a comparable ambition to modernize when planning his first Woolworth Building in Lancaster. "Modern America," he later recalled, "was growing up all around" the Pennsylvania city, "and it just had to move forward."[31] Woolworth, furthermore, had by 1890 pointed to New York as the day's quintessentially modern, vertical city. It claimed, as he put it, a large commercial harbor, elevated railroads, "lofty" buildings, crowds, and "life, push, and snap."[32] Perhaps most important, Woolworth participated in a retailing culture that linked the use of inventive construction techniques with the novel, the eye-catching, and the fashionable, as exemplified by Stewart's, Wanamaker's, and especially Boucicaut's spectacular department store interiors, the latter featuring a light-filled atrium, cantilevered staircases, and free-hanging balconies with construction in iron and glass (see fig. 1.13).

When the Edison Electric Illuminating Company completed the first electrical generating station in lower Manhattan in 1882, the Pearl Street Station, Woolworth and his contemporaries in retailing identified in electricity yet another modern tool with seemingly limitless market potential. Electrical illumination brought a new level of seductiveness to the display of ordinary commodities, elevating their appearances to "the level of the marvelous."[33] Electricity, moreover, had altered the pace of life; as Stephen Kern put it, "nothing moved faster than the electricity that raced through conduits, powering motors, and accelerating a variety of activities," among the latter the "liquidity of securities" through telephonic communication, inciting Wall Street's leap to dominance as a world financial center.[34] In 1902, *Harper's Weekly* described lower Manhattan's electrical power grid as a forceful signifier of the city's modernity: "The city is simply bursting its bonds. It is as if some mighty force were astir beneath the ground, hour by hour pushing up structures that a dozen years ago would have been inconceivable. . . . The distribution of electrical energy through the streets and the invention of the steam-drill, together with the use of skeleton frames for immense buildings, have transformed the outward appearance of the town."[35] If steel-framed construction and electricity functioned as the visible signs of modernity, then the "mighty force" to which *Harper's* referred also involved no less than the city's intensifying "trade" in three-dimensional urban space.[36] For Woolworth, these aspects of the new city growing up around lower Broadway represented "modern America."

For the writer and historian Henry Adams, lower Broadway's infrastructural modernization, electrification, and vertical drive skyward exemplified another social phenomenon entirely; he wrote of "new forces" that "must at any cost be brought under control."[37] To Adams, the skyscrapers' heights signified on the one hand a confusing, frightful, and extreme consolidation of industrially based financial power and on the other the city's seemingly inhuman capacity for competition, the growing insidiousness of its commercial values, and the whole disquieting process of change.[38] Adams condemned lower Broadway's skyscrapers as the metaphor for the darker side of modernity. For Woolworth and many of his business contemporaries, however, the very personifications of Adams's new forces, the modern city stood to the contrary as evidence of their ability to impose the latest market values on the urban surroundings—now as seemingly transitory as the processes of capitalism itself. Hence, lower Manhattan possessed an "extraordinary, almost electric sense of excitement."[39]

In distant views, lower Broadway's towering skyscrapers created a new urban identity for New York—that of the first "signature" skyline (fig. 2.6). "Skyline" had come into common use in the mid-1890s to describe the new profile view of the city's tall buildings; this view replaced the older harbor views as the accepted convention for picturing the city.[40] Illustrations in popular journals such as *Harper's Weekly* and *Scientific American* celebrated the city's new identity by contrasting its old and new skylines; skyscrapers, they emphasized, had replaced the steeples of churches to command the profile views.[41] In the eyes of many architectural critics, however, the new skyline had associations echoing Adams's condemnation of lower Broadway. Montgomery Schuyler, for example, wrote in 1897 that the view might not be "agreeable" but was nonetheless "tremendously forcible"; it impressively and exclusively "looked like business." Schuyler further lamented the skyline's lack of ensemble, noting that such a speculative, ad hoc composition limited even "artistic-minded designers" to a mere aestheticizing function: In imagining the silhouette from across the river, however, they might give the view "of spirit and picturesqueness."[42] In the same year, the architect and critic A. D. F. Hamlin advocated the design of skyscrapers as isolated towers; only then might the chaotic skyline attain such a desired quality of picturesqueness.[43]

FIGURE 2.6 *The Skyline of Buildings below Chambers Street, as Seen from the Hudson River*. From *Harper's Weekly*, vol. 31 (March 20, 1897), showing the skylines of 1881 and 1897. (Courtesy of the Trustees of the Boston Public Library.)

With the new explosion of construction in lower Manhattan around 1900 and the city's setting of a new record for height with the 391-foot Park Row Building (R. H. Robertson, 1896–99), the debate over the aesthetics and meanings of the skyline intensified. Many questioned the social implications of the new, towering mass of skyscrapers. On the one hand, they suggested a business community vigorously engaged in the shared activity of white-collar work. The Boston architect and planner Sylvester Baxter, for example, characterized the city's profile in 1906 as "the effect of collective activity" that accompanied "a common impulse in a given direction."[44] On the other hand, many thought that very activity inextricable from what amounted to a wholly new social order, described by Henry James during his 1904 visit to New York as "a vast, crude democracy of trade."[45] The single-minded pursuit of profits at any cost, architectural critics similarly argued, compromised the older, republican ideal of community for the singular objective of private gain. For Montgomery Schuyler, writing in 1907, the skyscrapers, regardless of the merits of the view, suggested individuals "merged in a riot." Altogether, they appeared "bewildering and stupefying in the mass, with no ensemble but that of strife and struggle."[46] The editors of *American Architect and Building News* echoed Schuyler, writing that the skyline represented no less than a "vaunting of sheer materialism."[47] While the skyline generated mixed feelings for many observers, for others, it also powerfully signified a peculiarly "American" character. The critic Mary Fanton Roberts argued in 1907 that it represented "the first absolutely genuine expression of an original American architecture." As a consequence, the new skyline had the capacity to convey potent messages about Americans as a "busy people" engaged in "fearlessly building" to suit the most ordinary of functional needs.[48]

Ernest Flagg's 612-foot Singer Tower, completed in 1908, nearly doubled the skyline's height. It represented the boldest expression to date of New York's increasingly ambitious dynamic of vertical construction, effecting a striking change in the city's profile. Critics acclaimed and commercial photographers celebrated the tower in picture postcard views (fig. 2.7). Schuyler judged it "among the most interesting of our experiments in skyscraping."[49] Van Dyke praised Flagg's design as both beautiful and outrageous in his *New New York*, and the editors of *Architectural Record* hailed it as a spectacular skyline feature, whose completion marked the "breaking through of another stratum of ether" to create a striking silhouette for the city.[50] For Harrison Rhodes, writing in the popular literary journal *Harper's Monthly*, such towers embodied "the romance of the future."[51] In a similar vein, Joseph B. Gilder confessed in *Putnam's Monthly* that although he opposed skyscrapers, they might if treated as towers number among "the chief architectural ornaments of the new New York."[52] The Singer's crown functioned effectively as a trademark, but critics focused their appreciation instead on the tower's artistic contribution to the distant skyline views. Van Dyke compared lower Manhattan's water approaches with those of Constantinople.[53] A writer for the *Living Age* responded in 1909 that such a "towered city" on the water, recalling Venice or ancient Tyre, would indeed provide New York with an unmistakable urban identity: "The dead skyline of the future city will not rise extravagantly high, but above it, like particular peaks in

FIGURE 2.7 New York from the Hudson River, 1908. Photograph by Irving Underhill (postcard view). Author's collection.

a chain of mountains, will be towers and domes and pinnacles, through which the sun may shine and the breezes blow. New York will be a towered city. And of course this style of architecture will be imitated all over the world. . . . The towers of New York will be reckoned as characteristic as the minarets of a Mohammedan city, as the bell towers of Russia, as the pillar-towers of India . . . or as the campaniles of Italy."[54] For locals and visitors alike, the startlingly vertical commercial tower, all dazzle, modernity, and show, pointed to a new urban identity for New York among the metropolises of the world.

CITY HALL PARK

The evolving skyline of lower Manhattan would provide visibility for Woolworth's skyscraper in the newly popular profile views, but Woolworth found City Hall Park, lower Manhattan's most prominent open space, of still greater value. The open expanse of the park, he argued, would provide the ideal environment for showcasing his skyscraper as a "giant signboard." The skyscraper's architectural elevation would have full frontal exposure in vistas across the park, and so would be seen in its entirety by spectators stationed at distant locations and, in particular, by the crowds crossing the Brooklyn Bridge (see figs. 2.1, 2.2). The effects of such architectural visibility would have been difficult to achieve on a site confined by the dense pattern of streets making up lower Manhattan's financial district.

Woolworth had ample time to study City Hall Park's potential as a setting for such a "giant signboard." Between 1888 and 1901, he numbered among the throng of approximately five hundred thousand commuters who poured into the park each day from the Brooklyn Bridge, departing for work by foot from his brownstone at 209 Jefferson Avenue in Brooklyn. By the early 1890s, the city's leading newspapers, notably the *World*, the *Tribune*, and the *Times*, had built a series of architecturally ostentatious towers on the park, bordering Park Row, known collectively as "Newspaper Row." For these, such a public park with benches and trees served effectively as the superb architectural "forecourt" (fig. 2.8). In competing ambitiously for the widest possible readership during the 1880s and 1890s, the newspapers may have anticipated, as one writer for *Scribner's* put it, that the crowds who observed and appreciated Newspaper Row would presume that "the length of their subscription lists [was] in proportion to the height of their towers."[55] The newspapers' choice of location also reflected their desire for geographic proximity to City Hall, the chief source of local news. In exploiting for advertising purposes the visibility afforded by the park, they collectively invested the competitive mass publishing industry with a glittering profile in one of the most densely populated regions of the city.

Joseph Pulitzer's World Building, the tallest and most flamboyant of the newspaper headquarters facing City Hall Park, may well have functioned as an instructive model for Woolworth. Pulitzer drew on techniques from the advertising industry to contrive during his rivalry with William Randolph Hearst a new brand of journalism, called "yellow journalism," which sensationalized the more strident and colorful elements of the city's mass culture. Just as Woolworth had designed his stores and show windows to catch the eye of the potential shopper, so Pulitzer designed his newspaper's bold graphics—with large headlines, multicolumn banners, cartoons, and illustrations enhancing the comprehension of written text—to command the

FIGURE 2.8 City Hall Park and Newspaper Row (Park Row), ca. 1900. Photograph by the Detroit Publishing Company. Prints and Photographs Division, Library of Congress.

attention of the widest, most diversified readership possible, among it the city's working classes and foreign immigrants.[56] As a consequence, the *World* prospered, boasting in 1886 a record-breaking circulation of two hundred fifty thousand. As if to cater to this new, visually attuned mass readership, Pulitzer began construction of his new headquarters, the World Building, three years later.

The World Building, at twenty-six stories the tallest skyscraper in the city, had a jarring red, buff, and gray exterior. Its architect, George Post, crowned that exterior with a gilded Baroque dome that visually dominated the City Hall's (see fig. 2.2). At the skyscraper's completion, Pulitzer enlisted both the mayor and the governor's participation in a splashy opening ceremony. A crowd of thousands filled City Hall Park to view the event. Afterward, Pulitzer invited the crowd to ride by elevator up to the skyscraper's top story and to take in the highest and hence the most spectacular views of the city—views that during the 1890s he would promote to tourists. As a consequence, the skyscraper became an overnight architectural sensation, commanding the attention of people in the park and highlighting the *World's* supremacy among its neighboring newspaper rivals.[57] Pulitzer had discovered architecture's potential for self-advertising.

As the showy architecture of Newspaper Row suggested, City Hall Park during the 1880s and 1890s functioned as a vibrant center of urban activity, a kind of outdoor stage for a range of civic-spirited mass spectacles, among them watching election returns and news of important events on large bulletin boards; bringing in the New Year with red, white, and blue incandescent illumination decorating City Hall; and in 1899, the city's official reception of Admiral Dewey after his military exploits in the Philippines (fig. 2.9).[58] The newspaper enterprises whose headquarters fronted the park may have found it advantageous to locate in such a civic-spirited center of major public events and their journalistic coverage. There, benefiting from the aura of municipal idealism surrounding the historic City Hall, they could pretend a public identity, decked out in the architectural regalia of historically sanctioned towers and domes.[59] Few spaces in lower Manhattan, Woolworth may well have surmised, supplied such a richness of opportunity for broad exposure among the city's crowds and for private profit through such public associations.

At the turn of the century, New York's Municipal Art Society began advocating a wholly contrasting vision for City Hall Park, one that emphasized the city as a dignified public realm as opposed to merely a colorful setting for mass spectacles. Inspired by the Senate Park Commission Plan for Washington of 1901–2, the Municipal Art Society—an elite, reform-minded organization composed of leaders in the city's government, professions, and the arts—imagined the park as a restored and rebuilt civic center, the focal point of a

WATCHING THE BULLETIN-BOARDS ON PARK ROW AT THE TIME OF DEWEY'S GREAT BATTLE OF MANILA BAY.

FIGURE 2.9 *Watching the Bulletin-Boards on Park Row at the Time of Dewey's Great Battle of Manila Bay*. From E. Idell Zeisloft, *The New Metropolis*, 1899. Milstein Division of United States History, Local History, and Genealogy, New York Public Library, Astor, Lenox, and Tilden Foundations.

FIGURE 2.10 George Post and Henry Hornbostel with Gustav Lindenthal, commissioner, New York City Department of Bridges, proposed civic center and Brooklyn Bridge terminal, City Hall Park, 1903. From Municipal Art Society of New York, *Report of the Committee on Civic Centers* (New York, 1905).

"city beautiful," and the heart of New York as a dignified and triumphant "imperial capital."[60] After the creation of five-borough greater New York in 1898, the society's president, John De Witt Warner, wrote in *Municipal Affairs* that New Yorkers now bore the responsibility for "building the world's capital for all time to come."[61] Herbert Croly, the noted progressive critic and, from 1900, editor of *Architectural Record*, similarly advised in 1903 that New York, having risen to the stature of "at least the financial and industrial metropolis of the United States," must now do something "to anticipate, to clarify, and to realize the best national ideals in politics, society, literature, and art."[62] Warner and Croly's ideas coincided with Charles Mulford Robinson's influential *Modern Civic Art* (1903), which championed the importance to the "city beautiful" of the dignified civic center: A grouped arrangement of public buildings inspired by European models, it would compose a city's monumental core; reflecting the pride of the citizenry, it would officially represent a city's inhabitants, institutions, and ideals.[63] New York's civic center at City Hall Park, not surprisingly, had become the focus of this new, publicly oriented municipal idealism.

Led by Warner, the Municipal Art Society developed a block plan in 1902, which distilled their ambitions for a redesigned City Hall Park. In 1903, at the behest of Mayor Seth Low and the New York Board of Estimate, and working in association with Gustav Lindenthal of the Department of Bridges, George Post and Henry Hornbostel revised the plan, as part of a broader effort to alleviate congestion at the terminus of the Brooklyn Bridge and to accommodate the needs of the city's transportation, engineering, and manufacturing interests (fig. 2.10). The earlier plan had isolated Mangin and McComb's jewel-like, neoclassical City Hall (1802–11) in a pristine open setting, cleared of the encroaching Tweed Court House (John Kellum and Leopold Eidlitz, 1861–81) and flanked by the city's key public buildings.[64] Post and Hornbostel, however, also proposed demolishing the Second Empire Post Office (Alfred Mullet, 1875), and, importantly, they proposed incorporating a 650-foot municipal campanile in a new terminal for the Brooklyn Bridge. The city intended to finance the campanile, which was to house municipal offices, by using interest on bonds equivalent to the amount they had spent on office rentals elsewhere in the city. As the tallest tower in New York at the time, it would unassailably command the lower Manhattan skyline.[65] It was Post and Hornbostel's purpose, journalists reported, to "dwarf" the skyscrapers of the neighborhood.[66] The New York skyline, consequently, would be dominated by a tower that belonged to the municipality as opposed to commerce.

Although the city's new mayor, George McClellan, chose not to build the campanile, the New York City Improvement Commission incorporated lessons from the civic center's design in its reports of 1904 and 1907.[67] Well before the publication of the reports, however, Robinson called City Hall Park, "the centre of the municipal life of the chief city of the United States," an "apparently lost opportunity."[68] In the same year, Croly denounced the city's neglect of City Hall Park as the setting for the City Hall, the one public building of "general interest and pride"; it had allowed the park to become "overrun with buildings, with no approaches, no vistas, very little atmosphere, and no disposition of any kind to give space, distinction, and dignity."[69] Van Dyke echoed Croly in 1909: "The small park about [City Hall] seems to hold off invasion year by year; but the skyscrapers near at hand—the lofty towers of the Park Row Building, the gilded dome of the World that repeats the City Hall cupola on a massive scale of impudence . . . seem to look over and glare at it as if wondering what it is doing there."[70] Any designer who aspired to give New York a proper civic center, both architectural critics and advocates of the City Beautiful movement suggested, faced eclipse by the city's market forces.

By the end of the decade, the Municipal Art Society's planning agenda had taken the character of a last-ditch effort to defiantly impose on the skyline the centrality of the progressive elite's municipal values. In 1910, the New York architect James Riely Gordon proposed a one-thousand-foot-high county courthouse to replace the spatially inadequate Tweed Court House on the northern edge of City Hall Park (fig. 2.11). Gordon, originally from Texas, specialized in courthouses; he had also recently designed the territorial capitol for Arizona (1899–1900). He responded to the Court House Board's call for a new design with a composition of four colossal Doric columns. Crowned with a 192-foot statue of Justice, which carried a Roman torch illuminated by a ten-foot-high electrical flame, Gordon's Court House would triumph over lower Manhattan's commercial skyscrapers, as if to reclaim with finality the identity of the municipal government on the skyline.[71]

To make a mark in America's economic capital, to be close to the heart of banking and finance, to build a modern skyscraper on lower Broadway, and to secure the highest possible visibility at City Hall Park—these were key siting considerations for Woolworth. Given such criteria, the Municipal Art Society's proposals for City Hall Park may have caught his attention. In 1895, he wrote to a friend from Paris to

FIGURE 2.11 James Riely Gordon, "Temple of Justice," project, 1910. James Riely Gordon Drawings and Papers, Alexander Architectural Archive, University of Texas Libraries, University of Texas, Austin.

jubilantly assert that he had discovered the "city beautiful" in the city's fountains, gardens, and architecture.[72] Yet regardless of his appreciation of the "city beautiful," and in all likelihood his knowledge of the idealism surrounding the Municipal Art Society's City Hall Park proposals, Woolworth still aimed first and foremost to advertise with his skyscraper as a spectacular "giant signboard."

Regardless of Woolworth's objective in choosing a site adjacent to City Hall Park, his decision to build a skyscraper at such a location aroused high skepticism among experts in the city's real estate circles.[73] "The real estate people said it was a gigantic gamble," Woolworth later recalled—"that it could never be filled."[74] For those experts, a skyscraper's raison d'être derived from its convenience of location to future rent-paying tenants. Richard Hurd's authoritative *Principles of City Land Values* (1903), for example, noted that the land values of lower Manhattan rose by a factor of approximately forty in the vicinity of the New York Stock Exchange: on Broadway between Cortlandt and Wall streets and on Wall Street between William Street and Broadway.[75] Consequently, the closer that Woolworth located his skyscraper to the financial nexus of Wall Street and the exchange, the greater its likelihood for commanding high rental rates. It was a maxim among investors well before Woolworth's day that the desirability and hence the commercial value of urban real estate hinged on its proximity to "where everybody else is."[76]

Despite the expert consensus on the city's real estate values, Woolworth believed that a skyscraper built adjacent to City Hall Park could be nonetheless financially profitable—particularly if as a landmark it had the advantage of great size and distinction.[77] As a new center of attraction, such a landmark had the potential to "create" land values. It would pull other commercial interests into its orbit, induce the city's leading corporate executives, entrepreneurs, and professionals to leave less glamorous office buildings and to relocate, and in doing so, enhance the value of surrounding property.[78] Woolworth had already pointed out to skeptics that his Lancaster Woolworth Building, a bold intervention on the "wrong" side of Queen Street, had the power to change the undesirable side of the street into a fashionable and prosperous "right" side of the street. He boasted to incredulous friends shortly after the project opened that the sidewalk's teeming pedestrian traffic had indeed proved his experiment succeeded.[79] Such a conception of his skyscraper as a landmark, above all else, influenced Woolworth's decision to locate at City Hall Park, or on the edge of New York's financial district, rather than at its heart and center. In standing perpetually free from the congestion of "where everybody else is," moreover, the landmark would be visible to crowds.

In 1911, Woolworth further argued that for several reasons City Hall Park, in fact, had begun to function within lower Manhattan as a second node of development, rivaling that of Wall Street and the Stock Exchange. First, in serving as the location for the municipal government's offices, it offered a larger rental market than speculators in urban real estate had typically assumed. The city's expanding government bureaucracy had already absorbed vast amounts of space in buildings situated around the park, and recently the city had proposed a new municipal office building as the future center of its affairs, along with yet another courthouse for the Stewart Building site, both of which would attract additional municipal government workers and trial lawyers to the area. Second, the Post Office had served as a magnet for that office space: On account of the huge volume of business conducted through the mail, it attracted important financial concerns to the area. Finally, City Hall Park had become in its own right an important transportation hub.[80] All, to Woolworth's thinking, pointed to a new vitality of white-collar office work in the vicinity of City Hall Park, suggesting in turn a desire for convenience and centrality on the part of future tenants seeking office space.

Woolworth never mentioned it, but in conceiving his skyscraper as a landmark he had yet another critical advantage over his competitors in the city's real estate industry, most of whom ceased planning new office buildings in times of oversupply and low rents. His financial clout as a corporate capitalist was such that he did not have to rely on his huge speculative investment to turn a quick profit. Nor did he as an investor feel compelled to "play it safe" by following the standard financial formulas. Consequently, he could afford to be impractical; he could take the time to build the project of his dreams. The strength of Woolworth's financial position, according to one contemporary, unnerved other speculative investors in the real estate field.[81]

Exactly where Woolworth sited his landmark skyscraper, then, was inextricably linked with his concept of what the project was going to be. On the one hand, the skyscraper would have an address on lower Broadway, the city's spine of high-style consumerism, the axis around which clustered skyscrapers whose crowns functioned like trademarks, and the site of a technological modernization so massive as to make New York unique among the cities of the world. On the other hand, the skyscraper would have a commanding architectural presence on the city's most important public open space, City Hall Park—a center of mass-market journalism, flamboyant architectural advertising, civic-spirited mass spectacles, and, more recently, catalyst for the municipal ideals and imperial strivings of the City Beautiful movement.

Above all else, Woolworth's choice of a site mirrored his vision for the skyscraper as a piece of spectacular advertising, or "giant signboard," a vision bound up with the modern world of consumerist seduction that he had in large part defined. In the process, Woolworth had perfected the art of enticing and manipulating the attention of crowds. No matter how those crowds happened to encounter his future skyscraper—from the axis of lower Broadway or the wide spatial expanse of City Hall Park—it would alter their perceptions of the city.

The Irving National Exchange Bank and the Broadway–Park Place Company

In identifying the site for his skyscraper, Woolworth relied on his own calculated analyses of New York land values, the circulation of sidewalk crowds, examples of earlier skyscrapers built for advertising purposes, and office needs at City Hall Park. Financing the skyscraper, however, presented a separate problem entirely. So did identifying the expected anchor tenant, ideally a major bank, to occupy its main story. Irving National Exchange Bank, Woolworth's bank, offered a solution that addressed both. Around 1907, Woolworth began discussions about the project's financing with Irving's president, Lewis E. Pierson. He proposed involving the bank with financing in three stages: first, with finalizing the acquisition of the project's site; second, as a partner in its development as a speculative office building; and third, with overseeing the completed skyscraper as a lucrative rental property. The bank, as a consequence, would assume a pivotal role in making Woolworth's skyscraper a financially viable enterprise. Indeed, as Montgomery Schuyler later noted, if Woolworth had not formed a partnership with Irving, which also sought a "new quarters," the Woolworth Building might not have been built at all.[82]

On March 1, 1910, Woolworth formed a joint stock corporation, the "Broadway–Park Place Company," officially establishing Irving National Exchange Bank as the project's financial partner. Earlier that February, he had begun acquiring the project's site. After discovering that Mercantile Bank intended to sell 237 Broadway, located directly across from the Post Office, he had his real estate agent for the project, Edward J. Hogan, investigate an adjacent parcel for sale to the south, at 233 and 235 Broadway (see figs. 2.1, 2.12).[83]

FIGURE 2.12 View of lower Broadway, from Park Row, ca. 1900. Photograph by George P. Hall and Son. Collection of the New-York Historical Society, negative 78901d.

Formerly the site of New York mayor Philip Hone's house, the parcel had more recently served as the site of Tracy and Erwin's Dry Goods Store. Across the street to the south stood the Astor House Hotel (Isaiah Rogers, 1834–36), historically renowned as the city's first luxury hotel. Woolworth asked Hogan to begin negotiations on both parcels immediately.[84] With the acquisition of the site decisively underway, Woolworth began outlining Irving National's financial stake in the project.

In 1907, Woolworth had facilitated a merger to create the Irving National Exchange Bank, bringing together New York National Exchange Bank—on whose board of directors he served—with Irving National Bank. Pierson, then New York National's president, had conceived the merger for the purpose of easing the two banks' stiff competition for depositors.[85] When Pierson's negotiations for the merger stalled, Woolworth acquired enough stock in Irving National to ensure the merger's success. At the same time, he stipulated that the new and larger Irving National Exchange Bank, with Pierson as president, lease offices in his proposed skyscraper. Boasting combined assets of over $24 million, the new bank would also function as a useful source of capital in what Woolworth at the time conceived as a limited joint venture.[86]

Shortly after the merger, Irving National Exchange Bank began seeking locations for its own new and larger headquarters. In 1908, its board of directors appointed Woolworth to a Committee on Quarters. Even though Woolworth had already stipulated that the bank occupy his future skyscraper, the committee argued instead that the bank should expand its existing offices on the third floor of the Gerkin Building at West Broadway, Hudson, and Reade streets. It also considered renting other properties. After briefly evaluating West Broadway and Reade as a site for the skyscraper, Woolworth argued strongly for the bank's relocation to a more prestigious Broadway address. Such an address, Woolworth maintained, would be critical if the bank intended to "gain about two million dollars in deposits" and to rank among the "great banks" of New York.[87] Even before the merger, Woolworth had tried to convince New York National that it should relocate to space adjacent to his own offices within the Stewart Building.[88]

In drafting the original prospectus for the Broadway–Park Place Company, Woolworth at first proposed putting up the initial capital for the skyscraper himself and then having Irving National Exchange Bank buy back the corporation's stock year by year until it owned both the corporation and the skyscraper outright. In the interim, Irving would assume the entire eighteen-story rental capacity of the planned $1 million office building on a twenty-five-year lease. Rents paid by F. W. Woolworth and Company and other tenants would allow the bank to occupy its own quarters rent free. The bank could nominate two of the Broadway–Park Place Company's five directors, but its president would be Woolworth.[89] Strangely, Woolworth's prospectus cast Irving in an extremely powerful role—as the future owner of "his" skyscraper.

As Woolworth and Irving National Exchange Bank hammered out the details of creating the Broadway–Park Place Company, Woolworth continued to acquire parcels at Broadway and Park Place. He investigated two new parcels bordering Park Place to the west of the two he had recently acquired on Broadway and authorized Hogan to begin negotiations with their owners. On April 15, 1910, Woolworth signed the agreements to purchase 6 and

8 Park Place. He combined the two new parcels with those he had already acquired at 233, 235, and 237 Broadway. The resulting rectangular site extended 80 feet along Broadway and 173 feet along Park Place (fig 2.13). Woolworth, in the end, spent a total of $1.65 million assembling the Woolworth Bank and Office Building's original site.[90]

Shortly after Woolworth finalized the purchase of the site's last two parcels, his plans for the Broadway–Park Place Company took a new and unexpected turn. On April 19, he totally reconfigured the corporation's original prospectus. The Broadway–Park Place Company would now construct a larger, twenty-story building, the cost of which Woolworth now estimated at $1.5 million. Woolworth's financial stake would dominate, and the bank, now but a minor partner, would underwrite only one-third of the project's total, or five hundred thousand dollars. Woolworth would underwrite the remainder. Significantly, Woolworth stipulated that Irving allow him to name the skyscraper after himself, as the "Woolworth Bank and Office Building," an assertion that reinforced his claim of a newly powerful financial role in the project. Irving agreed to lease for a twenty-five-year period the building's entire main story, a room for the bank's board of directors on the fourth floor, and vaults in the basement. Irving's board officially endorsed the new prospectus on April 20, 1910.[91]

Although Irving National Exchange Bank had much to offer Woolworth and his project in the way of financial security, the bank's visibility and presence on the skyscraper's main floor provided Woolworth and his F. W. Woolworth and Company with a mark of status and prestige difficult to calculate in rational economic terms. Leading banking houses had by the 1830s

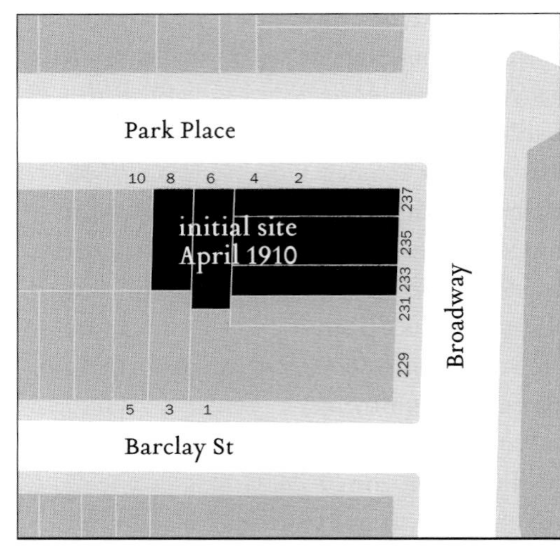

FIGURE 2.13 Woolworth Building site at Broadway and Park Place, April 15, 1910. Map by Dennis McClendon.

concentrated near the New York Stock Exchange and Merchant's Exchange on Wall Street—among them Bank of America, City Bank, Bank of New York, and Manhattan Bank—making the city the nation's indisputable banking capital. By 1900, the banks claimed 25 percent of the nation's financial resources. They continued to export capital to foreign offices abroad, a practice that had originated in the 1880s, leading John Jay Knox, the nation's comptroller of currency, to call lower Manhattan the "clearinghouse of the western world."[92] Significantly for Woolworth, New York's banks had also financed the turn of the century's wave of corporate consolidations, with his own and those of the nation's other mass retailing enterprises numbering prominently among them.

Ever since Woolworth's arrival in New York in 1886, the growth of his retailing enterprise had mirrored the growth of Irving National Exchange Bank. He began his relationship as a depositor at New York National Exchange Bank, but as he continued to expand his chain, the bank had in all probability served as the creditor for his manufacturers and wholesale suppliers and had thereby indirectly financed that expansion.[93] Perhaps most important, after Woolworth assisted New York National's merger with Irving, the newly enlarged bank had become an extremely powerful bank, in itself a formidable product of the early twentieth century's wave of corporate consolidations. The new Irving National Exchange Bank, now with twice the capital, or $2 million, and with assets of $32 million, had gained financial clout among investors on Wall Street.[94] Woolworth's own capital, in turn, accounted for a substantial portion of the bank's reserves.

Woolworth valued his long association with Irving National Exchange Bank. Such an association brought prestige to Woolworth's enterprise and to the Woolworth name. Later, it found a counterpart in his so-called binding provision, a legal document he had drawn up prohibiting a five- and ten-cent store from occupying the skyscraper's ground floor.[95] Woolworth's earlier Lancaster Woolworth Building and related speculative projects, by contrast, had featured ground-floor five-and-tens. Woolworth's stores, furthermore, constituted a formidable presence on the sidewalks of greater New York; he had opened twelve new stores in Manhattan alone since 1896, averaging one per year, creating a total of thirteen by 1910.[96] Yet between his Manhattan stores and his New York headquarters Woolworth set up a calculated distance. He placed greater importance on his relationship with the bank.

In choosing to locate the Woolworth Syndicate's headquarters in the Stewart Building, Woolworth had linked his identity as a merchant with that of New York's historically wealthiest merchant, A. T. Stewart. Subsequently, he had built a conspicuous French Renaissance chateau on Fifth Avenue, seeking social distinction among the city's prominent capitalists in industry and high finance. Now, as both the F. W. Woolworth and Company's controlling shareholder and also a major shareholder in Irving National Exchange Bank, Woolworth cemented his ties architecturally with the very institution that had supported the growth of his enterprise, and in which he had invested personally. Most important, Irving continued to shelter his own staggering accumulation of capital. Woolworth's business may have been five- and ten-cent retailing among the nation's sidewalk crowds. But Irving's presence in the Woolworth Building would establish his identity as a formidable capitalist in the nation's preeminent clearinghouse of capital, lower Manhattan's citadel of banking and finance.

Selecting Cass Gilbert as the Architect

Woolworth selected Cass Gilbert as the architect for the Woolworth Bank and Office Building in early April 1910, shortly after setting up the Broadway–Park Place Company and about a week before finalizing negotiations for the site's two remaining parcels bordering Park Place. Woolworth had already defined the many complex goals he aspired to fulfill with the construction of his skyscraper. Now, for obvious reasons, he sought an architect who would help him realize the project in his imagination. Yet Woolworth's choice of Gilbert, and Gilbert's method of securing the Woolworth Building commission in turn, also reflected a larger, albeit localized, social phenomenon: the degree to which the city's commercial impulses, among them aggressive salesmanship and heated speculation in land, had permeated all human encounters, even the professional architect-and-client relationship.

According to the builder Theodore Starrett, Woolworth aspired to construct a grander version of Gilbert's West Street Building, having "admired the Gothic style of that structure" (fig. 2.14).[97] The architect Guy Kirkham later recalled that "the West Street Building was largely responsible for attracting the interest of Mr. Woolworth of 'five and ten fame.'"[98] Completed in 1907, Gilbert's West Street Building stood at the intersection of West Street with Cedar and Albany streets, only a few blocks away from Woolworth's Stewart Building headquarters. In identifying the West Street Building as a model, Woolworth may have been thinking of his favorite retail architecture; this skyscraper, too, had modern, open, light-admitting facades. He also followed a familiar pattern in making his choice. As if buying one of the finely crafted commodities he planned for sale in his stores, Woolworth first selected an example of the product he intended to acquire—albeit through the processes of design and construction—and then identified its designer.

Woolworth may have also admired Gilbert's other works of Beaux-Arts architecture in lower Manhattan. Gilbert's Broadway Chambers Building rose to completion in 1900, directly across from his Stewart Building headquarters. More important, Woolworth had seen and experienced on a day-to-day basis Gilbert's monumental United States Custom House (1899–1907), sited at the foot of lower Broadway facing Bowling Green (fig. 2.15). By the early 1900s, Woolworth was reputed to be "the largest importer in the United States" in half of the lines he sold and a "name" that "figures most conspicuously in Custom House affairs."[99]

In 1904, Woolworth visited the Louisiana Purchase Exposition. At its architectural focal point stood Gilbert's Beaux-Arts Festival Hall. The same year, he may well have seen or visited Gilbert's Minnesota State Capitol (1895–1905) while inspecting stores in St. Paul and Minneapolis.[100] Equally important to Woolworth, Gilbert had earned in his estimation a national reputation as an architect: he called Gilbert "the greatest architect in the United States" after the Woolworth Building's completion, adding that he had designed "enormous and magnificent and artistic buildings" such as the West Street Building, the United States Custom House, and the Minnesota State Capitol.[101]

Little documentation of the early meetings between Woolworth and Gilbert survives. As late as March 12, 1910, the *Record and Guide* reported that regarding the Woolworth Building, "no plans have yet been prepared or architect selected."[102] After the completion of the project, however, Gilbert provided his own matter-of-fact explanation describing how he obtained the commission. "One day I received a telephone call. It was Mr. Woolworth. He asked me if I would consider a proposition to build a big structure for him. I said that was my business. He asked me if I could drop in some day and talk things over. . . . I happened to be going downtown that day. I visited his office. He outlined to me some idea of a skyscraper. There ensued many such conferences, but it wasn't until several weeks had elapsed that Mr. Woolworth told me to go ahead with the designs. . . . Mr. Woolworth had had an idea for the building for some time before he spoke to me about it."[103] Gilbert did not acknowledge any preliminary introduction to Woolworth. According to the architect Egerton Swartwout, however, Gilbert pursued Woolworth, coordinating a voyage to Europe with his and supposedly having Woolworth approve a preliminary

FIGURE 2.14 Cass Gilbert, West Street Building, at 90 West Street between Cedar and Albany streets, 1905–7. Photograph by Irving Underhill. Collection of the New-York Historical Society, negative 32071.

study for the skyscraper and sign the contract for his professional services in advance of the ship's meeting the opposite shore.[104] But as the project's documentation shows, Swartwout's account was apocryphal: It would have been impossible for Woolworth to leave New York for Europe in either March or April, due to his already heavy involvement with the planning of the Woolworth Bank and Office Building.[105]

Before Gilbert received Woolworth's telephone call, it is possible that Woolworth's real estate agent, Edward J. Hogan, served as the intermediary between the two men. Hogan had known Woolworth for almost ten years, having sold him the Fifth Avenue property for his French Renaissance chateau. Hogan also knew John Peirce, a builder with close ties to Gilbert, having been responsible for the United States Custom House's granite contract and, later, the West Street Building.[106] At the end of April, Hogan congratulated Gilbert, calling him the "lucky architect," adding that "I naturally have a great deal of interest in this transaction, having been with it from the start."[107]

Regardless of Hogan's having possibly introduced Woolworth and Gilbert, rumors about Woolworth's skyscraper had begun circulating years in advance of their meeting. In March 1910, for example, *Record and Guide* observed that "for a long time prior to 1906, it was a common report among financial interests that Irving National Bank [at the time, New York National Exchange Bank] was anxious to get hold of a plot on Broadway, on which to establish a headquarters."[108] According to both Louis Horowitz and Paul Starrett, the two builders who would later compete for the contract to construct the project, specula-

FIGURE 2.15 Cass Gilbert, United States Custom House, Bowling Green, 1899–1907. Photograph by George P. Hall and Son, 1908. Collection of the New-York Historical Society, negative 59216.

tion about the skyscraper had thrived in New York's building community for several years.[109] Gilbert, consequently, had good reason to have heard about such an attractive architectural commission.

Gilbert and Woolworth did not at all know each other, nor did they share a common circle of social acquaintances in New York. They had, rather, established independent social identities. These, in turn, were tied to their club memberships—New York City being "easily first among the cities of the new world" in the "number, variety, wealth, and importance" of clubs.[110] Gilbert belonged to the exclusive Union Club, the "wealthiest and most famous club in America," along with Stanford White and Charles McKim, for which he designed a new headquarters in association with John Du Fais in 1900. Established in 1836, the Union Club was known at the turn of the century for its strong Republican orientation as well as for its status as the city's oldest social club.[111] He also belonged to the Century Association, whose members included "authors, artists, and men of acknowledged position in professions akin to those pursuits" and whose headquarters Stanford White had designed at 7 West Forty-third Street in 1891.[112] Through his memberships in such socially desirable clubs, Gilbert had firmly established himself as an architect among the city's wealthy and cultivated elite.

Woolworth's club memberships suggested an elite status of another kind. Woolworth was known, first of all, as a longstanding member of the Hardware Club.[113] Founded in 1894 on an upper floor of the Postal Telegraph Building at 253 Broadway, the club had a membership composed largely of merchants and small manufacturers. Yet Woolworth also numbered among the "cultivated businessmen" and journalists who belonged to the new, less formal, but sprightly Lotos Club, founded in 1870 and known by 1900 as the "leading social-literary club of the city."[114] Only in 1915, after the completion of the Woolworth Building, did Woolworth become a member of the more socially desirable Union League Club.[115] Consequently, while Gilbert had firmly established his social identity through his professional accomplishments as an architect, Woolworth's was still fluid, and defined almost exclusively by his "new wealth."

New York in the early 1900s had a clearly defined urban "bourgeoisie," the historian Sven Beckert's term for the city's "self-conscious upper class," but among that elite, the social identities of various groups competitively jostled against each other in an "uneasy quest for precedence."[116] Whether they wanted to or not, neither Gilbert nor Woolworth participated in the social whirl associated with the most ostentatious of the groups, New York's frenetic, glittery, and "intellectually barren" high society—that is, Mrs. Astor and Ward McAllister's Four Hundred.[117] From 1901, moreover, the Gilberts' fashionable Upper East Side address, 45 East Seventy-eighth Street, appeared in New York's classic directory of elite identity, the *Social Register*. Frank Woolworth's name and address, by contrast, were never listed in the directory, regardless of his opulent Fifth Avenue mansion and his steadily expanding fortune.[118] Woolworth's fortune, furthermore, while honestly made, still came from what Wall Street bankers and investors considered the less respectable world of retailing.[119] Perhaps most important, Woolworth's identity as a merchant could not have contrasted more with those of A. T. Stewart or John Wanamaker; rather than catering to the city's financial elite, he catered instead to its immigrant and working-class shoppers.

Both Gilbert and Woolworth were descended from English families that arrived in North America in the seventeenth century, both were Protestant and Republican, and both venerated the United States' former president Theodore Roosevelt.[120] The whole of Woolworth's education, however, had consisted only of two winter sessions' instruction in bookkeeping and finance at a commercial college in Watertown, one of many that proliferated in the 1880s.[121] Unlike Andrew Carnegie, who dreamed of resigning from business to broaden himself with a few years' study at Oxford, Woolworth publicly and controversially asserted the uselessness of such a liberal arts education to a profitable business career.[122] Gilbert had spent most of his early life in the small city of St. Paul, Minnesota, which had a population of twenty-five thousand when he arrived in 1868. But by contrast to Woolworth, he had pursued a university education, albeit a single year of study as a "special student" at the Massachusetts Institute of Technology. Later, he recalled that Plato and Socrates "were my college . . . and they were my companions—they have guided me a great deal in my views of life and have often come to my aid now."[123] Members of the learned professions, moreover, counted among Gilbert's ancestors, and many had also pursued careers in government and the military.

Gilbert's father, Samuel Augustus Gilbert, worked as a surveyor for the United States Coast Survey and fought on the side of the Union during the Civil War, serving in the Twenty-fourth Ohio Volunteer Infantry. Having suffered from poor health after the war, he died when Gilbert was nine. Gilbert's paternal grandfather, Charles Champion Gilbert, graduated from Yale, was admitted to the bar, and then became the founding mayor of Zanesville, Ohio.[124] Gilbert's father's uncle and Cass Gilbert's namesake, Lewis Cass (1782–1866), however, counted among the most colorful of his ancestors. An attorney, a brigadier general in the Twenty-seventh Infantry during the War of 1812, secretary of war under Andrew Jackson, and secretary of state under James Buchanan, Cass ran twice as the Democratic candidate for president of the United States (1848 and 1852). He also served as a United States senator and as a governor of Michigan.[125] Gilbert owned a portrait of his great-uncle and spoke of him with pride throughout his career.

Given the clear differences between Woolworth and Gilbert's backgrounds and social identities in New York, the two men had little reason to have met as part of the same or overlapping social circles. Swartwout's apocryphal account of Gilbert's having pursued Woolworth across the Atlantic, then, may have been grounded on another actuality, that of the ever-present commercial environment of early twentieth-century New York. Gilbert had already tested an aggressive entrepreneurial form of architectural salesmanship on his earlier clients for skyscrapers. Prior to meeting Woolworth, he had discovered that designing the modern skyscraper in New York fostered a particular kind of architectural practice—the sales-oriented commercial practice.[126]

Gilbert's Broadway Chambers Building of 1896–1900, the commission that provided him with the financial wherewithal to establish his practice in New York, shows that in developing such a sales orientation for his practice, he had refined a method of deploying architectural sketches, watercolor renderings, and plans and elevations as "tools of persuasion."[127] These he coupled with his equally sophisticated skills in real estate development to land key commissions for skyscrapers. In November 1896,

Gilbert met the Broadway Chambers Building's client, Edward R. Andrews of Boston, through the Boston real estate broker Alexander Porter, who also represented Harry S. Black of Chicago's George A. Fuller Construction Company. Gilbert brought sketches to the meeting and shortly thereafter produced a complete set of plans and elevations illustrating Andrews's skyscraper; at the same time, he encouraged Andrews to lease the project's site to developers for a fixed percentage of the proposed project's net income. During the following weeks, Gilbert called on Black for detailed construction estimates and further advice on financing. Acting on the advice of Black, he approached several potential investors starting in early 1897, proposing that they subscribe to stock in a limited liability corporation.[128] That November, his office's Thomas G. Holyoke produced a seductive watercolor rendering that persuasively illustrated the project to those investors (fig. 2.16). Ultimately, Black's Fuller Construction Company financed the Broadway Chambers Building. Yet despite all this, Andrews procrastinated over officially awarding the commission for the skyscraper to Gilbert. As a consequence, Gilbert waited more than two years, until March 1899, before Andrews signed the contract for his architectural services.[129] Construction of the Broadway Chambers project would begin in May, based on a detailed set of working drawings, but Andrews had yet to pay Gilbert for any part of his professional work.

FIGURE 2.16 Cass Gilbert, Broadway Chambers Building, New York, 1896–1900, perspective drawn by Thomas G. Holyoke, November 3, 1897. Collection of the New-York Historical Society, negative 69616.

Gilbert's ambition to win other lucrative commissions for large-scale office buildings, in fact, had compelled him as an architect to at times assume the costs and entrepreneurial risks associated with speculative real estate development. He built up an extended network of relationships among real estate brokers, financiers, speculative investors, and builders and used their knowledge of the marketplace to fabricate his own commissions as potentially lucrative development schemes.[130] Among Gilbert's schemes were his detailed architectural studies and financial analyses from 1906 for a proposed loft building

FIGURE 2.17 *(left)* Cass Gilbert, preliminary design for the Woolworth Building in a classical style, ca. 1910. Collection of the New-York Historical Society, negative 57750.

FIGURE 2.18 *(right)* Cass Gilbert, preliminary design for the Woolworth Building in a Gothic style, ca. 1910. Collection of the New-York Historical Society, negative 57751.

in Newark, New Jersey, which he used to solicit a client, and his promotion in 1908 of a site near Pennsylvania Station, which he thought ripe for commercial development.[131] Enterprising Gilbert, then, had acquired the habit of initiating, managing, and even devising methods for financing speculative commercial projects himself, rather than waiting for a client—and possibly even for a Woolworth—to develop a project first and then bring it to him. Such methods of developing commissions suggested that the professional identity of the modern "commercial architect" had come to markedly diverge from that of the Renaissance ideal of the artist-architect or even the eighteenth-century English model of the gentleman-architect in advisory practice.[132]

Egerton Swartwout later recalled that "the Woolworth commission was the result of salesmanship." Swartwout envied Gilbert's skill at persuading clients. "The bulk of his work came from past performances plus his unique ability to convince his prospective clients. He was impressive and could handle his clients well, especially at first."[133] The young Hugh Ferriss confirmed Swartwout's observation. As a draftsman for Gilbert during 1912–15, Ferriss watched in awe as Gilbert swayed those prospective clients in the office's conference room: "After all the philosophical talk about the science and art of building, it was edifying to learn something of the science and art of salesmanship. The diplomat's iron hand and silk glove!—in those days an architect even wore a silk hat."[134] Paul Starrett later observed that Gilbert "made a deep impression on clients."[135] Although Gilbert would have never considered the extreme of advertising "plans," he nonetheless shaped his character as a salable item or architectural "personality," echoing the growing emphasis on the surface appearances and consumer enticements characteristic of his commercial surroundings.[136]

At critical junctures in the process of selling his professional services, Gilbert continued to practice his extraordinary skills in sketching and draftsmanship. He insisted on calling his drawings "instruments of service . . . not merchandise to be bought and sold."[137] But he and his office staff still produced all types of drawings rapidly and to great persuasive effect. Two of the Woolworth project's very early perspectives, which Gilbert identified simply as "Woolworth Building," show a twenty-story classical office building on an unspecified site and the same building on the same site in the Gothic style (figs. 2.17, 2.18).[138] Gilbert had produced the drawings before Woolworth finalized the acquisition of his site at Broadway and Park Place. Hence, he in all likelihood used the drawings as "tools of persuasion," providing Woolworth with the possibility of choosing between two alluring designs, which his office staff had accurately rendered in a specific urban setting with light, shadow, color, traffic, and people.

The architect Paul Revere Williams later noted that "Cass Gilbert got the Woolworth Building by drawing a sketch right in front of Mr. Woolworth, while all the other architects, after discussing the requirements, wanted at least two weeks."[139] Indeed, a remaining early but undated conceptual sketch by Gilbert, which is accompanied by preliminary cost figures, looks like the sketch to which Williams was referring (fig. 2.19). Besides Williams, Gilbert's clients and even building contractors were known to have been dazzled by such small but vivid conceptual sketches.[140] Strangely, Gilbert's Woolworth Building sketch shows accompanying cost figures and a more advanced design than that of the two early perspectives, suggesting a curious reversal of the expected order of the Beaux-Arts design process, a process that typically proceeded from a conceptual sketch to an accurate, finished perspective. Gilbert, apparently, viewed the two finished perspectives—which he in all likelihood presented to Woolworth upon their very first meeting—as even more effective sales tools.

As Gilbert's skills with speculative real estate development, salesmanship, and drawings as tools of persuasion show, he had thoroughly mastered a range of market-inspired methods for securing architectural commissions—and especially commissions for skyscrapers. Yet Gilbert continued to treasure the Beaux-Arts ideal of the artists' atelier. Indeed, the more the pressures of the marketplace threatened to dominate Gilbert's practice, the greater value he placed on the atelier as a symbol.[141] As a consequence, Gilbert kept his office small, never employing more than twenty-five assistants. He also conscientiously promoted the creative spirit of the atelier within its walls—whether through the Beaux-Arts-inspired process by which his office competed for major architectural projects or through the atelier's characteristic ambience of plaster casts and drawings. The British architectural journalist F. E. Bennett

FIGURE 2.19 Cass Gilbert, sketch for the Woolworth Building, 1910. Prints and Photographs Division, Library of Congress.

categorized Gilbert among the "great executives—men who are capable of daring enterprise" and who can direct with ease "all the forces of production combined" toward a building's realization.[142] But members of Gilbert's office staff, Francis Swales among them, also stood in awe of his "finding time to draw, while handling the business organization necessary to produce such designs and buildings."[143] Thus, Gilbert convincingly projected for even his closest associates the professional identity of an "artist."[144]

In support of his atelier and his identity as an artist, Gilbert traveled frequently in Europe. He made his first excursion overseas in 1880 and returned for extended periods during 1897–98, 1902, 1905, and 1906. Gilbert's letters from his trip of 1880 suggest those of another type of person—lighthearted, dreamy, and adventurous—when rambling among the architectural treasures of the Old World. "Every day I have reason to think that I am one of the most favored of mortals, for I wander perfectly free from care and at my own will, the whole time one peaceful, splendid holiday."[145] Much later, in 1909, Gilbert would write, "Of course I visited Europe a good many times and go there whenever I can, always gaining a fresh impulse toward good architectural work."[146] In an autobiography written at the time that he met Woolworth, Gilbert called himself "just an ordinary young fellow with his mind so bent on his art and so intent on it that everything else was second to it."[147]

The artist in the young Gilbert suggested the spirit of a romantic and a dreamer, and his atelier-like office the emblem of an artist, but in early twentieth-century New York, Gilbert still promoted in a wholly contrasting way the commercial side of his practice. As a consequence, he repeatedly complained about the long hours that he had to devote to the administrative and financial aspects of that practice. "Temperamentally I detest business; practically I have had to lick it into shape."[148] As a toiling executive, moreover, he seemed wholly consumed by the market realities of his big projects. Yet he still persisted in calling himself above all else an "artist."[149] Skyscrapers such as that proposed by Woolworth, particularly, presented Gilbert with a most difficult challenge. Beyond having to master the skills of salesmanship, Gilbert and his colleagues were thrust into the position of having to adopt new methods of office organization, to speed up the production of their designs, and to assume ever larger construction-related risks and responsibilities. "The requirements of today," Gilbert wrote in 1908, "are much more exacting than they were twenty years ago and are becoming more so from year to year."[150] Still, Gilbert adapted. His design for the West Street Building—his largest and most complex skyscraper to date—demonstrated his ability to meet those requirements while also producing a visually compelling—and certainly, for Woolworth, a wholly convincing—artistic result.

Woolworth's dreams for his skyscraper had entailed no less than the extension of his merchandising values and practices into the spatial realm of the city. He identified with Broadway as a site for elite consumption and as the preferred setting for a corporate headquarters' conspicuous trademark tower. He sought a site for his "giant signboard" at New York's City Hall Park. He used his partnership with Irving National Exchange Bank to assert his identity as a capitalist with clout among the bankers, brokers, and investors of Wall Street. Consequently, Woolworth's predilections as Gilbert's client already strongly mirrored the values of the expansive commercial emporium in which he and his retailing enterprise had prospered, flourished, and prevailed. That Gilbert should continue to idealize the professional identity of the architect as an artist within such a context may at first seem unusual. Yet when asked by a New Haven reporter about impressions of his own work in 1908, Gilbert also found it difficult to articulate a larger sense of purpose: "There is really nothing to say about myself. I have simply been a hard-working practicing architect for about 26 years . . . and I have not had much time to do anything else."[151] The entrepreneurial aggressiveness of Gilbert's practice, it appeared, in the end served his lofty and idealistic aspirations as an artist. Equally important, it served Woolworth's objectives as a retailing entrepreneur. With a curious mix of a trademark tower, giant signboard, and Gilbert's West Street Building, Woolworth aimed to assert his presence in the city.

CHAPTER THREE

Gilbert's Beaux-Arts Skyscrapers

When Gilbert and Woolworth began work on the Woolworth Bank and Office Building in April 1910, Gilbert's Beaux-Arts practice was well established on the fifteenth floor of the Metropolitan Life Insurance Company's annex on Madison Square.[1] Its reputation rivaled that of McKim, Mead and White or Ernest Flagg, or, from New York's preceding generation, Richard Morris Hunt or George Post. In contrast to the contemporary practices, however, Gilbert's was known for the diversity of its project types; for the sharply differing character of their Beaux-Arts imagery; and for the appeal of that imagery to a broad spectrum of urban observers. In major projects such as those admired by Woolworth—the Minnesota State Capitol, the United States Custom House, and the West Street Building—Gilbert exploited the imagery's pictorial capacities to fabricate vivid architectural identities for institutions of government and commercial enterprise.

In early twentieth-century New York, Gilbert also confronted the forces of the modernizing city, whether as represented by the skyscraper as a joint product of the speculative developer, engineer, and single-contract builder or by the city's many colorful consumer enticements and diversions—its grand department stores, elegant emporiums, roof gardens, restaurants, hotels, and theaters—with their accompanying modes of sidewalk spectatorship and visual display.[2] He conceived his pictorial imagery to compete visually within this setting, and in conjunction with the verticality of the new steel frame technology, used it to create skyscrapers with memorable, colorful, and distinctive skyline silhouettes. Yet in doing so, he also upheld the loftier aim of making the "high" culture of the western European tradition accessible and meaningful to his imagined audience of observers.[3] For this reason, the architecturally modern never became for Gilbert a profound artistic vision that engaged yet transcended a particular social context. It was within the city's modern, competitive visual environment, rather, that Gilbert shaped his identity as a Beaux-Arts architect.[4]

In making the skyscraper an important component of his practice, Gilbert followed the example of Richard Morris Hunt, who tackled the Tribune Building (1873–76) with the same skill he dedicated to major institutions such as the Lenox Library.[5] One of Hunt's students, George Post, trained as an engineer and then innovated with "cage" construction in the supporting structure of his New York Produce Exchange (1881–84) and true skeletal iron construction within its courtyard.[6] By the mid-1890s, however, both Hunt and Post had grown critical of the skyscraper's uncompromising modularity and of its adverse impact on city streets and city views.[7] After the completion of Bruce Price's completely steel-framed American Surety Building of 1894–95, at twenty stories the city's highest, the city's younger generation of Beaux-Arts practitioners, among them Charles McKim and Ernest Flagg, led a growing opposition to the building type. As late as 1909, McKim asserted that the skyline of New York "grows daily more hideous," and in 1911, Flagg noted, "We have a lurking inward consciousness" that tall buildings "do not belong to the highest type of art."[8]

For those architects and planners in New York who advocated the Beaux-Arts-inspired ideal of the "city beautiful," the repeated failures of municipal authorities to implement a height restriction—the equivalent of Chicago's 130-foot height restriction of 1893—made the urban effects of the skyscraper seem especially problematic, among them congestion, obstructing light and the circulation of fresh air in the city's streets, and the hazard of fire. They began vociferously debating the skyscraper in forums sponsored by the Architectural League in 1894 and then rekindled their debate throughout the ensuing two decades. As the Woolworth Building rose to completion, they reached a consensus on their recommendations for reform, integrating a range of proposals, among them height limitations as related to the width of a street, setbacks, and limitations on the percentage of site area above which a tower might be constructed to any height. They outlined their recommendations in *Report of the Height of Buildings Commission* of 1913, which served as the basis for the zoning resolution of 1916.[9]

During the same years, newspapers such as the *World*, along with *Harper's Weekly* and other mass-market journals, documented a growing popular interest in the skyscraper, and particularly in the new "signature" skyline.[10] In contrast to his more circumspect Beaux-Arts colleagues in New York, this popular interest Gilbert cultivated and understood. While designing and advocating the "city beautiful," he championed the skyscraper's capacity for enhancing its urban surroundings, conceiving the imagery of his designs to rival that of his widely accessible compositions for key institutions of government. Gilbert's faith in the skyscraper showed especially strongly in his imaginary designs for steel-framed towers that soared to extreme heights as loftier versions of his Broadway Chambers and West Street Buildings (fig. 3.1). Through such designs, he highlighted the skyscraper's capacity to

FIGURE 3.1 Cass Gilbert, "A 150-Story Office Building," 1905, project. Prints and Photographs Division, Library of Congress.

FIGURE 3.2 (*top*) Cass Gilbert at the Minnesota State Capitol during construction, St. Paul, 1901. Minnesota Historical Society.

FIGURE 3.3 (*middle*) Cass Gilbert, perspective sketch for the Minnesota State Capitol, St. Paul, 1891. Collection of the New-York Historical Society, negative 72828.

FIGURE 3.4 (*bottom*) Cass Gilbert, Minnesota State Capitol, St. Paul (1895), 1895–1905, view of exterior. Prints and Photographs Division, Library of Congress.

influence, if not to spectacularize, New York's emerging identity as a modern, twentieth-century world metropolis.

Gilbert's Beaux-Arts Imagery

When Gilbert set up his practice in New York in 1898, his Minnesota State Capitol (1895–1905) was approaching completion; he had begun his rise to national prominence in the architectural profession (figs. 3.2, 3.3, 3.4).[11] Gilbert's sketches for the capitol showed its dome crowning the St. Paul surroundings, superbly demonstrating in city views the pictorial capacities of his Beaux-Arts imagery, creating, in his words, "a bold and beautiful building, which will be representative of the broad intelligence and civilization of our state."[12] A year after his arrival in New York, Gilbert fabricated a more elaborate and colorful, but equally memorable, institutional identity for the United States Custom House (see fig. 2.15). The Custom House's main facade—with its hierarchically complex sculptural program and profusion of ornamental motifs—embodied by his own account "themes" of "great pictorial interest."[13] Gilbert's attention to architecture's pictorial capacities suggested that he had begun functioning in New York as a mediator between the Beaux-Arts architect's professional culture and the broader culture of visual spectacle and consumer enticement identified with the city's sidewalk crowds.

Gilbert's uniqueness of outlook as a Beaux-Arts architect, and in particular the pictorial qualities of his imagery, can be ascribed in part to the influence of Stanford White, and more generally McKim, Mead and White, the noted Beaux-Arts practice that by 1887 "had already reached a commanding position in the profession."[14] From Gilbert's apprenticeship in the atelier of McKim, Mead, and White during 1880–82, throughout his early years of practice in St. Paul, and finally to his arrival in New York, the firm continued to represent the artistic standard to which he aspired.[15]

In addition to his esteem for McKim, Mead, and White, Gilbert made repeated reference to a different architectural standard during his student years of 1878–79 in the Department of Architecture at MIT: that of the medieval past. He professed admiration for the Romanesque medievalism of Henry Hobson Richardson, for example, and for the writings of Eugène-Emmanuele Viollet-le-Duc, whom he called "an authority of the highest order in medieval work and history."[16] He also cited the writings of John Ruskin, finding in *The Seven Lamps of Architecture* an "antidote" to the architect's tendency to become cramped by "the narrow limits of style, correctness, usage, and tradition," as opposed to aspiring to "beauty, truth, and love of art."[17] The year that he received the commission for the Woolworth Building, Gilbert summed up his point of view as a student: An "enthusiastic follower of the Gothic," he "eagerly followed the romantic tendency of the time."[18]

Gilbert had expressed little interest in attending the École des Beaux-Arts in Paris, but while at MIT he experienced a curriculum strongly influenced by the Beaux-Arts teachings of the French architect Eugène Létang.[19] The department's founder, William Robert Ware, had persuaded Létang, an *élève* from the École's atelier Vaudremer (1865–69) and a winner of three medals, to establish in the Department of Architecture the École's method of design.[20] Gilbert respected Létang, but also resisted his efforts to "chasten and refine" students' tendencies toward "exuberance and fantasticality both in plan and design, which they fondly defended under the name of 'picturesqueness.'"[21] He refused to follow the Beaux-Arts logic of initiating composition with a ground plan, even while producing skillful Beaux-Arts projects, among them his "Pompeian Restoration" of 1879.[22] Instead, he sketched in perspective to aid his method of conceiving a building pictorially, emphasizing color, atmosphere, and scenographic effects.[23] Architecture, as Gilbert had already come to view it, should above all else respond to external criteria: to the ambience of its many urban or landscape settings or to the preferences of imagined observers.

At the basis of Gilbert's approach to Beaux-Arts composition—an approach that eventually distinguished his designs as vividly pictorial and pleasing to the eye of the spectator as well as stylistically distinctive according to building type—lay the elaborate repertory of architectural forms, motifs, and ornamental details he gleaned from his first European sketching tour of January through August in 1880 and later sketching tours.[24] The activity of sketching, it turned out, had an even greater influence over Gilbert's professional development as an architect than his experience at MIT. Gilbert's watercolors, *Southwest Tower, Amiens Cathedral* (1880) among them, illustrate his early mastery of architectural form and detail, a skill that won the admiration of his contemporaries (fig. 3.5).[25] His sketchbooks show that he carefully selected his subject matter and delineated it from viewpoints ranging from far, as city views, harbor and canal views, and street scenes, to near, as architectural details showing ornamental moldings, tracery patterns, or fragments of windows, doors, turrets, and stairs.[26] Through such sketches, paintings, and drawings, Gilbert took possession of the past, both artistically and intellectually: "Each day shows me something that improves and enlarges my stock of information."[27] Although his stated goal was to become knowledgeable about "all of the principal forms of architecture," his travel itinerary stressed the medieval traditions: "the English Gothic, French Decorated Gothic, Flamboyant, Romanesque, Byzantine, Italian Gothic, Venetian Gothic, Classic, Renaissance, varying styles of mixed classic, and Gothic of central France."[28] Throughout his career, there would exist a strong relationship between Gilbert's choice of a specific European subject matter while on tour and the uniqueness of historical imagery he employed to distinguish his varied designs.

During his first and later tours, Gilbert extolled in both his drawings and his letters the beauty of the medieval over the classical traditions. His watercolor of Amiens showed the ambient qualities of atmosphere and light pronounced in such a way that they seem to dissolve the cathedral's construction in stone (see fig. 3.5). He wrote rhapsodically about the Cathedral of Milan's "army of sculptures" and "wilderness of pinnacles." The vaulting of the cathedral's interior he described as a "mass of tracery delicate, intricate, almost fairy-like."[29] Nevers, he noted, was "such a one as I should like to build, in a great measure my ideal."[30] Notre Dame he called "without exception the most majestic and the most noble work of architecture I have ever seen . . . by far the most beautiful thing in Paris."[31] Soon enough, he would stress the pictorial capacities of such medieval exteriors—whether as viewed in silhouette, or as surface modeling, or as ornamental and textural detail. His watercolor drawing of the west tower of Ely Cathedral of 1905, for example, showed him studying the effect of natural light on the tower's mass, surfaces, and ornamental

FIGURE 3.5 Cass Gilbert, *Southwest Tower, Amiens Cathedral*, 1880. Smithsonian American Art Museum. Bequest of Emily Finch Gilbert through Julia Post Bastedo, executor.

projections (plate 1). Gilbert's method of sketching mirrored his way of seeing—sculpturally vigorous, ornamentally rich and colorful exteriors accounted for architecture's beauty. These qualities, his drawings suggested, had the capacity to stir the viewer emotionally.

In his passion for the Middle Ages, Gilbert found inspiration in Ruskin's aesthetic and ethical ideals. After following Ruskin's footsteps to St. Mark's in Venice in 1880, Gilbert in the fashion of Ruskin observed down to the minutest scale the sanctuary's hand-crafted surfaces and luminous color effects: "one vast mosaic of gold studded with bible history and monastic legends . . . of the most brilliant color" laid up in a surface that "reflects every ray of sunlight a thousand times."[32] Similarly, he wrote of the Cathedral of Milan: It is "built of beautiful marble which has assumed many tints and shades—rich yellow, pink, grey," and later at Durham he observed, "Old ivory, soft dull gold, low-toned lilac and violet are mellowed in marvelous combinations which time alone can perfect."[33] In 1885, Gilbert invoked Ruskin's principles to argue for architectural authenticity: "Of all things avoid a lie. . . . The very materials you use cry out against it. . . . Honesty, then, in my opinion is one of the first factors of good building."[34] But soon enough, Gilbert also recognized the capacity of such authenticity, especially as outwardly revealed in fine materials and craftsmanship—the intrinsic colors of stone carvings, figural reliefs, and polished inlays—to visually delight the eye of the spectator.

Besides his encounters with the historic architecture of Europe, Gilbert's exposure at McKim, Mead, and White to Stanford White's romantic, painterly approach to composition would be crucial: It nurtured what one contemporary called Gilbert's "natural bent" for the romantic and the picturesque.[35] Shortly after he arrived in the studio at 57 Broadway, Gilbert became known as one of "White's men," as opposed to "McKim's men," as the apprentices were later characterized. White, whom Howard Van Buren Magonigle described as a "painter born," began his career emulating J. M. W. Turner's landscapes, rather than training at the École as McKim had done. "He saw architecture as a painter of first rank sees it."[36] White, too, had traveled in Europe, sketched French cathedrals, churches, and chateaux, and lavished artistic passion on the intricacies of ornamentation and craft detail. "He could be classical when he chose," as Royal Cortissoz, the art critic and former apprentice at McKim, Mead, and White, later described him, but in reality he "was a romanticist at heart, a sworn devotee of the picturesque."[37]

At the time Gilbert apprenticed with White, the atelier's designs included the informal, medievalizing "shingle style" for country houses such as the Isaac Bell House in Newport, Rhode Island (1881–83). They also included a more formal Richardsonian urban style for city houses, which integrated French chateaux motifs and "Queen Anne" detailing, as shown by the Charles Barney (1880–82) and J. Coleman Drayton (1882–83) houses in New York, and by the Ross Winans house in Baltimore (1882–83). Gilbert assisted White with those houses and, by his own account, with the Newport Casino (1879–80).[38] Gilbert also worked with Joseph Morrill Wells on the Villard houses (1882–85) in New York, the bellwether of the firm's new orientation toward the order, balance, and decorum of Renaissance classicism.[39] But when Gilbert decided to set up his own practice in St. Paul in 1882, it was White who expressed disappointment, warmly thanking Gilbert for his "valuable help and faithful service" while reminding him that he would always be there should Gilbert need him.[40] Throughout his career, Gilbert continued to value the example of White's approach to composition, which he found supported and encouraged by the freewheeling, creative atmosphere of the McKim, Mead, and White atelier.[41]

During Gilbert's early years of practice in St. Paul, the McKim, Mead, and White atelier's example—and more particularly Stanford White's approach to composition—continued to function as the pacesetter for his own. But Gilbert's range of stylistic experimentation, grounded in his dedicated and consistent search for a memorable, pictorial imagery, also pointed to his pursuit of a more complex architectural objective. Rather than seeking a unified and characterizing language for his designs, such as the Renaissance classicism perfected by McKim, Mead, and White, Gilbert had become increasingly devoted to a wide range of historic precedents and to the crystallization of unique architectural identities that fulfilled the desires of a particular client, whether an individual or an institution.[42] His "Venetian" Crawford Livingston house (1898), for example, evidenced his indebtedness to the Doge's Palace in Venice and the tower of his "Romanesque–Early Gothic" First German Methodist Episcopal Church (1892) echoed those of Coutances Cathedral (fig. 3.6). At the same time, early designs such as his asymmetrically massed St. Clement's Episcopal Church (1894–95) and the extremely quaint German Bethlehem Presbyterian Church (1890–91) revealed his continued predilection for the picturesque (fig. 3.7).[43]

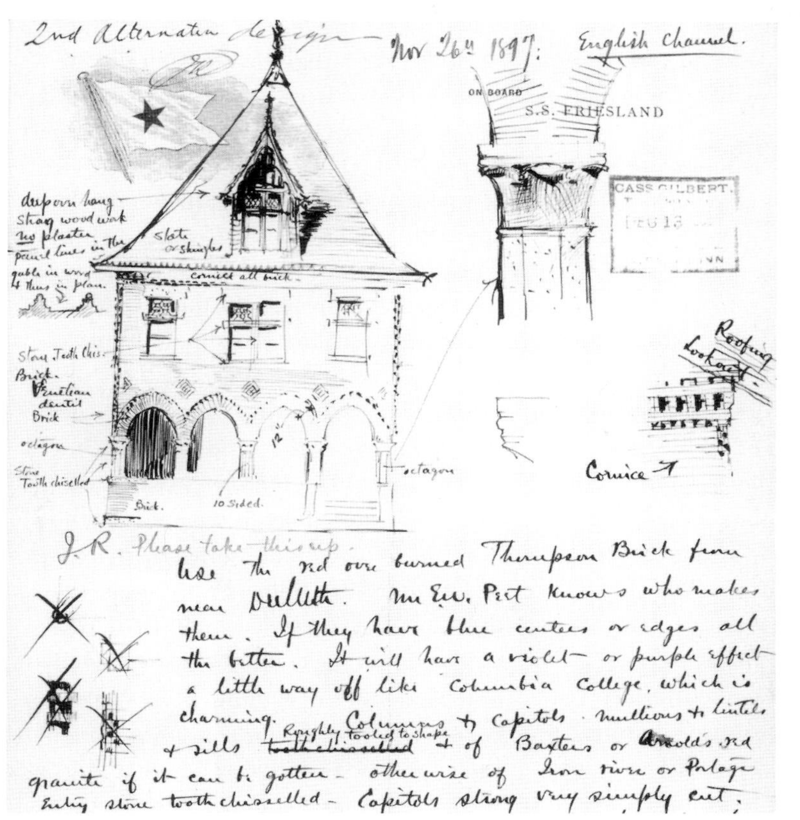

FIGURE 3.6 *(left)* Cass Gilbert, Crawford Livingston house, St. Paul, 1897, sketch of main elevation. Cass Gilbert Papers, Minnesota Historical Society.

FIGURE 3.7 *(below)* Cass Gilbert, St. Clement's Episcopal Church, St. Paul, 1894–95, view of exterior. Unidentified photographer. Minnesota Historical Society.

So did his A. Kirby Barnum house (White Bear Lake, 1884), with its casual assemblage of "shingle style" forms subservient to the goal of scenic effect.[44]

Gilbert's use of a Renaissance classicism for the Minnesota State Capitol (1895–1905) showed him responding to McKim, Mead, and White's recent shift toward the new standard of order, balance, and decorum identified with such a classicism. But more important, Gilbert's capitol showed him employing the lessons of his early career toward the end of forging a powerful compositional pictorialism and a memorable institutional identity for the relatively young state of Minnesota (see fig. 3.4).[45] Gilbert had subsumed his inclinations toward the romantic and picturesque under the framework of the Beaux-Arts compositional precepts he had initially absorbed at MIT.[46] The resulting pictorial but classical whole he infused with a Ruskinian sensitivity for surfaces, particularly as shown in the exterior's precise craftsmanship in marble and the interior's variegated colors in marbles, paintings, and mosaics. The capitol's composition recalled that of McKim, Mead, and White's recently designed Rhode Island State Capitol (1891–1903), but its skillful proportions, heightened pictorialism, and lavishness and intricacy of surface effects suggested that Gilbert had developed a new awareness of the many ways in which such a composition influenced the eye of the spectator.

The Minnesota Board of State Capitol Commissioners aspired to create through the capitol's design a strong institutional identity for the state of Minnesota. They reported in 1901 that "a canvass of public sentiment" dictated that the design should have a central dome, for "the people would not be satisfied with any other."[47] Gilbert's Beaux-Arts composition, crowned with a dome, sited high on a hill overlooking the Mississippi River and so visible in the city for miles, seemed destined from the outset to translate such a collectively held image of the ideal state capitol. To that end, Gilbert employed a widely understood repertory of architectural forms, conventions characteristic of European and American architectural masterworks, which had been handed down through historical time.[48]

Besides McKim, Mead, and White's Rhode Island State Capitol, Gilbert's references for the capitol ranged from the widely known compositions of the United States Capitol and McKim, Mead, and White's Rhode Island State House to the dome of St. Peter's in Rome and the wings of Jacques-Ange Gabriel's buildings for the place de la Concorde in Paris.[49] The design's references also included its primary material of construction, solid blocks of white, iridescent Georgia marble, which linked it by association with other temple-like monuments made of white marble dating from antiquity, and classical sculptures such as Daniel Chester French's gilded quadriga, *The Progress of the State*.[50] Regardless of the spectator's skill at deciphering such varied references in the capitol's design, Gilbert had exploited the full range of architecture's representational capacities to forcefully signify the state's identity. One contemporary called the design "an everlasting monument to the sovereignty of the state."[51] As such, Gilbert's capitol effectively represented the political ideals that he and the commissioners anticipated would be shared by "the people."

Gilbert, it could be argued, had designed the Minnesota State Capitol for an "imagined political community" whose ideals his composition was destined to crystallize and signify. Such a community, as described by Benedict Anderson, is "imagined" because many of its members do not know each other, much less see or hear of each other, yet in the mind of each there continues to persist an image of their shared identity as a community.[52] Although Gilbert never explicitly described his design in reference to such a community, his dome designed for "the people" makes it clear that he responded to a set of shared architectural values existing among its members. Minnesota's transformation from the "frontier" of Native American lands into an urban "civilization" in the eyes of Gilbert's contemporaries constituted a form of "progress" into which could be read, hypothetically, the Minnesota pioneer's life's effort, and so with it the citizen's stake in the community.[53] Given such a local historical context, Gilbert's capitol could not fail to promote the individual's membership within the framework of the state. It also exemplified Gilbert's skill at mastering the architectural sources required—in this case, mostly Renaissance and classical—for the effective projection such an identity.

Like the Minnesota State Capitol, Gilbert's commission for the United States Custom House (1899–1906) showed him crystallizing an institutional identity for an imagined political community, now comprising the citizens of New York, and more generally, those of the nation (fig. 3.8).

FIGURE 3.8 Cass Gilbert, United States Custom House, New York (1899), 1899–1906, exterior from Bowling Green, 1908. Photograph by George P. Hall and Son. Collection of the New-York Historical Society, negative 77519d.

It also marked a turning point in his professional practice.[54] With this key commission, his formerly Midwestern practice now became a well-established national practice, headquartered in New York.[55] In the early 1890s, Gilbert had attempted to form partnerships with McKim, Mead, and White, Carrère and Hastings, Peabody and Stearns, and Daniel Burnham, as a way of securing a professional presence in New York, Boston, or Chicago.[56] But now, as he put it, he "hailed" from New York.[57] Gilbert officially won the Custom House commission in a highly publicized national competition of 1899 after a sustained, bitter controversy among local architects and politicians.[58] Still, for Gilbert, the commission's size and importance served as reward enough. They augured future opportunities for his practice; he would design, as he put it, "bigger buildings and more of them."[59] The Custom House commission also linked Gilbert's name with one of the most wealthy and powerful institutions of government in the United States.

According to Gilbert, he conceived the United States Custom House's "rich and sumptuous" Beaux-Arts composition to symbolize "the wealth and luxury of the great port of New York." Its "exterior aspect," he added, "would tell of its purpose . . . would express the power and wealth of the United States."[60] He designed the facade's program of figural sculpture and ornamentation for, as he put it, "pictorial interest," but he also fully exploited the facade's potential for visibility—given what he called the Custom House's "conspicuous site," the terminus of the axis of lower Broadway, or "the beginning of the greatest street in the world."[61] The Custom House's composition, moreover, was to be in keeping with the "character which is appropriate to a great government building," for it had been financed by the steep protective tariffs that the federal government imposed on the nation's foreign trade.[62] At the turn of the century, the port of New York, in fact, controlled more than half the total volume of that trade, and the tariffs it collected constituted one-fifth of the United States treasury's total income.[63] Gilbert further contended that, given its site, the Custom House's scale should be "impressive by reason of the majesty of its composition," that is, "more imposing" than that of the skyscrapers, "the lighter, though higher buildings around it."[64]

Gilbert's design, isolated like an island in its urban surroundings, combined with the proportions and placement of the facade's sculptural groups to call to mind the exterior of Woolworth's favorite Beaux-Arts building, the Paris Opéra. The Custom House's blocklike outline, furthermore, pierced by a huge arched portal, suggested a triumphal urban gateway for receiving the world's commerce.

In the larger context of the world political economy, Gilbert's United States Custom House proclaimed with architecture and allegorical sculptures the nation's arrival in the international arena as the world's newest imperial power. The competition of 1899 coincided with the succession of political events that crystallized the United States' new sense of imperial destiny—the war with Spain over Cuba, the establishment of Cuba as an unofficial American protectorate, and Spain's yielding of the Philippines to the United States. Gilbert's design, selected within days of New York's 1899 triumphal celebration of Admiral Dewey's victory over Spain in the Battle of Manila Bay, dramatized the nation's new program of conquest and dominion. The United States had deployed military force to signal its competitive position in a world dominated by the empires of Spain, France, Germany, and England—a world those empires had already divided into protectionist blocks restricting free trade—in order to open its own new markets overseas.[65] The decision to seek new markets through force in part served the banking and financial institutions of Wall Street, which in turn had ties to investments in Cuba. It also coincided with the rise to dominance of corporate structure in the American economy.[66] In light of the century-old rhetoric of transcontinental expansion that "manifest destiny" had ingrained in the popular consciousness, the art and architecture of Gilbert's United States Custom House could not fail to promote before the city's sidewalk observers such a renewed quest for empire—albeit now bound up with the expansion of commerce by sea.[67]

The Custom House's main facade, designed by Gilbert for "pictorial interest," comprised a harmoniously proportioned architectural framework for displaying a four-part hierarchy of iconographic sculptures; these forcefully acclaimed the glories of the United States' new position of eminence among the empires of the world.[68] According to Gilbert, he commissioned "four great seated figures" by the noted sculptor Daniel Chester French to represent "the four great continents" that contributed to "the commerce of the world, namely America, Europe, Asia and Africa." At the attic story, he placed a line of twelve standing figures modeled by Frederick Ruckstull, Louis Saint-Gaudens, Albert Jaegers, and others to portray in historical sequence "the great commercial nations of the world," among them Greece, Rome, Venice, Germany, England, and France.[69] In the side elevations' main-story windows, he featured as keystones ethnological heads, comprising eight so-called racial types, modeled by Beuhler and Lauter, illustrating analogously the "commerce of every nation on the globe": these he ordered and classified like the official art of world's fairs to mirror his own and others' Anglo-Saxon racial assumptions.[70] The entire encyclopedic array of continents, nations, and peoples in maritime history Gilbert designed to represent New York's port as a gateway and host to the commerce of the world, crowning the whole with Karl Bitter's emblematic shield *America*. Above the shield there rose still higher—as if a symbol of absolute triumph and hegemony—the flag of the United States.

Gilbert's iconographic messages reverberated throughout the key public spaces of the Custom House's interior. He composed that interior around a great elliptical rotunda, which he placed sequentially on an axis with the facade's central arched portal and roofed with a structurally dazzling thin-shelled Guastavino vault, the central skylight of which he ringed with the names of famous explorers (fig. 3.9).[71] The rotunda functioned as the central focal point of the raised ground floor, the hub of all customs transactions, and the climax of the visitor's experience of the building. Arriving brokers, shipmasters, and merchants such as Woolworth, all of whom engaged in the import trade, proceeded through the central arched portal and groin-vaulted vestibule; there they greeted ships' prows, seashells, and other nautical motifs. From the vestibule, they could continue to the rotunda or, alternatively, to the Collector's Office, where Elmer Garnsey had painted scenes depicting the historic ports of the world. Gilbert said that he conceived the Custom House's interior's sculptural, mural, and ornamental decoration to "illustrate the commerce of ancient and modern times, both by land and sea."[72] Altogether, his synthesis of architecture with sculpture and painting

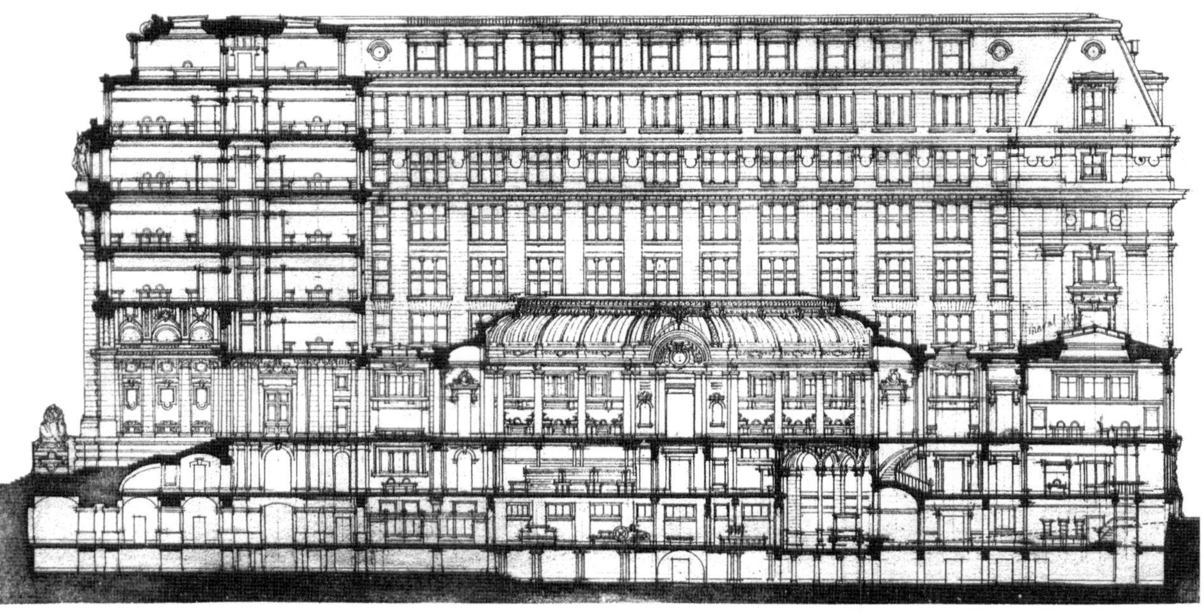

FIGURE 3.9 Cass Gilbert, United States Custom House, New York (1899), 1899–1906, section. From *American Architect and Building News*, vol. 67 (March 24, 1900).

promulgated the Custom House's aura of high nationalistic purpose and, more specifically, the global determination and quest for prosperity associated with New York's command of oceangoing commerce.

Gilbert's design for the United States Custom House coincided with the recent effort by New York's bourgeois class, along with the city's architectural professionals and artists, to foster a new social cohesiveness in a city they found severely fragmented by class divisions and ethnic heterogeneity.[73] By 1898, the Architectural League of New York, the National Sculpture Society, and the National Society of Mural Painters had joined the Merchant's Association, the Manufacturer's Association, and the New York Board of Trade and Transportation to further the objective of "civic improvement."[74] Together, the organizations promoted the Beaux-Arts ideal of the decorated public building, with the aim of inducting the city's immigrants and working classes into the symbolic rituals of American nationalism. They pointed to the virtues of art and architecture's capacity for public education, which they thought would foster social cohesion, and even effect social control, whether through the "humanization" of the city's ethnic crowds, and hence the reduction of ethnic tensions and class conflict, as the sculptor Frederick Stymetz Lamb put it, or, as Edwin Blashfield argued, through art's inherently democratic character as a medium: it was "the property of all men."[75] Whether or not the Custom House's messages actually reached their intended audience, Gilbert's design was opulent, visually engaging, and theatrical in its own right. On those grounds alone, it might well have appealed to sidewalk spectators as well as to regular visitors such as Woolworth.

After Gilbert completed the United States Custom House, he continued to emphasize in his Beaux-Arts compositions the theme of institutional identity, albeit rarely again as forcefully. Still, after 1900, Gilbert's designs for major public buildings were marked by an individuality and distinctiveness of European forms, with the design of each destined to vividly characterize the uniqueness of a particular institution. Projects as widely diverging as the Graeco-Roman Suffolk Savings Bank in Boston, the English Gothic Union Theological Seminary in New York, the Italian Renaissance St. Louis Public Library, and the Romanesque Finney Memorial Chapel at Oberlin College—all of which Gilbert conceived between 1905 and 1907—evidenced his desire to craft each of his new designs as specifically and memorably as possible. In a parallel vein, Gilbert refused to commit himself ideologically to any single direction for American architectural thought or practice, whether in his public lectures, interviews, or writings. Instead, he at once criticized Beaux-Arts doctrinaires such as Ernest Flagg, vigorously supported the American Academy in Rome, and in 1909, continued to advocate the revival of the Roman Renaissance as well as the Gothic past.[76]

The wide array of European and contemporary architectural vocabularies from which Gilbert fashioned his ever-changing Beaux-Arts imagery would serve him especially well as an architect practicing in early twentieth-century commercial New York. There, his vivid, opulent, and pictorial compositions not only would find respect and appreciation among his clients, the city's elite in business and government, but also had the potential to resonate over a wide spectrum of sidewalk spectators. In a city marked by ethnic heterogeneity and by huge disparities in wealth, Gilbert's architecture had the capacity to communicate across social divides. Woolworth may well have understood this. Beyond any doubt, he recognized the value of Gilbert's skillful distillation of European precedents to the public projection of his own identity as a merchant as well as to the identity of his enterprise as a consumer "institution." In decorating the Lancaster Woolworth Building's interior with historical iconography, Woolworth had already attempted to secure such an identity for his expanding retail empire. His "imagined community" consisted of little more than a "consumption community," however, or a loosely configured collectivity bound only by its purchases of his many inexpensive commodities.[77] Nonetheless, he would find of great importance Gilbert's skill at fabricating widely accessible institutional identities, which promulgated before the city's sidewalk crowds the imperial triumphs of a state or nation.

Gilbert and the Skyscraper

Gilbert's outlook as a Beaux-Arts architect conditioned him to see the problem of the skyscraper differently from the way many of his contemporaries in New York viewed it, Charles McKim and Stanford White among them. His experience as a Midwestern practitioner, furthermore, had from the outset of his career favorably disposed him to the skyscraper as a modern building type. While in St. Paul, Gilbert participated indirectly throughout the 1880s and early 1890s in Chicago's vigorous and interrelated professional cultures of architecture, engineering, and building, with their intensive exploration of new techniques, materials, and innovative methods for rationalized construction through the single-contract system—a system in which a general contractor, for a fee, took charge of all subcontracts to coordinate a project in its entirety, stipulating in advance its total cost and delivery date.[78] By 1885, the architects Holabird and Roche had conceived an entirely new type of construction for the Tacoma Building—a metal skeleton encased with a thin cladding of terra cotta—with the aim of minimizing the skyscraper's bulk and weight.[79] Gilbert also followed the development among the city's architects of a new theoretical approach to the skyscraper, which emphasized authenticity and realism in design. In 1890, John Wellborn Root argued for authenticity in conceiving tall office buildings as "sincere, noble, and enduring monuments to the broad and beneficent commerce of the age," and a few years later, Louis Sullivan would call the skyscraper a "fact" of American civilization and its representative building type.[80]

Gilbert, however, did not fully subscribe to the viewpoints of his Chicago contemporaries. He resisted their decisive commitment to seeking a constructional, philosophical, and, in the end, aesthetic equivalent for the modern industrial conditions identified with the emergence of the skyscraper. While aware of their concerns, he charted his own course, seeking instead to capitalize architecturally on the skyscraper's potential for monumentality and for catching the eye of the urban spectator. At the same time, he continued to seek an openness of dialogue between his own commitment to the Beaux-Arts tradition and the visual influence of a city's commercially oriented enticements. His "skyscraper Gothic" West Street Building, for example, claimed a Beaux-Arts monumentality and compositional pictorialism rivaling that of his public buildings. But it also sported a striking verticality, highlights of color, and engagingly picturesque ornamental detail—all of which caught the spectator's eye while embellishing the lower Manhattan skyline in views from the Hudson River.

In New York during the early twentieth century, Gilbert remained curiously silent about the architectural and urban problems presented by the skyscraper, at the very moment his most influential Beaux-Arts contemporaries engaged in vigorous architectural debates. During the same years, Beaux-Arts-influenced planners put forward countless City Beautiful proposals; these found especially vivid expression in their designs for City Hall Park of 1902–3. After Gilbert won the commission for the city's United States Custom House in 1899, he took the lead in designing City Beautiful plans for Washington, D.C., in 1900 and St. Paul, Minnesota, in 1902–3.[81] Yet in 1908, the year after he completed the West Street Building, he publicly championed the skyscraper, refusing to take part in the local efforts to reform the building type—in an unusual departure from the active stance assumed by the professional colleagues he held in highest esteem. He told a reporter that the plans to regulate the height of buildings in New York would be "unjust and impracticable."[82] In 1909, he described the skyscraper as "a story of enterprise, of activity, of farsighted judgement, prompt action—and of both mental and physical courage that must challenge your admiration."[83]

A MODERN BUILDING TYPE

As a young architect, Gilbert showed a predisposition to office, industrial, and store buildings as modern commercial building types, an interest that he would exploit during his practice in St. Paul of the 1880s and 1890s, based on his professional connections with the architects, engineers, and builders of Chicago. While working for the U.S. Coast and Geodetic Survey in New York during 1879, he noted a "factory office building" in Cold Spring and then immediately proceeded to design twenty improved versions.[84] Then, while traveling in London during 1880, he sketched "some very good modern store fronts," finding beauty in their "simple arrangement of forms," while noting that "the simplicity of the design was a lesson to me."[85] While in St. Paul, Gilbert's exploitation of Chicago's advances in engineering would be critical to his design of the Endicott Building (1888–90) and the Boston Clothing House Block (1895, demolished), his two key commercial designs in that city.[86] Chicago's engineers and its leading general contractor, the George A. Fuller Company, would contribute further essential expertise to the realization of Gilbert's first commercial skyscraper, the Brazer Building (1894, 1896–97) in Boston.

The Endicott Building's facade on East Fourth Street in St. Paul Gilbert modeled after Wells's "Renaissance" Villard houses, on which he assisted during his years at McKim, Mead, and White.[87] The Chicago engineer Louis E. Ritter designed the project's foundation and cage of iron.[88] Five years later, Gilbert's Boston Clothing House Block showed him experimenting with a totally new approach to commercial architecture, that of a steel-framed structure sheathed in glazed white terra cotta (fig. 3.10). Gilbert used broad expanses of glass to meet display requirements in the ground-floor show windows and to properly illuminate the loft stories rising above. He treated the loft stories' plate glass windows as tripartite "Chicago windows," not unlike those recently designed by Holabird and Roche for the Marquette Building (1893–95). The store's top story, however, featured a traditional arcade with ivory and blue terra cotta in figures and roundels, the decorative exuberance of which jarred with the gridlike formal clarity of the loft stories.[89] Gilbert, consequently, had been inspired by Chicago's rational approach but resisted its systematic integration throughout the project's design.

With his design for the eleven-story Brazer Building in Boston (1894, 1896–97), Gilbert produced his first true skyscraper (fig. 3.11). Located at State and Devonshire, catercorner from the recently restored old State House, the project demonstrated Gilbert's aim of reconciling his Beaux-Arts principles of composition with his knowledge of 1890s innovations in Chicago design, engineering, and construction. The project's client, Thomas H. Russell of the Brazer Building Trust, asked for a "bright, attractive" skyscraper, "classic" in style, which could "compete with the best of modern office buildings."[90] In fulfilling Russell's objective, Gilbert may have viewed as a suitable model a new and prominent New York skyscraper, Bruce Price's version of a Renaissance campanile, the American Surety Building (1894–96).[91] Yet for the Brazer's design he responded to the Boston surroundings, aligning the skyscraper's cornice and stringcourses with those of the adjacent Worthington Building (Carl Fehmer, 1894) and with the Stock Exchange (Peabody and Stearns, 1889–91) further down State Street. He chose off-white for the exterior's terra cotta cladding, to match that of the adjacent Worthington Building. Combined, the three light-colored buildings formed a neutral backdrop for Boston's venerated old State House.

Gilbert's Brazer Building had tripartite proportions suggesting a Renaissance campanile, but also a modern, skeletal openness. "Before making my preliminary studies for the exterior design, or even the plan, I laid out a diagram of the site, and platted what appeared to me the best arrangement of structural work."[92] The tall, two-story arcade of the skyscraper's

FIGURE 3.10 Cass Gilbert, Boston Clothing House Block (E. D. Chamberlain Building), St. Paul, 1895. From *American Architect and Building News*, vol. 51 (March 21, 1896).

base, the skeletal quality of the upper stories, or "capital," and the exterior's thin curtain wall of terra cotta emphasized that openness—as did the large curved windows of the corners, located precisely where the observer expected to find heavy piers concealing diagonal wind bracing and primary structural supports. The latter further proclaimed the curtain wall's constructional character as merely an envelope that performed none of the important structural work. At the project's outset, Gilbert had returned to Chicago's Louis E. Ritter for professional advice on the steel frame—and in particular, on its wind bracing.[93] Ritter, in turn, enlisted the advice of Henry S. Pritchard, an in-house engineer employed by the New Jersey Iron and Steel Company.

FIGURE 3.11 Cass Gilbert, Brazer Building, Boston, 1894, 1896–97. From *Prominent Buildings Erected by the George A. Fuller Company* (New York: George A. Fuller Co., 1904). (Courtesy of the Boston Public Library, Fine Arts Department.)

Together, the two engineers proposed a new type of portal bracing, the portal arch system, with the arches running crosswise in depth to the frame's orthogonal grid of columns. The portal arches freed up the elevations' corners structurally, and thereby allowed Gilbert's use of the curved corner windows.[94] After construction of the skyscraper began, Harry S. Black, vice president of the George A. Fuller Company, insisted on replacing Ritter with Corydon T. Purdy of Purdy and Henderson. Purdy, originally based in Chicago, but since 1894 headquartered in New York, had developed a still more economical version of Ritter's design.[95] As a consequence of his collaboration with the two Chicago-trained engineers, Gilbert achieved an unusual lightness of construction in the Brazer Building. Although a classical design, it portended the seemingly weightless verticality of his Gothic West Street Building, completed a decade later.

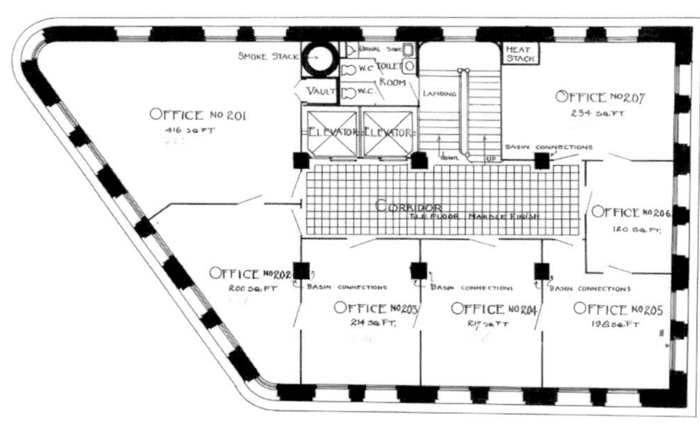

FIGURE 3.12 Cass Gilbert, Brazer Building, Boston, 1894, 1896–97, typical floor plan. Unidentified artist. Collection of the New-York Historical Society, negative 72883.

The Brazer Building stood out in Gilbert's career as an architect of the skyscraper for yet another key reason. It is here, working with his client Russell and the Brazer Building Trust, along with Black and the Fuller Company, that Gilbert first began to hone his understanding of the financial mechanisms for developing the modern building type as a profitable investment in urban real estate.[96] As a consequence, he came to deeply understand the primacy of the floor plan to the success of such an investment (fig. 3.12). As Russell put it, "It is very obvious that the inside of the building must dominate to some extent the outside."[97] Russell's view reflected that of 1890s real estate industry experts, the engineer and architect George Hill notable among them. If a skyscraper's offices were to appeal to tenants and, hence, to produce an income for an investor, the floor plan had to mirror the highest of tenant expectations. Such expectations dictated the size of individual offices, but also the quality of related amenities, among them natural illumination, adequate heating and ventilation, efficient elevators, and the proper number of toilet facilities.[98]

The Brazer Building's typical floor plan showed that Gilbert had completely mastered and even exceeded the criteria set forth by Hill and others regarding the design of a profitable office building. Six closely spaced structural steel columns defined the service core, around which Gilbert housed light-filled offices in wider structural bays. Every office, then, functioned as an "outside office," providing the generous exposure to the natural illumination that tenants had come to value. The skyscraper's ground-floor lobby had a dome of colored mosaic and offices for banking purposes; above it rose a tall main story boasting a spacious banking hall. The upper stories featured marble toilet rooms on every floor, with private access from stair landings, corridors with marble wainscots, and offices finished with "quartered oak."[99] Gilbert had produced one of the finest office buildings of his day.

In the course of designing the Brazer Building, Gilbert injected a rigorous understanding of the skyscraper as a financial investment into his Beaux-Arts preconceptions about the building type's compositional possibilities—whether as a work of architecture in its own right or as a distinctive feature within a larger urban composition. In 1900, Gilbert frankly acknowledged that the skyscraper's interior planning dimensions, whether in the height of stories or in the width and depth of its plan, both of which influenced composition, were *not* the prerogative of the architect. Instead, they were determined by "business expediency, probable income, and profitable investment."[100] By 1912, Gilbert would note that such seemingly intractable planning constraints posed especially thorny design problems: "In a business building . . . we cannot waste space for arches or colonnades or other architectural features, without sacrificing the rentable area, and we cannot project beyond the property line, therefore we have to deal with a perfectly flat surface without 'relief' which would give light and shade. We have also to provide windows at frequent and regular intervals both horizontal and vertical. It is these conditions that make the skyscraper problem so difficult of solution."[101]

Gilbert never wavered, however, in the certainty of his mission as a designer of skyscrapers. On the basis of his knowledge of the architectural, engineering, and construction innovations of Chicago, he respected the rigidity of the skyscraper's modern engineering and planning parameters. He also aspired, however, to ameliorate those parameters with his own measure of Beaux-Arts imagery, seeking architectural strategies for lightening construction while heightening textural effects. In doing so, he aimed to reconcile the skyscraper's aesthetically unruly dimensions with his Beaux-Arts principles of composition and, more generally, to bring those proportions in accord with the emerging "city beautiful" ideal of order and dignity in the broader public realm.

THE URBAN PICTURESQUE

Gilbert's earliest conceptual design for the Brazer Building was not Renaissance, but rather a highly picturesque "medieval" tower sporting projecting turrets, gables, and a steeply sloping roof. Such a design would have enlivened its Boston surroundings with a distinctive skyline silhouette (fig. 3.13). Gilbert may have conceived the tower's crown, which echoed in outline that of Henry Hobson Richardson's Trinity Church (1871–76), to associate the skyscraper with 1870s Boston—the older "medieval" Boston of Richardson and his years at MIT. After his client requested a classical design, however, Gilbert tamed the original design's high picturesque exuberance. Gilbert's final design for the Brazer's upper stories, both Baroque in ornamental flamboyance and modern in skeletal openness, had double-height pilasters sporting eagles perching on shields or ships' prows; these overlaid two stories of classicizing tripartite windows framing ornamental oval wreaths. As if to compensate for the Renaissance design's lack of a picturesque silhouette, then, Gilbert had deployed every architectural device at his command to infuse those upper stories with a vivid compositional pictorialism, aiming to rival in color and sculptural detail that of his Beaux-Arts public buildings.

FIGURE 3.13 Cass Gilbert, conceptual sketches for Brazer Building, Boston, 1894. Brazer Building, verso. Collection of the New-York Historical Society, negative 69631.

Gilbert's natural bent toward the picturesque had already evidenced itself during his education at MIT, his first and later sketching tours in Europe, and his designs for churches and houses in St. Paul. In the late 1890s, however, as Gilbert became more attuned to Beaux-Arts classicism in architecture and city planning as well as more deeply engaged with the skyscraper as a modern building type, he devoted increasing attention during his European sketching tours to the study of towers, campaniles, and the profile views of cities. Seeking more than the Brazer's simple reconciliation of the steel frame's unruly construction with the emerging City Beautiful planning paradigm, he began imagining how such vertical construction might enhance a city's profile view. During his European tour of 1898, for example, he produced several sketches of Italian towers and campaniles—among them the cathedral tower in Pistoia and the tower at the Cathedral of Torcello. During that tour, as well as during an earlier tour of 1897, he documented with watercolors a range of urban profile views, among them his *Zwinger Towers, Dresden* (1898) and his *Towers from the City Wall, Nuremberg* (1897) (fig. 3.14).[102] The architectural character of Dresden, Nuremberg, and other European cities, his sketches and watercolors demonstrated, hinged on the ways in which individually prominent buildings—often sporting angled roofs, pinnacles, and domes—enhanced such profile views.

FIGURE 3.14 Cass Gilbert, *Towers from the City Wall, Nuremberg*, 1897. Smithsonian American Art Museum. Bequest of Emily Finch Gilbert through Julia Post Bastedo, executor.

Gilbert's careful study and documentation of historical European towers would be essential to the design of his first skyscraper in New York, the Broadway Chambers Building (fig. 3.15). His early sketches showed that at the project's outset, he envisioned the skyscraper as a picturesque tower in the city; an image of the campanile of St. Mark's, Venice, appeared in the background as a design reference (fig. 3.16).[103] The steeply sloping roof of St. Mark's, however, could not be practicably built, so Gilbert focused instead on augmenting the pictorial capacities of the skyscraper as a tower in near and distant views. In the loggia of the capital he introduced darker, richer colors in terra cotta to suggest depth and shadow, and at key

FIGURE 3.15 Cass Gilbert, Broadway Chambers Building, New York, 1896–1900, view from the southeast showing buildings on west side of Broadway, north and south of Chambers Street, ca. 1905. Unidentified photographer. Collection of the New-York Historical Society, negative 58803.

FIGURE 3.16 Cass Gilbert, conceptual sketches for the Broadway Chambers Building, 1896. Collection of the New-York Historical Society, negative 69632.

points in cream-colored pilasters and paneling he added polychromatic overlays of light greens, blues, ivories, and yellows. The tower's elevations he modeled in high relief—using rusticated rose-colored granite for the "base" and dark red, rough-textured "Harvard brick" for the "shaft"—showing a Ruskinian sensitivity in his manipulation of materials and colors to receive light. In taking such a novel approach to materials and color—especially by contrast to the virtually monochromatic exterior he had earlier designed for the Brazer Building—Gilbert may have been inspired by the variegated brick and terra cotta elevations of Bruce Price's new St. James Building (1896–97) on Broadway at Twenty-sixth Street.[104] Gilbert's Broadway Chambers Building, however, showed a greater sophistication in the use of color, a heightened texture in materials, and in his embellishment of the capital's two-story loggia, a sculptural and even flamboyant ornamental exuberance.

Later, Gilbert would call attention to color as the architect's most essential modeling tool. Particularly in skyscraper exteriors, he argued, color compensated for the typically thin enclosing walls, the mere envelopes devoid of depth and shadow, or what he called the "third dimension, such as is so potent an element in the older forms of architecture." "Color," he added, "may be invoked to aid in the desperate need of thickness, by an architect if he be an artist . . . for the effect it may produce in emphasizing form."[105] Furthermore, for Gilbert the Ruskin-inspired watercolorist, color served as an effective device for relating New York's skyscrapers to the city's distinctive atmospheric setting—what the art historian John Van Dyke called a "brighter, more sparkling, more luminous" background of clouds and sky.[106] Gilbert also viewed color as a tool for catching the eye of the street spectator. In the Broadway Chambers Building's shaft and capital, he placed increasingly vivid colors at increasingly greater distances from the eye of that spectator, as if to compensate for the muting of colors by the distance—a clever optical strategy that caught the attention of the critic Herbert Croly. Croly further argued that Gilbert had recognized in such a liveliness of color architecture's possibilities for appealing to the "ordinary man." Architecture's more arcane nuances, such as fine proportions or "balance" in the composition of masses, he argued, required the discernment of the learned eye.[107]

In designing skyscrapers as colorful and picturesque towers, then, Gilbert aimed to improve the city's skyline silhouette and also to make that silhouette accessible—perhaps even entertaining—to the spectator, whether stationed near or afar. In such a use of color, Gilbert may well have been influenced by what William Leach has called the city's "extensive public environment of desire," in which "displaymen 'drenched' their goods in color to increase their appeal" and a "new advertising pictorialism" invaded visual space to entice the eye of the spectator.[108] Such colorful and pictorial skyscrapers, moreover, had the potential to distract the city's sidewalk observers with what Alan Trachtenberg has called "spectacles of style"—while at the same time tempering the discomforting realities of the city's modernization process.[109] In early twentieth-century New York, those realities were manifesting themselves in threatening, rarely understandable ways—not only in the intensive technological modernization identified with the skyscraper, electrification, and the new systems of infrastructural machinery and high-speed movement, but also in social modernization: the hardening of the rift between rich and poor, the continuing conflict between labor and capital, the swelling tide of immigration, and, with it, the city's unprecedented ethnic heterogeneity. Consequently, Gilbert's quest for a picturesque beauty, while unquestionably bound up with such "spectacles of style," still offered an architectural brightness and diversion amid an urban landscape in the process of fragmenting, even seemingly disintegrating under the forces of modernization.[110]

Gilbert's design for the Broadway Chambers Building rivaled that of the Brazer Building in up-to-date office planning and in the quality of the modern services it provided for tenants (fig. 3.17). It claimed amenities such as a mail chute for every story, washbasins in most offices, and an independent electric lighting.[111] More important, in engineering and construction the Broadway Chambers Building—the product of professionals trained in Chicago—counted among the most technologically sophisticated skyscrapers in contemporary New York. The engineers Purdy and Henderson designed the skyscraper's concrete-bedded steel grillage foundation and wind-braced steel frame using detailed calculations. They also produced the project's requisite shop drawings, as opposed to relying on the steel fabricator, and wrote a complete set of construction specifications.[112] Working as a single-contract builder, the George A. Fuller Company built the skyscraper rationally, systematically, and on schedule, completing its superstructure in less than four months, leaving Gilbert in awe of the builder's skills as a "triumph of organization."[113] Confronted with the very agents of the city's modernization, Gilbert may well have felt marginalized as an architect. He did, in fact, characterize his own contribution to the project as a mere "measure of beauty," or the subsidiary thin enclosure of brick and terra cotta that added ornamental enrichment and visual appeal to "the machine that makes the land

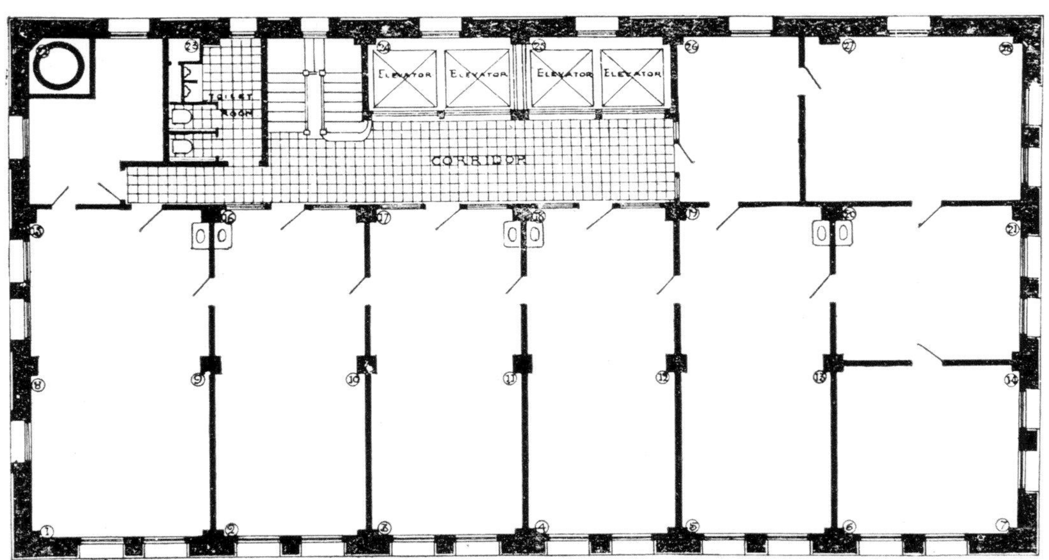

FIGURE 3.17 Cass Gilbert, Broadway Chambers Building, 1896–1900, typical floor plan. From George A. Fuller Company, *Broadway Chambers Building: A Modern Office Building* (New York: Andrew H. Kellogg, 1900). Collection of the New-York Historical Society, negative 72884.

pay."[114] Yet Gilbert had also discovered a way of exploiting to the end of visual effect the exigencies of such efficient engineering and rapid construction: His Europe-inspired towers would heighten the picturesqueness of the city.

Gilbert, like the speculative investors he served, had identified in eye-catching exteriors a distinctive architectural packaging for an otherwise ordinary urban commodity, generic office space. Such exteriors, furthermore, served the owners of skyscrapers as potent public relations tools, memorable theatrical diversions for urban crowds, and ravishing enticements for attracting desirable tenants. "Architectural beauty, judged even from the economic standpoint," Gilbert emphasized upon the Broadway Chambers Building's completion, "has an income-bearing value."[115] Above all else, Gilbert had discovered that the architectural quest for such distinctive exteriors need not conflict with the parameters of speculative real estate finance, that is, the market-driven planning and construction of "the machine that makes the land pay." His may have been an architecture of appearances, but the richness and warmth of a well-crafted exterior or a tower's picturesque outline, as Gilbert's skyscrapers seemed to demonstrate, would aesthetically enliven and romantically gild the frenetic silhouette of the early twentieth-century city.

The West Street Building and the Skyscraper Gothic

With his design for the twenty-three-story West Street Building of 1905, Gilbert invested the skyscraper with a new urban monumentality and compositional pictorialism, giving the type a commanding presence in the city (figs. 3.18, 3.19). His original composition for the West Street Building joined an office block to a majestic central tower. It rivaled in pictorial force his earlier Minnesota State Capitol and United States Custom House. At the same time, however, Gilbert continued to employ the lessons of Chicago. As shown in his treatment of the West Street Building's verticals, he had carefully studied the Chicago architect Louis Sullivan's noted example of architectural design in New York—the recently completed Bayard Building. Although Sullivan's intrinsically "organic" solution to the skyscraper ultimately eluded him, Gilbert still developed a convincing skyscraper Gothic idiom and, in doing so, marked the appearance in New York of a new and evocative imagery for vertical construction that fluctuated between the medieval and the modern.[116]

In his composition for the West Street Building, Gilbert sought nothing less than a powerful institutional identity for a New York commercial enterprise. In doing so, he chose a compositional prototype that evocatively recalled the Flemish free-trading cities of the Middle Ages, as shown by his models, the *hôtels des villes* in Brussels and Middelburg and, in particular, the *hôtel de ville* in Audenarde (fig. 3.20). Gilbert traveled to Flanders for the first time in 1897, and his continuing exploration of the region, as documented in his diaries, an essay, and travel drawings, would be well established by the time of the West Street Building commission in 1905.[117] Later, Gilbert would argue for the representational importance of such a "civic or commercial" compositional prototype.[118] According to contemporary historical accounts, Flemish *hôtels des villes*, market halls, and belfries, originally adaptations of the region's ecclesiastical buildings, signified for their builders the democratic independence and wealth of its free-

FIGURE 3.18 Cass Gilbert, sketch of West Street Building, New York, May 3, 1905. Prints and Photographs Division, Library of Congress.

FIGURE 3.19 Cass Gilbert, West Street Building, New York, 1905–7, original design. Perspective rendering by Birch Burdette Long. Museum of the City of New York.

trading cities, chief among them Bruges (fig. 3.21).[119] While in Bruges, Gilbert sketched a number of such buildings, devoting special attention to the composition of the belfry (fig. 3.22). Other Beaux-Arts-influenced critics and architects, from the editors of *American Architect and Building News* to the French Beaux-Arts theorist Julien Guadet, called attention during the same years to the "emblematic" connection between the towered structures of Flemish medieval cities and desirable urban qualities such as "municipal dignity," grandeur, and prosperity.[120]

In the late nineteenth century, American builders of headquarters for modern commercial enterprises had already put the Flemish medieval prototype widely and prominently in use in compositions integrating a block with a central tower, such as Richard Morris Hunt's Tribune Building (1873–75) in New York and Richard E. Schmidt's Montgomery Ward Company in Chicago (1898–99). Gilbert, however, in choosing such a prototype within the business environment of early twentieth-century New York romanticized, whether knowingly or not, the city's still newer and less palatable social reality: the rigid hierarchies and wide earnings disparities associated with large-scale corporate consolidation.[121]

During New York's earlier mercantile era of business, the city's merchants had engaged in "free-trade internationalism." As a consequence, they resisted the use of military aggressiveness in the regulation of markets overseas. But by the 1880s, the city's newly powerful financial elite began supporting militarization, viewing foreign expansion through force as a practical strategy for overcoming the economic setbacks caused by the depressions of the 1870s, 1880s, and 1890s. Seeking methods to secure the autonomy of the state, and

FIGURE 3.20 *(left)* *Hôtel de ville*, Audenarde, Belgium, 1527–30. Unidentified photographer. (Copyright Institut royal du Patrimoine Artistique and Koninklijk Instituut voor het Kunstpatrimonium, Brussels.)

FIGURE 3.21 *(below)* P. Claeissens the Elder (attributed to), *The Seven Wonders of Bruges*, 1550. (Copyright Institute royale du Patrimoine Artistique and Koninklijk Instituut voor het Kunstpatrimonium, Brussels.)

FIGURE 3.22 Cass Gilbert, sketch of the belfry and other buildings in Bruges, Belgium, ca. 1905. Prints and Photographs Division, Library of Congress.

advocating through the New York Chamber of Commerce a stronger United States Navy, they prepared the ground for the structuring, regulation, and expansion of the emerging corporate economy.[122] In choosing to show historic seagoing vessels such as a sloop and a clipper ship in one of his early sketches for the West Street Building, Gilbert identified his design not with such a recent past, but rather with New York's earlier mercantile era, and still further back historically, with the Middle Ages' free-trading cities, the latter characterized by their informal merchant communities, colonies of agents, and far-flung routes of commerce (see fig. 3.18).[123] Gilbert aimed at nothing less than romantically fabricating for the diversion of New York's early twentieth-century crowds this earlier, benign image of commerce.

The West Street Building's composition also may have been inspired by Gilbert's client. Howard Carroll, head of the West Street Improvement Company, initially called the project the Railroad and Iron Exchange Building. Carroll expected the skyscraper to house a tenantry that collectively suggested a "corporate" identity; together the tenants comprised interrelated coal, iron, rail, steamship, and ferry concerns. The Delaware, Lackawanna, and Western Railroad Company, the project's anchor tenant, was chief among them; it would prominently occupy the seventeenth through twentieth stories.[124] The building's tenants, including Carroll's own Sicilian Asphalt Paving Company and Starin Transportation Company, would have access to West Street and to the Hudson River. They would also have adjacency to the Coal and Iron Exchange at Church Street and Maiden Lane. Given that Carroll's Starin Transportation Company transported railroad cars on floats across the river, he envisioned the skyscraper catching the attention of ferry traffic.[125] Some one hundred thousand passengers also crossed daily, and at the docks and warehouses they merged with what Van Dyke called "that mob of humanity," or the shipping enterprises' "trucks, carts, cabs, trolleys," and their associated crowds.[126] Carroll's skyscraper, even as finally constructed without the tower, would stand out prominently on the skyline, given the richness of Gilbert's Beaux-Arts imagery and, in particular, the picturesqueness of its crown (fig. 3.23).[127] Gilbert, then, may well have been seeking a "corporate" architectural identity as well as a distinctiveness of "address" for both Carroll and the West Street Building's tenants.

The seemingly sudden and startling appearance of a marked verticality in Gilbert's West Street Building struck con-

FIGURE 3.23
Cass Gilbert, West Street Building, New York, 1905–7, view looking north. Unidentified photographer, ca. 1907. Collection of the New-York Historical Society, negative 74165.

temporaries as a wholly new approach to the design of the New York skyscraper. Van Dyke, for example, assessed Gilbert's design as a "more modern structure using the vertical instead of the horizontal line."[128] Montgomery Schuyler and others, not surprisingly, pointed out Gilbert's indebtedness to Louis Sullivan and in particular, to Sullivan's Bayard Building (1897–99) (fig. 3.24).[129] According to Schuyler, Gilbert's modeling of the West Street's verticals, like those of Sullivan, emphasized "the fact that they are mere envelopes and wrappages for a framed building," resulting in a treatment "at once practical, logical, and artistic." Even the West Street Building's picturesque crown, Schuyler argued, could be ascribed to Sullivan's notion that the treatment of an office building's upper stories "invites subordinate and reduced apartments."[130] Yet Gilbert's combination in the West Street Building of Sullivan-inspired verticals with a picturesque crown also suggested his continuing faith in the skyscraper's capacity for delighting the eye of the spectator and for visually enhancing urban profile views.

Gilbert recounted in a talk at West Point of 1909 that Sullivan's verticals called attention to the skyscraper as "the 'most *modern*' of architectural problems." Hence, he had by choice followed Sullivan's well-known dictum, "Form follows function." "Form adapts itself to the use it is intended to serve," Gilbert continued, and "the inevitable logic of design now bids us lift these huge masses in the air with aspiring verticals, accentuating rather than dissembling height."[131] In Sullivan's "aspiring verticals," moreover, Gilbert had identified a feature of crucial importance to his pictorial composition, that of defining the "character" of the skyscraper—in the Beaux-Arts sense of the term—as a modern building type.

FIGURE 3.24 Louis Sullivan, Bayard-Condict Building, New York, 1897–99. From *American Architect and Building News*, vol. 70 (October 6, 1900). (Courtesy of the Boston Public Library, Fine Arts Department.)

It was critical to the success of the West Street Building's skyscraper Gothic design that Gilbert consulted a well-established structural engineer, Gunvald Aus, while refining the details of its structure. Gilbert had met Aus in 1900 through his former partner in St. Paul, James Knox Taylor. Beginning in 1897, Taylor served as the supervising architect of the United States Department of the Treasury; within the same department Aus oversaw federal buildings nationwide as the chief construction engineer.[132] Aus had emigrated from Norway to the United States in 1883, after training at the Polytechnic Institute in Munich. Initially, he worked as a bridge engineer for the Long Island Railroad and then for the Phoenix Bridge Company in Pennsylvania.[133] In 1901, he advised Gilbert on the inventive triple-shell dome for the Minnesota State Capitol, and for the West Street Building, he conceived the foundation as an unconventional system of wooden supporting piles.[134] More important for Gilbert's skyscraper Gothic design, however, Aus engineered the West Street Building's steel frame in an aesthetically complementary relationship to his Sullivan-inspired verticals, aligning the frame's main structural supports with each of the strongest piers in Gilbert's elevations while allowing the openness of elevation essential for the skyscraper's impression of a light and soaring verticality. Beyond his discovery of Sullivan's Bayard Building, then, Gilbert's collaboration with Aus—and hence his release from designing the Broadway Chambers project's mere "measure of beauty"—contributed to the uniqueness within his architectural practice of the West Street Building's skyscraper Gothic design.

Sullivan's verticals and Aus's structural engineering solutions, for all of their importance to Gilbert, were but aspects of the West Street Building's skyscraper Gothic imagery. During his sketching tour in Flanders of 1897, Gilbert admired the soaring yet monumental verticality of the cathedral tower of St. Rombout in Malines, writing as if standing before the tower one of his most lucid and intoxicating descriptions of any work of architecture (fig. 3.25):[135] "The cathedral tower is remarkable for the effect of its *rise* or *uplift*—a sort of grand fling upward, this effect caused by the tower having many deep buttresses, giving vigorous vertical lines. These buttresses give a deep, cavernous, cliff-like aspect as though they had stood for ages and been washed into deep palisades by countless storms. The third dimension of this tower is *most* effective."[136] Gilbert had also recently toured English cathedrals near London, among them Ely, Lincoln, York, and Durham, in June through August of 1905. He visited

FIGURE 3.25 Cathedral of St. Rombout, Malines, Belgium, 1452–1546. Unidentified photographer. (Copyright Institute royale du patrimoine artistique and Koninklijk instituut voor het kunstpatrimonium, Brussels.)

the English cathedrals again in August 1906, traveling to them by automobile in the twilight with George Post and Francis D. Millet after attending a Royal Institute of British Architects banquet.[137] At Durham, Gilbert recalled the cathedral's "splendid effect of mass against the evening sky," and at Ely he and Millet roamed around the "romantic" cathedral in the moonlight.[138] This northern European Gothic tradition, it appears, historically legitimated for Gilbert his synthesis of a Beaux-Arts monumentality with a modern, Chicago-inspired verticality.

In his detailing of the West Street Building's monumental and grand, yet soaring and weightless ivory-colored terra cotta shaft, Gilbert began with the Bayard Building's alternating piers and colonnettes, then added his knowledge of St. Rombout's tower to vigorously model the West Street Building's piers, creating the illusion of depth, and hence of a historic Gothic monumentality. To this end, he employed color as a modeling tool. As he told his colleague R. Clipston Sturgis in 1906, the design represented "an effort to use terra cotta in a frank way, with the introduction of a certain amount of color."[139] He highlighted the skyscraper's main entrance with panels of polychrome terra cotta and diamond-shaped marble inlays. He set off the ivory-colored verticals with accents of dark blue and yellow and used green in the shaft's horizontal transoms to create the effect of a "thick" historical wall. He reinforced the effects of modeling with color by enclosing the shaft's corners to enhance the illusion of strong piers, and then increasingly chamfered those piers until they terminated in the hexagonal tourelles of the skyscraper's crown. He encrusted the crown with French-chateau-inspired projecting canopies, corbeled colonnettes, crockets, gables, and finials. All, in the end, heightened the composition's pictorialism. "The effect is to carry the eye upward," Van Dyke observed, "to increase the height; and finally, to allow definition to be lost in a mystery of ornamental wind caps, cornices, and terra cotta pinnacles."[140]

In the West Street Building's spacious, groin-vaulted lobby, Gilbert had the decorative arts firm Paris and Wiley design Perpendicular Gothic grillework, stenciling, and nautical motifs to evoke a medieval *hôtel de ville* (fig. 3.26). On the skyscraper's upper floors, he arranged flexible modern offices on the perimeter of the plan, around a central utilities core with a curved elevator lobby, stairs, and bathrooms, while opening office interiors to light and sweeping views of the Hudson River (fig. 3.27). Carroll installed the Garrett Restaurant on the top floor. Consequently, the West Street Building's tenants would have spread out before them, as Joseph Pennell illustrated in an etching of 1908, the city's industrial landscape of waterfront piers, terminals, and warehouses, which many of them owned and on which their shipping-related enterprises depended (fig. 3.28). These included the Delaware, Lackawanna, and Western Railroad Company's pier 13, owned jointly with the Starin Transportation Company, along with its rail and ferry terminal in Hoboken, across the Hudson River on the New Jersey shore.[141]

Critics instantly recognized the distinctiveness of Gilbert's skyscraper Gothic design—as both an architectural and an urban solution tailored exquisitely to its waterfront site. Schuyler called attention to Gilbert's skill with proportion, along with his expression of verticality in the "reeding of the twelve-story shafts." But it was the sight of the skyscraper's picturesque crown "from up or down the river," he emphasized, that above all else provided the city's crowds with "an

FIGURE 3.26 (*left*) Cass Gilbert, West Street Building, 1905–7, lobby. From *Architectural Record*, vol. 22 (August 1907). (Courtesy of the Boston Public Library, Fine Arts Department.)

FIGURE 3.27 (*below*) Cass Gilbert, West Street Building, 1905–7, typical upper floor plan. From *American Architect and Building News*, vol. 91 (January 19, 1907).

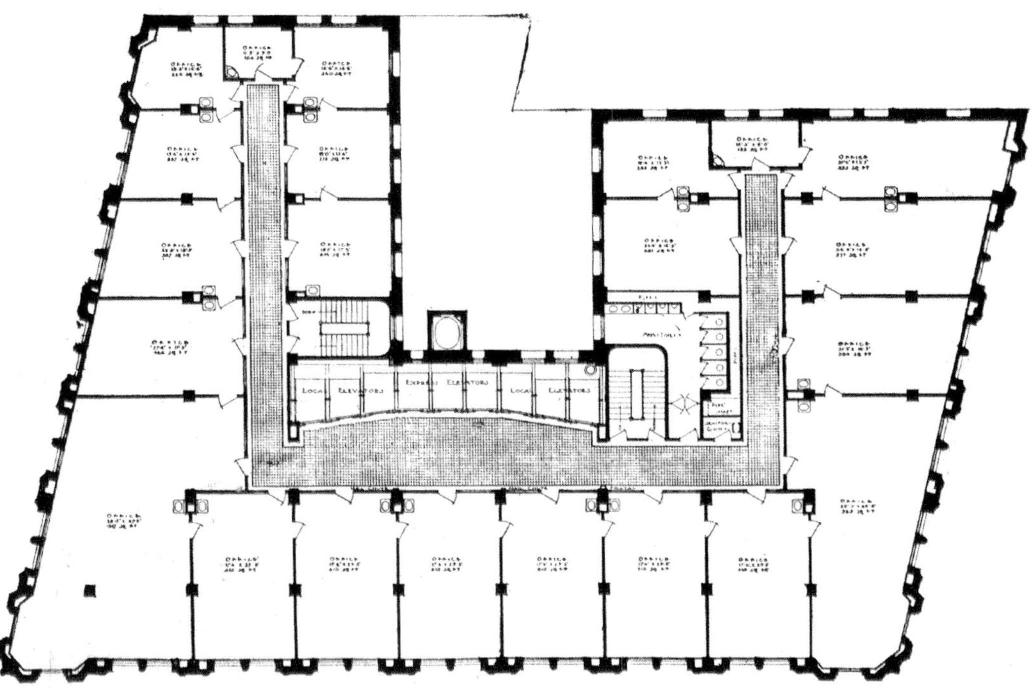

FIGURE 3.28 Joseph Pennell, *West Street Building from the Singer Building*, 1908. Author's collection.

inspiration."[142] The crown's "rich pinnacles relieved against the roof of sky" Schuyler called "the thing." "In the nearer or distant view," he wrote, it made the beholder "glad and grateful."[143] Claude Bragdon echoed Schuyler, pointing to the highly appealing pictorial qualities of the design, with its beauty "in mass, in outline, in color, in detail" favored by the crown's detachment against the "background of city and sky." For these reasons, Bragdon concluded that Gilbert's West Street Building stood out among his New York and Chicago contemporaries' earlier experiments. "The work of a master mind," the design marked "the last word in New York skyscraper architecture."[144]

It was Gilbert's intention that the West Street Building feel abreast of its times, if not be classified among the most stylistically advanced office buildings of the day. "While I do not maintain that it is by any means the last work on the subject," he wrote to Sturgis in 1908, "it is, for the moment, the latest word on the subject."[145] Gilbert showed an equal enthusiasm over the favorable reception of his design by Carroll. "It seems to have met a sort of popular approval. The owners are delighted with it."[146] Yet as the diversity of Gilbert's later designs for skyscrapers shows, among them his classical Kinney Building in Newark, New Jersey (1912–13), and the classical Union Central Life Insurance Company Building in Cincinnati, Ohio (1911–13), he continued seeking in his characteristic pattern what he called "the choice of style."[147] Such a predilection for choice served Gilbert's overarching objective of crafting a unique architectural identity for a particular client or a particular business enterprise. Such an approach may well have been reinforced by the social milieu of early twentieth-century New York. The city boasted the distinction of heterogeneity in architecture, with the architectural incongruities reflecting, as Van Dyke put it, "a million people with a million tastes and perfect freedom to express them as they please."[148]

Gilbert's stylistically distinctive exteriors, not-too-distant echoes of the contemporary works the critic H. W. Desmond ascribed to the city's architectural "scene painters," or "modistes," stood in contrast to the intellectual seriousness and conviction with which his contemporaries debated the skyscraper Gothic.[149] In 1905, Frederick Stymetz Lamb argued that modern skyscrapers in many ways resembled Gothic cathedrals. They carried weight on isolated points of support, or piers, their walls were screenlike and nonstructural, they admitted light through full-height vertical openings, and they subordinated ornamentation to structure.[150] Lamb's incisive comparison immediately elicited strong and opposing reactions from the New York critic A. D. F. Hamlin and from Louis Sullivan. Hamlin supported Lamb, emphasizing that modern architects should indeed carefully examine the Gothic style, for such "eclecticism" would "mark the progress of artistic design in the twentieth century."[151] Sullivan, on the other hand, reprimanded Lamb for viewing the Gothic "not as the living thing it *was*, but as a fetish within his own mind": such flaws in "current architectural reasoning" reflected the "moral degradation" of American thought and civilization. "Our real, live, American problems concern neither the classic nor the Gothic, they concern *us* here and now."[152] Such words demonstrated Sullivan's continued commitment to realism in architecture and, in turn, to its philosophical basis in nineteenth-century American Transcendentalist thought, with its reverence for the "profound side," as opposed to the merely fashionable side, of the new.[153]

Gilbert remained silent during the debate, but in an earlier letter to the architect Albert Kelsey, in 1899, he advocated what he called "progress" over "novelty" in design.[154] Architects, he argued, should adapt and modify received historical precedents to accord with contemporary conditions, following the pattern by which the styles had developed in history. Like his contemporary heirs of nineteenth-century "Darwinian" thought, Gilbert maintained that the natural law of evolution dictated incremental change in all realms of human endeavor—architecture along with language, art, and science—regardless of whether modern innovations such as electricity and steel had irreversibly transformed building practice.[155] Even after the New York City Armory Show of 1913, Gilbert persistently held this middle ground. As he put it, "the stimulus of the secessionist may well be balanced with the restraining influence of the conservative."[156] In arguing for "progress" and "balance," then, Gilbert respected the modern character of the skyscraper as a building type but also craved the grandeur of the Beaux-Arts tradition. He hoped that his architecture would fashionably reflect the moment but also stand up nobly in comparison to the great masterworks of the past.

Gilbert's larger objectives in practice were inextricable from his conception of New York as the capital of the world's newest "great civilization.[157] After receiving the commission for the United States Custom House, Gilbert began to identify with noted architects of similarly large-scale monuments in history, who served the wealthy elite in the major urban centers of their day. Besides Woolworth, Gilbert made the personal acquaintance of J. P. Morgan and of John D. Rockefeller and Andrew Carnegie, New York's magnates in oil and steel.[158] In 1912, he wrote to his children from the Norddeutscher Lloyd steamship *Bremen* about the first-cabin company he was enjoying, including that of Adolphus Busch, the brewer from St. Louis, and the Rockefeller family.[159] Gilbert admitted that such concentrated wealth had its drawbacks, perhaps with the characters of Carnegie or Rockefeller in mind. But early in his career he still managed to justify wealth's power in favorable social terms; as a "positive benefit to the community," it led to "improvements such as railroads, steamship lines, public libraries, hospitals, and a thousand charities and benefits of civilization."[160] Yet Gilbert, who also regularly contributed to charitable organizations such as the Fresh Air Fund, knew that over half of New York's total population—many of whom were recent immigrants—were living in substandard housing.[161] The city's heavily congested and ethnically contrasting neighborhoods, among them the Lower East Side, the Bowery, and Little Italy, however, had at best a minor prominence in Gilbert's personal panorama of New York. His New York was instead that of the nation's biggest port, the innumerable shipping piers bordering West Street, the towering skyscrapers of lower Broadway, and his triumphal United States Custom House commanding Bowling Green.

Gilbert's view of New York as a prospering world metropolis meshed well with his conception of architecture as "the permanent recorder of the histories of the various ages of man."[162] The New York of Gilbert's day, "the gateway to the western world," as he described it, crowned the vast western historical succession.[163] In the West Street Building, moreover, Gilbert had identified yet another opportunity after the Custom House to design one of the city's most grandly scaled, vividly pictorial, lavishly ornamented, and conspicuously sited works of monumental architecture.

Indeed, if built as originally designed, the West Street's tower, as Gilbert noted, would have commanded the skyline of New York in a fashion not unlike that of a *hôtel de ville* or belfry commanding a Flemish medieval city of trade: "To give you a comparative idea of [the West Street Building's] size, it is over twice as big on the ground as the Flatiron Building and the tower and roof will extend at least 50 feet higher. In other words, I think it will be one of the notable buildings of New York and I am very enthusiastic regarding it."[164]

Woolworth may well have appreciated the West Street Building's monumentality and urban presence. Beyond any doubt, he recognized its potential for a skyscraper with a still greater urban flamboyance and theatricality. Such may not have been the case if Gilbert had followed in the footsteps of Sullivan, seeking above all else authenticity in a quest for a modern, democratic architecture, or if he had been inspired on the eve of World War I, as had Europe's Vienna Secession and contemporary avant-gardes, to seek artistic truths that resonated with the momentous material, political, social, and intellectual forces disrupting and reshaping the modern world.

CHAPTER FOUR

Designing the Woolworth Building

Both Woolworth and Gilbert had already contributed to shaping New York's visual identity as a modern metropolis—Woolworth with show windows celebrating the city's consumer fantasy environment of sidewalk shopping, and Gilbert with monumental, pictorial, and lavishly decorated Beaux-Arts compositions. Now each envisioned the Woolworth Building as a still more noteworthy feat of design and construction: Woolworth would build to impress his department store competitors and to dazzle metropolitan audiences, and Gilbert to surpass the scale of his earlier West Street Building, further monumentalizing New York as "the gateway to the western world." Each would shape his destiny with a work of "star" architecture, exploiting the skyscraper's capacity for the spectacular and using printed media publicity to advertise the design throughout the metropolis and around the world.[1]

Woolworth's involvement with the design of the Woolworth Building, from conceptualization through development and construction, exceeded that of his corporate peers, among them Frederick G. Bourne of the Singer Manufacturing Company and John Rogers Hegeman of the Metropolitan Life Insurance Company. This involvement, Woolworth later acknowledged, precipitated his severe "neurasthenia"—fits of uncontrolled weeping and sleeplessness—diagnosed in April 1912.[2] The project presented a challenge for Gilbert as well, "such a tremendous undertaking that [he] began to talk in his sleep, a little sign that he was using too much mental fuel," his wife Julia Finch Gilbert later recalled.[3] Woolworth still viewed himself as the skyscraper's principal creator, however, a delusion that Gilbert, ever the diplomat with his clients, in no way discouraged. At the Woolworth Building's opening ceremony, Gilbert credited Woolworth as the project's "real architect."[4]

In choosing a site on the southwest corner of City Hall Park, adjacent to New York's Newspaper Row, Woolworth secured high visibility for his proposed "giant signboard." But as Gilbert's designs for the skyscraper progressed through four distinctive stages, they showed the increasing influence of Woolworth's desire to promote the project, using the theatrics of height coupled with sensational printed media publicity. Woolworth had discerned the value of such publicity to the success of his store openings, but now he went a step further to combine that publicity with visually enticing pictures. Gilbert's first "accepted" design, for example, filled the *New York Times* real estate section's front page on Sunday, November 13, 1910, and his taller, final design, the *Times*'s same section's front page on Sunday, May 7, 1911. Such eye-catching media publicity, while important to Woolworth, posed a challenge to Gilbert's method of design. It set up a tension between the aesthetic ideals of his historically sanctioned Beaux-Arts composition and the type of picture that mechanical image reproduction required for such publicity. This tension played itself out throughout the process and the public presentation of Woolworth's "accepted" and final designs. What had started out as a twenty-story office building became instead a skyscraper Gothic pictorial fantasy, a spectacular feat of engineering, and a sensational news event—Woolworth's "world's greatest skyscraper."[5]

New York in the early twentieth century, as William Taylor has pointed out, emerged as a "novel kind of city, a city designed as a showcase" and, as such, served as "at once a stimulus and a gratification to the mass of consumers."[6] The city's crowds, comprising a generation "both spectatorial and aggressive," had become sharply attuned to the competitive enticements of its sidewalk environment, which featured show windows, theatrical and cinematic spectacles, and other sensual visual displays.[7] Ubiquitous within this environment, as Vanessa Schwartz has suggested, the illustrated daily newspaper presented an equally powerful form of mass visual entertainment and diversion.[8] Quadrupling in production between 1870 and 1900, newspapers had increased during the same period almost sixfold in total circulation nationally.[9] In New York, they functioned as widely available transmitters of metropolitan culture, not only providing the news, but also through their saturation with images framing the "real thing" and, in doing so, instructing readers in the practices of urban spectatorship. As such, they served as a powerful vehicle for constituting a new form of urban collectivity. They created "the terms through which people might order and make sense of their experiences" and, in doing so, cultivated "the possibility that the everyday could be transformed into the spectacular and the sensational."[10] Woolworth, deeply attuned to the power of his commodities and show windows to excite consumer desire, may well have expected that an image of his skyscraper showcased in the city's newspapers would possess the same capacity for influence on a mass audience of readers.

Gilbert's Office during the Woolworth Building Project

From the Woolworth Building project's outset, a collision of values permeated the production of its design, those of a Beaux-

Arts architect who idealized the artist's atelier and those of a mass retailer devoted to the visual environment of storefronts, show windows, and signs, which served to catch the attention of sidewalk crowds. As the project progressed, Gilbert and his office staff confronted the vexing problem of producing a serious but accessible work of Beaux-Arts architecture in the face of Woolworth's increasing determination to spectacularize the design, that is, to exploit the printed media's capacity to reach a still larger audience of spectators. In addition, Woolworth specified detailed requirements for all aspects of the project, from his choice of the Victoria Tower as a model to the quality of its engineering and cladding materials and the planning of its lobby-arcade. To his advantage, Gilbert chose collaborators who adeptly and diplomatically accommodated Woolworth's changing objectives. They efficiently solved the project's countless, time-contingent practical problems, producing results that may well have exceeded Woolworth's expectations for architectural design. Thomas R. Johnson's perspectives made Gilbert's skyscraper Gothic imagery as accessible to crowds as the city's sidewalk entertainments, while Gunvald Aus's expertise with steel-framed construction made possible his goal of an eye-catching, theatrical, and publicity-generating height.

THE ARCHITECT-CLIENT COLLABORATION

Near the end of his career, Gilbert argued that the relationship between the client and his architect lay at the basis of any successful architectural undertaking, a perception informed by his experience with the Woolworth Building project: "It is necessary that the owner and the architect should be in entire harmony, should be loyal to one another and loyal to the enterprise. This spirit of mutual confidence and loyalty is of the utmost importance. It is essential to success."[11] Despite Gilbert's belief in such a harmonious ideal of client-architect relations, however, tensions arose during the course of the Woolworth Building project. Woolworth's objectives as a retailer at times conflicted with Gilbert's principles of design. The two men argued over fees; Woolworth obsessed over the project's details and procrastinated over determining the final scope of the project.[12] Gilbert did feel, nevertheless, that he and Woolworth seemed to be of one mind throughout the process of design: "Mr. Woolworth was so sympathetic, so enthusiastic, and so helpful in his attitude that he enlisted the enthusiasm of all connected with the work. In order to produce a good building the architect must have a sympathetic client. . . . Mr. Woolworth *was* a good client and a sympathetic client in every stage of the work."[13] While calling attention to Woolworth as an outstanding client, Gilbert might have had in mind his less successful relationship with James J. Hill of St. Paul, an experience that produced the St. Paul Seminary (1891), one of his least inspired designs.[14] Without Woolworth's "encouragement, faith, and complete backing," Gilbert later proclaimed, "the Woolworth Building could not have been built."[15]

Gilbert may have appreciated Woolworth as a client, but his wife, Julia Tappen Finch Gilbert, the daughter of a prosperous Milwaukee attorney, provided a different perspective on his collaboration with the five- and ten-cent entrepreneur.[16] During March 1911, Finch Gilbert arranged a winter vacation for her husband and herself in Ormond and Palm Beach, Florida. They were to stay for a week at Henry Morrison Flagler's fashionable coastal resort, the Poinciana Hotel.[17] When Gilbert had difficulty leaving Woolworth, the project, and New York, however, Finch Gilbert reluctantly allowed Woolworth and his daughter to join them (fig. 4.1). Later, she wrote about the social challenges that "vacationing" with Woolworth presented: "Mr. Woolworth as the possessor of an inventive brain is interesting and he was always scrupulously clean and well-groomed, to my never ending thankfulness, but from the standpoint of a polished gentleman, heaven protect us! I would stand it as long as I could and then I would fly to my room."[18] Finch Gilbert admitted to respecting Woolworth for "his integrity and honesty and his ability to hold his tongue" and judged him a "keen businessman." But she also found him "quite illiterate": his bad grammar she judged particularly offensive—an "atmosphere of nickel and dime slang," which caused her to "no longer feel sure of my 'dids' and 'dones.'"[19] Consequently, in social deportment, learning, and cultivation, Woolworth, the very personification of mass culture, had yet to become—at least for Finch Gilbert—a member of Gilbert's social class. Of far greater importance to Gilbert, however, the merchant had the means of financing the skyscraper he had for years dreamed of designing, as well as the ambition to see it built.

THE VICTORIA TOWER, HOUSES OF PARLIAMENT, AS WOOLWORTH'S MODEL

Shortly after his first meeting with Gilbert, Woolworth made the most important architectural decision about the Woolworth Building's design. It was to be conceived in the "Gothic style," as he told Gilbert, and more precisely, to have a "great tower" modeled on the Victoria Tower of the Houses of Parliament in London (fig. 4.2).[20] Woolworth may have assumed that his shoppers—enamored of his European imports to the point of mobbing his stores when they arrived, and so making them "scenes of riots"—would show an equal enthusiasm for such a giant replication of the famous and memorable English landmark.[21] Gilbert later told a reporter that "before the first sketch for his building was made," Woolworth "showed me a picture of [the Victoria Tower], although at the time he did not know where it was."[22] Woolworth had, in fact, seen the tower, when he visited the Houses of Parliament, or "at least looked at it from the outside," as he wrote his store managers in a "general letter" mailed from London in March 1890.[23] In any case, Woolworth may well have envisioned the tower functioning like a trademark and, in doing so, effectively advertising his chain of stores "around the world."[24]

Woolworth's choice of London's Victoria Tower—its architecture inextricable from the day's most expansive colonizing power—coincided with his ambition to establish the F. W. Woolworth and Company's five- and ten-cent stores in England. In 1909, he chose Liverpool as the company's first and primary transatlantic base of operations, and by 1913, he had opened twenty-eight "three-and-sixpence" stores in English cities and towns such as Preston, Manchester, Leeds, and Hull. He had also begun expanding his operations in Continental Europe. Before 1910, he set up buying headquarters and warehouses in Sonneberg, Germany, London, and in New York City, from which he stockpiled and exported commodities to stores in England and America. By 1912, he had also set up headquarters and warehouses in Paris as well as Fuerth, Germany, and Calais, France, for stockpiling and assembling lots of commodities and organizing

FIGURE 4.1
Frank Woolworth and Cass Gilbert in a chair at Palm Beach, Florida, March 1911. Photograph by Metcalfe. Collection of the Supreme Court of the United States.

FIGURE 4.2 Charles Barry and Augustus Welby Northmore Pugin, Houses of Parliament, London, 1836–ca. 1860. Photograph by George Washington Wilson, ca. 1880. (Courtesy of the Boston Public Library, Print Department.)

buying functions.[25] In 1924, the F. W. Woolworth Company opened a chain of stores in Cuba, and in 1926, in Germany, while promoting its strategy of international expansion in corporate literature as "more buying power for the small coins of the world."[26]

In suggesting the transposition of the Victoria Tower from its Thames waterfront site to a new site near the Hudson River in lower Manhattan, as if by magic, Woolworth also contrived to impress his rivals in the retailing world—the self-made Henry Siegels and John Wanamakers he admired—with his own brand of theatrical one-upmanship. He could not, like Siegel, build his small five-and-tens as gigantic palaces of consumer entertainment, with more than fifty departments, special restaurants, parlor rooms, and banks. Nor could he, like Wanamaker, convert a giant train depot in Philadelphia into a "Grand Depot" department store, build a new store in Philadelphia, and then acquire and build an addition to A. T. Stewart's cast-iron palace in New York.[27] But he could, as he put it, "build something bigger that any other merchant had"—a spectacular income-generating skyscraper resembling a memorable "European" landmark.[28] In doing so, he would also be presenting New York's crowds with a spectacle of architecture they expected to see—or in Gilbert's more conservative terms, a Gothic tower "noted for its beauty."[29]

Woolworth further instructed Gilbert that the Woolworth Building's offices were to be "first class," that is, they were to meet the most discriminating of tenants' requirements for natural illumination and flexibility: "He wanted many windows so divided that all of the offices should be well lighted and so that partitions might be placed at almost any location, subdividing the spaces into larger or smaller offices as tenants might require."[30] Woolworth also specified that Gilbert's design be structurally engineered without an excessive and expensive conservatism, that its materials be fabricated and assembled by the most efficient of methods, and that it be serviced with advanced electrical, heating, and ventilating equipment and systems: "You and I must look out for these engineers and see that we get the modern, up-to-date things."[31] Such equipment and systems, Woolworth expected, might rival in technological sophistication those he had recently seen on a basement tour of Francis H. Kimball's City Investing Building (1908). Gilbert assured Woolworth of a design "in accordance with the highest standard of modern office building construction."[32]

By the late 1890s, New York had become a haven for salespeople and publicity men, who molded their personalities "in the interest of forging profitable relationships" with customers.[33] Seeing his clients in a similar fashion, Gilbert later noted, "It is well to remember that his [the client's] needs and wishes govern. . . . You must recognize that he pays the bill, and he is going to use the building."[34] Indeed, Gilbert demonstrated his determination to please Woolworth as a client from the very outset of the project's design. He gave thorough study to the Victoria Tower, following Woolworth's first suggestion of using the tower as a model, even though he had earlier criticized the Houses of Parliament's Perpendicular Gothic exteriors as "copies of Westminster [Abbey]" that "may be left out of consideration."[35] In 1905, Gilbert proudly explained to Professor Warren Laird of the School of Architecture at the University of Pennsylvania that "I make for [clients] as many sketches as necessary to meet their views, trying one design after another."[36] It is likely that Woolworth, given his experience with pleasing shoppers, appreciated Gilbert's similarly accommodating and service-oriented approach to architectural design.

GILBERT'S ASSISTANTS AND COLLABORATORS

The smooth administrative efficiency with which Gilbert ran his office worked to his advantage in tackling the many complex and fluctuating parameters governing the Woolworth Building's process of design (fig. 4.3). Gilbert had a knack for choosing talented associates who followed his lead and to whom he felt comfortable delegating key design tasks.[37] As the architect Guy Kirkham later put it, "He must necessarily depend on assistants and collaborators, and the successful execution of his work lies largely in the success with which he chooses them and secures their loyal co-operation."[38] Gilbert, beyond any doubt, masterminded the Woolworth Building's design, but his delegation of key responsibilities to Thomas R. Johnson, Gunvald Aus, and later to other key associates, among them John Rockart and George Wells, would be essential to the timely realization of the project.

The architect Alexander Trowbridge called Thomas R. Johnson, Gilbert's key collaborator in design, "a designer of rare ability" and a "master of every form of architectural draughtsmanship."[39] Johnson's perspectives, in fact, seemed ideally suited to the development and, eventually, to the public presentation of Gilbert's many differing schemes for the project. As Gilbert later put it, Johnson's "facile pen and refined artistic genius" played "so

FIGURE 4.3 Cass Gilbert's office on East Twenty-fourth Street (Metropolitan Life Insurance Annex), drafting room, during the Woolworth Building project, New York, ca. 1911. Photograph by Wurts Brothers. Museum of the City of New York.

large a part in the creation of the design."[40] "Much of the work from Mr. Gilbert's office," the *Brickbuilder* similarly observed after the completion of the skyscraper in 1914, "is now designed in perspective [by Johnson], aided by Mr. Gilbert's criticism and suggestions."[41] Johnson, a Canadian by birth, arrived in Gilbert's office in April 1900, reportedly after a brief stint working for Ernest Flagg. He had studied painting, illustration, and architecture at the School of Science in Toronto and then apprenticed under the Toronto architect E. J. Lennox, known for the city's highly regarded "Richardsonian Romanesque" City Hall (1890–99).[42]

During the Woolworth Building project, Johnson's speed and expertise at producing large-scale perspectives—"not taking over six hours to draw, mount, and render"—echoed the time-contingent demands dictating Gilbert's process of finalizing and presenting to Woolworth his many differing designs.[43] What Trowbridge called Johnson's "quick and brilliant studies," combining "pencil, watercolor, and colored chalks with the most remarkable effectiveness and truth of representation," expedited the study of Gilbert's compositions. They also rapidly advanced Gilbert's process of design, with Johnson adding to Gilbert's conceptual sketches his own refinements in elevation and ornamental imagery.[44] In Gilbert's office, Johnson's perspectives took precedence over the more typical orthogonal plans, sections, and elevations favored by Beaux-Arts practitioners. The perspectives also happened to appeal visually, as one expert on architectural rendering noted, to a broad middle audience of observers: "Mr. Johnson's work in this way is undoubtedly adapted to popular use, since his colors please the popular as well as the educated taste, without disguising the sound architecture behind them."[45] Precise and accurate, they also persuaded that audience—many of whom would encounter Gilbert's design for the first time on the front pages of New York's newspapers—of the skyscraper's aesthetic distinction as well as its structural plausibility.

The engineer Gunvald Aus's role in the Woolworth project rivaled, if it did not surpass, that of Johnson's. In 1910, Gilbert described Gunvald Aus and Company to Woolworth and others as his office's "engineering department."[46] Gunvald Aus and Company did, in fact, have the same address as Gilbert's office, 11 East Twenty-fourth Street in the Metropolitan Life Insurance Annex, even though Aus consulted for other architects besides Gilbert after establishing his practice independently in New York in 1902. More important, Aus had achieved a significant professional reputation in his own right. He participated actively in meetings of the American Society of Civil Engineers and published articles in professional journals on topics ranging from reinforced concrete and fireproofing to building codes.[47] Aus's contribution of his engineering skills to the design of Gilbert's West Street Building attracted notice, but Woolworth's skyscraper, more than any other project, inspired his peers in engineering to call him "one of the greatest builders of the new America."[48]

One of Gilbert's Beaux-Arts contemporaries, the architect Robert Peabody of Boston, noted in 1901 that "it now takes several men to make a good architect."[49] Peabody's comment hinted at the commercial pressures and technological complexities imposed on the modern practitioner, and hence at the need for employing experts such as Johnson and Aus. Still, Gilbert continued to treasure the romantic ideal of the architect as the sole creator of masterworks within an independently functioning artist's atelier. He refused to form partnerships, relying instead on a succession of key talented designers and key engineering professionals. At the same time, however, the modernizing forces imposed on Gilbert's practice exceeded in scale those imposed on many Beaux-Arts practices. Woolworth's skyscraper, more than any other project, epitomized those forces. As a consequence, Johnson and Aus's contributions to the Woolworth Building's design—whether as shown by the quick, brilliant, and widely accessible perspective studies of an accomplished delineator or by the efficient and reliable calculations of a seasoned engineer—would rival in importance Gilbert's own.

Gilbert's Skyscraper Gothic Designs and Printed Media Publicity

By mid-April 1910, Gilbert, Johnson, and Gilbert's office staff were concentrating virtually all of their energies on Woolworth's skyscraper (see fig. 4.3). Still, they faced considerable obstacles. First, the size of the project increased in fits and starts, fueled by Woolworth's difficult-to-rein-in ambition to spectacularize through printed media publicity. Gilbert, Johnson, and their assistants responded with a total of four increasingly larger and more sophisticated designs. Second, Woolworth's requirement that the skyscraper generate rental returns as quickly as possible dictated not only that its design be produced, but also that it be constructed with the utmost speed and efficiency. Consequently, the project's architectural development reflected on the one hand an agility of responsiveness to Woolworth's ever-changing vision for the project. But on the other, it exhibited the tensions between Gilbert's Beaux-Arts methods of design and Woolworth's market-inspired requirements for the skyscraper—whether those of a speculative investor in real estate or those of a promoter keen to publicize a trademark tower with seductive, colorful pictures showcased in the news media. The office's drawings, as a consequence, vacillated throughout the process of design between meeting the demands imposed by Woolworth and his skyscraper's modernizing impulses and fulfilling the artistic potentials of Gilbert's time-honored repertory of medieval compositional models and motifs. In the final stages, the drawings exhibited a brightness, color, and a modern, linear quality of detail that set up an unusual counterpoint with Woolworth's esteemed historic model, the Victoria Tower.

THE FIRST DESIGN

Gilbert, Johnson, and the office's staff of assisting designers and draftsmen devoted intensive study to the Woolworth Building's first design during a short span of three weeks between April 21 and May 12, 1910. Gilbert's conceptual sketches, Johnson's exterior perspectives and elevations, and floor plans produced by junior designers such as Frederick Stickel and others show a low, blocky building joined with a tower that ranged between thirty and thirty-eight stories, or 420 and 550 feet, in height. The office's drawings, consistently entitled "Woolworth Bank and Office Building," reflected Woolworth's original prospectus for a joint project between the F. W. Woolworth and Company and Irving National Exchange Bank. No written record remains documenting Woolworth's communications with Gilbert during this early phase of the project. The rapid sequence of drawings dating from April 21, however, indicates that six days after Woolworth had acquired the 80 × 172-foot site at Broadway and Park Place, and one day after he signed a contract with Irving National Exchange Bank to create the Broadway–Park Place Company, he instructed Gilbert to begin design.

Johnson took Gilbert's Victoria Tower–inspired sketch as the starting point for the first design's series of perspectives (see fig. 2.19). His method entailed nothing less than grafting the Victoria Tower's Gothic imagery onto an open skeleton of steel. Johnson's earliest perspective, drawn on April 22, features the Victoria Tower's corner tourelles and thin, reticulated Perpendicular Gothic detail (plate 2). "Aspiring verticals, accentuating rather than dissembling height," as Gilbert had earlier described Sullivan's verticals, showed he and Johnson responding to Woolworth's request for "an inspired upward movement."[50] The verticals also incorporated Sullivan-influenced colonnettes while echoing the continuously rising moldings of the Perpendicular Gothic style. Woolworth had specified a twenty-story project, but Johnson's drawing showed the addition of ten new stories, creating a thirty-story tower. The new stories increased the building's cost from the originally projected $1.5 million to an anticipated $2 million.[51] The design now rivaled in height the adjacent thirty-two-story Park Row Building (1896–99)—the city's tallest prior to the completion of the Singer Tower—and so portended at the project's very outset Woolworth's pattern of steadily expanding ambition.

Three days later, on April 25, Johnson produced a second rendered watercolor perspective (plate 3). It showed him and Gilbert infusing the design with a higher

FIGURE 4.4 Cass Gilbert, Woolworth Building, first design, conceptual sketch, April 26, 1910. Graphite on tracing paper. Collection of the New-York Historical Society, negative 72148.

level of abstraction, replacing the rounded piers with flat, astylar piers and verticals. In doing so, they gave up the Victoria Tower's corner tourelles, which presented a thorny client-relations dilemma for Gilbert. In Woolworth's eyes, the tourelles suggested highly desirable office interiors: "He liked the corner bay windows ('tourelles,' I corrected) running from ground to top, where the occupants could sit at their desks and look out of the windows up and down the street."[52] Gilbert persuaded Woolworth that the tourelles' distinctive circular shape required setting the building nine feet back from the property line and, consequently, sacrificing valuable rental area.[53] His astylar corner piers, by contrast, maximized the site's economic value. Gilbert did not argue for the aesthetic virtues of the piers, but when combined with the verticals, they had an architectural merit in their own right. Their tense rigidity and soaring upward movement produced an exterior distinguished by a seeming lack of mass or weight. Johnson enhanced the piers' sense of uplift with sparkling highlights in "Chinese white," predicting the glistening verticals of the Woolworth Building's final design.

In a quick conceptual sketch of April 26, Gilbert seemed to be seeking a remedy for the new design's absence of high picturesqueness and depth-producing sculptural effects (fig. 4.4). The modern, astylar piers receded, and he reinvigorated the composition with a profusion of ornamental motifs concentrated at the skyscraper's base, the top of its twenty-story block, and its crown. These he derived from the same Flemish sources he had employed earlier in his West Street Building. The crown's deep arcade, boldly projecting canopies, bristling culmination, and especially its tourelles—striking protrusions on the skyline—fleshed out the skyscraper's typically austere and boxy construction, evoking the turreted and pinnacled monuments of medieval Flanders and so infusing the entire composition with a new monumentality.

Johnson produced a study of the Park Place elevation a week later, on May 3, taking his cues from Gilbert's conceptual sketch (fig. 4.5). He revised the proportional relationship between the composition's block and tower, increased the tower's height to thirty-five stories, and playfully toyed with a "Woolworth" advertising sign perched on the tower's highest stage. In a second Park Place elevation, of May 9, Johnson continued to refine the composition's proportional relationships, now extending the height of the tower three more stories, to 550 feet, and topping its projecting five-story crown with a steeply pitched, two-staged pyramidal roof, which housed an observatory within an open lantern (fig. 4.6). Vigorously scrubbed over with a blue pencil, perhaps belonging to Gilbert, Johnson's roof and lantern quoted key features almost verbatim from the Victoria Tower's neighbor, the Houses of Parliament's Clock Tower.

Johnson's rendering of both elevations' verticals as emphatically projecting, angular Gothic piers may have been inspired by the piers of Howells and Stokes's entry in the Municipal Building competition in 1908, a design indebted in turn to Gilbert's West Street Building (fig. 4.7).[54] The piers of Johnson's second elevation, however, showed a greater lightness and linearity. They echoed in profile a High Gothic cathedral's clustered piers—even though as supported by steel-framed construction they could not be truly lithic, much less the cathedral's decisively rotated clustered piers. Still, the bold character of their projection, which later inspired Schuyler to observe that "in a diagonal view of the side, even at a considerable angle, the openings quite disappear," created the illusion of a powerful yet light and energetic monumentality.[55] Sculptural on the one hand, yet linear and modern on the other, they animated the building's exterior with rhythmic sequences of reflected light and shadow. They also provided a vivid visual analogue for the structural steel columns' unequal loading conditions: Those piers supporting the tower had mass and strength while those modulating the elevations had slenderness and grace.

FIGURE 4.5 *(below)* Cass Gilbert, Woolworth Building, first design, Park Place elevation drawn at the scale of 1⁄32" = 1'0" by Thomas R. Johnson, May 3, 1910. Watercolor and Conté crayon over print, mounted on illustration board. Collection of the New York Historical Society.

FIGURE 4.6 *(above right)* Cass Gilbert, Woolworth Building, first design, Park Place elevation, drawn at the scale of 1⁄32" = 1'0" by Thomas R. Johnson, May 9, 1910. Graphite, watercolor, and Conté crayon over print, mounted on illustration board. Collection of the New-York Historical Society, negative 57530.

FIGURE 4.7 Howells and Stokes, Municipal Building, competition entry, 1908. From *American Architect and Building News*, vol. 93 (May 27, 1908).

As Johnson and Gilbert designed the skyscraper in perspective and elevation, one of the office's junior designers, Frederick Stickel, led other hands in developing several sets of floor plans.[56] Stickel and his assisting draftsmen drew plans of the ground floor, a typical upper story, and a typical tower story between April 26, 1910, and May 12, 1910. Most were unsigned, but the initials of Stickel appeared on a few. The first set of sketch plans, dated April 21, showed a ground floor with a single large store and a public lobby. In the subsequent sets of plans, Stickel and the draftsmen explored at least seven design variations on the first (figs. 4.8, 4.9). They enhanced the lobby's qualities of spaciousness, grandeur, and perspectival depth by enlarging the plan dimensions and by pushing the monumental stair—which led on an axis from the main entrance to Irving's banking hall—deeper into the space. In some drawings, they replaced the stair with two flanking stairs, and in others, they spanned the lobby with a bridge. They investigated elevators in a variety of arrangements, and in most plans they indicated a secondary entrance from Park Place.

Gilbert aimed to engage Woolworth's hopes for F. W. Woolworth and Company's identity with the project's first design. Its composition of a distinctive tower connected with a lower office block signified "corporate headquarters," by now in New York a widely recognized, generic type. As in his design for the West Street Building, Gilbert invoked the precedents of medieval Flanders. He also expressed with dynamic Gothic piers the skyscraper's modern character as a building type. Abstracted and modulated with slender colonnettes, the piers reflected Woolworth's barely articulated desire for a landmark headquarters that evoked the historical landmarks of Europe, but also presented before the city's spectators an imagery tantalizingly fashionable and new.

"SCHEME 17"

On May 17, only three weeks after Gilbert, Johnson, and their assistants had officially begun working on the project, Woolworth's ambitions took a new and astonishing turn. He abruptly judged the first design's rectangular site and thirty-five-story tower as less than adequate. In its place emerged a magnificent new composition, commanding the entire 152-foot Broadway block front. The composition incorporated a majestic central tower soaring 720 feet high.

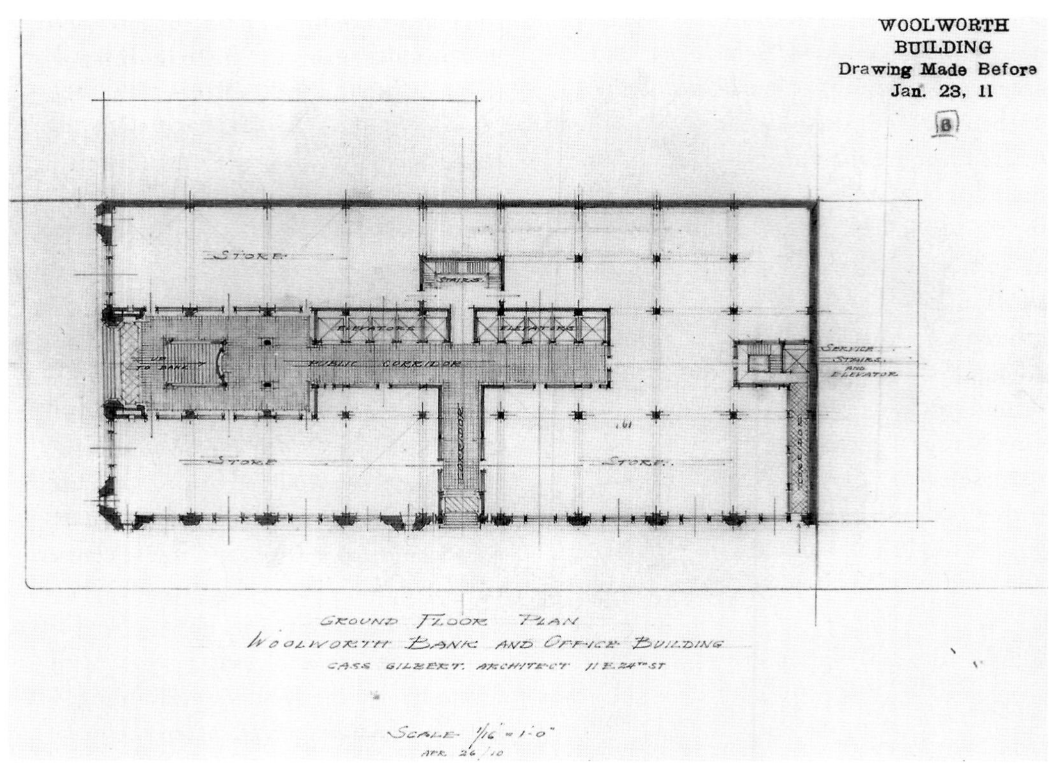

FIGURE 4.8 (*above*) Cass Gilbert, Woolworth Building, first design, plan of ground floor drawn at the scale of 1/16" = 1'0", April 26, 1910. Graphite on tracing paper. Collection of the New-York Historical Society, negative 69840.

FIGURE 4.9 (*below*) Cass Gilbert, Woolworth Building, first design, plan of ground floor drawn at the scale of 1/16" = 1'0", May 14, 1910. Graphite on tracing paper. Collection of the New-York Historical Society, negative 69838.

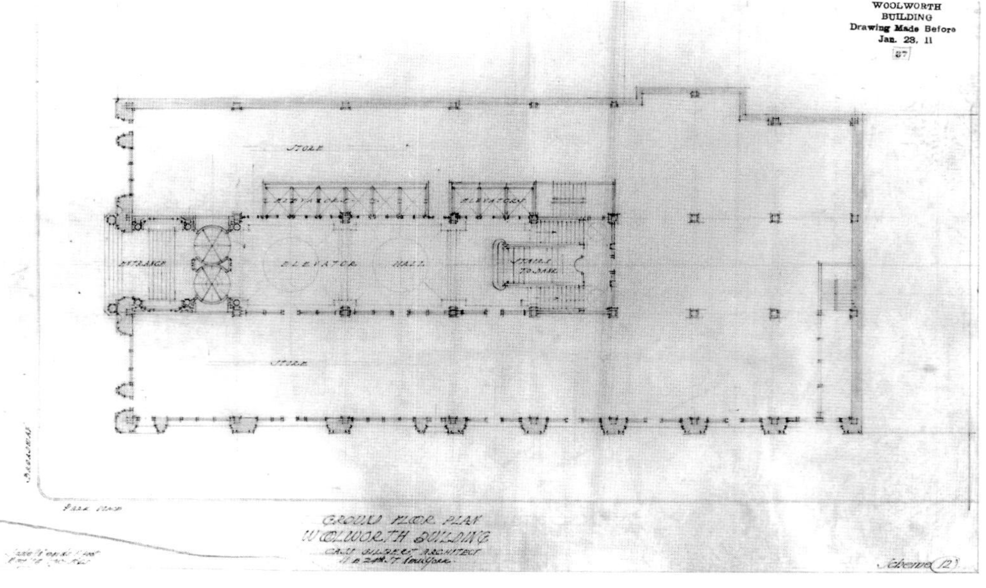

Gilbert and his staff documented the new design in plans entitled "Scheme 17," and seven weeks later in a perspective entitled "Scheme 26" (figs. 4.10, 4.11). Woolworth's desire for more than just an office building modeled on the Victoria Tower—that is, for the world's tallest skyscraper designed as a distinctive Gothic landmark—had now become the project's central goal. Gilbert offered a pragmatic explanation for his client's new ambitions: The skyscraper's second story could not accommodate Irving National Exchange Bank's growing spatial needs: "The rapid growth of the Irving National Bank required more space than could be conveniently provided on the plottage first secured, and Mr. Woolworth's ideas grew proportionally until he saw the possibility of erecting a building which would be of such proportions and character as to constitute a great landmark in the city."[57] But even Gilbert's matter-of-factness thinly veiled the more compelling reason behind the project's increasing size. Woolworth—no longer content with rivaling the adjacent Park Row Building—had broadened his arena of competition to incorporate the entire skyline panorama of lower Manhattan. Woolworth's new skyscraper, if built, would at 720 feet high surpass the Singer Tower and, in doing so, triumph as New York's dominant corpo-

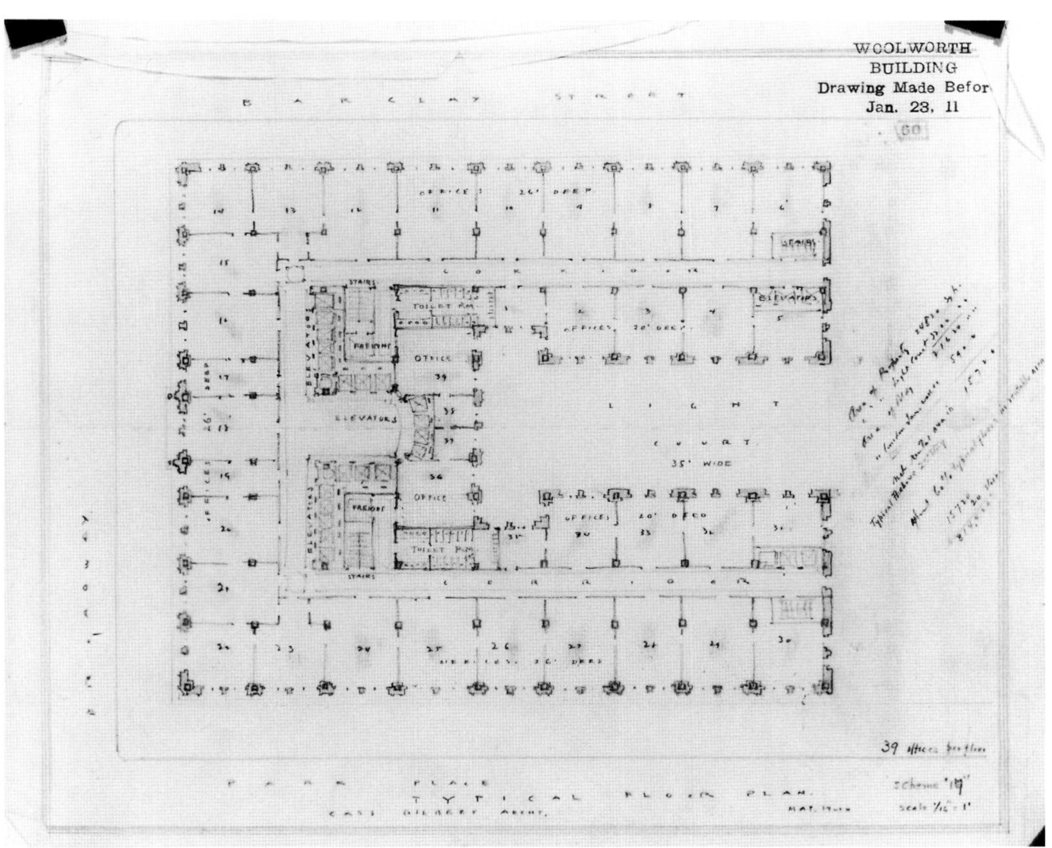

FIGURE 4.10 Cass Gilbert, Woolworth Building, second design, "Scheme 17," plan of typical story drawn at the scale of 1/16" = 1'0", May 17, 1910. Graphite and Conté crayon on tracing paper. Collection of the New-York Historical Society, negative 69839.

FIGURE 4.11
Cass Gilbert, Woolworth Building, second design, "Scheme 26," perspective drawn at the scale of $\frac{1}{32}$" = 1'0" by Thomas R. Johnson, July 6, 1910. Graphite and watercolor on illustration board. Collection of the New-York Historical Society, negative 45871.

rate trademark and skyline feature. Gilbert now called the project simply "Woolworth Building," suggesting that Woolworth had invested a decisive personal stake in the city's crowd-exhilarating, publicity-generating tower-building race.

Gilbert may have produced conceptual sketches for the exterior of "Scheme 17," but only the plans of "Scheme 17" remain—a lobby story, a typical upper story, and a typical tower story—all dated May 17. The plans for "Scheme 17" show a tower flanked by two attached twenty-story wings, together enframing a thirty-five-foot-wide central light court. A notation on the typical story of the tower indicated the project's proposed height of 720 feet. In all of its important features, then—the size of its site, its composition, and its new height—"Scheme 17" predicted with near accuracy the scope and character of the Woolworth Building's final design.[58]

"Scheme 17" also entailed a totally new method of conceptualizing the project financially. Woolworth no longer seemed interested in constructing merely a speculative bank and office building and memorable skyline feature. Instead, his new question might have been this: Could a magnificent and beautiful landmark that dominated its urban surroundings be supported financially with the mechanism of speculative office uses? Woolworth apparently thought so. Still, construction to the new 720-foot height required costly structural features, that is, a still larger foundation utilizing caissons carried to bedrock and a far more complex and elaborate system of wind bracing.[59] Woolworth, moreover, understood the sizable risk involved with adding acres of office space to a local market threatened since 1909 by overbuilding. Woolworth's new concept for the project, then, showed a streak of the irrational—regardless of the indirect returns originating from height's potential for publicity or appeal to tenants, or what one contemporary real estate expert called the "symbolism" of "financial opulence and stability."[60]

Tom Johnson's perspective of "Scheme 26," produced on July 6, mirrored Woolworth's new and altered vision for the skyscraper (see fig. 4.11). It showed a main office block rising twenty-eight stories and tower projecting skyward for an additional fourteen stories. The block and tower combined to create a total height of forty-two stories, or about 580 feet, as opposed to the 720 feet in "Scheme 17." Importantly, Gilbert had decided to extend the office block's wings upward by an additional eight stories. No explanation remains for the differences between "Scheme 17" and "Scheme 26." But in all likelihood, Woolworth and Gilbert had begun testing workable financial strategies for the newly enlarged project.

As Gilbert later put it, he based the composition of the Woolworth Building—like that of the West Street Building—on "many medieval civic buildings, with towers of proportionally great height," all of which were studied, but none copied.[61] He cited as specific examples the *hôtels des villes* in Compiègne and Brussels, the Cloth Hall at Ypres, and the town halls of Middelburg and Alkmaar in the Netherlands, the latter called "noble" by the English Victorian architect George Gilbert Scott.[62] By contrast, the Metropolitan Life and the Singer towers' Italian Renaissance and "modern French" exteriors, Gilbert wrote in 1909, offered him little in the way of inspiration: "The Metropolitan Tower is much admired, even though [Cyrus L. W.] Eidlitz thinks that it is weak and thin, everyone else has nothing but praise for it. Personally, I like its simplicity, but do not find myself very enthusiastic over the design, being however of the Italian rather than the French type it will have a better influence on taste than the Singer Tower."[63] In modeling the West Street Building on the *hôtels des villes*, cloth halls, and belfries of medieval Flanders, moreover, Gilbert had already discovered the capacity of such medieval precedents for a heightened compositional pictorialism. Equally important, the Flemish towers effectively expressed his desire to romantically and nostalgically associate New York's commercial enterprises with the free-trading cities of the Middle Ages.

The Woolworth project's "Scheme 17" and "Scheme 26," in their newly gargantuan size, had a bulk far more difficult to manage compositionally than that of the project's first design. In this most recent phase of the process Gilbert had begun struggling, as Montgomery Schuyler later put it, with "the subjugation of our strange new monster."[64] The problem he and Johnson confronted showed in the less-than-satisfactory relation of the office block to the height of the tower in "Scheme 26," as well as in what looked like a desperate effort to impart monumentality to the design's seemingly countless, repetitive office stories. They heavily modeled the elevations' verticals, markedly emphasizing those that supported the tower. They attached projecting canopies and outriggers to the upper stories of both the office block and the tower. All intensified the illusion of depth. Still, the skyscraper's requirements for openness and light continued to be in conflict with Gilbert's desire for monumentality. The cruder details of "Scheme 26," glaringly among them the awkward fenestration of its major verticals, highlighted the conflict. Gilbert recounted his awareness of the struggle: "We must be faithful to the problem of the time and give it beauty if we can. What was the problem? It was, in cold blood, to justify the existence of the tower by getting as much rentable floor space as possible within a given area. The logic of the balance sheet is inexorable. Ignoble, if it be, such is the essential fact of its being. There must be a rentable floor in every twelve feet six inches or fifteen feet of height and the whole area of the lot must be filled. Room for deep recessed windows or projecting buttresses here? . . . It is not a copy of Malines, beautiful as is Malines."[65] "Scheme 26," then, vividly demonstrated the project's central predicament. Later, Gilbert asked whether the skyscraper could "be solved in beauty" or whether it "must be the Caliban of buildings forever grossly struggling with materialism, forever thrusting an unlovely monstrous form aloft?"[66] He and Johnson had yet to synthesize Woolworth's desire for a Perpendicular Gothic grandeur with the speculative modern office uses that served as the project's financial justification.

The plans associated with "Scheme 26" showed Stickel and the office draftsmen enlarging the new design's ground-floor public space, imbuing it with a commensurate sense of monumentality and grandeur (fig. 4.12). Gilbert had expanded the former lobby for elevators to create a magnificent, cross-shaped lobby-arcade. The lobby-arcade's central axis, now a twenty-foot-high hall, dominated the plan.[67] The hall led past a pair of stairs rising to the bank, and then again past several stores to terminate in an apselike sculpture niche. Conceptually recalling the arcade of Gilbert's earlier Endicott Building, it featured show windows that extended through its interior the street's lively ambience of spectatorship and sidewalk crowds. As the salient feature of the ground floor, it dramatically altered the skyscraper's relationship with its urban surroundings.

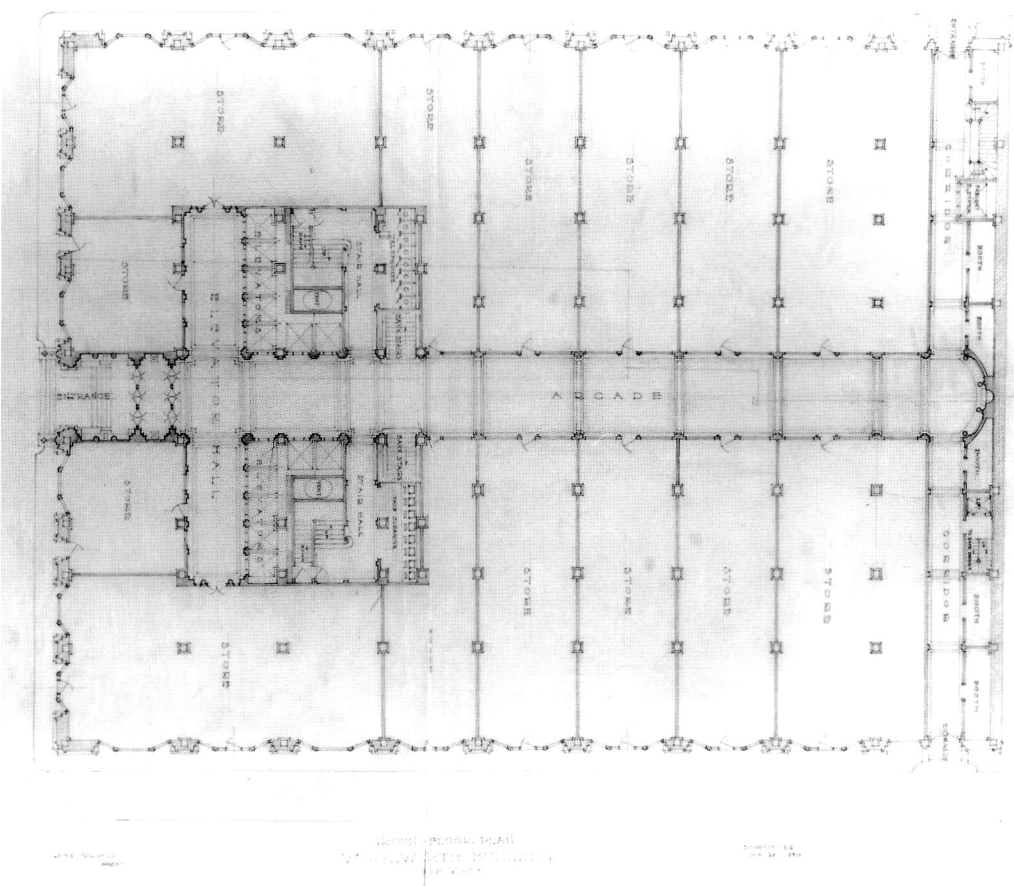

FIGURE 4.12 Cass Gilbert, Woolworth Building, second design, "Scheme 26," plan of ground floor drawn at the scale of 1/8" = 1'0", June 28, 1910. Graphite on tracing paper. Collection of the New-York Historical Society, negative 69837.

Soon enough, the realities of speculative real estate frustrated Woolworth and Gilbert's vision for the Woolworth Building's second, much larger design. Woolworth had failed to obtain the corner parcel he needed to complete the project's site at Broadway's intersection with Barclay Street—known today as a "holdout." The project's line of development, proceeding from "Scheme 17" to "Scheme 26," moreover, had already twice entailed a scaling back of the design to fit Woolworth's original 80 × 172-foot site.[68] Intricate sequences of numerical calculations, which initially appeared on the typical upper floor plan and tower of "Scheme 17," and then later in plan studies and office memorandums, reflected Gilbert's struggle to make the project work financially.[69] The later calculations, spread across a total of twenty-eight studies, showed a variety of scenarios aimed at increasing the net rentable areas on a typical office floor and a tower floor. Detailed analyses of specific office and corridor dimensions showed Gilbert exploring the trade-offs between the areas in the main building and those in a tower of varying heights. They also showed him

FIGURE 4.13
Cass Gilbert, Woolworth Building, third design, conceptual sketches, August 1910. Graphite on paper. Cass Gilbert Collection, Archives Center, National Museum of American History, Behring Center, Smithsonian Institution.

exploring the trade-offs between the areas of the light court and the building itself.[70] As Gilbert explained in his 1909 West Point lecture on the skyscraper, "The greater number of square feet of well-lit floor space that can be made available for rent, the greater the income."[71] Woolworth's ambition to build the spectacular "Scheme 17" continued to be challenged by the formulas governing speculative real estate finance.

In August 1910, Gilbert and Woolworth met in London to inspect the Victoria Tower and to discuss the skyscraper's design at the Carlton Hotel over drawings of "Scheme 26."[72] By then, Woolworth's level of frustration with acquiring the Barclay corner from its owners, the Adelaide and John Hamilton family, had reached a breaking point. Gilbert wrote to John Rockart, whom he had charged with managing the project in his absence,

"[Woolworth] tells me that he and the owner of the Barclay Street corner are only $50,000 apart on the price of the land." Gilbert added that Woolworth had decided to abandon "Scheme 26" entirely: "He told me that he had decided that the large building (extending to Barclay Street) was too big for him to undertake, that he did not want to tie up so much money in one enterprise."[73] Gilbert quickly conceptualized and sketched a new scaled-back version of the project—having during the same trip culled for his sketchbook key Gothic details—and sent it to Johnson for further development (figs. 4.13, 4.14).

Woolworth, Gilbert knew, intended to sail from Liverpool to New York on the *Lusitania* on August 6, returning well ahead of his own sailing scheduled for August 22. Consequently, he urged Rockart to tactfully encourage Woolworth in considering yet another option: building a revised version of the earlier "Scheme 26": "I would not have you urge the matter, however, so hard as to jeopardize the *whole* project, or to give him the idea that we are unwilling to go on with the smaller building or holding him up in any way; for we must loyally carry out his instructions and help all we can."[74] Woolworth, Gilbert added, might also be willing to pay whatever price necessary to acquire the Barclay Street corner, to create the larger site, and then to build a substantially scaled but financially less risky twenty-story, or even twenty-five-story, office block without a tower. Such a financially "safe" design, Gilbert may have reasoned, would at least yield a skyscraper comparable in size to his earlier West Street Building. But as Antonin Raymond, who at the time worked in association with Gilbert's office as a draftsman later recalled, "Mr. Gilbert had the genius and ability to exploit the ambition of Woolworth toward the realization of

FIGURE 4.14 Cass Gilbert, *Part of a Shrine in Cathedral, Cologne*, sketch, July 19, 1910. Cass Gilbert Collection, Archives Center, National Museum of American History, Behring Center, Smithsonian Institution.

a monumental architectural creation, without precedent."[75] Gilbert, as a consequence, may well have applied every technique of architectural salesmanship at his command to support Woolworth in undertaking the boldest feat of construction possible.

THE ACCEPTED DESIGN

Despite his difficulties with obtaining the Barclay Street corner, Woolworth continued to be haunted by the idea of dramatically altering lower Manhattan's skyline with the construction of a spectacular Gothic landmark. By August 22, he had firmly decided not to give up on the 720-foot height of "Scheme 17." Rockart reported that "Mr. Woolworth took up the large scheme; evidently he re-considered his determination since leaving London."[76]

Woolworth, it appears, had in the interim discovered his "giant signboard." He had identified a rational financial excuse that justified the irrationality of building to such an extreme height. He now counted himself among speculative builders of another type —the New York corporate moguls who had erected skyscrapers "with a keener eye to their advertising than to their investment qualities."[77]

For Woolworth, the trademarklike Singer Tower continued to function as the primary model of effective skyscraper advertising in its command of the skyline and through printed media publicity. In addition, Woolworth may have known that Metropolitan Life's vice president, Haley Fiske, viewed its tower as "an advertisement that didn't stand the company a cent because tenants footed the bill."[78] In any case, Woolworth had identified in such potential for advertising the supreme financial instrument for reconciling his unruly ambitions about height with his five- and ten-cent frugality. The shrewdness of such a strategy was not lost on his contemporaries. Louis Horowitz, the project's builder, hailed the "new factor of value in advertising that [the Woolworth Building] would give to the merchant's chain of stores. It was never hoped that it might yield, through rents, a fair return on Mr. Woolworth's big investment."[79]

By November 2, Woolworth had officially approved Gilbert's "Scheme 30," a new and taller third design, with a forty-five-story tower rising 625 feet. He had instructed Gilbert to top the height of the Singer Tower and to decisively crown the skyline of lower Manhattan.[80] That October, Johnson had illustrated the design in a watercolor perspective (plate 4). This new "accepted design" fell short of the 720-foot height of "Scheme 17." The project's confined site, moreover, had dictated vertical construction of the slenderest proportions. Woolworth, consequently, had decided to extend the Broadway frontage from 80 to 105 feet. In doing so, he provided an increased breadth of dimension at the skyscraper's base, thereby serving to counter the powerful stresses produced by wind forces pushing sideways on the tower.[81] He added a new parcel to the site, 231 Broadway, which he had originally purchased along with a parcel at 10 Park Place to guarantee an ambient environment of light and air (fig. 4.15).[82]

Johnson subjected "Scheme 30" to laborious study in his watercolor perspective as well as in two rough study models comprising the design's Broadway and Park Place elevations.[83] The scheme's height may have been suitably spectacular, but its composition was not resolved. The Broadway elevation's main entrance Gilbert had shifted off axis, and the composition's main block he had reduced to a tentative, awkward projection from the tower. The exterior's

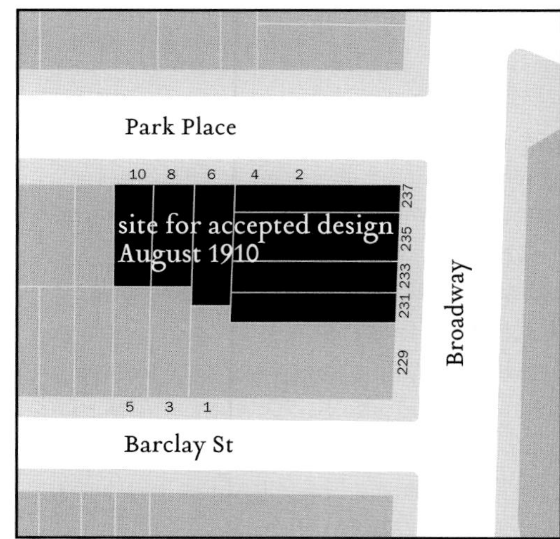

FIGURE 4.15 Woolworth Building, plan showing individual parcels acquired to create building site for third, or "accepted design," Broadway and Park Place, August 27, 1910. Map by Dennis McClendon.

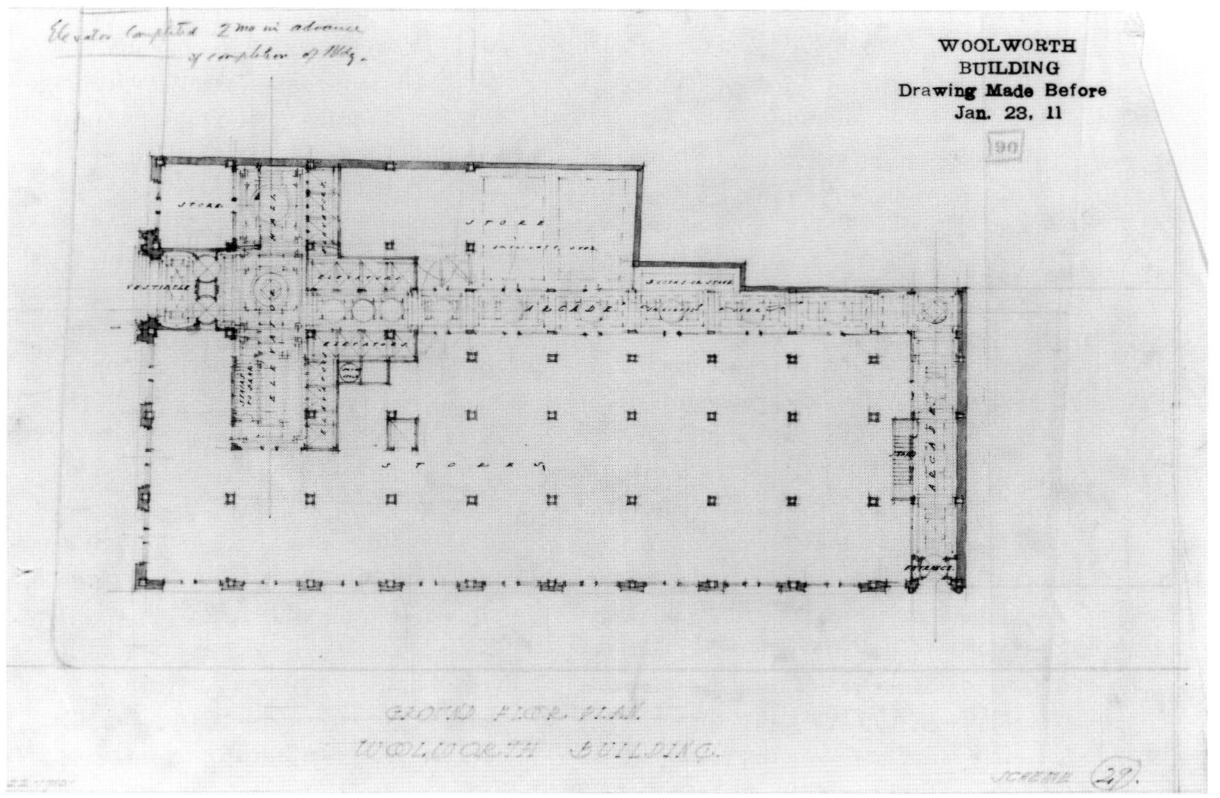

FIGURE 4.16 Cass Gilbert, Woolworth Building, third design, "Scheme 29," plan of ground floor drawn at the scale of 1/16" = 1'0", August 16, 1910. Graphite on paper. Collection of the New-York Historical Society, negative 69836.

Gothic ornamentation, and especially the canopies, seemed attached as if by afterthought and in its brittle Perpendicular Gothic–inspired fragility conflicted with the structure's gargantuan size. Yet for all of the design's "crude and lumpy" awkwardness, as Schuyler later described it, Gilbert had managed to preserve a composition inspired by the *hôtels des villes*, cloth halls, and belfries of medieval Flanders.[84]

In their compromise on the "ideal" site for "Scheme 26," the third design's plans betrayed the same awkward inelegance as the composition's gangly exterior (fig. 4.16). For "Scheme 29," of August 16, Gilbert had explored the idea of a twenty-five-story building without a tower, and then in the similar, undated "Scheme 30," probably of early September, he had proposed extending the tower upward by an additional sixteen stories.[85] Gilbert's dilemma manifested itself vividly in the ground-floor lobby-arcade in "Scheme 29." He had managed to preserve a vestige of the arcade from "Scheme 26," but the new arcade lacked the coherence and grandeur of the original. It jogged inelegantly off axis from a cross-shaped elevator lobby, then made an abrupt L-shaped turn to connect through a side entrance with Park Place. Altogether, the third design's compositional problems underscored Woolworth's willingness to make artistic sacrifices for the sake of advertising by means of a spectacular, media-publicity-generating height.

The editors of *Architectural Record* summed up the phenomenon of advertising with towers built to high altitudes, proclaiming upon the completion of the Singer Tower in 1908: "Now we possess genuine tower architecture as an advertising feature on a rental basis."[86] Business architecture of the mid- to late nineteenth century—particularly that of the fiercely competitive and publicity-seeking insurance industry—had effectively exploited opulent and lavishly ornamented exteriors for the purpose of image making and urban profile. But the impulse to construct slender towers whose outlines functioned in skyline views and in printed media publicity like advertising trademarks was new: "The tower, would, of course, be a striking and spectacular feature, the design of which in itself would offer a tempting opportunity, and in making such a design the architect would be emancipated from limitations which hamper him very much in the erection of ordinary skyscrapers."[87] Many architects questioned whether such showy construction had the capacity to engage nobler artistic sympathies—even though Charles McKim was known to have admitted that a beautiful commercial building could also function as good advertising.[88] Instead, there existed a continued commitment to the nineteenth-century's ethic of honest construction, based on Ruskin's principle of "truth to nature." In the early twentieth century, however, such a commitment provided little guidance for the fabrication of trademark towers with crowd-dazzling surface effects.

Given the standard set by the Woolworth Building project's original Park Place elevation, Gilbert's 625-foot third design, despite its height and dazzle, signaled a retreat as opposed to an advance in the project's line of artistic development. Still, for all its awkwardness as a composition and fussiness of detail, Gilbert had solved another equally important problem, albeit a problem of a wholly different kind. He had fully integrated the skyscraper's characteristically thin terra cotta cladding with its internal skeleton of structural steel. The tower's dynamic verticals, moreover, expressed in clear visual terms the functional distribution of its structural loads. Altogether, Gilbert's third design showed that the project had entered an advanced phase of architectural-constructional refinement.

Gunvald Aus had signed a formal contract with Gilbert outlining his professional services on September 23, 1910, shortly after Gilbert began working on the project's "accepted design."[89] In 1905, Corydon T. Purdy described the role the structural engineer had previously assumed in the design of the New York skyscraper: "Ten years ago . . . architects depended upon one of three or four great iron manufacturers of New York for their steel designing."[90] Aus, by contrast, brought the highest level of professional engineering expertise to the Woolworth project, based in part on his earlier design for the West Street Building, and now augmented by that of his new associates, S. F. Holtzman and Kort Berle.[91] Like Johnson, moreover, Aus demonstrated an extraordinary professional flexibility in the face of Woolworth's perpetually changing parameters of design. Aus's contribution to the Woolworth project, as Antonin Raymond later noted, strongly influenced its artistic resolution as a skyscraper: Gilbert owed credit "above all, to the engineer, Gunvald Aus."[92]

As shown by Gilbert's designs for the United States Custom House and the West Street Building, his method of Beaux-Arts composition had typically entailed conceiving exteriors pictorially. Aus, by contrast, believed that the skyscraper's internal framework of steel and, most significantly, its vertical uprights, should receive the strongest emphasis visually: "From an engineering point of view, no structure is beautiful where the lines of strength were not apparent, where one cannot follow the distribution of loads from the top of the structure to its foundations."[93] Aus's views suggested those of a committed structural rationalist; he may well have understood the rational theories of Eugène-Emmanuele Viollet-le-Duc. Still, Aus put Gilbert's compositional priorities first, in the spirit of a loyal consulting professional. He found the architectural requirements "of greatest importance" in determining "the engineering design."[94] This held especially true for the location of the structural steel columns in the tower. "In the tower proper, the column spacing was determined largely by the architectural requirements, that is to say, by the front elevation."[95] Gilbert and Aus, it appears, together sought the impression of a seamless unity between the Woolworth's skeletal steel framing and the rhythmic verticals so essential to the character of the design.

The design of the Woolworth's extremely tall, thin tower thrust Gilbert and Aus into a totally new and previously unexplored structural engineering domain. There they found particularly troublesome the problems of how to rigidly brace and to clad the tower to withstand the powerful lateral forces of the wind. In late September 1910, they began evaluating a variety of cross-bracing and knee bracing systems, both of which provided through triangulation the rigidity required for resisting such forces. Then, on October 19, Aus recommended "after considerable discussion" the portal arch system as the solution to the Woolworth Building's wind-bracing problem.[96] Derived in principle from the portal or entrance frames of truss bridges, portal braces achieved rigidity through two or more points of connection, eliminating the need for the triangulation provided by diagonal bracing.[97] The more elaborate portal arch system, which Aus described as "a rather expensive form of wind bracing, as the material in the portals is not strained in direct tension and compression, as is the case with diagonal bracing," would be nonetheless extremely strong.[98] Gilbert understood the potential of the portal arches for visually lightening curtain wall construction, given his earlier experience with the Brazer Building. The Woolworth's portal arch system, however, would accomplish more than simply providing the internal bracing required to free a corner structurally: It would serve as the Woolworth tower's primary and most extensive system of wind bracing.

"Fortunately architects are gradually recognizing that steel and stone should act together," Aus asserted after he completed the Woolworth Building's design. The portal arches, which allowed broad openings between structural supports, could also "generally be arranged so as not to interfere with window openings." The appearance of the Woolworth's verticals would therefore "be made very much lighter than would be possible with a system of diagonal braces."[99] The strength of the portal arch system derived ultimately from its individual arch units, each of which steel fabricators produced by the labor-intensive process of riveting heavy steel plates together to form a deep, solid, arch-shaped web. On the site, steelworkers riveted the webs in turn to adjoining columns and girders throughout their depth and breadth.[100] To Aus's credit, he deployed the portal arch system's method of solid steel plate construction in the Woolworth tower with the aim of achieving Gilbert's desired visual impression of a soaring verticality and screenlike delicacy.

Throughout September and early October, Gilbert and his office staff assessed the problem of choosing a suitable exterior cladding for the third design, seeking a system that would complement Aus's proposed systems of wind bracing. That November, however, Woolworth suddenly and inexplicably specified that the skyscraper be sheathed in marble. Gilbert solicited advice from two experts in stone construction, Paul Starrett of the George A. Fuller Company in New York and O. W. Norcross of the Norcross Brothers Company in Worcester, Massachusetts. Both Starrett and Norcross—perhaps to Gilbert's dismay—supported Woolworth's choice of marble.[101] Gilbert, consequently, proposed an alternative third design—not Gothic, as Woolworth had initially specified, but instead a striking classical composition clad in marble panels (fig. 4.17). With flat tripartite elevations and enclosed corner bays, the design masked an extensive system of diagonal knee bracing, which rose the full height of the tower. Johnson rendered the design in perspective on October 1. But regardless of the seriousness with which Gilbert and Johnson studied the new classical scheme, Aus reportedly balked at the added weight of the marble.[102] All of the project's subsequent designs, consequently, were terra cotta clad and skyscraper Gothic.

The Woolworth Building's "accepted design," it can be argued, would not have been successful without a shared sympathy of spirit between engineer and architect. Both Gilbert and Aus made a goal of successfully marrying the skyscraper's modern steel-framed engineering with its characteristically thin wall of cladding in terra cotta. Moreover, in his earlier pictorial compositions Gilbert had little use for soundness of "bones," but now in both the West Street Building and the Woolworth Building, Aus had stepped in to infuse his designs with a wholly new and convincing structural rationality. Without Aus's ingenious structural scaffolding of steel, Gilbert would have been, in fact, hard pressed to fabricate the Woolworth Building's sensational Gothic imagery. For this reason, advocates of Aus's profession applauded his contribution to the skyscraper's design, arguing that the professional engineer, whose structural feats "guaranteed that the building would stand forever," deserved as much recognition as the architect.[103]

THE FINAL DESIGN

Johnson's rendering of the Woolworth Building's third "accepted design" appeared in the real estate section of the *New York Times* on November 13, filling the front page under the banner "New Woolworth Building on Broadway Will Eclipse Singer Tower in Height" (fig. 4.18). The undertitle exemplified Woolworth's and the news media's penchant for the Barnumesque variety of showmanship: "$5,000,000 Structure to be Erected on Park Place Corner Will Be an Architectural Ornament to the Metropolis—Gothic in Treatment, Containing Forty-Five Stories, It Will Be the Third Loftiest Building in the World and the Second in America—Will Contain a Swimming Pool, Gymnasium, and Running Track on the Roof—Occupies a Historic Corner Made Famous by Mayor Hone's Residence Social Events—Its Many Novel Features."[104] Gilbert exhibited the design—now reported to cost $5 million—at the Architectural League of New York throughout December.[105] For the moment at least, Woolworth and Gilbert viewed the design as final. It was spectacular enough

FIGURE 4.17
Cass Gilbert, Woolworth Building, third design, perspective, classical alternative, drawn at the scale of 1⁄32" = 1'0" by Thomas R. Johnson, October 1, 1910. Graphite, watercolor, and Conté crayon on illustration board. Collection of the New-York Historical Society, negative 63313.

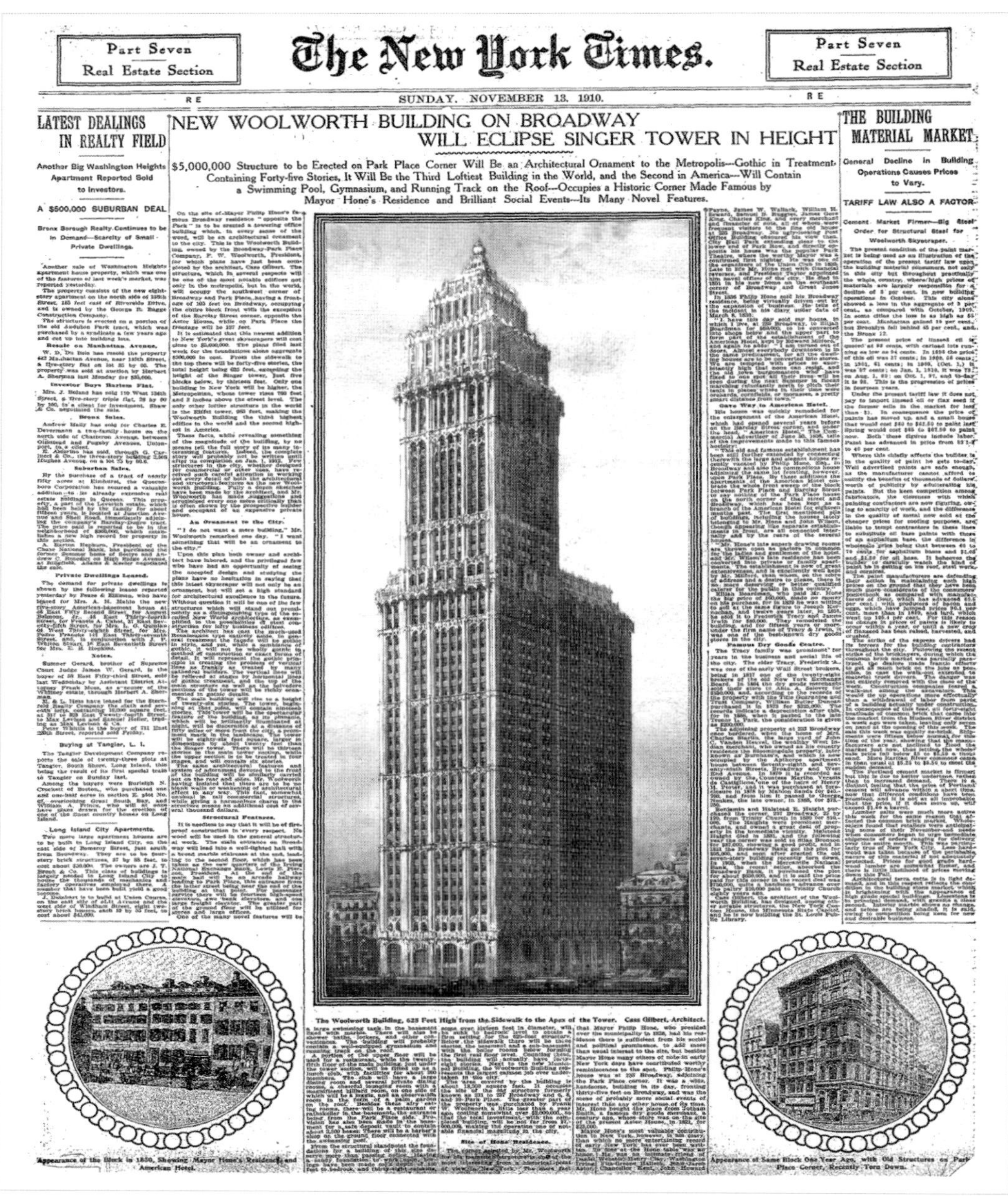

Part Seven
Real Estate Section

The New York Times.

Part Seven
Real Estate Section

SUNDAY, NOVEMBER 13, 1910.

LATEST DEALINGS IN REALTY FIELD

Another Big Washington Heights Apartment Reported Sold to Investors.

A $500,000 SUBURBAN DEAL

Bronx Borough Realty Continues to be in Demand—Scarcity of Small Private Dwellings.

NEW WOOLWORTH BUILDING ON BROADWAY WILL ECLIPSE SINGER TOWER IN HEIGHT

$5,000,000 Structure to be Erected on Park Place Corner Will Be an Architectural Ornament to the Metropolis—Gothic in Treatment. Containing Forty-five Stories, It Will Be the Third Loftiest Building in the World, and the Second in America—Will Contain a Swimming Pool, Gymnasium, and Running Track on the Roof—Occupies a Historic Corner Made Famous by Mayor Hone's Residence and Brilliant Social Events—Its Many Novel Features.

THE BUILDING MATERIAL MARKET

General Decline in Building Operations Causes Prices to Vary.

TARIFF LAW ALSO A FACTOR

The Woolworth Building, 625 Feet High from the Sidewalk to the Apex of the Tower. Cass Gilbert, Architect.

FIGURE 4.18 "New Woolworth Building on Broadway Will Eclipse Singer Tower in Height," *New York Times*, November 13, 1910. (Copyright 1910 *The New York Times*. Reprinted by permission.)

in engineering and sumptuous enough in style to fulfill Woolworth's objective of eye-catching advertising through printed media publicity.

Woolworth, however, continued to remain indecisive about the skyscraper's final height. On December 13, Gilbert wondered "whether he wanted me to design the tower of his building at a height of 625 feet or to carry it up to something over 700 feet . . . high enough to be the highest tower in the world."[106] Woolworth's level of personal involvement with the project's third design, moreover, had become heavy enough to elicit comment from the *New York Times*: "Fully a dozen sketches have been made by the architect, and Mr. Woolworth has made suggestions and scrutinized every one more critically than is often shown by the prospective builder and occupant of an expensive private house."[107] Yet in spite of Woolworth's ambivalence about the question of height, the pressures imposed by speculative real estate finance rapidly propelled the project forward.

On November 21, 1910, the Bureau of Buildings of the Borough of Manhattan issued the Woolworth Building's first construction permit. On November 4, workers had begun excavating the Broadway and Park Place site with pneumatic caissons.[108] Even a quick decision by Woolworth about the skyscraper's height would result in wasted design efforts—as it was, Gilbert's office expenses averaged three thousand dollars a week—and costly construction delays.[109] Yet Woolworth vacillated: "He continued to advocate the higher tower on the ground that it would be the greatest tower in the world and yet he was not finally determined upon doing it. He seems unable to make up his mind."[110] Significantly for Woolworth, the Metropolitan Life Insurance Tower stood isolated in midtown as the tallest pinnacle on Manhattan Island and as the tallest office building anywhere in the world (fig. 4.19).[111]

Metropolitan Life, too, sold "commodities," consisting largely of "weekly ten and twenty-five cent insurance premiums," to a mass market of millions of consumers, most of whom numbered among the city's new immigrant arrivals and working classes.[112] It, too, had an international profile as well as a strong national presence, with eleven district offices in the Northeast, the Midwest, and the South, along with Canada.[113] According to one contemporary story, Metropolitan Life insulted Woolworth by refusing a loan he solicited, inciting him to build taller in retaliation.[114] Woolworth had, in fact, approached Metropolitan Life regarding the project's financing that August, reportedly expressing shock over their interest rate of 5–6 percent.[115] Far more important to his decision about the skyscraper's height, however, Woolworth had simply found it impossibly difficult to settle for constructing the world's second-highest skyscraper. He had been deeply impressed as a tourist in Paris by Eiffel's "wonderful tower," and by the magnificent views afforded from the tower's "high altitude."[116] Woolworth could easily enough envision his own marvel of technology conquering equally vertiginous heights.

Woolworth's new ambition to build the tallest skyscraper in the world coincided with his preparations for the F. W. Woolworth and Company's merger of 1911, through which he created the much larger F. W. Woolworth Company, a $65 million private stock corporation that now boasted eight district offices and a total of 605 stores.[117] Woolworth took a controlling interest of more than 50 percent in the new, much larger corporation, and his partners, the vice presidents Charles Sumner Woolworth, Fred Morgan Kirby, Seymour Horace Knox, and Earle Perry Charlton—former partners, "friendly rivals," and at times collaborators as independent chain store owners—took the remainder.[118] Negotiations for the merger did not begin until April 1911, but Woolworth had already envisioned the world's tallest skyscraper as the executive headquarters of an expanded international empire. From his offices on high, he would oversee district offices and stores spread across all regions of America, in Canada, and across the Atlantic in Eng-

FIGURE 4.19 Pierre Le Brun, Napoleon Le Brun and Sons, Metropolitan Life Insurance Tower, New York, 1907–9. Prints and Photographs Division, Library of Congress.

land, along with warehouses in Germany and France (fig. 4.20).[119] The determination of Woolworth and other American corporate executives to establish outlets abroad had in the United States fueled the newest horizontal dynamic of imperial expansion, that is, in the wake of the closing of the American frontier, the renewed conquest of space overseas.[120] For this, Woolworth's ambition to boldly conquer vertical space served as an especially vivid metaphor.

Gilbert, for his own reasons as an architect, felt nearly as competitive as Woolworth. Julia Finch Gilbert explained the skyscraper's increasing height as the product of an architect-client collaboration: "Mr. Woolworth's inventive brain and my husband's equally inventive brain conspired together with the result that it was decided to make the skyscraper the highest office building in the world."[121] But for Gilbert, building the world's tallest skyscraper would be pointless if the skyscraper were not also the world's most beautiful. Montgomery Schuyler described the artistic standard established by Gilbert's competitive architectural milieu: "Meanwhile the competition is not only commercial, but in a measure artistic. No Gradgrind of a projector would dare attack 'the record' without some thought as to how his record beater was going to look."[122] Gilbert barely masked his competitive tone in a letter of December 9 to Metropolitan Life's architect, Pierre Le Brun, which he wrote shortly after the publication of the Woolworth Building's "accepted design" in the *New York Times*: "It is always a pleasure to see your great tower and I have little hope of rivaling its beauty, not only on account of its superb proportions, but on account of its beautiful material and unique simplicity."[123] Gilbert's words were but a quiet echo of Woolworth's increasing ambition. Only one week later, on December 20, Woolworth decisively resolved to top the Metropolitan Life Insurance Tower.

According to Louis Horowitz, Woolworth's seemingly spur-of-the-moment decision to surpass the height of the Metropolitan Life Insurance Tower reflected an earlier, rationally laid plan and could not be considered at all sudden. Woolworth was "determined to play a joke on the populace by keeping '100 feet up his sleeve.'"[124] A contemporary journalist, however, reported another story: "'How high do you want the tower now?' asked Mr. Gilbert. 'How high can you make it?' Woolworth asked in reply. 'It is for you to make the limit,' said Mr. Gilbert. 'Then make it fifty feet higher than the Metropolitan Tower.'"[125] The latter account corresponds more closely with the project's written record, for on December 20, Woolworth instructed Gilbert to accurately ascertain the height of the Metropolitan Life Tower. Gilbert retained the surveyor John Van Horne. Van Horne determined that the tower's roof, when measured at its apex on the tower's central axis, rose exactly seven hundred feet, two inches above the Madison Avenue curb.[126] Van Horne's measurement served as the benchmark for Gilbert's new and taller design. In a conceptual sketch of December 31, Gilbert refined the proportions of the tower's setbacks, taking cues from those of the Metropolitan Life Tower (fig. 4.21; see fig. 4.19). In doing so, he in effect transformed the entire composition's proportions into those of a slender and soaring Gothic campanile, its steeply rising roof tapering gracefully into a spire.

Gilbert's newest scheme for the Woolworth Building had a short life, however. On January 18, 1911, the Hamilton family "holding out" at the Barclay Street corner suddenly capitulated to Woolworth, offering their prized corner parcel at a price

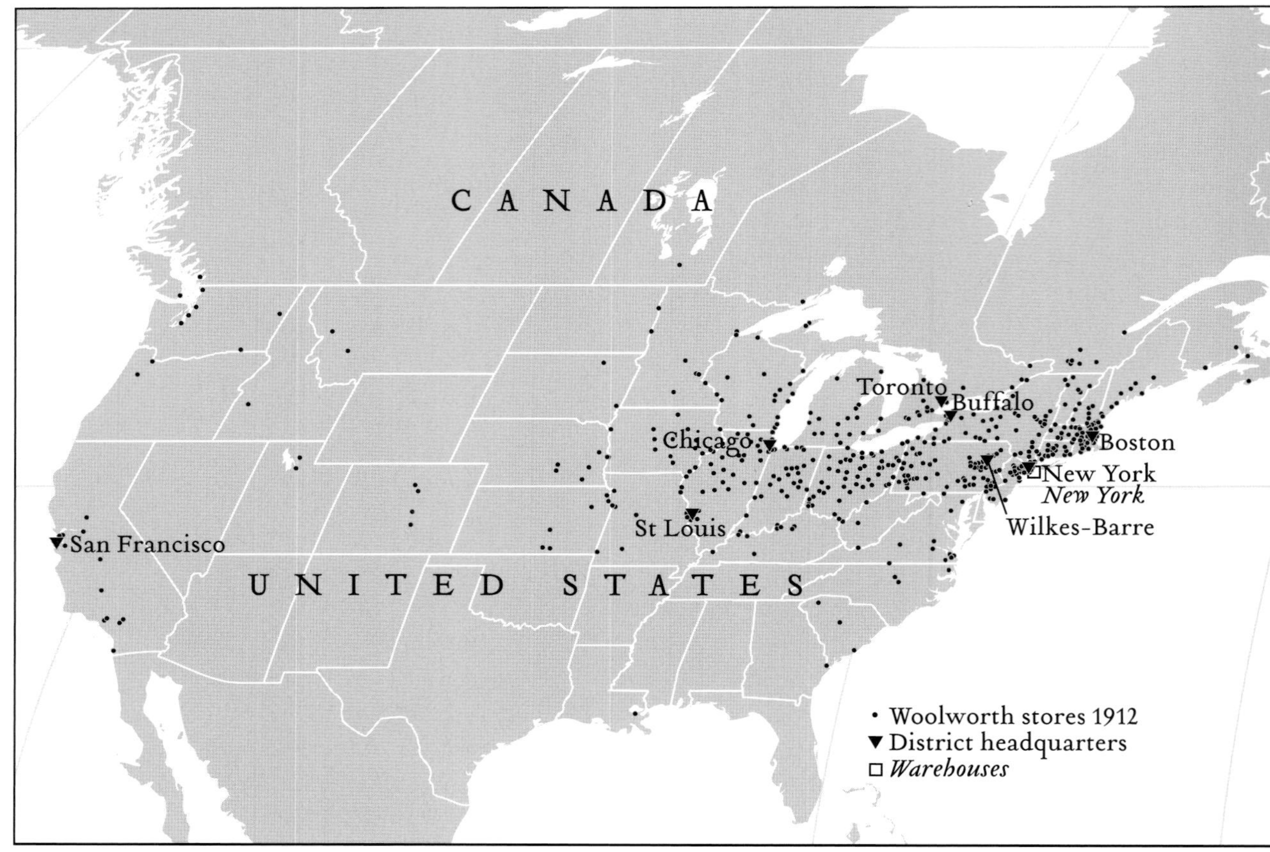

FIGURE 4.20 Location of Woolworth stores, national headquarters, and district headquarters in the United States, Canada, and England, 1912. Map by Dennis McClendon.

one hundred thousand dollars less than Woolworth had proposed only six months earlier.[127] Two weeks prior to the sale, Woolworth had purchased with Edward Hogan's assistance 3 and 5 Barclay Street from the estate of Mrs. Frederick Kennedy, which enabled him to strategically surround and isolate the corner parcel. The Hamilton family, already intimidated by the scale and shadow-casting potential of the "accepted design" so grandly illustrated in the *New York Times*, now feared losing the income-producing value of their small corner property altogether. Journalists applauded the conclusion of Woolworth's nine-month process of acquisition as one of the most formidable real estate transactions of the era. Furthermore, "no exorbitant prices [were paid] for any of the property" noted the *New York Times* in "A Realty Triumph in Assembling Plot" of January 22.[128] Now Woolworth boasted, after having invested a total of $4.5 million, the ownership of a totally reconfigured, reasonably priced, and finally complete full-block building site (fig. 4.22).

The Woolworth project's two last-minute changes—first, Woolworth's decision of December 20 to top the Metropolitan Life Insurance tower and, second, his enlargement of the site on January 18, 1911, after acquiring the Barclay street corner—

drastically altered the scope of Gilbert's third design. On January 19, Gilbert ordered the Foundation Company to halt construction on the project's concrete pier footings. "The Broadway–Park Place Company . . . is considering certain changes of the building with a view to increasing its size."[129] "My building ideas have enlarged," Woolworth explained a day later to the the *New York Times* journalist who reported "the tallest office building in the world."[130] By January 20, Gilbert's office staff had produced revised sketch plans and an elevation for a totally new design at fifty-five stories and 750 feet high, which they submitted to Woolworth for approval.[131] By early that February, Johnson had produced a detailed perspective of the design, which Gilbert sent later to the noted architectural renderer Hughson Hawley for "coloring" (fig. 4.23).

After Woolworth decided to top the Metropolitan Life Tower, Aus and his assistants had recalculated the stresses on the Woolworth Building's concrete pier footings and steel framework to take into account the tower's new height.[132] On January 8, however, Gilbert informed Aus of the project's second important change, the enlarged site. The foundation's piers, consequently, would have to be relocated southward to carry a centrally placed tower, now shifted from its original location on the Park Place

FIGURE 4.21
Cass Gilbert, Woolworth Building, third design, conceptual sketch, December 31, 1910. Graphite on tracing paper. Prints and Photographs Division, Library of Congress.

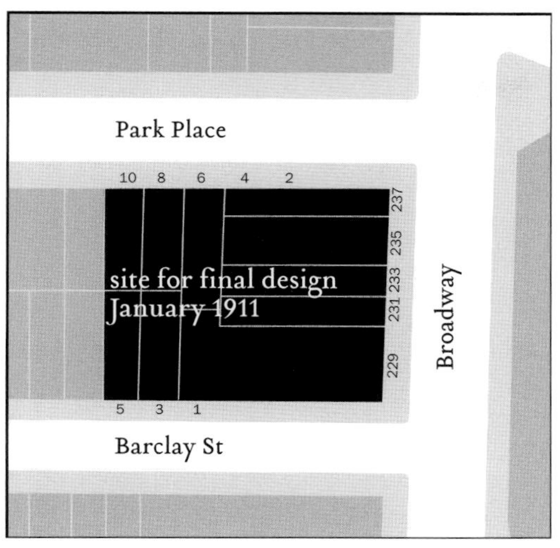

FIGURE 4.22 Woolworth Building, plan showing individual parcels acquired to create final building site, Broadway and Park Place, New York, January 18, 1911. Map by Dennis McClendon.

corner.[133] Aus had completed the project's shop drawings up to the twenty-sixth story, but he concluded on January 18 that the new design's central tower, given its potential for further stabilizing the entire building against wind forces, would make possible a wholly new structural economy. He could, furthermore, use the entire width of the building north to south to resist lateral forces. Consequently, he decided to discard his original set of shop drawings completely and to begin the project's structural design anew.[134]

Gilbert's final design for the Woolworth Building crystallized Woolworth's search for a world character, a goal he had identified at the project's outset through his choice of the Victoria Tower as a model. It also incorporated the medieval secular sources that he had esteemed from the project's earliest stages. To this basic secular repertory Gilbert added innumerable lesser motifs and details culled from a vast array of medieval buildings—many of which were churches and cathedrals. Gilbert especially admired the tower of Antwerp Cathedral (fig. 4.24). This inspired him to subdivide the Woolworth tower's upper stages with thin vertical mullions, which enhanced the visual effect of a skeletal delicacy and augmented the visual sensation of loftiness.[135] He based the tower's highest stage on the crossing tower of the Benedictine Abbey Church of Saint-Ouen in Rouen. He had visited the church in 1880 and while there had produced a detailed drawing of the tower (fig. 4.25).[136] Woolworth described Saint-Ouen while touring France in 1914 as a "fine cathedral" that "all architects adore and copy from."[137]

During the final stages of the Woolworth Building's design, Gilbert and Johnson began mixing the church and cathedral motifs with abandon, adding an array of lesser motifs while thoroughly collapsing the distinction between the sacred and the secular. They chose the roof of the Guild Hall in Cologne, Germany, for the Woolworth tower's steep octagonal roof. Johnson based a detailed study of September 1911 on the Guild Hall, perhaps relying on a photograph recently published in *American Architect* (figs. 4.26, 4.27).[138] Stickel then produced a measured version of Johnson's drawing, refining the tourelles and encrusting the whole with his own precisely rendered Flamboyant Gothic detail (fig. 4.28). Calling the tower's pinnacle "an impressive silhouette against the sky," Schuyler extolled its scenographic array of Gothic gables, canopies, crockets, and tourelles.[139]

In seeking the widest range of Gothic motifs, Gilbert and Johnson consulted Gilbert's sketchbooks, along with countless printed images, many of which Gilbert had stored in office scrapbooks, as photographs, illustrations from architectural journals, and picture postcards. As Gilbert put it, "The Palace of Jacques Coeur at Bourges, the Hotel de Cluny in Paris, the Town Hall

FIGURE 4.23
Cass Gilbert, Woolworth Building, final design, perspective, drawn by Thomas R. Johnson and rendered by Hughson Hawley, April 1911. From *National Architect*, vol. 1 (November 1912).

FIGURE 4.24 *(above)* View of Antwerp, Belgium, showing cathedral, 1352–1525. Unidentified photographer, ca. 1890. (Courtesy of the Boston Public Library, Print Department.)

FIGURE 4.25 *(left)* Cass Gilbert, *Saint-Ouen, Rouen*, July 2, 1880. Prints and Photographs Division, Library of Congress.

FIGURE 4.26 *(left)* Cass Gilbert, Woolworth Building, drawing of roof and lantern of tower by Thomas R. Johnson, September 28, 1911. Graphite on tracing paper. Collection of the New-York Historical Society, negative 72149.

FIGURE 4.27 *(right)* Guild Hall, Cologne, Germany, 1437–44. From *American Architect*, vol. 98 (November 9, 1910).

at Middelburg, Hotel de Ville, Compiègne, the towers of Reims, Antwerp, and Malines, and many others all contributed their quota of precedent and suggestion to the development of the detail."[140] Altogether the composition's complex but fluid synthesis—with some motifs sacred, some secular, some Perpendicular, or Norman, or Flamboyant—appeared stylistically unified insofar as it evocatively recalled "late Gothic" (see fig. 4.23).

If a skyscraper's chief attribute was its tallness, Gilbert later recalled, "its height should be recognized, insisted upon, and expressed by vertical lines."[141] In 1912, Gilbert quoted Sullivan's aphorism, "Form follows function," a second time in a lecture that he delivered at Harvard. He chose Sullivan's "simple formula," he argued, in an effort to resolve the skyscraper's most vexing problem of composition, that of the gridded monotony produced by uniform fenestration with "every window the same size; every window spaced equally." Such a choice he called "wholly in my case, for the moment, a sacrifice," while acknowledging that "my logic and my judgment told me it was the right thing to do," and "out of it grew a certain type, at least for me, and it was a decision fundamental to my practice."[142] Gilbert, then, had taken Sullivan's verticals as his starting point. Yet in his hands those verticals became an artful as well as truthful compositional device: Their syncopated rhythms evoked the experience of the modern while heightening the impact of his illusory effects.

Gilbert's ease with manipulating the Woolworth Building's panoply of medieval and Sullivan-inspired modern sources showed a sophisticated eye for compositional subtleties that defied logic. Beneath the elevations' gables, Gilbert visually "carved" away a tall section of the facade, leaving in its place verticals of extreme attenuation and slenderness. He enlarged the main building's culminating gable forms, so that they served effectively as transitional devices between the wings' steep roofs and the soaring shaft of the tower. Such compositional decisions were highly intuitive, if not frankly irrational. Treating the rhythmic verticals of each side elevation in a strictly logical fashion or designing a simple and straightforward transition from wing to tower would have undermined the elegance of the design.

Gilbert, in essence, contrived the Woolworth Building's composition as highly pictorial—to be seen in the city, from up and down lower Broadway, from across the Brooklyn Bridge and against the greenery of City Hall Park, from close at hand on the street, and from across the river on distant shores. Montgomery Schuyler extolled Gilbert's mind's-eye method of visualization: "There is no point of view from which it 'comes in wrong,' which means there is no point of view from which the designer had not been beforehand with the observer."[143] In drawing upon known medieval compositions, sacred and secular medieval vocabularies, and a wide array of medieval motifs both historically recent and distant, Gilbert's pictorial effects reverberated with countless memories of the treasured older buildings. He had crafted a tantalizingly novel and seductive skyscraper Gothic image with a uniqueness and visual force destined to resonate among the city's spectatorial crowds.

In January 1912, Gilbert finalized the plan for the Woolworth Building's lobby-arcade, showing a secondary cross-axis

FIGURE 4.28 Cass Gilbert, Woolworth Building, detailed pencil study of roof and lantern of tower by Frederick Stickel, 1911. From *Pencil Points*, vol. 8 (October 1927). (Courtesy of the Trustees of the Boston Public Library.)

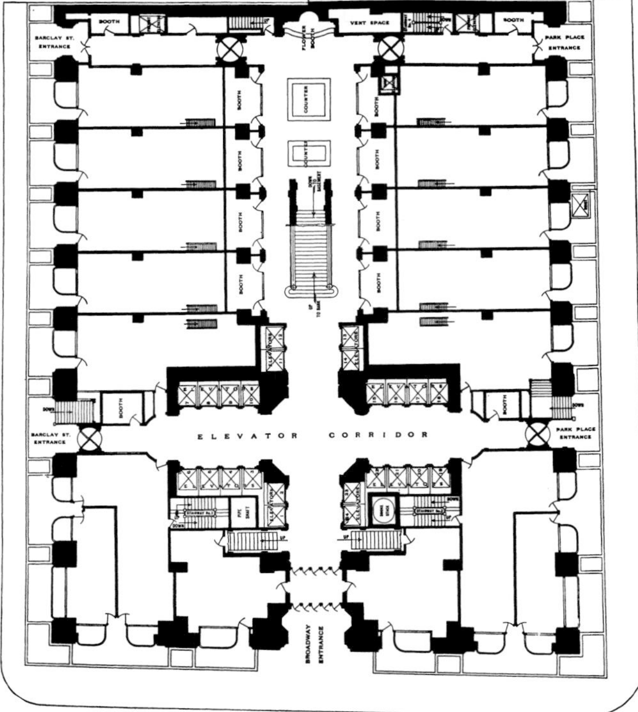

FIGURE 4.29 Cass Gilbert, Woolworth Building, final design, plan of lobby-arcade, 1912. From *National Architect*, vol. 1 (November 1912).

intersecting the main axis, connecting Park Place with Barclay Street, and so decisively linking the building's interior with all surrounding streets (fig. 4.29).[144] A year earlier, he had sketched a late Perpendicular Gothic hall of tall proportions with fan vaulting suggesting King's College Chapel in Cambridge (plate 5). But by April 1912, he had replaced the fan vaulting with a series of domical vaults, then a single barrel vault spanning a space of tall and narrow proportions, suggesting a Romanesque cathedral nave (plate 6). In June 1911, Woolworth indicated in a sketch of his own new show windows and sales booths at the easternmost Park Place entrance, as if elaborating on Gilbert's sketch of that February (figs. 4.30, 4.31).[145] In December, he continued to press for additional show windows, now at the Broadway entrance.[146] A few weeks later, he questioned the merits of the lobby-arcade's monumental stair, insisting that it detracted from the rental value of flanking shops.[147] But Gilbert prevailed. As finally designed, the stair, housed in a marble hall open to illumination from a ceiling light, set up a dazzling terminus for the interior's main axial vista—a vista extending from an unencumbered Broadway entrance into the full depth of the space.

Gilbert never acknowledged the affinities among the Woolworth Building's eye-catching skyscraper Gothic exterior, its spectacular lobby-arcade, and the city's ubiquitous consumer values. But as early as the American antebellum era, perceptive critics had noted the parallels between "the commodity's capacity to excite desire and embody deceit" and works of art tailored for modern commercial purposes.[148] By the end of the nineteenth century, followers of Ruskin's nature-inspired ethic of authenticity expressed fears that individuals of artistic genius working in a "commodity civilization" might turn into acute manipulators of surface effects.[149] Fresh experiences, "novel excitements," and the perception that "the future is bright, much brighter than the past, and that the new is desirable," furthermore, had already become the hallmarks of consumerism's emphasis on appearances.[150] Whether or not Gilbert recognized his own philosophical drift away from the Ruskinian principles of his youth, the Woolworth Building's high pictorialism, spine-tingling verticals, and ornamental flamboyance suggested the illusion of contemporaneity valued most by Woolworth, his shoppers, and the city's wide and varied audience of consumers—now visually attentive and visually attuned to its competitive array of colorful enticements and diversions.

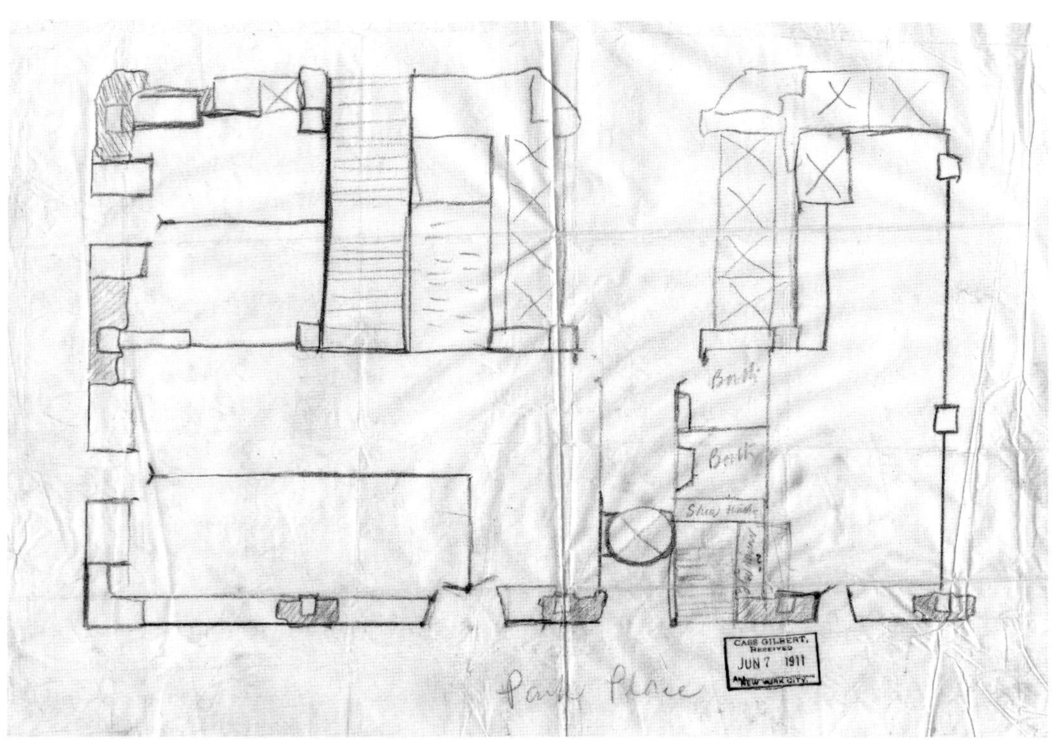

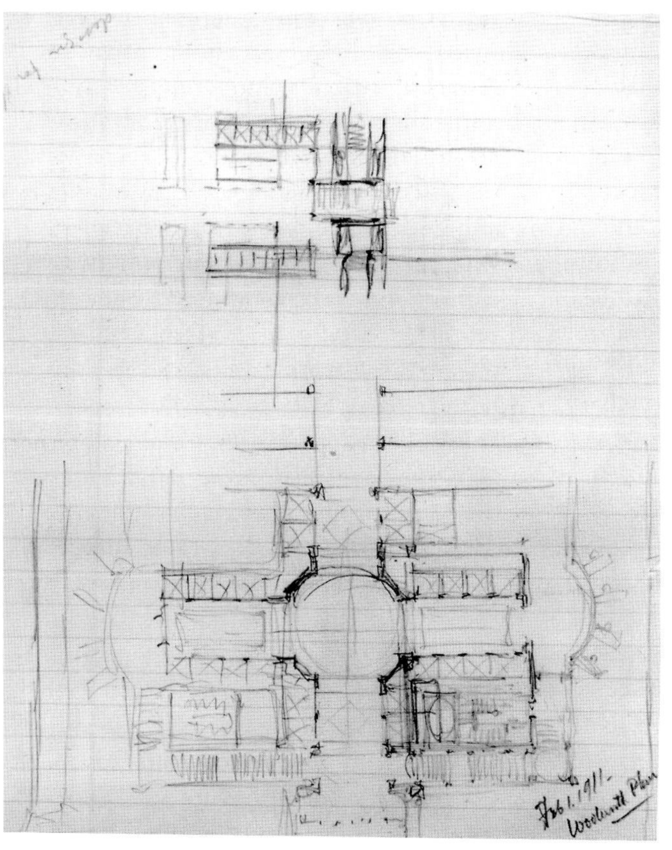

FIGURE 4.30 (*top*)
Frank Woolworth, Woolworth Building, final design, plan of lobby-arcade, sketch, June 1911. Graphite on tracing paper. Collection of the New-York Historical Society, negative 78894d.

FIGURE 4.31 (*bottom*)
Cass Gilbert, Woolworth Building, final design, plan of lobby-arcade, conceptual sketch, February 1, 1911. Graphite on paper. Prints and Photographs Division, Library of Congress.

The Release of Gilbert's Final Perspective as a News Media Event

At 12 noon on May 4, 1911, Woolworth copyrighted, photographed, and then distributed Thomas R. Johnson and the architectural renderer Hughson Hawley's colorful perspective of the Woolworth Building to the *New York Times*, the *Herald*, the *World*, the *Tribune*, and the *Post* with instructions for simultaneous publication—for the sake of impact—in their Sunday, May 7, editions (fig. 4.32).[151] As a consequence, the story of the Woolworth Building's expanding size, already closely followed by the *Times* and its newspaper rivals, now reached the expected climax—an image of the skyscraper presented in magnificent completeness, as if a giant consumable object, to the city's already tantalized mass readership. Woolworth's dramatic "unveiling" of Gilbert's Gothic design before such a mass audience of readers counted among the cleverest of his showmanship strategies. The photograph's accompanying headline in the *Times*, "Woolworth Building Will Be World's Greatest Skyscraper," was presented as if it were a self-fulfilling prophecy. Its undertitle, "Fifty-Five Stories High, Rising 750 Feet above Broadway, Overlooking Post Office—Rays of Electric Light in Tower Will Be Visible Ninety-six Miles Out to Sea—Operation Involves Millions of Dollars," effectively imparted the air of the spectacular surrounding the project.[152] Woolworth could have released the perspective in March, but instead he waited until after May 1, the date the leases for the city's office space expired and the new renting season began. In advertising his skyscraper as premium office space, Woolworth may well have contrived along with enterprising newspapermen to create a grand illusion such as this, an early version of the modern "media event."[153]

Gilbert, keenly aware of the printed news media's role in the public presentation of his designs, had Johnson and Hawley tailor their perspective for the maximum visual impact.[154] The day following the *New York Times*'s November 13 publication of Woolworth's "accepted design," in fact, Gilbert had attempted to control its further reproduction by limiting rights to the Hearst newspapers.[155] Equally concerned with how his final design would succeed as such a widely published picture, Gilbert described Hawley to Woolworth as "the most experienced artist in New York of this class."[156] Hawley, in fact, had begun his career as a theatrical scene painter in Exeter, England, followed by a stint at New York's Madison Square Garden. But soon enough, New York's architects, among them Ernest Flagg, George Post, and Trowbridge and Livingston, discovered the effectiveness of his pictorial representations to the selling of their unbuilt designs—especially those designs whose sheer bigness had overwhelmed the traditional rendering techniques. Such effectiveness, beyond doubt, had inspired Gilbert to employ Hawley for his earlier Broadway Chambers Building and United States Custom House. Hawley's representations, moreover, appeared with frequency in the city's newspapers and nationally circulating mass-market literary journals, among them *Harper's Weekly* and the *Century*. Independently, he reproduced the drawings as color lithographs and picture postcards.[157] Woolworth, in turn, produced his own copyrighted version of Hawley's rendering, which he had printed like a giant trade card for the widest possible distribution (plate 7). Hawley's Woolworth Building, sparkling white with gilded roofs set against a blue- and rose-colored and cloud-filled sky, cemented Gilbert's design, even before construction, as a widely

PLATE 1 Cass Gilbert, watercolor sketch of Ely Cathedral, west tower, 1905. Prints and Photographs Division, Library of Congress.

PLATE 2 Cass Gilbert, Woolworth Building, first design, perspective drawn at a scale of 1⁄32" = 1'0" by Thomas R. Johnson, April 22, 1910. Watercolor and gouache over graphite on illustration board. Collection of the New-York Historical Society, negative 57748.

PLATE 3 Cass Gilbert, Woolworth Building, first design, perspective, drawn at a scale of 1/32" = 1'0" by Thomas R. Johnson, April 25, 1910. Watercolor and gouache over graphite on illustration board. Collection of the New-York Historical Society, negative 71467T.

PLATE 4 Cass Gilbert, Woolworth Building, third design, perspective study drawn at a scale of 1⁄32" = 1'0" by Thomas R. Johnson, October 1910. Watercolor, Conté crayon, and gouache over graphite on illustration board. Collection of the New-York Historical Society, negative 32018.

PLATE 5 Cass Gilbert, Woolworth Building, final design, conceptual sketch perspective for lobby-arcade, January 1911. Watercolor, Conté crayon, and gouache over graphite on illustration board. Collection of the New-York Historical Society, negative 46313.

PLATE 6 Cass Gilbert, Woolworth Building, final design, final perspective of lobby-arcade, drawn by Z. N. Matteossian and Thomas R. Johnson, April 15, 1912. Watercolor and Conté crayon over graphite. Collection of the New-York Historical Society, negative 70876.

PLATE 7 Cass Gilbert, Woolworth Building, final design, perspective, drawn by Thomas R. Johnson, rendered by Hughson Hawley, and reproduced by F. W. Woolworth, May 1911. Author's collection.

PLATE 8 Unidentified artist, F. W. Woolworth's fortieth-story apartment, 1912. Watercolor over graphite on illustration board. Prints and Photographs Division, Library of Congress.

PLATE 9 Mack, Jenney, and Tyler Decorators, "Decoration of Swimming Pool in Sub-basement of Woolworth Building," 1912. Watercolor over graphite on illustration board. Collection of the New-York Historical Society, negative 78940d.

PLATE 10 John Marin, *Woolworth Building, No. 31*, 1912. Watercolor on paper. Gift of Eugene and Agnes E. Meyer. (© Board of Trustees, National Gallery of Art, Washington, D.C.)

PLATE 11 John Marin, *Lower Manhattan (Composing Derived from Top of Woolworth)*, 1922. Watercolor and charcoal with paper cutout attached with thread on paper. Acquired through Lillie P. Bliss Bequest. (© The Museum of Modern Art, New York.)

PLATE 12 Unidentified artist, *King's Views of New York*, 1926, cover illustration.

PART EIGHT

The New York Times.

Real Estate--Financial --Business News

XX SUNDAY, MAY 7, 1911. XX

LATEST DEALINGS IN REALTY FIELD

Breslin Hotel, Subject to Nearly $3,000,000 Mortgages, Transferred to New Company.

DEAL ON RIVERSIDE DRIVE

Realty Company Buys Apartment House Site on Washington Heights —An Active Bronx Market.

CO-OPERATIVE MANAGEMENT.

New Plan Adopted in Several Big Long Island Developments.

WOOLWORTH BUILDING WILL BE WORLD'S GREATEST SKYSCRAPER

Fifty-five Stories High, Rising 750 Feet Above Broadway, Overlooking the Post Office—Rays from Electric Light in Tower Will Be Visible Ninety-six Miles Out to Sea—Operation Involves Millions of Dollars.

Fifty-five Story Woolworth Building on Broadway Block Front Between Park Place and Barclay Street. Cass Gilbert, Architect. Photo Copyright by F. W. Woolworth.

BUSINESS MEN ORGANIZE.

A Special Meeting to be Held Next Wednesday.

QUEENS BUILDING BOOM.

Plans for 1,800 Structures Filed During First Four Months of 1911.

ADVICE TO HOMEBUILDERS.

An Interesting Feature of the Architecture and Building Show.

HISTORIC ESTATE IN AUCTION MARKET

Pinkney Property, Comprising the Old Watt Farm, to be Sold Next Week.

OLD HOMESTEAD STANDING

Estate Consists of Many Entire Blocks in Rapidly Growing Section — How It Was Acquired.

LEWIS & CONGER BUILDING

To Be Erected on the Southeast Corner of 45th Street and Sixth Avenue. Renwick, Aspinwall & Tucker, Architects.

The Old Pinkney Mansion, Located on 139th Street, Between Seventh and Lenox Avenues.

FIGURE 4.32 "Woolworth Building Will Be World's Greatest Skyscraper," *New York Times*, May 7, 1911. (Copyright 1911 *The New York Times*. Reprinted by permission.)

recognized visual phenomenon, now part high-style commodity and part popular visual entertainment.

The *New York Times*'s account of the Woolworth's completed design resounded along with those of its newspaper rivals across the United States in other cities and small towns—virtually all of which had main streets featuring Woolworth stores—among them Pittsburgh, Pennsylvania; Wilmington, Delaware; Fargo, North Dakota; Pueblo, Colorado; and Aurora, Illinois.[158] In showcasing and describing Gilbert's design within New York's and the nation's printed news media, Woolworth responded to the craving, as the contemporary literary critic Annie Russell Marble put it, for the "surface pleasure" of rarely edifying but ever more spectacular pictures.[159] Given the era's "excesses of fashion," the pictures Marble described fulfilled the "commercial demand for all grades of illustration," which like "the deeds that are conspicuous, the ideas that are garish, the literature that is episodic and pictorial" had gained "popular favor."[160] Only recently had newspapers such as the *New York Times* benefited from the forty-fold increase in the level of production made possible during the 1870s and 1880s by the invention of the stereotype, the web-perfecting press, and Linotype setting, along with the large-scale manufacture of cheap wood-pulp-based paper. By 1900, equally revolutionary techniques for reproducing works of art, among them photoengraving, had provided the modern newspaper with tools for disseminating images at a fantastic pace.[161] In utilizing New York's and the nation's newspapers to call attention to his as-yet-unbuilt skyscraper, Woolworth set the stage for still further news media publicity. He would advertise not only the Woolworth Building, but also the F. W. Woolworth Company, its stores, and the commodities they sold around the world.

Frank Woolworth's decision to build and to publicize "the highest skyscraper in the world" marked the project's decisive turning point. It also called attention to Woolworth as an individual with a wealth formidable enough to produce such a spectacular work of architecture and renowned news media phenomenon. As Julia Finch Gilbert put it in 1911, Woolworth had "amassed a fortune the interest on which, together with the income from nearly three hundred five and ten cent stores, yields an income of some millions of dollars."[162] The F. W. Woolworth Company, from which Woolworth in fact earned $2 million a year, had strong ties to Wall Street and the New York Stock Exchange.[163] Woolworth, moreover, commanded 1,794 shares of stock in Irving National Exchange Bank; in April 1912, he would use his own capital to assist the bank with a second, $50 million merger.[164] As the president of the Broadway–Park Place Company, Woolworth would also eventually capitalize handsomely on his big investment in the Woolworth Building—the estimated cost of which now stood at $8 million—parlaying his earlier Lancaster formula into one of the most financially risky and aggressive speculative ventures of the day.[165]

The image of Woolworth as a thrifty accumulator of nickels and dimes, the mythology that journalists had tailored for the readership of the day's newspapers and mass-market magazines, hardly portrayed the retailer's true and substantial financial status. Given the expansive scale of Woolworth's monetary endeavors—those of a capitalist, monopolizer, investor, and shrewd real estate operator, along with the geographically dispersed audiences of shoppers, store managers, and other merchant rivals that he intended to impress—his investing in the smaller, thirty-eight-story skyscraper illustrated by the project's first design simply would not have had the desired media impact. For the sake of effective advertising, Woolworth's skyscraper—even as an unbuilt project—had to be spectacular; it had to be international news.[166]

In 1897, Lincoln Steffens called Woolworth's type of advertising through printed media publicity "the mercantile equivalent of applause." The enterprise whose headquarters is "striking enough to be talked about, and pictured throughout the country," he added, "finds by actual experience that the investment, though a failure as a renting enterprise, pays astonishingly."[167] Woolworth's carefully timed release of Johnson and Hawley's giant, seductively rendered, and visually enticing perspective, however, also suggested that he viewed the news media, like his commodities, as a supreme stimulator and gratifier of desire. The day after the perspective's release, Hugh McAtamney, a New York press agent who may well have appreciated Woolworth's promotional strategy, wrote to offer his services to Woolworth and Gilbert, completely free of charge. By early July, the Broadway–Park Place Company, fully understanding the value of publicity, officially hired McAtamney as "director of advertising."[168] Gilbert—who had instructed the city's newspapers when releasing Johnson and Hawley's copyrighted perspective to allow its reproduction "as often and as broadly as they choose for news purposes"—may well have felt in command of the news media's capacity for reaching the widest audience possible.[169] Still, he may not have imagined his monumental Beaux-Arts skyscraper becoming a true mass cultural phenomenon, its image mass produced in New York's newspapers and then described in those across the nation, which were then in turn purchased and mass consumed by an untold number of readers.

CHAPTER FIVE

A Record-Breaking Feat of Modern Construction

Woolworth and Gilbert's determination to build the highest skyscraper in the world was rivaled only by the ambition of the men who vied to construct it, among the most vocal of proponents for modernizing the city. "From 1905 to 1914 . . . there seemed to be among modern builders an epidemic of heroic design, a veritable competition in lofty ambitions." New York's skyline was reshaping itself seemingly overnight, and from the perspective of the builder, "nothing man-made" produced "an equivalent thrill."[1] Such a context of competition, described in the builder Paul Starrett's autobiographical account of enterprise and "can-do," *Changing the Skyline*, may have inspired Gilbert to assert his professional authority as an architect among New York's most noted builders. Starrett, he warned, should not enter the Union Club through the front door, but instead through the tradesman's entrance.[2] But Gilbert also knew that Starrett, as president of the George A. Fuller Company, signified an economically powerful, thoroughly twentieth-century phenomenon. Starrett headed one of New York's two giant, recently incorporated general contracting firms, two among the few big enough to compete for the contract to build the Woolworth Building.

Regardless of Gilbert's view of Starrett, the builder wielded tremendous power as the chief protagonist in the creation of the Woolworth Building once construction began. Louis Horowitz, president of the Thompson-Starrett Company, the firm that ultimately triumphed over Starrett's Fuller Company to secure the project's contract, later asserted that "an architect could dream and plan, but we could make the dream come true."[3] Both Thompson-Starrett and Fuller had recently ascended to their position of dominance in the industry as "national builders," prevailing during an extended period of labor conflict in New York—an outgrowth of the tens of thousands of industrial strikes nationwide. During the 1880s and 1890s, the conflict had left the body politic reeling from the shock, and especially from the violence of the Haymarket (1886) and Homestead (1892) strikes, throwing up a seemingly impassable barrier between capital and labor.[4] In reaction, Fuller promoted strategies of "peaceful" labor conciliation, designed to mask the day's deep division between the employer and the employed. The Woolworth Building's promotional literature supported and furthered the deception: It was not the "national builder," but rather "master builders" and their force of artisanal "free labor" that collaborated to construct New York as a modern skyscraper metropolis.[5] In actuality, however, Thompson-Starrett and Fuller had thoroughly reorganized the construction industry in the effort to circumvent such conflict. They had employed their own forces of construction labor along with that of subcontractors under the new single-contract system. In aiming to complete large-scale projects in record time, they had imposed a new level of modern rationalization, efficiency, and financial control over the entire construction process.

Horowitz later elucidated the builders' enterprising zeal and conviction about changing the skylines of major American cities, his spirit of conquest resonating with the widespread enthusiasm for technology and for feats of daring construction.[6] "Everyone of us in the company felt himself to be an adventurer. We visioned the cities of America rising to dizzy, gleaming heights. We dreamed of unshaped inventions that would become part of the fabulous, mechanistic structures we were going to build."[7] "New York was the place for the man who wanted to build skyscrapers," Paul Starrett added.[8] It offered the optimal economic and geographic conditions for conquering vertical space in the open "frontier" of sky. Popular magazines such as *Everybody's* similarly lauded the builders' force of structural ironworkers as "cowboys of the skies," a reference to the heroic masculinity identified with Theodore Roosevelt's "rough riders" of 1898, the self-taught regiment of cowboys who charged up Cuba's Kettle Hill toward San Juan Ridge during the Spanish-American War (fig. 5.1).[9] The enterprise of constructing skyscrapers, the magazine further suggested, reflected the nation's preparedness for battle, its persisting belief in manifest destiny, and its current policy of expansion overseas.

In competing for the contract to construct the Woolworth Building, builders such as Paul Starrett and Louis Horowitz were, in fact, reacting to the localized, speculative market pressures inciting expansion skyward—pressures that Woolworth had likewise exploited as a source of capital and an instrument for attaining his headquarters' visibility. They and their contemporaries in the building industry had invented new mechanical devices, techniques, and methods of construction, besides systematizing the entire process toward the end of modernizing the city at a breathtaking pace. Exemplary of this modernization, during what Thomas Hughes has called the "era of technological enthusiasm," the Woolworth Building was characterized by extremes.[10] These were evident in the depth of its caisson-constructed foundation and the record-breaking height of its structural steel as well as in the workers' assembly of that steel in record time. Such evidence of modern-

FIGURE 5.1 *Cowboys of the Skies*, showing steelworkers on the Metropolitan Life Insurance Tower, New York. From *Everybody's Magazine*, vol. 19 (November 1908). Photograph by Arthur Hewitt and Frederick Colburn Clarke.

ization presented a stark contrast to the City Beautiful movement's highly esteemed horizontal landscape of axial planning, gardens, and Beaux-Arts monuments.[11] But by the time the New York City Improvement Commission published its first large-scale plan, in 1905, New York's real estate speculators, bankers, and financiers had already identified the city's audacious, vertical skyline with its stature as a world financial center.

The Single-Contract System and the Rise of the "National Builder"

The George A. Fuller Company, founded in Chicago in 1882, pioneered the single-contract system of general contract construction in the Tacoma Building project of 1886–89. For the first time, Fuller built a skyscraper within a contractually predetermined frame of time for a predetermined price, then "delivered" it as a product to its owner, the Chicago lawyer and businessman Wirt D. Walker, ready to occupy. Subsequently, the Fuller Company built up its reputation on taking full financial responsibility for such projects, either on its own or through letting subcontracts to others.[12] It incorporated in 1890 and by 1896, set up an office in New York. In 1899, Theodore Starrett founded with Henry S. Thompson a rival organization modeled on Fuller, the Thompson-Starrett Company.[13] Fuller moved its headquarters to New York in 1900, and shortly thereafter, both the Fuller Company and the Thompson-Starrett Company boasted reputations as "national builders" that worked on several big projects in several big cities at once.[14]

William Aiken Starrett, the vice president of the Thompson-Starrett Company during the Woolworth Building project, later recounted that national builders had pioneered an "administrative revolution in construction," and so "raised contracting from a limited trade to both an industry and a profession" by "visualizing the building problem in its entirety."[15] Theodore Starrett and Paul Starrett, brothers of William Aiken, apprenticed with the Chicago architect Daniel Burnham in the late 1880s and early 1890s. Both admired Burnham's organizational capacities and largeness of vision.[16] Theodore served as president of the Thompson-Starrett Company from its founding in 1899, and Paul became president of the Fuller Company in 1905.[17] Well before competing for the Woolworth Building contract, both Thompson-Starrett and Fuller had taken charge of and, for a fixed percentage fee, had systematically organized all aspects of the large-scale construction process: planning, financing, and engineering, along with the subcontracts required to assemble labor and materials, chief among them the big contracts for structural steel.

Thompson-Starrett and Fuller predicated their growth nationally as corporations on procuring big projects through strategic salesmanship, that is, on their ability to convince a speculator of a proposed project's future income-earning capacity.[18] This markedly distinguished both firms from the mid-nineteenth century's local builders, that is, the small, independent, and skilled tradesmen renowned for their artisanal orientation. Strategic salesmanship generated volume, and volume facilitated the rapid expansion of Thompson-Starrett and Fuller across the country in branch offices after they set up headquarters in New York.[19] Before 1909, Thompson-Starrett had founded offices in Chicago, San Francisco, Philadelphia, Washington, Pittsburgh, Salt Lake City, and Portland—and steel-framed speculative office-building projects composed by far the largest proportion of the firm's total volume of construction.[20] Similarly, Fuller had established offices in Chicago, Boston, Pittsburgh, Baltimore, Washington, D.C., San Francisco, Chattanooga, Kansas City, and Philadelphia.[21] By 1911, Horowitz had developed Thompson-Starrett into what he called a "modern building organization": a still larger, more systematized, and more efficient variation of Fuller's original single-contract system.[22] Regardless of Thompson-Starrett's and Fuller's new national scope, however, New York remained the industry's dominant center. If we are to believe Starrett, Fuller constructed 80 percent of Manhattan's new buildings during the years around 1910 alone.[23] Within such a context, Woolworth's skyscraper offered not only a profitable contract, but also the potential for advertising that contract, and with it, the builders' skills, organization, and modern methods of construction in record time.

THE WOOLWORTH BUILDING CONTRACT

Even before Woolworth began discussing his project with Irving National Bank's board of directors in 1908, several of New York's largest builders—the George A. Fuller Company and the Thompson-Starrett Company among them—began aggressively competing for the contract to construct his skyscraper. Word of Woolworth's intentions had leaked out early, Paul Starrett later recalled, and the building community was electrified. "The rumor had been about for a long time that

F. W. Woolworth was playing with the idea of a gigantic skyscraper in New York, to bear his name, and all the leading builders had their ears pricked up. This would be a prize worth fighting for!"[24] Horowitz later reminisced, "I schemed with all my power, during several years, to get the contract for the vast project." He described such projects as "a masonry of chance encounters, vague ambitions, and even less substantial things."[25] But as the architect H. A. Shreve more directly put it, Horowitz was "aggressive in conceiving projects himself and then in cajoling into partnership necessary human elements possessing desire and site and capital to the end that there would be another big building against the skyline."[26] Horowitz, in fact, called himself a "contract hunter": he targeted big, lucrative projects during the years he headed Thompson-Starrett, when the company completed $600 million worth of projects. These, he claimed, represented "a conspicuous part of the skylines" of the nation's major cities, but "most of all, New York."[27]

Woolworth's choice of a builder involved a tedious, excruciatingly drawn-out process of investigation and interviewing, as Horowitz later recounted: "All my nightmares had to do with the black despair of failing to get that mighty contract. Woolworth's method of selection was extremely aggravating for those of us who waited for his decision. It was a slow process of elimination. He talked to everybody; and time and time again he seemed to have his mind made up, only to change it and begin to hunt all over again. Some of his meetings with me and with my rivals were in his office; some were in the office of Cass Gilbert, the architect, where the excitement was enough to keep me on fire with hunger for the job."[28] Woolworth narrowed down the group of competing builders slowly, Horowitz added, and "after three years," dropped those that were, in his view, "not big enough for this job," with the Metropolitan Life Insurance Tower's V. J. Hedden and Sons probably counting among them, to focus strictly on the Thompson-Starrett Company and the George A. Fuller Company.[29] Thompson-Starrett had constructed large office buildings in New York: Clinton and Russell's Atlantic Mutual Life Insurance Company Building (1900–1901) and the U.S. Express Building (1905–7). But by 1910 the Fuller Company—although formerly branded a "Chicago operation"—clearly had the competitive edge. Fuller had built some of Chicago's largest skyscrapers during the boom of 1889–94, among them Burnham and Root's Woman's Temple and the Reliance Building, as well as some of New York's during the boom of the early 1900s, among them the Flatiron (1903) and the New York Times (1903–5) buildings and, later, the Hudson Terminal Buildings (1907–9).[30] Fuller's record in New York, however, may well have made Horowitz feel even more determined to seize for Thompson Starrett the city's newest and biggest contract for a skyscraper.

Woolworth later explained the criteria guiding his choice of the skyscraper's builder: He "not only had to be the best in his field, have the best material at his disposal, the best talent at his service, but it was also essential that he have an organization back of him which was thoroughly adequate and had reached the maximum of efficiency."[31] Woolworth announced his project in New York's *Record and Guide* on November 19, 1910, which remarked that "the general contract has been practically closed and awarded."[32] Nevertheless, "the matter rested for several months," according to Horowitz, "because Woolworth just could not make up his mind."[33]

Woolworth eventually signed a contract with Horowitz and the Thompson-Starrett Company five months later, on April 20, 1911.[34]

As an architect, Gilbert had the clout to decisively influence Woolworth's selection of a builder, and both Paul Starrett and Louis Horowitz knew it. After Starrett discovered that Horowitz and his Thompson-Starrett Company had indeed won the contract to construct the Woolworth Building, he instantly sent his competitor a congratulatory note, adding that he was "heartbroken" and blaming Gilbert—"Woolworth told me Gilbert wouldn't have me."[35] Earlier, Starrett had mailed Gilbert a copy of the sales letter he wrote to Woolworth, noting that he "would appreciate very much any assistance you feel warranted in giving to me in this matter."[36] Unfortunately for Starrett, Gilbert had already made up his mind; he had developed a mistrustful view of Fuller's new parent organization, the United States Realty and Construction Company.

After the death of Fuller in 1901, Fuller's son-in-law, Harry S. Black, took over the George A. Fuller Company, making it part of his new venture, the United States Realty and Construction Company, a giant, consolidated corporate enterprise that he capitalized at $66 million. Black aimed to control all aspects of acquiring, financing, constructing, and leasing space in the largest New York properties.[37] Paul Starrett observed that "Black loved to amalgamate and expand": he knew little about construction, but he had reportedly built up the Fuller Company into a $15 million corporation from a mere fifty-thousand-dollar enterprise in just a few years. Starrett characterized Black as "a business genius, a gambler, a financial juggler"; as a person he was "bighearted and selfish . . . and rather unscrupulous."[38]

In 1909, during his term as president of the American Institute of Architects, Gilbert argued vociferously against the very phenomenon in construction represented by Black and the United States Realty and Construction Company. Such big, amalgamated corporations aimed to monopolize all aspects of large-scale construction and so presented a "serious menace to the interests of the architect." Gilbert proposed as a solution that architects return to the nineteenth-century's "old-fashioned system" of letting certain contracts for large-scale projects to minor contractors.[39] Gilbert may have read the accounts about the Fuller Company's having hired in-house draftsmen with the objective of controlling all aspects of design and construction, among them the architect's function of "drawing up the plans."[40] The Fuller Company and the Purdy and Henderson team had already put Gilbert's professional role as an architect to a severe test during the Broadway Chambers project. Now, beyond question, Gilbert aspired to reinstate the architect in the central function of administering all aspects of a building's design and construction.

Besides viewing corporations such as United States Realty as a "menace," Gilbert had little trust in Black's business practices. Julia Finch Gilbert described Gilbert's encounter with the construction tycoon in Palm Beach in March 1911: Black, Finch Gilbert wrote, was "working the East Coast" with the ambition of acquiring the Woolworth Building and other big construction contracts for the Fuller Company. Knowing that Black had been previously "untrue" to Gilbert—a reference, perhaps, to the Broadway Chambers project—Finch Gilbert performed "social gymnastics" to keep Black from "having heart to heart talks with Mr. Woolworth," hoping to see Black "beautifully turned down."[41] Woolworth did, in fact, turn down the Fuller Company, as Paul Starrett, while blaming Gilbert, lamented. Horowitz and Thompson-Starrett, as a consequence, would build Woolworth's skyscraper, securing not only a big and lucrative construction contract, but also a decisive stake in the modernization of New York.

LOUIS HOROWITZ AND THE "MODERN BUILDING ORGANIZATION"

Horowitz published *The Modern Building Organization* in 1911, the year that he secured the Woolworth Building contract. An essay in booklet form, it described a still newer version of the single-contract system. Horowitz's system would be more efficiently organized and its methods of construction still further rationalized. It would have a corporate structure geared toward erecting with unprecedented speed and all at once many skyscrapers rivaling the Woolworth's technological sophistication and scale (fig. 5.2). Theodore Starrett had recently led Thompson-Starrett through a period of rapid growth, but by 1903 Theodore's "nerves were shot," as Paul Starrett later put it; the "competition for jobs and the speed on jobs . . . were killing."[42] By 1905, consequently, Thompson-Starrett's board of directors had elected Horowitz the company's vice president and general manager. Horowitz took charge of the company's finances, steering it through the panic of 1907, and in 1908, when Starrett officially resigned, Thompson-Starrett, by Horowitz's own account, boasted over $15 million in business annually.[43] When elected in March 1910 as president, Horowitz credited his rise within Thompson-Starrett to the nearly completed $6 million Gimbel Brothers Department Store in New York (D. H. Burnham and Company), a project known for its rapid construction and during which he functioned all at once as the owner, developer, and general contractor.[44] Such a job for a major retailing concern, more importantly, may have helped Horowitz seal the Woolworth Building contract. Bernard Gimbel, Horowitz later recalled, "put on his hat" and went to see Woolworth for him.[45]

Horowitz defined the "modern building organization" as "a machine that can take contracts at a fixed figure, for a fixed fee, and deliver the buildings to their owners in a guaranteed time, as methodically as a tailor handles an order for a suit of clothes."[46] Railroad builders had by the mid-nineteenth century achieved unprecedented rates of speed by building several railroad lines at once and by employing interchangeable work gangs or "machines" of men.[47] More recently, both Fuller and Thompson-Starrett had utilized the single-contract system to similarly construct several large office buildings in several cities at once with the objective of a comparable rationalization and speed. But in Horowitz's view, both big contractors still unfortunately practiced "brokerage pure and simple:" They still hired out major portions of the typical large building's construction to subcontractors, each of whom had a profit to make. Such a method of cobbling together too many subcontractors and the fees for their work slowed down the process of construction and increased expenditures, and given the real estate speculator's requirement of rapid completion and a timely financial return, it unnecessarily augmented a project's total cost.[48]

Horowitz further argued that the administration of the modern building organization must be as systematized and efficient in its component parts as the current state of the construction industry would permit—an industry still known for its labor disputes, craft practices, and the diversity of its building trades. Managed from a central office, the organization comprised "in-house departments" responsible for key lines of work. The central office established the project's comprehensive time schedule and, through the schedule, aimed to impose a rational and systematic order from start to finish over all lines of work.[49] The in-house departments estimated project costs, awarded contracts for labor and materials, purchased materials in bulk, expedited the delivery of materials, and coordinated shop drawings. After construction began, the central office enforced the comprehensive time schedule by tracking weekly progress and costs and through the authority of the construction superintendent and the superintendent's daily reports. Horowitz acknowledged that the uniqueness among the thirty to fifty trades typically employed on a given construction site—"too diverse to be welded into a whole"—presented a challenge, but he still anticipated that his organization would facilitate a systematic, orderly, and harmonious relationship among all lines of work.[50]

Horowitz's organizational methods resembled those recently proposed by his New York contemporary, the mechanical engineer and building contractor Frank Bunker Gilbreth. Gilbreth's "System in Contracting" (1905) and *Field System* (1906) similarly defined the departmental functions housed within the contractor's central managerial office and similarly called for clear lines of communication with the building site.[51] Gilbreth's effort to rationalize the work process and the work site traced its origins in turn to the principles of Frederick Winslow Taylor, whose "Piece Rate System" of 1895 pioneered "scientific management." Taylor based his time and motion studies on observations from the shop floor of the steel industry; he aimed to improve the speed and the efficiency of the individual worker.[52] While less focused

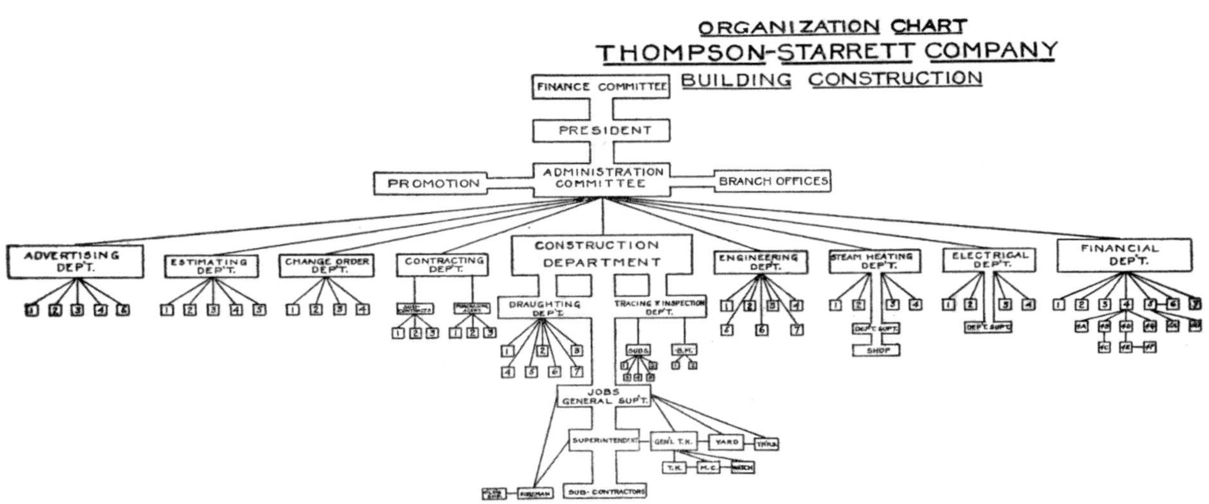

FIGURE 5.2 "Organization Chart, Thompson-Starrett Company Building Construction." From *The Modern Building Organization* (New York: The Alexander Hamilton Institute, 1911). Science, Industry and Business Library, New York Public Library, Astor, Lenox and Tilden Foundations.

on the worker, Horowitz's "modern building organization," like Gilbreth's "system in contracting," emphasized the rationalization of both the work process and the work site.

Horowitz's self-described mission as a builder was "get the order, and then put up the building, so that it is done in the shortest possible time."[53] Paul Starrett likewise stressed the centrality of speed to the financial success of any big construction project: "Time is important in building. Equipment is tied up, other jobs wait, tenants are ready to move in, the owner stands on the sidelines counting the days. Speed pleases everybody and is money in the pocket. Speed gets jobs."[54] When campaigning for the Woolworth Building's contract, Starrett told Woolworth, "You watch that building across the street; see it shoot up! You'll see what speed we get," pointing to the East River Savings Bank, at the time starting construction catercorner across Broadway from Woolworth's Stewart Building headquarters.[55] In the railroad construction industry, Benjamin Franklin's notion that "time is money" had already become a truism on rationalized work sites by the mid-nineteenth century, but for Starrett and Horowitz speed in its own right had risen to precedence as the industry's overarching, all-pervasive credo.

Speed mattered especially to Woolworth. After the Woolworth Building's construction began, he frequently worried about whether Thompson-Starrett could, in fact, complete the skyscraper on time, his fear fueled by "evasive answers from Horowitz," as he anxiously told Gilbert in December 1911. Woolworth anticipated losing fourteen thousand to fifteen thousand dollars a month in potential rental income if confronted with construction delays.[56] Gilbert, not surprisingly, had reason to be sympathetic. In his "Financial Importance of Rapid Building" (1900), he had outlined one of the most convincing arguments of his day for rapidly constructing a skyscraper. Using the example of a $1.5 million office building and a full set of detailed numerical calculations to illustrate his argument, Gilbert concluded that, ideally, a medium-sized office building should be built within a single year. "The reasons for rapid construction . . . are of course economic," he asserted.[57] The sooner a skyscraper reached completion, the sooner it paid its owner, and the sooner it could effectively compete in a market rapidly filling up with comparably attractive, modern office space.

Equally important, Horowitz, Gilbert, and Woolworth knew that achieving speed during construction required that potential labor conflicts be resolved or, still better, altogether avoided. Strikes had crippled Fuller Company building sites between 1900 and 1903, and across the New York building industry, strikes and lockouts had come to a head in 1902–3, with 432 industrial actions involving 2,268 buildings.[58] "The labor question constantly arose," Gilbert wrote in 1900, during the construction of the Broadway Chambers Building.[59] Within the next five years, however, the industry had achieved an unusual level of stability. The city's General Arbitration Board, established in 1904, settled labor disputes. For a brief period, it also gave workers a closed shop, or the right to stipulate that the whole of a particular organization be protected by a union. Although Fuller and employer's associations challenged the right in 1906, they settled for employing union alongside nonunion labor.[60] In addition, the Fuller Company adopted a position of conciliation among the unions. After Black took control, it devised methods for defusing labor actions in advance: It paid workers reliably and well, but it also bribed union leaders to ensure peaceful labor conditions.[61]

Regardless of the New York building industry's having reached a new level of stability and order, Gilbert continued to worry about a major disabling strike at the Woolworth project site; work on his United States Custom House had been halted repeatedly by strikes. When sending the Woolworth Building's specifications out for bid, Gilbert advised "the use of such a class of labor that will not occasion strikes."[62] With the exceptions of a painters' strike in March 1912, a five-day strike in the shops of the Atlantic Terra Cotta Company in June, and last-minute negotiations with the Reliance Labor Club over the carving of the interior marble in September 1912, the Woolworth project remained remarkably free of labor conflict throughout the course of construction, to the relief of Horowitz, Gilbert, and Woolworth.[63] After completion, Gilbert applauded the site's "peaceful" labor conditions, which he thought offered a broader social lesson: "It is only by the combination of the interests of capital and labor that organized society can successfully exist."[64] Both sets of interests, Gilbert had come to believe, contributed to the timely realization of his costly, opulent, and skillfully crafted Beaux-Arts designs.

Besides the threat of strikes, Horowitz and the Thompson-Starrett Company faced another complication in their goal of thoroughly rationalizing and speeding up the construction process—New York's increasingly diversifying labor community. Between 1890 and 1910, immigrants from Southern Italy and Eastern Europe flooded the city, along with Chinese and African-Americans from the southern United States. By 1900, three-quarters of the city's population consisted of foreign-born immigrants.[65] The Metropolitan Life Tower's steel erectors, one writer reported in 1908, comprised "Americans, English, Irish, French-Canadians, Swedes, now and then an Italian," and "two full-blooded Indians."[66] That year, *Bricklayer and Mason* compared building a skyscraper to building the Tower of Babel, given the confusion of languages arising from the integration of native-born workers with the new immigrant groups.[67] Gilbreth argued that the problem of confusion could be obviated altogether, and speed thereby increased, through the segregation of construction crews into groups by nationality.[68] But regardless of such racial and ethic differences among the workers, by the mid-1890s many of the New York building trades had achieved a new solidarity; they had isolated themselves from party politics and had begun adhering to Samuel Gompers's "pure and simple unionism."[69]

New York's building trades unions, the membership of which increased twofold between 1897 and 1910, enforced standards of safety while promoting equality among all members.[70] By 1910, moreover, the city's structural ironworkers had achieved still greater solidarity through their swelling numbers in the Housesmiths' and Bridgemen's Union of New York and Vicinity and, as consequence, the status of a "labor aristocracy," or a well-paid working-class elite.[71] Still, control over the workers' livelihoods remained vested in the hands of their giant corporate employers, the founders of an industry that viewed them no longer as skilled, independent artisans, but instead as employees, and in doing so, enforced above all else the criterion of speed.

ARCHITECT, BUILDER, AND CLIENT

As construction of the Woolworth Building began, Gilbert's office, organized hierarchically but still functioning as something of a Beaux-Arts atelier, faced coordinating one of the most complex, daunting, and rigorously scheduled architectural projects of the day (see fig. 4.3). To that end, Gilbert tailored his office methods to synchronize with the expectations of Thompson-Starrett's "modern building organization."[72] Gilbert's relatively small staff of twenty to twenty-five assistants produced the project's hundreds of working drawings to accord with Thompson-Starrett's construction schedule and, afterward, supervised assembly and craftsmanship on the site with efficiency.

Gilbert organized the lines of command between his office and those of his engineering consultants and manufacturers to resemble those existing between the general contractor's central office, related departments, and subcontractors. Gunvald Aus and Company, with thirty engineers and draftsmen, produced the Woolworth Building's structural steel shop drawings in an office adjacent to Gilbert's within the Metropolitan Life Insurance Annex. Long before completing the drawings, it sent batches of them directly to the project's steel fabricator, the American Bridge Company.[73] In a similar fashion, the Atlantic Terra Cotta Company's twenty-five draftsmen produced detailed drawings for the process of fabrication in a temporary office on the annex's tenth floor, five stories below Gilbert's, under the supervision of Thomas R. Johnson.[74] The project's heating engineer, Nygren, Tenney, and Ohmes; electrical engineer and elevator expert, Mailloux and Knox; and sanitary engineer, Albert Webster, all prepared similar sets of detailed drawings for the project's subcontractors and related manufacturers.[75] Gilbert's many consultants effectively extended his own reach over the project's many interlocking processes of producing detailed drawings for construction and so facilitated his organization of the project's disparate design efforts simultaneously.

Gilbert had not departmentalized his office like that of the Thompson-Starrett Company, but the current obsession with system and organization permeated his thinking as much as it did theirs. Of this Gilbert was deeply aware: "The architect of today conducting great building enterprises must of necessity maintain a large organization. It is physically impossible for any one man to do all of the things that the architect is required and expected to do. It is his function to design the building in every sense of the word, but necessarily he must use many assistants in accomplishing this. Skilled designers and draftsmen, structural experts, mechanical, electrical, heating, ventilating and sanitary experts . . . must take their part in the organization of a great building. . . . It naturally follows, then, that the architect, being the designer and master builder, must be the one to coordinate the work of all those engaged in the enterprise."[76] Contemporaries admired the Gilbert office's "able and systemizing deputizing effort, without which works of the magnitude of Mr. Gilbert's could not be achieved."[77] Like the Woolworth project, each of the office's earlier projects had presented a wide array of unique and unprecedented construction-related problems. The time pressures imposed by Thompson-Starrett's "modern building organization" only exacerbated the challenges.

Gilbert told Woolworth in August 1912, "This high speed business and the extraordinary character of the propositions we have had to solve sometimes forces us all to nearly a killing pace."[78] By 1907, Gilbert had attempted to combat such pressures by establishing within his office a secondary tier of key associates. John Rockart and George Wells had joined Johnson in becoming the office's highest-paid employees. In 1909, all received three hundred dollars a month, about three times the average draftsman's salary.[79] Still, Gilbert refused to let Johnson's, Rockart's, or Wells's names grace the office's letterhead, reinforcing the impression to clients and to the public alike that his creative works were his alone.[80] The preparedness and efficiency with which Gilbert's office was able to tackle projects as large and complex as Woolworth's skyscraper can be ascribed largely to Gilbert's careful selection and promotion of Johnson, Rockart, and Wells.

Johnson, having already fulfilled a pivotal role in the project's conceptual design process, now oversaw the office staff's production of all craft details, including the full-scale drawings for ornamentation; he "directed the overall design of the Woolworth Building," recalled Antonin Raymond, who drew some of those details.[81] Johnson also approved the full-scale shop drawings produced by the Atlantic Terra Cotta Company's in-house draftsmen and, later, Donnelly and Ricci's models for the project's ornamental terra cotta, stone, and copper.[82] As Gilbert's project manager for the Woolworth Building, Rockart supervised the office staff's production of drawings for construction and coordinated all project meetings.[83]

After construction began, Wells oversaw the project's progress in the office and on the job site. He collaborated with Horowitz to supervise the signing of all contracts between the building's subcontractors and the Broadway–Park Place Company. He also wrote and updated construction specifications, inspected the quality of the structural steel and all other materials and their fabrication, approved on-site assembly and craftsmanship, and with Thompson-Starrett synchronized the timing of steel, terra cotta, and stone deliveries. Later, he coordinated the subcontractors' installation of the building's mechanical and electrical equipment.[84]

At the construction site, Gilbert instructed Wells to rigorously enforce his own high standards of craftsmanship while also cultivating a climate of goodwill: "As long as you maintain your good temper, keep free from personalities, and do your duty, as I believe you have done in the past, I will sustain you. Do not under any circumstances lose temper or enter into any personal feeling. . . . Your position is a difficult one and it would not be an unnatural trick for them [the foremen] to quarrel with you if possible, and to claim that your decisions were influenced by spite. . . . Hold them strictly to the contract, and no matter how many times you have a thing done over, insist upon it until it is right. Do this no matter how much they protest."[85] Gilbert valued solid craftsmanship, and Wells's supervision of construction distanced him from some of the project's most important craft details.[86] But it also allowed him to focus on developing the identity of his firm as a Beaux-Arts atelier—through effective administration, skillful salesmanship, and the production of the vivid conceptual sketches and seductive perspectives that won support for his designs.

Gilbert's office, with its two associated corps of "structural" and "ornamental" draftsmen—totaling about eighty in his own employ and that of Gunvald Aus and Company and the Atlantic Terra Cotta Company combined—produced virtually all the Woolworth Building's construction drawings within about three months, between January 22, 1911, and April 29, 1911 (figs. 5.3, 5.4, 5.5). Sometime after April, however, Gilbert increased the height of the tower to 792 feet, causing revisions to continue until the end of July.[87] The drawings produced by Gilbert's draftsmen,

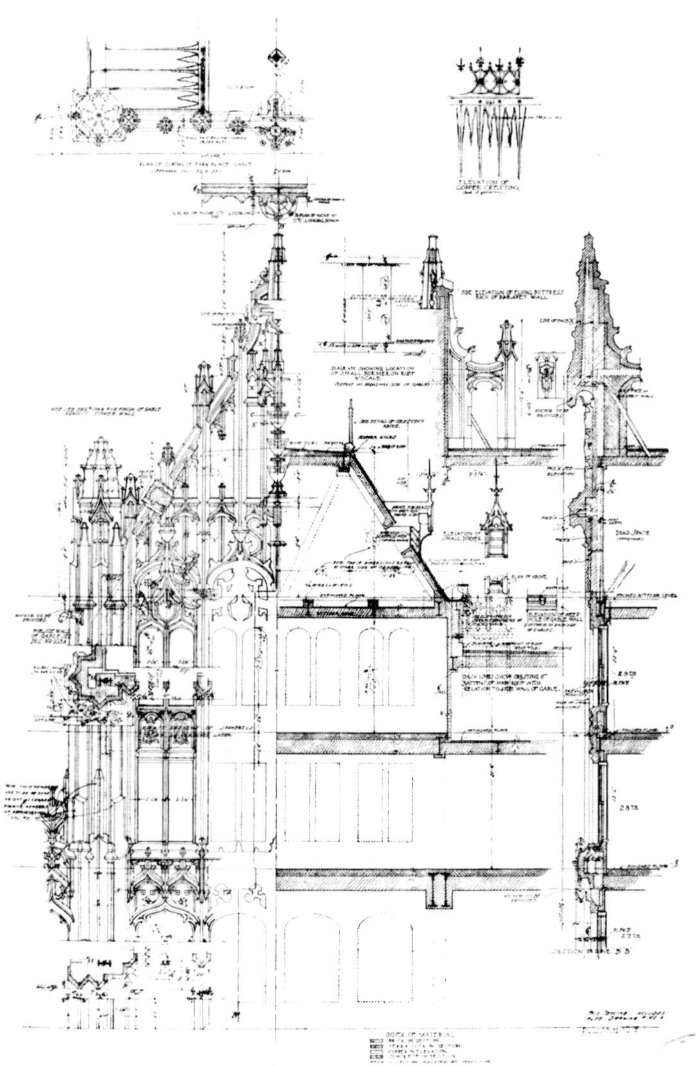

FIGURE 5.3 Woolworth Building, construction drawings, Park Place elevation, gable at twenty-eighth to thirtieth stories, 1911. From *National Architect* 1 (November 1912).

when added together with the drawings produced by the project's consulting engineers, brought the total to 1,550.[88] Given the sky-scraper's gigantic size and the urgency of completing the drawings, Gilbert, who treasured the ideal of the architect as an artist, nonetheless found himself at the mercy of the countless impersonal hands that methodically translated his original conceptual sketches and Johnson's perspectives into documents for construction. "The principal of a large practice has many difficulties. If I had the physical and mental ability to make the drawings for the Woolworth Building, it would have taken me ten years."[89] Still, at Gilbert's behest, Thomas R. Johnson led the office's junior designers and draftsmen in the production of the skyscraper's many plans and elevations, choosing Stickel for the important Broadway elevation, and guided their refinement of intricate ornamental details in limestone, terra cotta, copper, and marble: spandrels, canopies, tourelles, buttresses,

FIGURE 5.4 Woolworth Building, construction drawings, forty-sixth to fifty-first stories, showing buttresses and tourelles, 1911. From *National Architect*, vol. 1 (November 1912).

pinnacles, and gables.[90] Some of the ornamental details they studied at full scale, among them the interior's metal screens, woodwork, and plaster cornices. These Johnson treated as designs from which a fabricator could produce shop drawings directly.

Hierarchy, delegation, and specialization had already characterized the organization of large-scale architectural practices in New York and Chicago by the turn of the century, notable among them D. H. Burnham and Company's office with 180 employees and McKim, Mead, and White's with approximately 100.[91] Gilbert distinguished his practice from such practices, however, by keeping his staff of assisting designers and draftsmen comparatively small, rarely exceeding the Woolworth Building project's total of 25. In doing so, he resisted creating D. H. Burnham and Company's so-called large manufacturing plant, which in the view of H. Van Buren Magonigle produced "cold and lifeless syndicated

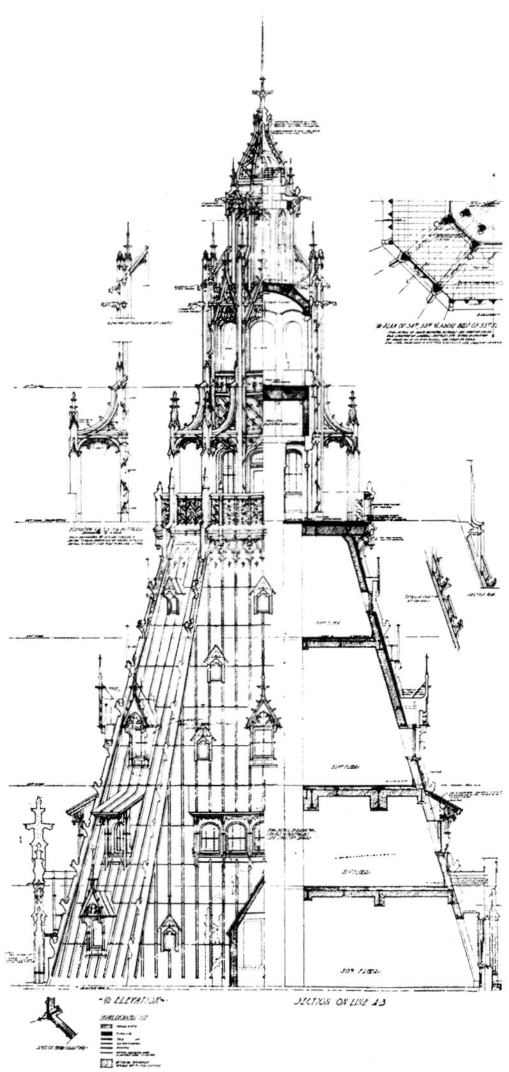

FIGURE 5.5 Woolworth Building, construction drawings, tower roof and observatory, 1911. From *National Architect*, vol. 1 (November 1912).

work."[92] In this, his office more closely resembled that of New York's Beaux-Arts-trained George Post or Ernest Flagg, both of whom also designed skyscrapers and both of whom also relied on a secondary tier of key associates, with Post's office numbering close to 60 at the time of the St. Paul Building (1896–99) and Flagg's 47 at the time of the Singer Tower (1906–8). Both offices, however, also incorporated departments of engineering, with Post serving as his own chief engineer and Flagg employing Otto Francis Semsch. Flagg, furthermore, had added a department of construction in 1907.[93] Gilbert, by contrast, utilized the combined capacities of outside consultants, draftsmen, and construction contractors. In doing so, he aspired to keep intact the identity of his practice as a small, independently functioning Beaux-Arts atelier.

Despite Gilbert's "able and systematizing deputizing effort," the Woolworth Building was nonetheless "carried through under the personal direction of Woolworth," as Gilbert put it. "There was no detail that did not have Frank Woolworth's personal supervision . . . somewhat to my temporary distress."[94] Horowitz recalled Woolworth's "close watch of the operations."[95] Woolworth, in fact, competed with both Horowitz and Gilbert for control of the project, at times commandeering Horowitz's position, tracking and recording the project's labor costs week by week, and at times pestering Gilbert about whether the project's consulting engineers had indeed met the highest standards of design.[96] Woolworth kept especially careful watch over Aus, whom Gilbert had appointed during construction as the steel inspection engineer, fearing that he might start "bossing the job" and giving steel contracts to his friends.[97]

Woolworth, furthermore, imposed cost-saving methods of his own accord, frequently requested changes, and vacillated over minute materials- and equipment-related decisions, all of which delayed construction.[98] Horowitz characterized Woolworth's methods as his "customary way of buying goods for his five-and-ten-cent stores."[99] In January 1911, for example,

Woolworth accused Thompson-Starrett of charging the Broadway–Park Place Company three-quarters of a cent more than the typical price of new rope for "second-hand rope" from other jobs, and in February, he haggled with Gilbert over "details of a more or less immaterial character": pneumatic pivot door checks, metal trim, elevator signal service, locks on elevators, bulletin boards, and mail chutes.[100] Earlier, Woolworth had solicited an "astonishingly low" bid from Elbert Gary of United States Steel for the project's total of more than twenty-four thousand tons of structural steel—its highest-priced contract—on the grounds that supplying steel for the Woolworth Building had advertising value.[101] After Horowitz locked in the price of the steel's fabrication at almost two hundred thousand dollars less than the American Bridge Company had originally proposed, however, Woolworth reportedly changed his stance and became "more cooperative."[102]

In his severest effort at cost cutting, Woolworth attempted to slash both Horowitz's fee for managing the project's construction and Gilbert's professional fee, arguing that the publicity associated with the world's tallest skyscraper would bring "a fortune in the shape of fame." Horowitz recalled arguing to Woolworth that he would not handle all aspects of the building's construction "for nothing": he could not "afford to put up [Woolworth's] building for the sake of prestige, because we already have earned an abundance of prestige."[103] As for Gilbert, he reportedly told Woolworth that he was "just another millionaire" until his own architectural design for the Woolworth Building had made him famous.[104] Gilbert, in fact, sent Woolworth the bill for his professional services, $61,000 for the project's three earliest designs, on April 20, 1911.[105] The project's design phase had ended four months earlier, the office had virtually completed detailed working drawings, construction of the foundation also neared completion, and within two weeks, Woolworth would release Johnson and Hawley's colorful perspective for simultaneous publication in the Sunday editions of New York's newspapers. Still, Woolworth disputed Gilbert's fee.[106] In response, Gilbert argued that his office had totally redesigned the skyscraper between January 23, 1911, and April 23, 1911, producing a complete set of construction documents within ninety calendar days. More critically, after working "night and day" it had filed those documents at the Manhattan Bureau of Buildings.[107] In the end, Woolworth paid Gilbert the expected 5 percent professional fee on a project cost of approximately $8.5 million, or $426,000.[108] Gilbert's refusal to give in to Woolworth during the arguments over fees, the secretary and treasurer of the American Institute of Architects, Glenn Brown, later proudly asserted, "won a victory for the Institute Schedule and a handsome remuneration for himself."[109]

Despite the obvious stresses in their architect-builder-client relationship, Gilbert, Horowitz, and Woolworth remained effective collaborators throughout the course of the project. In October 1912, Gilbert wrote to his children while sailing for Europe aboard the Norddeutscher Lloyd steamship *Bremen*, describing gifts from Woolworth, a "handsome clock which folds flat in a travelling case; my name is engraved on it; it looks expensive," and from Horowitz, "boxes of rare cigars."[110] Horowitz later recalled that he became "devoted" to Woolworth during the years of the Woolworth Building's construction. After meeting at Gilbert's office several times a week and at other times informally, "the three of us began to find companionship in these conferences."[111] Woolworth frequently invited Horowitz to his Fifth Avenue chateau. Gilbert rode downtown in Woolworth's automobile for lunch at the Hardware Club and dined with Woolworth at the Waldorf Astoria Hotel, spending the evening afterward in Garden City discussing business and then returning with him to New York the next day.[112] Regardless of their many individual disagreements, then, Horowitz, Woolworth, and Gilbert recognized the importance of their own shared stake in the shaping of New York as a modern skyscraper city.

Building the Woolworth Building

The construction techniques and methods Thompson-Starrett employed to build the Woolworth Building represented the culmination of two and a half decades in the development of the skyscraper's foundation, steel framing, wind bracing, and cladding technologies. They also tested the limits of those technologies. Workers excavated the concrete piers of the Woolworth's foundation to some of the deepest bedrock in the city. The skyscraper's steel frame, the highest in the world, reached the greatest level of intricacy in its individual bracing members, and its exterior, sheathed throughout in terra cotta, represented the day's most extensive system of ornamental cladding. From a purely technological standpoint, however, the Woolworth Building was a conservative design, reflecting the restrictive stipulations of New York's 1899 building code.[113] The skyscraper had "few if any absolutely new features of importance," reported *Engineering Record* in 1912.[114] But on account of its unusually large scale, rationalized process of construction, sophistication as a work of engineering, and inclusion as well as multiplication to an unprecedented degree of the many new technological developments preceding it, the Woolworth Building epitomized the skyscraper as a building type. For this reason, it anticipated the great, iconic New York setback skyscrapers of the 1920s, the Chrysler Building and the Empire State Building among them, leading the structural engineer Mario Salvadori to call it a "first" in reference to the later skyscrapers.[115]

THE CONSTRUCTION SITE

The Thompson-Starrett Company had considerable experience with building tall, steel-framed skyscrapers, but the unusual size of Woolworth's project presented a host of new challenges (fig. 5.6). *Engineering Record* and *Scientific American* emphasized how Thompson-Starrett organized the site for efficiency and how by ingenious methods they raised the project's steel, brick, and terra cotta to previously unconquered heights. New derricks and steam-powered cranes lifted "loads which never before had been lifted," among them twelve-ton members of steel.[116] Hod hoists delivered tile, brick, and terra cotta to the skyscraper's upper stories at a speed of one thousand feet per minute.[117] To increase speed, Thompson-Starrett developed a special two-stage vertical hoisting process, along with a method for shifting sets of guy derricks upward two stories at a time. It invented new electrically powered hoisting engines and new safety devices for special types of electrically powered scaffolding, or the temporary, open platforms that supported workmen and materials as construction progressed.[118] To produce steam of the high pressure required for rapid hoisting, it employed a battery of three boilers that consumed twenty tons of anthracite coal in twenty-four hours.[119]

FIGURE 5.6 Woolworth Building, construction site, May 1, 1911. From *Photographic Views of the Construction of the Woolworth Building, 233 Broadway, New York City, 1911–12, Irving Underhill, Photographer* (New York, 1911–12). Milstein Division of United States History, Local History, and Genealogy, New York Public Library, Astor, Lenox and Tilden Foundations.

According to *Engineering Record*, the Woolworth project stood out as remarkable for "the organization, administration, and execution of the complicated and difficult construction work with numerous diverse operations, simultaneously prosecuted by an army of workmen in a very restricted space." The site's confined area for storage, contained by sidewalk boundaries, imposed severe limitations on the delivery and removal of the project's nearly two hundred thousand tons of materials, some of which trucks hauled in gigantic, fifty-ton masses. As the skyscraper's steel skeleton mounted higher, and as successive batches of new materials and new subcontractors arrived at the site, the human and mechanical energy intensified; "a large number of freight and passenger elevators [moved] materials and men."[120]

The superintendent for the Woolworth project, William Sunter—whom Gilbert called "the most efficient man on the job"—requisitioned materials two or three days in advance, so that they flowed to the site systematically, and precisely at the moment specified by the schedule.[121] Thompson-Starrett had not planned the skyscraper as a "fast-track project" in the present-day sense of the term, but the frame's more than twenty-three thousand tons of structural steel—three times the amount used to construct the Metropolitan Life Tower—it had fabricated in the American Bridge Company's plants in Philadelphia and Pittsburgh as rapidly as Gunvald Aus and Company could supply the shop drawings.[122] American Bridge then shipped the fabricated steel by rail to the Pennsylvania Railroad Company's yards in Greenville, New Jersey. Sunter ordered the steel from the yards in three-hundred- to five-hundred-ton lots; after being shipped by lighter to New York, the lots were carted to the site by the comparatively simple method of horse-drawn truck (fig. 5.7).[123] The Atlantic Terra Cotta's shops in Perth Amboy, New Jersey, shipped the skyscraper's terra cotta cladding directly to lower Manhattan around Staten Island via the upper bay and the Hudson River. Once workers began attaching terra cotta, Sunter had batches sent from the factory at the rate of one truckload every fifteen minutes.[124] When the batches arrived on the site, workers hoisted the terra cotta to ever higher stories as construction progressed.

At the project site, there existed a "spirit of cooperation which pervaded the work from the beginning," according to Gilbert's later description of the peaceful labor conditions.[125] Woolworth likewise applauded the ease with which "each contractor worked as a unit in cooperation with the other contractors," comparing the unity with the "deep and rich communal spirit" of the cathedral builders.[126] Both men, however, refused to recognize the contradictions between such a "communal spirit" and the early twentieth-century reality of a labor force totally at the mercy of speed, or a "well systematized organization" working in "record time." The average size of the project's labor force was approximately two thousand, with about one thousand employed directly by Thompson-Starrett and about one thousand by the project's ninety subcontractors, most of whom worked in single eight-hour shifts. A total of twenty-six subcontractors fabricated, assembled, and installed the building's electrical, heating, and ventilating systems alone.[127] That such a vast array of trades and individuals should fall into place systematically and on time can be attributed above all else to Thompson-Starrett's rationalized control over the project's seventy classified items or "principal operations" through its comprehensive time schedule.[128] As interchangeable work units, the project's gangs of men functioned something like cogs in a giant machine, methodically advancing a quasi-industrialized sequence of construction, a time- and money-driven process that would reach its most systematic state of efficiency and order in the Empire State Building's construction almost twenty years later.

William Sunter and George Wells supervised construction from offices poised on a sidewalk bridge bordering the edge of the site. Thompson-Starrett supplied the office with a forty-plug switchboard, wired to seven telephones throughout the building and to the offices of the project's subcontractors, each of which fell under the direction of a foreman and, in some cases, several deputy foremen. Sunter's staff, comprising a civil engineer, a chief timekeeper, three time clerks, and a materials clerk assisted by two checkers, rigorously enforced the project's schedule in their daily inspections of all lines of construction.[129] Both Sunter and Wells sent Gilbert's office daily progress reports.[130] Wurts Brothers photographers systematically documented the project daily, for Gilbert's reference as an architect, but, more important, also to establish a visual record of the project's construction should a disagreement arise.[131]

FIGURE 5.7 Delivery of terra cotta to construction site by the Atlantic Terra Cotta Company, near the Hudson River docks, June 1912. Unidentified photographer. Collection of the New-York Historical Society, negative 53451.

Altogether, the Foundation Company and the Thompson-Starrett Company constructed the Woolworth Building within a period totaling twenty-nine months. Preparation of the site began in April 1910, when Gilbert engaged Phillips and Worthington to investigate the area's surface geology with test borings. That July, the E. H. Southard Wrecking and Trucking Company, followed by the Volk House Wrecking Company, razed the five existing commercial buildings that bordered Broadway and Park Place.[132] On November 1, the Foundation Company demolished and removed the buildings' remaining walls, footings, and floors below grade and then three days later began excavation with pneumatic caissons (see fig. 5.6). In May 1911, four months after Woolworth acquired the Barclay corner, Volk House demolished the existing structures bordering Barclay Street, which opened up the entire 152-foot Broadway frontage.[133] Although the Foundation Company had begun excavation in November, it took another ten months before its labor force sank the last of the foundation's caissons. It completed the skyscraper's foundation on August 26, 1911.

Thompson-Starrett's structural ironworkers set the Woolworth Building's first steel grillage on August 15, and by October 11, the skyscraper's skeletal steel superstructure began to rise in the city. In late November, the superstructure reached the sidewalk level, and then it climbed incrementally upward through the following winter and spring at a rate of nearly a story and a half per week (fig. 5.8). Bricklayers attaching terra cotta cladding followed closely behind. By April 6, 1912, steel erectors had carried the frame up to the thirtieth story, the top of the main block, and by May 30, to the forty-seventh story of the tower (fig. 5.9). On July 1, 1912, less than nine months later, they drove the frame's final rivet in place, topping off the tower's 792-foot pinnacle (fig. 5.10).[134] "The highest piece of steel was erected on schedule time," Gilbert wrote to Woolworth, adding that "the other work has been following along with extraordinary speed and system, and it is a matter of constant remark all over the city and in fact all over the country that it has been wonderfully well handled."[135] Thompson-Starrett's original schedule had specified a completion date of December 31, 1912. That July, Sunter pointed out that certain trades had completed work in advance of the schedule but others, unfortunately, had lagged significantly behind.[136] Horowitz revised the schedule and designated April 1, 1913, as the project's new completion date.[137] By comparison to the length of time it took to build a major public building—Gilbert's United States Custom House, for instance, took more than six years to construct—the Woolworth Building's three-month delay was minor; thousands of workers had fabricated and assembled its structural steel and terra cotta with speed and efficiency.

CAISSONS

Next to the Municipal Building, the Woolworth Building represented the largest architectural caisson job ever undertaken anywhere (figs. 5.11, 5.12).[138] As such, it challenged the conventional practices of caisson construction and put to the test the newest caisson technologies. These had significantly matured since Charles-Jean Triger's fabrication of the earliest caisson for a coal mine, in 1839, a pressurized cast-iron enclosure with a sharp cutting edge for excavation underwater, featuring an air lock that permitted communication with the outside.[139] Still, the Woolworth job imposed new demands; it pressed caisson

FIGURE 5.8 Woolworth Building, erection of structural steel, December 28, 1911. From *Photographic Views of the Construction of the Woolworth Building, 233 Broadway, New York City, 1911–12, Irving Underhill, Photographer* (New York, 1911–12). Milstein Division of United States History, Local History, and Genealogy, New York Public Library, Astor, Lenox and Tilden Foundations.

FIGURE 5.9 Woolworth Building, erection of structural steel, April 4, 1912. From *Photographic Views of the Construction of the Woolworth Building, 233 Broadway, New York City, 1911–12, Irving Underhill, Photographer* (New York, 1911–12). Milstein Division of United States History, Local History, and Genealogy, New York Public Library, Astor, Lenox and Tilden Foundations.

FIGURE 5.10 Woolworth Building, erection of structural steel, July 1, 1912. From *Photographic Views of the Construction of the Woolworth Building, 233 Broadway, New York City, 1911–12, Irving Underhill, Photographer* (New York, 1911–12). Milstein Division of United States History, Local History, and Genealogy, New York Public Library, Astor, Lenox and Tilden Foundations.

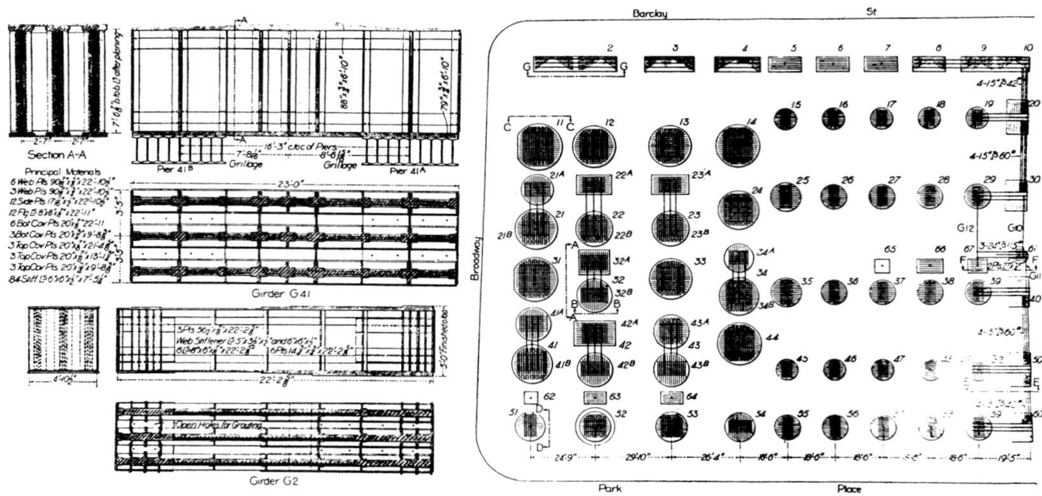

FIGURE 5.11 Woolworth Building, plan showing foundation, Gunvald Aus and Company, 1911. *Engineering Record*, vol. 65 (February 17, 1912).

workers into shafts of unusual vertical depths, where they charted unknown subterranean territory and, despite the latest technologies, grappled with all the attendant risks.

After the Foundation Company arrived on the Woolworth Building site on November 1, 1910, caisson workers drove wood and interlocking steel sheet piling with steam hammers along the site's street edges and underpinned the walls of adjacent buildings with new concrete footings. On November 4, they began excavating shafts for the skyscraper's thirty-eight reinforced concrete piers, and when Woolworth enlarged the site on February 3, they excavated the thirty-one new shafts required for the project's total of sixty-nine piers. The site's bedrock, lying deep beneath waterlogged quicksand, gravel, and hardpan, varied in profile from 110 to 120 feet below surface grade. Where the bedrock inclined steeply, workers carved out horizontal offsets to provide suitable bearing strata.[140] Inside the caissons, the workers labored around the clock in three eight-hour shifts of two hundred men, digging the shafts completely by hand. A half-dozen men crowded into confined chambers with at best six feet of headroom and faced poor ventilation and stifling heat.[141] At night, the excavation continued under electric lamps, the poet John Reed's "thousand candle flares."[142] As many as nine caissons the workers at once sealed and placed under air pressure equal to the surrounding water pressure.

Each shaft took an average of two weeks to construct, with wagons carting away the excavation spoil throughout the day and night.[143] As excavation by caisson proceeded, other teams of workers poured and sank concrete piers in sections while at times reducing the air pressure in the caissons' steel working chambers. They loaded the piers with "ballast," or huge quantities of one- and two-ton cast-iron blocks, frequently totaling up to eight hundred tons. One of the piers, caisson number 61 (six feet, six inches in diameter), they sank eighty feet in twenty consecutive hours. The larger caisson number 34 (nine feet, nine inches in diameter) took twelve days to excavate, pour, and sink.[144]

FIGURE 5.12
Woolworth Building, detail of caisson, May 16, 1911. Photograph by Wurts Brothers. Woolworth Collection, National Building Museum.

The Foundation Company provided the Woolworth site with its own steel air lock for "hospital purposes" and kept a physician and nurse constantly in attendance.[145] Although experts in Germany and France had determined the cause of "caisson disease," or "the bends," around 1861, it had yet to be fully understood; workers continued to suffer from the sudden decompression caused by the changes in atmospheric pressure, or "the effects of dissolved gases 'boiling' in the bloodstream," with 110 cases of the sickness and four of the Brooklyn Bridge's estimated twenty deaths during construction attributed to the disease.[146] Reportedly, fewer than 80 percent of the applicants for the Woolworth's caisson construction qualified after on-site medical examinations for the rigors of the work. During the Municipal Building project of only a few months earlier, which required excavations as deep as 178 feet below grade, experts judged an atmospheric pressure of forty-five pounds per square inch the limit of human tolerance. At the Woolworth's site, the men excavated the shafts in forty-minute shifts, spent an equivalent amount of time decompressing in the caisson's air lock, and repeated the process just one more time before finishing for the day.[147]

Gilbert and his contemporaries described the rigors of caisson work as an important rite of masculinity: "The courage of a soldier under fire is not more heroic," Gilbert exclaimed. In "the excavation or the caisson" there lurked "imminent and terrible physical dangers every hour of the day": such work "is quoted as 'extra hazardous,' for it is so in every sense of the word."[148] William Aiken Starrett similarly compared the building of a skyscraper to the waging of a war, with workers deployed like an army in a risk-filled field operation.[149] Rather than banding together as Gilbert and Starrett's troops in a battle, however, the Woolworth's caisson workers achieved solidarity through their fight to secure safe and survivable conditions of work. Their union, the International Compressed Air Workers of America, defended and protected that solidarity.

The Foundation Company, headquartered adjacent to the Woolworth's construction site at 115 Broadway, boasted patents on caisson technology, among them the sturdy and efficient air lock developed by its vice president, the civil engineer Daniel E. Moran. The company's reputation rested largely on the achievements of its professional engineering staff, which continued to refine excavation equipment and procedures. For the Woolworth project, it specially prefabricated the caissons' steel forms, air locks, and cofferdams in its own yards near Newark, New Jersey, and in other shops in the vicinity. On the construction site, it installed batteries of steam boilers and air compressors and set up movable derricks with long booms that manipulated ten- and twelve-ton caisson sections with rapidity and ease.[150] After completing the Woolworth's foundation, it proudly advertised itself as the provider of pneumatic caissons for "twenty-six of the tallest and most costly buildings in New York City," with the Singer Tower and the Municipal Building also numbering among them.[151]

The Woolworth Building's sixty-nine reinforced concrete piers functioned like giant tubular roots extending downward through water-saturated soil to bedrock. Their odd arrangement and two-staged process of construction—hardly a "pure" solution for the design of a concrete pier foundation—reflected instead Woolworth's disjointed process of acquiring parcels to create the project's final site. Aus designed most of the piers as circular, ranging in diameter from six feet, six inches up to eighteen feet, nine inches. Along the skyscraper's Barclay Street edge, however, he shaped the piers instead as long and narrow rectangles, permitting a tight adjacency against the property line, and so utilizing the site to the very fullest.[152] After Woolworth enlarged the site, Aus joined eight of the project's original thirty eight piers to the project's new piers with enormous transfer girders. The girders carried at their midspan enormous concentrated point loads, which shot straight downward from the main columns of the tower.

The largest of the Woolworth's transfer girders, G41, spanned two piers underneath tower column 41. Probably the heaviest ever used in building construction, G41 was eight feet deep, six feet, nine inches wide, and twenty-three feet long. Built up from three separate girders, and finished with solid web and side plates, it weighed sixty-five tons. At its center, it carried a concentrated point load of four thousand seven hundred tons. On account of its size, G41 required a forty-two-horse team and a one-hundred-ton truck to haul its bulky mass to the building site. After grappling with girder G41, the Foundation Company chose to cut apart the project's remaining seven transfer girders while still in transport aboard a lighter; at the construction site, it had workers rivet the pieces back together again.[153] Along the project's western property line, a special type of transfer girder, the cantilever girder, carried the column loads eccentric with the building's main foundation piers, supporting those loads as closely as possible to the existing adjacent construction.[154] Unusually elaborate steel grillages distributed the tower columns' concentrated point loads over the top of each concrete pier, utilizing four separate tiers of steel I beams, each laid crosswise—contrasting with the simpler two-way grillages typically found in New York's skyscrapers.[155] Altogether, Aus's design for the Woolworth Building's cumbersome system of oddly shaped concrete piers, huge transfer girders, cantilever girders, and complex grillages illogically transferred down to bedrock the skyscraper's combined column loads of 136,000 tons. Still, it effectively exploited every square inch of Woolworth's property.[156]

STEEL

The extreme depth of the Woolworth Building's concrete pier foundation was exceeded only by the extreme height of the tower's structural steel. The project's huge quantity of steel pointed to the high volume of production made possible by the size of United States Steel, the recently consolidated, vertically integrated, and now largest industrial corporation yet to appear in the United States. As the parent company of the Carnegie Company and the American Bridge Company, United States Steel produced as well as fabricated all the structural steel for the Woolworth Building.[157] United States Steel's great size, however, also engendered a particular type of product, its Carnegie Company's massive and overdesigned steel I beam. The Carnegie Company, furthermore, had continued to build up I-beam sections using plates and angles at the very moment that its competitor, Bethlehem Steel, began producing the innovative, labor-saving wide-flanged H-beam, a product of the new "universal" rolling method devised by Henry Grey.[158] Corresponding to the Carnegie Company's conservative method of creating built-up sections, United States Steel's American Bridge Company had continued to employ the steel fabrication technique known as "heavy bridge construction" for its structural members, which reportedly increased the total weight of the Woolworth project's steel by at least one-third.[159] The massiveness and structural conservatism of the Woolworth Building's steel frame, then, can be explained in part by a corporation that in becoming so large, and indeed, so inflexible as an industrial system, could no longer maintain its position at the forefront of technological innovation.

The rapidity and efficiency with which the steel erectors assembled the Woolworth Building's steel frame, by contrast, pointed to an antithetical phenomenon—Thompson-Starrett's modern, rationalized system of construction, in which speed reigned paramount. In addition to fabricating the project's steel, the American Bridge Company also served as the structural steel subcontractor, employing a total of 180 structural ironworkers in single eight-hour shifts (fig. 5.13). Antonin Raymond later recalled, "The workers of that time on the whole were excellent, and I learned more from them than I had ever learned in the office."[160] Organized in teams of erectors and riveting gangs, the ironworkers averaged a pace of two stories per week while constructing the skyscraper's twenty-eight-story main structure, setting in the process a new record for the largest amount of structural steel ever assembled—1,153 tons—within six consecutive eight-hour days.[161]

FIGURE 5.13 Woolworth Building, structural ironworkers hoisting a beam in place, 1912. Photograph by Brown Brothers.

As the steel arrived at the site, between thirty and forty structural ironworkers unloaded, sorted, and began erecting the frame's individual steel components, assisted by large stiff-legged derricks. A team of ten erectors followed two stories behind, "fitting up" and plumbing the steel columns, girders, beams, and portal arch wind bracing to a tolerance of three-eighths of an inch (fig. 5.14). Four-man gangs of riveters, twenty-two in all, accompanied the erectors. Concentrated in groups around the frame's column splices, portal and knee braces, and girder intersections, the gangs drove an average of three hundred rivets per eight-hour day using pneumatic hammers operated from the basement by two electrically powered air compressors. A force of thirty-five steel painters followed one story behind the riveters, applying the code-required field coat of red lead paint. The floor-arch builders followed still another story behind.[162]

Gilbert spoke of "the hazardous height to be scaled by the workmen erecting the structural steel," and Horowitz of the chilling experience of working high on a steel skeleton "so high from the ground [that] on wet mornings, its upper half was lost to view in clouds."[163] The steel erectors, Horowitz added, "seem not to know the meaning of fear" (fig. 5.15). They stood on the edges of beams, leaning their bodies outward against the wind, and swarmed "like flies onto the chain of the hoisting mechanism," by which they were lowered, "almost as swiftly as falling, to the street," finding the elevators too slow.[164] Journalists hailed the steel erectors' risk taking, while knowing full well that the risks were all too real. At the project's outset, a derrick's steel cable broke, crashing down over the sidewalk and, in Gilbert's words, "killing a man and badly wounding, probably mortally, a boy while passing."[165] As the frame approached the twenty-eighth story, the riveter Peter Gushue of Brooklyn fell down an elevator shaft, and several hundred fellow workers mourned his death, refusing to work for twenty-four hours afterward.[166] Liability insurance inspectors reported the accidents and injuries, which ranged from minor to severe, at least once a week.[167] New York's unions continued to demand safer building methods and equipment, given the industry's national average of 12 fatalities and more than 350 serious injuries per 1,000 workers a year—among them the stabilizing of scaffolding and ladders, the placement of guardrails around openings, and the covering of floors as a skyscraper's skeleton rose—and backed those demands with strikes. Still, they found their demands at best infrequently acknowledged.[168] Paul Starrett frankly admitted that a worker should join a union to protect himself, but also applauded the site's foremen who "made a game of it, a race against time."[169]

FIGURE 5.14 Woolworth Building, structural ironworkers, 1912. Unidentified photographer. Cass Gilbert Collection, Archives Center, National Museum of American History, Behring Center, Smithsonian Institution.

FIGURE 5.15 Woolworth Building, structural ironworkers, 1912. Photograph by Brown Brothers.

In 1902, the editors of *American Architect and Building News* called attention to the rapidity of the day's steel-framed construction, arguing that it demonstrated the virtues of a modern method of assembly: "The advantage of the modern steel-frame construction over the older style in point of rapidity has been strikingly shown of late. It is obvious that, while every portion of a steel-frame structure takes as long to make as the corresponding part of a building of masonry, it is possible, in the former, to prepare parts outside, and when they are ready, to 'assemble' them . . . with a rapidity which is out of the question in masonry structures."[170] In assuming such a preconceived relationship among the steel frame's component parts, the method of assembly suited Thompson-Starrett's objective of rationalizing the process of construction. As early as the 1840s, James Bogardus had pioneered a modular system of cast-iron construction, but not until 1851 did the method of assembly triumph—in London's Crystal Palace. Its builders, Fox and Henderson, had the design's individual cast- and wrought-iron members prefabricated as modular, interchangeable parts and in turn erected by a rationalized, linear method that portended later industrial assembly lines.[171] Horowitz would go on to declare that "our mighty skyscrapers all have been assembled out of factories."[172] Steel, in use for skyscrapers in New York since the mid-1890s, comprised modular components not unlike the earlier cast- and wrought-iron systems—albeit with the added advantage of increased strength in both tension and compression. Horowitz found steel ideally suited to a comparable type of prefabrication off site, where the final location of each member could be predetermined by the fabricator's setting plan. The Woolworth's steel members could not "have either been fabricated, properly finished, shipped, handled, or erected in the ordinary course of events," *Engineering Record* reported in 1912, suggesting Thompson-Starrett's recent advances in the scale of assembly.[173] The process of assembly, moreover, ensured predictability and accuracy in the scheduling of construction and so made the company's goals of rationalized construction and rapid completion achievable.

As constructed, the Woolworth Building's steel frame possessed not only a visual massiveness that betrayed its conservative design, but also a complexity among its component parts unprecedented in earlier skyscrapers. Column, girder, and bracing members the American Bridge Company built up in accordance with Aus's design for the structural steel, by joining many large pieces using hundreds of rivets, following the methods of heavy bridge fabrication.[174] Columns 11 and 14 of the tower, the heaviest ever used in building construction, required box sections at their bases (fig. 5.16). At seven hundred square inches of material in cross-sectional area and approximately three feet by four feet in plan dimension, each column carried a

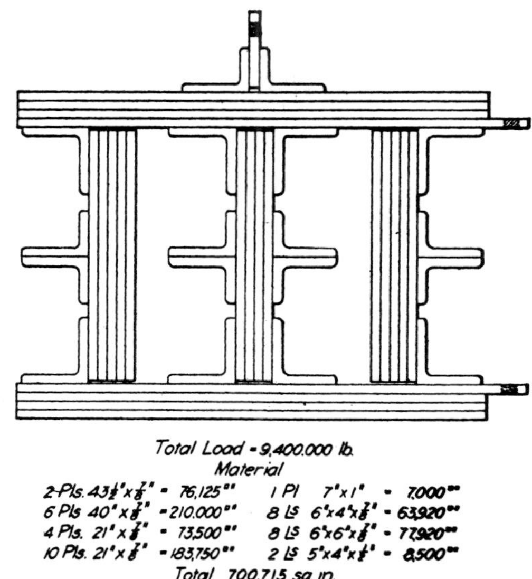

FIGURE 5.16 Woolworth Building, detail of columns 11 and 14, Gunvald Aus and Company, 1911. From *Engineering Record*, vol. 67 (July 5, 1913).

cumulative vertical load of 4,700 tons. Of that total, about 750 tons constituted the weight of the column itself.[175] Horowitz later recalled that columns 11 and 14 and other heavy structural members had to be hauled to the building site along a special route laid out by Thompson-Starrett, to avoid the caving in of streets honeycombed with a "complex mechanical jungle" and of the tunnels he characterized as "vaulted sewers through which a coach and four might be driven."[176] Despite the virtues of assembly, then, the massiveness and complexity required of the Woolworth Building's structural steel contradicted Horowitz's effort to streamline, rationalize, and speed up the entire process of construction.

The Woolworth Building's system of wind bracing, the final design of which Aus assigned to his associate S. F. Holtzman, had a level of elaboration never reached before or since in steel-framed construction (figs. 5.17, 5.18, 5.19).[177] First of all, the

FIGURE 5.17 Woolworth Building, wind bracing for tower, Gunvald Aus and Company, 1911. *Engineering Record*, vol. 63 (May 27, 1911).

system integrated a wide catalog of bracing types: portal arch and double portal arch bracing, full-story diagonal bracing, and knee bracing, or the low diagonals joining corner girders and columns. It also incorporated the more common stiff, moment-resisting connections made by joining triangular gusset plates to girders and columns.[178] Second, the tower's lower twenty-eight stories featured the most extensive use of portal arches ever to appear in tall building construction.[179] In the tower's frontal elevation, the portal arches made possible an unusual degree of openness between the main structural columns, precisely in the places the eye would have expected to find either full-bay diagonals or, in masonry construction, the greatest massiveness and weight. The portal arch system, in essence, made possible the architectural impression desired by Gilbert, that of a screenlike ethereality.

The Woolworth's tall and thin central tower functioned structurally as a highly rigid vertical cantilever: Totally self-supporting, it stabilized the entire building.[180] From the tower's fifty-fifth-story pinnacle down to its fiftieth floor, inclined roof members counteracted the lateral forces of the wind. Then, from the fiftieth floor down to the forty-seventh floor, four interior columns joined to floor girders resisted the forces, and from the forty-seventh floor downward, outer columns connected to wall girders. From the forty-second floor down to the twenty-eighth floor, Aus reinforced the tower's system of columns and wall girders with diagonal knee bracing. Finally, from the tower's intersection with the building's flanking wings at the twenty-eighth story, and all of the way down to the building's base, Aus's portal arches spanned each structural bay and every story in the tower's front and back elevations. In addition, Aus set por-

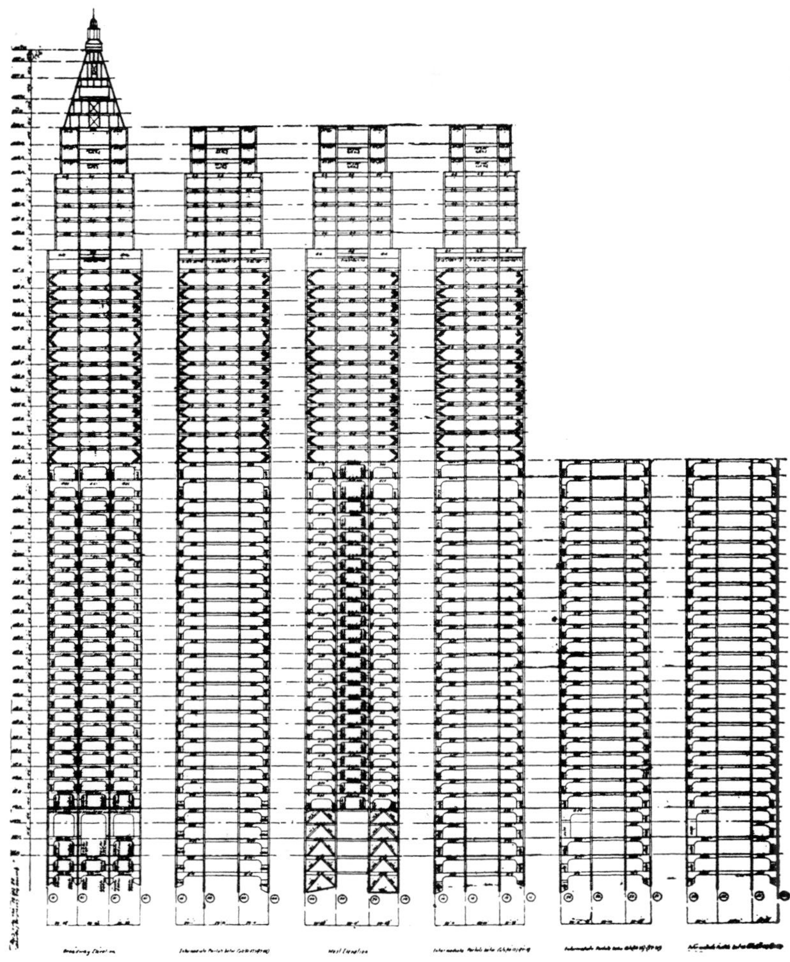

FIGURE 5.18
Woolworth Building, elevations of wind bracing planes in tower, Gunvald Aus and Company, 1911. From *American Architect*, vol. 103 (March 26, 1913). (Courtesy of the Trustees of the Boston Public Library.)

tal arches in bracing planes, which extended perpendicularly back from the Broadway elevation through the tower's full depth of three bays. On the Woolworth's lowest four floors, he doubled the portal arches, and for its basement as well as its first floor, he designed each reinforced concrete floor as a horizontal diaphragm, or what he called "a continuous sheet of great strength," to provide additional rigidity in resisting the lateral forces of the wind.[181]

Aus designed the Woolworth Building's lower flanking wings to be structurally self-supporting—their massive vertical loads exceeded the potential lateral loads—but he also combined them with the central tower to ensure the building's lateral stability. He secured the wings' rigidity by joining them in tandem with gracefully arched portal struts spanning the skyscraper's light court. Due to the intricacy of the skyscraper's full catalog of bracing components, and to their integration with the steel skeleton as a system, Aus could assert with complete confidence that "not the slightest tremor can be observed on top of the tower, even in a very heavy wind."[182]

The scale and complexity of the Woolworth Building's wind-braced steel frame required that Gilbert rely heavily on the

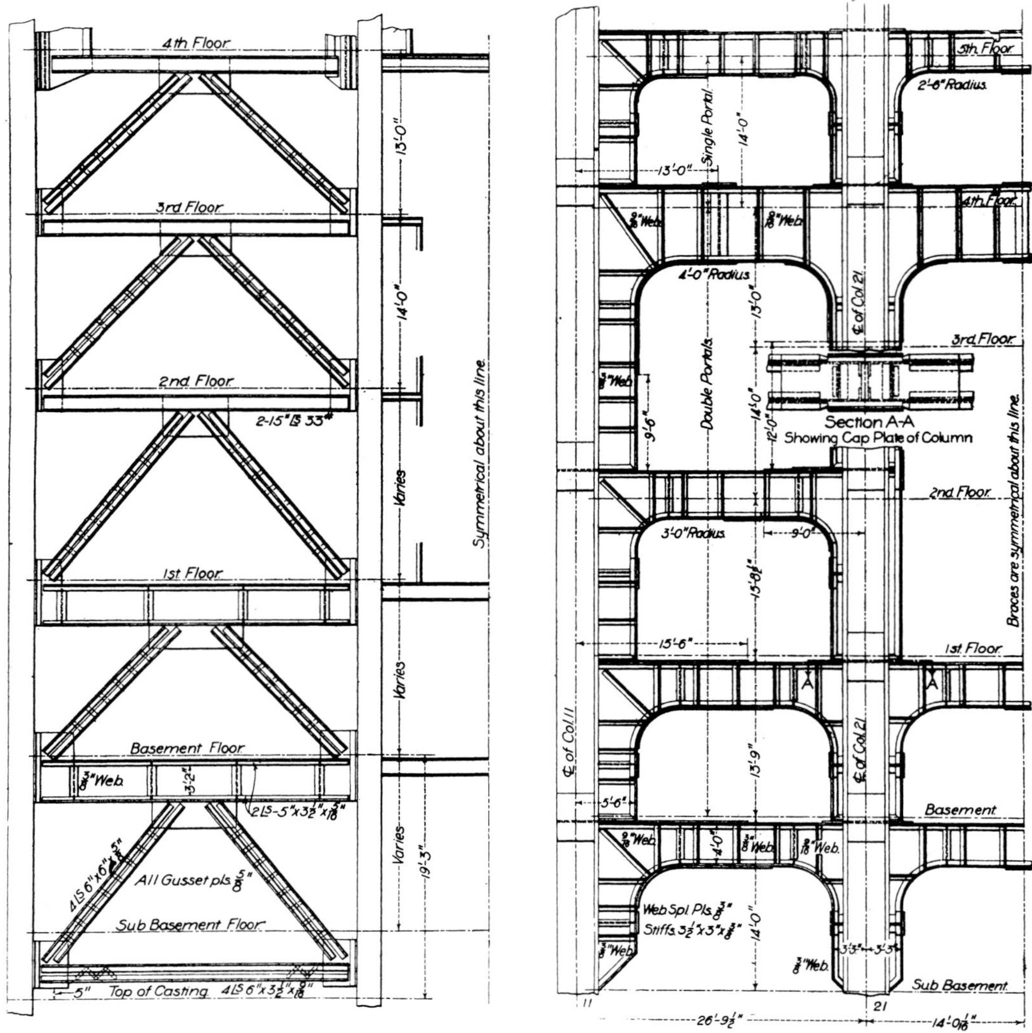

FIGURE 5.19 Woolworth Building, details of wind bracing in tower, Gunvald Aus and Company, 1911. From *Engineering Record*, vol. 65 (February 24, 1912).

engineering expertise of Aus. Still, Gilbert instructed Aus to be "extremely careful and conservative" with his structural calculations.[183] Gilbert also advised Woolworth that Aus's design be checked by "an outside engineer" as an "additional precaution" and recommended Boller and Hodgé, the structural engineers who had checked Otto Francis Semsch's design for the Singer Tower and more recently Purdy and Henderson's design for the Metropolitan Life Tower.[184] Woolworth, eager to trim expenses, countered that checking by United States Steel or the Manhattan Bureau of Buildings would be adequate.[185] Gilbert continued to advocate caution, nevertheless, choosing Thompson-Starrett's chief engineer, George Simpson, for the checking. He then emphasized to Simpson that while he had confidence in the engineering judgments of Aus, he also wanted to ascertain the Woolworth Building's absolute stability, given its "extraordinary height."[186] In 1912, Gilbert wrote proudly of the Woolworth Building's superior rigidity against the forces of the wind: "It has been the intention to provide the soundest, strongest, and most efficient construction."[187] Tests made by Aus during a "violent gale" on January 6, 1913, Gilbert felt comforted to know, revealed not the slightest tremor.[188] In 1923, Gilbert reasserted that the tower "*does not sway at all* so far as we can detect by the most careful measurements" and that "the structure is of the most substantial character; we did not dare take any risks that could be foreseen or avoided."[189] Although the tower did in all likelihood sway at least a fraction of an inch, Gilbert had it tested yet again the following year, to put to rest once and for all recurring myths about its swaying.[190]

Aus, in marked contrast to Gilbert, strongly criticized the Woolworth Building's structural redundancies and wasteful conservatism, publicly calling attention to its absence of structural engineering economy. This he blamed on the 1899 New York City building code's excessively high figures for wind loads and live loads. Skyscrapers, he insisted, could beyond any question be built to a height of one thousand two hundred feet—but only if engineers and officials reevaluated the code's requirement for wind loads and live loads. Under the current code, it would be impossible to ever build much higher than the Woolworth Building, at least without the closer spacing of major columns and the consequent loss of valuable floor area.[191] Other engineers called New York's building code archaic and urged that it be amended. They cited Chicago's building code as the desired model.[192]

The Woolworth Building's rapid, rationalized process of construction and record-setting height may have exemplified Thompson-Starrett's ambition to modernize the city, but the massiveness and conservatism of its structural design pointed instead to the outmoded stipulations of the firmly entrenched 1899 New York City building code. Even the giantism of United States Steel, with its stagnant methods of design and reliance upon heavy bridge fabrication techniques in the end served the dictates of the code. Those who attempted to revise the code, in particular the New York Building Code Revision Commission in 1909, confronted the vicissitudes of city politics in addition to the competition between local building trades and professional interests. The code's stipulations remained in force until 1916, when the city finally adopted a new code.[193] Only in later skyscrapers such as the Empire State Building would engineers use fewer structural pieces and connections of increased rigidity to serve the same ends with greater economy. Consequently, the most innovative aspect of the Woolworth's construction would be identified instead with Horowitz and the Thompson-Starrett Company's "modern building organization" and, in particular, with the organization's rationalized method for assembling the skyscraper's intricate skeleton of steel in record time.

TERRA COTTA

The Woolworth Building's steel frame asserted itself audaciously during construction as a bold feat of modern technology, but the application of its handcrafted terra cotta cladding suggested by contrast a kinship with the great stone monuments of the Middle Ages (see figs. 5.9, 5.10). Terra cotta invested Aus's steel-framed engineering with a human scale, delicacy, and soaring, aerial lightness; without such an intricacy of ornamental detail,

FIGURE 5.20 *Woolworth Building Tower*, showing installation of terra cotta cladding on the first two floors of the tower as it rises above the main building, 1912. From *Atlantic Terra Cotta*, vol. 2 (April 1915). Unidentified photographer. Collection of the New-York Historical Society, negative 78898d.

the skyscraper might have appeared cold and overpowering to the street spectator. The main challenge he faced, Gilbert told a reporter in 1912, was "how to combine height with architectural distinction."[194] In the large-scale industrial manufacture of terra cotta—the largest single use of architectural terra cotta to date—Gilbert had identified a modern method for recreating the character of a Ruskin-inspired handcrafted and polychromatic design and, with it, a modern method of hierarchically integrating types of ornamentation that rivaled his medieval models.

Bricklayers began attaching the Woolworth Building's terra cotta cladding on February 1, 1912, after the structural ironworkers had completed the riveting of its skeleton up to the eighteenth story. That day, about one hundred men positioned on scaffolds encircling the building's entire sixth story began tying the pieces of terra cotta to steel members with steel anchors, fastening each numbered piece to reflect its numbered location on the drawings. Subsequently, they backfilled the cladding with common red brick and mortar, employing a craft technique the industry had developed fully by 1910 (figs 5.20, 5.21).[195] Although working within the oldest tradition of their craft, the bricklayers found themselves subject to the dictates of Thompson-Starrett's comprehensive time schedule and to the concomitant rigging of the building site for efficiency and speed. Thompson-Starrett kept the Woolworth project's 120 scaffolds, suspended completely around the building by seven-story ropes, under the constant supervision of five men, who raised them on schedule methodically, abruptly, and all at once, to keep the top of the terra cotta cladding continually at waist height for the workmen. On the skyscraper's lower floors, work advanced at the rate of one and a half stories per week. Still, the speed of the terra cotta's application wholly depended on the rates of its production and shipment by the Atlantic Terra Cotta Company.[196]

On April 10, 1912, after the bricklayers had finished attaching fourteen stories of the Woolworth Building's terra cotta cladding, thirty stonemasons began dressing, setting, and anchoring carved Bedford limestone to its three-story base (fig. 5.22).[197] The skyscraper's steel-framed construction facilitated speed by allowing workers to proceed with such typically discrete cladding operations simultaneously.[198] It also allowed the building to remain open

FIGURE 5.21
Woolworth Building, detail showing the installation of terra cotta cladding, May 18, 1912. Photograph by Wurts Brothers. Collection of the New-York Historical Society, negative 70852.

below the sixth story until it received the approximately 150 loads of terra cotta, 50 loads of stone, and 80 loads of brick delivered to the site, deposited on the sidewalk bridges, and then handed over to the workmen or stored in designated areas elsewhere within the structure.[199]

On September 4, 1912, seven months after the first batch of terra cotta arrived, construction suddenly came to a standstill. The intricate Gothic ornamentation of the crown's projecting canopies and the tower's three setback stages required further labor and time to craft in the factory by hand. Almost two months later, on October 31, Atlantic Terra Cotta shipped its last cargo of ornamental cladding to the site.[200]

The manufacture of the Woolworth Building's seven thousand five hundred tons of architectural terra cotta by the Atlantic Terra Cotta Company's Perth Amboy, New Jersey, industrial works had begun in December 1911.[201] Only four years earlier, Atlantic Terra Cotta had merged with three

FIGURE 5.22 Woolworth Building, lower stories under construction, showing the setting and the anchoring of limestone at the three-story base, June 10, 1912. Photograph by Wurts Brothers. Collection of the New-York Historical Society, negative 54751.

other large terra cotta companies, among them the Perth Amboy Terra Company, to become the largest terra cotta manufacturer in the world.[202] Given the volume of production required for the accelerating pace of office building construction, Atlantic Terra Cotta employed "efficiency experts" at its Perth Amboy plant to oversee a newly standardized and mechanized system of production.[203] As a result of such practices, terra cotta's production, which had already doubled on a national scale between 1890 and 1900, had almost quadrupled by 1910.[204] In 1912, Atlantic Terra Cotta publicized the product it supplied for the Woolworth Building as "one of the largest contracts in terra cotta ever given for a single structure in the world."[205]

The Atlantic Terra Cotta Company's production of individual terra cotta units for the Woolworth's cladding followed the industry's conventional practices, with two key exceptions. First, Gilbert required that the company's draftsmen produce the project's hundreds of full-size detailed drawings in an office adjacent to his own under the supervision of Johnson. Its construction department then produced yet another set of detailed drawings, or shop drawings, at "shrinkage scale."[206] Second, Wells's specifications stipulated that the full-size models of the Woolworth's handcrafted and costly "foliate or intricate ornamental parts"—its terra cotta tracery, crockets, pinnacles, and gargoyles—be modeled by an outside firm of Gilbert's choice, which he later identified as Donnelly and Ricci.[207] Donnelly and Ricci, Gilbert further stipulated, were to sculpt the models at Atlantic Terra Cotta's Perth Amboy factory rather than in their own shops.[208]

Many of Donnelly and Ricci's modelers had trained as architectural sculptors in European art schools before departing to the United States. Elisio Ricci, the firm's partner in charge of the Woolworth project, studied sculpture in Florence before emigrating to America in the 1890s.[209] Ricci either modeled himself or supervised the modeling of all terra cotta ornamentation for the Woolworth Building.[210] After Ricci and the modelers sculpted the project's full-scale "foliate or intricate ornamental parts," they presented their work to Johnson for approval.[211] Johnson authorized the models, and then factory workers cut them up to make plaster molds. Shortly thereafter, the manufacture of the terra cotta began.[212]

Gilbert had few reservations about assigning the design of the Woolworth Building's structural steel to Aus. He jealously guarded the ornamental character of its terra cotta cladding, however, as his own métier. For Gilbert, terra cotta offered new possibilities for surface textures, for colors, for "authentic" craftsmanship, and for rivaling the colorful stone facings and veneers he admired in the Florentine and Venetian architecture of the Middle Ages.[213] Even more important, terra cotta had the capacity to compensate architecturally for what Gilbert continued to view as the structural steel frame's problematically thin and repetitive construction.

Woolworth intended, Gilbert emphasized, to build the Woolworth Building not as "a purely commercial structure," but rather "to clothe it with beauty," and "to make it a worthy ornament to the great city of New York" (fig. 5.23). Woolworth, he added, was willing to pay for such a structure "enriched and beautified" with ornamentation and color, and terra cotta cladding provided the means.[214] Gilbert gave all elevations of the Woolworth Building an equally elaborate ornamental treatment, even the lustrous, fully glazed, and highly reflective light court.[215] For the

FIGURE 5.23 Woolworth building, view from Barclay Street, ca. 1915. Photograph by Apeda Studios. Collection of the New-York Historical Society, negative 71981.

FIGURE 5.24
Woolworth Building, detail of terra cotta showing color in ogee arches and recessed spandrels at twenty-seventh story, 1912. Photograph by Tebbs-Hymans. Collection of the New-York Historical Society, negative 78892d.

Woolworth Building's general color, Gilbert chose a combination of warm cream and ivory shades, which he combined in a matte-glazed surface that suggested the patina of age. Against this background, he tinted the building's transoms with a darker tone of buff, to deepen the illusion of recession between the verticals; he intended to attract and to lead the eye upward with "the light lines and planes of the piers."[216]

Gilbert used a far bolder, varied palette of color to "accent both the highlights and shadows" in the Woolworth's Flamboyant Gothic ornamentation (fig. 5.24; see fig. 5.23). Against the dark blue undersides of crowning canopies, he applied touches of bright gold glaze as highlights in ornamental shields, setting these off against "denser shadows." When caught by sunlight, their sparkle emphasized "by contrast the depth of shadow."[217] Just below the projecting canopies at the twenty-sixth and the forty-second stories, Gilbert set the terra cotta transoms more deeply and colored them more darkly in bronze green. In their juxtaposition with the dark blue tones lining the canopies' undersides, they intensified the illusion of shadowy depth and cavernous recess beneath a crown. In the backgrounds of the transoms'

FIGURE 5.25 Woolworth Building, detail of terra cotta and copper roof at gable, 1912. Photograph by Tebbs-Hymans. Collection of the New-York Historical Society, negative 78893d.

FIGURE 5.26 Woolworth Building, detail of terra cotta, buttress at forty-third story, 1912. Photograph by Tebbs-Hymans. Collection of the New-York Historical Society, negative 78891d.

Flamboyant Gothic tracery patterns, Gilbert applied golden yellow, sienna, bronze green, and light and dark blues as polychromatic accents to throw the tracery's delicate outlines into sharper detachment and relief. Although the eye of the street spectator could barely distinguish such background colors on the building's higher floors, they grew stronger in depth, and appeared across larger areas of surface as their distance from the ground increased.[218]

In his choice of colors, Gilbert gave special consideration to how the Woolworth's picturesque tower would look against the city's atmospheric background of sky and clouds. As if he were recreating through his choice of colors one of his many sun-filled watercolors of European towers and campaniles, he wanted, he said, to "apparently increase the height of the tower" and to "relate it to the color of the sky, whether blue or grey."[219] In the transoms of the tower's higher setback stories, he colored panels light green, and for the highest stories, he used white against blue. As for the spire, Gilbert later recalled that he "studied for many months" the "color of the roofs and especially of the apex of the tower, with its delicate gilding . . . before it was finally determined."[220] Gilbert eventually decided to gild the ribs of the roof and observation story. He highlighted the copper roofs of the main building with their Gothic pinnacles, cresting, and tracery patterns in a pale blue green (fig. 5.25).[221] Little in the Woolworth's bright and sunny color scheme could be traced to Gilbert's original, and darker, medieval sources, whether those of the sacred or secular Low Countries Gothic, or the English Perpendicular and French Flamboyant Gothic traditions. Gilbert, rather, continued to view colored terra cotta through a nineteenth-century Ruskinian Gothic lens. In place of the Ruskinians' authenticity of "constructional polychromy," however, he exploited instead the illusory capacities of terra cotta's colorful surface glazes. In doing so, he strengthened the vividness of the Woolworth tower in the eye of the street spectator while also highlighting its shape as an eye-catching ornamental feature in distant street and skyline views.

Besides terra cotta's suitability for color, Gilbert exploited its technical capacities to the fullest: its potential for the clarification of form through sculptural detachment, tolerance for deep undercutting, facility in attenuation, and susceptibility to modeling in high relief. Linear Flamboyant Gothic ornamentation in terra cotta enlivened the surfaces of the Woolworth's gables, culminating tourelles, spandrels beneath ogee arches, and horizontal belt courses. It vigorously projected in Gothic canopies—Schuyler's "efflorescence" of "buds and blossoms"—in the gargoyles of the tourelles, and in the finials and crockets of the crown.[222] Large flying buttresses of terra cotta effected skillful transitions at the tower's setbacks (fig. 5.26). Freestanding verticals projected from outriggers in the tower's upper stages, attenuated to the point of weightlessness. As if inspired by the writings of Ruskin, Gilbert found in terra cotta the ideal medium by which to calibrate the proportions of the tower's Flamboyant Gothic ornamentation, thereby reducing the skyscraper's colossal size in the eye of the street spectator.[223] "As the parts were reduced in size and increased in number," wrote Gilbert, "they were also increased in *relative* size, so as to make some allowance for the optical reduction due to their distance from the eye" (fig. 5.27; see fig. 5.23).[224] The large-scale ornamentation Gilbert designed for the tower's highest stages, particularly—"by no means . . . a process of mere 'monstrification,'" as Schuyler put it—augmented its legibility from a distance while retaining the material's characteristic clarity of outline for all beholders to appreciate, whether stationed near or far.[225]

Along with its lightness, grace, and subtleties of color, the Woolworth Building's terra cotta cladding had a peculiarly delicate, lean, and brittle character that made it stand out as a specifically modern material among Gilbert's earlier Beaux-Arts monuments in stone, notably the United States Custom House. The Woolworth's terra cotta pieces, moreover—already stylized and factory made—Gilbert designed in repetitive patterns, as groupings of four stories about the central axis of the tower. Gilbert, it appears, had little immunity to the modern, industrial tendency that an 1890s critic had already identified in the terra cotta ornamentation of Chicago skyscrapers, which he called the "machine-lace of the present day."[226] Still, few contemporary critics could find any artistic shortcoming in the Woolworth Building's modern version of the Gothic ornamental tradition—they called attention, rather, to its remarkable authenticity. Schuyler compared the Woolworth's ornamentation favorably with that of a medieval cathedral's. "One has seen photographic 'bits' of famous minsters in comparison with which this brand new American Gothic loses nothing."[227] And if *Engineering Record* and *Scientific American* hailed the Woolworth Building as a feat of structural engineering, art critics such as Clarence Ward attributed its success as a skyscraper to the beauty embodied in the scale, poetry—indeed, in the "Gothicness" of its "lacelike and beautifully proportioned" terra cotta detail.[228] In architectural terra cotta, consequently, Gilbert and Woolworth had discerned the ideal material for reconciling their desire for a European, handcrafted exterior with the city's forces of modernization.

The Highest Building in the World

Well before the Woolworth Building's steel frame began to rise visibly in the city, Woolworth hired the commercial photographer Irving Underhill—whose studio directly fronted the building site—to document its construction at regularly timed intervals. He then mailed Underhill's photographs to his store managers and agents throughout the country and abroad, with the recommendation that they be distributed and published as "widely as possible" (see figs. 5.6, 5.8, 5.9, 5.10).[229] The construction of the Woolworth Building, like that of other major skyscrapers and noted works of engineering of the day, inspired a widespread enthusiasm for what David Nye has called the "technological sublime."[230] This enthusiasm Woolworth appreciated. He would both exploit it and celebrate it through Underhill's photographs and other forms of publicity, continuing his program of strategically promoting his project, thereby calling still greater attention to his "world's greatest skyscaper."

As the Woolworth Building rose skyward, New York's newspaper reporters recorded its progress and in the process transformed its construction into a form of urban theater. In their well-timed sequence of stories they interwove the epic of the skyscraper's ascent with human drama. The reporters' accounts reached the expected climax on July 1, 1912, with the tower's topping off as a noon whistle blew. Charley Campbell, Thompson-Starrett's steel superintendent, hoisted a twelve-by-twenty-four-foot flag to the top of a thirty-foot flagpole (fig. 5.28). Thousands of people in the streets, the reporters noted, "paused to pay tribute to the highest building in the world."[231] "The upper stories were crowded with ironworkers, steamfitters, plumbers, reporters, photographers,

FIGURE 5.27 Woolworth Building, detail of terra cotta, crockets at fifty-fifth story, 1912. Photograph by Tebbs-Hymans. Collection of the New-York Historical Society, negative 73191.

FIGURE 5.28 Woolworth Building, topping off the steel frame, July 1, 1912. (© Bettmann/Corbis.)

and other curiosity seekers," the Gilbert office's G. F. Shaffer more accurately explained, "while far below could be seen the upward gazing throng of Broadway's noon thousands."[232] The denouement of the newspaper drama took place on December 12, 1913, with the exceedingly spectacular and some thought "wholly unnecessary and daredevil performance," of the craftsman Niels Nelson, who inched his way to the top of the tower's flagpole to gild its summit with a glint of gold.[233]

In June 1911, Hugh McAtamney reported to Gilbert that he had succeeded in getting news items about the as-yet-unbuilt Woolworth Building printed in two hundred newspapers around the world, and that "clippings are now coming in from France and Germany."[234] In all likelihood, it was McAtamney who broached to reporters in May that the roof of the Woolworth's twenty-eighth story might serve as an "aerial wharf" for airships, and its tower sport an electric beacon at its peak, transforming it into an "aerial lighthouse."[235] And as the tower's frame neared climax and completion in June 1912, it was probably McAtamney who apprised the city's reporters of the exploits of the aviator Frank Goodale. Goodale piloted a balloon contraption out of the haze over the Hudson River, encircled the pinnacle of the tower, and waved at the structural ironworkers. He then headed south to Battery Park, "to the wonder of gaping thousands from the streets, roofs, and windows of skyscrapers."[236]

The capstone of McAtamney's publicity program for the Woolworth's construction, his commemorative *The Master Builders: A Record of the Construction of the World's Highest Commercial Structure* (1913), exalted the skyscraper as well as its builders (fig. 5.29): "The United States of America has set the pace for building construction of the entire civilized world," the book triumphantly pronounced in its opening line, linking the project with the day's popular and widely trumpeted themes of western expansion and dominance. "There may never be a building in New York City which will tower away so high skyward."[237] Woolworth and Gilbert wrote introductions, with Woolworth proclaiming his skyscraper "the greatest structure in the world" and Gilbert calling his own design a "worthy ornament to the great city of New York."[238] The embossed blue cover of *The Master Builders*, with its gilded lettering and tinted photographs showing the completed Woolworth Building and the new New York skyline, functioned as a superb piece of visual boosterism for the Thompson-Starrett Company, Woolworth, and for the city. It also functioned as eye-catching advertising for the project's subcontractors, craftsmen, and manufacturers, who in giving to prospective customers such an account of "the greatest structure in the world" furthered Woolworth and McAtamney's objectives for publicity.

Burrelle's Press Clipping Bureau culled accounts of the project's construction from newspapers around the world and mounted them in scrapbooks designed for Gilbert and Woolworth.[239] McAtamney, in the end, spent approximately one hundred thousand dollars publicizing the construction of the Woolworth Building—perhaps the first public relations campaign on such a scale for a single building.[240] In the process, he further sensationalized an already sensational skyscraper. Yet after a certain point, McAtamney's program of publicity threatened to destroy the air of high seriousness that Gilbert, Horowitz, and Woolworth brought to the construction of the project. In late July 1912, Gilbert cautioned that "spectacular advertising of the building must not be permitted,"

THE MASTER BUILDERS

A RECORD OF THE CONSTRUCTION OF THE WORLD'S HIGHEST COM-MERCIAL STRUCTURE

PUBLISHED BY
HUGH McATAMNEY & COMPANY
NEW YORK
1913

FIGURE 5.29 *The Master Builders: A Record of the Construction of the World's Highest Commercial Structure* (New York: Hugh McAtamney & Co., 1913).

SKY-LINE OF NEW YORK CITY

Arrows indicate a number of buildings erected by Thompson-Starrett Company, forming part of the sky-line of lower New York.

1. Atlantic Trust Building.
2. United States Express Building.
3. Kuhn-Loeb Building.
4. Equitable Building.
5. 68 William Street Building.
6. 80 Maiden Lane Building.
7. Wyllys Building.
8. Hilliard Building.
9. Frankel Building.
10. 123 William Street Building.
11. 134 William Street Building.
12. Woolworth Building.
13. Municipal Building.
14. Chapel Court Building.
15. Schieren Building.

FIGURE 5.30 *Sky-Line of New York City.* From *Thompson-Starrett Company: Building and Industrial Construction* (Montreal: Thompson-Starrett Co., 1922). Science, Industry, and Business Library, New York Public Library, Astor, Lenox and Tilden Foundations.

and later, Edward Hogan asserted as the skyscraper's rental agent that "if you get too spectacular, you don't get the tenants you want."[241]

By 1910, skyscrapers, along with long-spanning bridges, subway tunnels, and great railway stations, had become powerful and awe-inspiring emblems of the modernizing city. As the Thompson-Starrett Company's William Aiken Starrett later put it, "when a great building starts, all the world is a builder," and "the whole citizenry of a metropolis takes to its heart the swift and skillful accomplishment."[242] Horowitz, not surprisigly, viewed the Woolworth Building as a superior work of construction in its own right, as the defining project in his career as a builder, and the lower Manhattan skyline as a "three-dimensional memoir" (fig. 5.30).[243] As innovators in the construction industry, Horowitz and his Thompson-Starrett Company took pride in participating as builders in the nations's larger ethos of technological experimentation, innovation, and achievement.

Hughes has written that in the United States the "character-forming achievement for almost three centuries has been to transform a wilderness into a building site."[244] The New York skyline, which Paul Starrett later described as "more skyscrapers per acre and taller skyscrapers than any spot on earth," signified the early twentieth century's most pronounced architectural manifestation of such an achievement.[245] Equating those skyscrapers with recent advances in the construction industry, William Aiken Starrett proclaimed that historians of the future "will of surety say that we were a nation of builders, great builders, the greatest the world has ever seen."[246] For Gilbert's contemporaries in construction, then, the Woolworth Building—at its completion New York and the world's tallest, its height the product of a newly systematized building organization and a rationalized process of assembly in record time—marked a turning point in the history of construction. Such height and speed of assembly they chose to celebrate, despite the building code's conservatism, the historicizing features of Gilbert's skyscraper Gothic design, the realities of the construction industry, or even Woolworth's exploitation of the project toward the ends of spectacular urban theatrics and printed media publicity. For this reason, skyscrapers such as the Woolworth galvanized for those who watched or read about its rise in the city a still newer belief in the nation's seemingly predestined technological greatness.[247]

CHAPTER SIX

The Skyscraper as a "City"

Besides promoting the completed Woolworth Building as the headquarters of his retailing empire, Woolworth promoted it as the most prestigious of modern office buildings and as a "city within a city" (fig. 6.1). In doing so, he exploited Hugh McAtamney's skills with publicity to orchestrate a splashy media campaign. The campaign began with President Woodrow Wilson's official opening of the skyscraper in April 1913, which hailed Woolworth's career as an ethically exemplary rags-to-riches success story, and culminated in the Broadway–Park Place Company's widely circulated publicity brochure *The Cathedral of Commerce* (1916). Woolworth used *The Cathedral of Commerce* to showcase the skyscraper's interior as a "city" as well as an ethically superior place of work, knowing that he had to compete for tenants in a market already overbuilt with space. He was determined to capitalize financially and raise the Woolworth profile internationally with his theatrical vision of the "world's greatest skyscraper."

By 1910, Woolworth's concept of his skyscraper as a "city within a city" was hardly new. In 1893, the novelist Henry Blake Fuller described Chicago's Clifton Building, the setting for his *Cliff Dwellers* of 1893, as a small city.[1] Ray Stannard Baker pointed out a few years later that "a great office building is really a city under one roof."[2] Some owners of Chicago skyscrapers, as Daniel Bluestone has shown, employed ingenious methods to enforce the idea of the skyscraper as a city; the Masonic Temple featured individual stories for office and shopping uses named after city streets.[3] Woolworth distinguished his skyscraper's interior from those of his predecessors, however, with an elaborate array of attractions designed for his own use, for the use of his executive circle, and for tenants. These rivaled the city's most fashionable settings for high-style consumption. Besides fine office space, the settings included the F. W. Woolworth Company's headquarters along with an array of distinctive semipublic spaces of European-inspired historical design. The spaces suggested for their occupants the experience of cosmopolitan travel, and along with it associations of escapism, fantasy, and seeming mastery over historical space and time.

Like the best of the city's stylish consumer enterprises, the Woolworth Building emphasized service: The skyscraper

FIGURE 6.1 Woolworth Building on City Hall Park, ca. 1915. Unidentified photographer. Prints and Photographs Division, Library of Congress.

featured the latest electrical, plumbing, ventilating, and fire protection technologies. Also like those enterprises, the skyscraper kept its interior sequestered from the urban surroundings. Yet as a retailer, Woolworth also understood the economic importance of connecting with those surroundings, whether through a visually engaging sidewalk approach toward the skyscraper's distinctive Tudor Gothic portal or through providing tenants and their visitors convenience of access via high-speed elevators to lower Broadway's newly completed express and local subway lines.

Ultimately, Woolworth aimed to achieve nothing less than distilling for his tenants the entire metropolitan experience within the interior of the Woolworth Building, and in doing so, making that interior so attractive and desirable that the skyscraper "created" its own land values in the modern urban marketplace. As a consequence, the Woolworth Building would radiate its prestige outward into the city, as had Woolworth's earlier Lancaster Woolworth Building, and thereby increase the market value of its urban surroundings.

The Opening as a Theatrical Spectacle

President Wilson's opening of the Woolworth Building on April 24, 1913, celebrated the completion of the "biggest building ever built for practical use" while also spectacularly announcing the availability of its interior as a "city" for rental to tenants.[4] McAtamney devised the opening as a clever piece of theatrical promotion, which he disguised as a "public event of importance to the whole nation."[5] To that end, he appropriated the conventions of public pageantry identified with the nationalistic crowd spectacles recently staged in New York, among them the Admiral George Dewey and Hudson-Fulton celebrations. For Woolworth, the skyscraper's opening—a dazzling electrical spectacle set within the showcase of New York's City Hall Park—crowned his earlier experiments with theatrical store openings and commemorative celebratory extravaganzas.

In accordance with McAtamney's script for the opening, President Wilson pushed a telegraphic button on his desk in Washington, D.C., at 7:30 in the evening. By doing so, he instantaneously closed an electrical circuit, caused a bell to ring in the skyscraper's engine room, and activated electricity-generating dynamos. Expectant spectators had filled City Hall Park and lower Broadway and lined the New Jersey shore. The skyscraper's eighty thousand incandescent bulbs flashed on at once, causing all fifty-five stories to leap into view as a brightly shimmering vertical object against the evening darkness (fig. 6.2). Altogether, thousands witnessed the event, which reportedly reached observers one hundred miles out to sea.[6]

For the Admiral George Dewey Celebration of 1899, New Yorkers had suspended a thirty-six-foot-tall, fully electrified "Welcome Dewey" sign 370 feet across the Brooklyn Bridge, its giant *W* sparkling with one thousand electric lights.[7] During the week-long Hudson-Fulton Celebration of 1909, engineers devised a futuristic "incandescent phantasmagoria" for more than a million visitors, featuring experimental electrical devices, signs, and batteries of searchlights that highlighted skyscrapers and bridges, all brightening the city's nocturnal landscape of rivers, streets, and public squares.[8] The nation's earliest example of a fully electrified tower, the 1893 World's Columbian Exposition's Edison Tower of Light, a so-called shrine of illumination, stood eighty-two feet high in

FIGURE 6.2 Woolworth Building, opening, April 24, 1913. Photograph by Detroit Publishing Company. Prints and Photographs Division, Library of Congress.

the center of its Electricity Building and counted among the exposition's most popular attractions.[9] But the drama of the Woolworth Building's spellbinding electrical flash, and City Hall Park's sublime transition from darkness to brilliant light, was new.[10]

McAtamney sent news of the Woolworth's opening from the Marconi wireless telegraph apparatus stationed atop its tower to the Eiffel Tower's wireless station in Paris and from there to all European capitals. He persuaded the Associated Press to transmit the news worldwide and told special foreign correspondents to send it out along their cables. In the words of one contemporary, McAtamney's opening, "the premier publicity stunt of this or any other day," made the Woolworth Building "the most widely known office building in the world."[11] Comparable schemes of architectural publicity dated to the early 1890s; the Chicago World's Columbian Exposition's Department of Publicity, for example, spent more than $190,000 to distribute more than two hundred thousand printed illustrations and related materials by mail.[12] The Woolworth Building's opening, however, stood out for its peculiar use of a modern, vertical strategy to inaugurate the "abstract image" of "Woolworth" as a brand name. According to William Taylor, Woolworth and McAtamney in effect exploited the world's most notable feat of steel-framed construction as a modern communications tower. Woolworth had typically advertised his commodities in show windows along the "horizontal access route" of a city or town's main street. But in choosing to deploy such a vertical strategy, he presaged 1920s purpose-built communications towers and the transmission of news via radio.[13]

To the end of highlighting "the national significance of the occasion," McAtamney secured President Wilson's participation in the opening by making "journey after journey to Washington."[14] The recently elected Wilson, who had occupied the White House for only a month as a Progressive Democrat, had criticized the hegemony of the nation's big businesses and resolved to shore up faltering antitrust legislation. That is perhaps why some journalists criticized his involvement with McAtamney's publicity scheme.[15] Woolworth, however, had cultivated the public image of a retailer who had reduced "many and many an item from the luxury class to a staple within the reach of anybody who has a nickel or dime," thereby making available to all classes high-quality but inexpensive commodities, many of which were the necessities of life.[16] Wilson, consequently, may well have been promoting a larger, patriotic American dream, that of abundance, good things, and progress.

McAtamney invited more than eight hundred men to the Woolworth Building's opening ceremony, many of whom had achieved prominence in the nation's affairs.[17] At least three United States senators participated, the populist Thomas Gore of Oklahoma and the Democrats Joseph Ransdell of Louisiana and Ollie James of Kentucky, and so did seventy-eight congressmen. "Others prominent in the life of the nation's capital" also joined in, among them the "moderately progressive" governor of Arkansas, Joseph Robinson; a former governor of New York, Horace White; and a former governor of Rhode Island, Abram J. Pothier. So did the minister plenipotentiary from Ecuador, Don Gonzalo S. Córdova.[18] Woolworth had listed among McAtamney's representatives of states and the nation his own mentor and first employer, William H. Moore, along with the company's executives, its vice president and general manager,

Carson Peck, and its new vice presidents after the merger of 1912, Charles Sumner Woolworth, Seymour Horace Knox, and Fred Morgan Kirby.[19]

McAtamney also invited a number of Woolworth's contemporaries from the business world, among them the banker Otto Kahn, who sat on the board of the Metropolitan Opera Company, the industrialist Charles M. Schwab, the former president of United States Steel and from 1903 the president of the Bethlehem Steel Company, and the lawyer and industrialist Elbert H. Gary, who had reorganized United States Steel for J. P. Morgan. In honor of Gilbert, McAtamney also involved an array of leading lights from architecture and the related fields of art, science, literature, and even muckraking journalism—Glenn Brown, Ernest Flagg, Daniel Chester French, Edwin Blashfield, Charles Rollinson Lamb, Charles Dana Gibson, Nikola Tesla, Montgomery Schuyler, and Ray Stannard Baker. The men identified with the skyscraper's construction occupied a prominent place on the list, notably Horowitz—whom McAtamney seated at the main table with Woolworth and Gilbert—along with Aus, Johnson, Rockart, Wells, Sunter, and Donnelly and Ricci. McAtamney's roster of men summed up virtually all aspects of the nation's contemporary political, economic, and cultural life.

McAtamney transported Woolworth's guests to New York from Boston and Washington, D.C., on special trains dispatched by the Pennsylvania Railroad—trains luxuriously equipped with dining cars for lunch and with sleeping cars for an uninterrupted postdinner return. Upon their arrival in New York, automobiles took the guests to the Waldorf-Astoria Hotel, where they dressed for the occasion, and then to the skyscraper's lobby-arcade, where Woolworth and Gilbert received them and guides described architectural highlights. After McAtamney seated the guests on the twenty-seventh floor, in a room he had decorated with palms, roses, American flags, and seals of the City of New York, the State of New York, and the United States of America, President Wilson's electrification of the building's exterior kicked off "probably the highest skyscraper dinner in the world" (fig. 6.3).[20] On cue, an orchestra struck up "The Star Spangled Banner" and the eight-hundred-plus guests stood, toasted President Wilson, Woolworth, and Gilbert, and cheered.

The Woolworth Building's lofty dinner gathering, the climax of McAtamney's opening celebration, featured Woolworth's presentation to Gilbert, "as much my friend today as he ever was," of a silver bowl, engraved by Tiffany and Company with his name and an image of the Woolworth Building.[21] Francis Hopkinson Smith—a novelist and artist as well as a prominent engineer, contractor, and businessman—served as the master of ceremonies. Gilbert had known Smith since at least 1897, probably recommended him, and read his novels. Smith, reputed to be "possibly the best raconteur and cleanest after-dinner talker at men's dinners in the city," set the tone for the evening's celebration.[22] He declared that the Woolworth Building's spectacular opening merited such observance on a national scale. The project represented "the world-wide belief in the integrity of the American character," as "exemplified in [Woolworth's] own stern, relentless, uncompromisingly honest life." Smith extolled Woolworth as the classic rags-to-riches Horatio Alger success story, "a plain farmer boy who kept ahead of the procession, close up to the band," and as "an example to every American lad to go and do likewise."[23]

FIGURE 6.3 Woolworth Building, opening dinner celebration, twenty-seventh story, April 24, 1913. Unidentified photographer. Collection of Franklin and Alex McCann.

Other speakers at the opening similarly highlighted the national significance of Woolworth's skyscraper while also linking its design with laudatory presentations of the retailer's life and career. William Hensel, Woolworth's lawyer in Lancaster and the former Democratic attorney general of Pennsylvania, remarked that Woolworth had built the skyscraper, a "contribution to the art treasures of this country," not for the select few, but rather for the millions. He built it especially for "immigrants from all lands."[24] Hensel then further proposed that Woolworth and his retailing enterprise offered an instructive example for solving the industrial-era conflict between labor and capital, still fresh in the city's public memory from the 1880s and 1890s.[25] "If students of our social system, if critics of our business order, will study the career for the last thirty years of the man whom architect and builder have testified here tonight is first of all and most of all responsible for this magnificent structure, they will find that in his dealings with the general public, in his relations with his business competitors, and above all, in his relations with his employees, he has better, to my mind, than any other individual solved those vexed problems which seem to disturb and confuse and perplex and complicate our legislators and the critics of our social system."[26] Hensel continued that Woolworth, moreover, had not "enforced against the public an odious trust." His career illustrated, rather, that the solution to the conflict between labor and capital could not be found in ordinances or statutes, but rather in "the individual character of the man who conducts the business, and stands between his business and the public."[27] During an era in which the concentrated power of trusts represented "a standing danger to democracy"—a power against which the enterprise of the individual seemed hopeless—Hensel presented Woolworth's career as an instructive exemplar for every man and especially the penniless man: that of the hardworking, self-made entrepreneur.[28]

Gilbert, in his own opening speech, reiterated Hensel's points about industrial-era relations between labor and capital and the ethical dimension of Woolworth's self-made success: "[The Woolworth Building] shows that this is a land of equal opportunity, and that under our laws and under our government a man may start in life with nothing of this world's goods, and, single-handedly, achieve success; that this opportunity is open to all and that it is not through agitation and unrest our people will prosper, but by the good, old-fashioned virtues of honesty, clean-dealing, industry, and thrift."[29] Gilbert based his presentation of Woolworth's career on the economic elite's Spencerian belief in the "survival of the fittest." Woolworth had demonstrated such survival through the construction of a giant, $65 million retail corporation from the building block of a single store. Gilbert also invoked the Protestant work ethic, attempting to justify Woolworth's staggering wealth in the context of a city heavily populated with immigrants living in scandalous poverty. In essence, he argued that Woolworth's skyscraper functioned as an apt architectural metaphor for the retailer's wholly ethical rise in the business world.

Neither Hensel nor Gilbert, nor any of the opening's speakers, mentioned Woolworth's determination to make a personal profit on the Woolworth Building as a speculative office building or to use its record-breaking altitude to spectacularly advertise his chain of stores around the world. Nor did they question whether Woolworth's retailing career indeed offered a solution to the industrial-era conflict between labor and capital—particularly given that Woolworth had continued to pay his salesgirls excruciatingly low wages, placing their total earnings well below the poverty line, and that he had risen to dominance in the fashion of his largest corporate contemporaries, through consolidation and merger. To the contrary, for the speakers the United States' thriving capitalistic economy and the larger mood of national expansion and prosperity seemed to have explained exactly this sort of celebratory extravaganza and theatrical opening as an audacious electrical display. For the millions overwhelmed by the skyscraper's arresting flash of light, moreover, McAtamney's promotion of Woolworth, his stores, his honestly made wealth, and the whole Protestant myth of individual success through hard work suddenly took on a newly seductive aura. Woolworth's great, twinkling object in the city seemed to signify a peculiarly American sense of unbounded possibility.[30]

A Skyscraper That Creates Its Own Land Values

The New York real estate environment in which Woolworth spectacularly celebrated his "greatest income-producing property" was highly competitive, totally unregulated, and, as noted by Woolworth's contemporaries, severely overbuilt. Between 1905 and 1915, the phenomenon of building increasingly larger and finer office buildings in order to compete for tenants—a phenomenon of which Woolworth's skyscraper followed by the Equitable Building represented the final stage—precipitated an unexpected destabilization of land values in New York's financial district. Later, experts reported that typically "the production of office space had closely paralleled the need for it." After 1905, however, "the headlong development of tower buildings and the haste to capitalize on their advertising value produced a condition of overbuilding and severe rental competition."[31] Harry S. Black declared in 1911 that "the difficulties which have been encountered by many large office structures below the City Hall in showing a fair return on their investment, in addition to the strong competition occasioned by the many new buildings within the last year or two, have demonstrated that . . . New York is overbuilt."[32] The *Real Estate Record and Builder's Guide* echoed Black's sentiment: "At present there appears to be more office space on the market than can be readily absorbed," a condition that "has prevailed since the panic of 1907."[33]

Overbuilding in New York's financial district had become so extreme that the supply of newer, costlier space exceeded the demand for it and the prices of the new space also fell. At the time Woolworth conceived his big skyscraper, tenants were paying a mere $2.00 per square foot for first-class space actually worth $3.00 or more. Many of the city's exasperated speculators, meanwhile, faced watching their built investments revert after foreclosure to the "unwilling hands of the lender."[34] Such a localized condition of severe overbuilding and rental competition made Woolworth's determination to construct "the highest in the world" seem especially unusual. But Woolworth remained undeterred. In February 1911, he had an advertising sign painted at the construction site, "Highest in the World: The Magnificent Woolworth Building," which reflected his ambitions (see fig. 5.6). That May, tenants began applying for space in the skyscraper through Woolworth's Broadway–Park Place Company.[35] Woolworth had already envisioned securing a total tenant population of between seven thousand five hundred and eight thousand.[36]

On top of the challenges presented by New York's overheated speculative environment, Woolworth faced competition from projects as large and attractive as his own, notable among them the new Municipal Building, as he observed in December 1911: "The Municipal Building, which is about completed now, will be finished and ready for occupancy, I am assured, on May 1, 1913, and this will empty a good many offices already taken by the city departments in various buildings near the Woolworth Building, and create a vacant space in their buildings which I will have to compete with."[37] As a countermeasure, Woolworth had Hogan begin a program of aggressively soliciting tenants from nearby office buildings. Among these were Beach and Pierson, a law firm headquartered in the Singer Tower, which eventually abandoned its offices there to pay Woolworth's Broadway–Park Place Company still higher rental rates.[38] By March 1915, Woolworth could write confidently to his store managers that skeptical real estate agents at first thought "it would be impossible to fill such a large building with tenants." They "predicted ruin for 'yours truly' and they never expected the building would be a success." Today, however, "it is one of the most popular buildings in downtown New York, without any exception."[39]

To Woolworth's advantage, the New York environment in which he conceived "the magnificent Woolworth Building" had yet to be legally regulated—by contrast to that of Chicago. In 1908, New York's Building Code Revision Commission appointed a committee to study anew the possibility of restricting building heights; their work yielded two highly esteemed proposals: Ernest Flagg's "tower solution" and the Philadelphia architect David Knickerbacker Boyd's setback scheme.[40] During the economic boom of that year, however, a mood of optimism and expansiveness fostered the urge to build anew at record-breaking altitudes. By 1913, buildings costing in total over $100 million in New York "had been erected with a keener eye towards their advertising than their investment qualities," and according to the mechanical and civil engineer Reginald Pelham Bolton, certain skyscrapers were "monuments of uselessness."[41] Speculators railed against "the mania for freak advertising that had prevailed," fearing the further destabilization of their initially secure investments. Not surprisingly, the construction of the giant, forty-story Equitable Building at Broadway between Cedar and Pine streets in 1913–15 catalyzed "a storm of protest": it boasted over twice the total rentable floor area of the Woolworth.[42] The consequences of such a totally unregulated urban environment precipitated the zoning resolution of 1916, but it also gave Woolworth complete freedom, as he put it, to "create" his own land values—that is, to finance a "city within a city" of such a spectacular height, architectural distinction, and printed news media renown that no other rental property could compete with it.

Inside the Skyscraper

Gilbert's first design for the Woolworth Building housed speculative office space along with a few small shops and the quarters of Irving National Exchange Bank. After Woolworth decided to top the Singer Tower six months later, however, the design expanded to become a "city within a city," incorporating a complex array of internal activities unprecedented in the day's typical speculative office buildings (fig. 6.4). As the *New York Times* described the Woolworth Building in November 1910, it would have "many novel features," and as a Brooklyn reporter later pointed out, the skyscraper "will contain in itself a small city."[43] Gilbert had alluded to Woolworth's new reasoning about the project that October. "He stated that he was constantly thinking of new things to make the building attractive to tenants, and that he wanted nothing left undone to make it so. He wanted to give them more than anybody else, as he was bound to fill the building."[44] In February 1911, Woolworth told a reporter that his intentions for the Woolworth Building as a small city were "purely commercial": He had recently discovered "the possibility of making the skyscraper the greatest income-producing property in which he could invest his money."[45]

Gilbert's final design for the Woolworth Building's interior incorporated a Tudor Gothic portal and lobby-arcade decorated with Early Christian, Byzantine, and Gothic motifs. On the twenty-fourth floor, he designed the F. W. Woolworth Company's headquarters as French Empire, and on the tower's fortieth floor, Woolworth's private office and apartment as Italian Renaissance.[46] In the first level below grade, he conceived a complete health club with a marble-lined "Pompeiian" swimming pool, a barbershop, and a "German" rathskeller. For the skyscraper's twenty-sixth, twenty-seventh, and twenty-eighth stories, he proposed in consultation with Woolworth a "New Amsterdam-inspired" downtown lunch club.[47] After construction

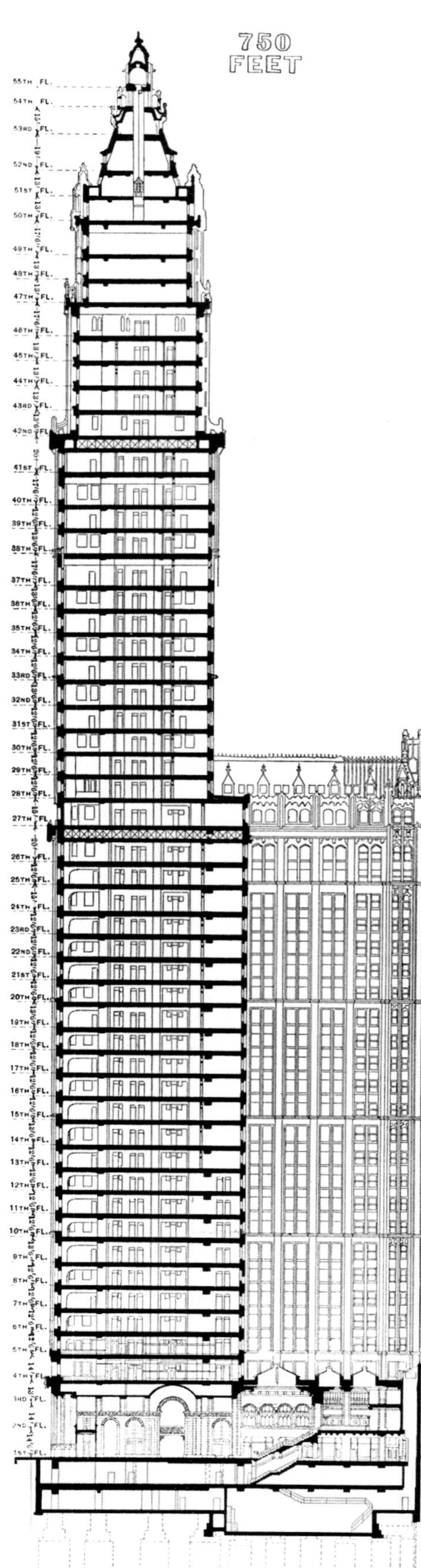

FIGURE 6.4 Woolworth Building, section. From *The Woolworth Building (Highest in the World)* (New York, 1912). Collection of the New-York Historical Society, negative 72150.

began, Woolworth had Gilbert expand the basement's health club, adding adjoining shower baths, lockers, and other conveniences, as well as the upper stories' downtown club, to incorporate a modern kitchen, dining rooms, and a billiard room. Above the club, Woolworth requested a fully equipped gymnasium with access to a running track on the roof. Finally, at the peak of the tower, he had Gilbert design a lofty observatory with a palm garden. None of the Woolworth Building's uses and conveniences represented anything especially new in their own right, but their number, variety, sophistication, and quality of publicness within a single office building was unprecedented.[48]

Woolworth's own Lancaster Woolworth Building served as one model for the Woolworth Building's complex and architecturally varied interior; it, too, had incorporated a diverse array of uses—offices, a store, restaurant, and a roof garden. Equally important, however, spectacular recent projects such as Samuel Friede's seven-hundred-foot "Globe Tower," designed for Coney Island in 1906, featured a roof garden with a restaurant and vaudeville theater, a hippodrome with four rings for continuous circuses, the largest ballroom in the world, a restaurant, a public observatory with automatic telescopes, and at the top, a station for the United States Weather Bureau and the world's largest revolving searchlight.[49] In midtown Manhattan, the Metropolitan Life Insurance Company's newly enlarged office complex offered Woolworth a more realistic model of the spatially varied interior. It provided the company's "family" of employees with an array of supporting facilities that echoed the full spectrum of leisure activity afforded by city life: an exercise gym, an auditorium, library, medical and dental clinics, and a dining hall. All were "tightly regulated" and private, however—that is, closed to the public above the first floor.[50]

Woolworth aspired to a level of architectural refinement surpassing that of Friede's imaginary project and to a degree of publicness exceeding that of the Metropolitan Life's officially regulated, sequestered interior. The Woolworth Building's interior as "city" would be not only architecturally, decoratively, and spatially opulent, but also would be noted for the evocations of pleasure and quality of service offered to tenants within its discrete European-inspired interiors, each designed around a theme, like the new and *de rigueur* "adult fantasy environments" of New York's finest hotels, theaters, department stores, restaurants, and roof garden hideaways.[51]

THE ENTRANCE PORTAL AND LOBBY-ARCADE

Gilbert introduced the sidewalk spectator to Woolworth's skyscraper as a particular kind of "city" with his design for its Tudor Gothic portal and monumental lobby-arcade. In doing so, he freely appropriated for commercial use the Beaux-Arts model of the decorated public building. This he had elaborated earlier in his Minnesota State Capitol and United States Custom House. He added spatial precedents and decorative iconography from the Christian masterworks of the Middle Ages. Altogether, he aimed to impress the spectator with visually engaging, didactic, and spiritually uplifting themes. The themes highlighted Woolworth's stature as a merchant, identified the world headquarters of the F. W. Woolworth Company, and projected an ethical image for Woolworth's recently merged, gigantic retailing corporation.

Gilbert accentuated the sidewalk path toward the Tudor Gothic portal with the skyscraper's rhythmic sequences of supporting piers (fig. 6.5). The piers featured allegorical masks representing the four continents—America, Europe, Africa, and Asia—echoing those gracing his United States Custom House. At the portal, Gilbert's decorative iconography reached a climax (fig. 6.6). Small grotesque figures in connected niches engaged in various types of work. They recalled the figures of cathedral portals, but in their new context suggested an homage to the Protestant work ethic. At the corners of the portal, large "Ws" in Gothic script appeared, and in spandrel panels Mercury symbolized commerce and Ceres, abundance. On axis directly above the portal stood an eagle with a shield, recalling that of the Custom House, an adaptation of the seal of the United States.[52] For its flanking niches, Gilbert proposed life-size figures of Jacques Coeur of Bourges and Jean Ango of Dieppe, the French shipping magnates of the fifteenth and sixteenth centuries, Woolworth's supposed progenitors in the history of world trade.[53]

After passing through the Tudor Gothic portal and entering the Woolworth's lobby-arcade, the visitor encountered a space with the monumental proportions and architectural character of a Christian cathedral

FIGURE 6.5 Woolworth Building, view along Broadway showing lower stories with storefronts, ca. 1915. Photograph by Wurts Brothers. Museum of the City of New York.

FIGURE 6.6 Woolworth Building, main entrance showing passersby, April 1913. Unidentified photographer. Collection of the New-York Historical Society, negative 46308.

nave (figs. 6.7, 6.8). In its key features, Gilbert intermingled the Christian masterworks of Europe with Woolworth's favorite consumer settings. His tantalizing arrangement of stairs, balconies and overlooks, for example, echoed those of Woolworth's two favorite Parisian landmarks, the Opéra, and more important, Au Bon Marché. Within the Park Place and Barclay Street entrances, Woolworth had Gilbert insert revolving doors, an early instance of their use in an office building, adapting a strategy used by retailers for easing pedestrian traffic flow.[54] Altogether, the lobby-arcade suggested that Woolworth, like his merchant-rival John Wanamaker, sought to reconcile the

FIGURE 6.7 Woolworth Building, lobby-arcade, looking toward main entrance. Photograph by Wurts Brothers. Museum of the City of New York.

FIGURE 6.8 Woolworth Building, lobby-arcade, view from rotunda showing marble hall. Unidentified photographer. Collection of the New-York Historical Society, negative 78896d.

FIGURE 6.9 Woolworth Building, lobby-arcade, looking from north balcony across rotunda. Photograph by Wurts Brothers. Wurts Collection, Museum of the City of New York.

new, wholly secular culture of consumption with the spiritual ethos of traditional Christianity or, in the words of Wanamaker's partner, Robert Ogden, "practical affairs" with "Christian ideals."[55]

The lobby-arcade's mosaics, crafted by Heinigke and Bowen with blue, red, and gold as predominating colors, recalled those of Woolworth and his competitors' retailing environments—from his own gilded and carmine red signage and faux-ruby jewelry decorating counters to the department stores' iridescent, sparkling mosaics in murals and domes. In the words of Woolworth's own publicity literature, Heinigke and Bowen's mosaics suggested "a flood of dazzling jewels glittering in the sunlight. . . . a riot of harmonious colors, all spread out in golden settings, and arranged in exquisite designs."[56] Such a depth of color, incorporating gilding, light, and reflected light—what William Leach has called the "visual materials of desire"—had become in Gilbert and Woolworth's hands a complex alchemy of signifiers evoking "otherworldly paradises."[57]

The lobby-arcade's cruciform plan and domed central rotunda strongly resembled the early Christian Mausoleum of Galla Placidia in Ravenna (figs. 6.9, 6.10). Its mosaics called to mind the mausoleum—in nature-derived, geometric patterns, stylized flowers, and exotic parrots—along with Gilbert's related sources in the Peacock Throne of Persia and the Church of Santa Costanza in Rome.[58] In 1880, Gilbert produced a watercolor showing the crossing of St. Mark's in Venice, but as his office refined the lobby-arcade's design in 1912, he made a special sketching trip to Venice and Ravenna, writing back to his wife, "I got what I wanted," referring to his studies of Byzantine mosaics.[59] Woolworth, who may well have viewed Gilbert's original Gothic design for the lobby-arcade as too dark and mysterious, appreciated Gilbert's newest studies; he described the design to his managers as "beautiful beyond description," a rival of Hagia Sophia in Constantinople.[60] Gilbert sheathed the lobby-arcade's walls in golden and pink-veined marble from the Greek island of Skyros, and crowned them with lacelike tracery cornices carved by Donnelly and Ricci. Incandescent lighting

FIGURE 6.10 Mausoleum of Galla Placidia, Ravenna, Italy, 425–50. Photograph by Alinari, ca. 1870s. (Courtesy of the Boston Public Library, Print Department.)

washing the undersides of the vaults further enhanced the depth of color and sparkle in the mosaics. Gilded Gothic tracery outlined balustrades and elevator surrounds. The elevator doors, designed by Tiffany Studios, Gilbert had adorned with arabesque tracery patterns in etched steel set off against a gold-plated background.

Like the Woolworth Building's skyscraper Gothic exterior, the lobby-arcade's iconographic decoration hearkened back to the city's antebellum years, that is, to the mercantile era of small-scale enterprise preceding the large-scale industrial corporation's rise to power and dominance. Gilbert had the German immigrant artist C. Paul Jennewein paint two prominent lunette murals, "Labor" and "Commerce," for a conspicuous cross-axial locations over the balconies of the lobby-arcade's two flanking cross arms (figs. 6.11, 6.12).[61] Jennewein's paintings, with their Christian triptych formats and gilded tracery surrounds, reinforced more than any other feature the interior's romantic nostalgia about world commerce. "Labor," positioned high over the balcony to the north, showed a central female figure on a throne, holding a distaff and spindle of flax, and flanked by two kneeling boys offering a sheaf of grain and flax and cluster of fruit. "Commerce," to the south, showed another female figure holding a globe, flanked by two boys bearing a clipper ship and a locomotive.[62] In representing the simpler, preindustrial worlds of agricultural labor and mercantile commerce, the murals distracted the viewer from the less than benign realities identified with contemporary labor and commerce: the wrenching turmoil of the industrial strikes and the cold dynamic of interdependency between the nation's big industrial corporations and its imperialistic policies abroad. They also identified the practices of Woolworth's big corporation with those simpler preindustrial worlds.

On the decorative corbels of cross beams, Gilbert strategically placed whimsical grotesques portraying key figures involved with the skyscraper's design and construction. "Delightfully gay exaggerations without being the least unkind," Donnelly and Ricci modeled the grotesques on caricature sketches by Johnson.[63] At the south flanking cross arm, Woolworth counted the nickels and dimes on which he built his business, and looked straight across the elevator lobby to Gilbert, who carried a miniature model of the Woolworth Building (figs. 6.13, 6.14). Other grotesques showed Aus inspecting a steel beam; Horowitz making a telephone call; Pierson operating a ticker tape machine, its tape inscribed with miniature Woolworth Buildings; and Hogan counting on his fingers, perhaps finalizing a deal. Similar portraits of modern personages posing as medieval saints had appeared in churches, chapels, and seminaries, but the Woolworth's grotesques portrayed instead the capitalist client, architect, builder, and engineer of a commercial skyscraper that surpassed in height the greatest of medieval cathedrals.[64]

For the lobby-arcade's tall and baronial marble hall, Gilbert designed in collaboration with Heinigke and Bowen an allegorical stained-glass ceiling light (see fig. 6.8).[65] The light featured the names and the seals of the world's "great mercantile nations"—Spain, China, Japan, Russia, Italy, the German Empire, Austria, Argentina, Brazil, France, Great Britain, and the United States—and so linked Woolworth's modern enterprise with historic sites of preindustrial wealth. The trademark letter *W* appeared, along with the dates "1879," the year that Woolworth opened

FIGURE 6.11
Woolworth Building, lobby-arcade, view of north balcony showing *Labor*, by C. Paul Jennewein. Photograph by J. C. Maugans, 1913. Collection of the New-York Historical Society, negative 46307a.

FIGURE 6.12
Woolworth Building, lobby-arcade, view of south balcony showing *Commerce,* by C. Paul Jennewein. Photograph by Wurts Brothers. Wurts Collection, Museum of the City of New York.

FIGURE 6.13 Woolworth Building, lobby-arcade, grotesque of Frank Woolworth. Photograph by Franz Jantzen. Collection of the Supreme Court of the United States.

FIGURE 6.14 Woolworth Building, lobby-arcade, grotesque of Cass Gilbert. Photograph by Franz Jantzen. Collection of the Supreme Court of the United States.

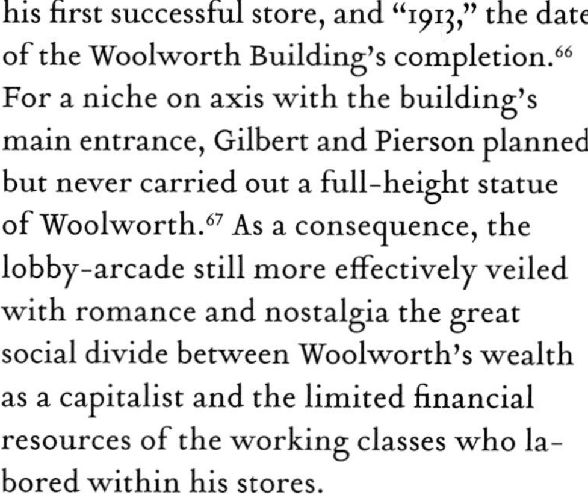

his first successful store, and "1913," the date of the Woolworth Building's completion.[66] For a niche on axis with the building's main entrance, Gilbert and Pierson planned but never carried out a full-height statue of Woolworth.[67] As a consequence, the lobby-arcade still more effectively veiled with romance and nostalgia the great social divide between Woolworth's wealth as a capitalist and the limited financial resources of the working classes who labored within his stores.

Woolworth understood quite well that if his retailing enterprise were to yield profits, its growth and continuity required not just the resource of his own work, but also that of countless others. Thousands of salesgirls worked in his stores and legions of manufacturers and cottage industries supplied the millions of five- and ten-cent goods those stores distributed with an unprecedented speed and efficiency throughout the country and abroad. The lobby-arcade's quasi-religious atmosphere, consequently, not only promoted an ethical image for Woolworth and his enterprise, but exalted the Protestant work ethic. It also suggested that the success of Woolworth's big, industrial-era retailing corporation depended on the ethos of an earlier world of work, that of the slower-paced, preindustrial merchant and agrarian economy—free of labor conflict.

The City Beautiful movement's accepted principle that works of public art could bring an "image before the eye in some concrete form [and] fix the thought in the mind" convincingly expressed Gilbert's larger objective for the decoration of public buildings such as the Minnesota State Capitol and the United States Custom House as well as for the Woolworth's lobby-arcade.[68] In 1914, Gilbert argued that only an "enlightened," and by implication Anglo-Saxon elite, could through cultural means shape an "American" social identity. Its capacity for doing so depended on the indoctrination of the city's immigrant masses with inspirational works of art. "The average man cannot afford to buy and own important works of art. He must, therefore, look to public collections for such things; naturally, then, public buildings furnish an opportunity for this very important educational feature."[69] Gilbert added that once any community became prosperous, there emerged a desire for the "instruction" which came "from the consummation of beautiful works of art."[70] Gilbert's contemporary, the social reformer Benjamin Marsh, by contrast, had by 1908 voiced skepticism about the potential of the City Beautiful movement's decorated public buildings to improve the lives of New York's impoverished immigrant groups. The city's substandard housing conditions, in particular, called for deeper, societally based planning solutions.[71] Gilbert's designs, by contrast, spoke to his and others' persisting belief in their own and the progressive elite's commitment to social uplift and "public improvement" through such works of art.

To Woolworth's advantage, Gilbert's design for the Woolworth Building's lobby-arcade abounded with human scale and interest in its own right. Its medieval imagery had a spiritual aura, standard of craftsmanship, and atmosphere of fantasy that could not fail to impress any visitor. For this reason, it set the stage for the lavish sparkle of ornamentation, color, and metallic facings that distinguished the city's 1920s Art Deco skyscrapers. In his quest for such imagery, Woolworth was hardly seeking an elitist art or architecture reputed for its aristocratic reserve. His broad and populist vision embraced, rather, the nation's small-town main streets and sidewalk shoppers, rural farmers, and urban neighborhoods teeming with immigrant crowds. Their nickels and dimes had spurred the extremely rapid growth of his "consumption community." Consequently, he used every imaginable device to heighten his skyscraper's popularity; he aimed to win over not the few, but rather the many.

TRANSPORTATION NEXUS

In April 1912, Woolworth had the engineering firm Jacobs and Davies explore linking the Woolworth Building's basement story to the new Interborough Rapid Transit Company (IRT) and the Brooklyn Rapid Transit Company (BRT) subway lines with the objective of providing an alternative entrance for tenants and visitors besides the traditional sidewalk path.[72] In choosing to forge a link with the mechanical traffic of lower Broadway—in effect creating his own transportation nexus—Woolworth made his skyscraper an active presence within the traffic patterns of the city. He envisioned its population of tenants and visitors alike traveling to and from its offices with an unparalleled mechanical rapidity and ease.

In forging such a transportation link, Woolworth extended his earlier retailing principle of siting stores near transportation lines into the complex infrastructure supporting lower Broadway's "skyscraper city." He may have been inspired by Clinton and Russell's Mercantile Building (1904) at Fourth Avenue and Twenty-third Street, which featured the city's first "underground sidewalk"; described by one contemporary as a "dream of the future," it led past underground shops to the Fourth Avenue subway station.[73] The Times Building (1903–5) and Hudson Terminal Buildings (1907–9) similarly featured direct access to rail and subway lines. Woolworth's skyscraper as a transportation nexus, however, would stand out as the earliest full-fledged instance of the phenomenon on lower Broadway.

In August 1912, Gilbert conferred with the city's Rapid Transit Commission and then asked the engineers Jacobs and Davies to complete detailed drawings for the skyscraper's underground entrance from both the Interborough's Park Place station and the Brooklyn Rapid Transit's Broadway, or City Hall, Station. By November 1913, after

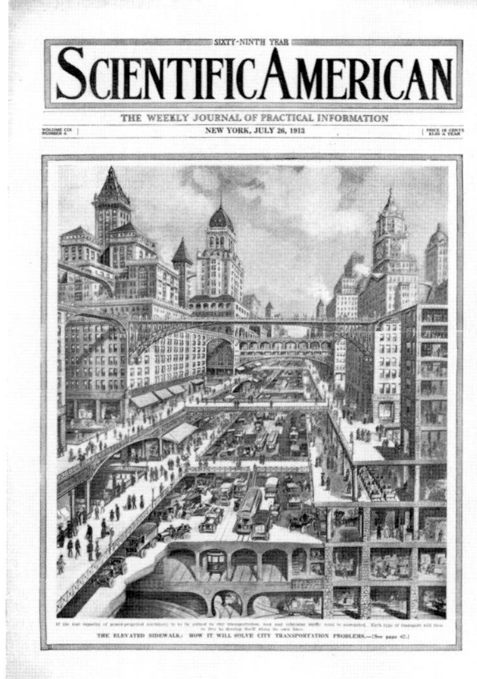
SIXTY-NINTH YEAR

SCIENTIFIC AMERICAN

THE WEEKLY JOURNAL OF PRACTICAL INFORMATION

NEW YORK, JULY 26, 1913

THE ELEVATED SIDEWALK: HOW IT WILL SOLVE CITY TRANSPORTATION PROBLEMS.—(See page 67.)

FIGURE 6.15 Harvey Wiley Corbett, *City of the Future*. From *Scientific American* 109 (July 26, 1913).

negotiating with the city's Public Service Commission regarding a "joint station," Jacobs and Davies proposed designing an underground passageway that connected the two stations.[74] A path leading southward from the west platform of the City Hall Station would direct tenants and visitors beneath Broadway, and then into the skyscraper on its main axis through monumental bronze gates. Once visitors were inside, their path intersected the elevator lobby, rose up the marble stair, and culminated in the lobby-arcade. Jacobs and Davies also provided a second, side entrance beneath Park Place. Woolworth's skyscraper as transportation nexus, then, would feature direct access to two new stations on the city's two principal subway lines.

Woolworth may have been inspired by the popular imagery illustrating lower Broadway as a multilevel transportation center: proliferating skyscrapers and systems of movement rose above the street in Harry M. Pettit's "King's Dream of New York" of 1908 and Richard Rummell's "Future New York" of 1911, both of which illustrated *King's Views of New York*.[75] Harvey Wiley Corbett's imaginary "City of the Future" (1913) showed comparable systems of transportation segregated in levels below ground according to type, with direct access to the systems from the lower stories of adjacent buildings (fig. 6.15). Woolworth's design preceded Corbett's by over a year. All inspired European avant-garde projects such as Antonio Sant'Elia's *Città nuova* (1914).[76] They also set the stage for rail traffic's further elaboration in the late 1920s in the city's most noted complex of skyscrapers, Rockefeller Center (1929–40).

In addition to connecting the Woolworth Building with New York's broader dynamic of infrastructural movement, Woolworth envisioned extending that dynamic of movement vertically. Perhaps inspired by the city's new subway system, he distinguished the skyscraper's system of elevators by its high speeds, large number of cars, and "express" and "local" service (fig. 6.16). Real estate experts ranked efficient elevator service among the most marketable of tenant conveniences. As such, it strongly influenced a skyscraper's "earning possibilities."[77] Gilbert's elevator consultant, Charles E. Knox of the engineers Mailloux and Knox, noted that he faced "an extremely knotty problem considered from every standpoint," given that Woolworth expected the skyscraper to receive some forty-two thousand visitors a day.[78] Knox's solution comprised a total of twenty-eight Otis Company electric elevators, twenty-four of which were designated for use by tenants. All employed the company's high-speed electric gearless traction technology, which it had developed in 1902, with the exception of the observatory's four-story shuttle elevator.[79] For the Woolworth's tower, Knox proposed three express elevators, all of which operated at the record-breaking speed of seven hunred feet per minute, a speed for which he had to seek special approval from the Manhattan Bureau of Buildings.[80] After the elevators made their first stop at the twenty-eighth story, they would travel nonstop to the fifty-first story, with each cab rising a total height of 696 feet. The skyscraper's other elevators would run at the near equally high speed of six hundred feet per minute.

FIGURE 6.16 Woolworth Building, system of twenty-nine Otis Company electric elevators. From *The Master Builders: A Record of the Construction of the World's Highest Commercial Structure* (New York: Hugh McAtamney & Co., 1913). Author's collection.

Besides seeking the efficiencies of speed, Gilbert and Knox designed the Woolworth Building's system of elevators for the highest efficiency in transporting tenants and visitors. When completed, the system carried up to 6,000 passengers per hour.[81] Gilbert attributed the efficiency to Knox's reduction of the floor area served by each elevator car from the typical 40,000 square feet to an area of between 13,500 and 18,000 square feet. The resulting large number of small cars, as opposed to a small number of large cars, Gilbert argued, provided multiple options for vertical travel per passenger and so reduced both waiting time and congestion.[82] Knox enhanced the system's efficiency still further with his rationalized time schedule, similar to that of train dispatching, which employed a method that

FIGURE 6.17
Woolworth Building, elevator dispatcher's desk in south balcony, lobby-arcade. Avery Architectural and Fine Arts Library, Columbia University.

one contemporary judged a worthy example of Taylor-inspired "scientific management."[83] From the lobby's mezzanine, an elevator dispatcher seated before a panel with lights indicating each car's position of speed and travel controlled the entire system (fig. 6.17). The dispatcher communicated with individual cars by telephone, in case "any operator, who by intention or neglect, should develop a habit of disregarding the up and down signals, and thus give the tenant reason for complaint."[84]

To assuage tenants' fears about elevator travel to unprecedented heights at record-breaking speeds, Woolworth aimed to make his elevators "accident proof": he had Gilbert equip all cars with the most reliable of safety devices, notable among them the highly touted, but exotic and costly "air cushions."[85] Elevator accidents, although rare and reportedly one-sixteenth as frequent as surface rail accidents in Manhattan in 1911, had nonetheless continued to be a cause of public fear.[86] The air cushion technology, patented by F. T. Ellithorpe and described by one contemporary as "nothing more than an enclosed hatchway with properly graduated air escapes," had been in use since 1879 when tested publicly in the Board of Trade Building in Chicago.[87] During an elevator accident of any kind, the air cushions would cause a falling car to function like a loose-fitting piston within the elevator shaft, gradually bouncing to a stop on a pressurized volume of air, and so preserving the lives of the occupants trapped within.

Woolworth decided to install the Woolworth Building's air cushions well after Thompson-Starrett had finished constructing the elevator shafts, and as a consequence, he complicated the expected sequence of completion with additional shop drawings and "night work" by Thompson-Starrett's construction crew.[88] The crew sealed and strengthened the elevator shafts to withstand the immense pressures created by the technology, adding heavy steel plates and reinforced concrete extending upward in height to the skyscraper's fourth, fifth, seventh, eighth, and eleventh stories, with the number of stories depending on the total distance each particular car traveled.[89] New York's newspapers reported in advance that Ellithorpe would be accompanying Thomas E. Brown, Jr., the Otis consulting engineer responsible for the cushions, to test their effectiveness by occupying a car plummeting in free fall.[90] Instead, on October 16, Ellithorpe's associates loaded elevator car number one with a ballast of 7500 pounds to mimic the weight of several passengers, and then dropped the car for the first time from the skyscraper's fifteenth story and for the second time from its forty-sixth story, while George Wells of Gilbert's office carefully watched and recorded what he saw. "The shock when [the car] reached the air cushion was very strong, and the air whistled out through every crevice, and there was considerable noise when it struck the bottom. There was no indication when examined later that any damage had been done to the car or its contents. . . . The engineers who had seen other tests stated that this was what they called a 'very beautiful landing,' and that there is no doubt whatever that if this had been a car filled with passengers, it would have saved their lives."[91] That was probably the news Woolworth wanted to hear. He and Gilbert aimed to provide not only the fastest and finest, but also the safest of high-speed vertical railways.

Altogether, Woolworth's vision of his skyscraper as a transportation nexus, incorporating access to electrified systems of subway travel as well as to high-speed elevator transportation featuring up-to-date safety devices, epitomized in microcosm the dynamism and the modernity of the new "skyscraper city" concentrated around lower Broadway. It offered tenants all that could be expected with regard to speed and efficiency when moving to, from, and through the interior of his big skyscraper. In this, the Woolworth Building had few rivals among the New York office buildings of its day.

THE F. W. WOOLWORTH COMPANY HEADQUARTERS

The F. W. Woolworth Company's corporate headquarters—a short trip vertically by Tiffany-decorated elevator to the skyscraper's twenty-fourth story—functioned hierarchically as the single most important architectural interior of his "city within a city." For Woolworth, its purpose for receiving an imagined audience of visitors rivaled that of a city hall (fig. 6.18). At the headquarters' heart stood his own marble-clad executive office or "Empire Room," which Gilbert had Baumgarten and Company furnish in a Napoleonic "Empire style" (fig. 6.19). Adjacent offices housed Woolworth's "inner New York circle," as he called it, or the company's vice presidents along with its corporate treasurer

FIGURE 6.18 *(above)* Woolworth Building, F. W. Woolworth Company, twenty-fourth-story headquarters, view from elevator lobby. Photograph by Wurts Brothers. Wurts Collection, Museum of the City of New York.

FIGURE 6.19 *(below)* Woolworth Building, Empire Room, F. W. Woolworth's executive office, twenty-fourth story. Unidentified photographer. Woolworth Collection, National Building Museum.

and secretary, and meeting rooms for its executive committee and board of directors.[92] Like other corporate chiefs—among them the *World's* Joseph Pulitzer, who occupied an executive office in the World Building's domed rotunda, or the Singer Manufacturing Company's Frederick G. Bourne, who established his headquarters on the Singer Tower's thirty-fourth floor—Woolworth chose a hierarchically prominent location for his own chief executive office along with those of his assisting executives.

Such "power locations" within skyscrapers—with height, light, space, and commanding urban views—had since the early 1890s symbolized their occupants' ascendancy, financially and socially, within the city. Woolworth, perhaps seeking to surpass Pulitzer and Bourne's single "power locations," asked Gilbert to design at least three such locations within his skyscraper. Besides the "Empire Room," Gilbert and his office designed a fortieth-story private apartment for Woolworth in the Renaissance style (plate 8, fig. 6.20). One contemporary journalist called the apartment the world's highest and "most desirable location."[93] Its decoration suggested the domestic setting of a Renaissance "merchant prince," complete with a Flemish Renaissance tapestry and an Italian Renaissance fireplace mantle. It is not known whether Woolworth had a mistress or mistresses, but in addition to his Renaissance apartment, he asked Gilbert to create a "private suite of rooms" in the twenty-fifth story's south wing, among them his own "extra sleeping room so I would not be obliged to remain there alone at night."[94] Whether by day or by night, then, Woolworth's skyscraper had begun to take on the character of a luxurious men's club, albeit a club commanded independently by Woolworth from his various locations on high.

Woolworth lavished special care on every detail of his "Empire Room." He described his executive office to his store managers in 1914 as the "handsomest office of any corporation in this country, and possibly the world," adding that his 1912 visits to Napoleon's palaces in Compiègne and Fountainebleu and to Napoleon's Chateau of Malmaison inspired its design.[95] Besides the room's "Empire style" furnishings, Baumgarten and Company crafted two copies of what Woolworth called Napoleon's "famous throne chair in the Palace of Fountainbleu."[96] Of greatest significance to Woolworth, Baumgarten and Company's "Empire Room" functioned as a museum-like setting for his own private "exhibition" of Napoleonic memorabilia, most of which he had recently acquired in Paris. The memorabilia included a large portrait of Napoleon in his coronation robes, copied from an original at Versailles, a bronze inkwell depicting Napoleon on horseback, a clock supposedly given to Napoleon by Czar Alexander I of Russia, and a life-sized bust in bronze of Napoleon posing as Julius Caesar.[97] Woolworth complained to Gilbert about Baumgarten and Company's "too elaborate" design, finding its dominant use of red "too gaudy and too luxurious for a business office."[98] But still he, like his elite contemporaries who shopped in the city's finest consumer emporiums, had used the Empire Room to fashion his own social identity as Napoleon-like through his conspicuous consumption of Napoleonic objects and memorabilia.

Woolworth outlined for his corporate managers the ideological objectives underlying his choice of Napoleon's "Empire style." First of all, "the business of the F. W. Woolworth Company is an empire in itself," and second, the style belonged to Napoleon as his "own" style. Napoleon,

FIGURE 6.20 Woolworth Building, F. W. Woolworth's private apartment, fortieth story. Unidentified photographer. Woolworth Collection, National Building Museum.

more than just a general, Woolworth added, had also achieved a reputation as a "wonderful businessman" and "an originator in nearly everything." Napoleon's style, consequently, visually crystallized for Woolworth the F. W. Woolworth Company's postmerger corporate ideology. "We have done things on entirely original lines. Our originality is the principal cause of our success. We did not adhere to the old methods formerly used by various merchants throughout the country. . . . Furthermore, the Woolworth Building stands alone among all buildings of the world as the most beautiful erected by man, and the building is practically original. . . . Could there be anything more appropriate for an office of this character than to copy the works of a man who did original things?"[99] Woolworth's desire to be at once both original and to copy sounds contradictory, but he was, in fact, faced as a chief executive with fabricating a full-fledged "corporate culture" where no such culture had previously existed. Napoleon's military model, with its allusions of territorial conquest and grandeur, served as an especially useful tool for building loyalty and inculcating devotion among his "lieutenants" and "generals," that is, Woolworth's core audience in the internal promotion of the company's corporate mission. To that end, Woolworth instructed his regional executives and store managers to visit the Woolworth Building, to call on the chief executive, and to inspect the Napoleonic items in the miniature museum of his "Empire Room." In 1915, he reported to them all that the Empire Room had won "the admiration of everyone who has had the chance to visit it."[100] Consequently, in a grandly artificial manifestation of what the historian Eric Hobsbawm has called the "invented tradition," Woolworth's Napoleonic ritual furthered his purpose of constructing a corporate community among his wholly new, and still yet to be fully initiated, postmerger managerial hierarchy.[101]

Beyond his bold utilization of Napoleonic imagery for crafting a corporate identity with the architecture of his executive offices, Woolworth promoted the Woolworth Building among his executive hierarchy and store managers as a national headquarters and type of "imperial capital." Corporate literature illustrated the skyscraper surrounded by speculative office blocks housing the F. W. Woolworth Company's district headquarters, among them the Rialto Building in San Francisco, the Blake Building in Boston, and the McCormick Building in Chicago (fig. 6.21).[102] The F. W. Woolworth Company's twenty-fourth-story executive offices and Woolworth's "empire room" could be identified in illustrations as housed within the topmost running arcade of the skyscraper's main office block, just beneath its architecturally elaborated crown. Such a depiction of the F. W. Woolworth Company's architectural holdings, with the landmark skyscraper standing at the center of a composition surrounded by the district headquarters in tall office blocks, visually reinforced the

FIGURE 6.21 Woolworth Building surrounded by office buildings housing regional headquarters. From F. W. Woolworth Co., *Fortieth Anniversary Souvenir, 1879–1919* (New York, 1919).

strongly pyramidal character of the company's corporate hierarchy. It also suggested that Woolworth's conception of himself and his managers as "one big united family," which dated from the early 1890s, had now succeeded as his preferred strategy for inculcating among the men a shared sense of mission.

OFFICE INTERIORS AND TENANT NEIGHBORHOODS

Given New York's frenzy of overbuilding and the keen competition for tenants, Woolworth and his rental agent Edward Hogan relied heavily on newspaper publicity, which they and others called "free advertisements," for the purpose of promoting the Woolworth Building's offices to tenants.[103] The handsomely illustrated booklet entitled *The Woolworth Building (Highest in the World)* (1912), which they directed toward the prospective tenant who happened to inquire about space, served as their most lavish piece of formal advertising.[104] Woolworth and Hogan also paid for print advertising in the city's real estate journals and newspapers, and in March 1912, they placed a full-page advertisement in *Record and Guide*, which touted the Woolworth Building as "the highest, safest, and most perfectly appointed office structure in the world." They also noted that the Broadway–Park Place Company had secured for the skyscraper's offices "permanent light and air" because it faced three streets and embraced a sizable light court, and because no new skyscrapers would rise beside its end walls.[105] Then, in a series of notices printed in the *New York Times* during 1912 and 1913, Hogan heralded the Woolworth Building's accessibility—"close to the City Hall, to the courts, and to the new Municipal Building" and at "the converging point of nearly 50 transportation lines" (fig. 6.22).[106] Of greatest

THE NEW YORK TIMES, SUNDAY, APRIL 27, 1913.

MONTCLAIR

Furnished

F. M. Crawley & Bros.

WOOLWORTH BUILDING

Edward J. Hogan
Agent
Woolworth
Building
Phone
Barclay

YOUR OFFICE, YOUR STORE, YOUR SHOWROOM IN THE WOOLWORTH BUILDING IS THE CONVERGING POINT OF NEARLY 50 TRANSPORTATION LINES—2 SUBWAYS; 4 ELEVATED LINES; 2 TUNNELS; JERSEY, BROOKLYN AND STATEN ISLAND FERRIES; 2 BRIDGES AND DOZENS OF SURFACE LINES COVERING BOTH MANHATTAN AND BROOKLYN.

EVERY MODERN DEVICE IS INCORPORATED IN THE BUILDING TO MAKE THE TRANSACTION OF BUSINESS MORE EFFICIENT. WHETHER YOU OCCUPY AN ENTIRE FLOOR OR A SUITE OF ROOMS OR A SINGLE OFFICE, YOU RECEIVE THE BENEFIT OF THE WOOLWORTH BUILDING'S COMFORT, SAFETY AND CONVENIENCE.

RAILROADS, INDUSTRIAL CORPORATIONS, MEMBERS OF THE BAR, ARCHITECTS AND BUSINESS MEN DESIRING HIGH CLASS OFFICES SHOULD INSPECT THOSE IN THE WOOLWORTH BUILDING BEFORE RENEWING THEIR PRESENT LEASES.

Offices and Studios For Rent

The best advertised and most exclusive office building in New York. To those whose business needs are best served by having quarters in a well-known and superb edifice, the opportunity is offered to secure an office, or studio in

Aeolian Hall
29-31-33 West 42nd St.

Considering its unequalled advantages, rents are exceedingly reasonable.
Send for descriptive book.
Renting office on premises.

PEASE & ELLIMAN
340 Madison Ave. Tel. 6200 Murray Hill

Seashore and Country
Red Bank Estates

Red Bank Estates

Exclusive Suburban Homes Located in the Garden Spot of Northern New Jersey
$4,500 — BUY A HOME — $10,000

HILLSDALE ESTATES.

W. J. RICH, 802 Singer Bldg

MONTVALE, N. J.

7-ROOM BUNGALOW.
HAYES & REARDON,

NEW FURNISHED COTTAGE

Lease Your Tenements
We Have Clients.
J. ROMAINE BROWN CO.,

"THE HEART OF NEW YORK"

Vanderbilt Avenue Building
Vanderbilt Avenue, 42nd to 43rd Street
Facing Grand Central Terminal

The stores in the Vanderbilt Avenue Building will do phenomenal business—in the course of a year they will be constantly before the eyes of millions of people. The ideal location for a Jeweler, Optician, Haberdasher, Florist, Hatter, Milliner or Boot and Shoe Dealer.

The office floors have light on all four sides. They are particularly desirable as New York headquarters for out-of-town concerns and as offices of business men who live along the

ARCHITECTS BVILDING
NORTHEAST CORNER OF 40th STREET & PARK AVE.

THIS admirably located office building will open Thursday, May 1st. Desirable offices and larger space at extremely reasonable rentals. ARCHITECTS, BUILDING TRADES, AND GENERAL LINES of business will find the building especially adapted. Maximum light and air. Within four hundred feet of the new Grand Central Terminal and Subway Express Station. An immediate inspection of this unusual building in the new uptown professional and business centre will prove advantageous to you.

Ewing, Bacon & Henry, Agent
101 Park Av. Phone Murray Hill 2500

FIGURE 6.22
"Woolworth Building," advertisement. From *New York Times*, Sunday, April 27, 1913. (Copyright 1913 *The New York Times*. Reprinted by permission.)

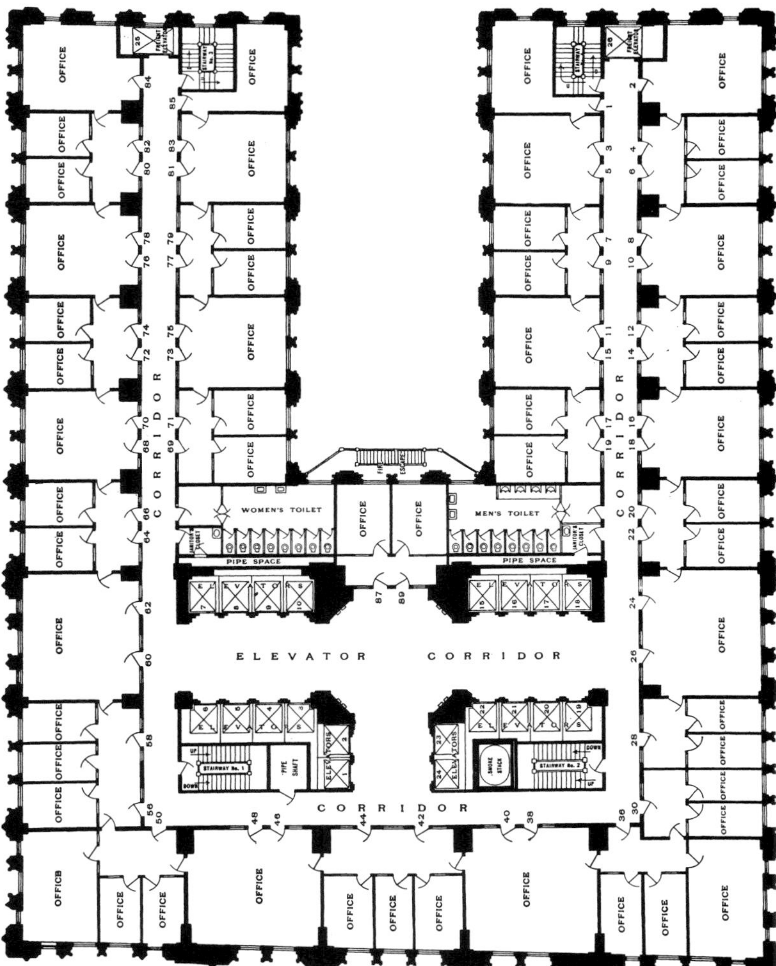

FIGURE 6.23
Woolworth Building, typical floor plan. From *National Architect*, vol. 1 (November 1912).

importance, Hogan's advertisements suggested, the skyscraper's fame and beauty reflected well upon "the highest type of businessman." Such a businessman identified his enterprise with an image of the Woolworth Building in letterheads and brochures, "a building whose reputation adds prestige to his prestige in the commercial world."[107]

The Woolworth Building offered prospective tenants a total of 563,150 square feet of office space, or nearly thirteen acres, boasting the city's largest total floor area when it opened, with 15,600 on each floor of the twenty-eight-story main office block and an average of 3,900 on each floor of the tower (figs. 6.23, 6.24). The Broadway–Park Place Company charged the highest rental rates for the tower offices, $4.00 a square foot, arguing that they cost the most to build and maintain. They priced the offices facing Broadway nearly as steeply—such "front" offices provided desirable and prestigious views of City Hall Park, the East River, and the Brooklyn Bridge.[108] They offered space within the Woolworth's ground-floor arcade at twice the price of the average office story and graded the rates in the main office block to rise in cost in accordance with the distance of each story from the sidewalk.[109]

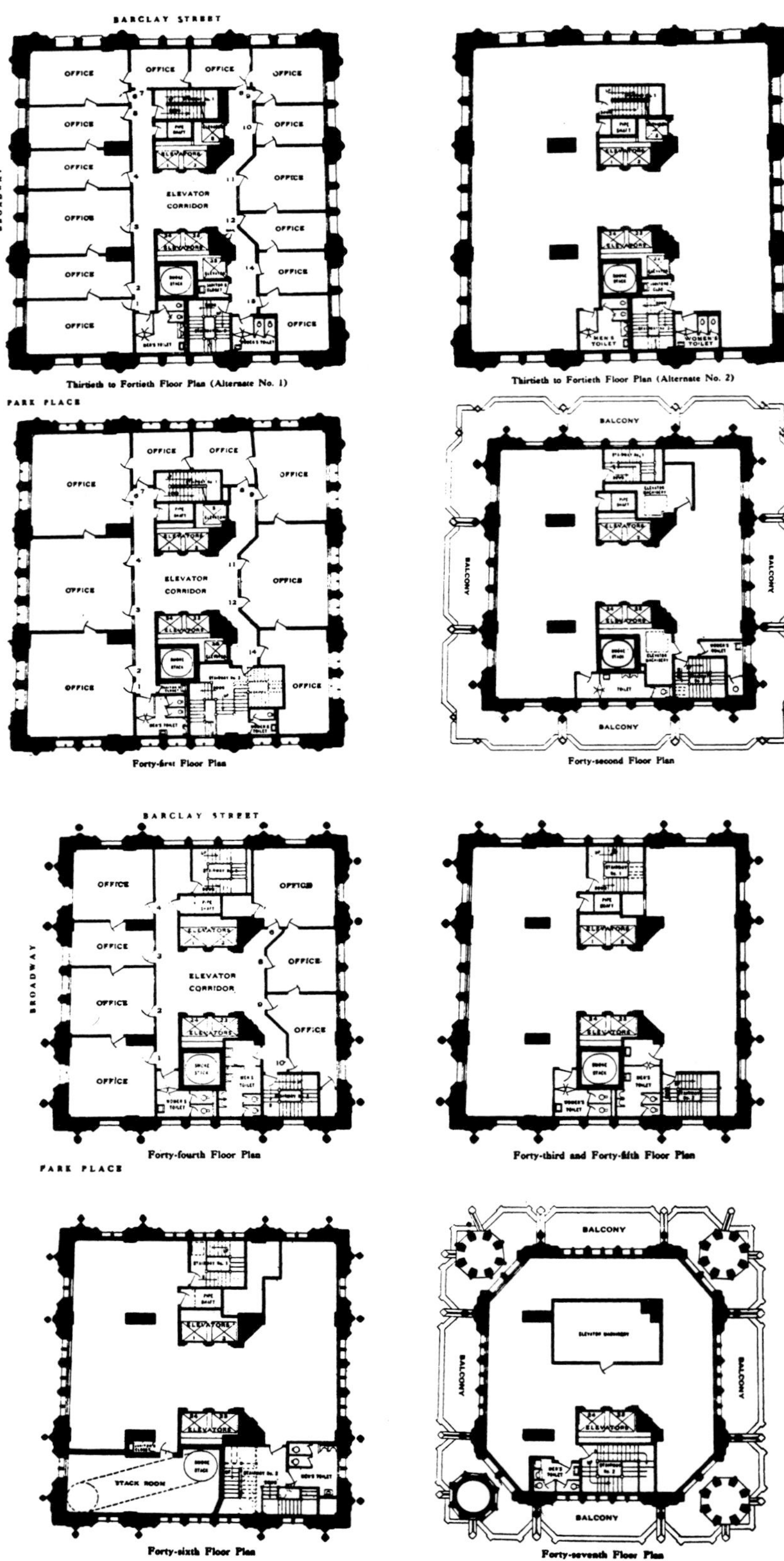

FIGURE 6.24
Woolworth Building, tower, floor plans. From *National Architect*, vol. 1 (November 1912).

The skyscraper attracted enough tenants to open and operate on a paying basis by May 1, 1913, and one year later, a reporter observed, "[The] fact that [the Woolworth Building] is tolerably well-filled is due to publicity given it."[110]

In *The Woolworth Building (Highest in the World)* and related advertisements, Hogan promoted the tower—once it soared free of the main office block—for the unusually high quality of its office interiors. As a "large building in itself" with "permanently unobstructed light and air," the tower provided "the most desirable offices in the world." Its height of 792 feet, taller than originally planned, may have inspired Woolworth to claim at the skyscraper's opening ceremony a sixty-story building as opposed to fifty-five. He arrived at the new count by adding to the skyscraper's two basement floors three "new" stories in the tower, two of which he created from the mezzanine stories, and the third from the observatory's crowning lantern.[111]

The *New York Times* had already noted in 1910 that a tenant housed in such a tall tower would gain a special distinction within the city, "as its pinnacle, which will be brilliantly illuminated at night, will be discernible at a distance of fifty miles or more from the city, a prominent mark in the landscape."[112] Then, in May 1911, Gilbert told the *Times* that Woolworth had just received an early application for "the highest office space to be rented . . . one or more rooms a few feet below the apex of the tower."[113] Such tower offices indeed attracted what Lincoln Steffens called "high livers," or tenants "who will not have an office unless it is up where the air is cool and fresh, the outlook broad and beautiful, and where there is silence in the heart of business."[114] Still, most of the offices in the Woolworth Building's tower, with the exception of those on the thirty-seventh, thirty-eighth, and thirty-ninth floors, rented last.[115] In December 1913, a reporter for the *Wall Street Journal* attributed the tower's checkered rental performance to the "long elevator journey" required to reach its offices, to the "comparative isolation" of those offices, and to skeptical tenants "honest enough to admit a shade of dread or doubt."[116] By May 1914, however, the tower offices did indeed begin to fill up, suggesting that they had won a special status as preferred locations within the city.[117]

In soliciting the skyscraper's tenants, Woolworth and his rental agent Hogan understood quite well the contemporary perception that an office building, "like a neighborhood," possessed a distinctive social character: "One's neighbors in an office building," Hogan advised prospective tenants, "should not differ in character from the neighbors in a home center."[118] The charm of one enterprise, he had privately reasoned, could be used to draw others, so that as Steffens had put it, an owner might establish the social reputation necessary for "permanent success."[119] In May 1915, Woolworth proudly reported to his executives and store managers that lawyers, publishers, manufacturers, contractors, and consulting engineers—a white-collar community reflecting well on his skyscraper as a rental enterprise—numbered among the Woolworth Building's new and prominent tenants.[120] That August, he told Gilbert that the skyscraper, on account of its tenantry's high caliber, had become a "success financially."[121] By 1924, the F. W. Woolworth Company's president, Hubert T. Parson, described the skyscraper as fully occupied and reaping the prestige of a first-class, luxury office building.[122]

In designing for such an elite class of tenants, Gilbert invested the Woolworth Building's interior with a spaciousness and grandeur that surpassed the day's typical office building. As he put it in Beaux-Arts compositional terms, "We have endeavored to express the plan."[123] On the typical upper floor, he joined a cross-shaped elevator lobby with symmetrically disposed corridors to suggest a monumentality and elegance that vied with those of the day's public buildings (see fig. 6.23). The lobbies' grand, octagonal centers echoed the lobby-arcade's great, domed rotunda.[124] Marble terrazzo floors and wainscots of Italian marble, the type of marble varying story to story, further heightened the interior's aura of opulence and grandeur. Still, Gilbert never lost sight of spatial economy in office planning: "I have endeavored to make a straightforward, simple plan, so that every part of the building can be reached by the most direct lines of communication, so that every office is well lighted, well ventilated, and well equipped."[125] Woolworth, ever in search of the magnificent as well as the modern, may well have felt confident that he and Gilbert had produced one of the most competitive office interiors in the city.

Throughout the interiors of the Woolworth's typical office stories, light filtered through internal glass partitions into corridors. The typical office depth of about twenty-six feet fell within the standard dimensional range for good natural illumination, and the typical height from floor to floor rose to a generous twelve and one-half feet (see fig. 6.4).[126] The spatial graciousness of such typical office interiors is evident in a June 1917 view of the American Steel Export Company's purchasing department (fig. 6.25). Stories housing distinctive establishments rose still higher, among them the fifteen-foot-high twenty-fourth story, housing the F. W. Woolworth Company's headquarters, and the twenty-foot-high twenty-sixth story, which was

FIGURE 6.25 Woolworth Building, American Steel Export Company, purchasing department. Photograph by Wurts Brothers. Museum of the City of New York.

to house the proposed New Amsterdam Club. The offices in the tower had extraordinary qualities of space and light (see fig. 6.24). Fulfilling the claims of Hogan's advertising, they boasted floor-to-floor heights of typically twelve and one-half to thirteen and one-half feet, but on the thirty-seventh, forty-seventh, and fifty-first floors the heights rose to seventeen and one-half feet, and on the forty-first floor, to twenty feet. The offices had, moreover, advantageously shallower depths. No tenant had to face a light court, and every office claimed a spectacular view. On the forty-third and forty-ninth floors, they opened via tall windows onto airy terraces high above the city, with red-tiled floors and flanking buttresses of a gigantic scale.

The social composition of the Woolworth Building's tenantry around 1915 reflected that of comparably big office buildings built in New York prior to World War I. Not a single one of the skyscraper's original tenants occupied an entire floor. In choosing the Woolworth Building, the tenants also chose a specific location within the city, for reasons of what is currently known as efficiency of "spatial proximity."[127] The building's many lawyers, for example, sought the advantages of locating near their clients in the financial district or near the courthouses of the civic center. Its consulting engineers, similarly, may well have appreciated their nearness to lower Manhatttan's flurry of construction activity. Within the building itself, moreover, tenants formed in their spatial arrangements independent neighborhoods, echoing and reaffirming the metaphor of the skyscraper as a small city.[128] Even as early as 1913, a group of railroad-related publishing concerns had clustered together on the twenty-second floor, gramophone and dictaphone interests on the twentieth floor, and railroad and telegraph businesses on the eighteenth floor. Petroleum, paving, and asphalt interests occupied the sixteenth story, construction-related enterprises the tenth story, and real estate agents the eighth story.[129] Businesses that benefited economically from mutual interaction or from their associations with the same types of customers found it advantageous to group together in such neighborhoods.

Once the Woolworth Building's tenants established their offices or suites of offices, their spatial domains expanded or contracted over subsequent years in response to their economic fortunes. In 1914, for example, the Union Bag and Paper Company chose offices in the south wing of the skyscraper's nineteenth story, the Foundation Company in the north wing, and the Nestle's Food Company in the south wing of the twenty-fifth story.[130] By 1924, the Union Bag and Paper Company had expanded into the north wing of the nineteenth story, the Foundation Company had left the building, and Nestle's remained in its original quarters. The Woolworth's largest tenants at the time comprised the Union Bag and Paper Company, the Radio Corporation of America, the Merchant's Association, Fordham University, and the New York State Tax Commission.[131] Small professional firms, mostly lawyers and accountants, rented the offices in the tower.

As an enthusiast of the railroads during his youth and a self-professed admirer of "the great big railroad corporations," Woolworth boasted to his store managers in 1915 that fifteen railroads had established themselves within his skyscraper.[132] The Woolworth Building also housed tenants renowned for innovations in communications technologies, noted among them the Italian inventor Guglielmo Marconi, who took a suite of offices on the eighteenth floor. Marconi's Wireless Telegraph Company of America, the precursor of the Radio Corporation of America, had patented in 1897 a radio set, or "Marconi set," for marine transportation communication. On January 19, 1903, Marconi sent the world's first transatlantic radio message from President Theodore Roosevelt to King Edward VII of England. By 1912, his company had linked several land stations with ships out at sea to form a single, instantaneous worldwide web of communication. As part of the Woolworth Building's opening celebration in 1913, Marconi transmitted news of the event across the Atlantic.[133] The Woolworth Building attracted related news media enterprises as well, among them the American Association of Foreign Language Newspapers, the Hartford City Paper Company, the *Hardware Review*, and the *Railway Age Gazette*.[134]

Important for Woolworth, in 1914 the New York's Merchants' Association set up a headquarters on the Woolworth Building's ninth floor. Organized in 1897 and formerly located at 54 Lafayette Street, the association's membership comprised leading New York businessmen and professionals, Woolworth and Gilbert among them; soon enough, it was reputed to be "a prime mover of civic advertisement."[135] Just prior to relocating in the Woolworth Building, the association had surveyed the city "from every trade and commercial angle," seeking to do away with "lost motion" in an "era of scientific management."[136] It promoted business travel as well as tourism to the city by securing special excursion rates from the railroads, selling the city as a summer resort, and otherwise calling attention to the city's cultural attractions. Given its mission, it is not unusual that the association spoke with pride about its new headquarters in Woolworth's skyscraper. "No other office building in this city or in any other city will surpass the Woolworth Building," it boasted in its *Bulletin* of November 1912.[137] Aspects of the association's mission resonated with Woolworth's: He, too, had built his skyscraper as a form of advertising, and he, too, reaped financial advantages from celebrating its location in New York.

Woolworth proudly spoke of a tenant's having received a letter from Germany addressed with "nothing but the party's name and 'Woolworth Building,'" and of his own secretary's having received a postcard addressed merely "The Highest Building in the World."[138] The Woolworth Building's fame as a skyscraper served as a magnet for certain classes of elite tenants. By 1921, more than two-hundred export firms had reportedly chosen the skyscraper for its ability to raise their profile internationally.[139] A "Miss Anna Morgan," the daughter of J. P. Morgan, asked Woolworth for an office in which to carry out her social work.[140] Four federal courts along with judge's chambers set up quarters on the Woolworth Building's twelfth floor, and so did the comptroller of the State of New York.[141]

Altogether, the tenants who occupied the Woolworth Building comprised a variegated and ever-changing mosaic of prominent individuals, firms, and related smaller neighborhoods. The Broadway–Park Place Company placed at their service a staff that reportedly numbered nearly four hundred in 1921, including maintenance workers, a police force, and a night watchman who made hourly patrols.[142] Secure in their white-collar status, the Woolworth's tenants represented little of the city's actual ethnic diversity. Still, together with the staff that served them they formed a social hierarchy echoing that of a small city. As Steffens put it, the modern high building, "distinctly of this day and of this country," constituted an enterprise in and of itself that contained "all the other modes of enterprise," and so was "comprehensively typical."[143] No other building type mirrored so accurately the social reality of the white-collar working experience.

SEMIPUBLIC SETTINGS FOR FANTASY AND CONSUMPTION

Within the tall volume of space on the Woolworth Building's main floor, Woolworth had Gilbert design Irving National Bank's spacious banking hall to suggest old Elizabethan halls and houses. Gilbert used the same style for the bank president's office, the conference room, and the Broadway Trust Company's private offices (figs. 6.26, 6.27). The skyscraper's basement rathskeller Gilbert patterned after the cellars of medieval German *Rathäuser*, or city halls, in which merchants originally gathered and beer was sold, choosing as his specific source the medieval rathaus in Lüneburg (fig. 6.28).[144] For the basement swimming pool, Gilbert hired the decorating firm Mack, Jenney, and Tyler to paint wall panels suggesting a "Pompeiian" bath; earlier, Hogan sought his advice regarding which style, Russian or Turkish, might have the greatest appeal to prospective tenants (plate 9).[145] At the top of the main office block, Woolworth had Gilbert organize the New Amsterdam Club around a central grill reminiscent of "Old Amsterdam."[146] In conceiving such settings, Woolworth and Gilbert skillfully crafted architectural illusions evoking cosmopolitanism and

FIGURE 6.26 Woolworth Building, Irving National Bank, banking hall. Unidentified photographer. Woolworth Collection, National Building Museum.

FIGURE 6.27 Woolworth Building, Broadway Trust Company, offices. Unidentified photographer. Woolworth Collection, National Building Museum.

European travel. These they supported with "every necessary comfort and convenience."[147] Woolworth expected the most fastidious of tenants. His skyscraper would rival if not surpass in opulence and sophistication the most splendid of New York's settings for elite consumption.

In March 1913, Wells reported that Mack, Jenney, and Tyler had twenty-six artists and craftsmen at work in the Woolworth's lobby-arcade, applying colorful stencil patterns and pure gold leaf. In the basement's German rathskeller, Frederick J. Wiley and more than a dozen artist-assistants painted detailed medieval hunting scenes showing castles, horsemen, troubadours, and galleons in the lunettes of the vaults, along with nature-inspired motifs and medieval German adages.[148] Woolworth appreciated such standards of craft integrity, whether as demonstrated by the quality of the handcrafted commodities he purchased from European cottage industries or by the fine architectural workmanship he associated with European landmarks such as the Paris Opéra. He understood their relation to the public perceptions of his own ethics as well as those of his retailing enterprise.[149] But he also understood the value of craftsmanship to the projection of "authenticity" within his envisioned illusory settings.

Just as department store retailers aimed to "eliminate the store" by "weaving through it some central ideas," so, too, did Woolworth attempt to eliminate the office building as an ordinary work environment by weaving through it architectural-theatrical settings that fulfilled his imagined tenants' most fantastic consumer longings.[150] Matthew Arnold, Charles Eliot Norton, and other nineteenth-century literary critics had long ago identified high culture, or knowledge of "the best which has been thought and said in the world," with the cultivation of a high moral character, but by the early twentieth century, Woolworth and other modern retailers had appropriated the trappings of that high culture with a wholly contrasting purpose in mind.[151] They along with New York's hoteliers and restaurateurs furthered its commodification through the production for customers of the finest but also the most convincingly illusory historical settings, in a trend that peaked in the 1920s.[152] In doing so, they offered the city's economic elite a means of escaping the streets' grimmer realities, and so becoming free of "ugliness" or "pain" in their retreat within such secluded and evocative illusory worlds.[153] The Woolworth Building's European-inspired interiors, moreover, like those of the city's most elegant settings for consumption, supported that elite's long-held fantasy of "owning" the best in the world.

Woolworth had experienced the city's full array of prominent sites for high-style consumption, but in comfort, opulence, and refinement, the Woolworth Building's

FIGURE 6.28 Woolworth Building, rathskeller. Unidentified photographer. Woolworth Collection, National Building Museum.

semipublic spaces most closely rivaled those of its elegant "palace" hotels: the Waldorf-Astoria, the Astor Hotel, and the Hotel Savoy, the latter Woolworth's own place of residence prior to occupying his Fifth Avenue mansion. The Waldorf-Astoria, completed in 1897, featured a German Renaissance café, an Italian Renaissance dining room, and a gallery in the rococo style modeled on Paris's Hôtel de Soubise. Similarly, the Astor Hotel of 1904–9 featured an Old New York Lobby, American Indian Grill Room, Flemish Smoking Room, and Pompeiian Billiard Room.[154] Accompanied by Gilbert, Woolworth had experienced similar interiors in Flagler's Poinciana Hotel while on vacation in Palm Beach in March 1911. During the same years, moreover, he may have watched New York's theater entrepreneurs add a new dimension to this illusory European repertory by spectacularizing such settings through the aggrandizement of scale and superposition of dazzling electrical effects, as shown at the performances in the Madison Square Garden and the Hippodrome.[155] Woolworth—already a seasoned tourist and theatergoer—fully expected to rival these historical-theatrical settings within the confines of his own ambitious office building.

The wide-ranging stylistic diversity of New York's European-inspired fantasy settings traced its origins to the interiors of New York's opulent Fifth Avenue mansions of the 1890s, the contrasting period rooms of which Woolworth had emulated in his own mansion of 1901.[156] By the early 1900s, however, savvy entertainment entrepreneurs had extended the elite's private patterns of consumption to a still broader, public class of wealthy consumers, while continuing to identify the city's culture of leisure with western civilization's earlier heights of wealth and power. In doing so, they fulfilled a more generalized yearning for the elite's pattern of cultivation and trappings of cosmopolitanism.[157] At the end of the decade, New York restaurants such as Martin's, Sherry's, and the Holland House rivaled the Waldorf-Astoria's Peacock Alley and Palm Garden as settings for a rarefied form of social interaction, situating evening diners among stylish replications of Imperial Roman, French, and Egyptian interiors. In conceiving comparable settings for his skyscraper's interior, Woolworth participated in the city's larger culture of fantasy and cosmopolitanism.

FIGURE 6.29 Woolworth Building, "hospital room," fourth story. Unidentified photographer. Woolworth Collection, National Building Museum.

In addition to such European, style-based trappings of cosmopolitanism, Woolworth aspired to provide his white-collar tenants with every possible consumer convenience. Small commodities they might want to purchase without leaving the premises he had retailers offer for sale in the lobby-arcade's eighteen shops and twelve arcade booths, including candies, shoes, optical goods, cameras, hats, and fountain pens. Gorham and Company, the Dr. Reed Cushion Shoe Company, C. Klauberg and Brothers, and National Drug Stores counted among the lobby-arcade's retailers in 1924. He also placed on hand the expected cigar store, news stand, bootblack's stand, and complete telephone, telegraph, and messenger services.[158] Tenants could make a daily visit to the barber shop in the basement, which boasted "all the latest sanitary appliances," along with manicure parlors and a chiropodist, or descend by stair to the health club's swimming pool in the subbasement, which its owner officially opened with a "water carnival" in May 1913, and which featured Turkish bath equipment and rubbing rooms.[159] A tenant's valuables might be deposited in one of the basement's one thousand seven hundred safe-deposit boxes, where they would be protected by a state-of-the-art electrical alarm system. For lunch and dinner, tenants could gather in the German rathskeller, which seated five hundred, or more informally in an adjacent café that seated seventy-five.

To further ensure his tenants' comfort, Woolworth provided a miniature hospital, or "hospital room," on the skyscraper's fourth floor, which he staffed with a nurse; the skyscraper's rental literature pointed out that female tenants, mostly clerks and stenographers, would be provided there with "first-aid treatment" or quiet rest from what was described as "the mental or physical strain attendant upon their work" (fig. 6.29).[160] On all of the skyscraper's upper office floors, Gilbert designed bright and spacious men's and women's toilet rooms, the surfaces of which craftsmen sheathed with white Carrara glass. In Woolworth and Gilbert's original vision for the skyscraper's pinnacle, a tenant seeking respite from work might have retreated to the tower's lofty tea room, where "light refreshments could be served." Johnson designed the room, nestled in the the tower's steeply sloping octagonal roof, as a "Victorian," gazebo-inspired shelter with terraces that opened to circumambient vistas (fig. 6.30).[161] Although never realized, this design might have been found clinging to a rugged landscape garden or crowning an isolated mountaintop.

FIGURE 6.30 Woolworth Building, study for "tea room" and observatory, Thomas R. Johnson, 1912. Collection of The New-York Historical Society, negative 46312.

Determined to fill his big skyscraper with a broad but elite class of white-collar tenants, Woolworth aimed to bring the experiences of worldly cultivation as well as comfort to the skyscraper's typically quotidian office domain. His European-inspired fantasy settings would fulfill the tenants' desire for escape from the ordinary while supporting an ambience of the extraordinary, that is, the cosmopolitan fiction of commanding the wealth and splendor of the world's greatest civilizations. Socially more lively, such settings would offer the welcome contrast of pleasure to the secluded routine of white-collar work. They would also call attention to Woolworth's own wealth, sophistication, and cosmopolitanism as the merchant-capitalist who conceived, financed, and provided his most fastidious of "customers" with such an incomparably seductive array of attractions.

A MARVEL OF TECHNOLOGY

Woolworth reasoned that the newest office building technologies, which he considered "fine fixtures" surpassing those of his stores, along with their associated ambience of comfort and safety could also function as a powerful means of enticing his tenants as customers.[162] Consequently, he brought the same high standard of design to those technologies, insisting upon state-of-the-art systems of electric lighting, heating, ventilating, and plumbing as well as a sophisticated system of fire protection. Collectively, the Woolworth Building's services represented the convergence of more than two decades of experimentation in equipping the modern office building and, as such, were widely documented and illustrated in engineering and scientific journals, among them *Engineering Record*, *Power*, *Fire and Water Engineering*, and *Scientific American*. Their hierarchical complexity as systems ensured the smooth and reliable functioning of Woolworth's "city." It also posed, however, new engineering challenges: The skyscraper's water supply Horowitz described as a "vast fountain" and its vertical sewer system as "large as that of a small town."[163] Still, such state-of-the-art engineering Woolworth viewed as desirable to tenants and more: it would be essential to the public image as well as the public promotion of his "world's greatest skyscraper."

In the Woolworth Building's subbasement engine room, an independent electrical power-generating station with "four mighty engines and dynamos," all of the "Corliss type" and boasting a capacity of one thousand four hundred kilowatts, produced electricity for the skyscraper's twenty-seven high-speed electric elevators, thousands of incandescent lights, ventilating fans, and 850 electric clocks (figs. 6.31, 6.32).[164] A generation earlier, the Mills Building (George Post, 1881–83) had incorporated the city's first such station, but the Woolworth took the concept to a wholly new scale.[165] Six coal-fired boilers generated the steam required to power the engines (fig. 6.33). Coal workers hand-fed the boilers without interruption around the clock from coal storage vaults below the surrounding sidewalks, the capacity of which totaled 750 tons of anthracite coal. Subbasement "settling chambers" separated smoke generated by the coal burning from particles and then exhausted it through a flue in the tower's northeast tourelle.[166]

For the design of the engine room, Woolworth instructed Gilbert to rival in "fine appearance" the engine room of the recently completed City Investing Building. Gilbert's design, which he had "handsomely finished" with white enameled brick, featured the Corliss-type dynamos displayed as if precious objects set within an all-white reliquary.[167] There they could be admired by Woolworth and visitors from a glass-enclosed observation gallery flanking the chief engineer's office. In accentuating the dynamos' display, Woolworth recalled the prominent featuring of dynamos at recent international expositions. But for others, Henry Adams notable among them, such an enthronement of the dynamo called attention not to virtues to be revered, but rather to the shortcomings of America's modern industrial system. For Adams, the dynamo at the World's Columbian Exposition functioned as a synecdoche for the whole of that system, and indeed, by comparison to the spiritually based society of the Middle Ages, for its utter soullessness.[168] Woolworth, by contrast, touted the skyscraper's dynamos in promotional literature, which called them "wondrous pieces of machinery," as the finest of modern industrial commodities.[169] As such, they epitomized the standard of service available during his modern industrial age.

The engine room's smooth functioning and the dynamos' reliability as providers of electrical power found its highest expression in the Woolworth Building's extensive system of synchronized electric clocks. Woolworth had all the clocks centrally regulated by a master clock, echoing the 1876 Philadelphia Centennial Exhibition's giant electrical pendulum master clock and twenty-six subordinate "slave" clocks.[170] By the turn of the century, however, such a synchronization of clocks also had come to reflect the recent introduction of standardized time, which engaged a wide array of enthusiasts, from astronomers

FIGURE 6.31 (*above*) Woolworth Building, engine room, subbasement. Avery Architectural and Fine Arts Library, Columbia University.

FIGURE 6.32 (*below*) Woolworth Building, electrical switchboard, subbasement. Photograph by Wurts Brothers. Museum of the City of New York.

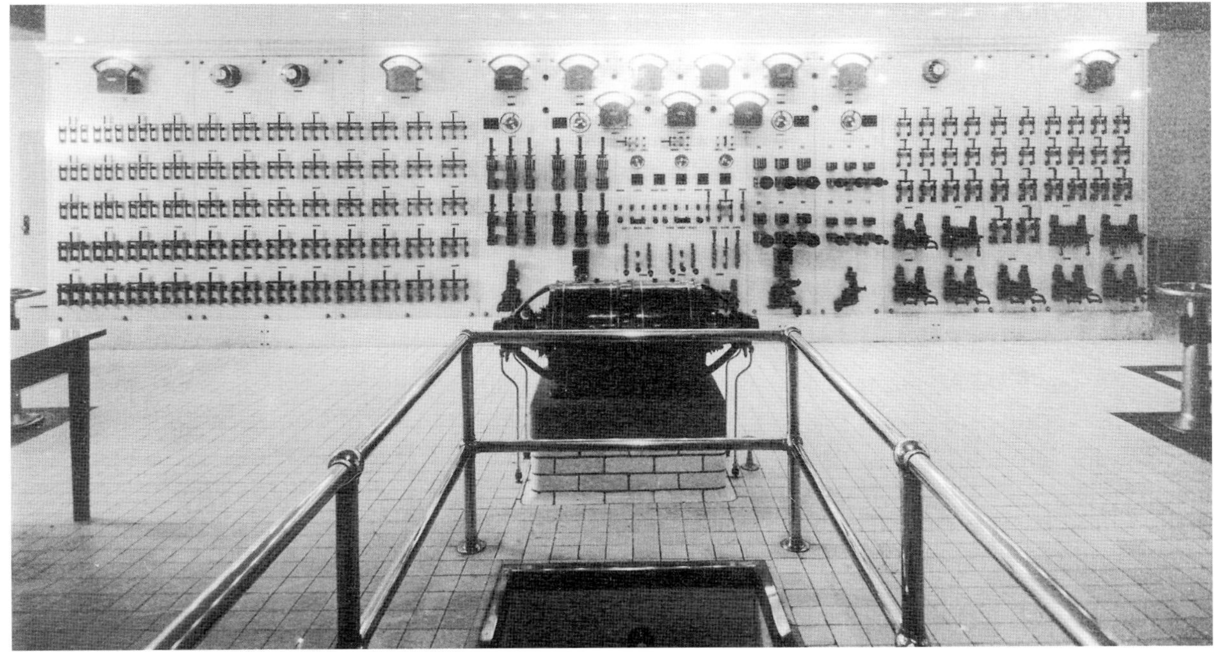

FIGURE 6.33 Woolworth Building, boiler room, showing workers shoveling coal. Photograph by Wurts Brothers. Wurts Collection, Museum of the City of New York.

to businessmen. At the Singer and Metropolitan Life Insurance's office complexes, corporate executives had imposed comparable centrally regulated systems for keeping track of time, with the aim of inculcating discipline and enforcing a strict work routine.[171] But for them as well as for Woolworth, such systems had come to signify not just managerial discipline and control, but more largely and indeed, as they viewed it, more romantically the pace of modern business life, with its increasing calculability, faster rhythms, and heightened demand for punctuality.[172]

The Woolworth Building's independent systems of heating and cooling represented little in the way of innovation, but when combined, the systems fulfilled Woolworth's ideal of a fully serviced office interior completely sequestered from the city's sooty and unsanitary street environment. Theodore Starrett had proposed a "made-to-order climate" for his gigantic, self-contained one-hundred-story skyscraper project of 1906—its temperature and atmosphere so precisely regulated as to produce conditions of "salt air," "dry salt air," "fresh air," and even "medicated air."[173] As if attempting to rival such an idealized standard of comfort, Woolworth and Gilbert instructed the engineers Nygren, Tenney, and Ohmes to design inventive, state-of-the-art heating and ventilating systems. Steam generated in subbasement boilers supplied a closed-circuit system that circulated steam by low pressure to radiators on the remotest upper floors. Huge electric blower fans cooled the basement and lowest four stories with a reliable method of evaporative air-cooling, using the sprays of an "air washer" to purify and chill outside air to twenty degrees below the summer temperature.[174] On the skyscraper's higher floors and in the tower, which the building's promotional literature described as "reveling in pure air," electric fans facilitated a continuous supply of fresh outside air.[175] Awnings protected office windows, which opened at a tenant's discretion to breezes, clouds, and sky.

The Woolworth Building's system of water supply—initially conceived to be sourced independently from an artesian well, but during construction connected with that of the city—was complicated on account of the building's tremendous size (fig. 6.34).[176] In totality, it consisted of seven completely separate piping and tank systems for fire protection, toilet rooms, offices with lavatories, washrooms, general hot water supply, the swimming pool, and the rathskeller and café. These separate systems could be in turn cross-connected as a much-enlarged single system in case of a fire-fighting emergency. Gilbert's consulting sanitary engineer, Albert Webster, designed a hierarchical network of gravity supply tanks for installation within five separate zones or mezzanines, to be located within the skyscraper's fourteenth, twenty-sixth, thirty-seventh, fiftieth, and fifty-third stories. In the American Surety and the St. Paul buildings, engineers had designed a single gravity supply tank for installation on a single intermediary floor. But in the Woolworth, each of the four intermediate tanks distributed water of the proper pressure to the next lowest tank, a standard practice today but a novel and sophisticated solution at the time.[177] Gilbert expressed in his design for the skyscraper's exterior the corresponding groupings of stories with continuous stringcourses running above tracery patterns and ogee arches, skillfully synthesizing the historicist features with the interior's modern mechanical requirements.

Like the big ocean liners with which it was illustrated and compared in the popular news media, among them the *Imperator*, the world's largest, and the notoriously "unsinkable" *Titanic*, the Woolworth Building functioned as a self-contained world of ambitious engineering—indeed, as a kind of "city"—in its own right (fig. 6.35).[178] As a consequence, the Broadway–Park Place Company's advertising stressed the skyscraper's absolute safety to prospective tenants, and, in particular, its construction as "fireproof beyond question."[179] For this reason, Woolworth asked Gilbert to design the most advanced system of fire protection.

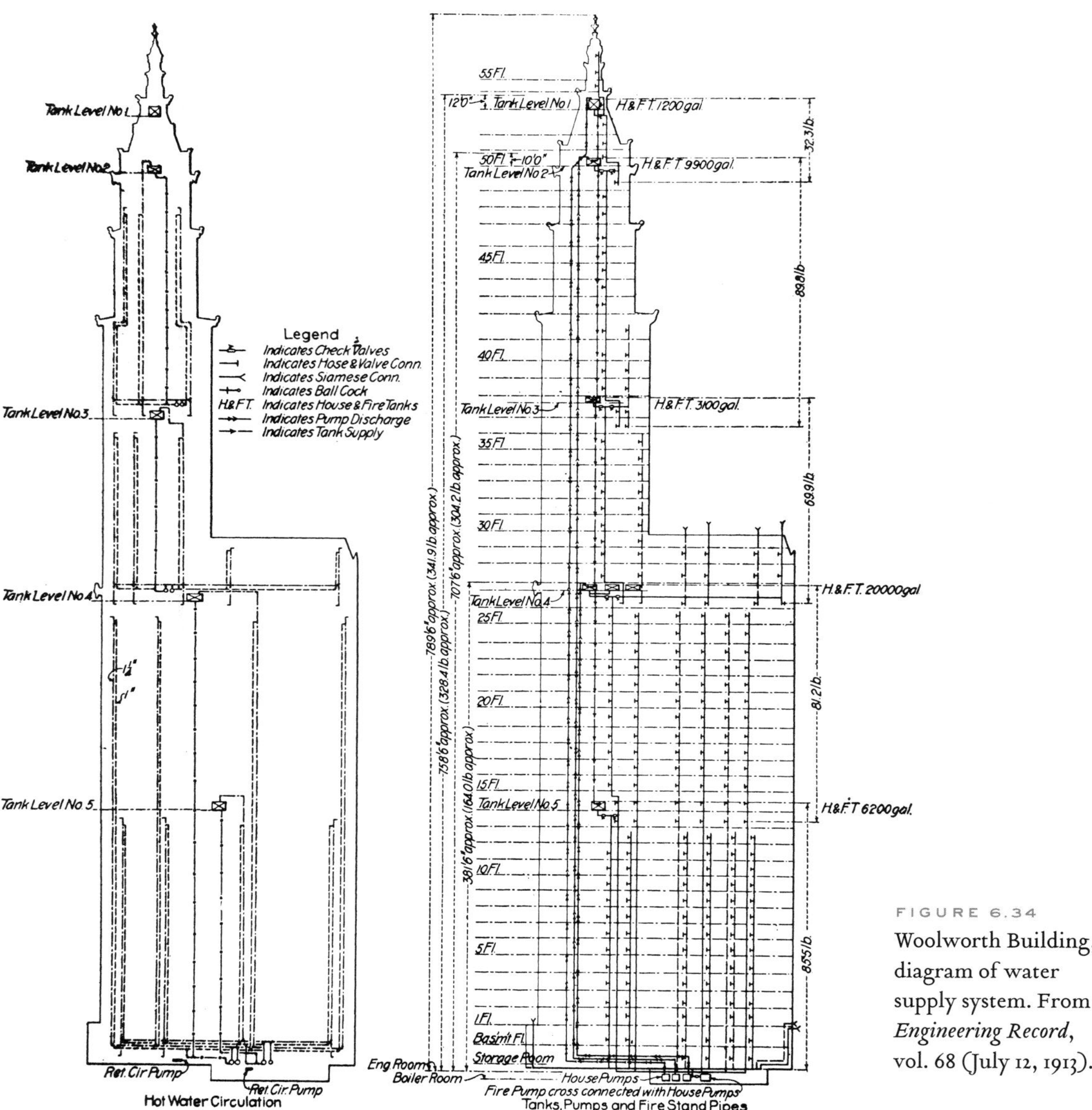

FIGURE 6.34
Woolworth Building, diagram of water supply system. From *Engineering Record*, vol. 68 (July 12, 1913).

To create the Woolworth's fire-fighting apparatus, Webster designed six standpipes, then cross-connected them with the intermediate water storage tanks and with as many as five seventy-five-foot fire hoses on each office floor. During a fire-fighting emergency, water delivered at five hundred gallons per minute from a powerful subbasement fire pump or from fire engines using the surrounding streets' siamese connections supplied the standpipes and, in turn, the fire hoses, which had the capacity when combined to thoroughly drench on demand any one or several of the stories.[180] Arthur T. Newman, representing Webster, conducted a spectacular test of the system's standpipes using the subbasement pump and the city's water supply for three hours on Sunday morning, June 9, 1913 (fig. 6.36). Jets of water shot out of the tower's

The "Imperator" 900 feet, Woolworth Building 750 feet.
THE LONGEST SHIP AND THE TALLEST BUILDING

FIGURE 6.35
Woolworth Building compared with the *Imperator*. From *Scientific American*, vol. 107 (September 14, 1912). (Courtesy of the Trustees of the Boston Public Library.)

fifty-seventh story, showering pedestrians from Fulton Street to Broadway with a "giant fountain" while spectators looking down from offices high in the Woolworth's tower enjoyed the "beautiful spectacle" of a breathtaking rainbow hovering over St. Paul's Chapel. Webster professed objectives both practical and symbolic: He asserted the need to determine how much pressure a fire pump could develop at a height of 780 feet, but also to publicly demonstrate that the Woolworth Building had the capacity to quench its own fires without the aid of ladders and crews from the New York City Fire Department.[181] Gilbert and his engineers' attention to such problems of safety contributed to the public perception of an interior that indeed rivaled a giant ocean liner sailing an open sea: fully serviced, virtually self-sufficient, and, in the face of danger, inviolably secure.

In addition to providing the Woolworth Building with an up-to-date fire-fighting apparatus, Gilbert assured Woolworth of "thoroughly fireproof construction."[182] He incorporated within the skyscraper's tower and wings four completely enclosed, smoke-proof, fire-escape stairways, and throughout the interior, he specified terra cotta partitions and floor slabs along with

FIGURE 6.36
Woolworth Building, test of fire protection system, June 9, 1913. From *Fire and Water Engineering*, vol. 53 (June 11, 1913). Collection of the New-York Historical Society, negative 78899d.

metal doors and trim.[183] The Baltimore conflagration of 1904 and the San Francisco conflagration and earthquake of 1906 had incited Gilbert's contemporaries, Ernest Flagg among them, to argue that skyscrapers with wood floors, windows, doors, and trim could be inflammable.[184] Equally important, Gilbert had responded to existing and widespread public perceptions regarding the skyscraper's potential safety for occupants during a fire. The recent horrific and widely reported fires of 1911, at the Asch Building's Triangle Shirtwaist Factory, near Washington Square, and of 1912, at the old Equitable Building on Broadway, had called public attention to the problems that the design of such interiors and, in particular, their stairways posed to the ability of people to escape during a fire.[185] Woolworth, then, would not only promote the self-sufficiency of his skyscraper as a "city," but would also reassure the potential tenant's perception of that safety with a complete, state-of-the-art system of fire protection.

Woolworth, like his contemporaries in the city's hotel industry, took pride in the new power of technology to guarantee for his tenants a perfected ambience of refinement, cleanliness, comfort, and security; he treated those tenants, like his store customers, as guests.[186] For this reason, the Woolworth Building's independence from the city's infrastructure—particularly its capacity to generate its own electricity and, given an adequate water supply, to fight its own fires—indeed made it technologically a virtually self-contained "city within a city." Yet at the same time the Woolworth Building as a transportation nexus both crowned and signified lower Broadway's intensity of development with towering steel-framed structures and systems of electrified high-speed movement—all of which celebrated New York as the "modern America" Woolworth had acclaimed as early as 1890. In distilling the entire metropolitan experience for his tenants, from the skyscraper's evocative settings for fantasy and consumption to its systems of high-speed travel—Woolworth demonstrated his own faith in New York as the world's "greatest" modern metropolis.

Cathedral of Commerce

Within two years of its completion, Woolworth's skyscraper had become a moderate success as a speculative real estate investment. During 1914, the estimated gross rental returns on the $13.5 million project came to $1.3 million for the year.[187] After paying maintenance and operating expenses, Woolworth's net rate would have added up to about 2½ to 3 percent, not quite the 5 percent that he had originally anticipated, but still falling within the range of 2½ to 6 percent that contemporary experts regarded as acceptable returns for a lower Manhattan office building.[188] In May 1914, Lewis Pierson reported that Woolworth had bought back all of Irving National Bank's five thousand shares in the Broadway–Park Place Company; Woolworth thereby owned the skyscraper outright and had reduced the bank's role to that of a mere tenant.[189]

As if seeking to guarantee the Woolworth Building's continuing appeal to tenants, the Broadway–Park Place Company commissioned a gilded, prayer-book-like booklet, *The Cathedral of Commerce,* in 1916, which promoted the skyscraper as a white-collar workplace and "city within a city" of a distinctive, sophisticated kind (figs. 6.37, 6.38). The booklet's principal author, Edwin A. Cochran, introduced his essay by calling the Woolworth Building "the tallest and most beautiful building in all the

FIGURE 6.37 (*left*) *The Cathedral of Commerce* (New York: Broadway–Park Place Co., 1916).

FIGURE 6.38 (*below*) *The Cathedral of Commerce* (New York: Broadway–Park Place Co., 1916), showing Woolworth Building at dawn and at dusk.

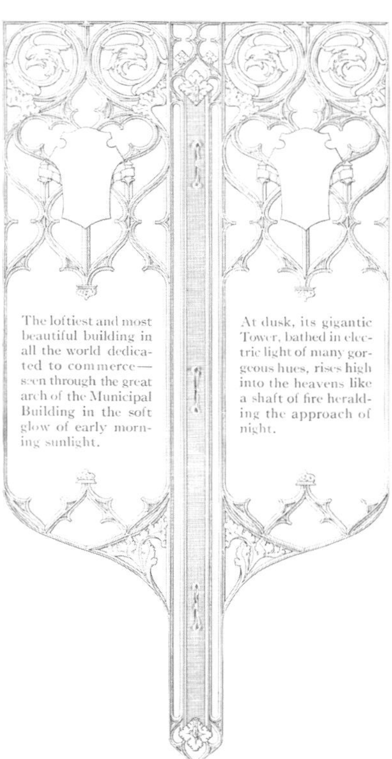

world erected to commerce." Continuing in this exalted vein, he noted that Woolworth's skyscraper housed "only tenants of the highest standard," each of whom met Woolworth's requirement for "personal integrity" and each of whom also "rank among our country's most prosperous, most progressive, and most reputable business and professional men." For these reasons, along with the excellence of Gilbert's "Gothic lines and tracery," Cochran contended that the appellation "Cathedral of Commerce" most fittingly described the Woolworth Building.[190]

Cochran's overt presentation of the Woolworth Building as a "cathedral" brought forward a starkly contrasting image to that suggested by the skyscraper's modern construction and other state-of-the-art mechanical marvels. Yet for the Broadway–Park Place Company, "cathedral" now assumed primacy in shaping the public image of the Woolworth Building. The skyscraper was to be known and publicized as the exclusive bastion of an ethical, even spiritually inspired, white-collar tenant elite, the elite with which Woolworth wished to identify himself and his enterprise. Woolworth and the Broadway–Park Place Company understood all too well the contemporary climate of hostility toward the unethical practices of big business enterprise. This had been clarified in the muckraking journalism of Lincoln Steffens and his contemporaries, and most recently in Herbert Croly's *Promise of American Life* (1909). Croly identified "rich men" and "big corporations" with "social disintegration."[191] Faced with such a climate of criticism, Woolworth repeatedly called attention to the company's "ethical" mission and to the "honesty" of the managers who made up its ranks, particularly after he incorporated F. W. Woolworth and Company in 1905.[192]

It was probably McAtamney who conceived the strategy of publicly presenting the Woolworth Building as a cathedral. Ever in search of publicity opportunities and ever aware of the positive tension between "high culture" and the popular imagination, he may have suggested inviting the popular divine Reverend S. Parkes Cadman to write the foreword that preceded and influenced Cochran's essay in *The Cathedral of Commerce*.[193] Cadman had immigrated to the United States from England in 1890 and by 1895 had become one of the most visible ministers of the Methodist Church in New York, serving from 1901 as the minister for the heavily attended Central Congregational Church in Brooklyn and working as a missionary in the city's immigrant neighborhoods.[194] Cadman's preaching reputation rested on his "moderate stand between the extremes of fundamentalism and modernism," that is, on his effort to reconcile religion with science, and on his advocacy of church unity as opposed to sectarianism.[195] Woolworth, who had been raised as a Methodist, probably attended Cadman's services. At the very least, he recognized in Cadman a potential for the type of broad public influence identified with his liturgical renown.[196]

The Cathedral of Commerce fell squarely within the genre of advertising booklet literature produced "for all classes."[197] Besides Cadman's preaching reputation, the Broadway–Park Place Company may have considered his writing talents—those of an essayist with a "wide newspaper-reading public"—essential for reaching an audience of readers seeking to invest the Woolworth Building with meanings that it could readily understand.[198] By contrast, the earlier commemorative art book that Woolworth had commissioned for himself, his friends, and his associates in 1913, *The Woolworth Building*, had comprised an essay by Montgomery Schuyler and twelve etchings by E. Horter.[199] Woolworth had tailored the privately printed and distributed art book for another sort of audience entirely—an elite, small audience of cultivated appreciators dedicated to the fine arts. Not surprisingly, the Broadway–Park Place Company's widely circulated *Cathedral of Commerce* had a greater impact on the public perceptions of the Woolworth Building. In the early 1920s, an authoritative New York guidebook described Gilbert's design as "an extremely original combination of an office building and a cathedral," and down to the 1960s, that is how the skyscraper continued to be known.[200]

Cadman's endorsement of the Woolworth Building by calling it "The Cathedral of Commerce"—while at the same time metaphorically baptizing it "a lofty example of the best possibilities in human nature, even when engaged in mercantile pursuits"—established Woolworth's skyscraper as part of a much broader, culturally based, and distinctively American effort to reconcile capitalism with Christianity.[201] As early as 1888, Henry Ward Beecher, the minister to the well-heeled congregation of Plymouth Church in Brooklyn, endorsed Pear's Soap with the pronouncement that "if cleanliness is next to Godliness," the soap could be recommended as "a means of grace."[202] William Lawrence, the Episcopal bishop of Massachusetts, defended in a similar vein the thesis of Andrew Carnegie's 1899 essay "Wealth" by arguing in his own "Relation of Wealth to Morals" of 1901 that "Godliness is in league with riches."[203] Such expressions of the desire for a rapprochement between capitalism and Christianity, aimed at restoring social order amid the marketplace's want of ethics, at times sinister competitiveness, and "questionable motives," reached a high point in the mid-1920s, when the advertising agent Bruce Barton presented Jesus as the ideal businessman in his bestseller *The Man Nobody Knows* (1925).[204]

To design the Woolworth Building as a "cathedral of commerce," however, reflected neither Woolworth's nor Gilbert's explicit intentions. Woolworth, in fact, had earlier criticized the Tudor portal's sculptures of Jacques Coeur and Jean Ango on the grounds that they "made the building still more of a cathedral."[205] Gilbert, more importantly, repeatedly defended the Woolworth's skyscraper Gothic exterior as a secular as opposed to a religious building. In 1923, he asserted that "the building has sometimes been called 'the Cathedral of Commerce'; I take this opportunity to say that there was no intention of making it anything like a cathedral, and in fact it bears no resemblance to a cathedral in the plan or exterior design or in any other respect."[206] Then, in 1927, Gilbert specifically described his composition as "civic." "The fact that most of the important buildings of the Middle Ages were cathedrals seems to have impressed the average mind that medieval architecture was only used in ecclesiastical structures. . . . Palaces, chateaux, town halls, and other civic or private buildings were very numerous and quite as beautiful in their way."[207] Gilbert, then, continued to view his design as part of the same architectural high culture represented by Woolworth's commemorative art book, despite the Broadway–Park Place Company's effort at publicizing and popularizing the skyscraper as a "cathedral."

Although Gilbert repeatedly denied that the Woolworth Building had been based directly on cathedral sources, he also frankly acknowledged that as an architect he harbored spiritual aspirations. In 1913, he received a poem that described the spiritual qualities of his design, "A Sermon in Stone" from C. F. Vandervoort. The poem, Gilbert wrote, "expressed in verse what I have often had in mind when making my designs, namely that the thing we are erecting for the material purpose of commerce and industry shall also inspire thoughts of a higher and more spiritual life."[208] Toward the end of his career, he recounted that when designing the Woolworth Building, "the mounting chords of the Stabat Mater kept sounding in my mind while I was piling up that building," and that its pinnacle "is not isolated, but is accompanied by other secondary points surrounding it, and imparting a sense of the ultimate rhythm, of the ultimate note of the mass gradually gaining in spirituality the higher it mounts."[209] Regardless of Gilbert's repeated insistence on the importance of the secular as opposed to ecclesiastical Gothic sources for his design, then, he clearly viewed the medieval past as the touchstone, both formally and philosophically, for the expression of architecture's spiritual possibilities.

Gilbert's contemporaries, Henry Adams and Ralph Adams Cram among others, had in the early twentieth century exalted the Middle Ages as a model of social unity, seeking a counterpoint to the social divisiveness characteristic of the modern industrial era. Their thought formed the substance of a strong antimodern intellectual current that had since the mid-nineteenth century idealized the Middle Ages. In his *Education of Henry Adams* of 1906, Adams expressed a profound ambivalence about his own fragmented, modern civilization as compared with that of the Middle Ages' more cohesive life of the spirit, asserting that "all the steam in the world could not, like the Virgin, build Chartres."[210] In Cram's view, the modern era had destroyed the Middle Ages' democratic social order and culture of an enlightened aristocracy, symbolized in the perfect organic unity of the Gothic cathedral.[211] More recently, steel-framed architecture, or what Cram called the "Iron City in America," had replaced the cathedral with a mere simulacrum of stone, that is, a false decorative mask or "second Chartres Cathedral" as opposed to the living thing.[212]

Ironically, the very presence in American intellectual thought of Adams and Cram's strongly antimodern ideology explains in part why advertising like *The Cathedral of Commerce* packed such a striking capacity for persuasion. As an idea "cathedral of commerce" operated on advertising's widely accepted premise that contradiction, deception, and "the bewilderment of identification" functioned as necessary steps in the processes of selling and consumption—in this case, the Broadway–Park Place Company's selling of office interiors in a highly competitive market for urban real estate. Insofar as the company wished to transform a prospective tenant for the Woolworth Building into a serious customer, then, *Cathedral of Commerce* served the end of enticing its targeted audience while also effectively beguiling it with images that contradicted the "true character" of the skyscraper.[213] Such publicity strategies, in essence, exploited a larger, localized culture of deception historically identified with the showman P. T. Barnum and New York's antebellum habit of casting trickery and fraud as highly popular entertainment. By the early twentieth century, Barnum's methods had found particularly fertile ground in the city's overheated environment of visual stimuli, market competition, and aggressive advertising.[214]

The Cathedral of Commerce, consequently, had little in the way of a direct relationship to either Gilbert's architectural intentions or to Adams and Cram's antimodern ideology. It functioned, rather, as an extremely effective advertising ploy and, as such, logically extended the reach of the Woolworth brand identity. McAtamney had already shaped and promulgated that identity by exploiting the Woolworth rags-to-riches success story during the skyscraper's spectacular opening. Now, however, Woolworth's Broadway–Park Place Company promoted the skyscraper on a higher ethical plane—as a "cathedral." Such a use of the architectural past for the most immediate of programmed ends had, in fact, from the outset pervaded the project as a whole—from Gilbert's development of a "Christian" imagery for the skyscraper's lobby-arcade, which cast the F. W. Woolworth Company as an ethical and benign capitalistic enterprise, to his and Woolworth's fabrication of the European-inspired fantasy settings situated throughout its interior, which cultivated for his white-collar tenant elite the safe and fully serviced romance of commanding the best of western civilization in historical space and time.

In New York, the "shock city" around 1900, such programmed deceptions fulfilled deeper social needs: they provided comforting and shared architectural illusions that diffused the tensions, conflicts, and uncertainties imposed by the social and technological upheavals of modernization and, more generally, identified with the experience of modernity. The Woolworth Building as a "cathedral," consequently, lifted Woolworth and its white-collar occupants high above the street into a putatively pure, ethical, indeed otherworldly "city within a city"—exalting the Protestant ethic of work while transcending the tumultous, darker life of the real city.

CHAPTER SEVEN

The Woolworth Building and Modern New York

In creating a major work of Beaux-Arts architecture, feat of engineering, and spectacular site for high-style consumption, Woolworth engaged audiences beyond those of his managerial hierarchy, his tenants, and the shoppers in his stores. Advocates of the City Beautiful movement, technological enthusiasts, tourists, critics, avant-garde artists, photographers, and illustrators, to name a few, invested the Woolworth Building with new meanings after its completion and opening. In doing so, they illuminated the complex cultural dynamic existing among Woolworth's skyscraper, modernity, and the city. That such an array of audiences should seek to experience and embrace Woolworth's project indicates that its reception reflected anything but the singular and unified. Instead, it highlighted the varieties of cultural experience that typified early twentieth-century New York.

Woolworth's objectives for his skyscraper had always been primarily commercial. But such an emphasis on the commercial would become especially clear in the F. W. Woolworth Company's use of Gilbert's design as a trademark—a graphic device with a visual power destined to resonate among Woolworth's "family" of executives and store managers as well as his vast "consumption community." Yet Woolworth and Gilbert also aspired to transcend the commercial. In projecting a monumental "civic" image for the Woolworth Building, Gilbert's Beaux-Arts composition coincided with the progressive elite's aspirations for a "city beautiful." Such a coincidence made it seem to confirm progressive values. Equally important, Woolworth aimed to build a landmark. In constructing the skyscraper's steel frame to an unprecedented height, he fired the spirit of a third, contrasting audience, the day's technological enthusiasts. The tower's innovative scheme of floodlighting, another product of the city's vibrant climate of technological experimentation, impressed this group as well. In addition to such clearly defined core audiences, Woolworth and Gilbert's project inspired the imaginations of other less specifically defined audiences. For the tourists and visitors to the tower's pinnacle observatory, the experience of panoramic viewing from the platform's high altitude forced confrontation in new experiential ways with the modern vertical city. Similarly, for the artists and photographers constituting the city's emerging avant-garde, the Woolworth's dynamic rhythms and energetic verticality altered conventional patterns of perception and suggested new ways of representing the city. Readers of the city's newspapers and mass-market magazines, a broad, general audience, found reflected in printed views of lower Manhattan's cluster of skyscrapers an emblematic tower among New York's "city of towers," the world's first signature skyline.

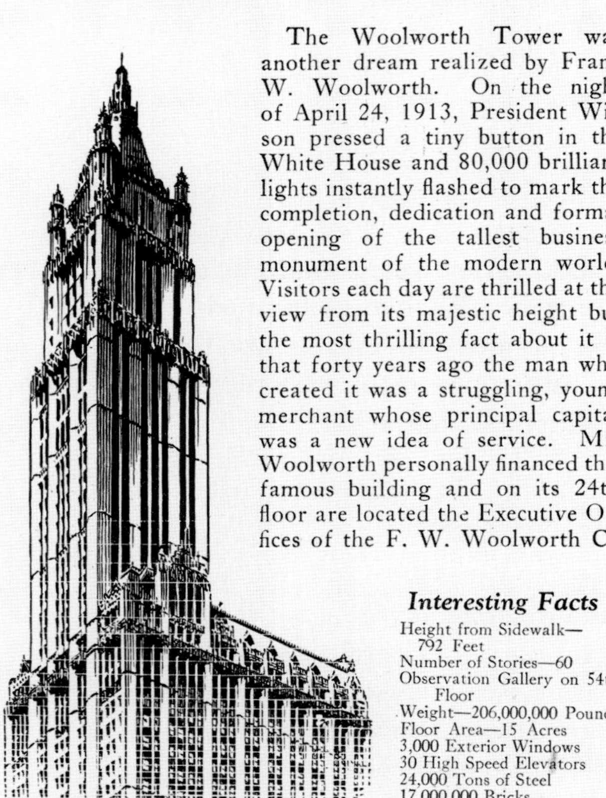

FIGURE 7.1 "Woolworth Building: Cathedral of Commerce." From *50 Years of Woolworth, 1879–1929* (New York: F. W. Woolworth Co., 1929).

The complexity of the Woolworth Building's reception shows that neither Woolworth nor Gilbert, and not even McAtamney's publicity machine, could meaningfully shape the skyscraper's "afterlife," much less control how the skyscraper would be perceived.[1] In the early 1920s, the professional journal *Architecture* posed the question "Who Was the Architect?" suggesting that Gilbert's identity as an artist had been eclipsed by the fame of his own creation.[2] The Woolworth Building—in the eyes of those who saw and appreciated it as well as in the experience of those who occupied and visited it—had indeed taken on a life of its own.

The Landmark as Trademark

Woolworth's insistence on copyrighting Gilbert's completed design for the Woolworth Building, and so giving it legal protection as a creative work within the competitive marketplace of the printed news media, now increasingly saturated with illustrations, graphics, and color, had marked a turning point in the project's development (see fig. 4.23). Woolworth had already recognized the design's potentials as a trademark. Certain skyscrapers functioned visually on the New York skyline as the equivalent of trademarks, but the Woolworth Building as a trademark would distinguish itself as unique among the earlier skyscrapers. Its image—and specifically the drawing by Johnson and Hawley published in the *New York Times*—would proliferate to a degree far eclipsing theirs. First, in corporate literature and advertising booklets, the F. W. Woolworth Company widely employed the skyscraper as a corporate symbol in conjunction with the "diamond W," the trademark Woolworth had developed by 1895. In one illustration, the Woolworth Building is coupled with the "diamond W" and is surrounded by the company's district headquarters (see fig. 6.21). Another shows the "diamond W" directly aligned with the skyscraper's pinnacle and flanked by the words "Cathedral of Commerce" (fig. 7.1). Second, the skyscraper appeared interchangeably with the "diamond W" on Woolworth's commodities—among them packages of sewing needles, handheld mirrors, and boxes of dominoes (fig. 7.2). In adding the Woolworth Building as a trademark to the company's visual repertory of commercial symbols and signs, Woolworth strengthened and sharpened the brand identity of Woolworth—both internally for his executives and store managers and externally for main street shoppers across the nation and abroad.

Trademarks such as Woolworth's "diamond W" had begun their proliferation in the 1880s and 1890s. By 1905, there reportedly existed at least ten thousand registered trademarks. These identified commodities ranging from crackers to fountain pens. Such symbols and signs merchants now relied upon to "stir up interest" in a particular commodity "at the very least, and devotion and loyalty at the most."[3] In using the Woolworth Building sometimes in association with the "diamond W" and sometimes in place of it, Woolworth ensured a prominent place for the skyscraper as a symbol within show windows and on the counters of his geographically vast and dispersed landscape of stores. Montgomery Ward, another mass retailing contemporary of Woolworth's, had similarly printed the image of its Chicago headquarters on mail order catalogs and souvenirs.[4] Woolworth, however, used the skyscraper as a trademark to individually identify his distincitve commodities as "Woolworth's." Woolworth's trademark, furthermore, associated the commodities with the elite values of high culture exemplified by Gilbert's Beaux-Arts design. As a result, even an inexpensive, mass-produced commodity could be made to seem more like the Woolworth Building: at once cosmopolitan, well-crafted, and superior in design. Such fashionable and seductive meanings transcended the commodities' ordinariness as necessities or appurtenances of everyday life.

FIGURE 7.2 "Woolworth Needle Book," ca. 1925, with an illustration of the Woolworth Building. Author's collection.

With the rise to dominance in the American economy of mass retailers such as Woolworth, loose collectivities of consumers began forming around the objects that people owned. These new collectivities competed for loyalty with older communities whose existence had been predicated on shared sets of religious or political beliefs.[5] The Woolworth Building as a trademark, consequently, signified for the modern purchaser of a Woolworth commodity fellowship within such a new and larger collectivity of consumers, for according to Daniel Boorstin, the members of such "consumption communities" were people "held together by their common use of objects so similar that they could not be distinguished even by their owners."[6] These modern consumption communities, furthermore, contrasted with the older communities in their quick formation, nonideological orientation, and rapidly changing character.[7] The image of the Woolworth Building as a trademark, then, effectively enticed Woolworth's consumers to join together in such a larger, loosely defined consumption community. It also functioned metaphorically as something of a giant home for that community. In doing so, it stimulated brand loyalty among Woolworth's shoppers and promoted a new iconography of group identity.

Boorstin has further pointed out the significance of "consumption communities" such as Woolworth's to the Americanization of arriving immigrants. After they purchased Woolworth's commodities, many of which were the most basic household essentials, the commodities began functioning for the purchasers as "vehicles of community."[8] Woolworth's shoppers could identify instantaneously with other shoppers who purchased the same commodities, and so through a shared pattern of consumption participate in a larger, more generalized experience of Americanness—an experience that acquired new importance during the nation's peak immigration years, 1903–14, when thirty thousand immigrants arrived through the port of New York each week. For the millions of new arrivals, such shared patterns of consumption also facilitated the processes of assimilation and acculturation.[9] Because Woolworth manufactured and purchased his goods in unprecedented quantities, moreover, he provided all prospective consumers, even the new arrivals in the nation's smallest towns, with the opportunity to participate in such a shared experience—regardless of how far-flung, widely dispersed, and rapidly changing the character of the Woolworth shoppers' collectivity. At the community's center stood the Woolworth Building, an easily identifiable landmark as well as trademark that served as a stable point of reference amid the continually shifting patterns of consumption.

Journalists writing for New York's new mass-market magazines, among them *American Magazine*, *Everybody's*, and *Hearst's*, presented the Woolworth Building to a broad audience of readers as an extension of Woolworth's "personality."[10] That personality they shaped in the wake of the Woolworth Building's dazzling opening ceremony and then trumpeted as the very incarnation of the Protestant work ethic and as America's newest rags-to-riches success story. When shoppers purchased a Woolworth commodity, then, they purchased not only the thing itself, but also through the trademark's chain of associations a piece of the skyscraper, and through the skyscraper, a piece of the Woolworth rags-to-riches dream.

Leach has emphasized the degree to which new collectivities of consumers such as Woolworth's shoppers had severed their connections to earlier family, religious, and republican values, or even to the historical concept of a "political democracy." Instead, they predicated their existence on the new, wholly secular, market-oriented culture.[11] Such loose collectivities of consumers stood in stark contrast to what Benedict Anderson called an "imagined political community," if only because they had no connection whatsoever to an established social-political framework of shared principles and ideals. Gilbert's designs for the Minnesota State Capitol and the United States Custom House, for this reason, could not have differed further from his thoroughly commercial Woolworth Building. In functioning as a trademark, the Woolworth Building's image, replicated countless times, moved fleetingly through the visual circuitry of market exchange. In the commodities' showcasing and display, from their appearances on main streets and counters to the interiors of their purchasers' apartments and houses, Gilbert's skyscraper as trademark proliferated so rapidly and widely as to take on a life of its own. In acquiring the status of a trademark shared by many, the Woolworth Building's Beaux-Arts composition, no longer an expression of timeless cultural ideals, had become instead a wholly modern, ephemeral form of advertising. Consequently, Gilbert's design—no longer really Gilbert's, but instead belonging to the F. W. Woolworth Company—achieved recognition of a sort and extent previously unknown for such a work of architecture.

A Catalyst for Community

Before receiving the commission for the Woolworth Building, Gilbert had time and again demonstrated his skill at single-handedly enhancing an entire urban district to which he contributed one of his own Beaux-Arts designs. With his composition for the Minnesota State Capitol, he exploited for stunning pictorial effect the capitol's site on a knoll. His United States Custom House "enclosed" New York's Bowling Green to create a harmoniously proportioned "outdoor room" and his Georgian Ives Memorial Library strengthened the "colonial" image of New Haven's historic green. Such new, prominently sited, and monumental public buildings, Gilbert asserted, should always be designed in harmony "with the traditions of their site."[12] This held particularly true for public buildings facing an open space as historically significant as New Haven's green.[13] When designing the Woolworth Building, Gilbert had, beyond any doubt, identified New York's civic center at City Hall Park as an open space of comparable historic importance.

Gilbert's Beaux-Arts contemporaries, as attuned as he to City Beautiful aesthetic principles, along with artists, photographers, and others, called attention to the Woolworth Building as an asset to New York's civic center and in particular to its relationship with the recently completed Municipal Building (fig. 7.3). Like Post and Hornbostel's municipal campanile of 1903, the Woolworth's slender tower and distinctive crown triumphed in height as well as beauty over lower Manhattan's cluster of humbler skyscrapers. According to Schuyler, the tower had "civic" associations that made it seem less commercial.[14] In 1912, New York's Bridge commissioner, Arthur J. O'Keeffe, published a civic center design showing a restored City Hall Park, completely cleared of buildings and obstructions and filled with fountains, statues, and greenery (fig. 7.4).[15] O'Keeffe's design suggested that the Woolworth Building had indeed succeeded as the proper

FIGURE 7.3 View of the Woolworth Building from the Municipal Building, 1913. From *Architecture and Building*, vol. 45 (July 1913). (Reproduced courtesy of the Trustees of the Boston Public Library.)

FIGURE 7.4 Arthur J. O'Keeffe, commissioner, New York Department of Bridges, proposal for New York's Civic Center, 1912. From *Scientific American*, vol. 106 (March 2, 1912).

architectural counterpart for the Municipal Building as well as in its contribution to the park as a public setting, regardless of its overtly commercial purpose. Gilbert, it appeared, had successfully reinterpreted Woolworth's "giant signboard" as a Beaux-Arts composition expressive of civic aspirations. Such a composition presented a welcome alternative to the city's proliferation of outdoor signboards, or "undesirable advertising," which in the interest of the "city beautiful" the Municipal Art Society had recently campaigned to banish from the streets (fig. 7.5).[16]

That Gilbert's Beaux-Arts design for the Woolworth Building suggested "civic" rather than strictly "commercial" values Werner Hegemann and Albert Peets made evident in their assessment of its composition in *American Vitruvius*, their 1922 handbook on civic art. Grouping the Woolworth Building together with New York's Municipal Building and Boston's Custom House, Hegemann and Peets classified Gilbert's design as "promising." The Woolworth Building's tower in particular, they noted, exemplified the advantages of such a design over the more conventional composition for a public building crowned with a dome. Given the aesthetic success of such "civic" towers, they concluded, "the intelligent use of the skyscraper in civic design" might become "America's most valuable contribution to civic art."[17]

In 1914, the architect and city planner George B. Ford, who served as secretary and director for the Heights of Buildings Commission and as a consultant to New York's Committee on the City Plan, similarly applauded the Woolworth Building in its setting on City Hall Park. For Ford, Gilbert's design served as an architectural benchmark in the city's progress toward a future "city beautiful": "Almost nowhere can we find a view that compares in charm and inspiration with that obtained by standing in front of the northwest door of the Municipal Building, looking up through its beautifully designed arch, over that gem of architecture, the City Hall, to the wonderful Woolworth Building rising beyond. It is a remarkable standard for the city to live up to in its future civic art."[18] Based on the Woolworth Building's enhancement of City Hall Park, Ford concluded that vistas could be found in New York rivaling those of any city in the world.[19]

In 1921, the artist Joseph Pennell etched the urban vista described by Ford, entitling it *Through the Arch* (fig. 7.6). Pennell lavished intricate detail on the Woolworth tower's telescoping stages and pinnacled crown, while reducing and simplifying the mass of the composition's main office block. In doing so, he effectively detached the Woolworth tower from the ordinary speculative office uses that served as its economic justification. Artists such as Pennell, along with critics such as Hegemann, Peets, and Ford, were engaging in a sensitive process of accommodation. All recognized in lower Manhattan's chaotic mass of skyscrapers the stridency and the ephemerality of modern commercial values. But if a critic could find the proper viewing point, or an artist render the Woolworth's Gothic pinnacle in the proper light, it might still be possible to see the commercial skyscraper as a civic tower. At the very least, a skyscraper could, like a giant *hôtel de ville* or a rathaus, calmly preside over its surroundings, introducing beauty, dignity, and order to the city.

Critics such as Schuyler, Hegemann, and Peets and artists such as Pennell had attempted to cast the Woolworth Building as an acceptable architectural substitute for

FIGURE 7.5 View of advertising signs at Thirty-fourth Street and Sixth Avenue, New York, 1910. From Reginald Pelham Bolton, *Building for Profit* (New York: De Vinne Press, 1911).

FIGURE 7.6
Joseph Pennell, *Through the Arch*, 1921. Author's collection.

an authentic work of public architecture at New York's civic center. But the president of the Borough of Manhattan, Markus M. Marks, went a step further. He applauded the significance of Gilbert's design to the city's public life. Beyond its value aesthetically to the "city beautiful," Marks argued that the Woolworth Building might serve as a catalyst in creating a community of citizens dedicated to his and the progressive elite's political agenda, or what he called the "joy of service." First, Gilbert had served as an exemplary "good citizen." He had enhanced the city with the Woolworth Building, a "noble monument," and had thereby demonstrated "the application of art to the daily lives of the people." Second, such a work of art signified the possibilities inherent in a coming together of "immigrants speaking so many tongues" with the city's "representatives in government." As a result, the inspired "good citizens," as opposed to "an apathetic and indifferent public completely absorbed in their own selfish interests" and "imposed upon by designing bosses," would be "alive to public issues, and cooperating actively in movements for betterment in government." In devoting themselves to civic service, they would "bring about the city pure, the city sound, the city prosperous, and the City Beautiful."[20] For Marks, then, the Woolworth Building, along with the progressive ideology of the "city beautiful" for which it stood, might catalyze a new, more publicly responsible, more ethically principled, and ultimately, more unified citizenry.

The political community that Marks imagined for Gilbert's design comprised citizens not unlike those Gilbert and Minnesota's capitol commissioners had imagined for the Minnesota State Capitol. Yet never had a major commercial skyscraper and corporate trademark been harnessed for the purpose of serving as such a shared, public emblem for a political community. In finding meaning in Gilbert's Beaux-Arts rendition of the progressive elite's vision of a single, unified community, Marks anticipated overcoming the city's deeper ethnic and class divides. Marks's imagined community, however—in his and the progressives' view sharing values established as official, hierarchical, and Anglo-Saxon—couldn't have contrasted more with the new "community" actually comprising Woolworth's consumers—an ethnically individuated, far-flung, kaleidoscopic, always-changing collectivity.

A Triumph of Modern Construction

In March 1913, the editors of *Scientific American* presented the Woolworth Building with a tone of intellectual gravity on the cover of their journal. Here stood a monument of superior technological achievement, they proposed, an exemplar of national progress (fig. 7.7). *Scientific American* had reported to a broad readership with enthusiasm since the mid-1890s on advances in the metal-framed structural technologies associated with the skyscraper. Such reporting enforced the journal's self-proclaimed mission "to record accurately, simply, and interestingly the world's progress in scientific knowledge and industrial achievement."[21] Now the spectacle of an American skyscraper rising to the unheard-of height of 792 feet, the highest in the world, epitomized for its editors the culmination of this two-decade-old scientific quest.

The Woolworth Building's latest height record, *Scientific American* further suggested, demonstrated that it took traditional American know-how along with recent advances in structural engineering and superior skills in construction to create the world's "loftiest office building." Aus's steel-framed design, as a consequence, inspired among the editors speculation about the American skyscrapers of the future. "As the eye ranges up through the multitudinous stories of the Woolworth Building to the pyramidal structure at its top," they asked, "the question arises as to what is the limit of height to which a habitable building can be carried."[22] They cited as their benchmark the world's tallest metal-framed structure, Paris's 1889 Eiffel Tower. At three hundred meters, or nearly one thousand feet feet, it alone surpassed the Woolworth Building in height.

The Eiffel Tower, in all likelihood, had influenced Woolworth's decision to build the world's tallest skyscraper (see fig. 1.14). On his European tour of 1890, Woolworth described "the world famous Eiffel Tower" as a signifier of Paris. He made a special visit to see the tower and to analyze its

SIXTY-NINTH YEAR

SCIENTIFIC AMERICAN

THE WEEKLY JOURNAL OF PRACTICAL INFORMATION

VOLUME CVIII. NUMBER 10. | NEW YORK, MARCH 8, 1913. | 10 CENTS A COPY $3.00 A YEAR

Removal of old buildings commenced, September, 1910; excavation of site, November, 1910; sinking foundation caissons, December, 1910; first steel column erected, October, 1911; steel work completed, June, 1912; the above photograph taken, November 25th, 1912. Height above street, 785 feet. Weight of steel, 23,000 tons.

THE TALLEST OFFICE BUILDING IN THE WORLD.—[See page 224.]

FIGURE 7.7 Woolworth Building on cover of *Scientific American*, vol. 108 (March 8, 1913).

construction in portentous detail, paying close attention to its arrangement of four main piers joined by lattice girders and to its system of hydraulic elevators.[23] In the United States, earlier nineteenth-century schemes for comparably high iron towers had remained unrealized projects, notable among them the one-thousand-foot cylindrical cast- and wrought-iron tower that Clark Reeves and Company had proposed for Philadelphia's Centennial Exhibition of 1876.[24] By the early 1890s, however, the Eiffel Tower suggested for American architects and engineers an example to be rivaled by building to such new and extreme altitudes. The *Chicago Tribune* had formally solicited proposals for the rival tower in 1889 and had identified a site for the project at the World's Columbian Exposition of 1893.[25] Professional architectural journals subsequently published at least five of the forty designs received by the *Tribune*, which ranged in height from one thousand to two thousand feet.[26]

The exposition's organizers chose not to construct the Eiffel Tower's American rivals, and later, they reportedly turned down a proposal from Eiffel himself for a taller version of his own design. Still, the Eiffel Tower continued to serve as a provocation to engineers and builders. It also inspired among American architects a new confidence in the capacity of metal-framed construction. As Francisco Mujica later pointed out, "In the discussions raised during the early years of the skyscraper, the Eiffel Tower was often cited as a point of support for demonstrating the possibilities of metal structures and the trust they merited."[27] Indeed, *Scientific American* had asserted in 1907: "Judging from the standpoint of structural engineering, there is no reason why . . . an office building should not be run up to a height of 1,000 feet."[28] After the turn of the century, architects did, in fact, propose such unusually tall designs. Ernest Flagg envisioned a one-thousand-foot tower at Broad Street and Exchange Place in 1908, opposite the Stock Exchange, and D. H. Burnham and Company proposed a nearly as tall 909-foot skyscraper for the Equitable Life Assurance Society at 120 Broadway in 1909, which reportedly contained the largest floor area of any building in the world.[29] The *New York Times* called Flagg's skyscraper "the newest development in the race skyward" while proclaiming that "the Eiffel Tower soon may be compelled to give up its place as the world's loftiest structure."[30]

Given the sense of competition that the new height record set by the Eiffel Tower fostered among American builders of skyscrapers, *Scientific American's* 1913 assertion in reference to the Woolworth Building may well have been expected: "America can take from France the prestige of the Tour Eiffel, the tallest structure raised by the hand of man, and outdo it in every form and feature."[31] The Woolworth did not rise as high as the Eiffel Tower, one newspaper reporter similarly declared, but it had other ways of measuring up.[32] Still another contended that "the Eiffel Tower . . . does not count for much, except to look at, whereas the Woolworth Building will house 10,000 tenants."[33] Regardless of such comparisons, the Eiffel Tower's extraordinarily delicate, airy tensile lightness—the product of systems logic, economy, and prefabrication from a well-ordered catalog of wrought-iron components with nine essential connection gussets—presented viewers with a structural character of a type totally antithetical to the Woolworth's far more ponderous height.[34] The Woolworth's cobbled-together arrangement of concrete piers, overdesigned steel skeleton, and varied catalog of wind bracing types indeed contradicted the ideals of the structural engineer: simplicity, efficiency, and absolute harmony among component parts. Yet both structures presented urban audiences with spectacular feats of structural engineering. In both Paris and New York, the modern city had become a theater, and the spectacle of iron construction that rose in well-timed increments to command the urban terrain excited observers. As David Nye has put it, such giant "man-made objects" inspired "awe and wonder" in the face of technological achievement, a form of popular admiration for sheer size or vastness that since the completion of the Erie Canal in 1825 and, more recently, the railway's conquest of the landscape, had characterized "the emergent cultural nationalism of the United States."[35] And now, at the turn of the century, that nationalism found its newest expression in the impulse toward expansion abroad. Few feats of construction made so visible the coincidence of such an impulse with the belief in technological progress.

A Great Lighting Spectacle

Woolworth and Gilbert's proposal to illuminate the Woolworth tower after dark further sharpened the public perception of its construction as a modern technological achievement (figs. 7.8, 7.9). In 1912, Woolworth requested for the tower "a large sign . . . that could be read from a distance away," which Gilbert and Johnson immediately translated into four illuminated *W*s worked into the four sides of its roof.[36] The four illuminated *W*s visually linked Woolworth's tower to the mass phenomenon of illuminated advertising signs newly punctuating Broadway's "Great White Way," famous among them H. J. Heinz's forty-five-foot-long sparkling green pickle set against an orange background in Madison Square and the Hotel Normandie's seventy-two-foot high "illuminated Roman chariot race," in which twenty thousand light bulbs showed galloping horses advertising ten different corporations.[37] On the Fourth of July in 1914, Woolworth and Gilbert draped strings of light over the Woolworth tower's setbacks, creating the glimmering pinpoints of light characteristic of dazzling mass amusement schemes such as that of Coney Island's Luna Park (fig. 7.10).[38] The Singer Tower had served as a rival and inspiration for their scheme; it sported a comparable lighting arrangement—one thousand six hundred incandescent lamps outlined its mansarded dome with pinpoints of light in addition to the thirty searchlights casting beams at full height against the tower's shaft.[39]

The Woolworth Building's advertising signs and strings of light were but two of the many lighting schemes proposed by Gilbert, Woolworth, and their electrical engineers, Mailloux and Knox. Others included a large flashing and revolving light in the crown's pinnacle; reflectors placed inside the building over each window of the tower, which washed light against white window shades; and batteries of search lights stationed at points nearby, atop the Park Row Building, the Postal Telegraph Building, and the rear of the Woolworth Building, all of which would cast beams as a "flood of white light" toward the tower.[40] Ultimately, Woolworth and Gilbert found the advertising signs, strings of light, and reflectors too reminiscent of Broadway's Great White Way and amusement parks such as those of Coney Island and so not befitting "the beauty and dignity of the Woolworth Building," as described by a writer for *Scientific American*.[41] As a consequence, on the New Year of 1915, they inaugurated the earliest known

FIGURE 7.8 Woolworth Building illuminated at night, with Singer Tower and World Building, 1915. Avery Architectural and Fine Arts Library, Columbia University.

scheme of permanent, even floodlighting for a work of architecture.[42] The Woolworth tower's floodlighting enhanced its quality of monumentality, and so as a consequence, further advanced the skyscraper's contribution to the City Beautiful movement's aesthetic ideals.

Gilbert employed Mailloux and Knox, forty assisting engineers, and a dozen electrical experts to work out the refinements of the Woolworth tower's floodlighting scheme. H. H. Magdsick of the General Electric Company numbered among the experts, one of the company's many specialists in lighting design. In the end, it was Magdsick who recommended the final floodlighting scheme, which the engineering department of the scheme's fabricator, National Lamp Works, further refined.[43] Woolworth personally oversaw the installation at strategic locations on the tower of 550 "ordinary automobile lamps of the largest size" with mirrored glass reflectors arranged in batteries and hidden by screens from the pedestrian's view.[44] Rays shot upward at different angles from the tower's thirtieth, forty-third, forty-ninth, and fifty-eighth stories to complement equally powerful rays shooting downward, creating across the tower's surface one even and continuous diffusion of light and so transforming its composition after dark into a "shaft of glistening alabaster against the blackness of the night."[45] Additional projectors with "the highest intensity of light" obtained direct reflection at various angles from the gold-leafed observation balcony and lantern, according to Magdsick, adding "life and sparkle to the spectacle."[46]

In the tower's sixtieth-story lantern, Mailloux and Knox designed a cluster of twenty one-thousand-watt lamps to create an "immense ball of fire," giving the effect of a scintillating jewel, emphasized *The Cathedral of Commerce*, "resplendent in its setting of rich gold."[47] *Scientific American* reported "a great crystal of flaming light" that caused "the other lighting spectacles of the metropolis to fade away before it." The "most novel feature of the whole installation," an automatic dimmer, altered the intensity of the lantern's light on an irregular cycle, causing the "jewelled effect of a deep red glow" to flare to a "bright white light of fifty times this intensity." On a typical night, the Woolworth tower consumed a total of 175 kilowatts of power, more light, *Scientific American* noted, "than is usually employed in lighting the streets of a city with 30,000 inhabitants." The continuous floodlighting of the tower may have befitted what the journal described

FIGURE 7.9 *Night View of New York*, from the Metropolitan Life Insurance Tower. From *New York in MCMXXIII* (New York: New York Edison Co., 1923).

FIGURE 7.10 Luna Park, Coney Island, ca. 1910 (postcard view). Author's collection.

as the Woolworth Building's "beauty and dignity."[48] Yet in the fluctuating intensity of the deep red "jewel" crowning the tower's pinnacle, Woolworth had also identified an acceptable means of competing with the Great White Way's brightly studded, blinking, and exceedingly colorful signs.

Woolworth's tower became the site of other fantastic illumination proposals as well, which if actually carried through, would have augmented its already prodigious capacity for urban theater. A number of New York newspapers, among them the *New York American*, *Evening Globe*, and the *New York Herald*, asked Woolworth about the possibilities of installing a giant revolving searchlight in the tower's pinnacle, with beams coded for instantaneously signaling election returns to evening crowds.[49] In 1911, an engineer from Thomas Edison's Experimental Laboratories, M. R. Hutchinson, proposed writing the name Woolworth in bright white light against a cloudy or clear sky by means of his newly patented "spectroscope."[50] Among the most intriguing of the lighting proposals was Hogan's scheme for a giant, sparkling, community lighthouse—which recalled the famous archetype, the Pharos at Alexandria—to be operated by the Barge Office of New York under the auspices of the U.S. Department of Commerce and Labor, Bureau of Lighthouses. The Woolworth tower-as-lighthouse would have incorporated a sixty-inch searchlight at its summit, which revolved once an hour with 163,000 candlepower, projecting as a beacon to ships on the East River, on the North River, and one hundred miles out to sea.[51] In 1912, Mailloux and Knox enlisted Barbier, Benard, and Turenne of Paris, probably "the largest builder of lighthouses in the world," to prepare detailed drawings that showed the roof's crowning cupola as a lantern housing a revolving and tilting beam of light.[52] The Bureau of Lighthouses had approved the scheme, but in the end, it was never carried out.[53] Still, the Woolworth tower's final illumination scheme, which culminated in a single, blazing beacon of light, recalled the earlier vision of a lighthouse.

Woolworth wrote to his store managers in March 1915, "The tower looks much handsomer at night than it does at any time during the day." Lighting, from Woolworth's perspective, further enhanced the tower's beauty—"no illuminating effects ever made at a World's Exposition could compare with it"—but more important, it augmented the tower's advertising clout: "The crowned jewel effect that they have inaugurated at the top of the tower is a sight in itself. The big light . . . is 400,000 candlepower and can be seen for 50 miles around on a clear night. . . . There have been a great many articles written in newspapers in regard to the light, and all of these things have been putting new life into the advertising features of the building."[54] Woolworth keenly understood the advertising potentials of the tower's illumination scheme. Later, he exclaimed to his store managers that "in fact a building is a standing advertisement" and that "one of the newspapers stated that if a newspaper had a circulation of 500,000, it could not reach as many people as the lights on the tower of the building at night."[55] Like the electrical lights that illuminated his counters and show window displays, Woolworth's skyscraper as a great lighting spectacle had the potential to seize and command the viewer's attention, to intensify awareness of the Woolworth brand, and to heighten consumer desire. By the turn of the century, moreover, electricity had taken on a new metaphorical importance, with associations of novelty, excitement, and glamour.[56] Electric light, in taking away the "fear of shadows" and disguising "unpleasant sights which might be revealed in the cold light of day," drew out into the nighttime streets the crowds of spectators Woolworth imagined as his monumental lighting scheme's most ardent appreciators.[57] Woolworth's floodlighting scheme as advertising feature had effectively transcended the city's garishly commercial signs to present its surroundings with an image of beauty. It enhanced the status of New York as a "city beautiful" while also fostering the consumer's "collective sense of life in a dream world."[58]

An Inspiration for the Avant-Garde

Gilbert did not have to incorporate into the Woolworth Building's design the setbacks later prescribed by the zoning resolution of 1916, so in views from up and down Broadway, the Woolworth tower's seemingly unstoppable, glistening verticals triumphed exuberantly over gravity. They shot straight upward from the edge of the sidewalk for forty-two stories, and then, after telescopic recessions, higher still. When seen from the street, they awed the spectator's senses (fig. 7.11).

For the American avant-garde artist John Marin, the Woolworth Building's verticals signified the modern city's dynamism and futurity. Marin painted four watercolors of the skyscraper, among them *Woolworth Building, No. 31* of 1912, which he chose for exhibition at Alfred Stieglitz's Photo-Secession Gallery and then at New York's heavily publicized and fiercely debated 1913 Armory Show (plate 10).[59] Stieglitz, who had introduced American audiences to the recent works of the European avant-garde, decided after seeing the Woolworth Building that the Flatiron Building no longer held his interest: this newest of skyscrapers exalted the form, making it "extraordinary" by its "shooting into the sky."[60] Marin's *Woolworth Building, No. 31* showed the Woolworth Building's verticals so tense with energy that they caused the entire mass of the building to fling itself vigorously skyward, "pushing, pulling, sideways, downwards, upwards," in the artist's words, as if to free itself totally from the city's historical surroundings.[61] "If these buildings move me," Marin told a reporter in 1913, "they, too, must have life. . . . It is the 'moving of me' that I try to express."[62] Gilbert, however, had little sympathy for Marin's spirited representations of the Woolworth Building, regardless of his having earlier acknowledged the intrinsically modern character of the skyscraper as a building type. According to Stieglitz, Gilbert "shook his head" upon viewing Marin's paintings in his Photo-Secession Gallery, looked "as though he had lost his last friend," and saddened, left the room.[63] But for Marin, the energy embodied in Gilbert's verticals pointed not only to a new future for the city, but also to a new future for art.[64]

During the same years, the Progressive critic Herbert Croly echoed in his writings Marin and Stieglitz's fascination with New York as an energetic, vertical city. As a consequence, he asserted in 1907 that the "city beautiful" could no longer function as a workable paradigm for ordering the city. Its broad, diagonal avenues might have relieved traffic congestion, but planners had found them impracticable to implement in the real city, particularly on account of its exorbitantly high land values.[65] As early as 1904, Croly noted that city officials had failed, in fact, to provide the funds required for carrying out the City Beautiful movement's planning proposals—modern

FIGURE 7.11 Woolworth Building, view from lower Broadway looking north from Maiden Lane, ca. 1915. Photograph by Robert Bracklow. Collection of the New-York Historical Society, negative 69835.

public works such as the city's extensive subway system had instead taken on an overarching urgency and importance. Besides, New York had already become too contrasting, too materialistic, and, indeed, too modern to accommodate what he now considered the City Beautiful movement's high-minded veneer of aestheticism, what he called a "pseudo-classic Beaux-Artist New Jerusalem," or a "bit of poetry out of place." Croly preferred instead "the skyscraper and the furnace stack."[66]

In a lecture of 1907, Gilbert expressed sentiments paralleling those of Croly. Although widely recognized as one of the City Beautiful movement's leading designers, Gilbert now began arguing instead for what he called the "city practical." The City Beautiful movement, he contended, suggested "the romantic, the sentimental, and the superficial"; because of that, it had failed to acquire significance for those who possessed the power, in fact, to change the city. The phrase "city beautiful," moreover, had failed to adequately express the vital role of material factors in city planning and, in particular, the American city's varied land uses and real estate economics.[67] Two years later, Gilbert argued before the Seattle chapter of the American Institute of Architects that the phrase "city beautiful" would almost certainly kill planning as a discipline in "the eyes of practical men." Seattle's location as a center of exchange and distribution in America's northwest region had demonstrated that "all great cities of modern times are great by reason of their commerce."[68] Gilbert might just as well have been speaking of New York. "Let us have the city useful, the city practical, the city livable, the city sensible, the city anything but the City Beautiful," Gilbert further proclaimed before applauding colleagues in 1910, as he retired from office as president of the AIA.[69]

By the end of the decade, New York had indeed projected itself to the world as the very antithesis of the "city beautiful"—a modern, vertical city.[70] The city's newest spate of skyscrapers, Gilbert's Woolworth Building and Flagg's Singer Tower striking among them, impressed that fact on New Yorkers and visitors alike. Those who depicted the city for popular audiences in colorful postcards, illustrations, and photographs continued to grapple with presenting the semblance of visual order (see fig. 2.7). But the city's architects and planning professionals had already begun to celebrate the skyscraper's verticality, incorporating it into their visions for the future of the city. The poster for New York's City Planning Exhibition of 1913 showed the Woolworth and Municipal towers, each gilded at their summits, combined to create a magnificent "portal" to the city (fig. 7.12). Striking in their extreme height, the two skyscrapers, which claimed towers appropriately scaled to the one-mile-long roadway of the Brooklyn Bridge, highlighted the exhilarating and thoroughly modern experience of entering the city. The confined topography of lower Manhattan Island had by the early twentieth century, furthermore, "enforced a standard of dizzy heights," and now architects and planners recognized that this new, vertical construction would indeed shape and dominate twentieth-century urban views.[71] In 1910, a writer for the *Independent* declared that New York had become not a city beautiful, but rather a "City Majestic."[72]

Even before the completion of the Woolworth Building, the themes of the skyscraper and urban verticality—as pictured in tourists' literature, widely published photographic reproductions, and the illustrated journalism of mass-market magazines—had acquired a visual power

FIGURE 7.12
Poster for New York's City Planning Exhibition, 1913. From *American City*, vol. 9 (December 1913).

that reverberated not only throughout the United States, but also in Europe and beyond. Strongly identified with modernity and "Americanism," the skyscraper reinforced among some Europeans "an insidious sense of backwardness vis-à-vis the New World."[73] More generally, the skyscraper's associated modern technologies and appurtenances, among them electrical, telephone, telegraph, and messenger services, along with its "protagonists"—engineers, builders, capitalists, adventurers, and "liberated ladies"—had come to represent across the Atlantic the appeal of an entirely modern, distinctively American way of life.[74] Gilbert seized the chance to exploit the European interest in the skyscraper. Shortly after the Woolworth Building's completion, he sent photographs, drawings, and plaster models to Paris's École des Beaux-Arts, the Deutsches Museum in Munich, the International Building Exhibition in Leipzig of 1913, the Anglo-American Exposition in London of 1914, and, upon request, to the English architectural historian Sir Banister Fletcher.[75] By the early 1920s, the skyscrapers of New York, combined with the city's infrastructural layers of traffic to create the world's first modern metropolis, had inspired a decisive perceptual shift among the architects of the European avant-garde—Le Corbusier, Ludwig Mies van der Rohe, and Ludwig Hilberseimer among them. All proposed future-oriented designs for European skyscrapers or cities of skyscrapers. Such visionary schemes, which exploited the potentials of height and infrastructural depth to reconfigure the city, would eventually make their American counterparts aware of the technologically audacious and indeed wholly modern world they had, in fact, invented.[76]

A Site for Panoramic Viewing

The Woolworth Building's pinnacle observatory, more than any other feature, firmly established Woolworth's skyscraper as a "wonder to tourists."[77] After purchasing tickets at a booth near the Barclay Street entrance, tourists could ride a high-speed elevator to the highest point of outlook in the city. The elevator stopped at the fifty-fourth floor, where they would find postcards, souvenirs, and ice cream stands. Then the tourists boarded a shuttle elevator or climbed a spiral stair up to the tower's fifty-eighth floor. There, from a circumambient terrace poised at a height of 750 feet, they confronted a breathtaking, thoroughly unrestricted panoramic view of Manhattan, the surrounding waterways, and the rolling country landscape in the distance beyond (figs. 7.13, 7.14).[78] Shortly after Woolworth decided to eclipse the height of the Singer Tower, he conceived the Woolworth Building's observatory as a competing sightseeing destination.[79] In transporting tourists to the tower's pinnacle for an all-embracing panoramic view, he would cement its status as a spectacular urban landmark among New Yorkers as well as visitors from around the world.

The F. W. Woolworth Company's promotional literature extolled the Woolworth Building's observatory: "Visitors each day are thrilled at the view from its majestic height."[80] In advertising his skyscraper as a sightseeing destination, Woolworth was engaging in the same orchestration of visual experience that had characterized his use of show windows and billlboardlike signs. He was also participating in the vibrant culture of visual spectacle historically associated with Broadway and Ladies' Mile. In addition to the department stores' extravagant show window displays, that culture of spectacle now incorporated elevated roof gardens with outdoor theaters. In encouraging the skyscraper's visitors to partake in such a modern and exhilarating way of seeing and experiencing the city, Woolworth aimed to rival if not surpass such new and enticing attractions.

In the 1890s, the 309-foot World Building served the public as one of the city's earliest such outlooks for panoramic viewing, "where the adjacent buildings are loftier, and the wide waters much nearer" to the spectator's eye, noted Mariana Griswold Van Rensselaer.[81] By the turn of the century, the twin cupolas of the Park Row Building housed observatories at an eleva-

FIGURE 7.13 Woolworth Building, observatory, ca. 1920. Photograph by Ewing Galloway Agency, New York. Avery Architectural and Fine Arts Library, Columbia University.

FIGURE 7.14 Bird's-eye view of lower Manhattan from the Woolworth Building's observatory, 1913. Photograph by Irving Underhill. Prints and Photographs Division, Library of Congress.

tion of about 375 feet, which served for a brief period of nine years as the city's highest.[82] Perhaps inspired by the observatories, in 1905 the artist Vernon Howe Bailey climbed a stair to the roof of the 307-foot Flatiron Building to produce eight sketches from a single vantage point, documenting the wholly new type of visual experience afforded by great height, "the most extraordinary panorama in the world."[83] Subsequently, the Singer Tower's fortieth story (at about 520 feet) and the Metropolitan Life Insurance Tower's fiftieth story (at about 660 feet) set a new standard for the height and spectacularity of publicly accessible panoramic viewing. But such skyscraper observatories, while celebrated among locals and visitors alike, had yet to be planned in advance and strategically promoted as unrivaled viewing destinations for travelers from around the world.

On his first trip to Europe in 1890, Woolworth showed more than the typical tourists' enthusiasm for Paris's Eiffel Tower as the city's preeminent site for panoramic viewing: "Paris never looked so beautiful as from the top of this tower. . . . The whole city and its surroundings for miles can be seen from this high altitude" (see fig. 1.14). He carefully observed the tower's elevators, which effortlessly lifted crowds to intermediate platform locations for viewing: "When the elevators are all at work, they can carry 2350 people per hour up to the first and second platform, and 750 up to the very summit." Of greatest importance to Woolworth, the Eiffel Tower's observatory produced a sizable financial return: "They claimed it paid for itself last year alone."[84] Woolworth beyond any doubt understood the process that Dean McCannell has characterized as "sight sacralization." It began with naming the sight and culminated in the mechanical reproduction of views that featured the site in prints and photographs. Such reproductions eventually incited the tourist to make a journey to find "the true object."[85] In February 1911, Woolworth told a reporter that his proposed Woolworth Building, the "tallest building in the world," would have a status not unlike that of the Eiffel Tower for "the millions who visit the city for business or for pleasure." Itineraries might include the City Hall, the New York Public Library, or other major New York icons, but when a tourist returned home, he or she would of course be asked, "Did you get to the top of the highest building in the world?"[86] The fame of the world's tallest tower in the eyes of tourists would bring prestige to his project, Woolworth contended, and their experience of it would only heighten the renown of New York.[87]

In 1916, the Woolworth tower's observatory drew more than 100,000 people a year, from more than sixty countries, and by 1921, it reportedly averaged 375,000 people a year—probably an exaggerated figure, as it would have been difficult for the tower to accommodate more than 1,000 people a day—but nonetheless an indication of the observatory's popularity as perceived in the eyes of contemporaries.[88] In charging an admission price of fifty cents, the equivalent of a single day's admission to the St. Louis World's Fair or ten times that to a nickelodeon, Woolworth may well have viewed his primary audiences as well-heeled tourists from abroad or alternatively locals who considered the destination a special experience for which the typical household would need to save. In 1923 alone, the F. W. Woolworth Company's profits from what it called the "observation business" totaled, after expenses, $111,000. Gilbert judged the profit "a very satisfactory showing, having exceeded all expectations that existed at the time the building was erected."[89] In 1931, one reporter noted that the observatory was currently averaging $136,000 each year. After seventeen years, its earnings had totaled $2,312,000, or about $3 million when inflation was factored in—around one-third of the building's original cost.[90] Woolworth's vision of entertaining the public with a modern, tantalizing way of seeing and experiencing the city had yielded a substantial financial dividend.

In 1915, Woolworth described the view from the top of the Woolworth tower. His words expressed the peculiarly modern experience of independence and power linked with the visual command of seemingly infinite surroundings:[91] "On the southeast you can on a clear day, see the ocean; on the east, along the skirts of Long Island; on the north as far as the Catskills; on the west, the orange mountains of New Jersey. I have been up in most all the towers of the world, and there is none so interesting as the top of the tower of the Woolworth Building."[92] Woolworth sent Gilbert special yearly passes to the observatory and told his store managers in a "general letter" that he had granted them unlimited free admission to the highest sightseeing destination in the city (fig. 7.15).[93] In treating the view from the observatory as a gift, Woolworth also fully understood its value. His earlier roof garden in Lancaster had coupled the experience of a lofty public belvedere with theatrical spectacle, but in New York, Woolworth exploited instead the thrill of extreme height coupled with the sensational geography of distance.

The source of the observatory's appeal to many visitors lay in its capacity for direct confrontation from on high with two novel types of viewing experiences: that treasured by Woolworth, the expansive, horizontal geography of the city, the surrounding waterways, and the distance beyond, and that presented just as forcefully by lower Manhattan's much more immediate vertical "city" of skyscrapers. In October 1913, the first type took precedence when members of the Architectural League christened the observatory and a reporter for the *New York Times* recorded the experience during a specially designated tour: "Entering the elevators, one arrives in one-and-three-quarter minutes, without stops, at the fifty-first story. From here, the winding staircase of the tower leads to the observation gallery on the fifty-fourth floor, from which on a clear day with glasses one may, according to the legend, see breakers at Sandy Hook. But yesterday was not a clear day, and there were no glasses, so the privileged observer was forced to content himself with an infinitely lovelier vision of the city, looking from that height small and white and clean, in its setting of river and bay, draped with gauzy mists, and altogether beautiful in the eyes of a faithful New Yorker."[94] From their lofty vantage point of 750 feet, the Architectural League viewers marveled at New York as a "shrunken city," pointing out in the nearer view Bradford Lee Gilbert's comparatively tiny metal-framed Tower Building, to which they traced the origins of the gigantic steel-framed structure on which they stood.[95]

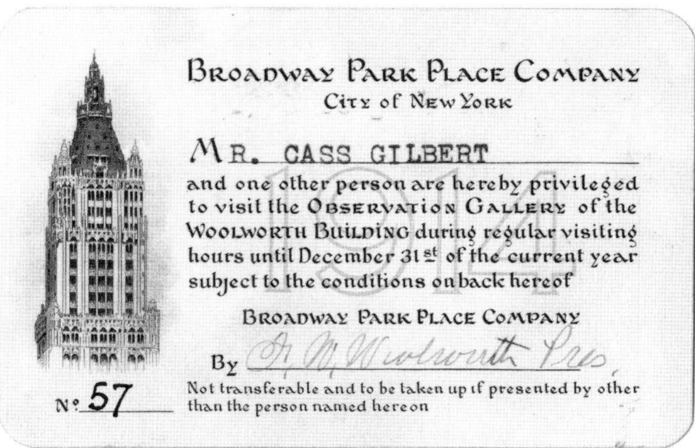
BROADWAY PARK PLACE COMPANY
CITY OF NEW YORK
MR. CASS GILBERT
and one other person are hereby privileged to visit the OBSERVATION GALLERY of the WOOLWORTH BUILDING during regular visiting hours until December 31st of the current year subject to the conditions on back hereof
1914
BROADWAY PARK PLACE COMPANY
By F. W. Woolworth Pres.
No. 57
Not transferable and to be taken up if presented by other than the person named hereon

FIGURE 7.15 Cass Gilbert's annual pass to the Woolworth Building's observatory, signed by F. W. Woolworth, 1913. Collection of the New-York Historical Society, negative 78895d.

If the observatory spectator shifted his or her focus when viewing to the closer, neighboring cityscape of lower Manhattan, the surrounding skyscrapers functioned in the immediate view as the space-defining structures of a futuristically vertical world—a "forest of towers" among which people could stand and interact and which they could experience as part of the city's peculiarly modern spatial personality (fig. 7.16). "Paris may have the Eiffel Tower," a writer for *Scientific American* asserted in 1896, "but for all ordinary purposes of observation, the high office building answers as well. . . . A better idea can be obtained of the true height of the office building by observing it from another high building than in any other way."[96] In the fan mail they sent to Gilbert, occupants of neighboring tall buildings made strikingly evident the wholly novel perceptual experience afforded by viewing such closely adjacent skyscrapers. From the windows of certain office interiors, those occupants looked out onto an urban scene now dramatically altered by the presence of Gilbert's lofty and ethereal Gothic tower. Among the

FIGURE 7.16 Singer and Woolworth Buildings, 1914. Photograph by Irving Underhill. Museum of the City of New York.

several who wrote to Gilbert, Edward S. Beach, whose office specializing in patent law framed a view of the Woolworth tower from the Singer Tower, described Gilbert's design as "majestic and superb. . . . In strong sunlight, it is a radiant joy to the eyes." H. Hobart Porter, from his quarters high in the Kuhn-Loeb Building, wrote to Gilbert, "What a real pleasure this view of the tower is, and how its beauty has grown on those of us who see it daily." An M. Stewart confessed that "I cannot resist the temptation . . . to tell you how much pleasure I get in looking out of my office window at your wonderful creation, the Woolworth Building."[97]

Such modern, elevated viewing experiences celebrated everyday life for many, but for the city's artists, they also transcended that everyday life. The unprecedented heights of the city's skyscrapers, in particular, intrigued the avant-garde photographer Alvin Langdon Coburn. Coburn, a member of Stieglitz's pictorialist circle who exhibited in Stieglitz's Photo-Secession Gallery, photographed the Woolworth Building one year after he produced pictures of elevated prospects in Yosemite and the Grand Canyon. As if seeing New York as a comparably craggy landscape, he aimed to render just as convincingly the uniqueness of visual experience afforded by the city's man-made peaks.[98] In a series of five photographs, which he called "New York from Its Pinnacles" and exhibited alongside photographs of the Grand Canyon at the Coupil Gallery on Regent Street, in London in 1913, Coburn showed the Woolworth Building as viewed from the Singer Tower (fig. 7.17). It rose above swirling plumes of smoke emanating from the tops of surrounding office buildings to occupy, as Merrill Schleier put it, "a separate realm" from the other buildings.[99] In London, Coburn exhibited with the Linked Ring, which Mary Woods has described as "a photographic society influenced by symbolist and Swedenborgian ideas of correspondence between physical and spiritual worlds." In Woods's view, Coburn's photograph might be considered a "symbolist representation of transcendence."[100] Yet Coburn was also participating in the broader set of everyday spatial practices identified with the modern city and with the peculiarly modern experience of singularity and detachment provided by the skyscrapers' newly extravagant heights.[101]

In the guidebooks of the early 1920s, the Woolworth Building, along with the City Hall, the Municipal Building, and the Brooklyn Bridge, received the highest ratings as landmarks desirable for tourists to visit in lower Manhattan.[102] Woolworth took pride in his skyscraper's inextricability from the tourist's classic itinerary of New York: "This building, as you all know, has been the talk of a great many people, not only in this country, but abroad, and whenever the name 'New York' is mentioned, the Woolworth Building is mentioned in connection with it. It is probably the best and most thoroughly advertised building in the world, and the beauty of its exterior architecture has been the cause of a great many photographs taken from various angles and sent to me, [and] in addition to photographs, words of praise, and admiration from all sources, and especially artists."[103] The "beauty" of Gilbert's design, Woolworth acknowledged, had contributed to the skyscraper's renown around the world. But like Eiffel, Woolworth aimed to link the Woolworth name—in his case, also a brand name—with a highly visited, widely acclaimed tourist destination. The tourists' sensational experience of panoramic viewing, more than any other factor, cemented the skyscraper's status as a landmark.

FIGURE 7.17
Alvin Langdon Coburn, *The Woolworth Building*, 1912. (Courtesy George Eastman House.)

In Woolworth's conception of his skyscraper as a tourist destination, McAtamney recognized yet another publicity opportunity and so commissioned H. Addington Bruce to write *Above the Clouds and Old New York* (1913) (fig. 7.18).[104] A popular, illustrated booklet designed especially for visitors to Woolworth's observatory, *Above the Clouds* juxtaposed the observatory's modern viewing experience with a simulated historical-archaeological excavation of the skyscraper's site, beginning with the founding of New Amsterdam and extending down to the present day's "many wonders of the Woolworth Building." To aid the reader in comprehending the Woolworth Building as a landmark, Bruce documented the skyscraper's total weight (206 million pounds), height (792 feet, 1 inch), number of electric lights (eighty thousand), amount of structural steel used in its construction (twenty-four thousand tons), and number of exterior windows (more than three thousand), then tallied the figures against those of the Singer and the Metropolitan Life Insurance towers. The city's tourists, many of whom habitually recorded the dimensions of the landmarks they visited, now had in *Above the Clouds* those dimensions gathered in a single factual source. Such dimensions reflected the new "romanticism of numbers" that Max Weber and others later associated with the American pursuit of "purely quantitative bigness."[105] The visitor's journey to the top of the tower, *Above the Clouds* made clear, offered all at once a means of conquering the city, nature, and historical time.

Regardless of Woolworth's objectives in promoting the Woolworth Building's observatory as a tourist destination, the experience of panoramic viewing from the top of the tower echoed the quickening pace of life in early twentieth-century New York. Rapid transit now ran the full length

FIGURE 7.18 *Above the Clouds and Old New York* (New York: Hugh McAtamney, 1913), cover illustration.

of Manhattan Island and to the boroughs beyond, electric lamps and illuminated signs brightened the city's streets at night, dynamic theatrical entertainments heightened the tempo of visual stimuli, and the modern consumer city had become "a vast and efficient emporium for the handling of goods."[106] This quickening pace Marin captured on paper in a panorama of 1922, *Lower Manhattan (Composing Derived from the Top of the Woolworth*), which released an explosion of energy in a collision of radiating streets and structures and crystallized in bold, seemingly spontaneous strokes of color the speed, dynamism, congestion, and cacophony identified with the city's newest vertical terrain (plate 11).[107] Marin, like Coburn, celebrated the Woolworth tower as the touchstone of modernity. For the city's white-collar workers, shoppers, spectators, and tourists in turn, experiencing Woolworth's theatrical orchestration of panoramic vision from the tower's pinnacle meant nothing less than participating fully, freely, and independently—as a part of the crowd yet standing out from the crowd—in the exhilarating atmosphere of the modern metropolis.[108]

An Emblem of New York

As New York's skyscrapers rose higher around the turn of the century, publishers of images tailored for tourists in guidebooks, in view books, and as picture postcards commissioned independent commercial illustrators and photographers to document images of the city's changing profile, the world's first "signature" skyline.[109] As shown by a 1926 cover illustration for *King's Views of New York*, the Woolworth tower coupled with the Singer Tower down to the 1920s dominated the skyline views (plate 12). At the same time, New York had become the nation's leading tourist attraction. As a destination in its own right, the city received up to two hundred thousand visitors a day.[110] Along with other essential stops on the tourist's itinerary such as the Statue of Liberty, the Brooklyn Bridge, and Grant's Tomb, the city's skyscrapers as presented in the views had by the mid-1890s begun to define a "symbolic landscape" of sights for visitation.[111] As McCannell has noted, the tourist's experience of such an itinerary, which entailed incorporating the fragments of discrete events into a unified totality, functioned as an effective means for overcoming the deep-felt sense of discontinuity identified with the experience of modernity.[112]

Renditions of the changing skyline also appeared with a clocklike frequency in the city's printed news media—newspapers, popular weeklies, and mass-market magazines, among them *Harper's Weekly* and *Putnam's Monthly*—published largely in response to what Annie Russell Marble, the contemporary literary critic, called the "craze for pictures."[113] In framing the skyline views, moreover, illustrators and photographers frequently employed the picturesque aesthetic.[114] In doing so, they linked a conventional, widely accepted mode of mid-nineteenth-century visual representation with the city's radically new, vertical forms and so made modernity seem less terrifying. Such representations accompanied a proliferating body of writing documenting the city's new and unusual heights. Journalists and critics aimed to explain for professional and lay audiences alike the startling changes the skyscraper had imposed on the individual's experience of the city.[115]

Beyond question, both Gilbert and Woolworth took notice of the ongoing process of imaging New York as a vertical city in the widely published skyline views. After the Woolworth Building's completion, both extolled the views. In 1928, Gilbert wrote in an introduction to the illustrator Vernon Howe Bailey's *Skyscrapers of New York* that "the changing skyline of New York is one of the marvels of a marvelous age. . . . Skyscrapers were born of the necessities of time and space, under the urge of modern life, and they are expres-

FIGURE 7.19 Ernest Flagg, sketch of the lower Manhattan as a "city of towers," 1908. O. F. Semsch, *A History of the Singer Building Construction: Its Progress from Foundation to Flagpole* (New York, 1908).

sive of its commercial conditions and the enterprise of our epoch."[116] After seeing a painting of the New York skyline during a trip abroad, Woolworth wrote more pointedly that his skyscraper brought fame not only to itself, but also to New York.[117] Gilbert, moreover, had documented numerous European cities in his own colorful profile views. More recently, he had aimed to shape the image of the Woolworth Building's design as represented in printed media such as the *New York Times*. That Gilbert should conceive the Woolworth Building as an integral piece of such a larger composition—a composition that, in turn, would be represented in the views—is, consequently, only logical. As for Woolworth, his membership in the New York Merchant's Association may well have heightened his appreciation for the skyline views' importance in the promotion of the city to tourists.[118]

During the years that Gilbert was designing the Woolworth Building, critics and writers frequently described New York's skyline view as a "city of towers."[119] In 1913, Gilbert declared that "I have seen and studied most of the great towers of Europe, and while copying none of them in the Woolworth Building, I endeavored to produce a tower which while meeting American conditions with modern materials would have beauty."[120] But Gilbert's conception of beauty, as shown by his compositions for the earlier United States Custom House and West Street Building, also owed its visual impact to a pictorial imagery of such force that it effectively competed for the eye of the urban spectator. In his watercolors illustrating profile views of European cities, moreover, Gilbert's capacities as a Beaux-Arts architect for creating such a vivid pictorialism had infused entire urban compositions. Hence, in Gilbert's perception of the skyline view, the Woolworth Building, even as a singular design, might invest that view with a heightened pictorial standard.

Ernest Flagg's Singer Tower, completed in 1908, constituted the most incisive expression to date of New York's ambitious dynamic of modern, vertical construction and, as such, served more than any earlier design to shape the profile view of New York as a "city of towers." Long an outspoken critic of the skyscraper, Flagg considered the Singer Tower a model for the skyline of the future. Such a skyline would be composed of similar tall, thin, campanile-like structures, "isolated pinnacles" occupying only one quarter of a site's buildable area and ascending upward to previously unconquerable heights, creating a "veritable city of towers," as described by the Singer's structural engineer, Otto Francis Semsch (fig. 7.19).[121] The office blocks above which the towers rose would form a coherent urban ensemble, but the isolated towers—memorable, unique, and artfully disposed—would suggest in their freer arrangement, as Flagg contended, a "picturesque, interesting, and beautiful" skyline with a European flavor. The towers' vertical construction in steel, moreover, would signify to spectators a thoroughly modern city in which the elevator and the steel frame had been carried to a logical conclusion—in Flagg's words, a "City of the Twentieth Century."[122]

FIGURE 7.20 Alfred Stieglitz, *City of Ambition*, 1910. From *Camera Work*, vol. 36 (October 1911). (Courtesy George Eastman House.)

As if inspired by Flagg, the avant-garde photographer Alfred Stieglitz treated the skycraper as a comparable typifier of the modern, energetic city in his 1910 photogravure showing the skyline, *City of Ambition* (fig. 7.20). But Stieglitz had little use for Flagg's "picturesque." Instead, he emphasized the competitiveness of modern building activity in the skyscrapers' hard-edged, geometric masses, using the backlighting of sky and clouds to set them off on the Hudson River against a boldly projecting, angular waterfront pier. Importantly, Stieglitz excluded half of Gilbert's West Street Building from his frame and, in doing so, compromised its picturesque crown. Picturesqueness, Stieglitz's art suggested, had in its superficiality and allegiance to the marketplace corrupted the viewer's experience of the authentic city.[123]

The emergence of the signature skyline as a powerful signifier of New York's early twentieth-century identity caused critics such as Montgomery Schuyler to express an equally powerful sense of regret over the loss in the views of formerly prominent, historical towers. Noted among them, as he wrote in his essay "American Towers" of 1910, was the spire of Trinity Church, *the* landmark of lower Manhattan, visible from distant points such as Brooklyn Heights and the Jersey Hills. The modern towers, unfortunately, had devalued through their extreme height and conspicuousness such older towers as treasured community symbols. Today's viewer found the spire of Trinity Church difficult to locate, even when close at hand: "There it is, surrounded, dominated, hustled, and bullied by stark, overbearing parallelopipeds, huge utilitarian erections, looking down upon it, bearing tier upon tier of tenants, and putting it to shame by their shapeless bulks. Just to the northward shoots up, twice or so as high as Trinity spire itself, the 'Singer

Tower,' having, to be sure, some form and comeliness, but pointing even more sharply than the shapeless bulks to the moral ascendancy of Mammon."[124] The "moral ascendancy of Mammon," Schuyler added, had preempted the historic spire, and now predicted its obsolescence. "The difference in effect of a monumental and utilitarian tower," Schuyler continued, "could hardly be better illustrated than by a comparison of the Metropolitan Life Insurance Company's tower in New York and the tower within sight of it, that of the Madison Square Garden, far from the tallest, but one of the most beautiful" (fig. 7.21). The older, smaller, ornamental tower suffered belittlement by its modern, skyscraping neighbor, but for Schuyler it could not be shamed: "How conducive to monumentality in a tower is inutility." Beauty in the smaller tower, furthermore, offered "its own excuse for being." Unfortunately, Schuyler despaired, the architects as well as the appreciators of the smaller, decorative towers faced their eclipse by the competitive activity of constructing ever higher modern commercial skyscrapers: "The campanile has outlived its practical usefulness, and its ideal use as well."[125]

FIGURE 7.21 Metropolitan Life and Madison Square Garden towers, 1910. From *American Architect*, vol. 96 (October 6, 1909).

With the completion of the Woolworth Building's tower, construction also neared completion on two of lower Manhattan's more prominent towers—Trowbridge and Livingston's Banker's Trust Building and William Kendall's Municipal Building. All contributed to the New York skyline's newest image, that of a modern, picturesque "city of towers" (fig. 7.22). Schuyler, now showing a curious reversal in his earlier position as a critic, lavished praise on this newest, towered skyline view; he considered it the fortuitous consequence of the inspired labors of many individual designers: "It will be admitted that all these towers are shapely, worthy of the attention which they compel, credits to their designers, ornaments to the city."[126] The skyline had become, as he saw it, a "tiara of proud towers."[127] Thankfully, Schuyler added, the builders of the towers had sacrificed otherwise rentable office space for the sake of enhancing the beauty of the skyline and had encouraged their architects "to detach an impressive silhouette against the sky to be far seen over either river." The Woolworth's tower Schuyler found especially worthy of its preeminence, "as in its white spectrality it 'shines over city and river'": it both "flatters and satisfies the eye."

Gilbert's design, moreover, had surpassed the "artistic as well as the altitudinous 'record.'" In the distant views, it struck the critic as "but a 'fair attitude,' a gracious and commanding shape, an overtopping peak in the jagged sierra which calls itself the skyline of lower Manhattan."[128]

Other critics and writers echoed Schuyler's praise of the Woolworth Building and of Gilbert's contribution to New York's newest skyline view. Mildred Stapley noted in her essay "City of Towers," for *Harper's Monthly Magazine* of 1911, that Gilbert had "concentrated his best efforts on the tower"—it would be silhouetted against the sky, and consequently would be his "greatest contribution to the wonderful picture." She added that the architects of New York, after having recognized a vestige of the city's identity in the great commercial cities of the Middle Ages—that is, in Paris, Rouen, Amiens, Brussels, Antwerp, and London—had now fortunately directed their creative energies toward the artistic design of these newest, modern towers. New York, as a consequence, had become "startlingly beautiful" and "completely and uniquely American." Stapley added that deriding the skyline had now fallen out of fashion, because the "commercial" had become "lost in the aesthetic."[129] A critic writing in the *Craftsman* added that New York's "towering monuments," among them the Woolworth Building, composed a "scene of vivacity, of unusualness, and modernness, the like of which cannot be found on the globe."[130] If the standard were the towered cities of Europe, the critics suggested, then lower Manhattan's skyline had at last succeeded on account of its picturesque beauty. If the standard were newness and futurity, its designers had prevailed on those grounds as well.

Gilbert, long a leading designer of the City Beautiful movement, and now arguing instead for the "city practical," had few reservations about envisioning New York's skyline as a picturesque as well as modern "city of towers."[131] He made a sketch of the skyline in 1912, as the Woolworth Building neared completion (fig. 7.23). In the letter of which the sketch formed a part, he wrote: "The view of New York as I saw it today is I believe the most picturesque

FIGURE 7.22 New York skyline from the East River, ca. 1913 (postcard view). Author's collection.

thing in the whole world. As we went farther and farther away it seemed to swim in the atmosphere like a dream city of towers and pinnacles—its color was fascinating and its silhouette enchanting."[132] Joseph Pennell chose a similar view for his etching *New York, from Brooklyn* of 1915 (fig. 7.24). Both Gilbert's and Pennell's skyline views masked the visual contradictions associated with the modern city's competitive frenzy of building activity. Instead, they accentuated the height of the Woolworth Building: to make it more towerlike, they placed it close to the center of the view, played down the height of the Singer Tower, and rearranged the city's other skyscrapers to further enhance the skyline's picturesqueness. Their drawings, while part of the same aestheticizing process, also reflected a larger desire to improve the architectural profile of the city, if only through the comparatively ephemeral device of the image. The isolated towers in both Gilbert's and Pennell's views complemented and contrasted with one another to enhance the impression of a European yet modern city on the water. As Gilbert put it, "These are masses seen nowhere else, and possible under no other conditions."[133] Still, both he and Pennell had refused to confront the city directly, as had Stieglitz or, soon enough, as would the avant-garde artist Charles Sheeler in 1920 with his technique of so-called straight photography (fig. 7.25). Tilting his camera downward, as Woods has noted, Sheeler flattened Gilbert's pictorial composition into an abstract pattern, making it a mere fragment among shadows in his view of the city as a "dense, cubist collage."[134] Gilbert and Pennell, by contrast, had emphasized the distant silhouette and thereby romanticized the city's modernity.

Significantly, Gilbert placed the Brooklyn Bridge adjacent to lower Manhattan's skyscrapers as a prominent feature in his skyline view. By contrast to the historic towers that structured compositions in his watercolors of European cities, Gilbert acknowledged the connection between the city's skyscrapers and such major works of modern, heroic engineering. His modern

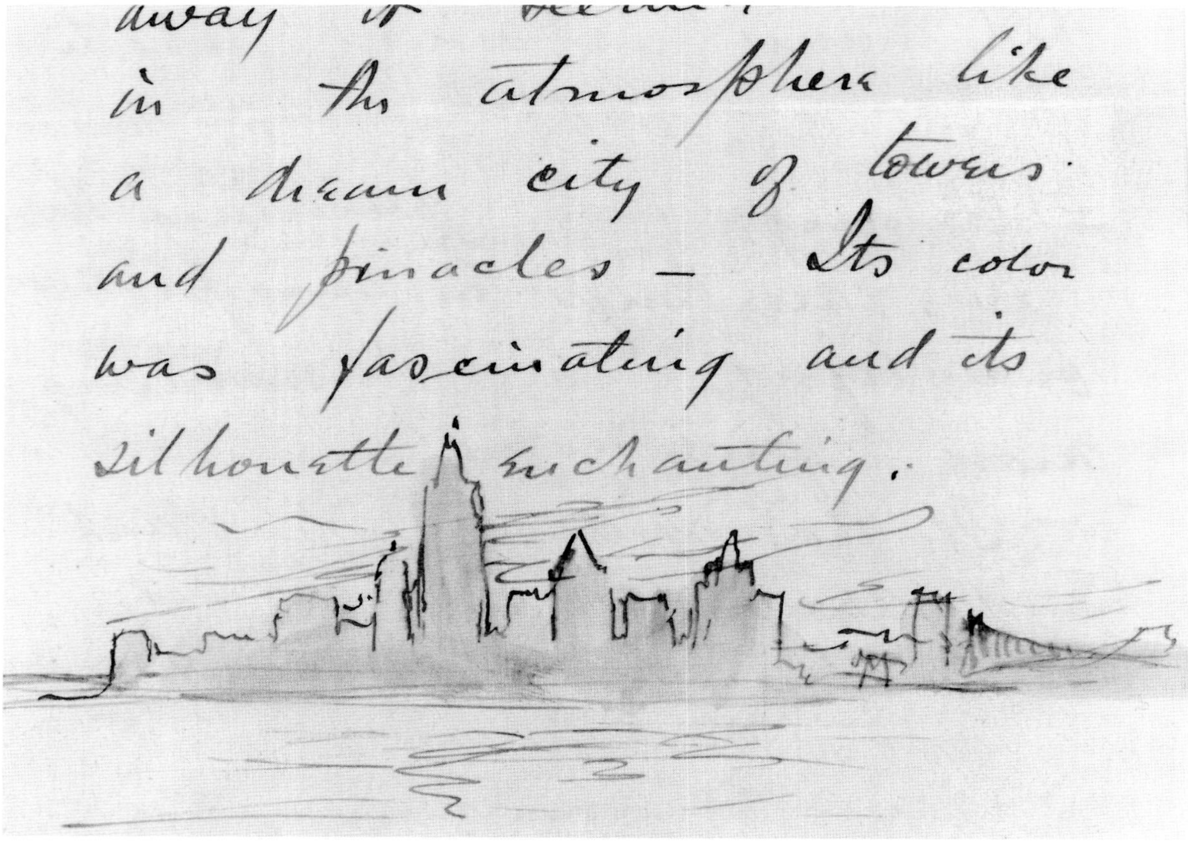

away
in the atmosphere like
a dream city of towers
and pinnacles — Its color
was fascinating and its
silhouette enchanting.

FIGURE 7.23 Cass Gilbert, sketch of New York skyline, October 1912. Manuscript Division, Library of Congress.

FIGURE 7.24 Joseph Pennell, *New York, from Brooklyn*, 1915. Author's collection.

FIGURE 7.25 Charles Sheeler, *New York, Buildings in Shadows and Smoke*, 1920. (© The Lane Collection. Photograph courtesy of the Museum of Fine Arts, Boston.)

FIGURE 7.26 Lower Manhattan skyline, 1912. Photograph by Irving Underhill. From *The Master Builders: A Record of the Construction of the World's Highest Commercial Structure* (New York: Hugh McAtamney & Co., 1913).

epoch, Gilbert reflected in 1928, had "produced the submarine boat and the airplane, the telegraph, the telephone and the radio in rapid succession; developed electric light and power, forged steel by machinery, spanned rivers and valleys with bridges and viaducts of unprecedented size, joined the Mediterranean to the Red Sea and the Atlantic Ocean to the Pacific, had explored the Arctic and the Antarctic."[135] New York's skyline embodied for Gilbert, as it had for the day's technological enthusiasts, the spirit of an American constructional daring, pragmatism, and can-do. In embodying that spirit, it served as an emblem of an authentic American character, or, in his words, the creation of a "bold, adventurous people."[136]

In investing the skyline with such meanings, Gilbert echoed the sentiments of President Theodore Roosevelt, who in a lecture of 1908 before the American Institute of Architects during Gilbert's term as president, linked New York's skyline with its "enormous size and height" and "unexampled picturesqueness" to America's "abounding material achievement; we have conquered a continent; we have laced it with railways, we have dotted it with cities."[137] Speaking as a historian in his own right and as a seasoned New York politician, Roosevelt's words recalled those of his own triumphantly narrated *Winning of the West* (1889). There he had described the territorial conquest and settlement of the continent, in accordance with the nineteenth-century policy of manifest destiny, as the "great work" of the nation.[138]

For Gilbert, the New York skyline as such an emblem of early twentieth-century progress—and particularly the form of material progress strongly identified with Roosevelt's program of imperial expansion—carried the most significant cultural meanings. Near the end of his career, the

Society of Arts and Sciences awarded Gilbert its gold medal for "his outstanding contribution to the sky-line view of New York," and upon his death in 1934, the *New York Times* praised him for making the New York skyline "one of the wonders of our time."[139] For Gilbert, New York's "city of towers" resonated as a signifier of the nation's new role in the world. In this sense, few architects besides Gilbert better understood New York's developing modern urban identity.

At the time of the Woolworth Building's completion, New York's signature skyline—both the physical totality and the representations of that totality—had achieved an emblematic status after more than a decade's worth of vigorous discussion and debate and the proliferation of representations in printed news media and literature tailored for tourists. But even as such a widely shared emblem, the skyline continued to project fragmented and conflicting meanings (fig. 7.26). Some observers might have been puzzled by how the large-scale corporate enterprises' collection of trademark towers, each directed toward a particular "consumption community," might also serve as a symbol of the nation's technological progress, that of Gilbert's "bold adventurous people," or even as the materialization of Roosevelt's euphoric proclamations about imperial destiny. Still others may have found it difficult to reconcile the avant-garde's depictions of the skyscrapers' willful and dynamic vertical terrain with the City Beautiful movement's continued search for an architectural order that signified its proponents' idealistic vision of civic unity. Ultimately, it could be argued that such contested and contradictory meanings echoed the discontinuities of cultural experience identified with early twentieth-century New York. Yet regardless of the disparities, the skyline as represented in the many views—consistently contained within clear outlines and bounded by water and sky—still projected with a profound pictorial force the semblance of a unity. In doing so, it triumphed over the realities of modernization to suggest all at once the values shared by the many: modernity, romanticism, excitement, glamour, and the exhilarating spectacle of the twentieth-century city.

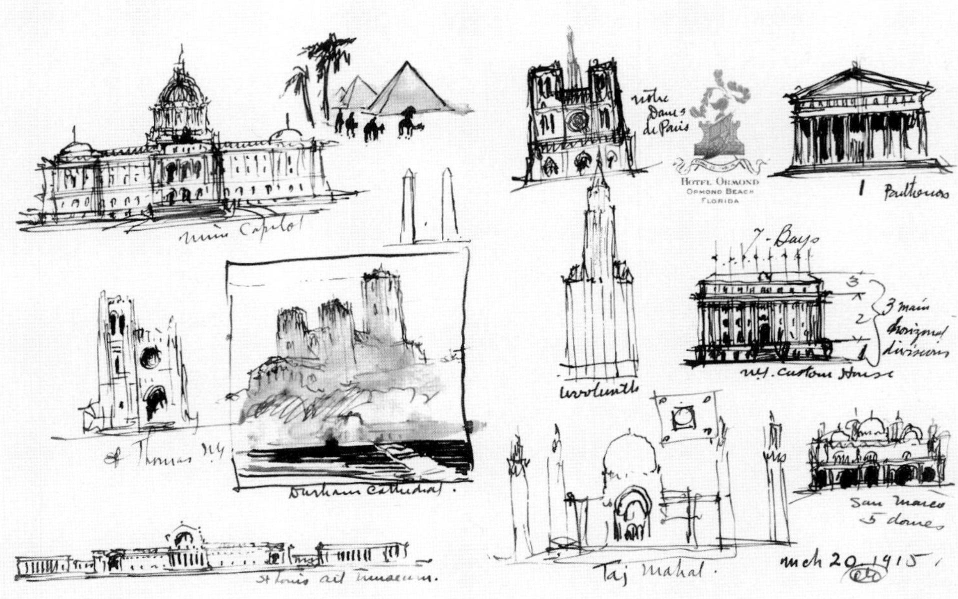

Cass Gilbert, sketch of world monuments with some of his designs, 1915. Monuments include the Minnesota State Capitol, St. Paul; Egyptian pyramids and obelisks; Notre Dame Cathedral, Paris; the Parthenon, Athens; St. Thomas Episcopal Church, New York (Cram, Goodhue, and Ferguson, 1913); Durham Cathedral, England; the Woolworth Building, New York; the United States Custom House, New York; the St. Louis Art Museum, expansion project; the Taj Mahal, Agra; and San Marco, Venice. Prints and Photographs Division, Library of Congress.

APPENDIX ONE

F. W. Woolworth and Company Stores, 1910

Albany, NY
Allentown, PA
Alliance, OH
Altoona, PA
Amesbury, MA
Amsterdam, NY
Anderson, IN
Appleton, WI
Arctic, RI
Asbury Park, NJ
Ashland, WI
Atchison, KS
Atlantic City, NJ (2 stores)
  1527 Boardwalk
  1520–22 Atlantic Ave.
Attleboro, MA
Aurora, IL
Barre, VT
Bellaire, OH
Belleville, IL
Bethlehem, PA
Beverly, MA
Biddeford, ME
Boston, MA (5 stores)
  Scollay Square
  558 Washington St.
  490 Washington St.
  2321 Washington St.
  1075 Washington St.
Braddock, PA
Bridgeport, CT
Brockton, MA
Brooklyn, NY (7 stores)
  532 Fulton St.
  755 Broadway
  1281 Broadway
  857 Manhattan Ave.
  458 Fifth Ave.
  5114 Third Ave.
  1039 Broadway
Burlington, VT
Butler, PA
Cambridge, MA
Camden, NJ
Canal Dover, OH
Carlisle, PA
Cedar Rapids, IA
Chambersburg, PA
Champaign, IL
Charleroi, PA
Charleston, WV
Chester, PA
Clinton, MA
Cohoes, NY
Colorado Springs, CO
Columbia, PA
Concord, NH
Conneaut, OH
Cortland, NY
Council Bluffs, IA
Cumberland, MD
Danbury, CT
Davenport, IA
Decatur, IL
Defiance, OH
Denver, CO
Des Moines, IA
Donora, PA
Dover, NH
Dover, NJ
Dubuque, IA
Duquesne, PA
East Boston, MA
East Liberty, PA
East St. Louis, IL
Easton, PA
Eau Claire, WI
Elizabeth, NJ

Everett, MA
Far Rockaway, NY
Fargo, ND
Fitchburg, MA
Flushing, NY
Fond du Lac, WI
Fort Dodge, IA
Fostoria, OH
Frankford, PA
Franklin, NH
Freeport, IL
Fremont, NE
Fremont, OH
Gardner, MA
Germantown, PA
Gloucester, MA
Goshen, IN
Grand Forks, ND
Grand Island, NE
Greenfield, MA
Hagerstown, MD
Harrisburg, PA
Hartford, CT
Hastings, NE
Hoboken, NJ
Holyoke, MA
Homestead, PA
Hudson, NY
Hull, England
Iowa City, IA
Ithaca, NY
Jacksonville, IL
Jamaica, NY
Janesville, WI
Jersey City, NJ (2 stores)
  145–47 Newark Ave.
  324–26 Jackson Ave.
Johnstown, PA
Joliet, IL
Joplin, MO
Kalamazoo, MI
Kankakee, IL
Keene, NH
Keokuk, IA
Kingston, NY
La Crosse, WI
La Porte, IN
Laconia, NH
Lafayette, IN
Lancaster, PA
Lawrence, MA
Leavenworth, KS
Leeds, England
Leominster, MA
Lewiston, ME
Lincoln, NE
Liverpool, England (2 stores)
  Church and Williamson Sts.
  London Road
Logansport, IN
London, England
Lynn, MA
Malden, MA
Manayunk, PA
Manchester, England
Manchester, NH
Mankato, MN
Marlboro, MA
Marshalltown, IA
Martins Ferry, OH
Mason City, IA
Massillon, OH
McKeesport, PA
Meriden, CT
Middletown, CT
Milford, MA
Minneapolis, MN (2 stores)
  509 Nicollet Ave.
  309 Central Ave.
Moline, IL
Monessen, PA
Monongahela, PA
Montclair, NJ
Montpelier, VT
Morristown, NJ
Mt. Vernon, NY
Mt. Vernon, OH
Muscatine, IA
Nashua, NH
New Bedford, MA (2 stores)
  70 Purchase St.
  1081 Acushnet Ave.
New Brunswick, NJ
New Castle, PA
New Haven, CT
New Philadelphia, OH
New Rockelle, NY
New York, NY (13 stores)
  258 Sixth Ave.
  22 E. Fourteenth St.
  208 W. 125th St.
  2925 Third Ave.
  585 Eighth Ave.
  830 Columbus Ave.
  2226 Third Ave.
  86th St. and Third Ave.
  1415 St. Nicholas Ave.
  741 Eighth Ave.
  209 Willis Ave.
  2042 Amsterdam Ave.
  184 E. 125 St.
Newark, NJ
Newburgh, NY
Newport, RI
Newport News, VA
Newton, KS
Norfolk, VA (2 stores)
  557 Church St.
  112–20 Main St.
Norristown, PA
North Adams, MA
Northampton, MA
Ogdensburg, NY
Omaha, NE
Orange, NJ
Oskaloosa, IA
Oswego, NY
Ottumwa, IA
Passaic, NJ
Paterson, NJ
Peekskill, NY
Perth Amboy, NJ
Petersburg, VA
Philadelphia, PA (6 stores)
  1020 Market St.
  43 N. Eighth St.
  1216 Chestnut St.
  2318 N. Front St.
  2627 Germantown Ave.
  4022 Lancaster Ave.

Phoenixville, PA
Pittsburgh, PA (3 stores)
  308 Fifth Ave.
  Pittsburgh Life Bldg.
  1323 Carson St.
Plainfield, NJ
Plattsburgh, NY
Port Jervis, NY
Portsmouth, NH
Portsmouth, VA
Pottstown, PA
Poughkeepsie, NY
Preston, England
Pueblo, CO
Putnam, CT
Quincy, MA
Reading, PA
Richmond, VA
Richmond Hill, NY
Rochester, NY
Rock Island, IL
Rockland, ME
Rome, NY
Rutland, VT
Salem, MA
Saratoga, NY
Sedalia, MO
Shelbyville, IN
Shenandoah, PA
Sioux City, IA
Somerville, MA
Somerville, NJ
South Bend, IN
South Bethlehem, PA
South Boston, MA
South Framingham, MA
South Norwalk, CT
Springfield, IL
Springfield, MA
Springfield, MO
Springfield, OH
St. Albans, VT
St. Johnsbury, VT
St. Joseph, MO
St. Paul, MN
Stamford, CT
Steelton, PA
Steubenville, OH
Syracuse, NY
Taunton, MA
Topeka, KS
Torrington, CT
Trenton, NJ
Troy, NY
Union Hill, NJ
Uniontown, PA
Utica, NY
Wallingford, CT
Waltham, MA
Warren, OH
Washington, DC (2 stores)
  410 Seventh St.
  923 Pennsylvania Ave.
Washington, PA
Waterbury, CT
Waterloo, IA
Waterville, ME
Waukegan, IL
Webster, MA
Westerly, RI
Westfield, MA
Wheeling, WV
White Plains, NY
Wilkinsburg, PA
Wilmington, DE
Winfield, KS
Woburn, MA
Worcester, MA
Yonkers, NY
York, PA

APPENDIX TWO

F. W. Woolworth Company Stores, 1912

Aberdeen, SD
Aberdeen, WA
Adrian, MI
Akron, OH
Albany, NY
Allentown, PA
Alliance, OH
Alpena, MI
Alton, IL
Altoona, PA
Amesbury, MA
Amherst, NS, Canada
Amsterdam, NY
Anderson, IN
Ann Arbor, MI
Appleton, WI
Arctic, RI
Asbury Park, NJ
Ashland, OH
Ashland, WI
Ashtabula, OH
Atchison, KS
Athol, MA
Atlantic City, NJ (2 stores)
  1527 Boardwalk
  1520–22 Atlantic Ave.
Attleboro, MA
Auburn, NY
Augusta, ME
Aurora, IL
Bakersfield, CA
Baltimore, MD (3 stores)
  223 W. Lexington St.
  525 N. Gay St.
  407 S. Broadway
Bangor, ME
Barre, VT
Batavia, NY
Battle Creek, MI
Bay City, MI
Beatrice, NE
Beaver Falls, PA
Bellaire, OH
Belleville, IL
Bellingham, WA
Berlin, NH
Berwick, PA
Bethlehem, PA
Beverly, MA
Biddeford, ME
Binghamton, NY
Bloomington, IL
Bloomsburg, PA
Bluefield, WV
Boise, ID
Boone, IA
Boston, MA (5 stores)
  Scollay Sq.
  558 Washington St.
  490 Washington St.
  2321 Washington St.
  1075 Washington St.
Boulder, CO
Bowling Green, KY
Braddock, PA
Bradford, PA
Brantford, ON, Canada
Brazil, IN
Bridgeport, CT
Bridgeton, NJ
Bristol, CT
Bristol, England
Brockton, MA
Brockville, ON, Canada
Brooklyn, NY (9 stores)
  532 Fulton
  755 Broadway
  1281 Broadway

857 Manhattan Ave.
458 Fifth Ave.
5114 Third Ave.
1039 Broadway
1026 Flatbush Ave.
5314 Fifth Ave.
Buffalo, NY (3 stores)
395 Main St.
448 Main St.
520 William St.
Burlington, LA
Burlington, VT
Butler, PA
Butte, MT
Calumet, MI
Cambridge, MA
Cambridge, OH
Camden, NJ
Canal Dover, OH
Canton, IL
Canton, OH
Carbondale, PA
Carlisle, PA
Cedar Rapids, IA
Chambersburg, PA
Champaign, IL
Charleroi, PA
Charleston, SC
Charleston, WV
Chatham, ON, Canada
Chelsea, MA
Chester, PA
Chicago, IL (6 stores)
38 S. State St.
219 S. State St.
4723 S. Ashland Ave.
518 W. North Ave.
1338 Milwaukee Ave.
3169 Lincoln Ave.
Chicago Heights, IL
Chillicothe, OH
Cincinnati, OH (2 stores)
26–30 West Fifth St.
1127–33 Main St.
Claremont, NH
Cleveland, OH (3 stores)
330–34 Euclid Ave.
1810 West 25th St.
2115–21 Ontario St.
Clinton, IA
Clinton, MA
Cohoes, NY
Colorado Springs, CO
Columbia, PA
Columbia, SC
Columbus, OH
Concord, NH
Conneaut, OH
Corning, NY
Corry, PA
Cortland, NY
Coshocton, OH
Council Bluffs, IA
Covington, KY (2 stores)
632 Madison Ave.
40 Pike Street
Crawfordsville, IN
Cumberland, MD
Danbury, CT
Danville, IL (2 stores)
8–10 N. Vermillon St.
51 N.Vermillon St.
Danville, PA
Danville, VA
Davenport, IA
Dayton. OH (2 stores)
135–37 S. Main St.
20–22 E. Third St.
De Kalb, IL
Decatur, IL
Defiance, OH
Delaware, OH
Deluth, MN
Denver, CO
Derby, CT
Des Moines, IA
Detroit, MI
Donora, PA
Dover, NH
Dover, NJ
Du Bois, PA
Dubuque, IA
Dunkirk, NY
Duquesne, PA
Durham, NC
East Boston, MA
East Liberty, PA
East St. Louis, IL
Easton, PA
Eau Claire, WI
Elgin, IL
Elizabeth, NJ
Elizabeth City, NC
Elkhart, IN
Elmira, NY
Elyria, OH
Erie, PA
Evanston, IL
Evansville, IN
Everett, MA
Everett, WA
Fall River, MA (2 stores)
93 S. Main St.
1353–59 Pleasant St.
Far Rockaway, NY
Fargo, ND
Findlay, OH
Fitchburg, MA
Flint, MI
Flushing, NY
Fond du Lac, WI
Fort Dodge, IA
Fort Madison, IA
Fort Wayne, IN
Fort William, ON, Canada
Fostoria, OH
Frankford, PA
Frankfort, IN
Frankfort, KY
Franklin, NH
Franklin, PA
Freeport, IL
Fremont, NE
Fremont, OH
Fresno, CA
Galesburg, IL
Galt, ON, Canada
Gardner, MA
Gary, IN
Geneva, NY
Germantown, PA

Glens Falls, NY
Gloucester, MA
Gloversville, NY
Goshen, IN
Grand Forks, ND
Grand Island, NE
Grand Rapids, MI
Green Bay, WI
Greenfield, MA
Greensburg, PA
Greenville, PA
Greenville, SC
Hackensack, NJ
Hagerstown, MD
Halifax, NS, Canada
Hamilton, OH
Hamilton, ON, Canada
Hammond, IN
Hannibal, MO
Harrisburg, PA
Hartford, CT
Hastings, NE
Haverhill, MA
Hazelton, PA
Henderson, KY
Hoboken, NJ
Holland, MI
Holyoke, MA
Homestead, PA
Hornell, NY
Houghton, MI
Hudson, NY
Huntington, IN
Huntington, WV
Hull, England
Indianapolis, IN
Iowa City, IA
Ironton, OH
Ithaca, NY
Jackson, MI
Jacksonville, IL
Jamaica, NY
Jamestown, NY
Janesville, WI
Jersey City, NJ (2 stores)
　145–47 Newark Ave.
　324–26 Jackson Ave.
Johnstown, PA
Joliet, IL
Joplin, MO
Kalamazoo, MI
Kankakee, IL
Kansas City, KS
Kansas City, MO
Keene, NH
Kenosha, WI
Kenton, OH
Keokuk, IA
Kewanee, IL
Kingston, NY
Kingston, ON, Canada
Kokomo, IN
La Crosse, WI
La Porte, IN
La Salle, IL
Laconia, NH
Lafayette, IN
Lancaster, OH
Lancaster, PA
Lansing, MI
Latrobe, PA
Lawrence, MA
Leavenworth, KS
Lebanon, NH
Lebanon, PA
Leeds, England
Leominster, MA
Lewiston, ME
Lexington, KY
Lima, OH
Lincoln, IL
Lincoln, NE
Liverpool, England (2 stores)
　25 Church St.
　135 London Rd.
Lockport, NY
Logansport, IN
London, England (3 stores)
　415 Brixton Rd.
　26 Hare St.
　37 High St.
London, ON, Canada
Lorain, OH
Los Angeles, CA (2 stores)
　431 S. Broadway
　113 N. Spring St.
Louisville, KY (2 stores)
　404 Fourth Ave.
　224 W. Market St.
Lowell, MA
Lynchburg, VA
Lynn, MA
Madison, WI
Mahanoy City, PA
Malden, MA
Manayunk, PA
Manchester, England
Manchester, NH
Manitowoc, WI
Mankato, MN
Mansfield, OH
Marinette, WI
Marion, IN (2 stores)
　121 W. Third St.
　304 S. Washington St.
Marion, OH
Marlboro, MA
Marshalltown, IA
Martins Ferry, OH
Mason City, IA
Massillon, OH
McKeesport, PA
Meadville, PA
Melrose, MA
Meriden, CT
Michigan City, IN
Middleboro, MA
Middlesborough, England
Middletown, CT
Middletown, NY
Middletown, OH
Milford, MA
Millville, NJ
Milton, PA
Milwaukee, WI (3 stores)
　222 Grand Ave.
　410 National Ave.
　779 Third St.
Minneapolis, MN (2 stores)
　509 Nicollet Ave.
　309 Central Ave.

Missoula, MT
Moline, IL
Moncton, NB, Canada
Monessen, PA
Monongahela, PA
Montclair, NJ
Montpelier, VT
Montreal, QC, Canada (3 stores)
 356 St. Laurence St.
 395 St. Catherine St., W.
 489 St. Catherine St., E.
Morristown, NJ
Mt. Carmel, PA
Mt. Vernon, NY
Mt. Vernon, OH
Muncie, IN
Muscatine, IA
Muskegon, MI
Nanticoke, PA
Nashua, NH
New Albany, IN
New Bedford, MA (2 stores)
 70 Purchase St.
 1081 Acushnet Ave.
New Britain, CT
New Brunswick, NJ
New Castle, IN
New Castle, PA
New Haven, CT
New London, CT
New Orleans, LA
New Philadelphia, OH
New Rockelle, NY
New York, NY (13 stores)
 258 Sixth Ave.
 22 E. Fourteenth St.
 208 W. 125th St.
 2925 Third Ave.
 585 Eighth Ave.
 830 Columbus Ave.
 2226 Third Ave.
 86th St. and Third Ave.
 1415 St. Nicholas Ave.
 741 Eighth Ave.
 209 Willis Ave.
 2042 Amsterdam Ave.
 443 Tremont Ave.
Newark, NJ
Newark, OH
Newburgh, NY
Newburyport, MA
Newport, KY
Newport, RI
Newport News, VA
Newton, KS
Newton, MA
Niagra Falls, NY
Norfolk, VA (2 stores)
 557 Church St.
 112–20 Main St.
Norristown, PA
North Adams, MA
Northampton, MA
Norwalk, OH
Norwich, CT
Oakland, CA
Ogden, UT
Ogdensburg, NY
Oil City, PA
Olean, NY
Omaha, NE
Oneonta, NY
Orange, NJ
Oshkosh, WI
Oskaloosa, IA
Oswego, NY
Ottawa, IL
Ottawa, ON, Canada
Ottumwa, IA
Owen Sound, ON, Canada
Owensboro, KY
Owosso, MI
Paducah, KY
Parkersburg, WV
Pasadena, CA
Passaic, NJ
Paterson, NJ
Pawtucket, RI
Peekskill, NY
Peoria, IL
Perth Amboy, NJ
Peru, IN
Peterborough, ON, Canada
Petersburg, VA
Philadelphia, PA (7 stores)
 1020 Market St.
 43 N. Eighth St.
 1216 Chestnut St.
 2318 N. Front St.
 2627 Germantown Ave.
 4022 Lancaster Ave.
 112 S. 52nd St.
Phoenixville, PA
Piqua, OH
Pittsburgh, PA (3 stores)
 308 Fifth Ave.
 Pittsburg Life Bldg.
 1323 Carson St.
Pittston, PA
Plainfield, NJ
Plattsburgh, NY
Plymouth, PA
Port Huron, MI
Port Jervis, NY
Portland, ME
Portland, OR
Portsmouth, NH
Portsmouth, OH
Portsmouth, VA
Pottstown, PA
Pottsville, PA
Poughkeepsie, NY
Preston, England
Providence, RI (2 stores)
 286 Westminster St.
 1920–30 Westminster St.
Pueblo, CO
Punxsutawney, PA
Putnam, CT
Quebec, QC, Canada
Quincy, IL
Quincy, MA
Racine, WI
Raleigh, NC
Reading, PA
Red Bank, NJ
Red Wing, MI
Richmond, IN
Richmond, VA
Richmond Hill, NY

Riverside, CA
Rochester, NY
Rock Island, IL
Rockford, IL
Rockland, ME
Rome, NY
Rumford Falls, ME
Rutland, VT
Sacramento, CA
Saginaw, MI
Salem, MA
Salem, OH
Salem, OR
Salt Lake City, UT
San Bernardino, CA
San Diego, CA
San Francisco, CA (3 stores)
  891 Market St.
  2554 Mission St.
  1347 Fillmore St.
San Jose, CA
Sandusky, OH
Saratoga, NY
Savannah, GA
Sayre, PA
Schenectady, NY
Scranton, PA (2 stores)
  317–19 Lackawanna Ave.
  1904–6 North Main St.
Seattle, WA
Sedalia, MO
Shamokin, PA
Sheboygan, WI
Shelbyville, IN
Shenandoah, PA
Sherbrooke, QC, Canada
Sioux City, IA
Sioux Falls, SD
Somerville, MA
Somerville, NJ
South Bend, IN
South Bethlehem, PA
South Boston, MA
South Chicago, IL
South Framingham, MA
South Norwalk, CT
Spokane, WA
Springfield, IL
Springfield, MA
Springfield, MO
Springfield, OH
St. Albans, VT
St. Cloud, MN
St. Hyacinthe, QC, Canada
St. John, NB, Canada
St. Johns, QC, Canada
St. Johnsbury, VT
St. Joseph, MO
St. Louis, MO (3 stores)
  510 Washington Ave.
  708 Franklin Ave.
  718 N. Broadway
St. Paul, MN
St. Thomas, ON, Canada
Stamford, CT
Steelton, PA
Steubenville, OH
Stockton, CA
Stratford, ON, Canada
Streator, IL
Suffolk, VA
Sunbury, PA
Superior, WI
Sydney, NS, Canada
Syracuse, NY (2 stores)
  327–29 South Salina St.
  242–44 North Salina St.
Tacoma, WA
Tamaqua, PA
Taunton, MA
Terre Haute, IN
Tiffin, OH
Toledo, OH
Tonawanda, NY
Topeka, KS
Toronto, ON, Canada
Torrington, CT
Traverse City, MI
Trenton, NJ
Troy, NY
Union Hill, NJ
Uniontown, PA
Utica, NY
Vancouver, BC, Canada
Victoria, BC, Canada
Vincennes, IN
Wabash, IN
Walla Walla, WA
Wallingford, CT
Waltham, MA
Ware, MA
Warren, OH
Warren, PA
Washington, DC (2 stores)
  410 Seventh St.
  923 Pennsylvania Ave.
Washington, PA
Waterbury, CT
Waterloo, IA
Watertown, NY
Waterville, ME
Waukegan, IL
Wausau, WI
Webster, MA
Wellington, KS
West Chester, PA
Westerly, RI
Westfield, MA
Wheeling, WV
White Plains, NY
Wilkes Barre, PA
Wilkinsburg, PA
Williamsport, PA
Willimantic, CT
Wilmington, DE
Winfield, KS
Winnipeg, MB, Canada
Winona, MN
Woburn, MA
Woodstock, ON, Canada
Woonsocket, RI
Worcester, MA
Xenia, OH
Yonkers, NY
York, PA
Youngstown, OH
Zanesville, OH

NOTES

ABBREVIATIONS

AAA. Archives of American Art, Smithsonian Institution
AIA. American Institute of Architects Archives
ALCU. Avery Architectural and Fine Arts Library, Columbia University
BNYA. Bank of New York Archives
LC. Manuscript Division, Library of Congress
LCHS. Lancaster County Historical Society
MHS. Manuscript Library, Minnesota Historical Society
NMAH. Archives Center, National Museum of American History, Smithsonian Institution
N-YHS. New-York Historical Society, Department of Prints, Photographs, and Architecture
OCA. Oberlin College Archives
NBM. National Building Museum
WDT. *Watertown Daily Times*

INTRODUCTION

1 Among recent books that examine the skyscraper as a building type within the urban cultures of New York and Chicago are Daniel Bluestone, *Constructing Chicago* (New Haven, Conn.: Yale University Press, 1991); Mona Domosh, *Invented Cities: The Creation of Landscape in Nineteenth-Century New York and Boston* (New Haven, Conn.: Yale University Press, 1996); and Katherine Solomonson, *The Chicago Tribune Tower Competition: Skyscraper Design and Cultural Change in the 1920s* (New York: Cambridge University Press, 2001); and Roberta Moudry, ed., *The American Skyscraper: Cultural Histories* (New York: Cambridge University Press, 2005).
2 Henry James, *The American Scene* (1907; reprint, Bloomington: Indiana University Press, 1968), 73.
3 Marshall Berman, *All That Is Solid Melts into Air: The Experience of Modernity*, 2nd ed. (New York: Penguin Books, 1988), 15–20, 16 (for quote).
4 See, for example, Kenneth T. Jackson, "The Capital of Capitalism: The New York Metropolitan Region, 1890–1940," in *Metropolis*, ed. Anthony Sutcliffe (London: Mansell, 1984), 319–53; and, more recently, Kenneth T. Jackson, ed., *The Encyclopedia of New York City* (New Haven, Conn.: Yale University Press; New York: New-York Historical Society); as well as Edwin G. Burrows and Mike Wallace, *Gotham: A History of New York City to 1898* (New York: Oxford University Press, 1999), 1039–1236.
5 William R. Taylor, "The Evolution of Public Space: The Commercial City as Showcase," in *In Pursuit of Gotham: Culture and Commerce in New York* (New York: Oxford University Press, 1992), 35–50; Sir Peter Hall, "The Apotheosis of the

Modern: New York, 1880–1940," in *Cities and Civilization* (New York: Pantheon Books, 1998), 746–802; Neil Harris, "Urban Tourism and the Commercial City," in *Inventing Times Square: Commerce and Culture at the Crossroads of the World,* ed. William R. Taylor (New York: Russell Sage Foundation, 1991; reprint, Baltimore: Johns Hopkins University Press, 1996), 66–82; and Alan Trachtenberg, "Image and Ideology: New York in the Photographer's Eye," *Journal of Urban History* 10 (August 1984): 453–64.

6 Charles Baudelaire, "The Painter of Modern Life" (1863), in *The Painter of Modern Life, and Other Essays by Charles Baudelaire,* trans. and ed. Jonathan Mayne (London: Phaidon Press, 1964), 13.

7 Berman, *All That Is Solid Melts into Air*, 17, 19, 22, 30.

8 William Leach, *Land of Desire: Merchants, Power, and the Rise of a New American Culture* (New York: Pantheon Books, 1993), xiii, xv, 3 (for quotes), 3–12.

9 Jackson Lears, *Fables of Abundance: A Cultural History of Advertising in America* (New York: Basic Books, 1994), 261–63.

10 M. Christine Boyer, *Manhattan Manners: Architecture and Style, 1850–1900* (New York: Rizzoli International Publications, 1985), 43, 88 (for quote), 88–90.

11 Vanessa R. Schwartz, *Spectacular Realities: Early Mass Culture in Fin-de-Siècle Paris* (Berkeley: University of California Press, 1998), 2–11; 2, 7, 8 (for quotes).

12 Ibid., 6, 11. Schwartz (4–5) notes that she extends the argument of T. J. Clark, *The Painting of Modern Life: Paris in the Art of Manet and His Followers* (Princeton, N.J.: Princeton University Press, 1984). Clark differentiates pre-1860s public life in Paris from the emerging "spectacular society." Before the 1860s, "the essential separation of public life from private, and the thorough invasion of both by capital, has not yet been effected." Clark, *The Painting of Modern Life*, 64 (for quote), 9, 63–64, 68–69.

13 John Kasson, *Amusing the Million: Coney Island at the Turn of the Century* (New York: Hill & Wang, 1978), 4 (for quote), 3–9.

14 Rem Koolhaas, *Delirious New York: A Retroactive Manifesto for Manhattan,* rev. ed. (New York: Monacelli Press, 1994), 32, 63 (for quote), 29–79.

15 David E. Nye, *Electrifying America: Social Meanings of a New Technology, 1880–1940* (Cambridge, Mass.: MIT Press, 1990), 29.

16 Dell Upton, "Inventing the Metropolis: Civilization and Urbanity in Antebellum New York," in *Art and the Empire City: New York, 1825–1861,* ed. Catherine Hoover Voorsanger and John K. Howat (New York: Metropolitan Museum of Art; New Haven, Conn.: Yale University Press, 2000), 3–4 (for quote).

17 Solomonson, *The Chicago Tribune Tower Competition*, 1, 4 (for quotes), 1–11.

18 Cass Gilbert, as quoted in Mary Beth Betts, "The Aesthetics of an Eclectic Architect," in *Cass Gilbert: Life and Work: Architect of the Public Domain,* ed. Barbara S. Christen and Steven Flanders (New York: W. W. Norton & Co., 2001), 84.

19 On Beaux-Arts principles of composition as they were understood by American architects at the time, see John Beverly Robinson, *Principles of Architectural Composition* (New York: Architectural Record Co., 1899); and John Vrendenburgh Van Pelt, *A Discussion of Composition* (New York: Macmillan & Co., 1902). On style, see A. D. F. Hamlin, "The Battle of the Styles," *Architectural Record* 1 (January–March 1892): 265–75; (April–June 1892): 405–13; and Hamlin, "Style in Architecture," *Craftsman* 8 (June 1905): 325–31.

20 Office memorandums dated June 22, 1910, to January 21, 1911, Woolworth Building, Cass Gilbert Collection, N-YHS. See also *The Woolworth Building (Highest in the World): Illustrated with Details from the Architect's Drawings and with Floor Plans* (New York: F. W. Woolworth, 1912).

21 Robert Bruegmann, *The Architects and the City: Holabird and Roche of Chicago, 1880–1918* (Chicago: University of Chicago Press, 1997), 65–99, documents and analyzes the origins of the single-contract system; Stephen Kern, *The Culture of Time and Space, 1880–1918* (Cambridge, Mass.: Harvard University Press, 1983), 10–20, 115–17.

22 Sarah Bradford Landau and Carl W. Condit, *Rise of the New York Skyscraper, 1865–1913* (New Haven, Conn.: Yale University Press, 1996), 381–91, highlight the level of sophistication and integration the New York skyscraper's technologies achieved in the Woolworth Building, which they call the "climax and conclusion"; Dietrich Neumann, *Architecture of the Night: The Illuminated Building* (Munich: Prestel, 2002), 102–3.

23 Thomas A. P. van Leeuwen, *The Skyward Trend of Thought: The Metaphysics of the American Skyscraper* (Cambridge, Mass.: MIT Press, 1988), 4, 39 (for quotes), 39–45.

24 Kern, *The Culture of Time and Space*, 226 (for quote), 223–40.
25 Burrows and Wallace, *Gotham*, 1212–18.
26 On the importance of the new technologies, and especially of electricity, to creating the desired ambience in consumer settings, see Rosalind Williams, *Dream Worlds: Mass Consumption in Late Nineteenth-Century France* (Berkeley: University of California Press, 1982), 84–90.
27 Carol Willis, *Form Follows Finance: Skyscrapers and Skylines in New York and Chicago* (New York: Princeton Architectural Press, 1995).
28 Montgomery Schuyler, *The Woolworth Building* (New York: privately printed by Munder-Thomsen Co. for F. W. Woolworth, 1913); Edwin A. Cochran, *The Cathedral of Commerce: Woolworth Building, New York* (Baltimore: Munder-Thomsen Co., 1916); and H. Addington Bruce, *Above the Clouds and Old New York: An Historical Sketch of the Site and a Description of the Many Wonders of the Woolworth Building, Published for Distribution among Visitors to the Woolworth Tower, New York* (Baltimore: Munder-Thomsen Press, 1913).
29 Neil Harris, *Building Lives: Constructing Rites and Passages* (New Haven, Conn.: Yale University Press, 1999).
30 Mary N. Woods argues in her recent account of nineteenth-century American architectural practice that attention to the architect's collaborators balances the existing and still-prevailing mythology of the "star architect." Mary N. Woods, *From Craft to Profession: The Practice of Architecture in Ninteenth-Century America* (Berkeley: University of California Press, 1999), 138–66.

CHAPTER ONE

1 On New York's urban crowds, public space as a "showcase," and Woolworth's perceptions of crowd behavior, see William R. Taylor, "The Evolution of Public Space: The Commercial City as Showcase," in *In Pursuit of Gotham: Culture and Commerce in New York* (New York: Oxford University Press, 1992), 35–50.
2 For the growing dominance of consumerism in American life from 1890, see William Leach, *Land of Desire: Merchants, Power, and the Rise of a New American Culture* (New York: Pantheon Books, 1993), 3–38.
3 "Frank Woolworth Dies Suddenly at L. I. Home," *Brooklyn Times*, April 8, 1919, in scrapbook, Woolworth Collection, NBM.
4 "Frank W. Woolworth Dies at Summer Home," *New York City Evening Post*, April 8, 1919, in scrapbook, Woolworth Collection, NBM.
5 Nina Baker, *Nickles and Dimes: The Story of F. W. Woolworth* (New York: Harcourt, Brace & World, 1954), is a good example of the Woolworth story as told in the Alger tradition. For a more balanced account of Woolworth's life and career, see his own autobiography, begun in 1919 and left uncompleted at his death: Frank W. Woolworth and Edward Mott Woolley, "From Dimes to Millions," *McClures' Magazine* 55 (December 1923): 8–18, 117–18; 56 (January 1924): 109–12, 114–16. See also Edwin Merton McBrier, *Genealogy of the Descendants of Henry McBrier and Kezia Sloan McBrier Who Migrated to the United States in 1827* (New York: privately printed, 1941); John K. Winkler, *Five and Ten: The Fabulous Life of F. W. Woolworth* (New York: Robert M. McBride & Co., 1940), 15–60; and John D. Nichols, "Milestones of Woolworth: A Compendium of Dates, Facts, and Data Skeletonizing Woolworth History through 1947," Woolworth Collection, NBM; and Nichols, "History of Woolworth (1879–1947)," Woolworth Collection, NBM.
6 Charles Sumner Woolworth, as quoted in F. W. Woolworth Co., *Celebrating 60 Years of An American Institution* (New York: Lord & Thomas, 1939), 5.
7 Woolworth's recollection of Emery J. Pennock is quoted in John D. Nichols, "History of Woolworth," n.p.
8 John D. Nichols, "History of Woolworth," n.p.
9 Woolworth and Woolley, "From Dimes to Millions," 12.
10 *Woolworth's First 75 Years: The Story of Everybody's Store, 1879–1954* (New York: F. W. Woolworth Co., 1954), 9, notes "the handicap of a poor location."
11 Woolworth and Woolley, "From Dimes to Millions," 16 (for quote), 114; and Ada Patterson, "A Man Who at 28 Suddenly Had a Great Idea," *American Magazine* 84 (October 1917): 53 (for quote). Five cents, at the time "shin plasters" or fractional currency, did not become a nickel coin until 1883, when the Treasury Department issued a five-cent piece. During the 1890s, the nickel gained purchasing clout in a wide array of settings: Consumers used the coin for nickel beer and nickel coffee, for amusement park rides, for the cheap entertainment offered by nickelodeons, or for nickel packs of cigarettes, a dozen roses, or a linen handkerchief. Thomas J. Schlereth,

Victorian America: Transformations of Everyday Life, 1876–1915 (New York: Harper Collins Publishers, 1991), 79–85.

12 Woolworth and Woolley, "From Dimes to Millions," 16; and Winkler, *Five and Ten*, 51–52.

13 Door-to-door peddlers sold "Yankee notions," as did department stores, which called them "fancy goods." For a list of the stock sold in Woolworth's Lancaster store, see F. W. Woolworth Co., *100th Anniversary: 1879–1979* (New York: F. W. Woolworth Co., 1979), 10.

14 Writing to his managers, Woolworth emphasized "the model of the big dry goods stores [with fixed cash prices], not the old country stores." Frank Woolworth, "General Letter to All Stores," September 24, 1891, Woolworth Collection, NBM.

15 The ninety-nine-cent-store phenomenon of the 1870s probably influenced Woolworth's single-price store; a ninety-nine-cent store reportedly opened in Watertown in 1874. John D. Nichols, "History of Woolworth," n.p.

16 Frank Woolworth, as quoted in "New Store Opens," *Lancaster Intelligencer*, June 21, 1879, Woolworth Collection, NBM.

17 Geoffrey M. Lebhar, *Chain Stores in America, 1859–1962*, 3rd ed. (New York: Chain Store Publishing Corp., 1963), 24–42.

18 Alfred D. Chandler, Jr., *The Visible Hand: The Managerial Revolution in American Business* (Cambridge, Mass.: Harvard University Press, Belknap Press, 1977), 233–34.

19 Frank Woolworth, as quoted in "F. W. Woolworth, Head of Chain of 1,038 Ten-Cent Stores, Dies," *St. Louis Star*, April 8, 1919, in scrapbook, Woolworth Collection, NBM.

20 *Woolworth's First 75 Years*, 16; and Winkler, *Five and Ten*, 102.

21 John D. Nichols, "History of Woolworth," n.p.

22 Ralph M. Hower, *History of Macy's of New York, 1858–1919: Chapters in the Evolution of the Department Store* (Cambridge, Mass.: Harvard University Press, 1946), 87–88; and Chandler, *The Visible Hand*, 215–16, 225.

23 See, for example, F. W. Woolworth to William Shimer Son and Company, December 28, 1894, Woolworth Collection, NBM. "You have our list, and we trust that you will be able to make many concessions from the old prices."

24 Glenn Porter, *The Rise of Big Business, 1860–1910* (Arlington Heights, Ill.: Harlan Davidson, 1973), 43–46.

25 Bernice L. Thomas, *America's 5 and 10 Cent Stores: The Kress Legacy* (New York: John Wiley & Sons, 1997), 5; and Winkler, *Five and Ten*, 162–82.

26 Woolworth fits the classic definition of the entrepreneur. See Joseph Schumpeter, *The Theory of Economic Development*, trans. Redvers Opie (Cambridge, Mass.: Harvard University Press, 1934), 74–94, which notes that the entrepreneur did new things or combined in a new way factors already available to others.

27 Frank Woolworth, as quoted in "F. W. Woolworth, Head of Chain"; and in "Frank Woolworth Dies Suddenly."

28 Alan Trachtenberg, *The Incorporation of America: Culture and Society in the Gilded Age* (New York: Hill & Wang, 1982), 39–40.

29 Woolworth described these economic conditions: "The first big boom in prices that I remember was in the fall of 1879, when it looked as though the whole five and ten cent business would be shoved right off the face of the earth. It was a hard struggle for me with my limited capital of less than $1,000, but the reaction came in the forepart of the year 1880 and prices continued to drop for several years. That is the time the five and ten cent business really got a foothold. In 1891 and 1892 there was another boom but the Financial Panic of 1893 struck the country with terrific force and we got another foothold and were able to secure large and fine goods to sell at our prices." Frank Woolworth, "Annual Letter," 1898, as quoted in Winkler, *Five and Ten*, 127.

30 Chandler, *The Visible Hand*, 79–80, 198, 204.

31 Ibid., 207–8, 224–39.

32 Between the 1870s and the 1930s, the United States "outdistanced other leading industrial economies in the growth of both population and per capita income—the two basic ingredients that determined overall consumer demand." Alfred D. Chandler, Jr., *Scale and Scope: The Dynamics of Industrial Capitalism* (Cambridge, Mass.: Harvard University Press, Belknap Press, 1990), 51–53.

33 On paper, F. W. Woolworth and Company actually comprised three corporations: F. W. Woolworth and Company of New York, the parent corporation; F. W. Woolworth and Company of Massachusetts; and F. W. Woolworth and Company of Pennsylvania. "Milestones" (unsigned chronology), Woolworth Collection, NBM.

34 Winkler, *Five and Ten*, 141–47.

35 Chandler, *The Visible Hand*, 7–8.

36 Andrew S. Dolkart, *Guide to New York City Landmarks* (New York: John Wiley & Sons, 1998), 23–24.

37 Frank Woolworth, as quoted in Winkler, *Five and Ten*, 146.

38 Ibid.

39 "Early Woolworth Statistics," Woolworth Collection, NBM; and *Woolworth's First 75 Years*, 16–17.

40 Frank Woolworth, "General Letter to All Stores," December 31, 1909, in John D. Nichols, "Milestones of Woolworth," 34.

41 Only one of the regional subheadquarters existed before Woolworth decided to incorporate in 1905, an office he set up in Chicago in 1904. F. W. Woolworth, "Ancient History of the Five and Ten Cent Business," in "Memorandum to the Officers, Office Managers, Buyers, Inspectors, and Store Managers of the F. W. Woolworth Co.," February 27, 1912, Woolworth Collection, NBM.

42 By 1919, Woolworth had relocated the Chicago office to the McCormick Building. F. W. Woolworth Co., *Fortieth Anniversary Souvenir, 1879–1919* (New York, 1919), 16.

43 Robert C. Kirkwood, "Personnel Entered in F. W. Woolworth Books as First Asset," *Christian Science Monitor*, March 31, 1959.

44 Frank Woolworth, "Annual Letter," 1898, in "Excerpts from Available F. W. Woolworth and Co. Annual Letters (1894–1911)," Woolworth Collection, NBM.

45 John D. Nichols, "History of Woolworth," n.p.; and Winkler, *Five and Ten*, 125–26.

46 Frank Woolworth, as quoted in G. A. Nichols, "How F. W. Woolworth Built His Wonderful Distributing Machine," *Printer's Ink* 107 (April 10, 1919), 27; and James Brough, *The Woolworths* (New York: McGraw-Hill Book Co., 1982), 99.

47 Frank Woolworth, as quoted in Winkler, *Five and Ten*, 125.

48 John D. Nichols, "History of Woolworth," n.p.; and Frank Woolworth, "Annual Letter," 1906, in "Excerpts from Available F. W. Woolworth and Co. Annual Letters (1894–1911)."

49 Managers in attendance at the convention of 1901 prepared such papers as "How to Meet Competition of All Kinds" and "How to Secure and Manage Employees to Get the Best Results." "Five and Ten Cent Store Convention," 1901, Woolworth Collection, NBM.

50 "First Five and Ten Cent Store: Twenty-Fifth Anniversary of Its Formation Properly Celebrated," *Watertown Daily Times*, February 23, 1904, in Frank Winfield Woolworth Press Clippings Files, WDT.

51 At the first seminar held in Washington, D.C., in 1907 managers discussed forty subjects related to five- and ten-cent retailing. "Milestones."

52 Frank Woolworth to Woolworth Syndicate (executive offices in New York), March 5, 1890, Woolworth Collection, NBM.

53 Mira Wilkins, *The Emergence of Multinational Enterprise: American Business Abroad from the Colonial Era to 1914* (Cambridge, Mass.: Harvard University Press, 1970), 35–36.

54 Frank Woolworth, as quoted in Bertie C. Forbes, "Frank W. Woolworth," in *Men Who Are Making America*, 2nd ed. (New York: Forbes Publishing Co., 1918), 421.

55 Alexis de Tocqueville, *Democracy in America* (1835), vol. 2, edited by Phillips Bradley (New York: Vintage Books, 1945), 261.

56 Frank Woolworth to Woolworth Syndicate, May 18, 1890, Woolworth Collection, NBM.

57 Eric Hobsbawn, *The Age of Empire: 1875–1914* (New York: Vintage Books, 1989), 9.

58 Walter La Feber, *The New Empire: An Interpretation of American Expansion, 1860–1898* (Ithaca, N.Y.: Cornell University Press, 1963), 1–61, 102–45, 161–66, 407–9; and Emily S. Rosenberg, *Spreading the American Dream: American Economic and Cultural Expansion, 1980–1945* (New York: Hill & Wang, 1982), 59–62.

59 Wilkins, *The Emergence of Multinational Enterprise*, 37–78.

60 Ralph Waldo Emerson, "Napoleon; or, The Man of the World," in *Selected Writings of Emerson,* ed. Donald McQuade (New York: Random House, 1981), 479.

61 Clarence J. Webster, *French Emigres in the Wilderness of the North* (Watertown, N.Y.: Watertown National Bank), n.p.; and Roger G. Kennedy, *Orders from France* (New York: Alfred A. Knopf, 1989), 353–57. The conjecture that Woolworth read a biography of Napoleon appears in Baker, *Nickles and Dimes*, 26–27.

62 Brough, *The Woolworths*, 146–47.

63 Louis J. Horowitz and Boyden Sparkes, *The Towers of New York: The Memoirs of a Master Builder* (New York: Simon & Schuster, 1937), 120.

64 Frank Woolworth to Woolworth Syndicate, March 21, April 6, April 10, April 19, April 25, April 26, April 30, 1890, Woolworth Collection, NBM.

65 Frank Woolworth, "General Letter To All Stores: United States, Canada, and Great Britain," February 20, 1914, Cass Gilbert Collection, N-YHS.

66 Forbes, "Frank W. Woolworth," 421; and F. W. Woolworth Co., *100th Anniversary*, 17.

67 Horowitz and Sparkes, *The Towers of New York*, 2.

68 Frank Woolworth, as quoted in Leo L. Redding, "Mr. F. W. Woolworth's Story," *World's Work* 25 (April 1913): 663. On the Singer Tower, see Mardges Bacon, *Ernest Flagg: Beaux-Arts Architect and Urban Reformer* (New York: Architectural History Foundation; Cambridge, Mass.: MIT Press, 1986), 209–33.

69 Katherine Solomonson, *The Chicago Tribune Tower Competition: Skyscraper Design and Cultural Change in the 1920s* (New York: Cambridge University Press, 2001), 103, analyzes how certain corporate headquarters functioned like trademarks.

70 Frank Woolworth, as quoted in Daniel J. Boorstin, *The Americans: The Democratic Experience* (New York: Random House, 1974), 114–15.

71 Winkler, *Five and Ten*, 102.

72 Schlereth, *Victorian America*, 141; Chandler, *The Visible Hand*, 5–6; and Chandler, *Scale and Scope*, 51–53.

73 Frank Woolworth to Woolworth Syndicate, April 6, 1890, Woolworth Collection, NBM.

74 Leach, *Land of Desire*, 40, 55.

75 Woolworth's "5 and 10 Cent Store Convention of the F. W. Woolworth and Company Stores," held in Lancaster on June 3–7, 1901, for instance, featured the presentations "The Necessity of the Proper Display of Goods on Counters, Show Cases, and Shelves" and "The Best and Most Effective Trim for Windows." Woolworth Collection, NBM.

76 F. W. Woolworth Co., *100th Anniversary*, 13.

77 John D. Nichols, "Milestones of Woolworth," 10; and Winkler, *Five and Ten*, 105.

78 On Woolworth's stores as an "institution," see Anthony W. Robins, "F. W. Woolworth Company: The '5 and 10' and the World's Highest Building," in "Woolworth Building, 233 Broadway, Borough of Manhattan," New York Landmarks Preservation Commission designation report, April 12, 1983, 4.

79 Frank Woolworth, "Opening Address," delivered at "5 and 10 Cent Store Convention of the F. W. Woolworth and Company Stores," June 3–7, 1901, Lancaster, Pennsylvania, Woolworth Collection, NBM.

80 Winkler, *Five and Ten*, 114–17; and F. W. Woolworth Co., *100th Anniversary*, 16–17.

81 *Rules for Management of Stores* (New York: F. W. Woolworth & Co., 1906), 3–16, Woolworth Collection, NBM.

82 Frank Woolworth, as quoted in Redding, "Mr. F. W. Woolworth's Story," 663.

83 Regarding the typical speculative office building, see Carol Willis, *Form Follows Finance: Skyscrapers and Skylines in New York and Chicago* (New York: Princeton Architectural Press, 1995), 19–33.

84 *The Woolworth Building, Lancaster, Pa.* (1900), n.p.; *Commerating 71 Years of Woolworth Service in Lancaster, Pennsylvania, 1879–1950* (1950), n.p.; and "Five and Dime Opened Here First in 1879," *Intelligencer Journal* (Lancaster, Pa.), June 11, 1979, 8, 26, Frank Winfield Woolworth Information Files, Woolworth Building, LCHS.

85 Leach, *Land of Desire*, 134–38.

86 Frank Woolworth, "Annual Letter," 1900, in "Excerpts from Available F. W. Woolworth and Co. Annual Letters (1894–1911)."

87 *The Woolworth Building, Lancaster, Pa.*, n.p. (for quote); and Karen Plunkett-Powell, *Remembering Woolworth's: A Nostalgic History of the World's Most Famous Five and Dime* (New York: St. Martin's Press, 1999), 188–89.

88 The roof garden manager kept a detailed account book documenting expenses, including the salaries of actors and musicians, Woolworth Collection, NBM.

89 On the importance of the Parisian example to American retailers, see Joseph Siry, *Carson Pirie Scott: Louis Sullivan and the Chicago Department Store* (Chicago: University of Chicago Press, 1988), 21, 32, 59, 101–4, 136, 204; and Rosalind Williams, *Dream Worlds: Mass Consumption in Late Nineteenth-Century France* (Berkeley: University of California Press, 1982), 8 (for quote), 9–12.

90 On Schickel and his designs, see H. Van Buren Magonigle, "A Half Century of Architecture," pt. 7, "A Biographical Review," *Pencil Points* 15 (March 1934): 564–65; and Robert A. M. Stern, Thomas Mellins, and David Fishman, *New York, 1880: Architecture and Urbanism in the Gilded Age* (New York: Monacelli Press, 1999), 202, 225, 261, 442, 485–86, 507–8, 541–42, 642–43, 714, 729–30, 826, 849.

91 The site cost $75,000 and the building about $225,000. Winkler, *Five and Ten*, 129.

92 John D. Nichols, "Milestones of Woolworth," 15.

93 "Milestones" (unsigned chronology), Woolworth Collection, NBM.

94 Woolworth, "Opening Address."

95 *The Woolworth Building, Lancaster, Pa.*, n.p.; and "Opening of F. W. Woolworth Company Store, July 19, 1950: Commemorating 71 Years of Woolworth Service in Lancaster, Pennsylvania, 1879–1950" (unidentified newspaper clipping), Frank Winfield Woolworth Information Files, Woolworth Building, LCHS.
96 *The Woolworth Building, Lancaster, Pa.*, n.p.
97 Ibid.
98 Leach, *Land of Desire*, 112–22.
99 Redding, "Mr. F. W. Woolworth's Story," 662.
100 Robert Bruce Davies, *Peacefully Working to Conquer the World: Singer Sewing Machines in Foreign Markets, 1854–1920* (New York: Arno Press, 1976), 42–44, 100, 334–36; and Gail Fenske and Deryck Holdsworth, "Corporate Identity and the New York Office Building, 1895–1915," in *The Landscape of Modernity: Essays on New York City, 1900–1940*, ed. David Ward and Olivier Zunz (New York: Russell Sage Foundation, 1992), 135–39.
101 "A Millionaire's Opinion of Education," *Outlook*, April 30, 1919, 731.
102 John D. Nichols, "History of Woolworth," n.p.
103 Frank Woolworth to Woolworth Syndicate, March 27–30, April 1, April 6, April 13, April 22, April 27, 1890, Woolworth Collection, NBM.
104 See "European Orders, 1891," Woolworth Collection, NBM.
105 Edward C. Rochette, "The Other Side of the Coin: The Five and Dime at Christmas Time," *Numismatist* 103 (December 1990): 1986. By 1902, Woolworth imported approximately 20 percent of his goods from abroad.
106 Woolworth and Woolley, "From Dimes to Millions," 118.
107 Frank Woolworth to Woolworth Syndicate, April 13, 1890, Woolworth Collection, NBM.
108 Williams, *Dream Worlds*, 8–12.
109 Frank Woolworth to the Woolworth Syndicate, April 26, 1890, Woolworth Collection, NBM.
110 Frank Woolworth to the Woolworth Syndicate, April 25, April 26, April 27, 1890, Woolworth Collection, NBM.
111 David Harvey, *Paris: Capital of Modernity* (New York: Routledge, 2003), 212–18.
112 Frank Woolworth to the Woolworth Syndicate, April 28, 1890, Woolworth Collection, NBM.
113 Frank Woolworth to the Woolworth Syndicate, April 27, 1890, Woolworth Collection, NBM.
114 Ibid.
115 Frank Woolworth to the Woolworth Syndicate, April 24, 1890, Woolworth Collection, NBM.
116 Frank Woolworth to the Woolworth Syndicate, April 27, 1890, Woolworth Collection, NBM.
117 Frank Woolworth to the Woolworth Syndicate, March 6, April 6, 1890, Woolworth Collection, NBM.
118 Frank Woolworth to the Woolworth Syndicate, March 6, March 7, April 27, 1890, Woolworth Collection, NBM.
119 Frank Woolworth, "General Letter to All Stores," March 26, 1892, Woolworth Collection, NBM.
120 Frank Woolworth, "General Letter to All Stores," September 15, 1893, Woolworth Collection, NBM; and John D. Nichols, "History of Woolworth," n.p.
121 Leach, *Land of Desire*, 32.
122 Franz K. Winkler [Montgomery Schuyler], "Architecture in the Billionaire District of New York City," *Architectural Record* 11 (October 1901): 679–99. On Fifth Avenue, see Stern, Mellins, and Fishman, *New York, 1880*, 570–601.
123 Isaac D. Fletcher was the president of the Barrett Manufacturing Company and the New York Coal Tar Company. John Tauranac, *Elegant New York: The Builders and Their Buildings* (New York: Abbeville Press, 1985), 181–83.
124 Thorstein Veblen, *The Theory of the Leisure Class* (1899; reprint, New York: Penguin Books, 1983), 29 (for quote). Frederic Cople Jaher, *The Urban Establishment: Upper Strata in Boston, New York, Charleston, Chicago, and Los Angeles* (Urbana: University of Illinois Press, 1982), 250–81; and Sven Beckert, *The Monied Metropolis: New York and the Consolidation of the American Bourgeoisie, 1850–1896* (Cambridge: Cambridge University Press, 2001), 207–334.
125 Winkler [Schuyler], "Architecture in the Billionaire District," 693.
126 Beckert, *The Monied Metropolis*, 258–61.
127 Herbert Croly, "A Contemporary New York Residence," *Architectural Record* 12 (December 1902): 720.
128 On Alva Smith Vanderbilt, see Mary Woods, *From Craft to Profession: The Practice of Architecture in Nineteenth-Century America* (Berkeley: University of California Press, 1999), 163–64.
129 Robert A. M. Stern, Gregory Gilmartin, and John Massengale, *New York, 1900: Architecture and Urbanism, 1890–1915* (New York: Rizzoli International Publications, 1983), 190–201.
130 Regarding Woolworth's social life, see "Woolworth's Original Salesgirl Recollects," in Frank Winfield Woolworth Information Files, LCHS. Louis Horowitz described a visit to Woolworth's mansion in Horowitz and Sparkes, *The Towers of New York*, 119 (for quote), 119–20.

131 Cleveland Amory, *Who Killed Society?* (New York: Harper & Row Publishers, 1960), 171–72.
132 Tauranac, *Elegant New York*, 183–85.
133 Frank Taft (vice president, Aeolian-Skinner Organ Company), as quoted in Winkler, *Five and Ten*, 134.
134 Plunkett-Powell, *Remembering Woolworth's*, 194; and Winkler, *Five and Ten*, 128.
135 Frank Woolworth to Woolworth Syndicate, March 27–30, April 1, April 6, April 13, April 20, April 22, April 27, 1890.
136 Jaher, *The Urban Establishment*, 237, 269–71; and Eric Homberger, *Mrs. Astor's New York: Money and Social Power in a Gilded Age* (New Haven, Conn.: Yale University Press, 2002), 232–33.
137 On the attitude of the city's old wealth toward skyscrapers, see Mona Domosh, *Invented Cities: The Creation of Landscape in Nineteenth-Century New York and Boston* (New Haven, Conn.: Yale University Press, 1996), 96.
138 Tauranac, *Elegant New York*, 16–18. For a description of Morgan's headquarters, see "Banking House of J. P. Morgan and Co.," *Architecture and Building* 47 (January 1915): 6–14.
139 "Frank Woolworth Dies Suddenly at L. I. Home."
140 *Rules for the Management of Stores* (New York: F. W. Woolworth & Co., 1906), 33, Woolworth Collection, NBM; and Frank Woolworth, "General Letter to All Stores," February 13, 1892, Woolworth Collection, NBM.
141 Frank Woolworth, "General Letter to All Stores," August 12, 1893, Woolworth Collection, NBM; and Woolworth, "Annual Letter," 1903, in "Excerpts from Available F. W. Woolworth and Co. Annual Letters (1894–1911)."
142 Frank Woolworth, "General Letter to All Stores," November 4, 1893, Woolworth Collection, NBM; and Woolworth, "Annual Letter," 1901, in "Excerpts from Available F. W. Woolworth and Co. Annual Letters (1894–1911)."
143 Winkler, *Five and Ten*, 110, 124, 136–37; Schlereth, *Victorian America*, 34, notes that the "poverty line indicator" moved from $506 per year in 1887 to $544 in 1893 to $660 in 1909.
144 Frank Woolworth, "General Letter to All Stores," February 13, December 13, 1892, Woolworth Collection, NBM. Woolworth justified his low wage scale with the argument that working in a store had more dignity than manufacturing or domestic work. To attract and retain a reliable work force, in spite of offering such low wages, he pioneered employment policies such as paid vacations and Christmas bonuses. *Rules for Management of Stores*, 29–31; and F. W. Woolworth Co., *100th Anniversary*, 17.
145 Frank Woolworth, "General Letter to All Stores," February 13, 1892, Woolworth Collection, NBM. Woolworth paid his male "learners," by contrast, a disproportionate share of the company's total salaries. Starting in the basement at six dollars per week, they earned an additional one dollar per week every month, and after five months at least ten dollars per week. Frank Woolworth, "General Letter to All Stores," March 29, 1905, in John D. Nichols, "Milestones of Woolworth," 25.
146 Frank Woolworth, as quoted in Ada Patterson, "A Man Who at 28 Suddenly Had a Great Idea," *American Magazine* 84 (October 1917): 53.
147 Woolworth and Woolley, "From Dimes to Millions," 111. Trachtenberg, *The Incorporation of America*, 115, argues that for mass retailers such as Woolworth small country towns provided "easy markets for mass-produced goods."
148 Frank Woolworth, as quoted in "Maxims of the Late F. W. Woolworth," *Watertown Daily Times*, April 11, 1919, in Frank Winfield Woolworth Press Clippings Files, WDT.

CHAPTER TWO

1 Frank Woolworth, "General Letter to All Stores," November 10, 1910, in John D. Nichols, "Milestones of Woolworth: A Compendium of Dates, Facts, and Data Skeletonizing Woolworth History through 1947," 37, Woolworth Collection, NBM.
2 John C. Van Dyke, *The New New York: A Commentary on the Place and the People* (New York: Macmillan Co., 1909), 8, 425 (for quote).
3 Ibid., 10.
4 "A Realty Triumph in Assembling Plot," *New York Times*, January 22, 1911; and Robert Holmes Elmendorf, "Evolution of Commercial Banking in New York City, 1851–1951, in Which Is Recorded the Story of the Irving Trust Company" (typescript, January 1951), 124.
5 Leo L. Redding, "Mr. F. W. Woolworth's Story," *World's Work* 25 (April 1913): 664. See also William R. Taylor, "The Evolution of Public Space: The Commercial City as Showcase," in *In Pursuit of Gotham: Culture and Commerce in New York*, ed. William R. Taylor (New York: Oxford University Press, 1992), 45–48.

6 "The Man Who Saw Millions in a Nickel," *Literary Digest* 61 (May 3, 1919): 78. See also Woolworth's "street locater map for stores," ca. 1900, Woolworth Collection, NBM.

7 Van Dyke, *The New New York*, 74.

8 William C. Conant, "Will New York Be the Final Metropolis?" *Century Magazine* 26 (September 1883): 688–91, 693.

9 "The Importance of New York," *Real Estate Record and Builders' Guide* 67 (January 5, 1901): 2 (for quote). See also Edwin G. Burrows and Mike Wallace, *Gotham: A History of New York City to 1898* (New York: Oxford University Press, 1999): 656–66, 939–41, 1041–49.

10 Conant, "Will New York Be the Final Metropolis?" 691 (for quote), 693; and Eric Lampard, "Introductory Essay," in *Inventing Times Square: Commerce and Culture at the Crossroads of the World*, ed. William R. Taylor (New York: Russell Sage Foundation, 1991; reprint, Baltimore: Johns Hopkins University Press, 1996), 17 (for quote).

11 "Large Corporations Moving to New York," *Real Estate Record and Builders' Guide* 66 (December 15, 1900): 822. On the Illinois law that restricted corporate investment in real estate (by prohibiting the construction of office buildings larger than needed for strictly corporate uses), see Katherine Solomonson, *The Chicago Tribune Tower Competition: Skyscraper Design and Cultural Change in the 1920s* (New York: Cambridge University Press, 2001), 32–33, 104.

12 Lampard, "Introductory Essay," 17–18.

13 Burrows and Wallace, *Gotham*, 1044–49, 1235–36; and Alfred D. Chandler, Jr., *Scale and Scope: The Dynamics of Industrial Capitalism* (Cambridge, Mass.: Harvard University Press, Belknap Press, 1990), 71–78.

14 Ibid., 61; and William Leach, *Land of Desire: Merchants, Power, and the Rise of a New American Culture* (New York: Pantheon Books, 1993), 24–25.

15 R. A. Oakes, *Genealogical and Family History of the County of Jefferson, New York* (New York: Lewis Publishing Co., 1905): 197–98.

16 Mona Domosh, *Invented Cities: The Creation of Landscape in Nineteenth-Century New York and Boston* (New Haven, Conn.: Yale University Press, 1996): 44–52.

17 Van Dyke, *The New New York*, 198.

18 *Scribner's Magazine* is quoted in "The Growth of Clubs in New York City," *Real Estate Record and Builders' Guide* 45, club number supplement (March 8, 1890): 1, as quoted in M. Christine Boyer, *Manhattan Manners: Architecture and Style, 1850–1900* (New York: Rizzoli International Publications, 1985), 88.

19 Burrows and Wallace, *Gotham*, 668.

20 Domosh, *Invented Cities*, 52–54, 55 (for quotes); and Harry E. Resseguie, "A. T. Stewart's Marble Palace: The Cradle of the Department Store," *New-York Historical Society Quarterly* 48 (April 1964): 131–62.

21 Domosh, *Invented Cities*, 57–64; and Boyer, *Manhattan Manners*, 92–96.

22 Leach, *Land of Desire*, 9; Burrows and Wallace, *Gotham*, 945–46; and Boyer, *Manhattan Manners*, 91.

23 John K. Winkler, *Five and Ten: The Fabulous Life of F. W. Woolworth* (New York: Robert McBride & Co., 1940), 117–18.

24 Carol Willis, *Form Follows Finance: Skyscrapers and Skylines in New York and Chicago* (New York: Princeton Architectural Press, 1995), 23.

25 Solomonson, *The Chicago Tribune Tower Compeition*, 103.

26 George French, *How to Advertise* (New York: Doubleday, Page & Co., 1917), 181, as quoted in Solomonson, *The Chicago Tribune Tower Competition*, 104.

27 "New York, the Unrivalled Business Centre," *Harper's Weekly* 46 (November 15, 1902): 1673.

28 "Executive Office," February 13, 1914, Woolworth Building, Cass Gilbert Collection, N-YHS; and Redding, "Mr. F. W. Woolworth's Story," 663.

29 Sir Peter Hall, "The Apotheosis of the Modern: New York, 1880–1940," in *Cities in Civilization* (New York: Pantheon Books, 1998), 746, 770 (for quotes), 746–49, 753–58.

30 Ibid., 754–68; Robert M. Fogelson, *Downtown: Its Rise and Fall, 1880–1950* (New Haven, Conn.: Yale University Press, 2001), 55–74; and *Interborough Rapid Transit: The New York Subway, Its Construction and Equipment* (New York: Interborough Rapid Transit Co., 1904), 23–35.

31 Frank Woolworth, as quoted in Redding, "Mr. F. W. Woolworth's Story," 662; and Taylor, "The Evolution of Public Space," 45–46.

32 Frank Woolworth to Woolworth Syndicate (executive offices in New York), April 19 (for quote), April 22, April 25, May 6, 1890, Woolworth Collection, NBM.

33 Thomas P. Hughes, *Networks of Power: Electrification in Western Society, 1880–1930* (Baltimore: Johns Hopkins University Press, 1983): 40–46; and Rosa-

lind H. Williams, *Dream Worlds: Mass Consumption in Late Nineteenth-Century France* (Berkeley: University of California Press, 1982), 84–90, 86 (for quote).

34 Stephen Kern, *The Culture of Time and Space, 1880–1918* (Cambridge, Mass.: Harvard University Press, 1983), 114.

35 "New York, the Unrivalled Business Centre," 1673.

36 Max Page, *The Creative Destruction of Manhattan, 1900–1940* (Chicago: University of Chicago Press, 1999), 24, 30.

37 Henry Adams, "Nunc Age (1905)," in *The Education of Henry Adams* (1907; reprint, New York: Library of America, 1983), 1176.

38 Alan Trachtenberg, "Image and Ideology: New York in the Photographer's Eye," *Journal of Urban History* 10 (August 1984): 455–58.

39 Page, *The Creative Destruction of Manhattan*, 2–3, 7; and Hall, *Cities in Civilization*, 746 (for quote).

40 William R. Taylor, "New York and the Origin of the Skyline: The Commercial City as Visual Text," in Taylor, *In Pursuit of Gotham*, 23, 27.

41 "The Skyline of Buildings below Chambers Street, as Seen from the Hudson River," *Harper's Weekly* 31 (March 20, 1897): 296–97; and "The Vertical Growth of New York City," *Scientific American* 84 (March 2, 1901): 136. *Harper's Weekly* contrasted the skylines of 1881 and 1897 and *Scientific American* the skylines of 1891 and 1901.

42 Montgomery Schuyler, "The Skyline of New York, 1881–1897," *Harper's Weekly* 41 (March 20, 1897): 295.

43 A. D. F. Hamlin, "The Tall Building from an American Point of View," *Engineering Magazine* 14 (December 1897): 441.

44 Sylvester Baxter, "The New New York," *Outlook* 83 (June 23, 1906): 415.

45 Henry James, as quoted in Leon Edel, "Introduction," in *The American Scene,* by Henry James (1907; reprint, Bloomington: Indiana University Press, 1969), vii.

46 Montgomery Schuyler, "Some Recent Skyscrapers," *Architectural Record* 22 (September 1907): 161.

47 "The Skyscraper and the Silhouette," *American Architect and Building News* 92 (September 21, 1907): 89.

48 Giles Edgerton [Mary Fanton Roberts], "How New York Has Redeemed Herself from Ugliness: An Artist's Revelation of the Beauty of the Skyscraper," *Craftsman* 11 (January 1907): 458, 471.

49 Montgomery Schuyler, "'The Towers of Manhattan' and Notes on the Woolworth Building," *Architectural Record* 33 (February 1913): 104.

50 John Van Dyke, *The New New York: A Commentary on the Place and the People* (New York: Macmillan Co., 1909), 148; and "Skyscraping up to Date," *Architectural Record* 23 (January 1908): 74.

51 Harrison Rhodes, "New York: City of Romance," *Harper's Monthly Magazine* 119 (November 1909): 914.

52 Joseph B. Gilder, "The City of Dreadful Height," *Putnam's Monthly Magazine* 5 (November 1908): 136, 141, 143 (for quote).

53 Van Dyke, *The New New York*, 4–5.

54 "Towered Cities," *Living Age* 42 (January 2, 1909): 47.

55 Richard Harding Davis, "Broadway," *Scribner's Magazine* 9 (1891): 588, as quoted in Domosh, *Invented Cities*, 86.

56 Domosh, *Invented Cities*, 83–87; and Burrows and Wallace, *Gotham*, 1151–54.

57 Ibid., 1051–52; Domosh, *Invented Cities*, 84; and Sarah Bradford Landau and Carl W. Condit, *Rise of the New York Skyscraper, 1865–1913* (New Haven, Conn.: Yale University Press, 1996), 197, 200–201.

58 Meyer Berger, *The Story of "The New York Times": 1851–1951* (New York: Simon & Schuster, 1951), 121, 134–35; and "The Programme for the Dewey Holidays," *Harper's Weekly* 43 (September 30, 1899): 986–88.

59 Pulitzer promoted the World Building as a monument to the newspaper's record of public service. Domosh, *Invented Cities*, 84.

60 Jon A. Peterson, *The Birth of City Planning in the United States, 1840–1917* (Baltimore: Johns Hopkins University Press, 2003), 102–8, 137–38, 202–6; and Harvey A. Kantor, "The City Beautiful in New York," *New-York Historical Society Quarterly* 58 (April 1973): 153–71.

61 John De Witt Warner, "Matters That Suggest Themselves," *Municipal Affairs* 2 (March 1898): 123.

62 Herbert Croly, "New York as the American Metropolis," *Architectural Record* 13 (March 1903): 195, 197. On Croly, see Thomas Bender, *New York Intellect: A History of the Intellectual Life in New York City from 1750 to the Beginnings of Our Own Time* (New York: Alfred A. Knopf, 1987), 222–27.

63 Charles Mulford Robinson, *Modern Civic Art* (New York: G. P. Putnam's Sons, 1903), 81–84.

64 *Memorial of the Municipal Art Society Relative to Proposed Changes in and about City Hall Square, New*

York City (New York: Municipal Art Society, 1902).

65 "Proposed Brooklyn Bridge Terminal and City Offices," *Architects and Builders' Magazine* 4 (August 1903): 483–89; and Gregory Gilmartin, *Shaping the City: New York and the Municipal Art Society* (New York: Clarkson Potter Publishers, 1995), 77–81.

66 "The Proposed Brooklyn Bridge Terminal Improvements," *American Architect and Building News* 81 (August 15, 1903): 50.

67 *The Report of the New York City Improvement Commission* (New York, 1904); and *The Report of the New York City Improvement Commssion* (New York, 1907). See also Kantor, "The City Beautiful in New York," 159–71.

68 Robinson, *Modern Civic Art*, 96.

69 Croly, "New York as the American Metropolis," 199.

70 Van Dyke, *The New New York*, 140.

71 "A Monumental Design for a Supreme Court House," *Architects and Builders' Magazine* 10 (August 1910): 427–29; "A Tower Building a Thousand Feet High," *Real Estate Record and Builder's Guide* 85 (April 30, 1910): 921–22; and "James Riely Gordon," *American Architect* 150 (April 1937): 143.

72 Frank Woolworth, as quoted in "F. W. Woolworth's Personality Revealed in European Letters," *Watertown Daily Times*, June 8, 1954, in Frank Winfield Woolworth Press Clippings Files, WDT.

73 Editorial, *Real Estate Record and Builders' Guide* 86 (October 15, 1910): 603; and "Surplus Office Space," *Real Estate Record and Builders' Guide* 88 (October 21, 1911): 590.

74 Frank Woolworth, as quoted in "F. W. Woolworth Dies Suddenly in L. I. Home," *Brooklyn Times*, April 8, 1919, in scrapbook, Woolworth Collection, NBM.

75 Richard M. Hurd, "Map Showing Value per Square Foot in Dollars of New York Real Estate," in *Principles of City Land Values* (New York: Record & Guide, 1903), 158; and Willis, *Form Follows Finance*, 157.

76 Peter Brooks (of Peter and Shepherd Brooks, real estate investors from Boston), as cited in Thomas A. P. Van Leeuwen, *The Skyward Trend of Thought: The Metaphysics of the American Skyscraper* (Cambridge, Mass.: MIT Press, 1986), 92; and Earle Shultz and Walter Simmons, *Offices in the Sky* (Indianapolis: Bobbs-Merrill Co., 1959), 21–22.

77 "Two-thirds of Woolworth Building Space Leased," *Wall Street Journal*, February 9, 1914, in scrapbook, Cass Gilbert Collection, N-YHS.

78 Later, W. A. Starrett, *Skyscrapers and the Men Who Build Them* (New York: Charles Scribner's Sons, 1928), 88, wrote that skyscrapers had the "power to move centers of cities. . . . Great structures can actually beckon the trends of population and traffic and, in a measure, can compel the shifting economic centers of gravity."

79 Redding, "Mr. F. W. Woolworth's Story," 662; and Taylor, "The Evolution of Public Space," 46.

80 "F. W. Woolworth Invests His Millions in Towering Broadway Office Building," *New York City American*, February 22, 1911, in scrapbook, Cass Gilbert Collection, N-YHS.

81 The anonymous author of "Surplus Office Space," 590, recounted in 1911: "Of late years it has been banks, insurance buildings, or individual investors like Mr. Woolworth who have been erecting skyscrapers; and inasmuch as they can afford to accept a smaller return on their investment, they are making the operations of speculative real estate companies in the field increasingly difficult."

82 Montgomery Schuyler, "The Woolworth Building" (1913), in *American Architecture and Other Writings by Montgomery Schuyler*, ed. William H. Jordy and Ralph Coe (Cambridge, Mass.: Harvard University Press, Belknap Press, 1961), 2:617. Banks had served as valued tenants in speculative office building projects from the mid-nineteenth century, although, from the 1880s, escalating land values encouraged many banks to speculate in their own office-building projects. Lee Edward Gray, "The Office Building in New York City, 1850–1880" (Ph.D. diss., Cornell University, 1993), 38–39.

83 Allen E. Beals, "Edward J. Hogan, Agent: The Inside Story of How the World's Tallest Structure Came to Be Built, and How the Site Was Procured," *Real Estate Record and Builders' Guide* 90 (November 9, 1912): 869–70. Hogan had recently assisted his employer, John N. Golding, with the assembly of the approximately one dozen blocks required for New York's Grand Central Terminal.

84 "Frank W. Woolworth," *Americana* 11 (October 1916): 355; and "$2,000,000 Broadway Building," *New York Times*, July 10, 1910.

85 Author's conversation with Chris McKay, archivist, BNYA, August 1996; and Elmendorf, "Evolution of Commercial Banking," 124.

86 "Frank W. Woolworth," *Americana*, 353–54.

87 Ibid., 354–55 (for quotes); and Redding, "Mr. F. W. Woolworth's Story," 664.

88 Author's conversation with Chris McKay, archivist, BNYA, August 1996; and Elmendorf, "Evolution of Commercial Banking," 124–25.

89 Elmendorf, "Evolution of Commercial Banking," 124; and Committee on Banking Quarters to Board of Directors, Irving National Exchange Bank, March 1, 1910, BNYA.

90 Committee on Banking Quarters to Board of Directors, Irving National Exchange Bank, April 12, 1910, BNYA. The deeds to the properties, indicating their dates of legal transfer, are housed in the Woolworth Collection, NBM.

91 Frank Woolworth to Board of Directors, Irving National Exchange Bank, April 19, 1910, BNYA; and Committee on Banking Quarters to Board of Directors, Irving National Exchange Bank, April 20, 1910, BNYA.

92 Benjamin J. Klebaner, "Commercial Banking," in *The Encyclopedia of New York City*, ed. Kenneth T. Jackson (New Haven, Conn.: Yale University Press; New York: New-York Historical Society), 264 (for quote), 261–65; David M. Scobey, *Empire City: The Making and Meaning of the New York City Landscape* (Philadelphia: Temple University Press, 2002), 24–25, 30, 99, 101; and Burrows and Wallace, *Gotham*, 445–46, 1038.

93 On Irving National Exchange Bank as a "bill of lading" bank, given its "extensive transactions with large wholesale firms that used bills of lading as credit," see Winkler, *Five and Ten*, 185.

94 For Irving National Bank's loans to Wall Street, see Elmendorf, "Evolution of Commercial Banking," 127.

95 "Human Nature as Seen in the World's Tallest Office Building," *Literary Digest* 68 (January 8, 1921): 56.

96 John D. Nichols, "History of Woolworth (1897–1947)," n.p., Woolworth Collection, NBM; and *Trow's Directory* (New York, 1909).

97 Theodore Starrett, "The Architecture of Louis H. Sullivan," *Architecture and Building* 44 (December 1912): 474.

98 Guy Kirkham, "Cass Gilbert, Master of Style," *Pencil Points* 15 (November 1934): 548.

99 Oakes, *Genealogical and Family History of the County of Jefferson*, 197.

100 John D. Nichols, "History of Woolworth," n.p.

101 Frank Woolworth to Reverend S. W. Brown, May 11, 1912, Cass Gilbert Collection, N-YHS (for quote); and *The Dinner Given to Cass Gilbert, Architect, by Frank W. Woolworth* (Baltimore: Munder-Thomsen Press, 1913), 38 (for quote).

102 "F. W. Woolworth to Build," *Real Estate Record and Builder's Guide* 85 (March 12, 1910): 546.

103 "Woolworth Building Idea Ridiculed," *Watertown Daily Times*, April 11, 1919, in Frank Winfield Woolworth Press Clippings Files, WDT.

104 Egerton Swartwout, "Cass Gilbert," in *Dictionary of American Biography*, vol. 11, ed. Harris E. Starr, suppl. 1 (New York: Charles Scribner's Sons, 1944), 342; and Robert Allen Jones, "Mr. Woolworth's Tower: The Skyscraper as Popular Icon," *Journal of Popular Culture* 7 (Fall 1973): 410.

105 Letters and memorandums housed in the BNYA, as cited above, document Woolworth's involvement with setting up the Broadway–Park Place Company during March and April 1910.

106 Edward J. Hogan, Jr., S.J., telephone conversation with author, September 1984; and Beals, "Edward J. Hogan, Agent," 869.

107 Edward J. Hogan to Cass Gilbert, April 30, 1910, Woolworth Building correspondence files, Cass Gilbert Collection, N-YHS.

108 "F. W. Woolworth to Build," 546.

109 Louis J. Horowitz and Boyden Sparkes, *The Towers of New York: The Memoirs of a Master Builder* (New York: Simon & Schuster, 1937), 1; and Paul Starrett, *Changing the Skyline* (New York: McGraw-Hill Book Co., 1938), 165.

110 *The Sun's Guide to New York* (New York: R. Wayne Wilson & Co., 1892), 88 (for quote). See also David C. Hammack, "Social Transformations," in *Power and Society: Greater New York at the Turn of the Century* (New York: Russell Sage Foundation, 1982), 72, which maintains that club memberships provided an index to social standing in New York.

111 *The Sun's Guide*, 93.

112 *The Sun's Guide*, 95. Writing to the English painter Sir Lawrence Alma-Tadema, Gilbert characterized the Century Association as "a rather select group of the best men." Cass Gilbert to Sir Lawrence Alma-Tadema, June 11, 1909, personal letterbooks, Cass Gilbert Collection, N-YHS.

113 References to Woolworth's membership in the Hardware Club appear frequently in biographical accounts. See especially Winkler, *Five and Ten*, 184, 185.

114 Oakes, *Genealogical and Family History of the County of Jefferson*, 197; and *The Sun's Guide*, 95–96. The Lotos Club organized art exhibitions and receptions for distinguished artists and literary personalities from around the world.

115 Winkler, *Five and Ten*, 214.

116 Sven Beckert, *The Monied Metropolis: New York City and the Consolidation of the American Bourgeoise, 1850–1896* (Cambridge: Cambridge University Press, 2001), 2; and Hammack, "Social Transformations," 59 (for quote). Beckert goes on to define "the United States bourgeoisie" (part of a western bourgeoisie including Europeans) as being dominated by "capital-owning New Yorkers," a group that formed "dense social networks," created "powerful social institutions," and articulated "an increasingly coherent view of the world and their place within it." Beckert, *The Monied Metropolis*, 3.

117 Frederic Cople Jaher, *The Urban Establishment: Upper Strata in Boston, New York, Charleston, Chicago, and Los Angeles* (Urbana, Ill.: University of Illinois Press, 1982), 270 (for quote), 269–79; and Hammack, "Social Transformations," 72, describe the Four Hundred. J. P. Morgan shunned the Four Hundred and "probably would have thought their balls prissy or vulgar," according to Ron Chernow, *The House of Morgan* (New York: Atlantic Monthly Press, 1990), 48.

118 *Social Register Locater 1914*, vol. 6 (New York: Social Register Association, 1914). On the *Social Register's* role in "class formation" as a "conscious project," see Beckert, *The Monied Metropolis*, 265. The *Social Register*, originally intended to be a list of names for commercial enterprises making advertising mailings, inadvertently turned into a blue book. Founded by Louis Keller in 1887, it was eventually published in twenty-one cities. Allen Churchill, *The Upper Crust: An Informal History of New York's Highest Society* (Englewood Cliffs, N.J.: Prentice-Hall, 1970), 157.

119 Chernow, *The House of Morgan*, 89. The city's older fortunes—those of Morgan, Vanderbilt, Rockefeller, and Carnegie—derived from banking, shipping, railroads, oil, and steel.

120 In Gilbert's own words, he "descended from that branch of Gilberts of Devonshire, England, who came to Connecticut in 1618." Cass Gilbert to Francis Swales (autobiographical letter), September 24, 1909, box 17, Cass Gilbert Papers, LC. Geoffrey Blodgett, *Cass Gilbert: The Early Years* (St. Paul: Minnesota Historical Society Press, 2001), 3, notes that Connecticut had not been settled at that time. Woolworth's colonial progenitor, known as Richard Wolley as well as Woolworth, arrived from England in 1678, to settle in Newburg, Massachusetts. Winkler, *Five and Ten*, 18.

121 Winkler, *Five and Ten*, 23; and John D. Nichols, "Milestones of Woolworth."

122 Abigail A. Van Slyck, "'The Utmost Amount of Effectiv (sic) Accommodation': Andrew Carnegie and the Reform of the American Library," *Society of Architectural Historians Journal* 50 (December 1991): 359, 364–65. Woolworth's sentiment, "the education I got in two terms in a business college at Watertown, New York, did me more good than any classical education I might have got," was widely published shortly after his death. See, for example, "A Millionaire's Opinion of Education," *Outlook*, April 30, 1919, 731–32.

123 Cass Gilbert to Julia Finch Gilbert, February 28, 1907, box 7, Cass Gilbert Papers, LC. Gilbert regretted not having attended Oxford, Cambridge, Yale, or Harvard. Cass Gilbert, untitled autobiography, ca. 1910, box 17, Cass Gilbert Papers, LC.

124 Cass Gilbert to Francis Swales (autobiographical letter), September 24, 1909, box 17, Cass Gilbert Papers, LC; and Norris F. Schneider, "Cass Gilbert," *Zanesville Times Signal*, October 4, 1959, reprinted in *Zanesville Stories*, vol. 4, ed. Norris Schneider (Zanesville, Ohio, 1965), n.p.

125 Cass Gilbert, untitled autobiography, ca. 1910; and "Lewis Cass" in *Dictionary of American Biography*, vol. 2, ed. Allen Johnson and Dumas Malone (New York: Charles Scribner's Sons, 1929, 1930): 562–64. In the Senate, Cass earned a reputation for his anti-British prejudice, for nationalism as a dominating principle in policy decisions, and for his imperialist stance toward Mexico.

126 On the use of commercial strategies in major Beaux-Arts practices, see Mary N. Woods, *From Craft to Profession: The Practice of Architecture in Nineteenth-Century America* (Berkeley: University of California Press, 1999), 116–37.

127 Mary Beth Betts, "From Sketch to Architecture: Drawings in the Cass Gilbert Office," in *Inventing the Skyline: The Architecture of Cass Gilbert*, ed. Margaret Heilbrun (New York: Columbia University Press, 2000), 67 (for quote), 67–79.

128 Harry S. Black to Cass Gilbert, November 11, 1896, and November 12, 1896, box 3, Cass Gilbert Papers, MHS; Cass Gilbert to Guaranty Construction Company, February 22, 1897, box 3, Cass Gilbert Papers, MHS; and E. W. Peet to R. A. Grannis, October 29, 1897, box 6, Cass Gilbert Papers, LC, introducing "Mr. Cass Gilbert of St. Paul and of Boston." See also Sharon Irish, "Cass Gilbert's Career in New York, 1899–1905" (Ph.D. diss., Northwestern University, 1985), 146–208.

129 Office memorandums by Cass Gilbert, February 20 to March 3, 1899, box 3, Cass Gilbert Papers, MHS; and Cass Gilbert to F. C. Gibbs, March 1, 1899 (telegram), box 18, Cass Gilbert Papers, MHS. Gilbert wrote: "Contract closed, I've got it."

130 Robert Bruegmann, *The Architects and the City: Holabird and Roche of Chicago, 1880–1918* (Chicago: University of Chicago Press, 1997), 19–20, describes William Holabird of Holabird and Roche as a "commercial architect." Gilbert's involvement with real estate can be compared to that of Holabird. Holabird, "who took charge of the business aspects of the firm," also invested in "parcels of land in Chicago for which the firm did innumerable development schemes" as well as "developments for which the firm served as architect." It appears that Gilbert, however, did not invest his personal funds in the development schemes.

131 For the Newark, N.J., project, see Cass Gilbert to Mr. C. Bierman, June 11, 1906, personal letterbooks, Cass Gilbert Collection, N-YHS. For the site near Pennsylvania Station, a $6 million parcel facing Broadway at Thirty-third Street, see Cass Gilbert to Mr. Northcote, September 9, 1908, personal letterbooks, Cass Gilbert Collection, N-YHS. Gilbert also met Northcote in London during summer 1905 regarding possible projects in that city. Aldis, Aldis, Northcote and Watson's precursor firm, Aldis, Aldis and Northcote, contemporaries viewed in the late 1880s as "the most important single player in Chicago real estate." Bruegmann, *The Architects and the City*, 488 n. 22.

132 Woods, *From Craft to Profession*, 5–6.

133 Swartwout, "Cass Gilbert," 343.

134 Hugh Ferris, *Power and Buildings: An Artist's View of Contemporary Architecture* (New York: Columbia University Press, 1953), 7–8.

135 Paul Starrett, *Changing the Skyline*, 272.

136 Woods, *From Craft to Profession*, 86–92; and Richard Wrightman Fox and T. J. Jackson Lears, "Introduction," in *The Culture of Consumption: Critical Essays in American History, 1880–1980*, ed. Richard Wrightman Fox and T. J. Jackson Lears (New York: Pantheon Books, 1983), xii.

137 Cass Gilbert to F. C. Gibbs, December 27, 1897, box 18, Cass Gilbert Papers, MHS, as quoted in Sharon Irish, "Cass Gilbert in Practice, 1882–1934," in Heilbrun, *Inventing the Skyline*, 27.

138 The perspectives are labeled on the verso as "Woolworth Building." Gilbert later characterized the twenty-story project as "Woolworth's original idea for a bank and office building." Cass Gilbert, "The Woolworth Building," in *Masterpieces of Architecture in the United States*, by Edward Warren Hoak and Humphrey Church (New York: Charles Scribner's Sons, 1930), 215.

139 Paul Revere Williams, as quoted in Anita Morris, "Recent Work of Paul R. Williams, Architect," *Architect and Engineer* 141 (June 1940): 24–25; and Wesley Howard Henderson, "Two Case Studies of African-American Architects' Careers in Los Angeles, 1890–1945: Paul R. Williams, FAIA, and James H. Garrott, AIA" (Ph.D. diss., UCLA, 1992), 168.

140 Paul Starrett, *Changing the Skyline*, 272, described one of Gilbert's sketches, completed in twenty minutes while in a meeting with a client, as a "wonderful performance."

141 On the atelier as an architectural ideal and symbol, see Woods, *From Craft to Profession*, 102–11.

142 F. E. Bennett, "Mr. Cass Gilbert," *Architect's Journal* 70 (June 8, 1927): 791–92. Glenn Brown, *1860–1930, Memories: A Winning Crusade to Revive George Washington's Vision of a Capital City* (Washington, D.C.: W. F. Roberts Co., 1931), 568, similarly described Gilbert as a "rare combination of executive and artist."

143 Francis S. Swales, "Master Draftsmen, XVIII: Cass Gilbert," *Pencil Points* 7 (October 1926): 585.

144 The Beaux-Arts-influenced curricula of American architectural schools in the late nineteenth century cultivated the ideal of the architect as an "artist," as did the American Institute of Architects. See Woods, *From Craft to Profession*, 44, 102.

145 Cass Gilbert to Elizabeth Fulton Wheeler Gilbert (mother), March 22, 1880, box 2, Cass Gilbert Papers, LC.

146 Cass Gilbert to Francis Swales (autobiographical letter), September 24, 1909.

147 Unpublished autobiographical essay by Cass Gilbert, ca. 1910, box 17, Cass Gilbert Papers, LC.

148 Unpublished autobiographical essay by Cass Gilbert, ca. 1910, box 17, Cass Gilbert Papers, LC.

149 At least one contemporary noted the seeming contradiction in Gilbert's character: "Unworldly, in an almost childlike way, he was at the same time shrewd, farseeing, and with a penetrating insight into the motives prompting action and reaction from the people with whom he came in contact." Mrs. Channing Seabury, Obituary (of Cass Gilbert), *St. Paul Pioneer Press*, May 24.

150 Cass Gilbert to Mrs. A. Pennington, March 26, 1908, box 20, Cass Gilbert Papers, MHS.

151 Cass Gilbert to C. H. Ryder, November 19, 1908, personal letterbooks, Cass Gilbert Collection, N-YHS.

CHAPTER THREE

1 Recent scholarship on the career of Cass Gilbert includes Geoffrey Blodgett, *Cass Gilbert: The Early Years* (St. Paul: Minnesota Historical Society Press, 2001); Sharon Irish, *Cass Gilbert, Architect: Modern Traditionalist* (New York: Monacelli Press, 1999); and two collections of essays: Barbara S. Christen and Steven Flanders, eds., *Cass Gilbert: Life and Work.: Architect of the Public Domain* (New York: W. W. Norton & Co., 2001); and Margaret Heilbrun, ed., *Inventing the Skyline: The Architecture of Cass Gilbert* (New York: Columbia University Press, 2000).

2 William R. Taylor, "The Evolution of Public Space: The Commercial City as Showcase," in *In Pursuit of Gotham: Culture and Commerce in New York,* ed. William R. Taylor (New York: Oxford University Press, 1992), 35–38.

3 For a comparable phenomenon in literature, see Joan Shelley Rubin, *The Making of Middlebrow Culture* (Chapel Hill: University of North Carolina Press, 1992), xi, xvii.

4 On the distinctive character of New York's visual environment around 1900, see Taylor, "The Evolution of Public Space," 35–50; Wanda M. Corn, "The New New York," *Art in America* 61 (July–August 1973): 58–65; and Rebecca Zurier, Robert W. Snyder, and Virginia Mecklenberg, *Metropolitan Lives: The Ashcan Artists and Their New York* (Washington, D.C.: National Museum of American Art; New York: W. W. Norton & Co., 1995).

5 Paul Baker, *Richard Morris Hunt* (Cambridge, Mass.: MIT Press, 1980), 181–85, 219–23, 460.

6 Sarah Bradford Landau and Carl W. Condit, *Rise of the New York Skyscraper, 1865–1913* (New Haven, Conn.: Yale University Press, 1996), 62–75, 78–83, and 116–25.

7 At a meeting of the Architectural League of New York in 1894, Hunt opposed skyscrapers and Post railed against them as "eyesores," resolving to enact a law against their construction. Francisco Mujica, *History of the Skyscraper* (Paris: Archaeology & Architecture Press, 1929), 45.

8 Charles McKim, personal letter, May 18, 1909, as quoted in Leland Roth, "The Urban Architecture of McKim, Mead and White" (Ph.D. diss., Yale University, 1973), 739; and Ernest Flagg, "Public Buildings," in *Proceedings of the Third National Conference on City Planning* (Boston, 1911), 48.

9 *Report of the Heights of Buildings Commission to the Committee on the Height, Size, and Arrangement of Buildings of the Board of Estimate and Apportionment of the City of New York, December 23, 1913* (New York: City of New York, 1913). On the various proposals for restricting building heights, see Gail Fenske, "The 'Skyscraper Problem' and the City Beautiful: The Woolworth Building" (Ph.D. diss, MIT, 1988), 28–42, 235–39 nn. 40–65.

10 William R. Taylor, "New York and the Origin of the Skyline: The Commercial City as Visual Text," in Taylor, *In Pursuit of Gotham*, 23–24.

11 Neil B. Thompson, *Minnesota's State Capitol: The Art and Politics of a Public Building* (St. Paul: Minnesota State Historical Society, 1974); and Thomas O'Sullivan, "The Minnesota State Capitol: Thinking Internationally, Designing Locally," in Christen and Flanders, *Cass Gilbert: Life and Work,* 87–99.

12 Cass Gilbert to Lucian Swift, September 2, 1897, as quoted in William Towner Morgan, "The Politics of Business in the Career of an American Architect: Cass Gilbert, 1878–1905" (Ph.D. diss.: University of Minnesota, 1972), 112.

13 Cass Gilbert, as quoted in "Cass Gilbert's New York Custom House Design," *Inland Architect and News Record* 35 (February 1900): 7.

14 H. Van Buren Magonigle, "A Half Century of Architecture," pt. 3, "A Biographical Review," *Pencil Points* 15 (March 1934): 115.

15 Gilbert wrote to Charles McKim in 1908: "You are the natural leader of our profession." Cass Gilbert to Charles McKim, August 4, 1908, personal letterbooks, Cass Gilbert Collection, N-YHS.

16 Cass Gilbert to Elizabeth Fulton Wheeler Gilbert, May 23, 1880, box 2, Cass Gilbert Papers, LC. Gilbert purchased both volumes of Henry Van Brunt's 1875 translation of Eugène-Emmanuel Viollet-le-Duc's *Discourses on Architecture.* He also owned Viollet-le-Duc's *Dictionnaire raisonné de l'architecture française du XIe au XVIe siècle*, 10 vols. (1858–68). List of books comprising Cass Gilbert's library, University of Maine at Orono, n.d., provided to the author by the University of Maine in 1986.

17 Cass Gilbert to Clarence Johnston, July 21, 1879, Clarence Johnston Papers, MHS. Cass Gilbert to Julia Tappen Finch, December 30, 1886, box 3, Cass Gilbert Papers, LC, states, "You may be surprised that I have not read Ruskin before, but such is the case." It is likely that Gilbert gained his knowledge of Ruskin through *American Architect and Building News* and his fellow students at MIT. Gilbert aspired to apprentice with George Edmund Street, whose church designs showed an indebtedness to the Ruskinian craft ideal of "constructional polychromy." Cass Gilbert to Clarence Johnston, June 22, 1879, and July 21, 1879, Clarence Johnston Papers, MHS.

18 Unpublished autobiographical essay by Cass Gilbert, ca. 1910, box 17, Cass Gilbert Papers, LC.

19 Gilbert wrote that Viollet-le-Duc had discouraged him from attending Paris's École des Beaux-Arts. Unpublished autobiographical essay by Cass Gilbert, ca. 1910. Gilbert's financial resources, however, may have limited the duration of his studies; the support from his father's estate ended when he was twenty-one. Robert Allen Jones, *Cass Gilbert: Midwestern Architect in New York* (New York: Arno Press, 1982), 31–32.

20 John A. Chewning, "William Robert Ware and the Beginnings of Architectural Education in the United States, 1861–1881" (Ph.D. diss., MIT, 1986), 129–35.

21 "Death of Professor Eugène Létang," *American Architect and Building News* 38 (December 3, 1892): 141.

22 Gilbert's "Pompeian Restoration" received "first mention." Gilbert received a 95, or an A, in Architectural Design; otherwise, his grades were average, a C in History and a "pass" in Ornament. Kimberly Alexander provided this information from the Architectural Collections at the MIT Museum. See also Jones, *Cass Gilbert*, 12–26.

23 Gilbert's letters to Clarence Johnston of January 5, February 5, May 29, and November 7, 1879, Clarence Johnston Papers, MHS, featured pictorial thumbnail sketches of his own designs, those of fellow students, and of buildings he encountered in Boston and on his travels.

24 Gilbert's 1880 itinerary can be reconstructed from his letters to Elizabeth Fulton Wheeler Gilbert, dated January 18, 1880, to August 11, 1880, box 2, Cass Gilbert Papers, LC. See also Paul Clifford Larson, *Cass Gilbert Abroad: The Young Architect's European Tour* (Afton, Minn.: Afton Historical Society Press, 2003).

25 According to H. Van Buren Magonigle, Gilbert and Francis Bacon "were publishing travel sketches transcending in merit those of most of their contemporaries about 1883–84." "A Half Century of Architecture," pt. 2, "A Biographical Review," *Pencil Points* 15 (January 1934): 9. Gilbert's sketches appeared in R. D. Andrews, E. M. Wheelwright, Cass Gilbert, and W. E. Chamberlain, eds., *Sketch Book of the Architectural Association of Boston* (Boston, 1883), and in 1889 were exhibited at Boston's St. Botolph Club. "Exhibition of the Boston Architectural Club," *American Architect and Building News* 64 (June 10, 1899): 83–84.

26 The Cass Gilbert Collection, N-YHS, houses one of the sketchbooks from Gilbert's 1880 tour, showing that he culled medieval details from Salisbury Cathedral, St. Mark's, Venice, the cathedral in Orvieto, houses in Ambert and Souvigny, France, and the cathedrals of Moulins and Bourges.

27 Cass Gilbert to Elizabeth Fulton Wheeler Gilbert, February 6, 1880, box 2, Cass Gilbert Papers, LC.

28 Cass Gilbert to Elizabeth Fulton Wheeler Gilbert, March 28, 1880, box 2, Cass Gilbert papers, LC. William Robert Ware's lectures on architectural history at MIT inspired his choices. Cass Gilbert to Clarence Johnston, January 16, 1879, Clarence Johnston Papers, MHS.

29 Cass Gilbert to Elizabeth Fulton Wheeler Gilbert, February 14, 1880, box 2, Cass Gilbert Papers, LC.

30 Cass Gilbert to Elizabeth Fulton Wheeler Gilbert, March 28, 1880, box 2, Cass Gilbert Papers, LC.

31 Cass Gilbert to Elizabeth Fulton Wheeler Gilbert, February 1, 1880, box 2, Cass Gilbert Papers, LC

32 Cass Gilbert to Elizabeth Fulton Wheeler Gilbert, February 14, 1880, box 2, Cass Gilbert Papers, LC.

33 Cass Gilbert to Elizabeth Fulton Wheeler Gilbert, February 14, 1880, box 2, Cass Gilbert Papers, LC; and Cass Gilbert to Julia Finch Gilbert, August 1, 1906, box 7, Cass Gilbert Papers, LC.

34 Cass Gilbert, "Church Building," unpublished essay, ca. 1885, box 17, Cass Gilbert Papers, LC.

35 Regarding White's compositional technique, see Royal Cortissoz, "Stanford White," in *American Artists* (New York: Charles Scribner's Sons, 1923), 301. On Gilbert, see H. Van Buren Magonigle, "A Half Century of Architecture," pt. 4, "A Biographical Review," *Pencil Points* 15 (May 1934): 224; and Egerton Swartwout, "Cass Gilbert" in *Dictionary of American Biography,* vol. 11, ed. Harris E. Starr, suppl. 1 (New York: Charles Scribner's Sons, 1944), 342.

36 Magonigle, "A Half Century of Architecture," pt. 3, 116–18.
37 Cortissoz, "Stanford White," 301.
38 "Contemporary Architects and Their Work: Mr. Cass Gilbert, of New York and St. Paul," *Builder* 102 (January 12, 1912): 31. Gilbert's own annotated copy of the article is housed in box 29, Cass Gilbert Papers, LC.
39 Gilbert later described Wells affectionately as a "purist" who was "tenacious in his opinions, modest of his ability, possibly a little narrow-minded," but also "deep-minded, very thoughtful," and "passionately fond of his profession." Cass Gilbert to Julia Tappen Finch, October 31, 1886, box 2, Cass Gilbert Papers, LC.
40 Stanford White to Cass Gilbert, November 1, 1882, box 2, Cass Gilbert Papers, LC.
41 Later, Gilbert spoke highly of his mentor: "The fellows I knew loved to work for Stanford White because of his great talents and because of the spirit of the man." Cass Gilbert to Cass Gilbert, Jr., August 12, 1924, as quoted in Sharon Irish, "Cass Gilbert's Career in New York, 1899–1905" (Ph.D. diss, Northwestern University, 1985), 118.
42 On Gilbert's early career in St. Paul, see Blodgett, *Cass Gilbert: The Early Years*; Patricia Anne Murphy, "Architectural Education and Minnesota Career," in Christen and Flanders, *Cass Gilbert: Life and Work*, 27–45; and Thomas R. Blanck and Charles Locks, "Launching a Career: Residential and Ecclesiastical Work from the St. Paul Office," in Christen and Flanders, *Cass Gilbert: Life and Work*, 46–61.
43 The *American Architect and Building News* judged the German Bethlehem Presbyterian Church a "picturesque design and a bad church." "Art in the Modern Church," pt. 6, *American Architect and Building News* 50 (November 16, 1895): 75.
44 The A. Kirby Barnum house caught the eye of a rationally minded French architect, who remarked on its "gables on top of gables. . . . How an architect must have to torture his mind to invent such things!" Editorial, *American Architect and Building News* 18 (November 14, 1885): 230.
45 In 1849, Minnesota became a territory, and in 1858, the thirty-second state of the United States. For contemporary evaluations of the Minnesota State Capitol, see Kenyon Cox, "The New State Capital of Minnesota," *Architectural Record* 18 (August 1905): 94–113; and Russell Sturgis, "Minnesota State Capitol," *Architectural Record* 19 (January 1906): 31–36.
46 Gilbert's surprising level of sophistication with the classical idiom can be attributed to his experience in the early 1890s with competitions for classical public buildings, none of which he won: the American Fine Arts Society Building (New York, 1890); the Minnesota Building at the World's Columbian Exposition (1892); the Baltimore courthouse (1894); and the Montana State Capitol (1894). Patricia Anne Murphy, "The Early Career of Cass Gilbert: 1878 to 1895" (master's thesis, University of Virginia, 1979), 103–5.
47 Board of State Capitol Commissioners, *Biennial Report*, 1901, 10, as quoted in Thompson, *Minnesota's State Capitol*, 2.
48 On architecture's capacity to suggest the authority of those who govern through the use of such conventions (among them a dome), see Lawrence Vale, *Architecture, Power, and National Identity* (New Haven, Conn.: Yale University Press, 1992), 3–16.
49 While designing the Minnesota State Capitol in 1895–96, Gilbert produced measured sketches on the sites of the Rhode Island State House, Boston Public Library, Low Library at Columbia University, United States Capitol, Library of Congress, and Corcoran Gallery of Art. Cass Gilbert, diaries, November 1895–May 1896, box 1, Cass Gilbert Papers, LC.
50 Gilbert insisted that the Minnesota State Capitol be built of white Georgia marble, like that of McKim, Mead and White's Rhode Island State House. In fighting for the marble, he made enemies of Minnesota stone producers. Thompson, *Minnesota's State Capitol*, 25–31.
51 *Minneapolis Tribune*, January 8, 1905, as cited in Thompson, *Minnesota's State Capitol*, 2.
52 Benedict Anderson, *Imagined Communities: Reflections on the Origin and Spread of Nationalism*, rev. ed. (London: Verso, 1991), 6–7.
53 Thompson, *Minnesota's State Capitol*, 65. The United States signed treaties with the Ojibwa and the Sioux in 1837, 1845, 1851, and 1855. Minnesota comprised lands from the Northwest Territory (the eastern part of the state) and the Louisiana Purchase (the western part of the state).
54 Irish, *Cass Gilbert, Architect*, 60–68; and Irish, "Cass Gilbert's Career in New York,"256–322. [Montgomery Schuyler], "The New Custom House at New York," *Architectural Record* 20 (July 1906): 10–14, provides a contemporary account of the project.

55 On the late nineteenth-century "national practice," see Mary N. Woods, *From Craft to Profession: The Practice of Architecture in Nineteenth-Century America* (Berkeley: University of California Press, 1999): 116–37.

56 On Gilbert's attempts to form partnerships with his prominent contemporaries, see William Rutherford Mead to Cass Gilbert, January 19, 1891, box 17, Cass Gilbert Papers, MHS; Robert S. Peabody to Cass Gilbert, July 8, 1893, box 17, Cass Gilbert Papers, MHS; and Cass Gilbert to John Mervyn Carrère, January 3, 1895, John Mervyn Carrère Papers, LC. Correspondence relating to the proposed partnership between Cass Gilbert and Daniel Burnham, which both Charles McKim and William Rutherford Mead encouraged, can be found in box 6, Cass Gilbert Papers, LC, and box 17, Cass Gilbert Papers, MHS.

57 Cass Gilbert to Julia Finch Gilbert, September 24, 1899, box 6, Cass Gilbert Papers, LC.

58 Irish, "Cass Gilbert's Career in New York," 262–82.

59 Cass Gilbert to Julia Finch Gilbert, April 5, 1900, box 6, Cass Gilbert Papers, LC.

60 Cass Gilbert, "New York Custom House" (unpublished manuscript), box 17, n.p., Cass Gilbert Papers, LC; and Cass Gilbert, as quoted in "Cass Gilbert's New York Custom House Design," 7.

61 Cass Gilbert, as quoted in "Cass Gilbert's New York Custom House Design," 7.

62 Ibid.

63 Irish, " Cass Gilbert's Career in New York," 260. After 1913, corporate and personal income taxes served as another important source of federal income. On the United States Customs Service, see Laurence F. Schmeckebier, *The Customs Service: Its History, Activities, and Organization* (Baltimore: Johns Hopkins University Press, 1924).

64 Cass Gilbert, as quoted in "Cass Gilbert's New York Custom House Design," 6, 7.

65 Geoffrey Blodgett, "The Politics of Public Architecture," in Christen and Flanders, *Cass Gilbert: Life and Work*, 66–69; and Stephen Kern, *The Culture of Time and Space, 1880–1918* (Cambridge, Mass.: Harvard University Press, 1983), 238–40.

66 Edwin G. Burrows and Mike Wallace, *Gotham: A History of New York City to 1898* (New York: Oxford University Press, 1999), 1209–18; and Sven Beckert, *The Monied Metropolis: New York City and the Consolidation of the American Bourgeoisie, 1850–1896* (Cambridge: Cambridge University Press, 2001), 329–30.

67 Kern, *The Culture of Time and Space*, 238–39.

68 P. T. Farnsworth, "The New York Custom House and Its Sculptural Decoration," *International Studio* 27 (November 1905): vii–x; and Charles De Kay, "The New York Custom House," *Century Magazine* 71 (March 1906): 733–43. See also Michele Bogart, *Public Sculpture and the Civic Ideal in New York City, 1890–1930* (Chicago: University of Chicago Press, 1989), 111–34.

69 Cass Gilbert, as quoted in "Cass Gilbert's New York Custom House Design," 7. According to De Kay, "The New York Custom House," 743, the historical sequence extended "from the Phoenicians in the dawn of history to the Germans, the last to seek colonies."

70 The "racial types" included "Hindu, Latin, Celt, Mongel, and Eskimo." Farnsworth, "The New York Custom House and Its Sculptural Decoration," vii.

71 In 1937, Reginald Marsh painted murals in the rotunda, as a Works Progress Administration project, showing views of ships entering the New York harbor and unloading cargoes at the city's docks.

72 Cass Gilbert, as quoted in "Cass Gilbert's New York Custom House Design," 7.

73 Rebecca Zurier and Robert W. Snyder, "Introduction," in Zurier, Snyder, and Mecklenberg, *Metropolitan Lives*, 13–27.

74 Barr Ferree, ed., *Year Book of the Art Societies of New York, 1898–99* (New York: Leonard Scott Publication Co., 1899), 46, 108, 146, 155; and Michelle H. Bogart, "In Search of a United Front: American Architectural Sculpture at the Turn of the Century," *Winterthur Portfolio* 19 (Summer/Autumn 1984): 162.

75 Frederick Stymetz Lamb, "Municipal Art," *Municipal Affairs* 1 (December 1897): 683–84; Edwin Howland Blashfield, "A Plea for Municipal Art," in Ferree, *Year Book*, 94–95, 96 (for quote); and Blashfield, "Mural Painting," *Municipal Affairs* 2 (March 1898), 100–109.

76 Cass Gilbert to Francis Swales (autobiographical letter), September 24, 1909, box 17, Cass Gilbert Papers, LC; Irish, "Cass Gilbert's Career in New York," 85; Donn Barber, "Charles Follen McKim," *New York Architect* 3 (September 1909): n.p.; and Cass Gilbert to William Eames, August 30, 1909, Cass Gilbert Collection, N-YHS.

77 Daniel Boorstin, *The Americans: The Democratic Experience* (New York: Random House, Vintage Books, 1974), 89–164.

78 Sibel Bozdagon Dostoglu, "Towards Professional Legitimacy and Power: An Inquiry into the Struggle, Achievements, and Dilemmas of the Architectural Profession though an Analysis of Chicago, 1871–1909" (Ph.D. diss., University of Pennsylvania, 1982), 89–114; and Robert Bruegmann, *The Architects and the City: Holabird and Roche of Chicago, 1880–1918* (Chicago: University of Chicago Press, 1997), 81–82.

79 Bruegmann, *The Architects and the City*, 73–76.

80 John Wellborn Root,"A Great Architectural Problem" (1890), in *The Meanings of Architecture: Buildings and Writings of John Wellborn Root*, ed. Donald Hoffmann (New York: Horizon Press, 1967), 142; and Louis Sullivan, "The Tall Office Building Artistically Considered" (1896), in *Kindergarten Chats and Other Writings* (1918; reprint, New York: Dover Publications, 1979), 202.

81 Cass Gilbert, "Grouping of Public Buildings and Development of Washington," in *Papers Relating to the Improvement of Washington, District of Columbia*, compiled by Glenn Brown (Washington, D.C.: Government Printing Office, 1901), 78–82; and Pierce Butler et al., *Report of the Capitol Approaches Commission to the Common Council of St. Paul* (St. Paul: Pioneer Press, 1906), n.p.

82 Cass Gilbert, as quoted in "Skyscrapers and the Skyline of the Future," *New York Times*, May 10, 1908.

83 Cass Gilbert, "The Architecture of Today" (lecture delivered at the West Point Military Academy), May 4, 1909, 10–12, box 16, Cass Gilbert Papers, LC.

84 Cass Gilbert to Clarence Johnston, November 17, 1879, Clarence Johnston Papers, MHS.

85 Gilbert to Johnston, January 30, 1880, Clarence Johnston Papers, MHS.

86 "Cass Gilbert," *Architectural Reviewer* 1 (June 1897): 44–48; and "Building Owned by E. D. Chamberlain, Esq., St. Paul, Minn.," *American Architect and Building News* 51 (March 21, 1896): 135, plate 1056. See also Sharon Irish, "West Hails East: Cass Gilbert in Minnesota," *Minnesota History* 53 (Spring 1993): 201–4.

87 Gilbert acknowledged his indebtedness to Wells's Villard houses for the Endicott's design in an annotated copy of Francis S. Swales, "Mr. Cass Gilbert of New York and St. Paul," *Builder* 102 (January 12, 1912): 32, box 29, Cass Gilbert Papers, LC.

88 Irish, "West Hails East," 202.

89 The sculptor Johannes Gelert of the American Terra Cotta and Ceramic Company of Chicago modeled the terra cotta. "Building Owned by E. D. Chamberlain," 135.

90 Harry J. Carlson to Cass Gilbert, October 9, 1894, box 17, Cass Gilbert Papers, MHS.

91 Gilbert could have observed the American Surety Building nearing completion during a trip to New York City in November 1895. See Gilbert's diaries, box 1, Cass Gilbert Papers, LC.

92 Cass Gilbert to Professor F. W. Chandler, June 14, 1897, box 2, Cass Gilbert Papers, MHS.

93 Daniel Burnham and William Le Baron Jenney recommended Ritter to Gilbert. See the Brazer Building correspondence, box 2, Cass Gilbert Papers, MHS.

94 Henry S. Pritchard, "Design of Structural Frame with an Explanation of Method of Determining Wind Stresses as Devised by Engineering Department of New Jersey Steel and Iron Company, Trenton, N.J., September 1896," box 2, Cass Gilbert Papers, MHS. Ritter and Pritchard's portal arch braces resembled those Corydon T. Purdy had recently designed by for Holabird and Roche's Old Colony Building in Chicago (1893–94).

95 Harry S. Black produced comparative cost estimates of Ritter and Purdy's designs. Louis E. Ritter to Cass Gilbert, October 7, 1896, box 2, Cass Gilbert Papers, MHS. George A. Fuller Company to Cass Gilbert, November 12, 1896, box 2, Cass Gilbert Papers, MHS, notes the selection of Purdy.

96 Henry Endicott, Gilbert's client for the Endicott Building in St. Paul, introduced Gilbert to Russell in June 1894. Gilbert signed the contract for his architectural services in June 1896, just before the skyscraper's construction began. Henry Endicott to Cass Gilbert, June 22, 1894, and Thomas H. Russell to Cass Gilbert, June 1, 1896, box 2, Cass Gilbert Papers, MHS.

97 Thomas H. Russell to Cass Gilbert, June 15, 1897, box 2, Cass Gilbert Papers, MHS.

98 George Hill, "Some Practical Limiting Conditions in the Design of the Modern Office Building," *Architectural Record* 2 (April–June 1893): 446–68. See also Carol Willis, *Form Follows Finance: Skyscrapers and Skylines in New York and Chicago* (New York: Princeton Architectural Press, 1995), 24–33.

99 "Brazer Building, Boston," *American Architect and Building News* 56 (May 22, 1897): 64, plate 1117.

100 Cass Gilbert, as quoted in "Building Skyscrapers—Described by Cass Gilbert," *Real Estate Record and Builders' Guide* 55 (June 23, 1900): 1091.

101 Cass Gilbert, "Architectural Design," in "The Woolworth Building, Most Modern Example of the Fire-Proof Skyscraper: How It Was Built," by George T. Mortimer, *Real Estate Magazine* 1 (July 1912): 56.

102 Also included among Gilbert's watercolors of towers from this period are *Tower at San Francisco Romano, Rome* (1898), *San Giorgio Maggiore, Venice* (1898; showing St. Mark's campanile), *Cathedral Tower, Pistoia, Italy* (1898), and *Church Tower, Italy* (1898), and of city views, *Lagoon, Venice* (1898), and *Mont Saint Michel*, France (1906), all of which are housed at the Smithsonian's American Art Museum.

103 The same sheet of sketches also shows a steeply sloping, picturesque roof that resembled Cyrus L. W. Eidlitz's new Washington Life Building (1897–98) on lower Broadway. Office memorandum by Cass Gilbert, February 24, 1899, box 3, Cass Gilbert Papers, MHS, cites the Washington Life Building as a model.

104 Sarah Bradford Landau compared Gilbert's Broadway Chambers Building with Price's St. James Building in "Cass Gilbert and the New York Skyscraper before 1914," a talk given at the symposium "Cass Gilbert, Life and Work: From Regional to National Architect," New York, November 13, 1998.

105 Cass Gilbert, "Response on the Occasion of the Presentation of the Gold Medal for Architecture to the Society of Arts and Sciences," in *Cass Gilbert: Reminiscences and Addresses*, ed. Julia Finch Gilbert (New York: privately printed, 1935), 51.

106 John C. Van Dyke, *The New New York: A Commentary on the Place and the People* (New York: Macmillan Co., 1909), 23.

107 Herbert Croly, "Glazed and Colored Terra Cotta," *Architectural Record* 19 (April 1906): 320–21 (for quotes), 322.

108 William Leach, *Land of Desire: Merchants, Power, and the Rise of a New American Culture* (New York: Pantheon Books, 1993), 40, 51, 65.

109 Alan Trachtenberg, *The Incorporation of America: Culture and Society in the Gilded Age* (New York: Hill & Wang, 1982), 119 (for quote), 117–21.

110 Alan Trachtenberg, "Image and Ideology: New York in the Photographer's Eye," *Journal of Urban History* 10 (August 1984): 454–55; and Max Page, *The Creative Destruction of Manhattan, 1900–1940* (Chicago: University of Chicago Press, 1999), 1–10.

111 "The Broadway Chambers, New York, N. Y.," *American Architect and Building News* 67 (February 24, 1900): 63, plate 1261.

112 George A. Fuller Company, *Broadway Chambers, a Modern Office Building: Exhibited by Models at the Paris Exposition*, 1900 (New York: George A. Fuller Co., 1900). See also Irish, "Cass Gilbert's Career in New York," 146–208; and Landau and Condit, *Rise of the New York Skyscraper*, 271–72. The skyscraper's engineering and construction made it a subject of interest at the Universal Exposition held in Paris in 1900; Gilbert, Corydon T. Purdy, and the Fuller Company all received medals. The projects specifications are housed in box 3, Cass Gilbert Papers, MHS.

113 Gilbert, "Building Skyscrapers," 1089.

114 Cass Gilbert, "Building Skyscrapers," 1091.

115 Ibid.

116 Gilbert's skyscraper Gothic incorporated many non-Gothic historical precedents. Contemporaries, the critic Montgomery Schuyler among them, nonetheless viewed it as Gothic. On the West Street Building, see Sharon Irish, "A 'Machine That Makes the Land Pay': The West Street Building in New York," *Technology and Culture* 30 (April 1989): 376–97.

117 Gilbert's 1897 trip to Flanders (at age thirty-nine) formed part of a four-month-long sketching tour. Gilbert's travel diary of November 7, 1897, to March 9, 1898, in box 1, Cass Gilbert Papers, LC, describes visits to Antwerp, Malines, Brussels, Ghent, and Bruges.

118 Cass Gilbert, "The Tenth Birthday of a Notable Structure," *Real Estate Magazine of New York* 11 (May 1923): 345.

119 Gilbert frequently traveled with Baedecker guides. *Baedecker's Belgium and Holland*, 10th ed. (Leipzig: Karl Baedecker, 1891), 12, describes Bruges as "one of the great marts of the Hanseatic League and of the English wool trade" in the early thirteenth century. "Richly-laden vessels from Venice, Genoa, and Constantinople might be seen simultaneously discharging their cargoes here, and the magazines of Bruges groaned underneath the weight of English wool, Flemish linen, and Persian silk." Bruges "attained the culminating point of its prosperity," the guide concluded, "during the first half of the 15th century, when the Dukes of Burgandy held their court there." A classic history of the region from Gilbert's era is Henri Pirenne, *Early Democracies in the Low Countries: Urban Society and Political Conflict in the Middle*

Ages and the Renaissance, trans. J. V. Saunders (New York: W. W. Norton & Co., 1963), 22–27, 68–74. It was published in 1910, and the first English translation was issued in 1915 by the Manchester University Press and Longmans, Green & Co., London.

120 "Architecture of the Low Countries," pt. 2, *American Architect and Building News* 39 (March 18, 1893): 163–67; and Julien Guadet, *Eléments et théories de l'architecture*, livre 8 (Paris: Libraire de la construction moderne, 1901–4), 455–60.

121 Trachtenberg, *The Incorporation of America*, 3–10.

122 Beckert, *The Monied Metropolis*, 329–32.

123 Peter Spufford, *Power and Profit: The Merchant in Medieval Europe* (New York: Thames & Hudson, 2002), 12–59.

124 West Street Building tenant list, West Street Building, incoming correspondence, Cass Gilbert Collection, N-YHS; and Hugh Bonner and Howard Constable to Cass Gilbert, April 29, 1905, West Street Building, incoming correspondence, Cass Gilbert Collection, N-YHS.

125 Irish, "A 'Machine That Makes Land Pay'," 378–80, 390–91; and Landau and Condit, *Rise of the New York Skyscraper*, 321.

126 Van Dyke, *The New New York*, 36–37.

127 "Original Scheme for the 'West Street Building,' New York, N.Y.," *American Architect and Building News*, vol. 91 (January 19, 1907). Plates illustrate the scheme.

128 Van Dyke, *The New New York*, 124.

129 [Montgomery Schuyler], "The West Street Building in New York City," *Architectural Record* 22 (August 1907): 103–9. See also Theodore Starrett, "The Architecture of Louis Sullivan," *Architecture and Building* 44 (December 1912): 474; and Guy Kirkham, "Cass Gilbert, Master of Style," *Pencil Points* 15 (November 1934): 548.

130 [Schuyler], "The West Street Building in New York City," 108, 109.

131 Cass Gilbert, "The Architecture of Today," 9. In describing Sullivan's functionalism, Gilbert added "that as in animal life, the bone, the tooth, claw . . . the form follows function as developed by the *need* and as in plant life the leaf, the petal, the root, the branch or the trunk itself takes shape from the nature and the function of the plant or tree," showing that he understood something of Sullivan's philosophical commitment to organicism.

132 Antoinette J. Lee, *Architects to the Nation: The Rise and Decline of the Supervising Architect's Office* (New York: Oxford University Press, 2000), 197–216; and Irish, "Cass Gilbert's Career in New York," 298.

133 Aus numbered among other Norwegian engineers in a larger migration to America. His and their arrival coincided with America's rapid urbanization and period of vigorous growth in the steel industry. "The Eastern Group: Gunvald Aus," *Norwegian American Technical Journal* 4 (April 1931): 5; and Kenneth Bjork, *Saga in Steel and Concrete* (Northfield, Minn.: Norwegian-American Historical Association, 1947), 24–39, 41–44. See also Irish, "Cass Gilbert's Career in New York," 298–300.

134 Thompson, *Minnesota's State Capitol*, 44–45; and Cass Gilbert to Gunvald Aus, October 4, 1905, West Street Building letterbooks, Cass Gilbert Collection, N-YHS. See also Irish, "A 'Machine That Makes the Land Pay,'" 380–86.

135 Gilbert recorded his trip in diaries dated November 17, 1897, to March 9, 1898, box 1, Cass Gilbert Papers, LC.

136 Unpublished essay written by Cass Gilbert on December 2, 1897, box 6, Cass Gilbert Papers, LC.

137 Gilbert recorded his 1905 trip to Europe in diaries dated June 13, 1905, to July 12, 1905, box 1, Cass Gilbert Papers, LC.

138 Cass Gilbert to Julia Finch Gilbert, August 1, 1906, box 8, Cass Gilbert Papers, LC.

139 Cass Gilbert to R. Clipston Sturgis, November 8, 1906, personal letterbooks, Cass Gilbert Collection, N-YHS.

140 Van Dyke, *The New New York*, 124.

141 Irish, "A 'Machine That Makes the Land Pay,'" 391.

142 [Schuyler], "The West Street Building in New York City," 109.

143 Ibid., 108, 109.

144 Claude Bragdon, "Architecture in the United States," pt. 3, "The Skyscraper," *Architectural Record* 26 (August 1909): 96.

145 Cass Gilbert to R. Clipston Sturgis, November 8, 1906, personal letterbooks, Cass Gilbert Collection, N-YHS.

146 Cass Gilbert to Julia Finch Gilbert, February 28, 1907, box 7, Cass Gilbert Papers, LC.

147 Cass Gilbert, "The Relation of the Architect to His Client, to the Builder, to His Brother-Architect, and the Organization of an Architect's Work" (lecture delivered at the Harvard School of Architecture on February 20, 1912), 5–6, box 16, Cass Gilbert Papers, LC.

148 Van Dyke, *The New New York*, 10.

149 H. W. Desmond, "A Rational Skyscraper," *Architectural Record* 15 (March 1904): 275.

150 Frederick Stymetz Lamb, "Modern Use of the Gothic: The Possibilities of a New Architectural Style," *Craftsman* 8 (May 1905): 150–70.

151 A. D. F. Hamlin, "Style in Architecture," *Craftsman* 8 (June 1905): 331 (for quote), 325–31.

152 Louis H. Sullivan, "Reply to Mr. Frederick Stymetz Lamb on 'Modern Use of the Gothic: The Possibility of New Architectural Style,'" *Craftsman* 8 (June 1905): 337 (for quote), 336–38.

153 Leach, *Land of Desire*, 4 (for quote), 4–5.

154 Albert Kelsey to Cass Gilbert, March 20, 1899, box 18, Cass Gilbert Papers, MHS. Kelsey wrote, quoting Gilbert: "I thoroughly agree with you in favoring 'progress rather than novelty in design.'" Kelsey edited the *Catalogue of the T-Square Club Exhibition and Architectural Annual for the Year 1898* (Philadelphia, 1899). The catalog included Gilbert's response among others to the question "An Unaffected School of Modern Architecture in America—Will It Come?" Gilbert wrote: "I should say that there are no signs of the formation of an American style, except in the way in which there have always been signs of development through the centuries of progress in any of the historic styles" (27). Louis Sullivan responded, by contrast: "There are American buildings that are fresh and original, and some of them are good from an artistic standpoint" (20).

155 On the importance of "evolutionary" theories in late nineteenth-century American art, see Lois Marie Fink, "19th Century Evolutionary Art," *American Art Review* 4 (January 1978): 74–81, 105–9.

156 Cass Gilbert, "President's Address, Architectural League Dinner," February 6, 1914, box 16, Cass Gilbert Papers, LC.

157 Richard Guy Wilson, "The Great Civilization: Expressions of Identity," in *The American Renaissance, 1876–1917*, by Richard Guy Wilson et al. (New York: Brooklyn Museum, 1979), 11–25.

158 Gilbert invited Morgan to a dinner party and memorial for Charles McKim, solicited Rockefeller's financial support for an unidentified building project of "general public interest and benefit," and asked Carnegie to contribute to the American Institute of Architects' educational programs. Cass Gilbert to J. P. Morgan, September 25, 1909, box 41, Correspondence Files, Office of the Secretary, AIA; Cass Gilbert to John D. Rockefeller, May 1, 1907, personal letterbooks, Cass Gilbert Collection, N-YHS; and Cass Gilbert to Andrew Carnegie, April 15, 1908, box 38, Correspondence Files, Office of the Secretary, AIA.

159 Cass Gilbert to Emily and Cass Gilbert, October 8, 1912, box 8, Cass Gilbert Papers, LC.

160 Cass Gilbert to [John Beverly] Robinson, September 25, 1891, box 17, Cass Gilbert Papers, MHS.

161 Gilbert's regular contributions to the Fresh Air Fund are recorded in his personal letterbooks, Cass Gilbert Collection, N-YHS.

162 Unpublished essay on architects of the late nineteenth century by Cass Gilbert, April 26, 1886, box 17, Cass Gilbert Papers, LC.

163 Cass Gilbert, as quoted in "Skyscrapers and the Skyline of the Future."

164 Cass Gilbert to Mr. Corliss, May 31, 1905, box 19, Cass Gilbert Papers, MHS.

CHAPTER FOUR

1 Ann Douglas, *Terrible Honesty: Mongrel Manhattan in the 1920s* (New York: Farrar, Straus and Giroux, 1995), 436, characterizes Manhattan's "star" skyline of the 1920s (after Wayne Attoe, *Skylines: Understanding and Molding Urban Silhouettes*): "Buildings compete with each other. . . . Buildings challenged each other directly."

2 Frank Woolworth to Cass Gilbert, July 27, 1914, Woolworth Building, Cass Gilbert Collection, N-YHS. Woolworth told Gilbert that two events in his life brought about his nervous condition: "the organization of our big corporation" and "the erection of the Woolworth Building," although he looked back "to New York and that building with pride in a great achievement." Earlier Woolworth wrote that doctors described him as "an overworked tired horse which has been whipped and whipped on." Frank Woolworth to Cass Gilbert, 14 July 1913, Woolworth Building, Cass Gilbert Collection, N-YHS. In 1912, Woolworth explained what he called "Americanitis" to his store managers, "a disease peculiar to Americans, which means 'nervous exhaustion.'" He had spent the summer recovering at spas in Karlsbad and Marienbad, receiving "massages, electricity, radium baths, and mud baths." Frank Woolworth, "Executive Office" (general letter to all stores), August 31, 1912. Woolworth Building, Cass Gilbert Collection, N-YHS. George M. Beard described "neurasthenia" in his *American Nervousness: Its*

Causes and Consequences of 1881. See Stephen Kern, *The Culture of Time and Space, 1880–1918* (Cambridge, Mass.: Harvard University Press, 1983), 124–25.

3 Julia Finch Gilbert, "An Experience" (1911), box 17, Cass Gilbert Papers, LC.

4 *The Dinner Given to Cass Gilbert, Architect, by Frank W. Woolworth* (Baltimore: Munder-Thomsen Press, 1913), 46.

5 "Woolworth Building Will Be World's Greatest Skyscraper," *New York Times*, May 7, 1911.

6 William R. Taylor, "The Evolution of Public Space: The Commercial City as Showcase," in *In Pursuit of Gotham: Culture and Commerce in New York*, ed. William R. Taylor (New York: Oxford University Press, 1992), 35.

7 Ibid., 47 (for quote), 47–48.

8 Vanessa R. Schwartz, *Spectacular Realities: Early Mass Culture in Fin-de-Siècle Paris* (Berkeley: University of California Press, 1998), 13–16.

9 Paul Starr, *The Creation of the Media: Political Origins of Modern Communications* (New York: Basic Books, 2004), 251–52.

10 Schwartz, *Spectacular Realities*, 26–28 (for quotes), 16 (for quote).

11 Cass Gilbert, "Response on the Occasion of the Presentation of the Gold Medal for Architecture of the Society of Arts and Sciences" (1931), in *Cass Gilbert: Reminiscences and Addresses*, ed. Julia Finch Gilbert (New York: privately printed, 1935), 46.

12 Correspondence and office memorandums in Woolworth Building, Cass Gilbert Collection, N-YHS, beginning May 5, 1910; and Louis J. Horowitz and Boyden Sparkes, *The Towers of New York: The Memoirs of a Master Builder* (New York: Simon & Schuster, 1937), 110.

13 Cass Gilbert, "The Tenth Birthday of a Notable Structure," *Real Estate Magazine of New York* 11 (May 1923): 344.

14 On Hill, see Leonard K. Eaton, "St. Paul and the Vision of James J. Hill," in *Gateway Cities and Other Essays* (Ames: Iowa State University Press, 1989): 39–44.

15 Cass Gilbert, "Regarding the Woolworth Building" (1927), box 17, Cass Gilbert Papers, LC.

16 On Julia Finch Gilbert, see "Mrs. Cass Gilbert Led in Philanthropy," *New York Times*, September 5, 1952.

17 The Poinciana Hotel numbered among a series of hotels that Henry Morrison Flagler established along the Florida coast and linked by rail.

18 Julia Finch Gilbert, "An Experience."

19 Ibid. Woolworth's wife, the former Jennie Creighton of Picton, Ontario, did not accompany him to Palm Beach. According to John K. Winkler, *Five and Ten: The Fabulous Life of F. W. Woolworth* (New York: Robert M. McBride & Co., 1940), 34, 132, 229, 245, she preferred to stay at home, in the background of her husband's affairs.

20 Cass Gilbert, "The Woolworth Building," in *Masterpieces of Architecture in the United States*, by Edward Warren Hoak and Humphrey Church (New York: Charles Scribner's Sons, 1930), 215.

21 According to F. W. Woolworth Co., *100th Anniversary: 1879–1979* (New York: F. W. Woolworth Co., 1979), 16, "several Woolworth stores became scenes of riots over these novel European goods." Woolworth began importing goods from Europe in 1893, and by 1896, his imports—from England, France, Germany, and Austria—reached the half million mark. Frank W. Woolworth, "General Letter to All Stores," February 11, 1897, Woolworth Collection, NBM.

22 Cass Gilbert, "The Tenth Birthday," 345.

23 Frank Woolworth to Woolworth Syndicate (executive offices in New York), March 6, 1890, Woolworth Collection, NBM.

24 Horowitz and Sparkes, *The Towers of New York*, 2.

25 Winkler, *Five and Ten*, 202–3; Woolworth, *War! War! War!* (letters from southern France and Switzerland written in 1914) (n.p.: David I. Nelke, 1914), 65; and John D. Nichols, "Milestones of Woolworth: A Compendium of Dates, Facts, and Data Skeletonizing Woolworth History through 1947," 31, 35, 41, 44, Woolworth Collection, NBM.

26 *50 Years of Woolworth, 1879–1929: F. W. Woolworth's 5 and 10 Cent Store* (New York: F. W. Woolworth Co., 1929), n.p.

27 William Leach, *Land of Desire: Merchants, Power, and the Rise of a New American Culture* (New York: Pantheon Books, 1993), 25, 33. For Wanamaker, see also Bruno Giberti, *Designing the Centennial: A History of the 1876 International Exhibition in Philadelphia* (Lexington: University Press of Kentucky, 2002), 204–19. D. H. Burnham and Company designed both Wanamaker's new store in Philadelphia (with John T. Windrim) and his addition to A. T. Stewart's cast-iron palace in New York.

28 Frank Woolworth, as quoted in "The 'Five and Ten'—an American Institution," in F. W. Woolworth Company, *100th Anniversary*, 24.

29 Cass Gilbert, "The Tenth Birthday," 344.

30 Office memorandum, October 19, 1910, Woolworth Building, Cass Gilbert Collection, N-YHS.

31 Frank Woolworth to Cass Gilbert, June 19, 1911, Woolworth Building correspondence files, Cass Gilbert Collection, N-YHS.

32 Cass Gilbert to Broadway–Park Place Company, August 31, 1911, Woolworth Building letterbooks, Cass Gilbert Collection, N-YHS.

33 Leach, *Land of Desire*, 11.

34 Cass Gilbert, "The Relation of the Architect to His Client, to the Builder, and to His Brother-Architect, and the Organization of an Architect's Work" (lecture delivered at the Harvard School of Architecture on February 20, 1912), 4, box 16, Cass Gilbert Papers, LC.

35 Cass Gilbert to Elizabeth Fulton Wheeler Gilbert, January 28, 1880, box 2, Cass Gilbert Papers, LC.

36 Cass Gilbert to Professor Warren P. Laird, May 17, 1905, box 20, Cass Gilbert Papers, MHS.

37 Like McKim, Mead and White's office, Gilbert's office attracted first-rate design talent—during the Woolworth Building project, for example, Antonin Raymond and Hugh Ferriss. But Gilbert also actively recruited that talent, as during the New York Custom House competition. Sharon Irish, "Beaux-Arts Teamwork in an American Architectural Office: Cass Gilbert's Entry to the New York Custom House Competition," *New Mexico Studies in the Fine Arts* 7 (1982): 10–11.

38 Guy Kirkham, "Cass Gilbert, Master of Style," *Pencil Points* 15 (November 1934): 541.

39 Alexander B. Trowbridge, "The Architectural League of New York Has Lost a Valued Member by the Death of Thomas R. Johnson," May 16, 1915, Thomas R. Johnson Papers, ALCU.

40 *The Dinner Given to Cass Gilbert*, 47–48.

41 "Monographs on Architectural Renderers: Being a Series of Articles on the Architectural Renderers of To-Day, Accompanied by Characteristic Examples of Their Work," pt. 5, "The Work of Thomas R. Johnson," *Brickbuilder* 23 (May 1914): 110. At the completion of the Woolworth Building project in 1913, Gilbert rewarded Johnson with a check for five thousand dollars. Cass Gilbert to Thomas R. Johnson, August 26, 1913, Thomas R. Johnson Papers, ALCU.

42 "Monographs on Architectural Renderers," 110; and obituary on Thomas R. Johnson, probably from a Toronto newspaper, in Thomas R. Johnson Papers, ALCU.

43 "Monographs on Architectural Renderers," 112.

44 Trowbridge, "The Architectural League of New York Has Lost a Valued Member."

45 "Monographs on Architectural Renderers," 112. Johnson's drawing skills were in demand outside Gilbert's office, particularly for competitions. See Charles Loring to Thomas R. Johnson, January 12, 1914, Thomas R. Johnson Papers, ALCU. Johnson had previously assisted Gilbert with design of the New Haven Railroad Station, the United States Custom House, the Union Club, the Louisiana Purchase Exposition's Festival Hall, and the West Street Building. Sharon Irish, "Cass Gilbert's Career in New York, 1899–1905" (Ph.D. diss., Northwestern University, 1985), 127–29, 239, 308–9, 356–59, 378.

46 Cass Gilbert to Torrance and Taylor, September 7, 1910, Woolworth Building letterbooks, Cass Gilbert Collection, N-YHS.

47 Articles written by Aus included "Special Fireproof Construction in the U.S. Appraiser's Warehouse, New York City," *Engineering News* 40 (November 3, 1898): 278–79; "Some Comments on Building Laws," *Engineering News* 51 (April 14, 1904): 361–63; "Reinforced-Concrete Construction," *American Architect and Building News* 91 (May 4, 1907): 177–78; and "Engineering Design of the Woolworth Building," *American Architect* 103 (March 26, 1913): 157–70.

48 "The Eastern Group: Gunvald Aus," *Norwegian American Technical Journal* 4 (April 1931): 5.

49 Peabody is quoted in Mary N. Woods, *From Craft to Profession: The Practice of Architecture in Ninetheenth-Century America* (Berkeley: University of California Press, 1999), 138.

50 Cass Gilbert, "The Architecture of Today" (lecture delivered at West Point Military Academy), May 4, 1909, 9, box 16, Cass Gilbert Papers, LC; "The Tenth Birthday," 344; and Cass Gilbert, "The Woolworth Building," 215.

51 "$2,000,000 Broadway Building," *New York Times*, July 10, 1910.

52 Cass Gilbert, "Relative to Designing a Skyscraper," 1–2, box 17, Cass Gilbert Papers, LC.

53 Ibid., 4.

54 "New York City Municipal Building Competition," *American Architect and Building News* 93 (May 27, 1908): plates. Gilbert was invited to enter the competition but declined. "Mr. Cass Gilbert's Withdrawal from the Competition for the New Municipal Building, New York, N.Y.," *American Architect and Building News* 93 (January 4, 1908): 7.

55 Montgomery Schuyler, "The Woolworth Building" (1913), in *American Architecture and Other Writings by Montgomery Schuyler*, ed. William H.

Jordy and Ralph Coe, (Cambridge, Mass.: Harvard University Press, Belknap Press, 1961), 2:618.

56 Stickel entered Gilbert's office in 1900. On Stickel, see Charles A. Johnson, "Silhouettes of American Designers and Draftsmen," pt. 4, *Pencil Points* 8 (October 1927): 589–600. Paul Starrett, *Changing the Skyline: An Autobiography* (New York: McGraw-Hill Book Co., 1938), 271, called Stickel "a remarkably competent man and a good designer."

57 Gilbert, "The Tenth Birthday," 344.

58 Howard Frederick Koeper emphasized this point in "The Gothic Skyscraper: A History of the Woolworth Building and Its Antecedents" (Ph.D. diss., Harvard University, 1969), 84.

59 On the expenses incurred by building higher than twenty stories, see George Hill, "The Economy of the Office Building," *Architectural Record* 15 (April 1904): 325–27; and Cecil C. Evers, *The Commercial Problem in Buildings* (New York: Record and Guide, 1912), 184, 188.

60 "Are We Putting Up Too Many Tall Buildings?" *Real Estate Record and Builders' Guide* 88 (July 1, 1911): 1244.

61 Cass Gilbert, "The Woolworth Building," 215.

62 Ibid.; and Cass Gilbert, "The Tenth Birthday," 344. Gilbert, who admired George Gilbert Scott, may have been familiar with Scott's views on the secular buildings of Flanders. In *Remarks on Secular and Domestic Architecture, Present and Future* (London: John Murray, 1857), 198, Scott wrote: "Next to churches, the finest medieval structures existing are, perhaps, the town-halls of Flanders, Germany, France, and some of the free cities of Italy; yet scarcely an attempt has been made to revive these noble buildings in England . . . to vie with the glories of Brussels, Louvain, or Ypres. Nothing can be more grievous than to see magnificent opportunities thus thrown away. . . . What character would a fine Hotel de Ville give one of our great seats of manufacture or commerce!"

63 Cass Gilbert to William Eames, August 30, 1909, personal letterbooks, Cass Gilbert Collection, N-YHS.

64 Schuyler, "The Woolworth Building," 609.

65 Cass Gilbert, untitled essay (on progress in the arts), December 26, 1921, 6, box 17, Cass Gilbert Papers, LC.

66 Cass Gilbert, "Response on the Occasion of the Presentation of the Gold Medal," 53.

67 An office memorandum dictated by Cass Gilbert on June 22, 1910, Woolworth Building, Cass Gilbert Collection, N-YHS, describes the proportions of the arcade.

68 "Schemes 18–20," plan studies of June 6–7 showed the Gilbert office returning to the smaller site, as did "Scheme 24," plan studies of July 7.

69 According to notations on the drawings, each office story of "Scheme 17" accommodated thirty-nine offices, with those facing the exterior twenty-six feet deep and those facing the light court twenty feet deep. Each story in the main office block totaled in net rentable area 14,125 square feet and each story in the tower, 4,300 square feet.

70 Gilbert's office produced the annotated plan studies associated with "Scheme 17" and "Scheme 26" between May 17 and June 28, 1910. See also office memorandum dictated by Cass Gilbert, June 22, 1910, Woolworth Building, Cass Gilbert Collection, N-YHS.

71 Cass Gilbert, "The Architecture of Today," 13.

72 Woolworth left for Europe on June 24, and Gilbert on July 5. Office memorandums dictated by Cass Gilbert, June 22, 1910, and September 16, 1910, Woolworth Building, Cass Gilbert Collection, N-YHS; and Frank Woolworth to Cass Gilbert, July 15, 1910, Woolworth Building correspondence files, Cass Gilbert Collection, N-YHS. While in London, Gilbert ordered two large prints from a photograph of the Victoria Tower, one of which still remains in the Cass Gilbert Collection, N-YHS.

73 Cass Gilbert to John Rockart, August 3, 1910, Woolworth Building correspondence files, Cass Gilbert Collection, N-YHS.

74 Ibid.

75 Antonin Raymond, as quoted in "One Hundred Years of Significant Office Buildings," in *Office Buildings: An Architectural Record Book* (New York: F. W. Dodge Corporation, 1961), 9.

76 Office memorandum dictated by John Rockart, August 22, 1910, Woolworth Building, Cass Gilbert Collection, N-YHS.

77 Earle Shultz and Walter Simmons, *Offices in the Sky* (Indianapolis: Bobbs-Merrill Co., 1959), 74.

78 Fiske is quoted in Marquis James, *The Metropolitan Life: A Study in Business Growth* (New York: Viking Press, 1947), 174; and cited in Shultz and Simmons, *Offices in the Sky*, 66.

79 Horowitz and Sparkes, *The Towers of New York*, 118.

80 Office memorandum dictated by Cass Gilbert, November 2, 1910, Woolworth Building, Cass Gilbert Collection, N-YHS.

81 According to Sarah Bradford Landau and Carl W. Condit, *Rise of the New York Skyscraper, 1865–1913* (New Haven, Conn.: Yale University Press, 1996), 291, in the early twentieth century, engineers understood that "the building acts as a vertical cantilever, with the bending moment induced by wind at its theoretical maximum at grade level."

82 Woolworth followed a practice well established in New York by 1910. See frontispiece to Richard M. Hurd, *Principles of City Land Values* (New York: Record & Guide, 1903). According to Shultz and Simmons, *Offices in the Sky*, 63, during the early twentieth century "owners of existing buildings bought up next-door properties at great expense to prevent competing skyscrapers from snuggling even closer."

83 Such study models typically played a minor role in the Gilbert office's design process. Irish, "Cass Gilbert's Career in New York," 124, states that "sometimes a model would be made of part of the elevation or a particular feature on the interior (like a rotunda)," when describing the process of design in Gilbert's office.

84 Montgomery Schuyler, "'The Towers of Manhattan' and Notes on the Woolworth Building," *Architectural Record* 33 (February 1913): 108.

85 Office memorandums by John Rockart, August 22, 1910, September 8, 1910, and September 16, 1910, Woolworth Building, Cass Gilbert Collection, N-YHS.

86 "Skyscraping Up to Date," *Architectural Record* 23 (January 1908): 74.

87 "The Newest Thing in Skyscrapers," *Architectural Record* 19 (May 1906), 399.

88 Charles McKim was writing to Daniel Burnham in 1897 about a design for the Illinois Trust and Savings Bank Building in Chicago, a two-story classical bank building. Charles Moore, *Daniel H. Burnham: Architect and Planner of Cities*, 2 vols. (Boston: Houghton Mifflin Co., 1921), 93.

89 Aus's professional fee for the Woolworth's "accepted design," which he described as a twenty-eight-story building incorporating a forty-story tower, was $7,000. On November 14, 1910, Gilbert increased Aus's fee to $7,500. See handwritten notation on Cass Gilbert to Gunvald Aus, September 23, 1910, Papers of Cass Gilbert, OCA.

90 Corydon T. Purdy, "The Relation of the Engineer to the Architect," *American Architect and Building News* 87 (February 11, 1905): 43. Purdy noted that in a few cases, New York architectural firms had employed an in-house engineer or engineers.

91 Aus made S. F. Holtzman and Kort Berle partners in his practice shortly before the Woolworth Building project began. Neither partner's name appears on the letterhead associated with the West Street Building project of 1905–7. Berle, like Aus an immigrant from Norway, had worked previously with Aus at the Phoenix Bridge Company and as a first assistant in the United States Department of the Treasury. Kenneth Bjork, *Saga in Steel and Concrete* (Northfield, Minn.: Norwegian-American Historical Association, 1947), 229. Much less is known about Holtzman.

92 Antonin Raymond, as quoted in "One Hundred Years of Significant Office Buildings," 9.

93 Aus, "Engineering Design of the Woolworth Building," 158. Aus's engineering drawings for the Woolworth Building, however, show that the centerlines of his structural steel verticals do not always align with the centerlines of Gilbert's Gothic piers. NMAH.

94 Aus, "Engineering Design of the Woolworth Building," 157.

95 Ibid., 159–60.

96 Ibid., 160. Aus's partner, S. F. Holtzman, collaborated on the design of the wind bracing.

97 Carl W. Condit, "The Wind Bracing of Buildings," *Scientific American* 230 (February 1974): 93–95, 98–99. Condit notes that engineers such as Aus, who trained as bridge designers, viewed the steel-framed office building as a metal truss bridge cantilevered vertically upward from the ground plane.

98 Aus, "Engineering Design of the Woolworth Building," 167.

99 Ibid., 158, 167.

100 Condit, "The Wind Bracing of Buildings," 98–99.

101 O. W. Norcross to Cass Gilbert, November 19, 1910, Woolworth Building correspondence files, and Cass Gilbert to O. W. Norcross, November 30, 1910, Woolworth Building letterbooks, Cass Gilbert Collection, N-YHS. Paul Starrett, *Changing the Skyline*, 165–67, recounts his opposition to terra cotta, given its fragility in withstanding the winds and weather typically endured by skyscrapers.

102 Winkler, *Five and Ten*, 191, notes that Woolworth was "enamored of marble," but that the engineers "shook their heads over the added weight" of the material, so Gilbert instead used terra cotta.

103 Bjork, *Saga in Steel and Concrete*, 231.

104 "New Woolworth Building on Broadway Will Eclipse Singer Tower in Height," *New York Times*, November 13, 1910.

105 Cass Gilbert to Arthur W. Page, February 9, 1911, Woolworth Building letterbooks, Cass Gilbert Collection, N-YHS. Gilbert also exhibited the design at the Chicago Architectural Club. "Woolworth Building Exhibited at the Chicago Architectural Club," *Chicago Post*, March 10, 1911, in scrapbook, Cass Gilbert Collection, N-YHS.

106 Office memorandum dictated by Cass Gilbert, December 13, 1910, Woolworth Building, Cass Gilbert Collection, N-YHS.

107 "New Woolworth Building on Broadway Will Eclipse Singer Tower in Height."

108 Gilbert applied for a building permit to proceed with construction on the foundation on November 7. Cass Gilbert to superintendent, Bureau of Buildings, New York City, November 7, 1910, Woolworth Building letterbooks, Cass Gilbert Collection, N-YHS.

109 Office memorandum dictated by Cass Gilbert, December 13, 1910, Woolworth Building, Cass Gilbert Collection, N-YHS.

110 Ibid.

111 The Metropolitan Life Insurance Company had also altered plans for the height of its tower well after design began. "Tower to Be 700 Feet: Metropolitan Changes Plans to Make Skyscraper of More Than 50 Stories," *New York Times*, April 19, 1908.

112 "Metropolitan Life Tower to Be Outdone," *Brooklyn Standard Union*, January 29, 1911, in scrapbook, Cass Gilbert Collection, N-YHS.

113 *The Metropolitan Life Insurance Company: Its History, Its Present Position in the Insurance World, Its Home Office Building and the Work Carried on Therein* (New York: Metropolitan Life Insurance Co., 1908), 5–15.

114 Shultz and Simmons, *Offices in the Sky*, 68.

115 John Rockart suggested that Woolworth call on Metropolitan Life regarding the financing of the larger scheme, after Woolworth failed to interest New York bankers. Office memorandum dictated by John Rockart, August 22, 1910, Woolworth Building, Cass Gilbert Collection, N-YHS. Gilbert subsequently wrote to Chicago's Arthur T. Aldis of Aldis and Northcote on Woolworth's behalf. "He will be in the market for such a loan provided the rate is made low enough." Cass Gilbert to Arthur T. Aldis, October 17, 1910, Papers of Cass Gilbert, OCA. When journalists reported much later in August 1911 that Woolworth had sent the real estate lawyer Robert McMaster Gillespie to Paris to obtain the financing required for Gilbert's final design, he accused them of spreading a "malicious rumor." "Obtains $8,000,000 for Big Skyscraper," *New York Times*, August 2, 1911, in scrapbook, Cass Gilbert Collection, N-YHS; and John Tauranac, *Elegant New York: The Builders and Their Buildings* (New York: Abbeville Press, 1985), 23.

116 Frank Woolworth to Woolworth Syndicate, April 28, 1890, Woolworth Collection, NBM.

117 Charles F. Phillips, "A History of the F. W. Woolworth Company," *Harvard Business Review* 13 (January 1935): 228; and Alfred D. Chandler, Jr., *Scale and Scope: The Dynamics of Industrial Capitalism* (Cambridge, Mass.: Harvard University Press, Belknap Press, 1990): 75.

118 Winkler, *Five and Ten*, 174–75; and F. W. Woolworth Company, *100th Anniversary*, 17–19. Woolworth's partners in the merger had collaborated in purchasing goods together under single orders and in pledging not to enter one another's territories. C. S. Woolworth, a former partner of F. W. Woolworth, had 15 stores; F. M. Kirby, a former partner of C. S. Woolworth, 96 stores; S. H. Knox, a former partner of F. W. Woolworth, 112 stores; and E. P. Charlton, a former partner of S. H. Knox, 53 stores. Woolworth's former employer, W. H. Moore, had 2 stores.

119 Winkler, *Five and Ten*, 172, 175, 178, 198–201; and John D. Nichols, "Milestones of Woolworth," 42. Goldman, Sachs and Company oversaw the transaction, the same firm that financed the expansion of Sears.

120 Kern, *The Culture of Time and Space*, 223–40.

121 Julia Finch Gilbert, "An Experience," 1–2.

122 Schuyler, "The Towers of Manhattan," 103.

123 Cass Gilbert to Pierre Le Brun, December 9, 1910, Woolworth Building letterbooks, Cass Gilbert Collection, N-YHS.

124 Horowitz and Sparkes, *The Towers of New York*, 109.

125 Leo L. Redding, "Mr. F. W. Woolworth's Story," *World's Work* 25 (April 1913): 665.

126 John G. Van Horne to Cass Gilbert, December 20, 1910, Woolworth Building correspondence files, Cass Gilbert Collection, N-YHS. Cass Gilbert to Broadway–Park Place Company, December 24, 1910, Woolworth Building letterbooks, N-YHS.

127 Deed for 229 Broadway, January 18, 1911, Woolworth Collection, NBM; and "A Realty Triumph in Assembling Plot," *New York Times*, January 22, 1911.

128 Ibid.

129 Cass Gilbert to the Foundation Company, January 19, 1911, Woolworth Building letterbooks, Cass Gilbert Collection, N-YHS.

130 Frank Woolworth, as quoted in "55-Story Building in Lower Broadway," *New York Times*, January 20, 1911.

131 Office memorandum dictated by Cass Gilbert, January 21, 1911, Woolworth Building, Cass Gilbert Collection, N-YHS: "I called at Mr. Woolworth's house last evening (January 20) with revised sketch plans and elevation showing the building extending from Barclay Street to Park Place on Broadway, the tower being 750 feet high from the sidewalk to the tip." The set of drawings to which Gilbert refers has not been located.

132 Gunvald Aus to Cass Gilbert, January 16, 1911, Woolworth Building correspondence files, Cass Gilbert Collection, N-YHS.

133 Gunvald Aus to Cass Gilbert, January 18, 1911, Woolworth Building correspondence files, Cass Gilbert Collection, N-YHS. Aus asked Gilbert for a two-thousand-dollar increase in his professional engineering fee, given the new height of the tower. He also billed Gilbert twenty-one thousand dollars for the shop drawings his office had already completed. He had employed all his draftsmen on the Woolworth project, had turned down other work, and had reached the limit of his resources.

134 Ibid. Aus argued that the savings in the dollar value of steel (less steel would be required in the new design) more than justified the cost of producing an entirely new set of drawings.

135 Cass Gilbert, "Regarding the Woolworth Building."

136 Henry Adams, *Mont-Saint-Michel and Chartres* (Boston: Houghton Mifflin Co.; Cambridge: Riverside Press, 1913; reprint, Princeton, N.J.: Princeton University Press, 1981), 46, observed that Saint-Ouen's crossing tower belonged to the same family of Norman Gothic crossing towers as Coutances, both of which stood along the same "architectural highway." Gilbert's English High Victorian Gothic predecessors, among them George Edmund Street, sought the origins of English Gothic and Romanesque architecture through antiquarian travel in Normandy, and this influenced contemporary designs. Gavin Stamp, "High Victorian Gothic and the Architecture of Normandy," *Journal of the Society of Architectural Historians* 64 (June 2003), 194–211.

137 Woolworth, *War! War! War!* 69. Woolworth equated churches with cathedrals.

138 See *American Architect* 98 (November 9, 1910): plate opposite p. 153.

139 Schuyler, "The Woolworth Building," 606.

140 Cass Gilbert, "Regarding the Woolworth Building."

141 Cass Gilbert, "The Tenth Birthday," 344.

142 Cass Gilbert, "The Relation of the Architect to His Client," 8.

143 Schuyler, "The Woolworth Building," 606.

144 Early plan studies for the Woolworth's lobby-arcade date from January 25, 1911, to February 20, 1911, and are housed in the Prints and Photographs Division, Library of Congress.

145 Frank Woolworth to Cass Gilbert June 6, 1911, Woolworth Building correspondence files, Cass Gilbert Collection, N-YHS. Woolworth wrote: "On the corner store, I suggest there be an outside door nearest to the entrance on Park Place and between the small store and the basement . . . a show window which can be seen from the street. I have drawn up a little sketch of my idea of how the plan should work out."

146 Office memorandum dictated by Cass Gilbert, December 20, 1911, Woolworth Building, Cass Gilbert Collection, N-YHS. Gilbert argued that too many shops would compromise the arcade's desired ambience of grandeur.

147 Frank Woolworth to Cass Gilbert, December 27, 1911, Woolworth Building correspondence files, Cass Gilbert Collection, N-YHS.

148 Jackson Lears, *Fables of Abundance: A Cultural History of Advertising in America* (New York: Basic Books, 1994), 264.

149 Ibid., 269.

150 Neil McKendrick, John Brewer, and J. H. Plumb, *The Birth of Consumer Society: The Commercialization of Eighteenth Century England* (London: Europa Publications, 1982), 316 (for quote); and Lears, *Fables of Abundance*, 270.

151 Cass Gilbert to Frank Woolworth, May 3, 1911; Cass Gilbert to Frank Woolworth, May 4, 1911; and Cass Gilbert to *Record and Guide*, May 4, 1911, Woolworth Building letterbooks, Cass Gilbert Collection, N-YHS. All published images of the Woolworth Building's final design featured the caption "Copyrighted by F. W. Woolworth." In some cases, a second line appeared: "All rights reserved; reproduction forbidden without written permission." See, for example, "Highest Building the World," *Real Estate Record and Builders' Guide* 87 (May 6, 1911): 844.

152 "Woolworth Building Will Be World's Greatest Skyscraper."

153 Daniel J. Boorstin, *The Image: A Guide to Pseudo-events in America*, 3rd ed. (New York: Random House, Vintage Books, 1992), 9–13.

154 During his early career, Gilbert aimed to publish as many drawings and designs as possible in *American Architect and Building News*. Geoffrey Blodgett, *Cass Gilbert: The Early Years* (St. Paul, Minn.: Minnesota Historical Society Press, 2001), 8, 13, 50.

155 C. A. Leidy to Cass Gilbert, November 14, 1910, Cass Gilbert Collection, N-YHS, as cited in Mary N. Woods, "In the Camera's Eye: The Woolworth Building and American Avant-Garde Photography and Film," in *Cass Gilbert: Life and Work: Architect of the Public Domain,* ed. Barbara S. Christen and Steven Flanders (New York: W. W. Norton & Co., 2001), 151, 302 n. 8.

156 Cass Gilbert to Frank Woolworth, April 13, 1911, Woolworth Building letterbooks, Cass Gilbert Collection, N-YHS. Gilbert wrote to Hawley, "I hope that you can complete the drawing very soon for it is in great demand." Cass Gilbert to Hughson Hawley, April 14, 1911, Woolworth Building letterbooks, Cass Gilbert Collection, N-YHS.

157 "Hughson Hawley: Scenic Artist and Architectural Painter," *Pencil Points* 9 (December 1928): 769, 773–74. Hawley reportedly colored more than eleven thousand architectural drawings by the end of his career. Janet Parks, "Hughson Hawley," in *New York on the Rise: Architectural Renderings by Hughson Hawley, 1880–1931* (New York: Museum of the City of New York; London: Lund Humphries Publishers, 1998), 7–17; and author's telephone conversation with Parks, July 2006.

158 For accounts of the design in newspapers other than those of New York, see scrapbooks, Cass Gilbert Collection, N-YHS.

159 Annie Russell Marble, "The Reign of the Spectacular," *Dial* 35 (November 1, 1903): 298.

160 Ibid., 297, 299.

161 Boorstin, *The Image*, 13; Starr, *The Creation of the Media*, 250–60; and Sir Peter Hall, "The Invention of Mass Culture," in *Cities in Civilization* (New York: Random House, Pantheon Books, 1998), 510, 515–16. Hall notes that with the older hand presses, it was possible to print two thousand sheets on one side in eight hours, which supported the distribution of a weekly paper, whereas by 1893, the new presses were capable of printing sixteen thousand copies of eight pages in one hour.

162 Julia Finch Gilbert, "An Experience."

163 Winkler, *Five and Ten*, 223, estimated Woolworth's own profits in 1915.

164 Woolworth facilitated the merger between Irving National Exchange Bank and Mercantile National Bank by purchasing with others a controlling interest in the Mercantile National Bank. "$50,000,000 Bank Merger," *New York City Commercial*, April 9, 1912, in scrapbook, Cass Gilbert Collection, N-YHS.

165 "Woolworth Building Will Be World's Greatest Skyscraper." Woolworth's Lancaster Woolworth Building had remained mortgage free since 1907 and continued to pay dividends. F. W. Woolworth Company, ledger book, 1907, Woolworth Collection, NBM.

166 Taylor, "The Evolution of Public Space," 46, notes that Woolworth made it a goal to create "a beacon of worldwide publicity."

167 Lincoln Steffens, "The Modern Business Building," *Scribner's* 22 (July 1897): 55.

168 Cass Gilbert to Frank Woolworth, May 5, 1911, Woolworth Building letterbooks, Cass Gilbert Collection, N-YHS. McAtamney, who had emigrated from Ireland, had worked for five years at the *New York Tribune* as the head of the proofroom and as a press agent for the McVickar-Gaillard Real Estate Company. "How McAtamney Climbed the Ladder," *New York City Press*, May 17, 1914, in scrapbook, Cass Gilbert Collection, N-YHS; and Spark, "How Hugh McAtamney Put the Woolworth Building on the International Map," *Real Estate Magazine* 2 (May 1913): 144–50. At the time of the Woolworth commission, publicity agencies were emerging to join the earlier-formed advertising agencies headquartered in New York. Edward L. Bernays, *Public Relations* (Norman: University of Oklahoma Press, 1952), 35–76.

169 Cass Gilbert to Frank Woolworth, May 4, 1911, Woolworth Building letterbooks, Cass Gilbert Collection, N-YHS.

CHAPTER FIVE

1 Bob Davis, "Foreword," in *Changing the Skyline: An Autobiography*, by Paul Starrett (New York: McGraw-Hill Book Co., 1938), viii–ix.

2 Paul Starrett, *Changing the Skyline*, 265.

3 Louis J. Horowitz and Boyden Sparkes, *The Towers of New York: The Memoirs of a Master Builder* (New York: Simon & Schuster, 1937), 128.

4 Alan Trachtenberg, *The Incorporation of America: Culture and Society in the Gilded Age* (New York: Hill & Wang, 1982), 74–100.

5 *The Master Builders: A Record of the Construction of the World's Highest Commercial Structure* (New York: Hugh McAtamney & Co., 1913), 11–12.

6 Thomas P. Hughes, *American Genesis: A Century of Invention and Technological Enthusiasm, 1870–1970* (New York: Viking Penguin, 1989), 1–2; and David E. Nye, *American Technological Sublime* (Cambridge, Mass.: MIT Press, 1994), xi–xx, 89–91.

7 Horowitz and Sparkes, *The Towers of New York*, 67.

8 Paul Starrett, *Changing the Skyline*, 85.

9 Ernest Poole, "Cowboys of the Skies," *Everybody's Magazine* 19 (November 1908): 641–53. Gail Bederman, *Manliness and Civilization: A Cultural History of Gender and Race in the United States, 1880–1917* (Chicago: University of Chicago Press, 1995), 170–71.

10 Hughes, *American Genesis*, 1.

11 See William R. Taylor and Thomas Bender, "Culture and Architecture: Some Aesthetic Tensions in the Shaping of New York," in *In Pursuit of Gotham: Culture and Commerce in New York*, ed. William R. Taylor (New York: Oxford University Press, 1992), 51–67.

12 Robert Bruegmann, *The Architects and the City: Holabird and Roche of Chicago, 1880–1918* (Chicago: University of Chicago Press, 1997), 80–82; and David Van Zanten, "The Nineteenth Century: The Projecting of Chicago as a Commercial City and the Rationalization of Design and Construction," in *Chicago and New York: Architectural Interactions* (Chicago: Art Institute of Chicago, 1984), 40–42.

13 Theodore Starrett began his career as a partner of Fuller in 1891 and from 1897 served as vice president and manager of the George A. Fuller Company's New York office under Harry S. Black. "Theodore Starrett Dead," *New York Times*, October 10, 1917; and "Theodore Starrett," in *The National Cyclopaedia of American Biography*, vol. 24 (1935; reprint, Ann Arbor, Mich.: University Microfilms, 1967), 41.

14 "The National Builder," *Supplement to the Real Estate Record and Builders' Guide* 64 (July 28, 1900), 1–4; and Timothy John Houlihan, "The New York City Building Trades, 1890–1910" (Ph. D. diss., State University of New York at Binghamton, 1994), 31–37. The Fuller Company was headquartered in the Fuller Building at 111 Broadway, and the Thompson-Starrett Company at 51 Wall Street.

15 W. A. Starrett, *Skyscrapers and the Men Who Build Them* (New York: Charles Scribner's Sons, 1928), 32–33.

16 Paul Starrett, *Changing the Skyline*, 29–43. According to Paul Starrett, Burnham told the Starretts "you have a genius for organization and leadership." Ibid., 43.

17 "Theodore Starrett," in *The National Cyclopaedia*, 41; and Horowitz and Sparkes, *The Towers of New York*, 66–68.

18 Earle Shultz and Walter Simmons, *Offices in the Sky* (Indianapolis: Bobbs-Merrill Co., 1959), 82–83.

19 Louis Jay Horowitz, *The Modern Building Organization* (New York: Alexander Hamilton Institute, 1911), 11, 15–17.

20 Thompson-Starrett advertised its branch offices in the *Architectural League of New York Yearbook, 1909*.

21 Fuller identified its branch offices on the company's letterhead. See Paul Starrett to Cass Gilbert, May 16, 1910, Woolworth Building correspondence files, Cass Gilbert Collection, N-YHS.

22 Horowitz, *The Modern Building Organization*, 6–13, 34–36.

23 Paul Starrett, *Changing the Skyline*, 130; and Van Zanten, "The Nineteenth Century," 42.

24 Paul Starrett, *Changing the Skyline*, 165.

25 Horowitz and Sparkes, *The Towers of New York*, 1, 97.

26 H. A. Shreve, "Foreword," in Horowitz and Sparkes, *The Towers of New York*, xii.

27 Horowitz and Sparkes, *The Towers of New York*, 4.

28 Ibid., 103.

29 Ibid., 104.

30 Sarah Bradford Landau and Carl W. Condit, *Rise of the New York Skyscraper, 1865–1913* (New Haven, Conn.: Yale University Press, 1996), 298–304, 309–13, 326–29.

31 Frank W. Woolworth, "Foreword," in *The Master Builders: A Record of the Construction of the World's Highest Commercial Structure* (Baltimore: Munder-Thomsen Press, 1913), 5.

32 "Advance Reports: Contract Practically Let for Third Highest Building in the World," *Real Estate Record and Builders' Guide* 86 (November 19, 1910): 833.

33 Horowitz and Sparkes, *The Towers of New York*, 104.

34 Ibid., 109.

35 Paul Starrett, *Changing the Skyline*, 167. Daniel Burnham had cautioned Starrett that "an unfriendly architect will see that the door is closed upon you." Ibid., 131. According to Horowitz and Sparkes, *The Towers of New York*, 106, Starrett insulted Woolworth, insisting he made a financial mistake in letting the almost eight-hundred-thouasnd-dollar contract for the caisson work to the Foundation Company. "When Paul Starrett won this argument, he lost the job."

36 Paul Starrett to Cass Gilbert, May 16, 1910, Woolworth Building correspondence files, Cass Gilbert Collection, N-YHS.

37 To create United States Realty and Construction Company, Black combined the assets of the George A. Fuller Company with those of the New York Realty Company, the Alliance Realty Corporation, and several other construction-related companies. Houlihan, "The New York City Building Trades," 35; and Landau and Condit, *Rise of the New York Skyscraper*, 302–3, 313.

38 Paul Starrett, *Changing the Skyline*, 69 (for quote), 115 (for quote), 116.

39 Cass Gilbert, "President's Address, American Institute of Architects" (1909), box 16, Cass Gilbert Papers, LC. Gilbert, according to rumor, considered organizing the construction of the Woolworth Building through his own office, letting the subcontracts himself. Paul Starrett, *Changing the Skyline*, 166.

40 "The Architect and the Builder," *Brickbuilder* 11 (December 1902): 257–58; and Houlihan, "The New York City Building Trades," 35 (for quote).

41 Julia Finch Gilbert, "An Experience," box 17, Cass Gilbert Papers, LC. Black also clashed with Daniel Burnham. Paul Starrett, *Changing the Skyline*, 88.

42 Paul Starrett, *Changing the Skyline*, 126.

43 Born in Częstochowa in 1875, Horowitz grew up poor in Poland and arrived in New York with his father in 1892 as a penniless immigrant. Horowitz and Sparkes, *The Towers of New York*, 5, 12–96; and Helen Christine Bennett, "The Greatest Builder of Skyscrapers in the World: Louis Horowitz—His Story and His Ideas," *American Magazine*, April 1920, 16, 176–77. According to Paul Starrett, *Changing the Skyline*, 128, "by great native intelligence and energy [he] had risen to a rather prominent place in New York real estate and finance."

44 Horowitz and Sparkes, *The Towers of New York*, 79–96.

45 Ibid., 103.

46 Horowitz, *The Modern Building Organization*, 11. On the machine as a widely used metaphor for industrial and organizational change, see Trachtenberg, *The Incorporation of America*, 42–52.

47 Alfred D. Chandler, *The Visible Hand: The Managerial Revolution in American Business* (Cambridge, Mass.: Harvard University Press, Belknap Press, 1977), 89–94; and Thomas J. Misa, *A Nation of Steel: The Making of Modern America, 1865–1925* (Baltimore: Johns Hopkins University Press, 1995), 1–5.

48 Horowitz, *The Modern Building Organization*, 8 (for quote), 8–9.

49 On the development of the comprehensive time schedule from the 1880s, see Landau and Condit, *Rise of the New York Skyscraper*, 179.

50 Horowitz, *The Modern Building Organization*, 9 (for quote), 10–34. For the Woolworth Building project, William Sunter's daily reports can be found in Woolworth Building, Cass Gilbert Collection, N-YHS.

51 [Frank Bunker Gilbreth], "System in Contracting," *Real Estate Record and Builders' Guide* 76 (August 19, 1905), 312; and Gilbreth, *Field System* (New York: Frank B. Gilbreth, 1906). See also Tom F. Peters, *Building the Nineteenth Century* (Cambridge, Mass.: MIT Press, 1996), 93–97.

52 Frederick Winslow Taylor, *A Piece Rate System: Being a Step toward Partial Solution of the Labor Problem* (n.p., n.p., 1895), reprint from the *Transactions of the ASME*, vol. 16. Gilbreth met Taylor in December 1907. Peters, *Building the Nineteenth Century*, 93.

53 Helen Christine Bennett, "The Greatest Builder of Skyscrapers in the World," 177.

54 Paul Starrett, *Changing the Skyline*, 172.

55 Ibid., 166.

56 Office memorandum dictated by J. R. Rockart, December 27, 1911, Woolworth Building, Cass Gilbert Collection, N-YHS.

57 Cass Gilbert, "Building Skyscrapers—Described by Cass Gilbert," *Real Estate Record and Builders' Guide* 55 (June 23, 1900): 1089 (for quote), 1091. Gilbert's essay was also published in *Construction News* 12 (July 7, 1900): 5–6, and in *Engineering Record* 41 (June 30, 1900): 623–24, as "The Financial Importance of Rapid Building." Gilbert based his analysis on his own experience with the Broadway Chambers project, having worked out the

project's financing with the Fuller Company's Harry S. Black.

58 Houlihan, "The New York City Building Trades," 156, 180, 186.

59 Cass Gilbert, "Building Skyscrapers," 1089.

60 Houlihan, "The New York City Building Trades," 50, 241, 286; and Jim Rasenberger, *High Steel: The Daring Men Who Built the World's Greatest Skyline* (New York: Harper Collins Publishers, 2004), 173–77.

61 Mary N. Woods, *From Craft to Profession: The Practice of Architecture in Ninetheenth-Century America* (Berkeley: University of California Press, 1999), 156–57; and Rasenberger, *High Steel*, 92–93. Some tradesmen, it was reported in 1904, valued working for Fuller because the company "provided steady employment, paid wages promptly, remedied grievances effectively and took on-site safety measures more seriously than other companies." Jeffrey W. Cody, "'Erecting Monuments to the God of Business and Trade': The Fuller Construction Company of the Orient, 1919–1926," *Construction History* 12 (1996): 68.

62 Office memorandums dictated by Cass Gilbert, December 13, 1910; January 3, 1911, Woolworth Building, Cass Gilbert Collection, N-YHS. On strikes at the United States Custom House during 1901, 1903, and 1905–6, see Sharon Irish, "Cass Gilbert's Career in New York, 1899–1905" (Ph.D. diss., Northwestern University, 1985), 288–89.

63 Office memorandums, February 6, 1912; March 1, 1912; June 20, 1912; September 4, 1912; September 12, 1912; and H. L. Marsh, general superintendent, Thompson-Starrett Company, to Cass Gilbert, January 28, 1913, Woolworth Building correspondence files, Cass Gilbert Collection, N-YHS.

64 Cass Gilbert, "The Architect's Approbation," in *The Master Builders*, 7.

65 On the "great immigration" and New York, see and Edwin G. Burrows and Mike Wallace, *Gotham: A History of New York City to 1898* (New York: Oxford University Press, 1999), 1111–31; and Sir Peter Hall, "The Apotheosis of the Modern: New York, 1880–1940, in *Cities and Civilization* (New York: Pantheon Books, 1998), 749–50.

66 Poole, "Cowboys of the Skies," 648. Native Americans also worked on the Singer Tower; no record remains documenting their involvement with the Woolworth Building.

67 *Bricklayer and Mason* 11 (November 1908): 169–70, as cited in Houlihan, "The New York City Building Trades," 72–73.

68 Peters, *Building the Nineteenth Century*, 95.

69 David C. Hammack, *Power and Society: Greater New York at the Turn of the Century* (New York: Russell Sage Foundation, 1982): 99–100.

70 Houlihan, "The New York City Building Trades," 50.

71 Hammack, *Power and Society*, 90, notes that the wage earned by a skilled worker in the organized building trades in greater New York "enabled a man to provide good food and decent clothing for his family, to pay union dues and purchase a little insurance, and to rent three or four rooms in a relatively new, clean, and comfortable tenement building or Brooklyn row house."

72 Gilbert kept close tabs on the schedule, so, as he explained it, his draftsmen would have the details prepared on time. Cass Gilbert to Thompson-Starrett Construction Company, May 3, 1911, Woolworth Building letterbooks, Cass Gilbert Collection, N-YHS. Still, the design of many details continued past mid-1912. Office memorandum dictated by John Rockart, July 25, 1912, Woolworth Building, Cass Gilbert Collection, N-YHS.

73 Office memorandum dictated by Cass Gilbert, December 13, 1910, Woolworth Building, Cass Gilbert Collection, N-YHS. Gunvald Aus and Company's shop drawings had to suit the fabrication of steel members directly without the preparation of new drawings and so had to conform to the American Bridge Company's standards. Frank W. Skinner, *Woolworth Building, New York City* (New York: American Bridge Co., n.d.), 33.

74 Office memorandums, June 3, 1911; October 2, 1911, Woolworth Building, Cass Gilbert Collection, N-YHS; and Hildegard J. Safford, "The Terra Cotta Industry and the Atlantic Terra Cotta Company," *Staten Island Historian* 31 (April–June 1974): 153, 161–62.

75 The project's steel alone yielded "thousands of drawings and blueprints . . . in the minutest details." "The Tallest Building," *Engineering Record* 66 (July 27, 1912): 86.

76 Cass Gilbert, untitled essay on the American Institute of Architects, the Architectural League of New York, and the practice of architecture, March 31, 1925, box 17, Cass Gilbert Papers, LC.

77 Walter Tittle, "The Creator of the Woolworth Tower," *World's Work* 54 (May 1927): 97.

78 Cass Gilbert to Frank Woolworth, August 1, 1912, Papers of Cass Gilbert, OCA.

79 Office ledgers, 1910–12, Cass Gilbert Collection, N-YHS.

80 In 1905, Gilbert mentioned that he wanted to make John Rockart and George Wells partners, along with the designers Samuel Stevens Haskell and Thomas Holyoke, but that his temperament prevented him from doing so. Irish, "Cass Gilbert's Career in New York," 135–36, 142.

81 Antonin Raymond, *Antonin Raymond: An Autobiography* (Rutland, Vt.: Charles E. Tuttle Co., 1973), 29.

82 Office memorandums by T. R. Johnson, October 20, 1911, through September 6, 1912, Woolworth Building, Cass Gilbert Collection, N-YHS.

83 See office memorandums by J. R. Rockart, August 1, 1909, through April 14, 1914, Woolworth Building, Cass Gilbert Collection, N-YHS. Born in St. Paul, John Rachac (from the Czech Roháč) began working for Gilbert in 1889. Gilbert, reportedly, made Rachac change his name to Rockart. "Transcript from Interview with John Rannells," October 4, 1979, Supreme Court Archives, Washington, D.C. See also "John Rockart Dies; Noted Architect," *New York Times*, October 14, 1951.

84 See office memorandums by G. H. Wells, December 30, 1910, through November 11, 1913, Woolworth Building, Cass Gilbert Collection, N-YHS. Gilbert hired Wells, who had previously worked in the New York City Office of Repairs in 1901, to write specifications and to oversee construction for the U.S. Custom House project. Irish, "Cass Gilbert's Career in New York," 300.

85 Cass Gilbert, as quoted in Irish, "Cass Gilbert's Career in New York," 300.

86 Ralph Adams Cram, by contrast, argued that "good results can best be accomplished through personal contact with the workmen themselves." Ralph Adams Cram, *My Life in Architecture* (Boston: Little, Brown & Co., 1936), 198.

87 Gilbert made the distinction between the project's "structural" and "ornamental" draftsmen in "Mr. Cass Gilbert and the Woolworth Building," *Architects' Journal* 51 (July 28, 1920): 90. Little in the way of documentation remains explaining the increase in the building's height from 750 feet to 792 feet, but it is likely that Gilbert added the height to improve the proportions of the tower. After construction, Gilbert had the height of the tower measured from five locations (given grade-level changes) to determine an average height of 792 feet 5½ inches. See office memorandums, June 1914 and July 10, 1914, Cass Gilbert Collection, NMAH.

88 "Woolworth Building" (office memorandum), May 1, 1915, Woolworth Building, Cass Gilbert Collection, N-YHS, documents the number of drawings produced for the project.

89 Cass Gilbert, as quoted in "Mr. Cass Gilbert and the Woolworth Building," 90.

90 The Woolworth Building's working drawings are housed in the Cass Gilbert Collection, N-YHS, and are also on file with the New York Department of Buildings. The structural steel shop drawings are housed in the Smithsonian Institution's National Museum of American History, Archives Center, and the shop drawings for the terra cotta in the Cass Gilbert Collection, N-YHS. The names of the junior designers and draftsmen who worked on the Woolworth Building appear on drawings and in memorandums and are listed in office ledgers, 1910–12, Cass Gilbert Collection, N-YHS: Harry K. Culver, G. F. Shaffer, Z. N. Matteossian, Franklin Keese, and William Foulds.

91 Woods, *From Craft to Profession*, 116–37.

92 H. Van Buren Magonigle, "A Half Century of Architecture," pt. 7, "A Biographical Review," *Pencil Points* 15 (November 1934): 563.

93 Sarah Bradford Landau, *George B. Post, Architect: Picturesque Designer and Determined Realist* (New York: Monacelli Press, 1998), 74; Landau and Condit, *Rise of the New York Skyscraper*, 238; and Mardges Bacon, *Ernest Flagg: Beaux-Arts Architect and Urban Reformer* (New York: Architectural History Foundation; Cambridge, Mass.: MIT Press), 219.

94 Cass Gilbert, personal note in own copy of Skinner, *Woolworth Building, New York City*, n.p.; and "The Address of Mr. Cass Gilbert," in *The Dinner Given to Cass Gilbert. Architect, by Frank W. Woolworth* (Baltimore: Munder-Thomsen Press, 1913), 46.

95 Horowitz and Sparkes, *The Towers of New York*, 108.

96 Woolworth's own week-by-week records of labor costs can be found in Woolworth Building, Cass Gilbert Collection, N-YHS. For Woolworth's view of the project's engineers, see Frank Woolworth to Cass Gilbert, June 19, 1911, Woolworth Building correspondence files, Cass Gilbert Collection, N-YHS.

97 Frank Woolworth to Cass Gilbert, June 5, 1911, Woolworth Building correspondence files, Cass Gilbert Collection, N-YHS.

98 Rockart wrote in a memorandum that "Mr. Woolworth insisted on the fact that he had not particularly delayed the building," but Gilbert later added a note to the memorandum, indicating that "in my opinion Woolworth is in error in these matters of delay—he has caused many delays." Office memorandum dictated by John Rockart, December 11, 1911, Woolworth Building, Cass Gilbert Collection, N-YHS.

99 Horowitz and Sparkes, *The Towers of New York*, 106.

100 Frank Woolworth to Cass Gilbert, January 3, 1911, Woolworth Building correspondence files, Cass Gilbert Collection, N-YHS; and office memorandum dictated by Cass Gilbert, February 3, 1911, Woolworth Building, Cass Gilbert Collection, N-YHS.

101 Leo L. Redding, "Mr. F. W. Woolworth's Story," *World's Work* 25 (April 1913): 664–65.

102 Horowitz and Sparkes, *The Towers of New York*, 111, 115 (for quote).

103 Ibid., 108. Horowitz questioned Woolworth's assumptions about the loading of responsibility for a construction job on "a man who would concede to you what should be worth $300,000?"

104 Gilbert added that he was already famous before Woolworth gave him the job; otherwise, Woolworth would not have considered him. Robert Allen Jones, "Cass Gilbert, Forgotten Giant," 10, box 26, Cass Gilbert Papers, LC; and Horowitz and Sparkes, *The Towers of New York*, 109.

105 Cass Gilbert to Frank Woolworth, April 20, 1911, Woolworth Building letterbooks, Cass Gilbert Collection, N-YHS. As with the Broadway Chambers project, Gilbert produced a complete set of design drawings before being officially compensated for his professional services. No record of a written contract between Gilbert and Woolworth remains.

106 Frank Woolworth to Cass Gilbert, April 24, 1911, Woolworth Building correspondence files, Cass Gilbert Collection, N-YHS. Gilbert argued that although he calculated the value of his designs at $61,000, he was willing to settle for $25,000. Cass Gilbert to Frank Woolworth, May 11, 1911, Woolworth Building letterbooks, Cass Gilbert Collection, N-YHS.

107 Cass Gilbert to Frank Woolworth, May 11, 1911, Woolworth Building letterbooks, Cass Gilbert Collection, N-YHS.

108 Office memorandum (project cost estimate), September 5, 1911, Woolworth Building, Cass Gilbert Collection, N-YHS. The fee represented Gilbert's largest to date. The United States Custom House, a $4.5 million project, earned his office $228,000. Cass Gilbert to Charles Gilbert, May 3, 1905, box 20, Cass Gilbert Papers, MHS.

109 Glenn Brown, *1860–1930, Memories: A Winning Crusade to Revive George Washington's Vision of a Capital City* (Washington, D.C.: W. F. Robers Co., 1931): 570.

110 Cass Gilbert to Emily and Cass (children), October 8, 1912, box 8, Cass Gilbert Papers, LC. Gilbert sent gifts to Woolworth as well, among them "fine flowers" and a bronze statuette sculpted by Frederick MacMonnies. Frank Woolworth to Cass Gilbert, June 30, 1911, May 17, 1912; and December 26, 1913, Woolworth Building correspondence files, Cass Gilbert Collection, N-YHS.

111 Horowitz and Sparkes, *The Towers of New York*, 119–20 (for quote).

112 Office memorandums, February 28, 1912, and October 19, 1910, Woolworth Building, Cass Gilbert Collection, N-YHS.

113 *The Building Code as Finally Adopted by the Building Code Commission of the City of New York* (1899). The New York Department of Buildings, which administered the code (initially adopted in 1892), preferred the "insurance" of high safety factors. Landau and Condit, *Rise of the New York Skyscraper*, 172, 183–84, 293.

114 "The Tallest Building," 86.

115 Mario Salvadori, *Why Buildings Stand Up: The Strength of Architecture* (New York: W. W. Norton & Co., 1980): 107. Salvadori writes, "They were called skyscrapers, a name to exalt the human mind. . . . In 1913, the first, the Woolworth Building dared to reach fifty-five stories, soaring up 791 feet." Salvadori's assessment stresses the Woolworth as a turning point in the development of the technologies required for the construction of the much larger skyscrapers. Architectural historians have emphasized the earliest skyscrapers, which appeared in New York and Chicago during the 1870s and 1880s. The literature on the origins of the skyscraper is large, but for a start, see Landau and Condit, *Rise of the New York Skyscraper*, 62, 71; Bruegmann, *The Architects and the City*, 65–69; and Rosemarie Haag Bletter, "The Inven-

tion of the Skyscraper: Notes on Its Diverse Histories," *Assemblage* 2 (February 1987): 110–17.

116 Horowitz and Sparkes, *The Towers of New York*, 118.

117 "Construction of the Woolworth Building," *Engineering Record* 66 (July 27, 1912): 98.

118 "Steel Erection for the Woolworth Building," *Engineering Record* 65 (June 29, 1912): 714–15; "Steel Derricks for Erecting Tall Buildings," *Engineering Record* 59 (March 27, 1909): 347–48; and Horowitz and Sparkes, *The Towers of New York*, 110–11, 118–19. Regarding the safety of scaffolding during the Woolworth project, see "The Tallest Office Building in the World: Erection of the Woolworth Building, New York," *Scientific American* 108 (March 8, 1913), 224. William J. Murray, who worked for Thompson-Starrett, was awarded the "Scientific American" Gold Medal for the scaffold by the American Museum of Safety in 1910. William J. Murray (grandson) to author, July 16, 2002.

119 "The Woolworth Building Foundations," *Engineering Record* 64 (August 26, 1911): 257.

120 "The Tallest Building," 86.

121 Cass Gilbert to Frank Woolworth, August 1, 1912, Papers of Cass Gilbert, OCA.

122 "Steel Erection for the Woolworth Building," 714; and "Lofty Steel Tower All Up" (on the Metropolitan Life Insurance Tower), *New York Times*, June 28, 1908.

123 "Steel Erection for the Woolworth Building," 714.

124 "A 52-Story Facade of Atlantic Terra Cotta," *Atlantic Terra Cotta* 2 (April 1915), n.p. Office memorandum, "Approximate Dates for Completing Details, Shipment and Fabrication of the Various Portions of the Woolworth Building," April 11, 1912, Woolworth Building, Cass Gilbert Collection, N-YHS.

125 Cass Gilbert, "The Architect's Approbation," 9.

126 Frank Woolworth, "Foreword," in *The Master Builders*, 5.

127 "Construction of the Woolworth Building," 100; and office memorandum, "List of Sub-contractors," July 20, 1914, Woolworth Building, Cass Gilbert Collection, N-YHS.

128 Skinner, *Woolworth Building, New York City*, 73–74; and "Construction of the Woolworth Building," 99 (for quotes).

129 "Construction of the Woolworth Building," 100.

130 For the reports, see Woolworth Building, Cass Gilbert Collection, N-YHS.

131 "General Conditions," in "Woolworth Building Specifications," vol. 1, 1913, Woolworth Building, Cass Gilbert Collection, N-YHS. Gilbert specified that an average of twenty photographs were to be taken each month and that these "shall be considered conclusive evidence of the condition of the work."

132 "$2,000,000 Broadway Building," *New York Times*, July 10, 1910.

133 "Staid Old Barclay Street to Change," *New York City World*, February 5, 1911, in scrapbook, Cass Gilbert Collection, N-YHS.

134 The inspection reports submitted by the Gunvald and Aus Company's J. Cornell to Cass Gilbert, Woolworth Building, Cass Gilbert Collection, N-YHS, document the progress of the steel frame's construction.

135 Cass Gilbert to Frank Woolworth, August 1, 1912, Papers of Cass Gilbert, OCA.

136 "Construction of the Woolworth Building," 99.

137 Office memorandum, "Woolworth Building," May 1, 1915, Woolworth Building, Cass Gilbert Collection, N-YHS.

138 "The Woolworth Building, New York," *Engineering Record* 63 (May 27, 1911): 591.

139 Peters, *Building the Nineteenth Century*, 126–30.

140 "The Woolworth Building Foundations," 257.

141 "How Caisson Work Feels in an Airtight Pit," *New York City Globe*, August 11, 1911, in scrapbook, Cass Gilbert Collection, N-YHS.

142 John Reed described this or a similar construction site in "The Foundations of a Skyscraper" (1911), in *The Complete Poetry of John Reed*, ed. Jack Alan Robins (Washington, D.C.: University Press of America, 1983), 33.

143 "The Woolworth Building Foundations," 257.

144 Ibid., 256–57; and Skinner, *Woolworth Building, New York City*, 20.

145 Skinner, *Woolworth Building, New York City*, 22.

146 Peters, *Building the Nineteenth Century*, 130 (for quote), 404 n. 108; Charles-Jean Triger identified the mysterious "caisson disease" in 1839. See also David McCullough, *The Great Bridge: The Epic Story of the Building of the Brooklyn Bridge* (New York: Simon & Schuster, 1972), 187–90, 207–11, 289–322, 506.

147 Robert Sloss, "Going Down," *Harper's Weekly* 55 (December 2, 1911): 17.

148 Cass Gilbert, "The Architect's Approbation," 7.

149 W. A. Starrett, *Skyscrapers and the Men Who Build Them*, 88.

150 "The Woolworth Building," *New York Times*, February 18, 1912; *The Master Builders*, 17; and Sloss, "Going Down," 17.

151 *Architectural League of New York Yearbook, 1920*, 213.

152 S. F. Holtzman (Gunvald Aus and Company), "Design of the Woolworth Building: Features of Substructure and Calculations for Wind Bracing of Tower," *Engineering Record* 68 (July 5, 1913): 22–23; and Gunvald Aus, "Engineering Design of the Woolworth Building," *American Architect* 103 (March 26, 1913): 160–65. Just prior to Gilbert's securing the project's final building permit, New York City's Board of Aldermen passed an ordinance prohibiting construction from extending past a site's property line and into the public domain. As a consequence, the wall columns of the Barclay Street elevation had to be moved back three feet to be concentric with the now-permitted narrow rectangular caissons, and a segment cut from the front of a caisson bordering Broadway.

153 Holtzman, "Design of the Woolworth Building," 23; "The Steel Substructure of the Woolworth Building in New York City," *Engineering Record* 65 (February 17, 1912): 177–78; and Horowitz and Sparkes, *The Towers of New York*, 110, 118.

154 "The Steel Substructure of the Woolworth Building in New York City," 177.

155 Ibid., 178. Outside the tower, Aus distributed most of the columns' point loads through two- and three-way grillages.

156 Skinner, *Woolworth Building, New York City*, 12.

157 The product of a merger of ten large companies, arranged by J. P. Morgan in 1901, United States Steel was capitalized at an unprecedented $1,404 million. It controlled 60 percent of the steel industry's output in sixty-one different plants, including seventy-three blast furnaces, one thousand miles of railroads, 112 steamships, and immense landholdings containing iron ore, coal, and limestone. Arundel Cotter, *Authentic History of United States Steel* (New York: Moody Magazine and Book Co., 1916): 21–22; and Misa, *A Nation of Steel*, 164–71.

158 Misa, *A Nation of Steel*, 170. See also Donald Friedman, *Historical Building Construction: Design, Materials, and Technology* (New York: W. W. Norton & Co., 1995), 71–73.

159 "Woolworth Building," *New York Journal of Commerce*, April 13, 1911, in scrapbook, Cass Gilbert Collection, N-YHS.

160 Raymond, *Antonin Raymond*, 30–31.

161 "Steel Erection for the Woolworth Building," 715. The workers' efficient pace saved Thompson-Starrett fifty thousand dollars. Cass Gilbert to Frank Woolworth, August 1, 1912, letterbooks, Papers of Cass Gilbert, OCA.

162 "Construction of the Woolworth Building," 97; and "Steel Erection for the Woolworth Building," 715.

163 Gilbert, "The Architect's Approbation," 7; and Horowitz and Sparkes, *The Towers of New York*, 119.

164 Horowitz and Sparkes, *The Towers of New York*, 119.

165 Office memorandum dictated by Cass Gilbert, December 13, 1910, Woolworth Building, Cass Gilbert Collection, N-YHS; and "Crane Falls, Man Killed, Boy Dying," *New York City Mail*, December 13, 1910, in scrapbook, Cass Gilbert Collection, N-YHS.

166 "First Life Lost," *New York City Evening Star*, March 25, 1912, in scrapbook, Cass Gilbert Collection, N-YHS. No fatal accidents occurred during the Singer Tower's construction. Bacon, *Ernest Flagg*, 220.

167 Inspectors from the Broadway–Park Place Company's insurer for the project, the Metropolitan Life Insurance Company, documented the accidents on a case-by-case basis. For example, a falling piece of tile hit William Burke on the head on April 23, 1912, and Louis Ackerno suffered two broken toes from a toppling radiator on December 17, 1912. The reports are filed in Woolworth Building, Cass Gilbert Collection, N-YHS.

168 Rasenberger, *High Steel*, 192; and Houlihan, "The New York City Building Trades," 19–20.

169 Paul Starrett, *Changing the Skyline*, 73.

170 "Rapid Erection of Steel-Frame Buildings," *American Architect and Building News* 76 (May 10, 1902): 40.

171 Peters, *Building the Nineteenth Century*, 226–53.

172 Horowitz and Sparkes, *The Towers of New York*, 180–81.

173 "The Tallest Building," 86.

174 "Woolworth Building," *New York Journal of Commerce*, April 13, 1911, in scrapbook, Cass Gilbert Collection, N-YHS.

175 Aus, "Engineering Design of the Woolworth Building," 165–66; and Skinner, *Woolworth Building, New York City*, 33–37.

176 Horowitz and Sparkes, *The Towers of New York*, 110.

177 Holtzman, "Design of the Woolworth Building," 22–23.
178 "The Woolworth Building, New York," 592.
179 Carl Condit, "The Wind Bracing of Buildings," *Scientific American* 230 (February 1974): 95, 98–99.
180 Aus, "Engineering Design of the Woolworth Building," 167.
181 Ibid., 160, 167; and "Wind Bracing in the Woolworth Building," *Engineering Record* 65 (February 24, 1912): 220–21.
182 Aus, "Engineering Design of the Woolworth Building," 167.
183 Cass Gilbert to Gunvald Aus, September 12, 1911, Woolworth Building letterbooks, Cass Gilbert Collection, N-YHS.
184 Cass Gilbert to Frank Woolworth, May 11, 1911, Woolworth Building letterbooks, Cass Gilbert Collection, N-YHS. Regarding the checking, Gilbert told Aus that "nothing would be further from my thought than to express doubt of your work, or infringe upon your professional dignity." Cass Gilbert to Gunvald Aus, September 12, 1911, Woolworth Building letterbooks, Cass Gilbert Collection, N-YHS.
185 Frank Woolworth to Cass Gilbert, May 15, 1911, Woolworth Building correspondence files, Cass Gilbert Collection, N-YHS.
186 Cass Gilbert to Thompson-Starrett Company, July 6, 1911, Woolworth Building letterbooks, Cass Gilbert Collection, N-YHS. Simpson reported to Gilbert in September that he had "gone through all the wind strains and found that they were correct in every respect, that he had not checked the live and dead loads, but that the work was in all respects of such high class so far as he had gone that he saw no occasion for proceeding any further." Office memorandum, September 12, 1911, Woolworth Building, Cass Gilbert Collection, N-YHS.
187 Cass Gilbert, "Architectural Design," in "The Woolworth Building, Most Modern Example of the Fire-Proof Skyscraper: How It Was Built," by George T. Mortimer, *Real Estate Magazine* 1 (July 1912): 56.
188 "Big Woolworth Tower Unshaken by Violent Gale," *Elizabeth New Jersey Journal*, March 6, 1913, in scrapbook, Cass Gilbert Collection, N-YHS. Gilbert requested the test from Aus, who set up instruments in offices located between the tower's fifty-second and fifty-fourth floors.
189 Cass Gilbert, "The Tenth Birthday of a Notable Structure," *Real Estate Magazine* 11 (May 1923): 345.
190 "Woolworth Tower Test: Measurements to Decide If It Sways in Next High Wind," *New York Times*, December 4, 1924.
191 Aus, "Engineering Design of the Woolworth Building," 165–67.
192 See, for example, Robins Fleming (engineer with the American Bridge Company), "Wind-Bracing Requirements in Municipal Building Codes," in *Six Monographs on Wind Stresses* (New York: Engineering News, 1915), 53–59.
193 Landau and Condit, *Rise of the New York Skyscraper*, 296, 352–53.
194 Cass Gilbert, as quoted in "Thousand Foot Skyscraper a Possibility," *Mt. Vernon Argus*, November 21, 1912, in scrapbook, Cass Gilbert Collection, N-YHS.
195 "Construction of the Woolworth Building," 99; and Theodore Henricus Maria Prudon, "Architectural Terra Cotta and Ceramic Veneer in the United States Prior to World War II: A History of Its Development and an Analysis of Its Deterioration Problems and Possible Repair Methodologies" (Ph.D. diss., Columbia University, 1981), 96.
196 "Construction of the Woolworth Building," 99.
197 Ibid.; and *The Master Builders*, 22.
198 Misa, *A Nation of Steel*, 87–88.
199 Skinner, *Woolworth Building, New York City*, 82.
200 Office memorandums dictated by George Wells, August 8, September 13, October 31, 1912, Woolworth Building, Cass Gilbert Collection, N-YHS; and "36 Stories on All the Outside and Court Elevations Were Set in Less Than Five Months," *Western Architect* 18 (August 1912).
201 According to *Atlantic Terra Cotta: A 52-Story Façade* (New York: Atlantic Terra Cotta Co., 1913), 7–8, Atlantic Terra Cotta's "plant number two" was founded in 1878 and known for "practically every important development in terra cotta." By 1901, it boasted twenty-two kilns. See also Susan Tunick, *Terra-Cotta Skyline* (New York: Princeton Architectural Press, 1997), 46–47, 54–56.
202 According to Walter Geer, *The Story of Terra Cotta* (New York: Tobias A. Wright, 1920), "The Atlantic Terra Cotta Company was incorporated in February 1907, being a consolidation of three former companies: Perth Amboy (1897), Excelsior (1894), and Atlantic (1897). The Standard Terra Cotta Works was purchased in 1907." Geer is quoted in Susan Tunick, *Friends of Terra Cotta* (newsletter) (March 2003): 2.

203 *Atlantic Terra Cotta: A 52-Story Façade*, 7–9.

204 Richard Veit, "Moving beyond the Factory Gates: The Industrial Archaeology of New Jersey's Terra Cotta Industry," *Industrial Archaeology* 25 (1999): 14.

205 "Artistic Terra Cotta Effects," *New York Times*, July 28, 1912.

206 Cass Gilbert to Thompson-Starrett Company, October 2, 1911, Woolworth Building letterbooks, Cass Gilbert Collection, N-YHS; and "Exterior Terra Cotta," in "Woolworth Building Specifications," vol. 4, 1913, Woolworth Building, Cass Gilbert Collection, N-YHS.

207 "Exterior Terra Cotta."

208 Cass Gilbert to Thompson-Starrett Company, October 27, 1911, Woolworth Building letterbooks, Cass Gilbert Collection, N-YHS.

209 "Elisio V. Ricci, 85, Building Sculptor," *New York Times*, September 24, 1955. Ricci's partner, John Donnelly, had trained as a stonemason in Ireland and then immigrated to the United States.

210 Cass Gilbert to Elisio Ricci, March 27, 1913, personal letterbooks, Cass Gilbert Collection, N-YHS. Gilbert thanked Ricci for "the very beautiful modeling you have done upon my works, including the St. Louis Public Library, University of Texas Library, and the Woolworth Building.

211 Office memorandums by T. R. Johnson, October 20, October 25, November 6, December 9, December 11, 1911, Woolworth Building, Cass Gilbert Collection, N-YHS.

212 On terra cotta's manufacture, see "Architectural Terra Cotta," in *International Library of Technology*, vol. 31D (Scranton, Pa.: International Textbook Co., 1922), 30–37; and Prudon, "Architectural Terra Cotta and Ceramic Veneer," 69–90.

213 Cass Gilbert, "The Architecture of Today" (lecture delivered at West Point Military Academy), May 4, 1909, box 16, Cass Gilbert Papers, LC.

214 Gilbert, "The Architect's Approbation," 9.

215 "A 52-Story Facade of Atlantic Terra Cotta," n.p.

216 Cass Gilbert, "Regarding the Woolworth Building" (1927), box 17, Cass Gilbert Papers, LC.

217 Ibid.

218 Cass Gilbert, "The Tenth Birthday," 345; *Atlantic Terra Cotta: A 52-Story Façade*, 5–6; and "A 52-Story Facade of Architectural Terra Cotta," *Western Architect* 18 (August 1912): 90–91.

219 Gilbert, "The Tenth Birthday," 345.

220 Ibid., 345.

221 Cass Gilbert to Hubert T. Parson, March 28, 1927, Woolworth Building, Cass Gilbert Collection, N-YHS

222 Montgomery Schuyler, "The Woolworth Building," in *American Architecture and Other Writings by Montgomery Schuyler*, ed. William H. Jordy and Ralph Coe (Cambridge, Mass.: Harvard University Press, Belknap Press, 1961), 2:619. Gilbert also tested terra cotta's technical capacities. The problems with splitting and cracking are documented in office memorandums dating from April 24, 1914, Woolworth Building, Cass Gilbert Collection, N-YHS. The cladding, tied integrally to the structure of the building, does not behave as a true curtain wall.

223 John Ruskin, "The Nature of Gothic," in *The Stones of Venice* (1853), ed. J. G. Links (New York: Hill & Wang, 1960), 190, wrote: "On a good building, the sculpture is always so set, and on such a scale, that at the ordinary distance from which the edifice is seen, the sculpture shall be thoroughly intelligible and interesting. In order to accomplish this . . . the upper ornamentation will be colossal."

224 Cass Gilbert, "Regarding the Woolworth Building."

225 Montgomery Schuyler, "'The Towers of Manhattan' and Notes on the Woolworth Building," *Architectural Record* 33 (February 1913): 112.

226 "Chicago: Gothic Detail in an Office Building," *American Architect and Building News* 51 (March 28, 1896): 145.

227 Schuyler, "The Towers of Manhattan," 114.

228 Clarence Ward, "The Woolworth Building in New York City," *American Magazine of Art* 8 (December 1916): 58.

229 John K. Winkler, *Five and Ten: The Fabulous Life of F. W. Woolworth* (New York: Robert M. McBride & Co., 1940): 190. Irving Underhill, *Photographic Views of the Construction of the Woolworth Building, 233 Broadway, New York City* (New York, 1911–12), is housed at the New York Public Library.

230 Nye, *American Technological Sublime*, 87–97.

231 "Stars and Stripes Flung into Breeze from Top of Tallest Building," *World*, July 2, 1912; and "Flag Is Floated," *Pittsburgh, Pennsylvania Post*, July 2, 1912, in scrapbook, Cass Gilbert Collection, N-YHS.

232 Office memorandum by G. F. Shaffer, July 1, 1912, Woolworth Building, Cass Gilbert Collection, N-YHS.

233 "Puts Gilding Nearest Sky," *New York Times*, December 13, 1912.

234 Cass Gilbert to Edward J. Hogan, June 26, 1911, Woolworth Building letterbooks, Cass Gilbert Collection, N-YHS, describes McAtamney's program of newspaper publicity.

235 "An Aerial Wharf," *New Haven, Connecticut Register*, May 9, 1911, in scrapbook, Cass Gilbert Collection, N-YHS.

236 "Bold Aerial Flight," *New York City People*, June 29, 1912, in scrapbook, Cass Gilbert Collection, N-YHS.

237 *The Master Builders*, 11 (for quote), 12.

238 Woolworth, "Foreword," in *The Master Builders*, 5; and Gilbert, "The Architect's Approbation," 9.

239 On Burrelle's Press Clipping Bureau, founded in New York in 1888, see Scott M. Cutlip, *Public Relations History: From the 17th to the 20th Century: The Antecedents* (Hillside, N.J.: Lawrence Erlbaum Associates, Publishers, 1995), 181.

240 "How McAtamney Climbed the Ladder," *New York City Press*, May 17, 1914, in scrapbook, Cass Gilbert Collection, N-YHS.

241 Office memorandum dictated by J. R. Rockart, June 25, 1912, Woolworth Building, Cass Gilbert Collection, N-YHS; and "Woolworth Building Built for Revenue and Not as Monument, Agent Believes," *New York Post*, July 17, 1925, in scrapbook, Cass Gilbert Collection, N-YHS.

242 W. A. Starrett, *Skyscrapers and the Men Who Build Them*, 2.

243 Horowitz and Sparkes, *The Towers of New York*, 4.

244 Hughes, *American Genesis*, 1.

245 Paul Starrett, *Changing the Skyline*, 85.

246 W. A. Starrett, *Skyscrapers and the Men Who Build Them*, 2.

247 Nye, *American Technological Sublime*, 43.

CHAPTER SIX

1 Henry Blake Fuller, *The Cliff Dwellers* (New York: Harper & Bros., 1893), 4–5.

2 Ray Stannard Baker, "The Modern Skyscraper," *Munsey's Magazine* 22 (October 1899): 48–58, 57 (for quote).

3 Daniel Bluestone, *Constructing Chicago* (New Haven, Conn.: Yale University Press, 1991), 145, 149.

4 Spark, "How Hugh McAtamney Put the Woolworth Building on the International Map," *Real Estate Magazine* 2 (May 1913): 50.

5 H. Addington Bruce, "Introduction," in *The Dinner Given to Cass Gilbert, Architect, by Frank W. Woolworth* (Baltimore: Munder-Thomsen Press, 1913), 19.

6 "55-Story Building Opens in a Flash," *New York Times*, April 25, 1913; and William R. Taylor, "The Evolution of Public Space: The Commercial City as Showcase," in *In Pursuit of Gotham: Culture and Commerce in New York*, ed. William R. Taylor (New York: Oxford University Press, 1992): 48.

7 "The Programme for the Dewey Holidays," *Harper's Weekly* 43 (September 30, 1899): 986.

8 David E. Nye, *American Technological Sublime* (Cambridge, Mass.: MIT Press, 1994), 164 (for quote), 153–71.

9 Carolyn Marvin, *When Old Technologies Were New: Thinking about Electric Communication in the Late Nineteenth Century* (New York: Oxford University Press, 1988), 171–72.

10 Nye, *American Technological Sublime*, 144–45.

11 Spark, "How Hugh McAtamney Put the Woolworth Building on the International Map," 48, 50.

12 Scott M. Cutlip, *Public Relations History: From the 17th to the 20th Century: The Antecedents* (Hillside, N.J.: Lawrence Erlbaum Associates, Publishers, 1995), 182–86.

13 Taylor, "The Evolution of Public Space," 37, 47–48.

14 Bruce, "Introduction," 20 (for quote); and Spark, "How Hugh McAtamney Put the Woolworth Building on the International Map," 50 (for quote). See also Hugh McAtamney to Cass Gilbert, July 31, 1912, and March 17, 1913. Woolworth Building correspondence files, Cass Gilbert Collection, N-YHS.

15 On the criticism of Wilson's involvement with the opening, see Bruce, "Introduction," 15; and John K. Winkler, *Five and Ten: The Fabulous Life of F. W. Woolworth* (New York: Robert M. McBride & Co., 1940), 192. Woodrow Wilson, "The New Freedom: A Call for the Emancipation of the Generous Energies of a People," pt. 4, "Benevolence or Justice?" *World's Work* 25 (April 1913): 634, 635, described the "master of the Government of the United States" as "those who in combination control the monopolies," adding that "when I am fighting monopolistic control, therefore, I am fighting for the liberty of every man in America, and I am fighting for the liberty of American industry."

16 F. W. Woolworth Co., *Fortieth Anniversary Souvenir, 1879–1919* (New York, 1919), 23.

17 Woolworth did not include women in the ceremony, even his pioneering woman manager, Mary Ann Creighton.

18 The guests are listed according to their seats in *The Dinner Given to Cass Gilbert*, 125–40. James B. Bell, compiler, *Official Congressional Directory, 63rd Congress, 1st Session, Beginning April 7, 1913* (Washington, D.C.: Government Printing Office, 1913), indicates that almost all of the congressmen were Democrats, which is unusual given Woolworth's and Gilbert's strong Republican orientation.

19 Some of the F. W. Woolworth Company's district managers also numbered among the guests: Ralph Connable (Toronto), Henry P. Knox (Buffalo), Frederick J. Neckesser (Wilkes-Barre), E. A. Bardoe (Boston), C. P. Case (New York), and C. C. Griswold (Chicago). Winkler, *Five and Ten*, 176.

20 "55-Story Building Opens in a Flash." Souvenirs for guests included a bronze replica of the building, the dinner's menu, a pot of four-leaf clover, and a brochure describing the skyscraper. Detectives masking as waiters provided security. Cass Gilbert to Col. C. N. Graves, American Legation, Stockholm, October 27, 1913, personal letterbooks, Cass Gilbert Collection, N-YHS.

21 Frank Woolworth, as quoted in "The Address of Mr. Cass Gilbert," in *The Dinner Given to Cass Gilbert*, 52.

22 "Francis Hopkinson Smith," in *Dictionary of American Biography*, vol. 9, ed. Dumas Malone (New York: Charles Scribner's Sons, 1935, 1936), 265–67. Cass Gilbert to Julia Finch Gilbert, November 8, 1897, box 6, Cass Gilbert Papers, LC, reports his having dined at Smith's house. Gilbert ordered Smith's novels directly from the publisher. Cass Gilbert to Charles Scribner's Sons, January 21, 1909, personal letterbooks, Cass Gilbert Collection, N-YHS.

23 "The Address of Mr. Hopkinson Smith, Toastmaster," in *The Dinner Given to Cass Gilbert*, 30–31.

24 "The Address of Hon. W. U. Hensel," in *The Dinner Given to Cass Gilbert*, 78–79. Regarding Hensel, see "Willliam Hensel," *American Biographical Index* (index to American Biographical Archive), vol. 3, ed. Laureen Baillee (London: K. G. Saur, 1993).

25 Sven Beckert, *The Monied Metropolis: New York City and the Consolidation of the American Bourgeoisie, 1850–1896* (Cambridge: Cambridge University Press, 2001), 324, 328.

26 "The Address of Hon. W. U. Hensel," 79–80.

27 Ibid., 80.

28 For a classic interpretation of the trusts within the day's economic context, see Edwin C. Rozwenc, ed., *Roosevelt, Wilson, and the Trusts* (Boston: D. C. Heath & Co., 1950), vii.

29 "The Address of Mr. Cass Gilbert," 49.

30 On the contemporary European view of America as a country identified with possibility, see H. G. Wells, *The Future of America* (1906), in *Britons View America: Travel Commentary, 1860–1935*, ed. Richard L. Rapson (Seattle: University of Washington Press, 1971), 166.

31 Earle Shultz and Walter Simmons, *Offices in the Sky* (Indianapolis: Bobbs-Merrill Co., 1959), 154. See also Carol Willis, *Form Follows Finance: Skyscrapers and Skylines in New York and Chicago* (New York: Princeton Architectural Press, 1995), 170 and 204, n. 70.

32 Harry S. Black, as quoted in Shultz and Simmons, *Offices in the Sky*, 73–74.

33 "Rents in Downtown Office Buildings," *Real Estate Record and Builders' Guide* 138 (July 29, 1911): 118.

34 Shultz and Simmons, *Offices in the Sky*, 75.

35 "Woolworth Building Will Be World's Greatest Skyscraper," *New York Times*, May 7, 1911.

36 "New Woolworth Building on Broadway Will Eclipse Singer Tower in Height," *New York Times*, November 13, 1910.

37 Frank Woolworth to Cass Gilbert, December 27, 1911, Woolworth Building correspondence files, Cass Gilbert Collection, N-YHS.

38 Edward Hogan to Cass Gilbert, September 13, 1913, Woolworth Building correspondence files, Cass Gilbert Collection, N-YHS.

39 Frank Woolworth, "Executive Office" (general letter to all stores), March 4, 1915, Woolworth Building, Cass Gilbert Collection, N-YHS.

40 Mardges Bacon, *Ernest Flagg: Beaux-Arts Architect and Urban Reformer* (New York: Architectural History Foundation; Cambridge, Mass.: MIT Pres, 1986), 220–23.

41 Reginald Pelham Bolton, as quoted in Shultz and Simmons, *Offices in the Sky*, 74.

42 Ibid., 75–76, 78 (for quote).

43 "New Woolworth Building on Broadway will Eclipse Singer Tower in Height"; and "Greatest of all Skyscrapers," *Brooklyn New York Citizen*, July 7, 1912, in scrapbook, Cass Gilbert Collection, N-YHS.

44 Office memorandum dictated by Cass Gilbert, October 19, 1910, Woolworth Building, Cass Gilbert Collection, N-YHS.

45 Frank Woolworth, as quoted in "F. W. Invests His Millions in Towering Broadway Office Building," *New York City American*, February 22, 1911, in scrapbook, Cass Gilbert Collection, N-YHS.

46 The array of stylistically distinctive spaces designed for the Woolworth's interior are described in the Gilbert office's memorandums dated 1912–15 and in Frank Woolworth's "General Letter to All Stores," March 4, 1915, both in Woolworth Building, Cass Gilbert Collection, N-YHS.

47 "Woolworth Building Will Be World's Greatest Skyscraper," *New York Times*, May 7, 1911.

48 Ibid.; and office memorandums, October 20, 1910; February 28, 1912 through June 4, 1913, Woolworth Building, Cass Gilbert Collection, N-YHS. For a comparison with the interiors of Chicago office buildings of the 1880s and 1890s, see Robert Bruegmann, *The Architects and the City; Holabird and Roche of Chicago, 1880–1918* (Chicago: University of Chicago Press, 1997), 93–99; and Bluestone, *Constructing Chicago*, 145–50. For the interiors of New York office buildings, see Sarah Bradford Landau and Carl W. Condit, *Rise of the New York Skyscraper, 1865–1913* (New Haven, Conn.: Yale University Press, 1996), 71–75, 312, 325, 360–61, 379.

49 Rem Koolhaas, *Delirious New York: A Retroactive Manifesto for Manhattan*, rev. ed. (New York: Monacelli Press, 1994): 71–75, 89–91. The project appeared in the *New York Herald* on May 6, 1906, in the *Brooklyn Union Standard* on May 27, 1906, and the *Brooklyn Daily Eagle* on May 19, 1907. Construction on its foundations began in 1906, but by 1908, Friede had decided not to go ahead.

50 Roberta Moudry, "Architecture as Cultural Design: The Architecture and Urbanism of the Metropolitan Life Insurance Company" (Ph.D. diss., Cornell University, 1995), 117 (for quote), 126, 135, 196; and Olivier Zunz, *Making America Corporate, 1870–1920* (Chicago: University of Chicago Press, 1990), 113–21.

51 William Leach, *Land of Desire: Merchants, Power, and the Rise of a New American Culture* (New York: Pantheon Books, 1993), 82.

52 On the Woolworth Building's sculptures, see Donald Martin Reynolds, *The Architecture of New York City*, rev. ed. (New York: John Wiley & Sons, 1994), 219–25.

53 Coeur (ca. 1395–1456), a French "merchant prince," served as the financial adviser to Charles VII while overseeing his own trading empire, which extended from Scotland to Palestine. Ango (ca. 1480–1551) owned a fleet of ships active in exploration under Francis I; he provisioned the ships used by Giovanni da Verrazano to explore the New York Bay. Gilbert asked Donnelly and Ricci to model the figures of Ango and Coeur in terra cotta and then to fire them with a gold glaze, but Woolworth opposed the figures as "too monkish," and they were never carried out. Office memorandums, April 14 and April 25, 1914, Woolworth Building, Cass Gilbert Collection, N-YHS.

54 Leach, *Land of Desire*, 72–73. Revolving doors were added at the front entrance by 1916.

55 Ibid., 35, 51 (for quote), 194–202.

56 Edwin A. Cochran, *The Cathedral of Commerce: Woolworth Building, New York* (New York: Broadway–Park Place Co., 1916), n.p.

57 Leach, *Land of Desire*, 9 (for quote), 65.

58 Vera Marie Siegar to author, August 1993. Siegar's father emigrated from Germany and worked for Heinigke and Bowen.

59 Cass Gilbert to Julia Finch Gilbert, October 25, 1912, Cass Gilbert Papers, LC.

60 Frank Woolworth, "Executive Office," March 4, 1915.

61 Carl Paul Jennewein, a sculptor and painter born in Stuttgart, Germany, emigrated to New York in 1907, apparently having been inspired by the work of McKim, Mead, and White. He apprenticed with Beuhler and Lauter, architectural sculptors, New York, in 1907–9, and then studied painting with Clinton Peters. He accepted the Woolworth commission in 1911, after Elmer Garnsey turned it down. Elmer Garnsey to Cass Gilbert, September 17, 1912, Woolworth Building correspondence files, Cass Gilbert Collection, N-YHS.

62 "Commerce" appeared frequently in American sculpture and mural painting of the 1890s and early 1900s. Daniel Chester French's "Commerce," for example, adorned the entrance to Arnold W. Brunner's Federal Building in Cleveland (1906–11).

63 "Monographs on Architectural Renderers: Being a Series of Articles on the Architectural Renderers of To-Day, Accompanied by Characteristic Examples of Their Work," pt. 5, "The Work of Thomas R. Johnson," *Brickbuilder* 23 (May 1914): 111.

64 Bernice L. Thomas, *Dean Hoffman's "Grand Design": The General Theological Seminary, 1879–1902* (New York: General Theological Seminary, 1988),

18, describes a "double portrait" of Saint Paul and the architect Charles Coolidge Haight, and Ralph Adams Cram, *My Life in Architecture* (Boston: Little, Brown & Co., 1936), 243, a portrait of a donor in St. George's Chapel, Newport, along with those of the architects and their representatives.

65 Heinigke and Bowen to Cass Gilbert, July 23, 1912, Woolworth Building correspondence files, Cass Gilbert Collection, N-YHS.

66 Office memorandum, February 6, 1913, Woolworth Building, and Heinigke and Bowen to Cass Gilbert, March 6, 1913, Woolworth Building correspondence files, Cass Gilbert Collection, N-YHS.

67 The sculptor Daniel Chester French advised Gilbert against the statue of Woolworth on the grounds that its "good taste" would be questioned by the public and so would convey the "wrong impression" of Woolworth. Daniel Chester French to Cass Gilbert, September 20, 1912, Woolworth Building correspondence files, and office memorandum dictated by Cass Gilbert, October 3, 1912, Woolworth Building, Cass Gilbert Collection, N-YHS.

68 William O. Partridge (National Sculpture Society), as quoted in Michele H. Bogart, "In Search of a United Front: American Architectural Sculpture at the Turn of the Century," *Winterthur Portfolio* 19 (Summer/Autumn 1984): 174.

69 Cass Gilbert, "Letter from Cass Gilbert to Governor Donaghey Relative to Mural Painting in the Capitol, October 12, 1914," in *Building a State Capitol* (Little Rock, Ark.: Parke-Harper Co., ca. 1937), 370.

70 Ibid., 369.

71 Marsh served as secretary of the Committee on the Congestion of Population in New York, which he founded with others in 1907. Bogart, "In Search of a United Front," 170.

72 J. V. Davies (Jacobs and Davies) to Louis Horowitz, April 14, 1912, Woolworth Building correspondence files, Cass Gilbert Collection, N-YHS.

73 "New York's First Underground Sidewalk," *Architects' and Builders' Magazine* 6 (October 1904): 31, 35 (for quote).

74 Office memorandums, August 8, August 28, August 29, September 4, September 13, 1912, Woolworth Building, Cass Gilbert Collection, N-YHS; and J. V. Davies (Jacobs and Davies) to Cass Gilbert, July 24, 1913, September 13, 1913, and November 18, 1913, Woolworth Building correspondence files, Cass Gilbert Collection, N-YHS.

75 Moses King, comp., *King's Views of New York, 1896–1915 and Brooklyn, 1905* (New York: Arno Press, 1974).

76 Jean-Louis Cohen, *Scenes of the World to Come: European Architecture and the American Challenge, 1893–1960* (Paris: Flammarion, 1995), 19–37.

77 Hermann Gumpel, "Running a Skyscraper Traction System," *Buildings and Building Management* 14 (January 1914): 22.

78 C. E. Knox to Cass Gilbert, May 10, 1911, Woolworth Building correspondence files, Cass Gilbert Collection, N-YHS. On Knox, the day's expert on elevators, see Sally A. Kitt Chappell, *Architecture and Planning of Graham, Anderson, Probst, and White, 1912–36: Transforming Tradition* (Chicago: University of Chicago Press, 1992), 104–6.

79 The Majestic Theater Building in Chicago of 1904 was probably the earliest permanent electric gearless traction installation. L. A. Petersen, *Elisha Graves Otis, 1811–1861, and His Influence upon Vertical Transportation* (New York: Newcomen Society of England, American Branch, 1945), 15–16; and "The History of Vertical Transportation," *American Architect* 129 (January 5, 1926): 24–25.

80 C. E. Knox to Cass Gilbert, May 10, 1911, Woolworth Building correspondence files, Cass Gilbert Collection, N-YHS. The Singer Tower's elevators, by contrast, traveled at 550 feet per minute, and the Metropolitan Life Tower's at 600 feet per minute. As built, the Woolworth's two high-speed elevators carried passengers to the fifty-fourth floor, according to Cochran, *The Cathedral of Commerce*, n.p.

81 "Six Hundred-Foot Drop Tests Woolworth Building Elevators," *Engineering Record* 70 (September 5, 1914): 266–67.

82 Cass Gilbert, "Architectural Design," in "The Woolworth Building, Most Modern Example of the Fire-Proof Skyscraper: How It was Built," by George T. Mortimer, *Real Estate Magazine* 1 (July 1912): 56.

83 "Running a Skyscraper Traction System," 21 (for quote), 20–22.

84 "Running a Skyscraper Traction System," 20.

85 McAtamney advertised the Woolworth's elevator system as "accident-proof." See, for example, "Woolworth Building" (advertisement), *Real Estate Record and Builders' Guide* 89 (March 23, 1912): 587: "Woolworth Building: Highest, Safest, Most Perfectly Appointed Office Structure in the World; Fireproof Beyond Question; Elevators Accident-Proof." Woolworth had previously used

air cushions in his five-story Lancaster Woolworth Building. *The Woolworth Building, Lancaster, Pa.* (1900), n.p.

86 Allen E. Beals, "The Elevator as an Enhancer of Land Values," *Real Estate Record and Builders' Guide* 88 (August 12, 1911): 208–9.

87 Mortimer, "The Woolworth Building, Most Modern Example of the Fire-Proof Skyscraper," 68 (for quote); and Cecil D. Elliott, *Technics and Architecture: The Development of Materials and Systems for Building* (Cambridge, Mass.: MIT Press, 1992), 352–53. By the 1920s, builders had abandoned the air cushion as an elevator safety device. But according to "Skyscrapers: Life on the Vertical," *Fortune* 11 (November 1930): 77, in 1930 "the Woolworth Building elevators still bounce confidently in a resilient column of air."

88 Louis Horowitz to Cass Gilbert, March 7, 1912, Woolworth Building correspondence files, Cass Gilbert Collection, N-YHS.

89 "Six Hundred-Foot Drop Tests Woolworth Building Elevators," 267; and Elliott, *Technics and Architecture*, 353.

90 "Bets His Life against Efficiency of His Emergency Elevator Stop," *New York Tribune*, July 28, 1912; and "Will Drop 676 feet in Elevator," *New York City Globe*, March 8, 1913, in scrapbook, Cass Gilbert Collection, N-YHS.

91 Office memorandum dictated by George Wells, October 15–16, 1913, Woolworth Building, Cass Gilbert Collection, N-YHS.

92 Winkler, *Five and Ten*, 151. The other office spaces of the F. W. Woolworth Company's headquarters Gilbert had designed by Theo Hofstatter and Company.

93 "Sky Suite for F. W. Woolworth," *New York City Herald*, July 12, 1914, in scrapbook, Cass Gilbert Collection, N-YHS. Woolworth's apartment was dismantled in 1927. Charles McCann to Cass Gilbert, December 1, 1927, Woolworth Building correspondence files, Cass Gilbert Collection, N-YHS.

94 Frank Woolworth to Cass Gilbert, January 31, 1913, Woolworth Building correspondence files, Cass Gilbert Collection, N-YHS. Woolworth's reputation for philandering was common knowledge among F. W. Woolworth Company and, later, Woolworth Corporation employees. Author's interview with Joseph Grabowski, vice president and director of facilities, Woolworth Corporation, February 1998.

95 Frank Woolworth, "General Letter to All Stores: United States, Canada, and Great Britain," February 20, 1914, Woolworth Building, Cass Gilbert Collection, N-YHS. The State Drawing Room in the Palace of Compiègne probably provided the model for the office, which had a working fireplace with a chimney that connected to the building's coal-burning exhaust flue.

96 Ibid.

97 Ibid. Woolworth also owned a portrait of Theodore Roosevelt. The portrait is housed in the Woolworth Collection, NBM.

98 Frank Woolworth, as quoted in L. Salter to Cass Gilbert, July 19, 1913, Woolworth Building correspondence files, Cass Gilbert Collection, N-YHS.

99 Woolworth, "General Letter to All Stores," February 20, 1914.

100 Frank Woolworth, "Executive Office," March 4, 1915. Although Woolworth did not call attention to it, the Empire Room also housed a vault containing documents from the opening of his first store. Frank W. Woolworth and Edward Mott Woolley, "From Dimes to Millions," *McClure's Magazine* 55 (December 1923), 13.

101 Eric Hobsbawn, "Introduction: Inventing Traditions," in *The Invention of Tradition*, ed. Eric Hobsbawm and Terence Ranger (Cambridge: Cambridge University Press, 1983), 1–14. Hobsbawm describes "invented" traditions as "responses to novel situations which take the form of reference to old situations." Among the purposes of such "invented traditions" are "establishing or symbolizing social cohesion or the membership of groups, real or artificial."

102 Woolworth Co., *Fortieth Anniversary Souvenir*, n.p.

103 Edward Hogan to Cass Gilbert, June 29, 1911, Woolworth Building correspondence files, Cass Gilbert Collection, N-YHS; and Lincoln Steffens, "The Modern Business Building," *Scribner's* 22 (July 1897): 59.

104 *The Woolworth Building (Highest in the World): Illustrated with Details from the Architect's Drawings and with Floor Plans* (New York: F. W. Woolworth, 1912) featured a complete set of floor plans, a section, renderings of the Broadway entrance and lobby-arcade, a section, and a site plan.

105 "Woolworth Building" (advertisement), *Real Estate Record and Builders' Guide* 89 (March 23, 1912): 587. Woolworth had purchased parcels adjacent to the end walls. The deed for one of the parcels, dated October 22, 1913, is housed in the Woolworth Collection, NBM.

106 "To Let for Business Purposes" (advertisement), *New York Times*, February 23, 1912; "To Let for Business Purposes" (advertisement), *New York Times*, April 10, 1912, in scrapbook, Cass Gilbert Collection, N-YHS; and "Woolworth Building" (advertisement), *New York Times*, April 27, 1913.

107 See, for example, "Woolworth Building" (advertisement), *New York Times*, April 24, 1913.

108 Office memorandum, "Woolworth Building," July 10, 1914, Cass Gilbert Collection, NMAH; and J. F. Springer, "The Tallest Building in the World," *Building Age* 34 (September 1912): 458. The total available square footage also included the basement and subbasement floors.

109 "List of Tenants, Woolworth Building—April 1, 1924," Woolworth Collection, NBM, identifies the terms of each tenants' lease (annual rental rate and expiration date). In 1913 the rental rate for the entire building averaged $2.30 per square foot. By 1924, the rents ranged from $3.60 a square foot to $4.50 a square foot. Office memorandum dictated by Cass Gilbert, January 28, 1924, Woolworth Building, Cass Gilbert Collection N-YHS.

110 "How McAtamney Climbed the Ladder," *New York City Press*, May 17, 1914, in scrapbook, Cass Gilbert Collection, N-YHS.

111 *The Woolworth Building (Highest in the World)*, n.p. The tower required at most six elevators, and on its highest floors, Gilbert reduced the number still further, which freed up even more light-filled space. Regarding Woolworth's conception of the tower as sixty stories, see *The Dinner Given to Cass Gilbert*, 41.

112 "New Woolworth Building on Broadway Will Eclipse Singer Tower in Height."

113 Cass Gilbert, as quoted in "Woolworth Building Will Be World's Greatest Skyscraper."

114 Steffens, "The Modern Business Building," 44 (for quote), 54–55.

115 Analysis by Deryck Holdsworth of the Woolworth Building's tenant list of April 1913, Woolworth Building, Cass Gilbert Collection, N-YHS. Holdsworth to author, June 8, 1990.

116 "Maximum Height Reached," *Wall Street Journal*, December 13, 1913, in scrapbook, Cass Gilbert Collection, N-YHS.

117 "How McAtamney Climbed the Ladder"; and office memorandum, "Woolworth Building: Data on Renting and Costs," August 12, 1914, Cass Gilbert Collection, NMAH.

118 "Woolworth Building," advertisement in *Real Estate Record and Builders' Guide* 89 (March 23, 1912): 587.

119 Steffens, "The Modern Business Building," 59.

120 Office memorandum, May 1, 1915, Woolworth Building, Cass Gilbert Collection, N-YHS.

121 Frank Woolworth to Cass Gilbert, August 17, 1915, Woolworth Building correspondence files, Cass Gilbert Collection, N-YHS.

122 Office memorandum dictated by Cass Gilbert, January 28, 1924, Woolworth Building, Cass Gilbert Collection, N-YHS. In 1962, the building continued to be fully rented, with a long waiting list. "Woolworth Building after 50 Years Is Still a 'Cathedral of Commerce,'" *New York Times*, February 11, 1962.

123 Gilbert, "Architectural Design," 56.

124 Office memorandum dictated by Cass Gilbert, February 3, 1911, Woolworth Building, Cass Gilbert Collection, N-YHS, describes the plans.

125 Gilbert, "Architectural Design," 56.

126 On the importance of natural lighting to the quality of office space, see Willis, *Form Follows Finance*, 24–27.

127 Larry Ford, *Cities and Buildings: Skyscrapers, Skid Rows and Suburbs* (Baltimore: Johns Hopkins University Press, 1994), 28 (for quote), 28–29.

128 According to Shultz and Simmons, *Offices in the Sky*, 13, "the great function of the office building is to make it possible for the businesses that deal with one another to be close together."

129 Analysis by Holdsworth of the Woolworth Building's tenant list of April 1913, Woolworth Building, Cass Gilbert Collection, N-YHS.

130 H. T. Parson (Broadway–Park Place Company) to Cass Gilbert, October 13, 1914.

131 "List of Tenants, Woolworth Building—April 1, 1924."

132 Frank Woolworth, "Executive Office," March 4, 1915, and "Executive Office: Business of 1913," Woolworth Building, Cass Gilbert Collection, N-YHS. In 1962, one-fifth of the building's total of 250 tenants were railroad companies. "Woolworth Building after 50 Years Is Still a 'Cathedral of Commerce,'" 1.

133 Thomas P. Hughes, *American Genesis: A Century of Invention and Technological Enthusiasm, 1870–1970* (New York: Viking Penguin, 1989): 23, 62–64, 112–13; and Stephen Kern, *The Culture of Time and Space, 1880–1918* (Cambridge, Mass.: Harvard University Press, 1983): 65–69. In 1924, the Radio Corporation of America occupied almost twice as much space on the eighteenth floor as the former Wireless Telegraph Company of America in 1913.

134 Woolworth Building's tenant list of April 1913, Woolworth Building, Cass Gilbert Collection, N-YHS.

135 "Purposes of the Merchants' Association in New York" in *Officers, Directors, Committees, Members, Annual Reports, By-Laws, Etc. of the Merchants' Association of New York* (New York, 1905); and Neil Harris, "Urban Tourism and the Commercial City," in *Inventing Times Square: Commerce and Culture at the Crossroads of the World*, ed. William R. Taylor (New York: Russell Sage Foundation, 1991; reprint, Baltimore: Johns Hopkins University Press, 1996), 75 (for quote), 78.

136 *Greater New York: Bulletin of the Merchant's Association of New York* 1 (November 18, 1912): 6.

137 Ibid., 11.

138 Frank Woolworth, as quoted in Bertie C. Forbes, "Frank W. Woolworth," in *Men Who Are Making America*, 2nd ed. (New York: Forbes Publishing Co., 1918), 433.

139 "Human Nature as Seen in the World's Tallest Office Building," *Literary Digest* 68 (January 8, 1921): 56.

140 Frank Woolworth, "Executive Office," October 16, 1914, Woolworth Building, Cass Gilbert Collection, N-YHS.

141 Frank Woolworth, "Executive Office," March 4, 1915.

142 Ibid.; and "Human Nature as Seen in the World's Tallest Office Building," 56.

143 Steffens, "The Modern Business Building," 38.

144 Photographs of the rathaus in Lüneburg's interior appear in Gilbert's office scrapbooks. The design also may have been inspired by Gilbert's own experience at the rathaus in Bremen in July 1910: "Bremen is an interesting town with a bully old Rathaus—big hall in second story—ceiling is beamed and painted—hanging from it are a number of models of full-rigged ships of ancient style." Cass Gilbert to Cass Gilbert, Jr., July 12, 1910, box 8, Cass Gilbert Papers, LC. Patrons criticized the German decorations of the Woolworth's rathskeller during World War I; Gilbert had them painted over with a watercolor paint, which he thought could be later easily removed. Office memorandum, April 23, 1918, Woolworth Building, Cass Gilbert Collection, N-YHS.

145 Edward J. Hogan to Cass Gilbert, August 2, 1912, Woolworth Building correspondence files, Cass Gilbert Collection, N-YHS. Woolworth never carried out the plan for the "Pompeiian" bath.

146 "Biggest Lunch Club in Tallest Building: Downtown Business Men to Lease Three Floors in the Woolworth," *New York Sun*, March 6, 1913, in scrapbook, Cass Gilbert Collection, N-YHS. Woolworth, the F. W. Woolworth Company vice president Hubert T. Parson, and the lawyer Charles McCann founded the New Amsterdam Club. Office memorandum, October 14, 1913, Woolworth Building, Cass Gilbert Collection, N-YHS. Gilbert produced plans for the club, but the project went unrealized.

147 Advertisement, *Real Estate Record and Builders' Guide* 89 (March 23, 1913): 587.

148 Office memorandum, March 13, 1913, Woolworth Building, and Mack, Jenney, and Tyler to Cass Gilbert, January 29, 1913, Woolworth Building correspondence files, Cass Gilbert Collection, N-YHS.

149 On fine materials and fine workmanship as a "character reference," see Bluestone, *Constructing Chicago*, 123.

150 Leach, *Land of Desire*, 83.

151 Alan Trachtenberg, *The Incorporation of America: Culture and Society in the Gilded Age* (New York: Hill & Wang, 1982), 154–55.

152 Katherine Solomonson, *The Chicago Tribune Tower Competition: Skyscraper Design and Cultural Change in the 1920s* (New York: Cambridge University Press, 2001), 60.

153 Leach, *Land of Desire*, 147 (for quotes); and Bluestone, *Constructing Chicago*, 149–50.

154 Robert A. M. Stern, Gregory Gilmartin, and John Massengale, *New York, 1900: Architecture and Urbanism, 1890–1915* (New York: Rizzoli International Publications, 1983), 253–72.

155 William Wood Register, Jr., "New York's Gigantic Toy," in Taylor, *Inventing Times Square*, 255–66.

156 Beckert, *The Monied Metropolis*, 258–61.

157 Lewis A. Erenberg, *Steppin' Out: New York Nightlife and the Transformation of American Culture* (Westport, Conn.: Greenwood Press, 1981), 33–45.

158 "List of Tenants, Woolworth Building—April 1, 1924"; and office memorandum, May 1, 1915, Woolworth Building, Cass Gilbert Collection, N-YHS.

159 "New Woolworth Pool: Natatorium to Be Opened in June With Water Carnival," *New York Times*, May 11, 1913, in scrapbook, Cass Gilbert Collection, N-YHS.

160 Edwin A. Cochran, *The Cathedral of Commerce*, n.p.

161 Office memorandum, June 4, 1913, Woolworth Building, Cass Gilbert Collection, N-YHS.

162 Office memorandums, October 19, 1919, and May 23, 1911, Woolworth Building, Cass Gilbert Col-

lection, N-YHS; and Woolworth and Woolley, "From Dimes to Millions," *McClure's Magazine* 55 (December 1923), 13.

163 Louis J. Horowitz and Boyden Sparkes, *The Towers of New York: The Memoirs of a Master Builder* (New York: Simon & Schuster, 1937), 110–11, 119; and Carl Condit, "Two Centuries of Technical Evolution Underlying the Skyscraper," in *Second Century of the Skyscraper*, ed. Lynn S. Beedle (New York: Van Nostrand Reinhold Co., 1988), 21.

164 Office memorandum dictated by Cass Gilbert, October 19, 1910, Woolworth Building, Cass Gilbert Collection, N-YHS.

165 Sarah Bradford Landau, *George B. Post, Architect: Picturesque Designer and Determined Realist* (New York: Monacelli Press, 1998), 53.

166 "Power Plant of the Woolworth Building," *Power* 37 (June 24, 1913): 885–88. The plant supplied direct current (DC). Today, transformers would have been placed at key locations throughout such a tall structure, to step down higher alternating current (AC) electrical loads from outside sources. Instead, the Woolworth's longest electrical feeder ran from its switchboard to a panel on the fifty-seventh floor, with total length of about 1,000 feet and a total rise of 740 feet.

167 Office memorandum dictated by Cass Gilbert, October 19, 1910, Woolworth Building, Cass Gilbert Collection, N-YHS.

168 Henry Adams, *The Education of Henry Adams* (1906), in *Novels, "Mont Saint Michel," "The Education,"* ed. Ernest Samuels and Jayne N. Samuels (New York: Library of America, 1983), 1066–74; and Kern, *The Culture of Time and Space*, 93–94.

169 *The Master Builders: A Record of the Construction of the World's Highest Commercial Structure* (New York: Hugh McAtamney & Co., 1913), 54, also notes that the dynamos were built by the Providence Engineering Works in Providence, Rhode Island, and like Edwin A. Cochran, *The Cathedral of Commerce*, n.p., highlights them with text and photographs.

170 Trachtenberg, *The Incorporation of America*, 41.

171 Kern, *The Culture of Time and Space*, 11–15, 110–11.

172 O. F. Semsch, ed., *A History of the Singer Building Construction: Its Progress from Foundation to Flagpole* (New York: Trow Press, 1908), 75; and Olivier Zunz, *Making America Corporate, 1870–1920* (Chicago: University of Chicago Press, 1990), 120.

173 Koolhaas, *Delirious New York*, 90–91.

174 Office memorandums, October 21, 1913, March 17, 1914, Woolworth Building, Cass Gilbert Collection, N-YHS.

175 *The Master Builders*, 56, 63 (for quote).

176 Office memorandum dictated by George Wells, September 13, 1912, Woolworth Building, Cass Gilbert Collection, N-YHS. Woolworth had engineers drill to one thousand five hundred feet below grade in search of a secondary supply of water. They found the water source brackish, of low pressure, and otherwise unsuitable.

177 Office memorandum showing locations of tanks and pipe galleries, ca. 1913, Woolworth Building, Cass Gilbert Collection, N-YHS; "Water-Supply System in the Fifty-Five-Story Woolworth Building, New York," *Engineering Record* 68 (July 12, 1913): 44; and Landau and Condit, *Rise of the New York Skyscraper*, 238–41, 386. As constructed, the mezzanines differ in design and height from Webster's original concept, but the supply tanks are located roughly as specified, albeit on different floors: the fourteenth, twenty-sixth, thirty-eighth, fifty-third, and fifty-seventh floors, according to Roy Suskin, the project manager for the current renovations.

178 John C. Van Dyke wrote in *The New New York: A Commentary on the Place and the People* (New York: Macmillan Co., 1909), 105: "The newspapers love . . . to show by pictorial illustration how much higher are the steel structures than, say, an ocean steamer placed on end."

179 See advertisement, *Real Estate Record and Builders' Guide* 89 (March 23, 1912): 587: "Woolworth Building: Highest, Safest, Most Perfectly Appointed Structure in the World: Fireproof Beyond Question, Elevators Accident-Proof."

180 "Office Buildings: Woolworth Building, New York City," *Insurance Engineering* 22 (December 1911): 403–10; and "Water-Supply System in the Fifty-Five-Story Woolworth Building," 44–45.

181 "Shooting Streams from the Woolworth's Pinnacle," *Fire and Water Engineering* 53 (June 11, 1913): 384–86; and "57th Story Tower Flooded on a Test," *New York Times*, June 9, 1913.

182 Cass Gilbert to Broadway–Park Place Company, August 31, 1911, Woolworth Building letterbooks, Cass Gilbert Collection, N-YHS.

183 Office memorandum, August 1, 1911, Woolworth Building, Cass Gilbert Collection, N-YHS. For contemporary views of fire-resistive and fireproof construction in the skyscraper, see Sara E.

Wermiel, *The Fireproof Building: Technology and Public Safety in the Nineteenth-Century American City* (Baltimore: Johns Hopkins University Press, 2000), 178–85.

184 Ernest Flagg, "Fire-Proof Buildings," *American Architect and Building News* 93 (April 29, 1908): 141–43.

185 Landau and Condit, *Rise of the New York Skyscraper*, 394; and Nancy L. Green, "Sweatshop Migrations: The Garment Industry between Home and Shop," in *The Landscape of Modernity: Essays on New York City, 1900–1940*, ed. David Ward and Olivier Zunz (New York: Russell Sage Foundation, 1992; reprint, Baltimore: Johns Hopkins University Press, 1997), 222. On the importance of proper egress to the fireproof building, see Wermiel, *The Fireproof Building*, 199–214.

186 Erenberg, *Steppin' Out*, 46.

187 "Two-thirds of Woolworth Building Space Leased," *Wall Street Journal*, February 9, 1914, in scrapbook, Cass Gilbert Collection, N-YHS. The Woolworth Building's total rental returns included returns from the offices, the Irving National Exchange Bank, and the stores of the lobby-arcade. The Equitable Building, by contrast, had a site valued at $14 million and construction at $15 million, for a total of $29 million, and was expected to garner $3 million a year in total rental returns.

188 "Rents in Downtown Office Buildings," 117, noted the acceptable returns. For the mainenance expenses, see "Human Nature, as Seen in the World's Tallest Office Building," 56. Woolworth privately told Irving National Bank that he expected at least a 3 percent return for the year 1914, which he further expected to rise gradually to 5 percent for 1922 and subsequent years. Robert Holmes Elmendorf, "Evolution of Commercial Banking in New York City, 1851–1951, in Which Is Recorded the Story of the Irving Trust Company" (typescript, January 1951) 125. See also Charles M. Nichols, comp., *Studies on Building Height Limitations in Large Cities with Special Reference to Conditions in Chicago* (Chicago: Real Estate Board Library, 1923), 24.

189 Elmendorf, "Evolution of Commercial Banking," 126. In 1924, F. W. Woolworth Company purchased the Woolworth Building from Frank Woolworth's heirs. Office memorandum, January 28, 1924, Woolworth Building, Cass Gilbert Collection, N-YHS.

190 Edwin A. Cochran, *The Cathedral of Commerce,* n.p. In the early 1920s, Cochran served as the Woolworth Building's manager. "Human Nature as Seen from the World's Tallest Office Building," 56. Cochran quoted the citation accompanying the gold medal the building received at California's Panama-Pacific Exposition in 1915. Broadway–Park Place Company to Cass Gilbert, January 15, 1916, Woolworth Building correspondence files, Cass Gilbert Collection, N-YHS, describes the objectives for the booklet.

191 Herbert Croly, as quoted in Kenneth Turney Gibbs, *Business Architectural Imagery in America, 1870–1930* (Ann Arbor, Mich.: UMI Research Press, 1984), 125–30, 130 (for quotes).

192 After Woolworth incorporated F. W. Woolworth and Company in 1905, he declared it an altruistic social "institution." "Did it ever occur to you that our business is an indirect charity and of benefit to the people at large? While we are in business for profit, we are also the means of making thousands of people happy. The more stores we create, the more good we do humanity." Frank Woolworth, as quoted in Winkler, *Five and Ten*, 150. In his annual letter to his store managers of January 16, 1912, Woolworth praised his managers for the "honesty" with which they conducted the business, "all of which has been free from graft." Frank Woolworth, "Annual Letter," 1911, in "Excerpts from Available F. W. Woolworth and Co. Annual Letters (1894–1911)," Woolworth Collection, NBM.

193 Broadway–Park Place Company to Cass Gilbert, January 15, 1916, Woolworth Building correpondence files, Cass Gilbert Collection, N-YHS; and S. Parkes Cadman, "Foreword," in Edwin A. Cochran, *The Cathedral of Commerce*, n.p.

194 "S[amuel] Parkes Cadman," in *The National Cyclopaedia of American Biography*, vol. 28 (New York: James T. White & Co., 1940), 192–94; and "S. Parkes Cadman Dies in Coma at 71," *New York Times*, July 13, 1936. Cadman was born in Shropshire to a family of Methodist ministers and graduated from Richmond (later Wesleyan) College of London University in 1899.

195 "S[amuel] Parkes Cadman," 193. See also S. Parkes Cadman, *Charles Darwin and Other English Thinkers: With Reference to Their Religious and Ethical Value* (Boston: Pilgrim Press, 1911).

196 S. Parkes Cadman, *A Prince in Commerce, a Master Builder: Address at the Funeral of the late Frank W. Woolworth* (Brooklyn, N.Y.), n.p., documents the relationship between Cadman and Woolworth. Cadman extolled Woolworth's life as a model of

enterprise, thrift, industry, unselfishness, and genuine concern for others, adding that the Woolworth Building would serve posterity as Woolworth's "parable and monument."

197 Thompson A. De Weese, *The Principles of Practical Publicity*, 2nd ed. (Philadelphia: George W. Jacobs & Co., 1906), 143.

198 "S[amuel] Parkes Cadman," 193. In 1923, Cadman also became one of the first preachers to address "an unseen audience of millions" by radio.

199 Montgomery Schuyler, *The Woolworth Building* (Baltimore: privately printed by Munder-Thomsen Co. for F. W. Woolworth, 1913). One thousand copies were printed for Frank Woolworth, intended for private distribution.

200 Fremont Rider, ed., *Rider's New York City: A Guide-Book for Travelers* (New York: Henry Holt & Co., 1923), 183; and "Woolworth Building after 50 Years Is Still a 'Cathedral of Commerce.'"

201 Cadman, "Foreword," n.p.

202 Trachtenberg, *The Incorporation of America*, 137.

203 William Lawrence, "The Relation of Wealth to Morals," *World's Work* 1 (January 1901), 286–92, 287 (for quote); and Andrew Carnegie, "Wealth," *North American Review* 148 (June 1889), 653–64. Both essays are reprinted in Gail Kennedy, ed., *Democracy and the Gospel of Wealth* (Boston: D. C. Heath & Co., 1949), 1–8, 68–76.

204 Trachtenberg, *The Incorporation of America*, 81 (for quote); Warren I. Susman, *Culture as History: The Transformation of American Society in the Twentieth Century* (New York: Pantheon Books, 1973), 129–30; and Solomonson, *The Chicago Tribune Tower Competition*, 232.

205 Frank Woolworth, as quoted in office memorandum, April 25, 1914, Woolworth Building, Cass Gilbert Collection, N-YHS.

206 Cass Gilbert, "The Tenth Birthday of a Notable Structure," *Real Estate Magazine of New York* 11 (May 1923): 344.

207 Cass Gilbert, "Regarding the Woolworth Building" (1927) box 17, Cass Gilbert Papers, LC.

208 Cass Gilbert to C. F. Vandervoort, March 1, 1913, personal letterbooks, Cass Gilbert Collection, N-YHS. Gilbert sent a copy of Vandervoort's poem to McAtamney; this may have inspired *The Cathedral of Commerce*.

209 Cass Gilbert, as quoted in Charles Moore, "Cass Gilbert, Architect, 1859–1934," *American Architect* 144 (July 1934): 20; and also in Francisco Mujica, *History of the Skyscraper* (Paris: Archaeology & Architecture Press, 1929), 34.

210 Adams, *The Education of Henry Adams*, 1074. See also Jackson Lears, *No Place of Grace: Antimodernism and the Transformation of American Culture, 1880–1920*, 2nd ed. (Chicago: University of Chicago Press, 1994), 262–97; and Solomonson, *The Chicago Tribune Tower Competition*, 179–81, 184–85.

211 Cram, *My Life in Architecture*, 156; and *The Significance of Gothic Art* (Boston: Marshall Jones Co., 1918), 19.

212 Ralph Adams Cram, "Editor's Note" in *Mont-Saint-Michel and Chartres*, by Henry Adams (Boston: Houghton Mifflin Co.; Cambridge: Riverside Press, 1913; reprint, Princeton, N.J.: Princeton University Press, 1981), viii; and Cram, "The Philosophy of the Gothic Restoration," in *Ministry of Art* (Boston: Houghton Mifflin Co., 1914), 34–36.

213 Trachtenberg, *The Incorporation of America*, 138.

214 Michael Leja, "Episodes from a Visual Culture of Suspicion" (lecture delivered at Harvard University, December 2, 2003).

CHAPTER SEVEN

1 Mary N. Woods, "In the Camera's Eye: The Woolworth Building in American Avant-Garde Photography and Film," in *Cass Gilbert: Life and Work: Architect of the Public Domain,* ed. Barbara S. Christen and Steven Flanders (New York: W. W. Norton & Co., 2001), 154–55, calls attention to the value of studying the "afterlife" of buildings such as the Woolworth "to construct a more inclusive history of the built environment."

2 "Who Was the Architect?" *Architecture* 47 (December 1923): 407.

3 William Leach, *Land of Desire: Merchants, Power, and the Rise of a New American Culture* (New York: Pantheon Books, 1993), 9 (for quote), 45–46.

4 Katherine Solomonson, *The Chicago Tribune Tower Competition: Skyscraper Design and Cultural Change in the 1920s* (New York: Cambridge University Press, 2001), 104.

5 Leach, *Land of Desire*, xiii, 8–9; and Daniel Boorstin, *The Americans: The Democratic Experience* (New York: Random House, 1974), 89–90, 148.

6 Boorstin, *The Americans*, 90.

7 Ibid.; Alan Trachtenberg, *The Incorporation of America: Culture and Society in the Gilded Age* (New York: Hill & Wang, 1982), 135–39.

8 Boorstin, *The Americans*, 89.

9 Ibid., 92, 100, 158; and Sharon Irish, *Cass Gilbert, Architect: Modern Traditionalist* (New York: Monacelli Press, 1999), 132–33.

10 Ada Patterson, "A Man Who at 28 Suddenly Had a Great Idea," *American Magazine* 84 (October 1917): 52–53; "Big Dreams That Came True," *Everybody's Magazine* 35 (November 1916): 607; and Edward Mott Woolley, "The Tower of Nickels and Dimes," *Hearst's Magazine* 22, October 1912, 17–19.

11 Leach, *Land of Desire*, 3–4.

12 Cass Gilbert, untitled lecture on American cities, the City Beautiful movement, and the grouping of public buildings, delivered at the Art School, Yale University, 1907, box 17, Cass Gilbert Papers, LC.

13 Barbara S. Christen, "The Architect as Planner: Cass Gilbert's Responses to Historic Open Space," in *Inventing the Skyline: The Architecture of Cass Gilbert,* ed. Margaret Heilbrun (New York: Columbia University Press, 2000), 206–11.

14 Montgomery Schuyler, "'The Towers of Manhattan' and Notes on the Woolworth Building," *Architectural Record* 33 (February 1913): 108; and Schuyler, "The Woolworth Building" (1913), in *American Architecture and Other Writings by Montgomery Schuyler*, ed. William H. Jordy and Ralph Coe (Cambridge, Mass.: Harvard University Press, Belknap Press, 1961), 2:609.

15 "The Creation of a Dignified Civic Center in New York: Restoration of City Hall Park by Removal of Unsightly Buildings," *Scientific American* 106 (March 2, 1912): 195.

16 Nathalie Dana, *The Municipal Art Society, 1892–1967: Seventy-Five Years of Service to New York* (New York: Municipal Art Society, ca. 1967), n.p.

17 Werner Hegemann and Albert Peets, *The American Vitruvius: An Architect's Handbook of Civic Art* (New York: Architectural Book Publishing Co., 1922), 135, 147.

18 George B. Ford, "Recreation, Civic Architecture, Building Districts and General Summary of Present City Planning Needs," in *Development and Present Status of City Planning in New York City*, by Committee on the City Plan (New York: Board of Estimate and Apportionment, 1914), 62.

19 Ibid.

20 "Address of Marcus M. Marks, President, Borough of Manhattan, at the Salamagundi Club in Honor of Mr. Cass Gilbert, December 7, 1915," 1–3, box 26, Cass Gilbert Papers, LC.

21 "The Tallest Office Building in the World: Erection of the Woolworth Building, New York," *Scientific American* 108 (March 8, 1913): 218 (for quote), 224–25, 233.

22 Ibid., 224. *Scientific American* answered that, theoretically, Manhattan bedrock could support foundations carrying the weight of a building two thousand feet high, assuming that it would be built according to the provisions of the New York City building code.

23 Frank Woolworth to Woolworth Syndicate (executive offices in New York), April 23, 1890, WCA.

24 Tom F. Peters, *Building the Nineteenth Century* (Cambridge, Mass.: MIT Press, 1996), 262–63.

25 Arnold Lewis, *An Early Encounter with Tomorrow: Europeans, Chicago's Loop, and the World's Columbian Exposition* (Urbana: University of Illinois Press, 1997), 167–75.

26 Notable among the designs were those of the engineer George Morison at one thousand feet, which had the financial backing of Andrew Carnegie, and of David Proctor at one thousand five hundred feet, which housed a four-thousand-room hotel. "The Columbian Tower," *Scientific American* 66 (January 2, 1892): 9; and editorial, *Inland Architecture and News Record* 4 (September 1889): 62. For the other proposals see editorial, *Real Estate Record and Builders' Guide* 44 (September 28, 1889): 1291; editorial, *American Architect and Building News* 26 (October 5, 1889): 153; editorial, *American Architect and Building News* 27 (March 22, 1890): 177; and editorial, *American Architect and Building News* 28 (May 31, 1890): 126.

27 Lewis, *An Early Encounter with Tomorrow*, 170–72; and Francisco Mujica, *History of the Skyscraper* (Paris: Archaeology & Architecture Press, 1929), caption, plate 19.

28 "A City of Towers," *Scientific American* 94 (March 30, 1907): 266.

29 "Tower 1,000 Feet High," *New York Times*, July 19, 1908; and Gregory F. Gilmartin, *Shaping the City: New York and the Municipal Art Society* (New York: Clarkson Potter Publishers, 1995), 174.

30 "Tower 1,000 Feet High."

31 David H. Ray, "The Skyscraper of the Future: A Retrospect and Forecast," *Scientific American* 75, suppl. 1940 (March 8, 1913): 149.

32 "Stars and Stripes Flung into Breeze from Top of Tallest Building," *World*, July 2, 1912, in scrapbook, Cass Gilbert Collection, N-YHS.

33 Editorial, *Brooklyn Eagle*, January 28, 1911, in scrapbook, Cass Gilbert Collection, N-YHS.

34 On the Eiffel's construction, see Peters, *Building the Nineteenth Century*, 264–65. Regarding America's culture of construction, see Peters, "An American Culture of Construction" *Perspecta* 25 (1989): 142–61.

35 David E. Nye, *American Technological Sublime* (Cambridge, Mass.: MIT Press, 1994), xvi, 32 (for quotes), 32–43, 77 (for quote), 87–94.

36 I. P. Frink Reflectors to Cass Gilbert, April 23, 1912, Woolworth Building correspondence files, Cass Gilbert Collection, N-YHS.

37 David E. Nye, *Electrifying America: Social Meanings of a New Technology, 1880–1940* (Cambridge, Mass.: MIT Press, 1990), 50–53.

38 Office memorandum, July 6, 1914, Woolworth Building, Cass Gilbert Collection, N-YHS.

39 "Highly Satisfactory Effect Produced by Illumination of Singer Building Tower," *American Architect and Building News* 94 (October 7, 1908): 120; and Mardges Bacon, *Ernest Flagg: Beaux-Arts Architect and Urban Reformer* (New York: Architectural History Foundation; Cambridge, Mass.: MIT Press, 1986), 229. In October 1910, Gilbert noted that the lighting must be "at least equal to the ornamental lighting of the Singer Tower." Office memoradum, October 20, 1910, Woolworth Building, Cass Gilbert Collection, N-YHS.

40 Mailloux and Knox to Cass Gilbert, May 22, 1912, Woolworth Building correspondence files, Cass Gilbert Collection, N-YHS.

41 Office memorandum, July 6, 1914, Woolworth Building, Cass Gilbert Collection, N-YHS; and Charles W. Person, "New York's Greatest Lighting Spectacle," *Scientific American* 112 (February 20, 1915), 171.

42 Dietrich Neumann, *Architecture of the Night: The Illuminated Building* (Munich: Prestel, 2002), 102–3. A few months later, the planners of the 1915 Panama-Pacific Exposition in San Francisco employed floodlighting to illuminate all of the exposition's structures.

43 H. H. Magdsick, "Floodlighting the World's Tallest Building," *Electrical World* 68 (August 26, 1916), 412–14.

44 In April 1914, Woolworth discussed the locations of the lighting and the reflectors in detail with G. F. Schaffer of Gilbert's office and the engineers Marks and Woodwell. Office memorandums, April 25 and April 27, 1914, Woolworth Building, Cass Gilbert Collection, N-YHS.

45 "Details of Woolworth Tower Lighting," *Electrical Review and Western Electrician* 66 (June 5, 1914): 1048–49; Person, "New York's Greatest Lighting Spectacle," 171; and Edwin A. Cochran, *The Cathedral of Commerce: Woolworth Building, New York* (New York: Broadway–Park Place Co., 1916), n.p. (for quote).

46 Magdsick, "Floodlighting the World's Tallest Building," 413.

47 Edwin A. Cochran, *The Cathedral of Commerce*, n.p.

48 Person, "New York's Greatest Lighting Spectacle," 171.

49 Frank Woolworth to Cass Gilbert, March 25, 1912, Woolworth Building correspondence files, Cass Gilbert Collection, N-YHS.

50 Office memorandum by Louis E. Eden to Cass Gilbert, October 25, 1911, and Thomas J. Murphy to Cass Gilbert, October 10, 1912, Woolworth Building correspondence files, Cass Gilbert Collection, N-YHS.

51 Edward J. Hogan to secretary of the treasury, Washington, D.C., March 16, 1911, and G. T. E. Putnam, commissioner, Bureau of Lighthouses, Department of Commerce and Labor, Washington, D.C., to Cass Gilbert, August 4, 1911, and October 28, 1911, Woolworth Building correspondence files, Cass Gilbert Collection, N-YHS; and office memorandum dictated by L. E. Eden, December 4, 1913, Woolworth Building, Cass Gilbert Collection, N-YHS.

52 C. O. Mailloux to Cass Gilbert, May 22, 1912, Woolworth Building correspondence files, Cass Gilbert Collection, N-YHS.

53 Department of Commerce and Labor, Bureau of Lighthouses, to Cass Gilbert, October 28, 1911, Woolworth Building correspondence files, Cass Gilbert Collection, N-YHS.

54 Frank Woolworth, "Executive Office," March 4, 1915, Woolworth Building, Cass Gilbert Collection, N-YHS.

55 Ibid.

56 Carolyn Marvin, *When Old Technologies Were New: Thinking about Electric Communication in the Late Nineteenth Century* (New York: Oxford University Press, 1988), 158–90; and Nye, *Electrifying America*, 56–58.

57 David Nasaw, "Cities of Light, Landscapes of Pleasure," in *The Landscape of Modernity: Essays on New York City, 1900–1940*, ed. David Ward and Olivier Zunz (New York: Russell Sage Foundation, 1992; reprint, Baltimore: Johns Hopkins University Press, 1997), 274–76.

58 Rosalind Williams, *Dream Worlds: Mass Consumption in Late Nineteenth-Century France* (Berkeley: University of California Press, 1982), 85.

59 Merrill Schleier, *The Skyscraper in American Art, 1890–1931* (Ann Arbor, Mich.: UMI Research Press, 1986), 56.

60 Alfred Stieglitz, as quoted in Dorothy Norman, *Alfred Stieglitz: An American Seer* (New York: Random House, 1973), 45. See also Schleier, *The Skyscraper in American Art*, 41–45; and Woods, "In the Camera's Eye," 155.

61 John Marin, as quoted in Ruth E. Fine, *John Marin* (Washington, D.C.: National Gallery of Art; New York: Abbeville Press, 1990), 126 (for quote), 119–41.

62 John Marin, as quoted in "The Futurist's New York," *World Magazine*, February 16, 1913, in scrapbook, Cass Gilbert Collection, N-YHS.

63 Alfred Stieglitz, as quoted in Norman, *Alfred Stieglitz*, 99. See also Matthew Josephson, "Profiles: Leprechaun in the Palisades," *New Yorker*, March 14, 1942, 30; Fine, *John Marin*, 126–27; and Woods, "In the Camera's Eye," 149.

64 Fine, *John Marin*, 123, 128. Marin began his career practicing architecture. Josephson, "Profiles," 29.

65 Herbert Croly, "'Civic Improvements': The Case of New York," *Architectural Record* 21 (May 1907): 347–52. Charles Mulford Robinson, the City Beautiful movement's leading theorist, wrote a rebuttal to Croly: "'Civic Improvements': A Reply," *Architectural Record* 22 (August 1907): 117–20.

66 Herbert Croly, "What Is Civic Art?" *Architectural Record* 16 (July 1904): 48, 50.

67 Cass Gilbert, untitled lecture on American cities, the City Beautiful movement, and the grouping of public buildings (delivered at the Art School, Yale University), 1907, box 17, Cass Gilbert Papers, LC.

68 Cass Gilbert, lecture on the City Beautiful movement (delivered to the Seattle Chapter, American Institute of Architects), 1909, box 17, Cass Gilbert Papers, LC.

69 Cass Gilbert, as quoted in "A Protest That Is Timely," *Architectural Record* 27 (February 1910): 202.

70 William R. Taylor and Thomas Bender, "Culture and Architecture: Some Aesthetic Tensions in the Shaping of New York," in *In Pursuit of Gotham: Culture and Commerce in New York*, ed. William R. Taylor (New York: Oxford University Press, 1992), 52.

71 Neil Harris, "Urban Tourism and the Commercial City," in *Inventing Times Square: Commerce and Culture at the Crossroads of the World*, ed. William R. Taylor (New York: Russell Sage Foundation, 1991; reprint, Baltimore: John Hopkins University Press, 1996), 82.

72 "The City Majestic," *Independent* 69 (September 15, 1910): 603–4.

73 Jean-Louis Cohen, *Scenes of the World to Come: European Architecture and the American Challenge, 1893–1960* (Paris: Flammarion, 1995), 14 (for quote), 15.

74 Ibid., 21–22, 26.

75 J. J. Jusserand to Cass Gilbert, January 17, 1914, Woolworth Building correspondence files, Cass Gilbert Collection, N-YHS. Regarding the Deutsches Museum and the exhibition in Leipzig, see Cass Gilbert to C. N. Graves, American Legation, Stockholm, Sweden, October 31, 1913, personal letterbooks, Cass Gilbert Collection, N-YHS. See also H. T. Parson, Secretary, Broadway–Park Place Company, to Cass Gilbert, February 2, 1914, Woolworth Building correspondence files, Cass Gilbert Collection, N-YHS; and Sir Bannister Fletcher to Cass Gilbert, September 14, 1920, Woolworth Building correspondence files, Cass Gilbert Collection, N-YHS. Gilbert also sent a plaster model (nearly twenty feet high) to the 1915 Panama-Pacific Exposition in San Francisco.

76 Angela Miller, "Balancing Acts: Writing American Art for the 21st Century" (lecture delivered at Roger Williams University, December 1, 2004).

77 "Frank Woolworth," in *Dictionary of American Biography*, vol. 20, ed. Dumas Malone (New York: Charles Scribner's Sons, 1936), 523.

78 K. D. Cook, "Hidden New York: The Woolworth Observatory," *New York Newsday*, February 21, 1994.

79 Office memorandum, December 13, 1910, Woolworth Building, Cass Gilbert Collection, N-YHS.

80 *50 Years of Woolworth, 1879–1929: F. W. Woolworth's 5 and 10 Cent Store* (New York: F. W. Woolworth Co., 1929), n.p.

81 Marianna Griswold Van Rensselaer, "Picturesque New York," *Century Magazine* 45 (December 1892): 168. The desire of sightseers to survey Manhattan panoramically has a still older history. As early as 1810, Joseph Holland painted a panoramic view of the city from a theater cupola near St. Paul's Church, for exhibition as a cyclorama, and engravings showing detailed views from the spires of St. Paul's Church and Trinity Church were produced in 1848 and 1849.

82 Van Rensselaer, "Picturesque New York," 168.

83 Vernon Howe Bailey's drawings illustrated Edgar Saltus, "New York from the Flatiron," *Munsey's Magazine* 33 (July 1905): 381–90.

84 Frank Woolworth to Woolworth Syndicate (executive offices in New York), April 28, 1890, WCA.

85 Dean McCannell, *The Tourist: A New Theory of the Leisure Class* (New York: Schocken Books, 1976), 44–45.

86 "F. W. Woolworth Invests His Millions in Towering Broadway Office Building," *New York American*, February 22, 1911, in scrapbook, Cass Gilbert Collection, N-YHS.

87 Ibid.

88 Edwin A. Cochran, *The Cathedral of Commerce*, n.p.; and "Human Nature as Seen in the World's Tallest Office Building," *Literary Digest* 68 (January 8, 1921): 56.

89 Office memorandum dictated by Cass Gilbert, January 28, 1924, Woolworth Building, Cass Gilbert Collection, N-YHS. Gilbert had originally told Woolworth that the observatory might earn fifty thousand dollars a year. The Singer Tower's observatory, the admission to which also cost fifty cents, around 1910 averaged twenty thousand dollars a year.

90 "Bonanza," May 21, 1931, unidentified newspaper clipping, collection of Edward Hogan, Jr. The United States Navy closed the tower in 1941 as a security precaution, after the Japanese attack on Pearl Harbor, because it afforded too clear a view of the New York harbor and the Brooklyn Navy Yard. See also "Woolworth Building after 50 Years Is Still a 'Cathedral of Commerce,'" *New York Times*, February 11, 1962; and Cook, "Hidden New York."

91 On the new perceptual experiences inspired by the heights of New York's skyscrapers, see Meir Wigoder, "The 'Solar Eye' of Vision: Emergence of the Skyscraper-Viewer in the Discourse on Heights in New York City, 1890–1920," *Journal of the Society of Architectural Historians* 61 (June 2002): 154–55; and Michel de Certeau, *The Practice of Everyday Life*, trans. Steven Rendall (Berkeley: University of California Press, 1984), 92–93.

92 Frank Woolworth, "Executive Office, March 4, 1915.

93 Frank Woolworth to Cass Gilbert, December 24, 1913, Woolworth Building correspondence files, Cass Gilbert Collection, N-YHS; and Frank Woolworth, "Executive Office," March 4, 1915.

94 "Visits Woolworth Tower: Architectural League Delegation Inspects World's Tallest Building," *New York Times*, October 20, 1913. The reporter did not account for Woolworth's recent decision to make the observatory the fifty-eighth floor.

95 Ibid.

96 "High Office Buildings in New York," *Scientific American* 41, suppl. 1053 (March 7, 1896): 16827.

97 Edward S. Beach to Cass Gilbert, January 27, 1913, H. Hobart Porter to Cass Gilbert, December 5, 1912, and M. Stewart to Cass Gilbert, November 21, 1912, Woolworth Building correspondence files, Cass Gilbert Collection, N-YHS.

98 Woods, "In the Camera's Eye," 156; and Wigoder, "The 'Solar Eye' of Vision," 152. Coburn wrote: "These five pictures were made from the towers of New York's highest buildings; how romantic, how exhilarating it is in these altitudes few of the denizens of the city realize." Alvin Langdon Coburn, *Alvin Langdon Coburn, Photographer* (1966; reprint, New York: Dover Publications, 1978), 86.

99 Schleier, *The Skyscraper in American Art*, 55.

100 Woods, "In the Camera's Eye," 157.

101 Wigoder, "The 'Solar Eye' of Vision," 154, 164.

102 See, for example, Fremont Rider, ed., *Rider's New York City: A Guide-Book for Travelers* (New York: Henry Holt & Co., 1923), 174–96.

103 Frank Woolworth, "Executive Office," March 4, 1915.

104 H. Addington Bruce, *Above the Clouds and Old New York: An Historical Sketch of the Site and a Description of the Many Wonders to the Woolworth Building, Published for Distribution among Visitors to the Woolworth Tower, New York* (Baltimore: Munder-Thomsen Press, 1913), n.p.

105 Max Weber, *The Protestant Ethic and the Spirit of Capitalism* (1904–5, revised 1920–21), trans. Talcott Parsons (New York: Charles Scribner's Sons, 1958), 71. Weber's work was translated into English in 1930.

106 William R. Taylor, "The Evolution of Public Space: The Commercial City as Showcase," in Taylor, *In Pursuit of Gotham*, 36; and "New York, the Unrivalled Business Centre," *Harper's Weekly* 46 (November 15, 1902): 1673–88.

107 Fine, *John Marin*, 141.

108 Wigoder, "The 'Solar Eye' of Vision," 154–55.

109 William R. Taylor, "New York and the Origin of the Skyline: The Commercial City as Visual Text," in Taylor, *In Pursuit of Gotham*, 23–33.

110 Harris, "Urban Tourism and the Commercial City," 66, 76.

111 Ibid., 69 (for quote), 72, 78.

112 Ibid., 66; and McCannell, *The Tourist*, 13.

113 Harris, "Urban Tourism and the Commercial City," 69–73; Taylor, "New York and the Origin of the Skyline," 26–28; and Annie Russell Marble, "The Reign of the Spectacular," *Dial* 35 (November 1, 1903): 297 (for quote).

114 On how the picturesque "completely saturated" the nineteenth-century urban marketplace, see Carrie Tirado Bramen, "The Urban Picturesque and the Spectacle of Americanization," *American Quarterly* 52 (September 2000): 444–77.
115 Wigoder, "The 'Solar Eye' of Vision," 155.
116 Cass Gilbert, "Introduction," in *Skyscrapers of New York*, by Vernon Howe Bailey (New York: William Edwin Rudge, 1928), n.p.
117 Frank Woolworth, "Executive Office," September 25, 1914, and March 4, 1915, Woolworth Building, Cass Gilbert Collection, N-YHS.
118 On the New York Merchant's Association's promotion of tourism, see Harris, "Urban Tourism and the Commercial City," 75–76.
119 See, for example, Schuyler, "The Towers of Manhattan," 99–119; and "Towered Cities," *Living Age* 42 (January 2, 1909), 45–47.
120 Cass Gilbert to Winthrop S. Gilman, March 21, 1913, personal letterbooks, Cass Gilbert Collection, N-YHS.
121 O. F. Semsch, ed., *A History of the Singer Building Construction: Its Progress from Foundation to Flagpole* (New York: Trow Press, 1908), 9. See also Bacon, *Ernest Flagg*, 220–23.
122 Ernest Flagg, "The Limitation of Height and Area of Buildings in New York," *American Architect and Building News* 93 (April 15, 1908): 126.
123 Jay Bochner, *An American Lens: Scenes from Alfred Stieglitz's New York Secession* (Cambridge, Mass.: MIT Press, 2005), 11–13, 21, 120–21.
124 Montgomery Schuyler, "American Towers," *Art and Progress* 1 (September 1911): 311.
125 Ibid., 312, 314.
126 Schuyler, "The Towers of Manhattan," 104.
127 Schuyler, "The Woolworth Building," 608.
128 Ibid., 606, 608, 609.
129 Mildred Stapley, "The City of Towers," *Harper's Monthly Magazine* 123 (October 1911): 698, 702, 706.
130 "The American Skyscraper: The Giant in Architecture: Its Purpose, Beauty, and Development," *Craftsman* 24 (April 1913): 10.
131 Cass Gilbert, as quoted in "A Protest That Is Timely," 202.
132 Cass Gilbert to Emily Gilbert, October 8, 1912, box 8, Cass Gilbert Papers, LC.
133 Ibid.
134 Woods, "In the Camera's Eye," 161, 162 (for quote); and Theodore Stebbins, Jr., "Sheeler and Photography," in *The Photography of Charles Sheeler, American Modernist*, by Theodore Stebbins, Jr., Gilles Mora, and Karen E. Haas (Boston: Bulfinch Press, 2002), 15–16.
135 Cass Gilbert, "Introduction," n.p.
136 Ibid.
137 "The Forty-second Annual Convention of the American Institute of Architects, Held at Washington, D.C., December 15, 16, and 17, 1908: The First Day's Proceedings," *American Architect and Building News* 94 (December 23, 1903): 210–11.
138 Joy Kasson, "The Wild West and the Frontier Thesis," in *Buffalo Bill's Wild West: Celebrity, Memory, and Popular History* (New York: Hill and Wang, 2000), 115; and Theodore Roosevelt, *The Winning of the West* (1889; reprint, New York: Current Literature Publishing Co., 1905), 1:40.
139 *Cass Gilbert: Reminiscences and Addresses*, ed. Julia Finch Gilbert (New York: privately printed, 1935), 44; and "Cass Gilbert Dead: Eminent Architect," *New York Times*, May 18, 1934.

SELECTED BIBLIOGRAPHY

ARCHIVES

American Institute of Architects, Washington, D.C., American Institute of Architects Archives
Correspondence Files, Office of the Secretary
Bank of New York Archives, New York
Columbia University, New York, Avery Architectural and Fine Arts Library
Thomas Robert Johnson Architectural Drawings and Papers
Lancaster Historical Society, Lancaster, Pa.
Frank Winfield Woolworth Information Files
Library of Congress, Washington, D.C., Manuscript Division
Cass Gilbert Papers
Library of Congress, Washington, D.C., Prints and Photographs Division
Minnesota State Historical Society, St. Paul, Minn., Manuscript Library
Cass Gilbert Papers
Clarence Howard Johnston Papers
Museum of the City of New York, New York
Prints, Drawings, and Photographs Collection
National Building Museum, Washington, D.C.
Woolworth Collection
New-York Historical Society, New York, Department of Prints, Photographs, and Architecture
Cass Gilbert Collection
Oberlin College Archives
Papers of Cass Gilbert
Smithsonian Institution, Washington, D.C., American Art Museum
Graphic Arts Collection
Smithsonian Institution, Washington. D.C., Archives of American Art
Cass Gilbert Papers
Smithsonian Institution, Washington, D.C., National Museum of American History, Archives Center
Cass Gilbert Collection
Gunvald Aus Engineering Drawings
Watertown Daily Times, Watertown, N.Y.
Frank Winfield Woolworth Press Clippings Files

PUBLISHED WORKS

Abramson, Daniel. *Skyscraper Rivals: The AIG Building and the Architecture of Wall Street.* New York: Princeton Architectural Press, 2001.

Anderson, Benedict. *Imagined Communities: Reflections on the Origin and Spread of Nationalism.* Rev. ed. London: Verso, 1991.

Atlantic Terra Cotta: A 52-Story Façade. New York: Atlantic Terra Cotta Co., 1913.

Aus, Gunvald. "Engineering Design of the Woolworth Building." *American Architect* 103 (March 26, 1913): 157–70.

Bacon, Mardges. *Ernest Flagg: Beaux-Arts Architect and Urban Reformer*. New York: Architectural History Foundation; Cambridge, Mass.: MIT Press, 1986.

Balmori, Diana. "George B. Post: The Process of Design and the New American Architectural Office (1868–1913)." *Society of Architectural Historians Journal* 46 (December 1987): 342–55.

Beals, Allen E. "Edward J. Hogan, Agent: The Inside Story of How the World's Tallest Structure Came to Be Built, and How the Site Was Procured." *Real Estate Record and Builder's Guide* 90 (November 9, 1912): 869–70.

Beckert, Sven. *The Monied Metropolis: New York and the Consolidation of the American Bourgeoisie, 1850–1896*. Cambridge: Cambridge University Press, 2001.

Bender, Thomas. *The Unfinished City: New York and the Metropolitan Idea*. New York: New Press, 2002.

Berman, Marshall. *All That Is Solid Melts into Air: The Experience of Modernity*. 2nd ed. New York: Penguin Books, 1988.

Birkmire, William. *Skeleton Construction in Buildings*. 3rd ed. New York: John Wiley & Sons, 1900.

Blodgett, Geoffrey. *Cass Gilbert: The Early Years*. St. Paul: Minnesota Historical Society Press, 2001.

Bluestone, Daniel. *Constructing Chicago*. New Haven, Conn.: Yale University Press, 1991.

Bogart, Michele H., *Artists, Advertising, and the Borders of Art*. Chicago: University of Chicago Press, 1995.

———. "In Search of a United Front: American Architectural Sculpture at the Turn of the Century." *Winterthur Portfolio* 19 (Summer/Autumn 1984): 151–76.

———. *Public Sculpture and the Civic Ideal in New York City, 1890–1930*. Chicago: University of Chicago Press, 1989.

Boorstin, Daniel J. *The Americans: The Democratic Experience*. New York: Random House, 1974.

———. *The Image: A Guide to Pseudo-events in America*. 3rd ed. New York: Random House, Vintage Books, 1992.

Boyer, M. Christine. *Manhattan Manners: Architecture and Style, 1850–1900*. New York: Rizzoli International Publications, 1985.

Brough, James. *The Woolworths*. New York: McGraw-Hill Book Co., 1982.

Bruce, H. Addington. *Above the Clouds and Old New York: An Historical Sketch of the Site and a Description of the Many Wonders of the Woolworth Building, Published for Distribution among the Visitors to the Woolworth Tower, New York*. Baltimore: Munder-Thomsen Press, 1913.

Bruegmann, Robert. *The Architects and the City: Holabird and Roche of Chicago, 1880–1918*. Chicago: University of Chicago Press, 1997.

"Building Skyscrapers—Described by Cass Gilbert." *Real Estate Record and Builders' Guide* 65 (June 23, 1900): 1085, 1091.

Burrows Edwin G., and Mike Wallace. *Gotham: A History of New York City to 1898*. New York: Oxford University Press, 1999.

Chandler, Alfred D., Jr. *Scale and Scope: The Dynamics of Industrial Capitalism*. Cambridge, Mass.: Harvard University Press, Belknap Press, 1990.

———. *The Visible Hand: The Managerial Revolution in American Business*. Cambridge, Mass.: Harvard University Press, Belknap Press, 1977.

Christen, Barbara Snowden. "Cass Gilbert and the Ideal of the City Beautiful: Campus and City Plans, 1900–1916." Ph.D. diss., City University of New York, 1997.

Christen, Barbara S., and Steven Flanders, eds. *Cass Gilbert: Life and Work.: Architect of the Public Domain*. New York: W. W. Norton & Co., 2001.

Cochran, Edwin A. *The Cathedral of Commerce: Woolworth Building, New York*. New York, Broadway–Park Place Co., 1916.

Cochran, Thomas C. *Business in American Life*. New York: McGraw-Hill, 1972.

Cohen, Jean-Louis. *Scenes of the World to Come: European Architecture and the American Challenge, 1893–1960*. Paris: Flammarion, 1995.

Condit, Carl. *American Building*. Chicago: University of Chicago Press, 1968.

———. "The Wind Bracing of Buildings." *Scientific American* 230 (February 1974): 93–105.

"Construction of the Woolworth Building." *Engineering Record* 66 (July 27, 1912): 97–100.

Corn, Wanda M. "The New New York." *Art in America* 61 (July–August 1973): 58–65.

Croly, Herbert. "New York as the American Metropolis." *Architectural Record* 13 (March 1903): 193–206.

The Dinner Given to Cass Gilbert, Architect, by Frank W. Woolworth. Baltimore: Munder-Thomsen Press, 1913.

Dolkart, Andrew. *Biography of a Tenement House in New York City: An Architectural History of 97 Orchard Street*. Santa Fe: Center for American Places, 2006.

Domosh, Mona. *Invented Cities: The Creation of Landscape in Nineteenth-Century New York and Boston*. New Haven, Conn.: Yale University Press, 1996.

Elliott, Cecil D. *Technics and Architecture: The Development of Materials and Systems for Buildings*. Cambridge, Mass.: MIT Press, 1992.

Erenberg, Lewis A. *Steppin' Out: New York Nightlife and the Transformation of American Culture*. Westport, Conn.: Greenwood Press, 1981.

Fogelson, Robert. *Downtown: Its Rise and Fall, 1880–1950*. New Haven, Conn.: Yale University Press, 2001.

Friedman, Donald. *Historical Building Construction: Design, Materials, and Technology*. New York: W. W. Norton & Co., 1995.

F. W. Woolworth Co. *Fortieth Anniversary Souvenir, 1879–1919*. New York, 1919.

Gibbs, Kenneth Turney. *Business Architectural Imagery in America, 1870–1930*. Ann Arbor, Mich.: UMI Research Press, 1984.

Gilbert, Cass. "Architectural Design." In "The Woolworth Building, Most Modern Example of the Fire-Proof Skyscraper: How It Was Built," by George T. Mortimer. *Real Estate Magazine* 1 (July 1912): 52–68.

———. *Cass Gilbert: Reminiscences and Addresses*. Edited by Julia Finch Gilbert. New York: privately printed, 1935.

———. "Introduction." In *Skyscrapers of New York*, by Vernon Howe Bailey. New York: William Edwin Rudge, 1928.

———. "The Tenth Birthday of a Notable Structure." *Real Estate Magazine of New York* 11 (May 1923): 344–45.

———. "The Woolworth Building." In *Masterpieces of Architecture in the United States*, by Edward Warren Hoak and Humphrey Church. New York: Charles Scribner's Sons, 1930.

Gilmartin, Gregory F. *Shaping the City: New York and the Municipal Art Society*. New York: Clarkson Potter Publishers, 1995.

Girouard, Mark. *Cities and People: A Social and Architectural History*. New Haven, Conn.: Yale University Press, 1985.

Goldberger, Paul. *The Skyscraper*. New York: Alfred A. Knopf, 1982.

Gordon, James Steele. "Woolworth's Cathedral." *American Heritage* 40 (July/August 1989): 16, 18.

Hall, Sir Peter. *Cities and Civilization*. New York: Random House, Pantheon Books, 1998.

Harris, Neil. *Building Lives: Constructing Rites and Passages*. New Haven, Conn.: Yale University Press, 1999.

———. *Cultural Excursions: Marketing Appetites and Cultural Tastes in Modern America*. Chicago: University of Chicago Press, 1990.

———. "Urban Tourism and the Commercial City." In *Inventing Times Square: Commerce and Culture at the Crossroads of the World*, edited by William R. Taylor. New York: Russell Sage Foundation, 1991; reprint, Baltimore: Johns Hopkins University Press, 1996.

Heilbrun, Margaret, ed. *Inventing the Skyline: The Architecture of Cass Gilbert*. New York: Columbia University Press, 2000.

Hill, George. "The Economy of the Office Building." *Architectural Record* 15 (April 1904): 313–27.

———. "Office Building." In *A Dictionary of Architecture and Building*, vol. 3, edited by Russell Sturgis. London: Macmillan & Co., 1902.

Hines, Thomas H. *Burnham of Chicago: Architect and Planner*, 2nd ed. Chicago: University of Chicago Press, 1979.

Hobsbawn, Eric. *The Age of Empire: 1875—1914*. New York: Vintage Books, 1989.

Hobsbawn, Eric, and Terence Ranger. *The Invention of Tradition*. Cambridge: Cambridge University Press, 1983.

———. *Nations and Nationalism: Programme, Myth, and Reality*, 2nd ed. Cambridge University Press, 1990.

Holtzman, S. F. "Design of the Woolworth Building: Features of Substructure and Calculations for Wind Bracing of Tower." *Engineering Record* 68 (July 5, 1913): 22–24.

Horowitz, Louis Jay. *The Modern Building Organization*. New York: Alexander Hamilton Institute, 1911.

Horowitz, Louis J., and Boyden Sparkes. *The Towers of New York: The Memoirs of a Master Builder*. New York: Simon & Schuster, 1937.

Houlihan, Timothy J. "The New York City Building Trades, 1890–1910." Ph.D. diss., State University of New York at Bimington, 1994.

Hughes, Thomas P. *American Genesis: A Century of Invention and Technological Enthusiasm, 1870–1970*. New York: Viking Penguin, 1989.

"Hughson Hawley: Scenic Artist and Architectural Painter." *Pencil Points* 9 (December 1928): 761–74.

Hurd, Richard M. *Principles of City Land Values*. New York: Record & Guide, 1903.

Huxtable, Ada Louise. "The Death of the Five and Ten." In *Architecture Anyone?* New York: Random House, 1986.

———. *The Tall Building Artistically Reconsidered: The Search for a Skyscraper Style*. New York: Pantheon Books, 1985.

Irish, Sharon. "Beaux-Arts Teamwork in an American Architectural Office: Cass Gilbert's Entry to the New York Custom House Competition." *New Mexico Studies in the Fine Arts* 7 (1982): 10–13.

———. *Cass Gilbert, Architect: Modern Traditionalist*. New York: Monacelli Press, 1999.

———. "Cass Gilbert's Career in New York, 1899–1905." Ph.D. diss., Northwestern University, 1985.

———. "A 'Machine That Makes the Land Pay': The West Street Building in New York." *Technology and Culture* 30 (April 1989): 376–97.

Jaher, Frederic Cople. *The Urban Establishment: Upper Strata in Boston, New York, Charleston, Chicago, and Los Angeles*. Urbana: University of Illinois Press, 1982.

Jones, Robert Allen. *Cass Gilbert: Midwestern Architect in New York*. New York: Arno Press, 1982.

———. "Mr. Woolworth's Tower: The Skyscraper as Popular Icon." *Journal of Popular Culture* 7 (Fall 1973): 408–24.

Kantor, Harvey A. "The City Beautiful in New York." *New-York Historical Society Quarterly* 58 (April 1973): 149–71.

Kasson, John. *Amusing the Million: Coney Island at the Turn of the Century*. New York: Hill & Wang, 1978.

Kern, Stephen. *The Culture of Time and Space, 1880–1918*. Cambridge, Mass.: Harvard University Press, 1983.

King, Moses, comp. *King's Views of New York, 1896–1905 and Brooklyn, 1905*. New York: Arno Press, 1974.

Kirkham, Guy. "Cass Gilbert, Master of Style." *Pencil Points* 15 (November 1934): 541–56.

Koeper, Howard Frederick. "The Gothic Skyscraper: A History of the Woolworth Building and Its Antecedents." Ph.D. diss., Harvard University, 1969.

Koolhaas, Rem. *Delirious New York: A Retroactive Manifesto for Manhattan*. Rev. ed. New York: Monacelli Press, 1994.

Krinsky, Carol Herselle. "Sister Cities: Architecture and Planning in the Twentieth Century." In *Chicago and New York: Architectural Interactions*. Chicago: Art Institute of Chicago, 1984.

La Feber, Walter. *The New Empire: An Interpretation of American Expansion, 1860–1898*. Ithaca, N.Y.: Cornell University Press, 1963.

Lamb, Frederick Stymetz. "Modern Use of the Gothic: The Possibilities of a New Architectural Style." *Craftsman* 8 (May 1905): 150–70.

Landau, Sarah Bradford, and Carl W. Condit. *Rise of the New York Skyscraper, 1865–1913*. New Haven, Conn.: Yale University Press, 1996.

Leach, William. *Land of Desire: Merchants, Power, and the Rise of a New American Culture*. New York: Pantheon Books, 1993.

Lears, Jackson. *Fables of Abundance: A Cultural History of Advertising in America*. New York: Basic Books, 1994.

———. *No Place of Grace: Antimodernism and the Transformation of American Culture, 1880–1920*. 2nd ed. Chicago: University of Chicago Press, 1994.

Magonigle, H. Van Buren. "A Half Century of Architecture." Pt. 3, "A Biographical Review." *Pencil Points* 15 (March 1934): 115–18.

Marble, Annie Russell. "The Reign of the Spectacular." *Dial* 35 (November 1, 1903): 297–99.

The Master Builders: A Record of the Construction of the World's Highest Commercial Structure. Baltimore: Munder-Thomsen Press, 1913.

McBrier, Edwin Merton. *Genealogy of the Descendants of Henry McBrier and Kezia Sloan McBrier Who Migrated to the United States in 1827*. New York: privately printed, 1941.

McCannell, Dean. *The Tourist: A New Theory of the Leisure Class*. New York: Schocken Books, 1976.

Misa, Thomas J. *A Nation of Steel: The Making of Modern America, 1865–1925*. Baltimore: Johns Hopkins University Press, 1995.

Moudry, Roberta. "Architecture as Cultural Design: The Architecture and Urbanism of the Metropolitan Life Insurance Company." Ph.D. diss., Cornell University, 1995.

———, ed. *The American Skyscraper: Cultural Histories*. New York: Cambridge University Press, 2005.

Mujica, Francisco. *History of the Skyscraper*. Paris: Archaeology & Architecture Press, 1929.

Murphy, Patricia Anne. "The Early Career of Cass Gilbert: 1878 to 1895." Master's thesis, University of Virginia, 1979.

"The National Builder." *Supplement to the Real Estate Record and Builders' Guide* 44 (July 28, 1900): 1–4.

Neumann, Dietrich. *Architecture of the Night: The Illuminated Building*. Munich: Prestel, 2002.

"New Woolworth Building on Broadway Will Eclipse Singer Tower in Height." *New York Times*, November 13, 1910.

Nye, David E. *American Technological Sublime*. Cambridge, Mass.: MIT Press, 1994.

———. *Electrifying America: Social Meanings of a New Technology, 1880–1940*. Cambridge, Mass.: MIT Press, 1990.

Page, Max. *The Creative Destruction of Manhattan, 1900–1940*. Chicago: University of Chicago Press, 1999.

Parks, Janet. "Hughson Hawley." In *New York on the Rise: Architectural Renderings by Hughson Hawley, 1880–1931*. New York: Museum of the City of New York; London: Lund Humphries Publishers, 1998.

Peters, Tom F. *Building the Nineteenth Century*. Cambridge, Mass.: MIT Press, 1996.

Peterson, Jon A. *The Birth of City Planning in the United States, 1840–1917*. Baltimore: Johns Hopkins University Press, 2003.

Phillips, Charles F. "A History of the F. W. Woolworth Company." *Harvard Business Review* 13 (January 1935): 225–36.

Plunkett-Powell, Karen. *Remembering Woolworth's: A Nostalgic History of the World's Most Famous Five and Dime*. New York: St. Martin's Press, 1999.

Poole, Ernest. "Cowboys of the Skies." *Everybody's Magazine* 19 (November 1908): 641–53.

Prudon, Theodore Henricus Maria. "Architectural Terra Cotta and Ceramic Veneer in the United States Prior to World War II: A History of Its Development and an Analysis of Its Deterioration Problems and Possible Repair Methodologies." Ph.D. diss., Columbia University, 1981.

Purdy, Corydon T. "The Relation of the Engineer to the Architect." *American Architect and Building News* 87 (February 11, 1905): 43–46.

Rasenberger, Jim. *High Steel: The Daring Men Who Built the World's Greatest Skyline*. New York: Harper Collins Publishers, 2004.

"A Realty Triumph in Assembling Plot." *New York Times*, January 22, 1911.

Redding, Leo L. "Mr. F. W. Woolworth's Story." *World's Work* 25 (April 1913): 659–65.

Robins, Anthony W. "Woolworth Building, 233 Broadway, Borough of Manhattan." New York City Landmarks Preservation Commission designation report, April 12, 1983.

———. "Woolworth Building, First Floor Interior . . ." New York City Landmarks Preservation Commission designation report, April 12, 1983.

Robinson, Charles Mulford. *Modern Civic Art*. New York: G. P. Putnam's Sons, 1903.

Roth, Leland M. *McKim, Mead and White, Architects*. New York: Harper & Row Publishers, 1983.

Rydell, Robert W. *All the World's a Fair: Visions of Empire at American International Expositions, 1876–1916*. Chicago: University of Chicago Press, 1984.

Safford, Hildegard J. "The Terra Cotta Industry and the Atlantic Terra Cotta Company." *Staten Island Historian* 31 (April–June 1974): 153–66.

Salvadori, Mario. *Why Buildings Stand Up: The Strength of Architecture*. New York: W. W. Norton & Co., 1980.

Schleier, Merrill. *The Skyscraper in American Art, 1890–1931*. Ann Arbor, Mich.: UMI Research Press, 1986.

Schlereth, Thomas J. *Victorian America: Transformations in Everyday Life, 1876–1915*. New York: Harper Collins Publishers, 1991.

Schuyler, Montgomery. "'The Towers of Manhattan' and Notes on the Woolworth Building." *Architectural Record* 33 (February 1913): 98–122.

———. *The Woolworth Building*. Baltimore: privately printed by Munder-Thomsen Co. for F. W. Woolworth, 1913.

Schwartz, Vanessa R. *Spectacular Realities: Early Mass Culture in Fin-de-Siècle Paris*. Berkeley: University of California Press, 1998.

Scobey, David M. *Empire City: The Making and Meaning of the New York City Landscape*. Philadelphia: Temple University Press, 2002.

Semsch, O. F., ed. *A History of the Singer Building Construction: Its Progress from Foundation to Flagpole*. New York: Trow Press, 1908.

Shultz, Earle, and Walter Simmons. *Offices in the Sky*. Indianapolis: Bobbs-Merrill Co., 1959.

Skinner, Frank W. *Woolworth Building, New York City*. New York: American Bridge Co., n.d.

Solomonson, Katherine. *The Chicago Tribune Tower Competition: Skyscraper Design and Cultural Change in the 1920s*. New York: Cambridge University Press, 2001.

Stapley, Mildred. "The City of Towers." *Harper's Monthly Magazine* 123 (October 1911): 697–706.

Starr, Paul. *The Creation of the Media: Political Origins of Modern Communications*. New York: Basic Books, 2004.

Starrett, Paul. *Changing the Skyline: An Autobiography*. New York: McGraw-Hill Book Co., 1938.

Starrett, W. A. *Skyscrapers and the Men Who Build Them*. New York: Charles Scribner's Sons, 1928.

Steffens, Lincoln. "The Modern Business Building." *Scribner's* 22 (July 1897): 37–61.

Stern, Robert A. M., Gregory Gilmartin, and John Massengale, *New York, 1900: Metropolitan Architecure and Urbanism, 1890–1915*. New York: Rizzoli International Publications, 1983.

Stern, Robert A. M., Thomas Mellins, and David Fishman, *New York, 1880: Architecture and Urbanism in the Gilded Age*. New York: Monacelli Press, 1999.

Sullivan, Louis H. "Reply to Mr. Frederick Stymetz Lamb on 'Modern Use of the Gothic: The Possibility of New Architectural Style.'" *Craftsman* 8 (June 1905): 336–38.

Susman, Warren. *Culture as History: The Transformation of American Society in the Twentieth Century*. New York: Pantheon Books, 1973.

"System in Contracting" (Gilbreth, Frank Bunker). *Real Estate Record and Builders' Guide* 76 (August 19, 1905): 312.

Swales, Francis S. "Master Draftsmen, XVIII: Cass Gilbert." *Pencil Points* 7 (October 1926): 583–98.

——. "The Work of Cass Gilbert." *Architectural Review* 31 (January–June, 1912): 2–16.

"The Tallest Office Building in the World: Erection of the Woolworth Building, New York." *Scientific American* 108 (March 8, 1913): 224–25, 233.

Tauranac, John. *Elegant New York: The Builders and Their Buildings*. New York: Abbeville Press, 1985.

——. *The Empire State Building: The Making of a Landmark*. New York: Scribner, 1995.

Taylor, William R. "The Evolution of Public Space: The Commercial City as Showcase." In *In Pursuit of Gotham: Culture and Commerce in New York*. New York: Oxford University Press, 1992.

——. "New York and the Origin of the Skyline: The Commercial City as Visual Text." In *In Pursuit of Gotham: Culture and Commerce in New York*. New York: Oxford University Press, 1992.

Thompson-Starrett Company: Building and Industrial Construction. New York: Thompson-Starrett Co., 1919.

Toll, Seymour I. *Zoned American*. New York: Grossman Publishers, 1969.

Trachtenberg, Alan. "Image and Ideology: New York in the Photographer's Eye." *Journal of Urban History* 10 (August 1984): 453–65.

——. *The Incorporation of America: Culture and Society in the Gilded Age*. New York: Hill & Wang, 1982.

Tunick, Susan. *Terra-Cotta Skyline*. New York: Princeton Architectural Press, 1997.

Upton, Dell. "Inventing the Metropolis: Civilization and Urbanity in Antebellum New York." In *Art and the Empire City: New York, 1825–1861*, edited by Catherine Hoover Voorsanger and John K. Howat. New York: Metropolitan Museum of Art; New Haven, Conn.: Yale University Press, 2000.

Van Dyke, John C. *The New New York: A Commentary on the Place and the People*. New York: Macmillan Co., 1909.

van Leeuwen, Thomas A. P. *The Skyward Trend of Thought: The Metaphysics of the American Skyscraper.* Cambridge, Mass.: MIT Press, 1986.

Van Zanten, David. "The Nineteenth Century: The Projecting of Chicago as a Commercial City and the Rationalization of Design and Construction." In *Chicago and New York: Architectural Interactions*. Chicago: Art Institute of Chicago, 1984.

——. "Twenties Gothic." *New Mexico Studies in the Fine Arts* 8 (1983): 19–23.

Veit, Richard. "Moving beyond the Factory Gates: The Industrial Archaeology of New Jersey's Terra Cotta Industry." *Industrial Archaeology* 25 (1999): 5–27.

Ward, David, and Olivier Zunz, eds. *The Landscape of Modernity: Essays on New York City, 1900–1940*. New York: Russell Sage Foundation, 1992.

Wermiel, Sara E. *The Fireproof Building: Technology and Public Safety in the Nineteenth-Century American City*. Baltimore: Johns Hopkins University Press, 2000.

——. "Norcross, Fuller, and the Rise of the General Contractor in the United States in the Nineteenth Century." In *Proceedings of the Second International Congress of Construction History* 3 (2006): 3297–3133.

Wigoder, Meir. "The 'Solar Eye' of Vision: Emergence of the Skyscraper-Viewer in the Discourse on Heights in New York City, 1890–1920." *Journal of the Society of Architectural Historians* 61 (June 2002): 152–69.

Wilkins, Mira. *The Emergence of Multinational Enterprise: American Business Abroad from the Colonial Era to 1914*. Cambridge, Mass.: Harvard University Press, 1970.

Williams, Rosalind. *Dream Worlds: Mass Consumption in Late Nineteenth-Century France*. Berkeley: University of California Press, 1982.

Willis, Carol, ed. *Building the Empire State: A Rediscovered 1930s Notebook Charts the Construction of the Empire State Building*. New York: W. W. Norton & Co.; and The Skyscraper Musem, 1998.

———. *Form Follows Finance: Skyscrapers and Skylines in New York and Chicago*. New York: Princeton Architectural Press, 1995.

Wilson, Richard Guy. "Architecture, Landscape, and City Planning." In *American Renaissance: 1876–1917*, by Richard Guy Wilson et al. New York: Brooklyn Museum; and Pantheon Books, 1979.

———. *McKim, Mead and White, Architects*. New York: Rizzoli, 1983.

Winkler, John K. *Five and Ten: The Fabulous Life of F. W. Woolworth*. New York: Robert M. McBride & Co., 1940.

Woods, Mary N. *From Craft to Profession: The Practice of Architecture in Nineteenth-Century America*. Berkeley: University of California Press, 1999.

———. "In the Camera's Eye: The Woolworth Building in American Avant-Garde Photography and Film." In *Cass Gilbert: Life and Work*, edited by Barbara S. Christen and Steven Flanders. New York: W. W. Norton & Co., 2001.

Woolworth, Frank W., and Edward Mott Woolley. "From Dimes to Millions." *McClure's Magazine* 55 (December 1923): 8–18, 117–18; 56 (January 1924): 109–12, 114–16.

The Woolworth Building (Highest in the World): Illustrated with Details from the Architect's Drawings and Floor Plans. New York: F. W. Woolworth, 1912.

"Woolworth Building Will Be World's Greatest Skyscraper." *New York Times*, May 7, 1911.

Zunz, Olivier. *Making America Corporate, 1870–1920*. Chicago: University of Chicago Press, 1990.

INDEX

NOTE: Page numbers in italics indicate figures; color plates are indicated by pl. and the plate number (e.g., pl. 1).